DASHBOARDS THAT DELIVER

DASHBOARDS THAT DELIVER

How to Design, Develop, and Deploy
Dashboards That Work

ANDY COTGREAVE | AMANDA MAKULEC |
JEFFREY SHAFFER | STEVE WEXLER

WILEY

Published by John Wiley & Sons, Inc., Hoboken, New Jersey.
Published simultaneously in Canada.

For general information on our other products and services or for technical support, please contact our Customer Care Department within the United States at (800) 762-2974, outside the United States at (317) 572-3993 or fax (317) 572-4002.

Wiley also publishes its books in a variety of electronic formats. Some content that appears in print may not be available in electronic formats. For more information about Wiley products, visit our web site at www.wiley.com.

Library of Congress Cataloging-in-Publication Data is Available:

ISBN 9781394281831 (Paperback)
ISBN 9781394393565 (FF ePub)
ISBN 9781394281824 (ePDF)
ISBN 9781394389186 (Print Replica)

Cover Design: Wiley
Cover Image: © Splash International

SKY10123774_080825

Contents

Part II: Scenarios Visual Table of Contents

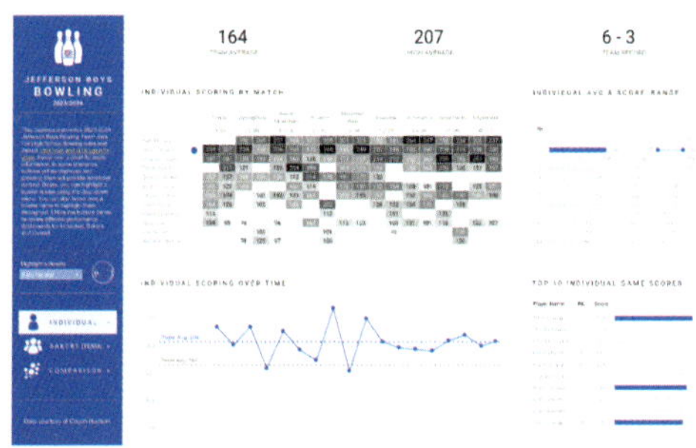

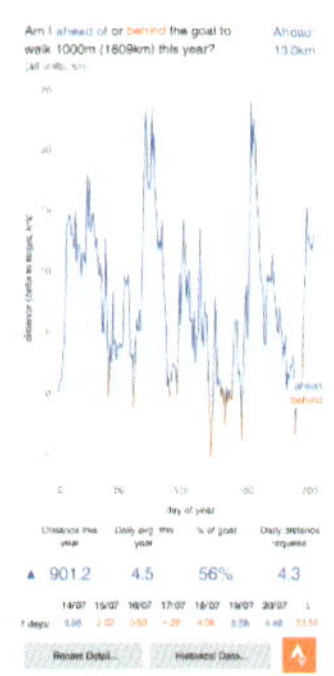

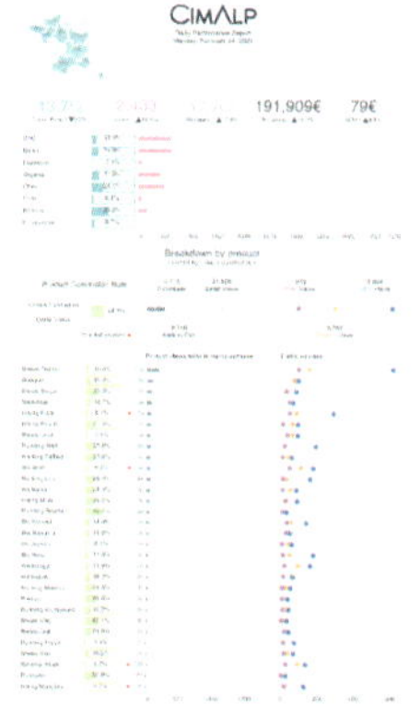

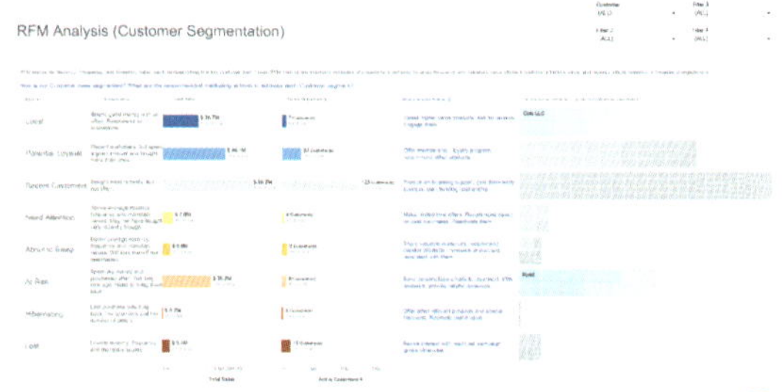

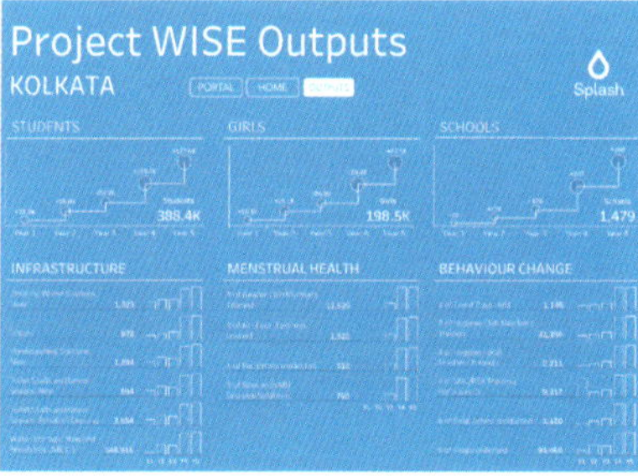

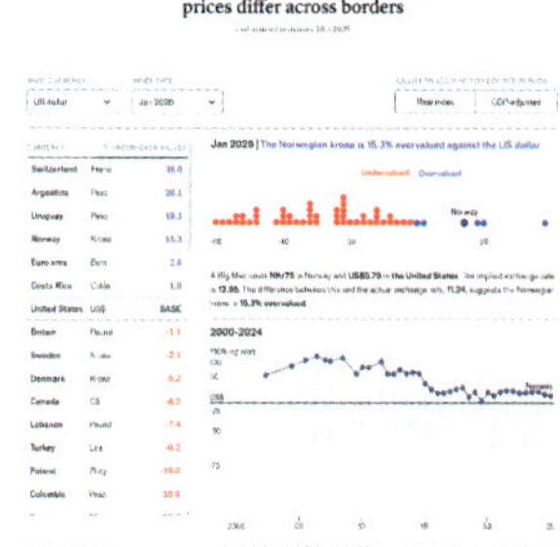

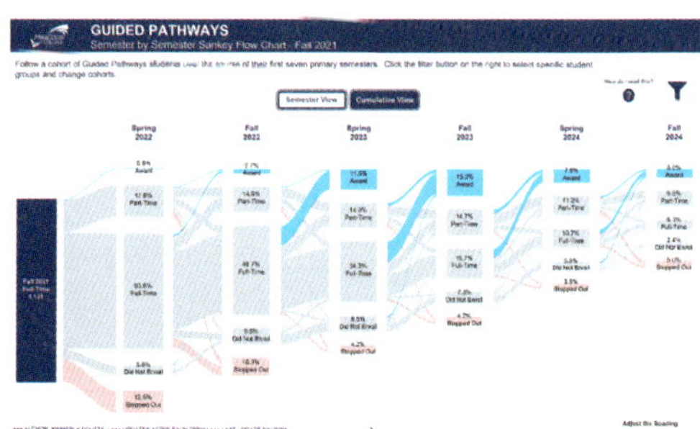

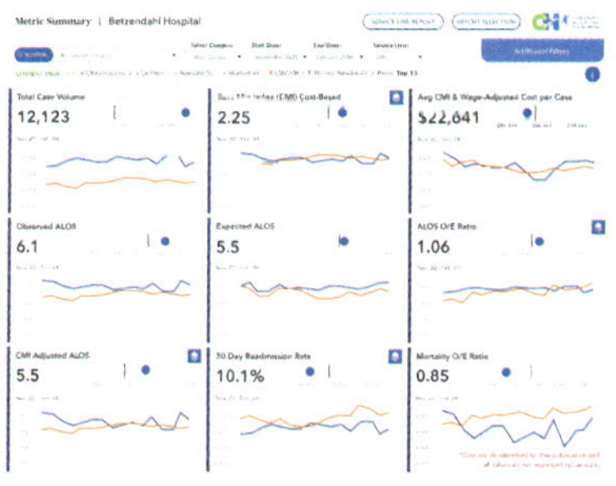

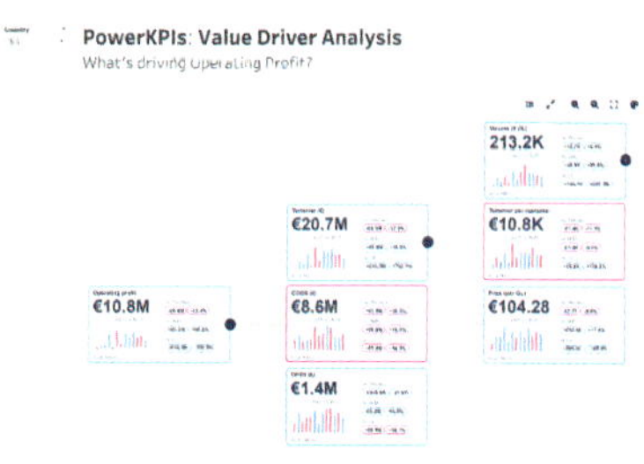

INSURANCE | BROKER PORTFOLIO 2019 Q3

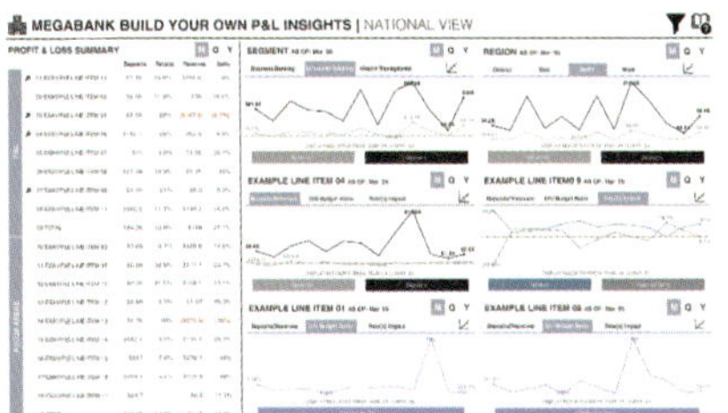
MEGABANK BUILD YOUR OWN P&L INSIGHTS | NATIONAL VIEW

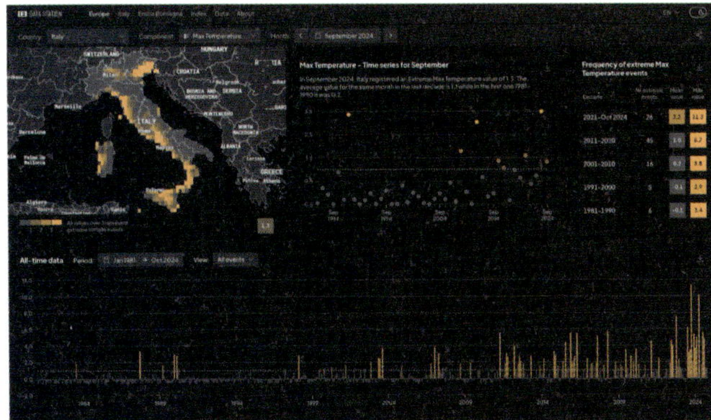

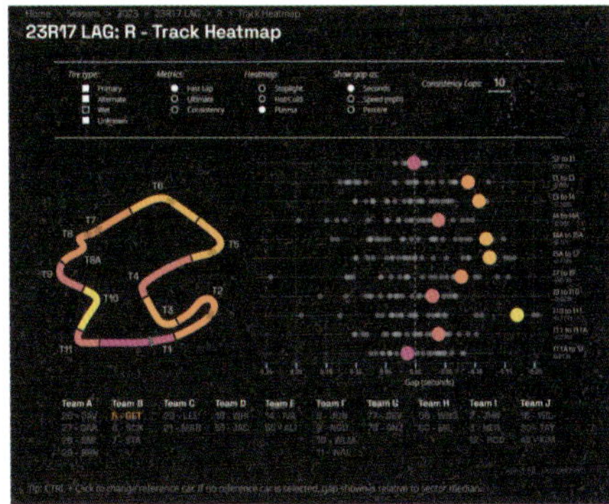
23R17 LAG: R - Track Heatmap

COVID-19 Dashboard
3/10/2023, 8:21 AM
676,609,955
6,881,955
13,338,833,198
4,035,254
28,018
28,156,730

Earth Now
Earth Observing Fleet

About the Authors

Andy Cotgreave

Andy Cotgreave is a data visualization expert and advocate for data literacy. He has 20 years of experience in data visualization and business intelligence.

He began his data analyst career at the University of Oxford before joining Tableau in 2011. He became their first Technical Evangelist in 2016, a role focused on helping people understand the value of data and how to effectively communicate insights. In this capacity, he has inspired thousands of people with his writing and presentations.

Andy is a passionate speaker and has presented at conferences around the world, sharing his insights on data visualization and the importance of data culture. He has hosted the Iron Viz keynote since 2018, a centerpiece of Tableau's annual conference that celebrates the best in data storytelling. He has also delivered keynotes at leading events such as Big Data London, Outlier, and Data Decoded.

Andy is the co-author of the best-selling book *The Big Book of Dashboards*. He writes the How To Speak Data newsletter, in which he shares his thoughts about the latest trends in data, including AI.

Amanda Makulec

Amanda Makulec is a data visualization leader and expert in public health data visualization. She has worked with clients in the public, private, and nonprofit sectors to design effective health data graphics, develop health data dashboards, and build cross-functional data teams. Her work emphasizes visualizing data responsibly, particularly when communicating health information and designing analytical tools that inform decisions about access, delivery, and quality of healthcare services.

Amanda has led data visualization workshops and courses for thousands of people around the world, from Boston to Zimbabwe. She also serves as adjunct faculty at the Maryland Institute College of Art and frequently guest lectures on data visualization design in public health and analytics programs. She hosts Chart Chat with her co-authors and writes about data visualization in publications including Nightingale, the *New York Times*, *Fast Company*, and her Viz Responsibly newsletter. Amanda serves on the Advisory Council for the global Data Visualization Society, where she is a founding board member and served as executive director (2021–2024) and operations director (2019–2020).

Jeffrey Shaffer

Jeffrey Shaffer is the director of the Applied AI Lab and the Kirk and Jacki Perry Professor of Analytics and Assistant Professor-Educator at the University of Cincinnati in the Carl H. Lindner College of Business. He received the 2025 Michael L. Dean Excellence in Classroom Education and Learning Graduate Teaching award and the 2021 and 2016 Outstanding Adjunct Professor of the Year awards. He previously served as the chief operating officer and vice president of Information Technology and Analytics at Recovery Decision Science and Unifund.

He is a regular speaker on the topic of data visualization, artificial intelligence, generative AI, and Tableau training at conferences, symposiums, workshops, universities, and corporate training programs. He is a 5× Tableau Visionary and in 2021 was inducted into the Tableau Visionary Hall of Fame. His data visualization blog was on the shortlist award for the 2016 Kantar Information is Beautiful Awards. He is also the co-author of *The Big Book of Dashboards*.

Steve Wexler

Steve Wexler is the founder and chief chart looker-atter for Data Revelations. He is also the author of *The Big Picture: How to Use Data Visualization to Make Better Decisions – Faster* (winner of Data Literacy's Most Insightful Data Book) and co-author of *The Big Book of Dashboards: Visualizing Your Data Using Real-World Business Scenarios*.

Steve has worked with ADP, Gallup, Johnson & Johnson, Deloitte, ACLU, Convergys, Consumer Reports, *The Economist*, SurveyMonkey, Con Edison, D&B, Marist, Cornell University, Stanford University, Tradeweb, Tiffany, McKinsey & Company, Fidelity, and many other organizations to help them understand and visualize their data. A Tableau Visionary (Hall of Fame) and Iron Viz winner, Steve also serves on the advisory board to the Data Visualization Society. Steve is also widely recognized as one of the world's experts in visualizing survey data.

His presentations and training classes combine an extraordinary level of product mastery with the real-world experience gained through developing thousands of visualizations for dozens of clients. Steve has taught thousands of people in both large and small organizations and is known for conducting his workshops and presentations with clarity, patience, and humor.

Chart Chat

The four of us present Chart Chat, a show about dashboards, charts and data literacy. We started the show after writing *The Big Book of Dashboards* because we got so much value out of the debates we had while writing that book. You are encouraged to join the debate: find out more at https://ChartChat.Live

PART I

PROCESS

In this part, we describe why some dashboards fail and how to make them succeed by providing a reusable framework built on:

- Our own experience designing dashboards across dozens of industries and sectors
- Interviews with experts in the field
- Adapting concepts and methods found in Agile (an iterative approach to software development and project management)
- Principles of user-centered design

Whether you're a novice or an expert in Agile and user-centered design and whether you are a solo practitioner or manage a large team, we're confident you will find value in this section.

Chapter 1

Dashboards Matter

Steve Wexler,
Jeffrey Shaffer,
Andy Cotgreave, and
Amanda Makulec

What Is a Dashboard?

If you were to ask 10 people who build dashboards and 10 people who use dashboards to define the term *dashboard*, you would probably get 20 different definitions.

Here's how we defined the term in *The Big Book of Dashboards*, and we'll continue to rely on this definition:

> A dashboard is a visual display of data used to monitor conditions and/or facilitate understanding.

Yes, it's a broad definition. As with our first book, there will probably be some protests about it. Andy covers these probable objections in Chapter 30, "What the Heck Is a Dashboard?"

Nick Desbarats, author of *Practical Charts* and an expert in dashboard design, created a taxonomy of 13 different types of data displays that all fit under the umbrella term *dashboard*. Each one has a distinct use case and design.

He makes a good point. Think of a vehicle. Literally, imagine one right now. What did you come up with? Truck? Train? Sports car? Bus? Helicopter?

Dashboards are the same.

We don't think your stakeholders need to understand this dashboard taxonomy or the names of all the different display types. *But you and your stakeholders must be in complete agreement as to what the deliverable you're creating will look like and how it's going to work.*

We cover this alignment of expectations in depth in the discovery chapters (Chapters 5 and 6).

Don't Be One of the 71% of People Who Fail

As we were writing this book, we conducted a survey of more than 450 dashboard creators and users and asked them this question:

> *To what degree do you agree with the statement "most dashboards fail."*

71% indicated that they agree or strongly agree with this statement (Figure 1.1).

That's a *lot* of failure.

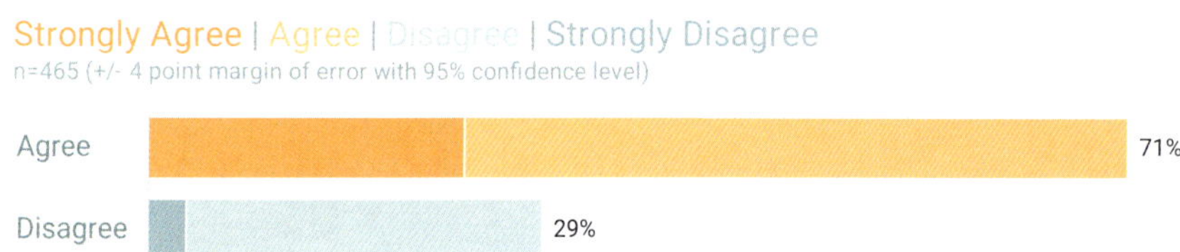

FIGURE 1.1 Percentage of people who agree or disagree that most dashboards fail.

If There's So Much Failure, Why Create Dashboards?

IF 71% of dashboard creators and users indicate that most dashboards fail, why bother to make them?

It's because companies that are effective at dashboarding outperform companies that aren't.

That was the finding of a 2022 MIT Sloan School of Management study, which stated that companies with top-quartile dashboard effectiveness *significantly* outperformed bottom-quartile companies on five internal and five external measures of performance.[1]

This aligns with our own experiences. The four of us have each helped build dashboards that have completely transformed organizations for the better.

But just what do we mean by failure? In our survey, we said failure occurs when the intended users don't adopt the dashboard at all or stop using it before it fulfills its purpose.

There are many reasons why people won't use a dashboard. Maybe the charts were too confusing. Perhaps the metrics on the dashboard were of no interest to the stakeholders. Maybe the performance was too sluggish, or the data was obsolete. Maybe users didn't even know there was a dashboard.

Reflect a bit on the last dashboard project you worked on that didn't have the impact you hoped, and then answer the following questions:

- How closely did you work with your stakeholders? Were they only involved peripherally, or were they active collaborators?
- Did you agree ahead of time on a way to measure whether your dashboard was successful?

[1] dtdbook.com/link1

- Did you set up a system for modifying the dashboard as users' needs changed?
- Were the business leaders behind the project charismatic champions who pushed for widespread adoption?

If you answered *no* to any of these questions, then that beautiful dashboard you and your team created was probably weighted toward failure.

We don't want you to be part of the 71% that fail. That's why we wrote this book.

But How?

"Know your audience."

"Design for your user."

"Get feedback early and often."

Okay great, but how?

If you create dashboards and occasionally read blogs, books, or LinkedIn carousels of well-intentioned advice around building better dashboards, you may have seen at least one of those recommendations.

No objection to those big ideas, but if you're new to dashboard design, how exactly are you supposed to *do* any of those things? And if you do find ways to *do them*, how do you know when you have enough feedback or have gone through enough iterations to click Publish on your new dashboard?

This book was born out of a gap in the dashboarding world. We love to admire dashboards that inspire an "ooh-ah" response for their elegance *and* spark an "ah-ha" by effectively answering a question. But we seldom dive into just how these dashboards get built. Books and blogs talk big picture ("Know your audience!") or get into the weeds of how to do *one thing*, often within a particular set of tools. But the list of resources that walk through, step-by-step, on how to deliver on these user-centered dashboards is...limited.

Filling that information gap – which will help you avoid dashboard failure – was another reason we wrote this book.

The Big Questions We Address

We wrote our first book, *The Big Book of Dashboards*, to answer this question:

> *Given this business predicament, what kind of dashboard should I create?*

We tackled this question by presenting 28 different scenarios, each with an accompanying dashboard that addressed the challenges of each scenario.

In *Dashboards That Deliver* we offer 15 new scenarios and address another critical question:

> *How do I make sure people use the dashboards I create, and get value from them?*

For that question, we'll delve into the *process* of building dashboards. Part I will dive deep into a framework we've created based on our own combined 50+ years' experience, along with interviews with dozens of people who build dashboards for organizations of all sizes. It's a process that addresses what you need to make dashboards that people will want to use, that will make people think differently, and that will make people act.

Should You Read *The Big Book of Dashboards* First?

You do not have to read *The Big Book of Dashboards* before reading this book. In fact, you don't have to read it at all (although we certainly would like you to). While complementary, both books stand on their own.

However, if you are brand new to data visualization, then we recommend either reading the first section of *The Big Book of Dashboards* or reading one of the myriad primers on data visualization. We share a list in Chapter 8.

We wrote this book so that you can learn from our successes and failures as you embark on developing new dashboards and learn from other experts across the field who contributed their thoughts in our interviews and dashboard scenarios.

If you're a dashboard developer, we know you'll find practical advice over the next 34 chapters around how to understand your audience, fail fast, and deliver a great product. We also encourage you to use this framework in your conversations with your stakeholders around ways to build connections between the data team and dashboard users.

If you're a data leader or team member, we hope you'll find ways to take a step back, take stock of your current delivery process, and think through how some of our ideas can help you deliver on the promise of impact every company aspires to with their data.

We all benefit from tools that help us analyze data more efficiently. Whether you call them dashboards, data apps, or "algorithmic cockpits" as we saw referenced by one AI company, they still have the potential to transform how we use data in our work.

This Book Is Tool Agnostic

The book is agnostic about what tools you use to create dashboards. You won't find step-by-step instructions about how to make anything. This goes for artificial intelligence (AI) tools as well. As we'll explore in Chapter 32, AI will play a big part in dashboard design, beyond exploratory data analysis, and its capabilities are changing rapidly.

Will AI replace many if not all the human factors that go into making a dashboard succeed? We'd never say never, but at the time of this writing you still need humans who know what good looks like to direct and drive the decisions. So, no matter the tool and no matter your reliance on, or avoidance of, AI, we'll show you what you should build, why you should build it, and the process that should go into designing, developing, and deploying it.

Downloadable Dashboards and Additional Resources

For downloadable dashboards, additional examples, information about workshops, and other resources, please visit DashboardsThatDeliver.com.

A Path Toward Fewer Failures and More Successes

The four of us have probably failed more than many of you in designing and launching different dashboards, and through those failures, we've refined and improved our own approaches. We've learned a lot from those failures, and we want to do what we can to help you avoid the missteps and failures we and many other practitioners have made.

In *Dashboards That Deliver*, we give you scenarios and coping-with-the-real-world essays. But more importantly, we arm you with a comprehensive, comprehensible, and customizable process – a process that will help you succeed.

Chapter 2

The Dashboards That Deliver Framework

Amanda Makulec and
Andy Cotgreave

Why Have a Framework?

You're on vacation, in your rental car, and it's time to take the family home. What do you do? Ask Google Maps for directions back to the airport, stopping at a gas station on the way? Or pull out and drive in whatever direction you fancy?

We suspect most of you would choose the GPS option. You can plan your time, set expectations with your kids on when they'll get a break, everyone in the car knows how far you've got to go. If you need to find a rest area with your favorite fast-food restaurant on the way, you can make the change en route.

You're a dashboard developer, and someone's asked you for a dashboard. What do you do? Create a shared plan, with checkpoints along the way? Or just dive into your dashboard development tool and build whatever takes your fancy?

We hope that after reading this book, you'll choose the first option.

As our research shows, a lot of dashboards fail. Too often it's because dashboards are spun up with chart choices based on the preferences of the creator, rather than the user, who feels like an outsider in the process rather than being part of the team. Without a framework, the team doesn't have a clear idea of where they're going, nor can anyone see how close they are to a finished product.

Based on our experiences and research for this book, we've defined a framework you can follow to build dashboards that deliver. Thinking in phases from the framework will help you:

- Build and maintain momentum throughout your dashboard's development, working toward success criteria for a dashboard.
- Share and delegate tasks among your team while setting expectations with your users.
- Build a culture and shared language of data and dashboards that helps people use data for decision-making.

Our Guiding Principles

In developing our framework for *Dashboards That Deliver*, we identified three guiding principles that focus on mindset, not technology:

1. **Adaptability and flexibility.** Our framework must be adaptable to different team sizes, timelines, and business contexts. You should be able to borrow and adjust the parts that serve your needs.
2. **Dashboards as applications.** Building a dashboard has many similarities to software development, particularly as dashboards include increasingly sophisticated features. The framework should use established techniques from that world, including Agile and user-centric design methodologies.
3. **Improvement over perfection.** You don't need to overhaul your team or process to improve dashboard development within an organization. Don't let the pursuit of an ideal process stop you from using parts of the framework to make incremental improvements to your work.

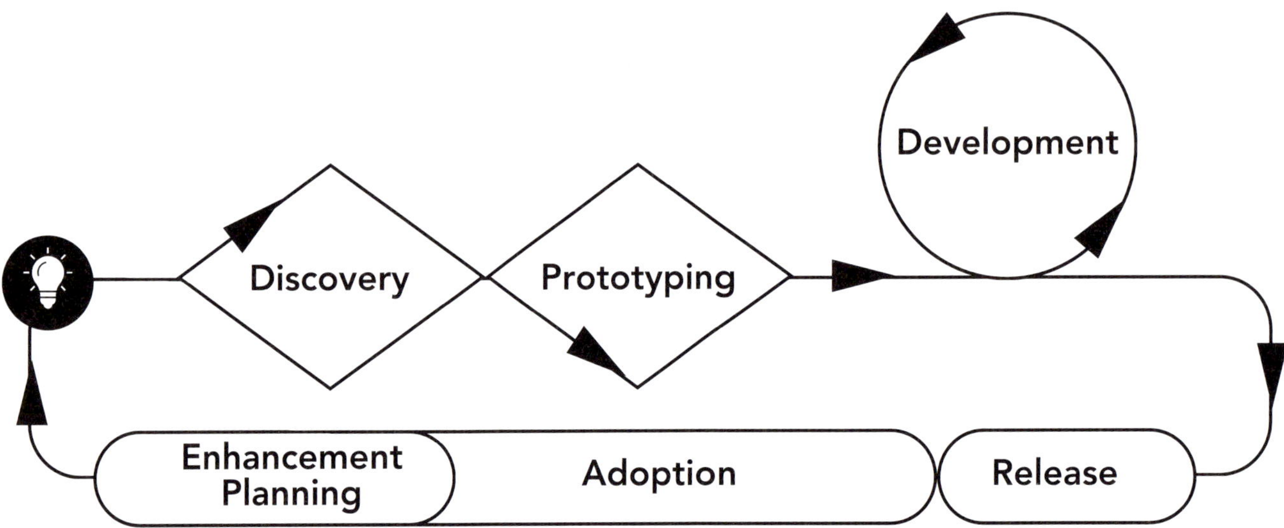

FIGURE 2.1 Dashboards that Deliver framework.

The Dashboards That Deliver Framework

Our framework (Figure 2.1) has seven phases:

1. **Spark:** Recognize the catalyst for building the dashboard.
2. **Discovery:** Define the audience and purpose for building the dashboard through engagement with users and mapping the specific use cases for the dashboard. Clearly define the presentation medium, like a laptop screen, a PDF, tablet, or even a 30-foot long display. Then, be specific in breaking down big goals into specific requirements. Define what success looks like for the launch of this dashboard.
3. **Prototyping:** Brainstorm different design approaches to address user needs, including developing early design concepts and finalizing the mockup. Get feedback from users before moving to development.
4. **Development and User Testing:** Build your design in your dashboarding tool. Get usability feedback from users via dedicated feedback loops.
5. **Release:** Launch the dashboard for end users, with a schedule for data refreshes and maintenance.
6. **Adoption:** Create a training plan and promote continued adoption. Solicit user feedback and monitor usage.
7. **Managing Enhancements:** Define the plan for managing enhancements and set boundaries around how often you will make updates.

The amount of time you spend in each phase will vary depending on complexity and your team size. You may spend time iterating in one phase or running through the whole cycle multiple times over the life of a dashboard.

But don't get stuck in one phase waiting for three levels of sign-off just to check a box stating you got the requirements "right": you need just enough discovery to avoid going off in the wrong direction, just enough prototyping to get something real into the users' hands, and continuous ways to get feedback from your users.

While we cannot guarantee success, we want to arm you with an approach that will greatly reduce the likelihood of failure.

A Practical Example: A Chart Chat Dashboard

In *Part 2 – Scenarios* we'll explore 15 different dashboards and how they applied the framework.

Instead of waiting until the end of this section to dive into a practical example, let's start with a hypothetical case study of how we would apply our own framework if we were co-designing a dashboard.

Since 2018, we've hosted a monthly livestream called Chart Chat (Figure 2.2). Like all good content creators, we want analytics! We need a consolidated view of our data, rather than having to scrabble around all the platforms (YouTube, Eventbrite, LinkedIn, etc.) to get an idea of what's going on.

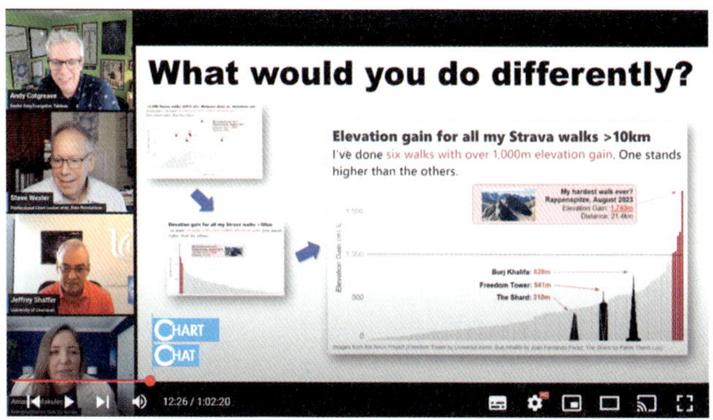

FIGURE 2.2 Chart Chat is our monthly video series about bringing data to life.

Sounds like a good opportunity for a *dashboard*, right?

Let's walk through what following our framework could look like in practice:

Spark: Each month we look for different ad hoc analytics on Chart Chat from the previous month, posting quick updates in our shared Slack channels or flagging on planning calls. Because we each manage different parts of Chart Chat – Steve needs to pull registration data, Jeff pulls YouTube analytics, Andy explores different ways to market and promote, and Amanda tallies data from Streamyard – there was no combined view. We decided we needed a dashboard to consolidate our data.

Discovery: We start by thinking through the analytics tasks we will use the dashboard for, rather than diving directly into what the available data tables will look like. Based on our analytics needs, we map out two personas (Figure 2.3) who represent different sets of needs:

- The Planner is responsible for promoting registrations.
- The Optimizer identifies popular topics and segment types from previous episodes.

Defining personas allows us to make the needs and pain points a bit less personal. Plus, each of

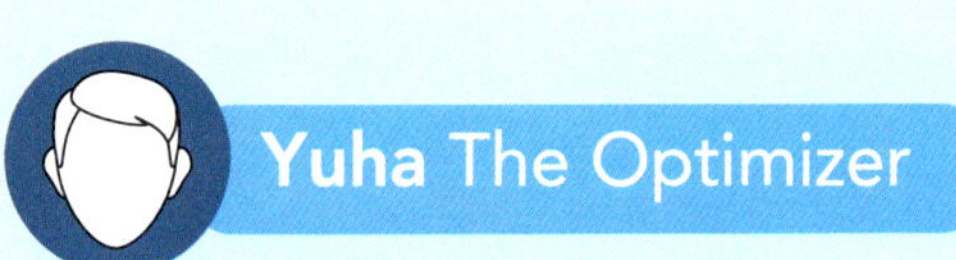

FIGURE 2.3 Persona cards for our Chart Chat dashboard.

us may step into either role, depending on the month. For each persona, we can brainstorm more detailed analytical questions and requirements (Figure 2.4).

The Planner needs data on traffic sources to our registration page and registration trends to assess if we're growing our audience. The Optimizer needs to know which type of content is best performing. For example, do episodes with guests do better than when it's just the four of us?

We define success during this phase. First, simply being able to see the data in one place is a success, as it saves much wasted time each month collecting the data from multiple sites. A second, longer-term measure, will be an increase in registrations and views based on insights from the dashboard.

Prototyping: Considering the two users and their needs, we map out a wireframe with a three-page structure:

1. **Summary Metrics.** This page combines data from across the watch funnel (i.e., from registrations to live attendees to post-show on-demand views)
2. **Registration Trends.** This is a detailed view of registration trends and details for each episode.
3. **YouTube and LinkedIn Live Analytics.** These show details of views, watch time, engagement, etc.

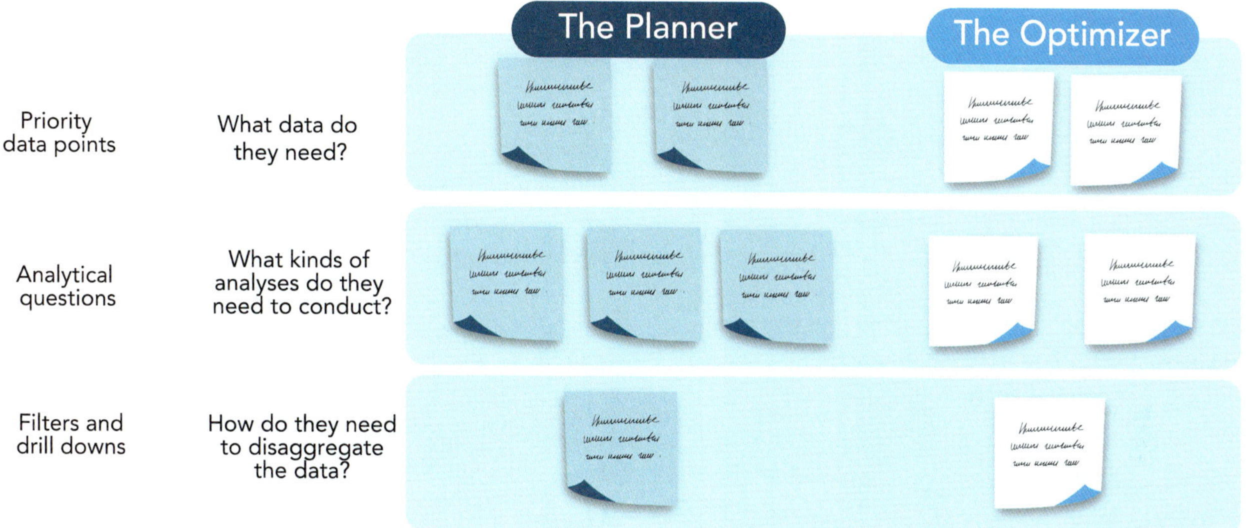

FIGURE 2.4 Mapping user needs across two personas.

We need to iterate with the mockup multiple times and construct a dataset that suits our needs. We could leverage APIs, Gen AI tools, and more to get the data into the shape we need. Depending on how the ideas shape up, we may also need to add metadata for episodes such as if there was a guest.

We go back and forth a few times on the mockups, debating the necessity of including the data on views by segment, and decide that it's likely not going to be terribly insightful to see that level of detail. We do, however, care how long people stick around within each episode. We also realize we need data on the performance of social media promotions. Figure 2.5 shows the progression of the first page of the dashboard.

Development and User Testing: At this point we have mockup for each page of the dashboard. The sketches have key performance indicators, specific chart types, annotations, and design directions. Now we can map out who has access to and can source the different data we need – including considering where we can automate that data refresh and what would need to be done manually. We agree to hand off the development to Andy, knowing that the debates and iteration with the mockup have us in a good place.

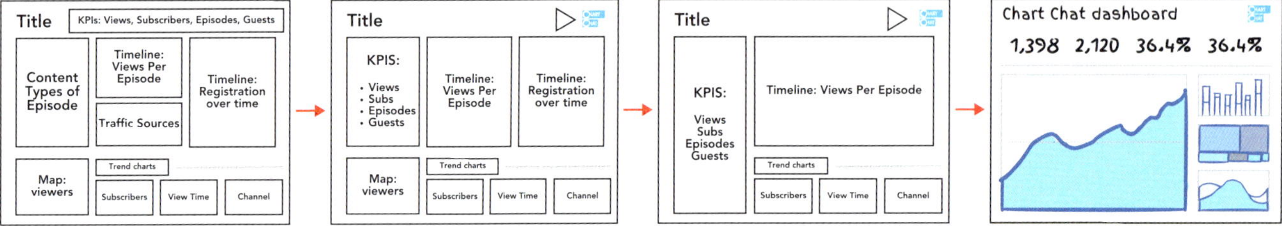

FIGURE 2.5 A progression from wireframe to prototype for the main page of the dashboard.

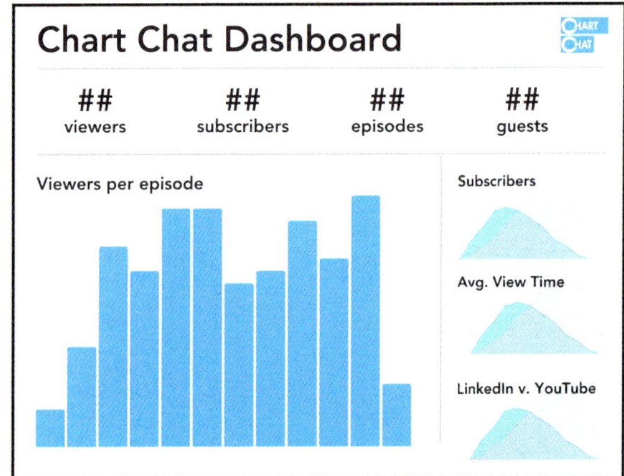

FIGURE 2.6 The final look for our main page.

Release: Once the dashboard is developed and tested, including quality assurance checks for accuracy, we agree on a cadence for refreshing the data and consolidating documentation and notes. See Figure 2.6.

Adoption: Since we're our own primary users, adoption is more straightforward than in some environments. We can share the dashboard over email or Slack. We'll need to make sure to measure something related to how it gets used to inform decisions, and identify a period – perhaps three months, since the livestream is monthly – at which point we'll evaluate if we're finding the dashboard useful and if we should continue.

Managing Enhancements: Luckily, we're all pretty adept at using the same tools, so we have some flexibility on who will make updates. It's important we set up a shared space to log ideas for changes, particularly as we evolve new use cases for the dashboard, like informing a new sponsorship request. Then, we can estimate the effort and impact each request will take and create our prioritized backlog of changes, as illustrated in Figure 2.7. Here, we're adopting the language from Agile with a backlog referring to a central list of tasks to complete, not an indication that you're behind on completing work.

We decide to make changes every three months and pull up the dashboard on our prep call each month to check how the numbers are faring.

Following our framework, we'd have a dashboard tracking the success of Chart Chat. Had we not used

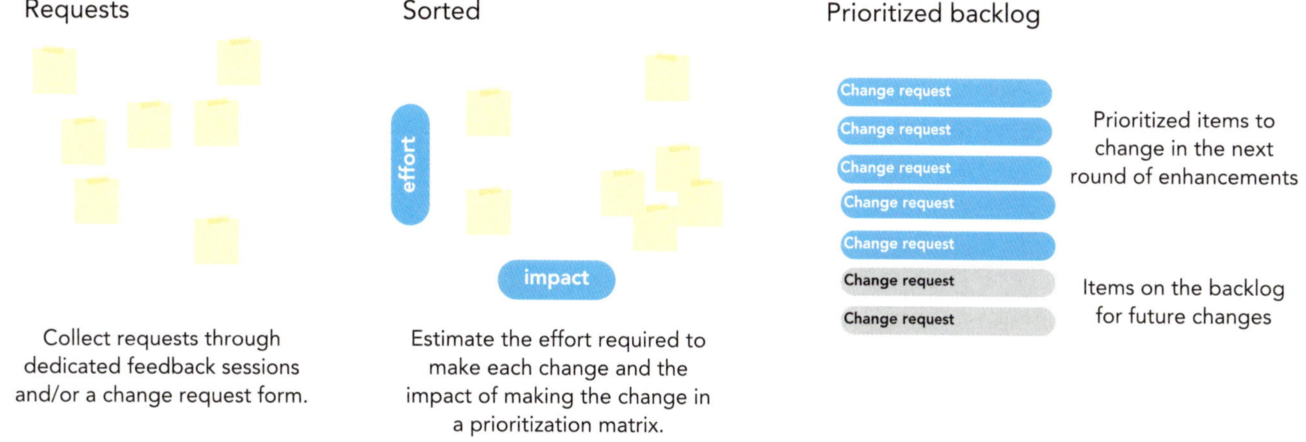

FIGURE 2.7 Steps in compiling a backlog of changes to implement.

our framework, how would it have gone? We'd probably each build something in isolation, focusing on our own personal needs, rather than those of the group. We may have gotten a great Chart Chat episode out of sharing and critiquing our different concepts, but it wouldn't have been nearly as focused or efficient.

Finalizing a single dashboard without a unified goal would be a nightmare. If you've ever seen an episode of Chart Chat, you'll know that we are all willing to debate (argue over?) every tiny detail of every chart. Apply that to a dashboard with no clear goal, and we'd be arguing forever. Plus, any attempt to merge different designs would probably have failed due to different goals, designs, and data models.

Using the framework helps us, and will help you, maintain a focus on the goals of your users.

Methodologies That Inspired Our Framework

Our approach isn't an earth-shattering new approach to dashboard design. Instead, it looks to the most relevant principles from software development, design, and our own experiences, combining tactics and approaches that we've seen work.

We make specific references to three methods in our framework: Agile, user-centered design, and the design double diamond. Those methodologies all value user engagement, feedback, and rapid prototyping (to enable quick feedback from users).

Let's unpack those three methods in a bit more detail, including how they informed this book.

Agile Software Development

Software developers have dealt with plenty of the same issues we have as dashboard developers. They learned through experience that hypothesizing about what a customer wants, going behind closed doors, building a solution, and then launching a final product often didn't work. Developers shifted away from stage-gated, waterfall processes toward a method that prioritizes small increments and continuous improvement.

Agile is a mindset centered on breaking projects down into smaller pieces guided by a shared set of values. There are four core tenets, summarized in Figure 2.8.

Agile values these...		more than these...
Individuals and interactions	>	**Processes and tools**
Working code	>	**Documentation**
Customer collaborations	>	**Contract negotiation**
Responding to change	>	**Following a plan**

FIGURE 2.8 List of values from the Agile Manifesto.

This isn't to say the latter items *don't* have value but instead that they are less important. Each tenet emphasizes the benefit of *collaboration with users* and *a working product* – tenets that are as valuable for dashboard development as they are for software.

Practically, Agile teams break down big projects into smaller pieces, delivered incrementally. Agile ways of working include clear team roles, defined collaboration approaches, and prioritizing making work visible often through a shared backlog and routine retrospectives.

If you've had some experience with Agile, you've likely heard references to scrum and kanban – both specific methods for implementing an Agile approach. *Scrum* defines a series of several phases of work, commonly known as *sprints*, with a focus and commitment to tight feedback cycles and continuous improvement. *Kanban* focuses on having a tightly managed backlog of tasks grouped by status – backlog, in-progress (WIP), and done – where teams work to minimize WIP or the number of WIP tasks at a given point in time. Instead, teams focus on closing out tasks to deliver incremental parts of the final product.

We've found value in our own projects adapting some of these ways of working to dashboards. Getting into the weeds of what methods to use when is beyond the scope of this book though; while we'll share some broad recommendations around tricks and tools that could be useful in adopting this framework in Chapter 3, part of the work of a dashboard designer is to set your working norms with your team.

User-Centered Design

User-centered design focuses on empathizing with and understanding your audience. Applied to dashboards, the approach gives developers the tools to dig deeply to understand the challenges users face, and how your dashboard will solve them.

An example is the design thinking process defined by d.school, a design institute at Stanford University. It defines five phases, as outlined in Figure 2.9 and covered in the following chapters.

Many of the techniques we outline Chapter 6, "Discovery Techniques," are rooted in user-centered design, which has a deep toolbox of methods for understanding user needs. It helps to have more creative approaches than just asking, "What do you want us to put on this dashboard?" But design thinking is more than a set of techniques; it's a method rooted in continuous engagement with and feedback from our users.

The Design Double Diamond

Also borrowing from the world of design thinking, both discovery and prototyping are framed as a pair of diamonds in our framework – a reference to the "double diamond" framework popularized by the British Design Council in 2005. The model focuses on the principles of divergence

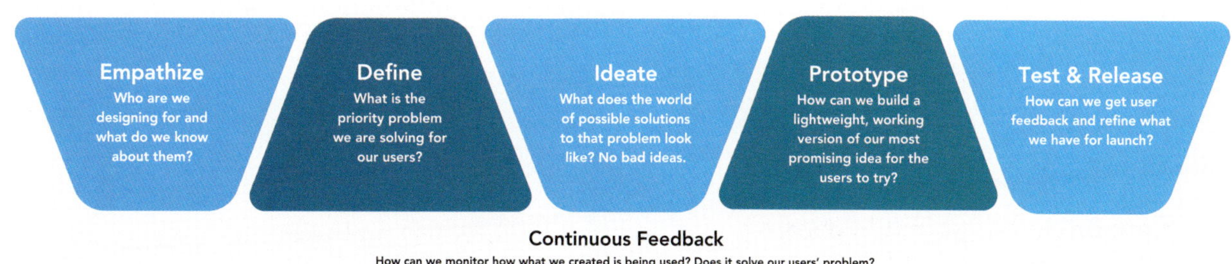

FIGURE 2.9 Process and feedback look within a user-centered design approach.

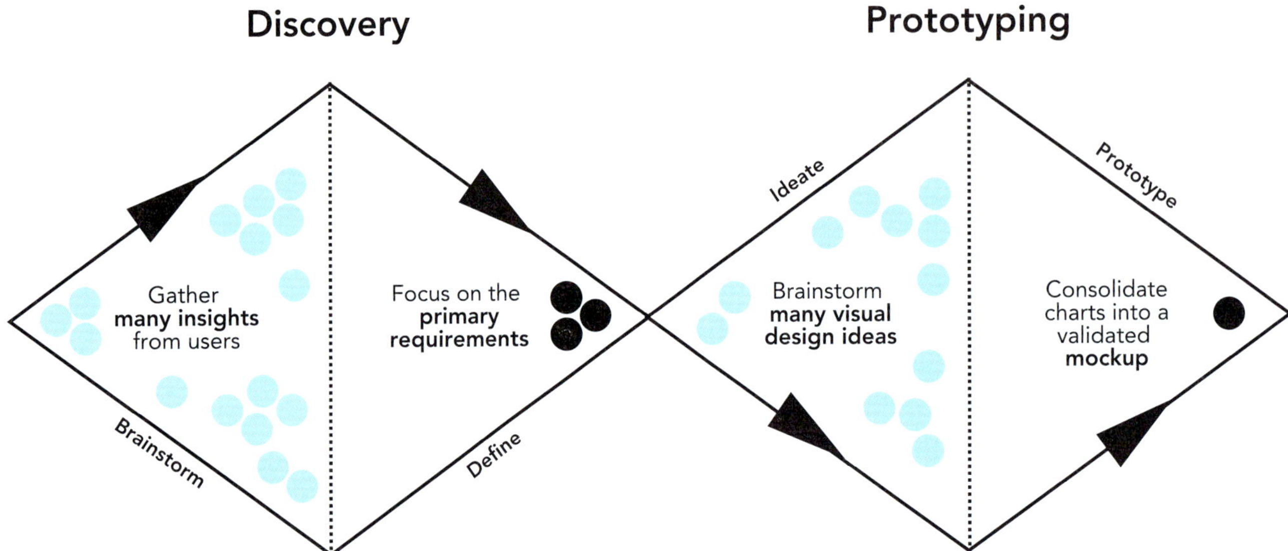

FIGURE 2.10 Design double diamond framework for dashboard discovery (gathering insights and focusing on priority requirements) and later, prototyping adapted to dashboard development.

(brainstorming many possible problems and solutions) and convergence (then narrowing into focus on solving a specific problem for a user in a specific way).

You'll use this same approach in your dashboard process: gathering many insights, trying out lots of ideas, and then narrowing down to a final prototype, as illustrated in Figure 2.10.

Find Out More About Development Methodologies

Agile's core goal is to get working software in the hands of users. The 4-point Agile Manifesto and further 12 principles are useful for dashboard developers to understand. You can find full details of Agile at dtdbook.com/link2.

Stanford's d.school has a User-Centered Design toolkit that provides details on how each stage of their process works. See dtdbook.com/link3.

The British Design Council's Double Diamond is a visual representation of the steps taken in design projects. You can find more resources at dtdbook.com/link4.

Chapter 3

Dashboard Teams and Roles

Amanda Makulec and Andy Cotgreave

Before we dive into our framework for building dashboards that deliver, we want to use this chapter to talk about a few of the practical considerations for who builds dashboards and the project management tools that can help you use the framework successfully.

The Skills

When you're a dashboard designer, you may function as a data engineer, UX designer, data visualization developer, business analyst, change management advisor, and more.

In large teams, experts in each of those domains manage one part of the development. But in smaller organizations, team members wear multiple hats, often switching between roles throughout development.

So, what skills do you need? Table 3.1 shows the list of skills we think you'll need on most dashboard projects.

Don't feel overwhelmed, even if the list feels long. This mix of "soft" skills and more technical skills likely connect to tasks you're already thinking about when you work on a dashboard. Note that we're focusing on *skills* and not people. This should give you the shared language you need to identify learning resources for domains where you're not as experienced.

The Team

As you read through the scenarios in Part II, you'll see many different team structures. While you may not be able to replicate the team from another organization, you can bring together collaborators who care deeply about the problem you want to solve.

When you're scoping a new dashboard, think about your team size, roles, and how you will engage users as you design and build the dashboard.

TABLE 3.1 Skills needed for successful dashboards

Skill	Description
Data engineering	Automates data pipelines, stands up new data infrastructure, and works on sticky data integration and interoperability issues. Leads development of data architecture such as data lakes, lakehouses, and data warehouses
Business analysis	Defines and develops requirements though an understanding of the business needs
Data analysis	Translates business requirements into data requirements (mapping metrics to the underlying sources)
User experience (UX) design	Informs interactivity design, layouts, and how to best enable users to explore the data
Data visualization design	Guides designers with science-backed approaches to chart selection, design, and fundamental principles of information design
Change management and communications	Plans for how to support adoption and use, particularly with large-scale analytics ecosystems or new analytical products
Project management	Keeps the whole development process on time and budget
Subject-matter expertise	Influences decision-making around what metrics and benchmarks to display, meaningful aggregations and analytics, and added context
User engagement	Provides feedback throughout the design process

Do I Need to Be a GenAI Expert Too?

At the time of writing this book, software companies seem to be releasing new AI features each week, with the promise of taking away some of the hand-chiseling work we often do when building a new dashboard. While tech firms make big promises around the ways AI components will help users more quickly engage with information, these tools rely heavily on well-governed data sources that an AI model can glean insight from.

You, as a dashboard designer, will continue to play a critical role in ensuring that what you create meets user needs, answers real analytical questions, and addresses the challenges of trusting charts and analyses generated by computer models with the added context and insight *you* bring to the table.

For more reflections on the ways GenAI is reshaping some of our work, see Chapter 32, "Generative AI and Data Analytics."

Team Size

The four of us have worked as dashboard developers, team leaders, and consultants with organizations of widely varying sizes. The team size and resources dedicated to dashboard development across these organizations looked remarkably different. For example:

- A small community organization in rural Zimbabwe had one monitoring and evaluation advisor responsible for every task related to data, including survey design, data collection, data management, visualization, and reporting. Reporting was managed using Excel spreadsheets.
- A Fortune 100 company had a mix of more than two dozen consultants and full-time staff dedicated to analytics and report development for the digital services part of the organization alone. Dashboards and reports were developed using complex data architecture and software platforms, including Tableau and PowerBI.
- A government agency had more than 20 staff with responsibilities for dashboard development as one part of their lengthy job descriptions. Reporting quarterly or annual data was managed with Tableau dashboards. As another mechanism for delivering information to stakeholders, presenters often copied, annotated, and pasted charts from these dashboards into slide decks.

There isn't one "right" team structure: despite their very different sizes and resources, each of these teams successfully adopted user-centered approaches to build better dashboards.

Team Roles

Two critical functions for keeping the work on track and making prioritization choices are:

- **Product owner:** This person is responsible for representing the stakeholder perspective and prioritizing feature requests. They may also act as a champion for the dashboard within the organization.
- **Project manager/scrum leader.** This person is responsible for leading team meetings, supporting the team to resolve impediments, and ensuring the backlog is up to date.

Users as Part of the Team

Even if you're a solo dashboard developer, you're not really working alone: when users share insights and give feedback, they become part of the team.

Starting with discovery for defining the user requirements, you can identify specific stakeholders to interview as part of a core group of users. We'll discuss this in detail in Chapter 5.

Let's consider two examples of how dashboard creators and users collaborate:

- At the pharmaceutical company Moderna, each business unit has a digital partner (data expert) in service of their data needs. The digital partner is already adept at analyzing and visualizing data, allowing the team members (users) to focus on clarifying their goals and providing subject-matter expertise.

Why Do I Need a Product Owner for My Dashboard?

THE product owner is a role borrowed from Agile software development. This person is responsible for representing the perspective of the end users, making prioritization decisions when you have more requirements that you can address within the timeline for developing the dashboard and, ideally, leading development of the project roadmap and refining requirements through use cases and user stories (more on those in Chapter 5, "Discovery").

Prioritization matters, particularly balancing user needs and feature feasibility. Working with your product owner to prioritize requests helps ensure the design focuses on the *most important* features, not just those that are the *easiest* to implement.

Ideally, the product owner also serves as a champion for your dashboard when it is released, advising on adoption strategies and being a vocal advocate of the ways in which the dashboard can help users. That can mean sharing insights at the start of demo meetings, sharing how they're using the dashboard, and sending launch emails, particularly if they're a person of influence within the organization.

- Rob Radburn, Business Intelligence Development team leader at Leicestershire County Council in the United Kingdom, said the service sets up the teams so that the data analysts act as "business partners" for each major department. Radburn said.

  "These analysts don't just parachute in, wireframe something, and move on. The analysts are a permanent link between the business intelligence team and the end user's department. The analysts are a permanent link between the business intelligence team and the end user's department."

Most importantly, be respectful of your users' time. Recognize that they have other responsibilities, and you can't expect them to be on constant call to look at and vet every issue that comes up.

Instead, be specific about your expectations and when the most important moments are for them to engage and share insights. Be transparent about how much time you expect them to commit, including setting meetings in advance with a clear purpose and agenda so that they know what to expect and their time is well spent.

Organizational Ownership

The ways many organizations structure data teams have evolved. Data isn't just an IT function; it's a core part of how decisions are made across departments, each with their own subject-matter expertise. We've seen that change in practice as more organizations shift away from housing their data and analytics team *within* the IT department, instead having dedicated data teams distributed across business units (Figure 3.1).

Who has overall responsibility for building and maintaining dashboards at your organization? Do you have a command-and-control structure with a central business intelligence or IT team governing what gets published, or do distributed teams across the organization have the flexibility to build their own dashboards? Is dashboard design seen as a technology function or a decision enablement function? Who is responsible for managing dashboards once they're released?

In our interviews with leaders in the field, Simon Beaumont, Business Intelligence director at real estate firm JLL, reflected on their holistic approach to building a data team. Data engineers and analysts collaborate to cover the full spectrum of dashboard requests, from simple data requests to complex dashboard design. In contrast with the structures of technology and data teams in past decades, the JLL data team specifically identifies *not* as an IT organization, but as a client-enabling team.

This mindset shift from analytics as an information technology entity to customer-serving entity is one of the biggest enablers of success for dashboards that deliver: user engagement is key.

In our user research, Beaumont (JLL) framed this challenge around analytics teams fulfilling an *enablement* function:

> As a data person, you could go to a department leader with insights to inform a decision.

Centralized Data Team

Data teams manage requests as part of a central IT department

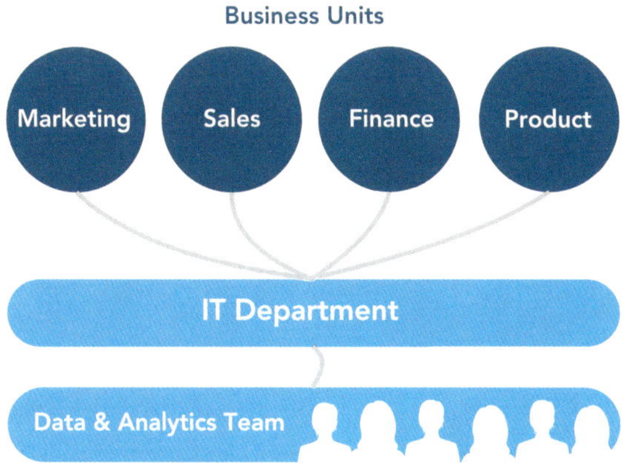

Distributed Data Teams

Data and analytics teams within business units for more integration with subject-matter expertise

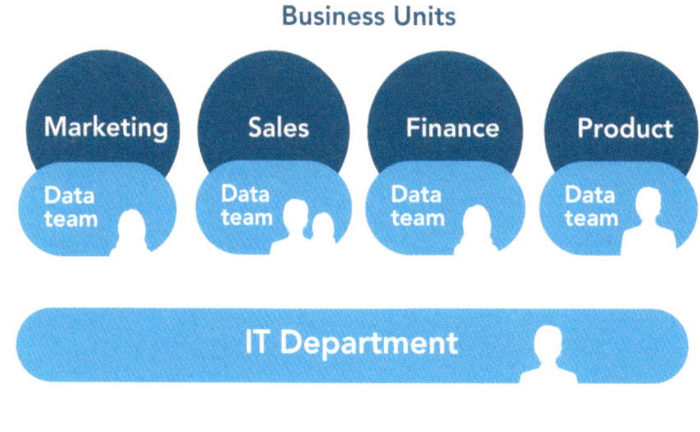

Each represents a data person within the organization

FIGURE 3.1 Comparison of two common organizational structures for data teams.

The projected results of implementing that choice should cut 20% of costs, driving the choice. The dashboard alone can't decide whether to implement the recommendation; it's just a report. You need the business appetite and the business culture to be able to drive that change. As data people, we always think about the business owner and how they will use the data, not just assuming that building tools like dashboards will have an impact.

Fundamentally we see ourselves as an enablement function, but it's not a *data enablement* function. It's a *business enablement* function. If you're a successful BI team, you are enabling the business to act on their data.

Enablement is a reference to how the dashboards and broader analytics work serve the organization. The goal of a dashboard isn't just to *enable access to information; successful dashboards help someone do something with that data*. That's where we bring in the critical skills that go beyond the technical knowledge of building a dashboard, such as communications and change management.

Managing Dashboard Development

This chapter isn't meant to be an exhaustive dive into how to manage a dashboard project, particularly because what works for you will depend on your own working norms.

That said, if you're building a new approach to dashboard development as a team, there are a few key things we've found useful.

Planning

Create a *dashboard roadmap*. Map out the phases of work, using the framework we walked through in Chapter 2 as a guide. If you're working within a specific timeline, take that into account when mapping out phases of work, as you see in Figure 3.2.

Your roadmap should include a high-level overview of the timeline and process for developing the dashboard. It will be more detailed for the earlier phases of development, as your timelines and plans may change based on what you learn during your discovery work.

Building a Backlog

Document the various tasks and features on a *development backlog*. A backlog is a more granular, actionable list of tasks connected to the roadmap. This list is useful for breaking down the dashboard into smaller pieces (more on that in a bit!) and helps team members pick up different responsibilities. Listing smaller tasks lets you see the progress you're making and set expectations with your users.

It can be tempting to make a long list of big items to tackle (like "Conduct Interviews" or "Build Dashboard"). As a result, you can't see the incremental progress as easily, and a team may find it harder to delegate pieces of work since the specifics aren't clearly defined.

As you manage the backlog, think about making the tasks more granular for milestones that come sooner (Figure 3.3). By all means, list the "big picture" thing you know you'll need to do later in the project, but don't worry (yet) about the details.

Backlogs are often managed at an enterprise level in tools like Confluence or JIRA, but you can also build a scrappy backlog in Excel, Google Sheets,

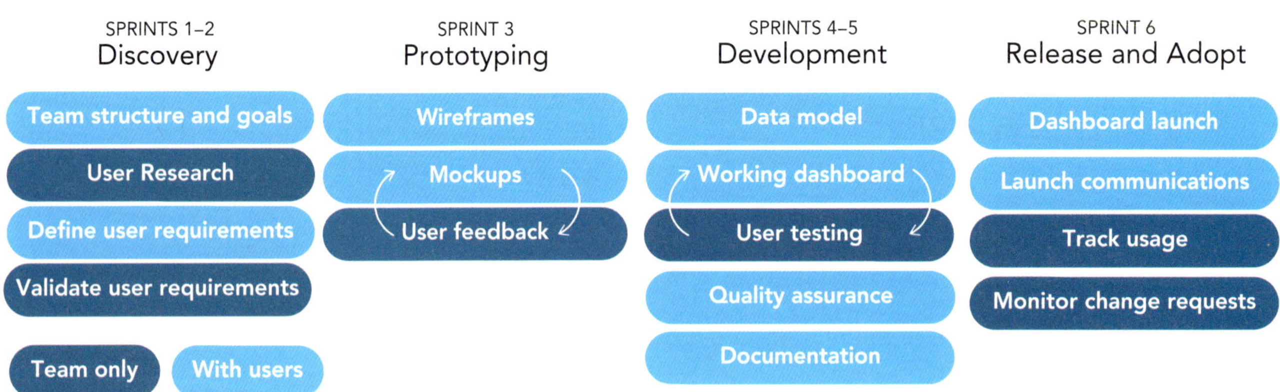

FIGURE 3.2 Sample dashboard roadmap.

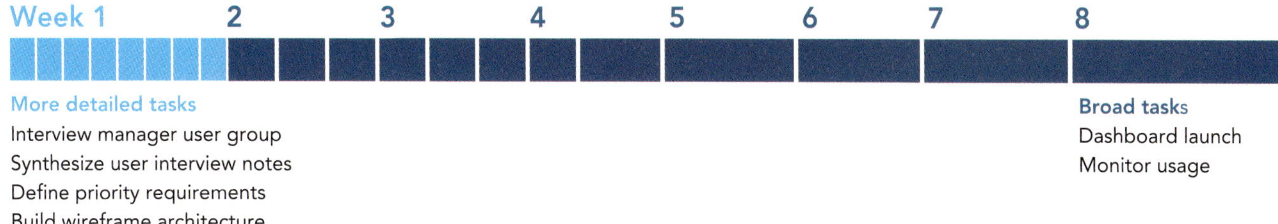

FIGURE 3.3 The level of detail on a backlog by week of the dashboard development timeline, where the level of detail is increasingly vague as you map tasks to do much later in the process.

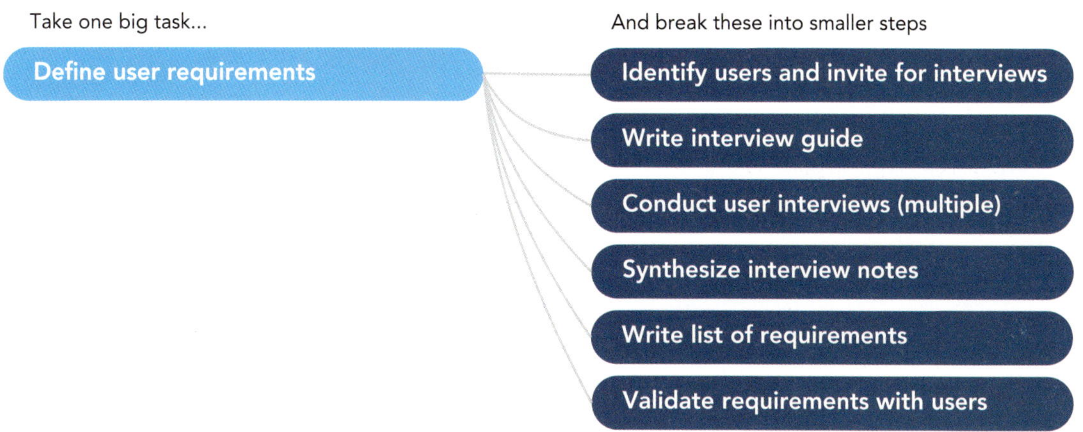

FIGURE 3.4 Breaking one big task into many smaller ones for easier estimation.

or even Trello. To be useful, the whole team needs to use the tools and keep the status of items up-to-date.

Ask your team to *estimate* the effort needed to complete backlog items. The benefit of breaking big projects into small pieces is that it's easier to estimate the effort necessary to complete something small (write interview guide) than something big (define user requirements), as illustrated in Figure 3.4.

Estimating the effort required for each part of the build helps you:

- Set realistic expectations with users about your progress.
- Plan which team members will handle each task.
- Spot places where team members might disagree on how much work is needed – an indication that you might not share the same understanding of a task.

Estimating effort needed to complete different parts of the build helps you set realistic expectations with users around the progress you'll make. For your team, estimation help you plan who from the team will take on different pieces of the project and identify where members of the team may have different opinions of the effort required, which could be a signal that you're not on the same page around a task (Figure 3.5).

At JLL they distinguish between simple projects (one to two people) and solutions (more people, more time), which can help with planning and setting expectations with clients. When starting a new dashboard, determine the scale by asking yourself, or your team, these questions:

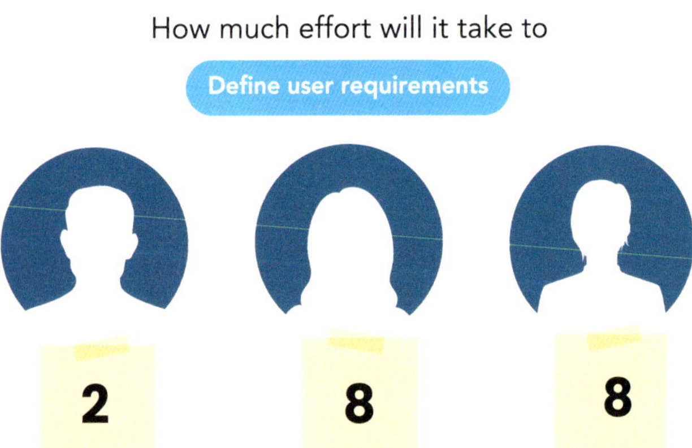
How much effort will it take to
Define user requirements
2
8
8
The much lower estimate for one of the team members is an opportunity to talk through the team's understanding of the tasks, complexity, and effort in order to come to a consensus.

FIGURE 3.5 Team members may estimate different levels of effort for the same task.

- **What information do the users need?** Consider the complexity of the request. Are you trying to communicate a snapshot of metrics or enable deeper analysis?
- **Is the data currently available?** Are there clearly defined data sources or metrics that can be used to address the analysis need? Dashboards leveraging existing data can be delivered more quickly than those that require setting up new data structures or reshaping tables.
- **What is the timeline for development?** When do the stakeholders need to have a dashboard?
- **How long will this dashboard be used?** Is the dashboard measuring a specific, time-bound campaign or will it be tracking KPIs over a longer arc of time? If the latter, you should expect to make enhancements.
- **How big is the audience using this dashboard?** Will the dashboard serve a small group of people or will it be accessed throughout the organization? Dashboards that have to serve larger audiences with differing needs will take longer to develop as interviews and feedback will take longer.

Managing the Work

Set *work cycles* with the team. How frequently are you expected to finish a phase of work on the dashboard? These time-bound increments are sometimes called *sprints* in Agile and are typically two or three weeks long. They enable the team to break the larger roadmap into smaller periods. Within each cycle, work together to identify which items from

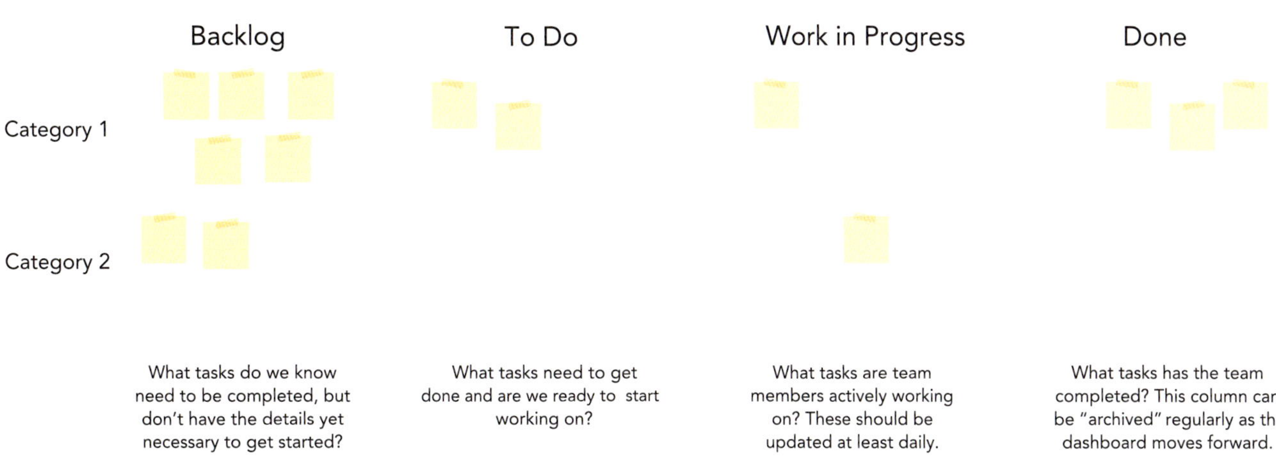

FIGURE 3.6 Kanban board where tasks are classified by status and category (e.g., team responsible or task type).

the backlog should be completed. These regular planning conversations help your team align on expectations.

Alternatively, if the dashboard development will be done in stages over an extended period, you could use a *kanban* management approach. This is a visual method to limit work in progress (WIP) and improve workflow, using a simple board to visualize the work (illustrated in Figure 3.6).

Instead of defining specific work cycles, progress continues over a longer time frame. You still maintain a shared backlog where tasks are marked as planned, in progress, or complete. However, rather than focusing on fixed milestones, the team limits WIP by finishing items already started before taking on new ones, reducing context switching.

We've summarized common benefits and challenges for dashboard developers across the two approaches in Figure 3.7.

Last, determine which *meetings* your team needs and who should attend. Schedule regular, brief stand-up meetings to discuss the current work and any impediments to include everyone on the team, prioritizing those heads down doing the work.

If there's a planning or prioritization decision to be made, make sure to invite your product owner to attend and weigh in. Use longer planning sessions to update the backlog and plan new work cycles, and hold routine retrospectives to reflect on the team's performance. Planning and retrospectives should be inclusive of anyone working on the team.

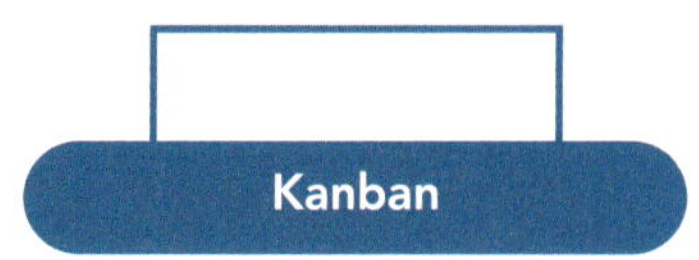

	Scrum	Kanban
Benefits	• Breaks work down into dedicated periods with the goal of releasing *something* each cycle • Works well when you have a dedicated team working on the dashboard build • Defined roles for scrum leader, product owner, and developer and dedicated meetings (Agile "ceremonies") support incremental progress	• Focuses on ongoing progress, moving work between status categories: to-do, in-progress, and done • Emphasizes focusing on completing one task at a time, minimizing the volume of tasks in "work in progress" • Less pressure to show incremental progress without having the dedicated sprint cycles
Challenges	• If the dashboard is one of many projects for the team members, availability to work on the dashboard may not align well with the work cycles • Ceremonies and roles may feel overwhelming for those new to Agile methods	• Board can be too simple to be useful or get too complicated to be manageable • Need to enforce "WIP limits" can be challenging for a new team used to multitasking

FIGURE 3.7 Comparison of challenges and benefits for dashboard developers across two common implementations of Agile.

You don't want to get stuck in a cycle where you're spending more time *managing* than actively building the dashboard. That's where your backlog of tasks comes in as a central source of truth for what the team is working on, and what still needs to be done.

Managing Scope Creep

One downside of gathering input from many users is that it can generate a long list of requirements. These may be difficult to accommodate in a single dashboard, leading to compromises on design, information density, and performance (rendering time).

Our job, as dashboard designers, is to work with our audience to understand their needs *and* help them prioritize their needs. That may mean breaking up what started as one request into multiple deliverables.

When a client asks Playfair Data, a leading dashboard and data visualization training studio, to build a dashboard, they first work to identify the key business questions and audience, scope the data needs, and *determine if the request is for one or many dashboards*. The team focuses on *quality over quantity*. One insightful dashboard is better than many unfocused ones, with the goal to guide clients away from "dashboard overload."

After building hundreds of dashboards, we've seen there isn't a single *right* way to build dashboards. However, having a shared set of expectations and breaking a large project into smaller pieces can help address many of the common challenges we face when crafting *dashboards that deliver*.

Chapter 4

Spark

Amanda Makulec and Andy Cotgreave

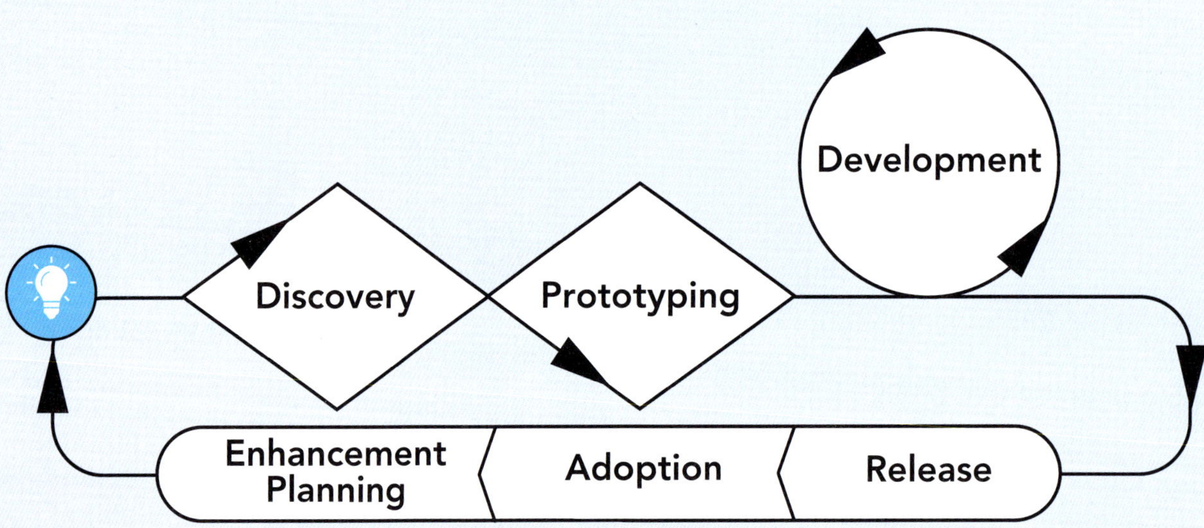

What is the Spark?

Every dashboard starts with some kind of spark (Figure 4.1). It's a catalyst: a moment, an idea, or a challenge that needs a solution.

The spark may be a question from an executive who needs real-time access to information. Or it may be an analyst, seeing the same ad hoc request show up in their inbox for a fourth week in a row who thinks, "How could we make answering that question easier?" Or even, as in the case of the NASA Earth Information Center featured in Chapter 26, it might be a public blog post by the NASA administrator!

Here are common scenarios we heard when interviewing leaders in the field around when and why to build a new dashboard:

- We have clear business questions and hypotheses and want to be able to explore them. The spark? *We need to see answers to known questions.*
- It takes two analysts three weeks to produce the reports we need to review every month. The spark? *We need to automate repetitive, time-wasting processes.*
- We ran a hackathon allowing anyone to find new insights in our data. There were some incredible outcomes we can capitalize on. The spark? *What useful ad hoc insights can we find and then automate to drive change?*

My Very First Dashboard: An Unusual "Spark"? (Andy)

When I look back to the first ever dashboard I built, I realize my spark was somewhat unusual: "How could I keep a tyrannical boss off my back?"

That was more than 20 years ago; I was working at a small company that researched fast-growing companies and published league tables ranking their growth. It was great fun interviewing CEOs of exciting companies, but the job had one problem: the company boss behaved like a sociopath.

At any time of any day, he might walk into the researchers' room and launch into a raging tirade focused on one person. Woe to anyone unable to answer a question instantly about their league table, even if caught off-guard. Never have I worked somewhere where I saw so many people reduced to tears.

I needed a means of defense from these unprovoked attacks.

The data for all our league tables was held in Excel spreadsheets. They were cumbersome because they had scores of columns. Since it was not a company that employed people for their data skills, information management was a bit of a mess.

I, however, was fascinated by Excel and enjoyed goofing around with formulae and macros. So, I figured I could make some charts and assemble them on a different worksheet. I laid them out so they'd fit onto a single sheet of paper. Now, any time the manager's anger might be directed toward me, I could simply hand him my printout and turn back to my screen.

It worked. It kept him off my back.

I showed colleagues they could do the same. Life improved.

Significantly buoyed by this success, I did some research around Excel charting and discovered that I had built was commonly called a "business dashboard." Who knew? The only name I'd given what I'd built was the "Get The Boss Off My Back" page.

That terrible boss led me to "dashboards" and changed my career. Grudgingly, I thank him.

Reflecting on this 20 years later, this is also a manifestation of the challenge I talk about in Chapter 30. What to call the thing I built was irrelevant to my situation.

A Spark for a Dashboard...and a Book! (Steve)

Two years after I founded Data Revelations, a prospective client contacted me to see if I could help them automate how they reported survey data findings. They had three analysts working full time for three weeks to produce a monthly report for their client, a major cable TV provider.

That's a lot of people working a lot of hours, and this was to serve just one big client.

The spark: Would a dashboard be able to automate the visualizations and allow the analysts do more analyzing and less busy work?

That's a very good spark.

During discovery I found out they were using Excel to create pages and pages of red, yellow, and green color-coded tables.

Yikes.

I remember having a conversation along these lines:

Me: Instead of just automating things would you be open to seeing a different way to visualize the data?

My client: Why? The tables are the way we do things and the way our client expects us to do things. They're the industry norms.

Me: Yes, but isn't your goal to make it easier and faster to make comparisons, see trends, spot outliers, and so on? Would you be open to seeing a few different ways to do this?

My client: Of course! If there really is a better way, we'd love to see it.

Me: Great! I'll build several prototypes, and we'll see which works best.

I built several prototypes. My client and I agreed that one of them was best and was considerably better than the "industry norms" approach. I also wrote a document explaining the merits of the new approach as I wanted to arm my client with something that would help them convince the VP at the cable company.[1]

How did things turn out?

My client *loved* the new approach, but that VP (who I never met but was apparently difficult to work with) stubbornly insisted on staying with what they had been using, despite all its drawbacks.

So, yes, we ended up with a lot of red, yellow, and green dashboards. But at least my client would have a better approach they could use with other clients.

[1]This document was the spark for *The Big Book of Dashboards*.

Why the Spark Matters

We know we shouldn't build dashboards for the sake of putting more charts into the world. We build them to inform, to enable decision-making, and to give someone the information they need to do something. But how do we design *dashboards that deliver* on that promise?

The process we outline in the subsequent chapters will help get you there, but you *need* a spark that starts the conversation around the dashboard's purpose and goals.

The spark is less about specific requirements and goals and more about *why* the dashboard needs to exist. Let your sparks be touchstones in the dashboard design process that you can go back to; don't let them become anchors that hold you back from iterating and shifting course when new ideas and directions emerge in the discovery process that we'll dive into next.

Chapter 5

Discovery

Amanda Makulec and Andy Cotgreave

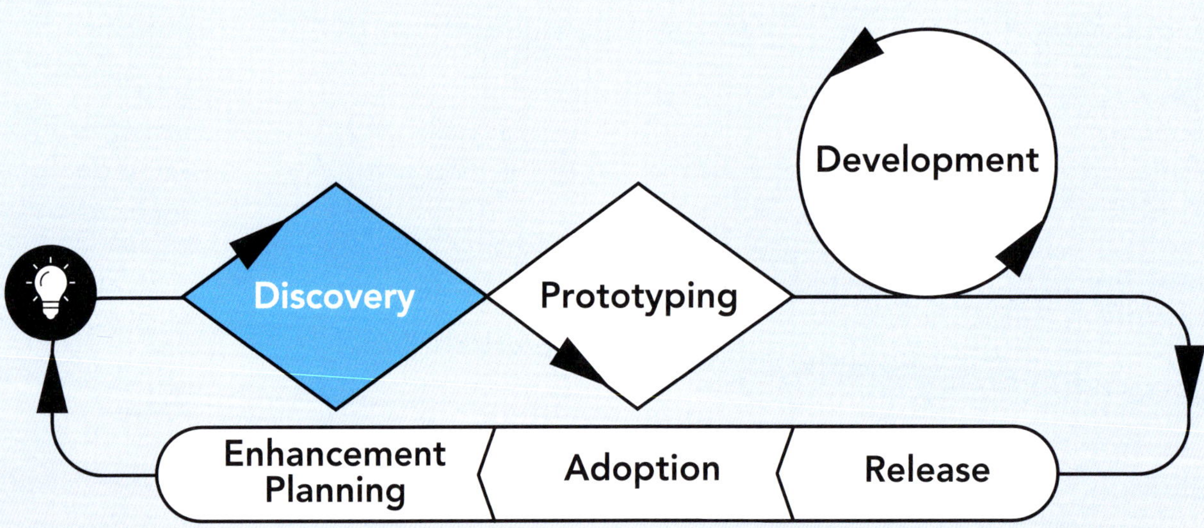

When we start a new dashboard, connecting to data and spinning up charts might seem like the quickest way to make progress. It's not. Diving in too fast is a route to an unfocused, unused dashboard that will require many overhauls.

You'll *save* time in the long run by doing two things first: define a clear purpose for the dashboard, including how to measure its success. That may include specific goals around creating a dashboard to eliminate a process or streamline tasks. Then, gather insights from users with a focused list of requirements.

The days or weeks at the start of your build are your opportunity for discovery, where techniques from design thinking and qualitative research help you understand your users. First, *diverge* to brainstorm with your users around the many data needs they have. Think broadly about their challenges. This helps surface unexpected ideas and opportunities. Then, *converge* on priority requirements for this specific dashboard. This helps you narrow the scope and prioritize users' needs.

This process will guide you to three key outcomes:

1. Define requirements.
2. Get feedback.
3. Create something meaningful.

You do this by working with end users, not delivering a product in isolation. Conversations from the start help build the relationship and trust between the development team and end users that can lead to greater enthusiasm and adoption later.

For simple dashboards designed for a focused group of users, discovery could take a few hours. For more complex dashboards with different user groups, plan for at least a week or two. You'll need time to listen to your users and synthesize what they share into a defined scope.

Let's walk through some of the practical tactics for using discovery to get those three key outcomes.

Define the Purpose

Having a **spark** is a start for a dashboard, but an enthusiastic spark doesn't always come with a clear goal.

Identify the business or organizational need for this dashboard. What will be different about how the organization uses data because this dashboard exists? It's critical to get this right and to revisit as you design the dashboard.

Consider three goals when defining the purpose with your users:

1. **Be clear.** Write down the purpose: Why does this dashboard exist? You will continue to expand on user needs throughout development, but narrow in on two to three sentences that define the dashboard's reason for being. This is particularly important if you're working with new stakeholders or clients and need to understand how the tool fits in the organization.

2. **Be specific.** Who is going to use this dashboard, and how do the business needs translate into measurable metrics? How will you know if a dashboard is successful, and what data will you track to monitor that success? Identifying the metrics you'll display in your BANs (Big-Ass Numbers) and charts will be an ongoing process, but having specific recommendations for key performance indicators from the start can help to focus conversations.
3. **Be achievable.** Stay focused and ensure the size/scale of the dashboard is reasonable based on the time, technology, and budget constraints you have.

Don't worry about limiting the scope for your first release. That doesn't mean you'll never add new features. Think of a dashboard as an evolving piece of software; there are features you'll build *now* in your first release, *soon* (perhaps in the second release), and in later stages of the framework. You want to make sure that your users also understand that *not now* doesn't always mean *never*.

Gather Insights from Users

To create a dashboard that delivers, you need to spend time listening to your users. It's not just dashboard designers who'll tell you that, but great product designers, engineers, marketers – all roles where design starts with understanding your user.

Even if you've been working building dashboards for your company for a while and have some understanding of your users' needs, each new dashboard presents a new opportunity to engage.

Great advice, sure, but how do you go about it?

First, identify who you expect your dashboard users to be. This could be people in specific departments or roles, or even specific names. Create meaningful groups who you expect to have similar data needs. Then, create space to listen to users' talk about their needs and preferences through structured approaches, rather than long, open-ended conversations. Let's dig into some of those techniques.

Discovery Techniques

We want to help you build your toolbox for facilitating conversations, gathering information, and codifying what you hear into concrete, specific outcomes.

While there are many techniques you can borrow from design, ethnography, and qualitative research to explore user needs, we've narrowed the list to five different methods we've used to understand our dashboard users better.

In Table 5.1, we summarize those five approaches, and in the next chapter, we'll dive deep into what they are and how you can use them. We'll finish walking through the discovery steps before getting into the weeds, though.

Where to Find More Details on Discovery Techniques

You can also find downloadable supplemental materials for facilitating these processes on DashboardsthatDeliver.com.

TABLE 5.1 Discovery techniques and why we use them.

Method	What you do	What information it gives us
Interviews	Conduct a series of one-on-one and group interviews with users who represent different stakeholder groups and needs.	An understanding of how people will use the dashboard, and user preferences.
User Personas	Using interview insights, create illustrative personas representing the needs and preferences of your different user groups, prioritizing the groups that represent the majority of your users.	A portrait of your users that is a bit more human (and easier to empathize with) than job titles.
User Stories	For each persona and their representative groups, define what kind of information is needed and how that information will be used. You can use the same user story structure we used before; just be more granular.	Defined requirements on a more granular level for each stakeholder group.
Journey Maps	For each persona, map when they access data across an applicable time period (month, quarter), including routine team meetings, reporting deadlines, and how they feel about existing data tools.	Metrics on how often people access data, what data they access, and if they are satisfied with the tools and systems they have.
Continuum Maps	Map your personas' levels of data literacy, subject-matter expertise, current engagement with data, and level of granularity needed in the data. Determine if the needs across groups are different enough to merit building separate dashboards instead of one big one.	A comparison of user needs beyond metrics, including users' data fluency. This can help you decide whether multiple dashboards are warranted or if one dashboard can satisfy the needs of all the users who will be accessing it.

Synthesizing Insights

You've gathered all of this information and have a folder of notes and transcripts. Now shift into the second part of the discovery double diamond: converging on the specific user needs for this dashboard.

The different pieces – persona, user story, journey map, and continuum – provide a shared snapshot of your users. You can go back to them and ask, "Does what we've designed meet these needs?" You're likely to have more than one user profile at this stage in your process. See Figure 5.1.

Synthesizing insights about your users into something you can look at serves two purposes. Users can review and provide feedback on the needs you've captured and synthesized. You also create visual progress toward a working dashboard, which can be particularly helpful when working with clients who want to *see* progress.

We've seen ways that user personas and other discovery outcomes aren't just a nice visual asset in a slide set. Chapter 19, "Children's Hospital Association Dashboard," describes a situation where user portraits were vital to the success of the dashboard.

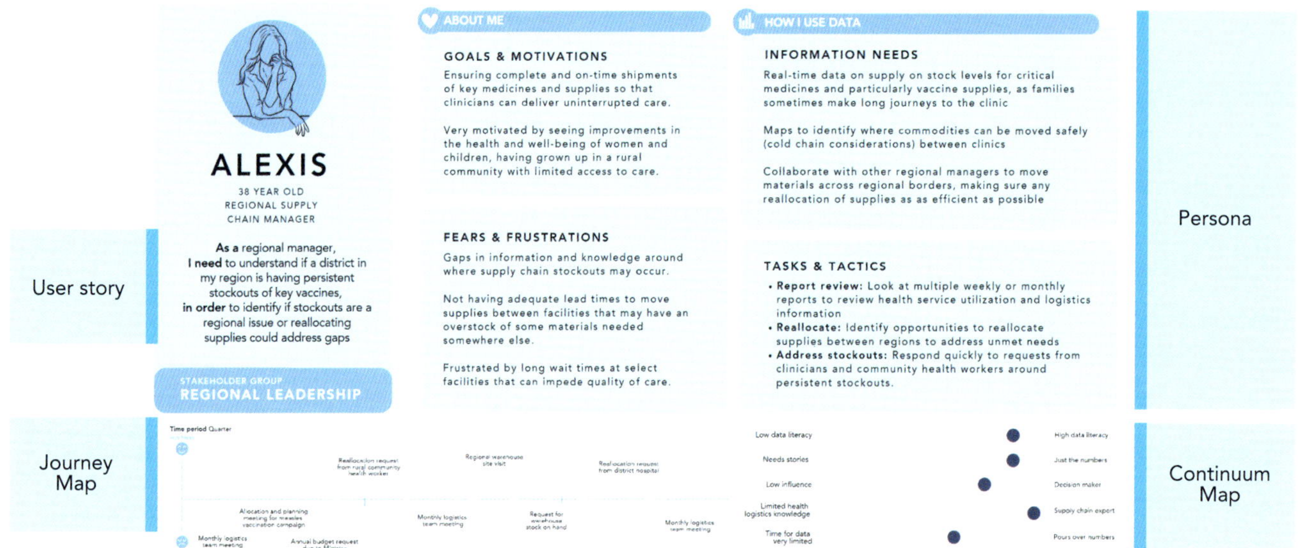

FIGURE 5.1 Illustrative portrait of a user, including a persona, priority user story, journey map, and continuum map to compare with other stakeholders.

With a clearer picture of who our users are, what information they need, how and when they'll use that information, and other insights you've picked up along the way, you can sit down and translate those needs into clear requirements and revisit these user profiles throughout the design process.

Defining Requirements

Armed with a clear purpose for the dashboard and a better understanding of who your users are, it's time to get more specific. What are the shared needs across your different stakeholder groups, and how will those translate into charts and features on the dashboard? We call these *requirements*.

What Are *Requirements*?

Requirements are the specific features a dashboard needs to have for the end users to find the dashboard useful.

Requirements answer how we'll achieve the dashboard's purpose. Functionally, they're a list of features synthesized from your discovery work, specific enough to translate into components on the dashboard.

I've worked on many different public health dashboards that were developed by plotting data for prescriptive lists of key metrics – for example, the number of instances where a commodity wasn't available (stockouts) by month and facility. If the metrics are useful to the users, the dashboard is usually *fine* but not great. Instead, we want our requirements for a dashboard that delivers to include more specifics on how the user will act on the data.

Let's stick with the example of a logistics dashboard. One user could be the regional manager. We can craft a more specific requirement with our user story structure. Instead of our list of requirements just saying "data on stockouts," we describe who will use the data and how:

> *As a regional manager, I need to understand if a district in my region is having persistent stockouts of key vaccines in order to identify if stockouts are a regional issue or if reallocating supplies could address gaps.*

For your dashboard, review your discovery insights. Identify shared needs and write down a list of requirements that will be the start of your development backlog. This may include specific data needs (like the earlier user story) and analysis needs (like drilling down from state to county level data). Find a tool that allows you to create cards, list requirements in a spreadsheet, or keep things simple by writing down ideas for requirements with pen and paper so you can sort and prioritize.

Defining specific requirements for the dashboard helps you focus and avoid adding charts or features that feel nice to have but don't serve a clear need. You often won't be able to address every requirement in a new dashboard, which is why ruthless prioritization is key.

Once you have a starting list of requirements, make time for team discussions. Include your product owner and developers, balancing user needs and feasibility within the project timeline. Discuss which requirements are the highest priority and must be included to deliver a successful dashboard. Which would be nice to have or could be postponed to a future release? Consider which of the requirements serves multiple stakeholders' needs or serves the needs of a high priority stakeholder (like an executive).

What you learn during discovery informs the design and development going forward. You'll keep revisiting the requirements you've defined in discovery throughout prototyping and development.

Documenting Basic Requirements

From your discovery work with users, you'll gather insights on how and where the dashboard will be accessed. These are necessary for determining the specifications for this particular dashboard.

Think of this as building out your design brief. Identify:

- Where will the dashboard be accessed? On a computer screen? A mobile device? Email? Slack? Print? This will determine the dimensions and sizing of the dashboard.
- Will it be embedded? This also may impact dimensions and functionality.
- How often will the data be updated?
- What security considerations are there, if any? Are there different user groups who should have different levels of access?

Mapping Requirements to Metrics

Your requirements, which typically focus on a business need for the data, need to be translated into data-speak. That means reading through each requirement and defining:

- What **metrics (calculations)** do I need to include to address this need?
- What **data (fields)** do I need for my charts, filters, and calculations?
- How **granular** does the data source need to be? Be mindful that more granular data typically means larger data volume, which can influence rendering time and performance.
- **Does this data already exist,** or do I need to collect new information? Are the existing sources in tidy tables or will additional data cleaning or transformation be required?

Let's revisit our sample user story:

> *As a regional manager, I need to understand if a district in my region is having persistent stockouts of key vaccines in order to identify if stockouts are a regional issue or reallocating supplies could address gaps.*

To address this requirement, we'll need:

- **Metrics:** Percent stock on hand, full stock availability (these are often defined through organizational or industry standards).
- **Data:** Date, facility, region, vaccine name, product specific stockouts or closing balance at end of resupply period.
- **Granularity:** Daily, health facility level.
- **Does the data exist?** Maybe. We would need to confirm access to facility level data tables.

Building Your Data Model

As you plan the front-end design and requirements, it's important to consider what data is available or should be collected to address key user needs.

In smaller projects or personal dashboards, you may need only a single data table (see Chapter 13, "Fitness Goal Tracker"). On the other hand, larger projects might require sourcing information and chart components from various entities, agencies and collaborators (see Chapter 26, "NASA's Earth Information Center | earth.gov").

Most enterprise reporting dashboards fall somewhere in between, typically drawing from existing data warehouses or data collection infrastructure.

Regardless of your dashboard's scale, don't wait until development to assess data availability. You don't want to present prototypes or design concepts that promise data you cannot deliver. Consider what the minimum viable dataset looks like, focusing on a data structure with the smallest volume *and* the granularity required.

More Details on Data Projects

If you're interested in exploring the data foundations of dashboards further, read Christine Haskell's *Driving Data Projects*, (dtdbook.com/link6).

Set Measures for Dashboard Success

Why We Think About Success at the Start

How will you know if your dashboard delivers for your users? You should set clear metrics for success as part of discovery.

When you're supporting a new team on a dashboard project and you ask someone early on what success looks like, they may not know.

Work in partnership with your users and build that trust early on, and you'll find that people are more likely to let their guard down and let you know what success looks like. Sometimes, it even helps to have an outsider asking, "What does success look like?" That outsider could be you as the dashboard designer, if you're not part of the core team.

Instead of proposing a specific list of metrics for every dashboard to use, we suggest thinking about two *types* of success for your dashboard:

- **Little "s" success** captures things you can count like the number of unique users or number of views, often available in near real time (*outputs* from launching the dashboard)
- **Big "S" success** focuses on the ways the dashboard informs decisions and impacts the organization in bigger ways (the *impact* of launching the dashboard)

These two types of measures have their own value. Document them as you define them, along with how you'll collect the necessary data: planning from the start ensures you have access to the information you need to assess success after launch.

Let's unpack what kinds of measures fall in each category.

Little "s" Success Measures

We often jump to dashboard usage as a benchmark for success. Usage statistics can give clues about how often people use the dashboard but often tell an incomplete story.

Where usage data *can* be particularly helpful is identifying who is using the dashboard. In many tools where a dashboard is published to the cloud or a server, you can identify who is viewing the dashboard and how frequently. Frequent users would be a great cohort to follow up with as "super users" to gather feedback or engage as champions for wider adoption.

From our interviews, here are three common examples of tracking little "s" measures of success, including:

- **Number of users or views:** Track usage of dashboards as a starting place and weight usage by user type, which could include segmenting by role, new/repeat users, or other categories
- **Change requests:** If a CEO or other key stakeholders keep requesting changes and additions it means they are using the dashboard. (see Chapter 16, "Splash Project WISE Dashboard," and Chapter 24, "Professional Racing Team Race Strategy Dashboard," for examples)

- **New users:** Track new users who request access or are added to the user list. If a CEO or key stakeholder is actively requesting to add more people to the distribution list over time for the dashboard, it is even better.

Big "S" Success Measures

When an executive asks you how the dashboard impacted the organization, you need more than a count of visits to the dashboard to make the case for continuing to invest in analytics and dashboard development. This is where our Big "S" measures come into play.

Ryan Sleeper, CEO of Playfair Data, made the case that *quality* of usage is more important the *quantity*. That could mean monitoring how two or three key decision makers refer to a dashboard to inform a million-dollar investment decision each quarter, or logging how a website analytics dashboard flagged an ecommerce website outage where every hour of downtime costs the company thousands in lost revenue.

Capturing these bigger impacts of a dashboard requires a more qualitative approach. The more you've engaged your users as partners in the design process, the more likely they are to share moments where the dashboard had an impact.

While you could be lucky enough to get an email bursting with excitement about how *your dashboard* made a difference, make a point to reach out regularly to your users to ask for specific examples. Consider three common ways dashboards have an impact:

- **Enabling decision-making.** This could translate into impacts ranging from operational efficiencies to lives saved. Ask your users what decisions the dashboard enabled over the last period. Focus on the business or organizational value.
- **Making data analytics more self-service.** You can monitor how frequently you have to say "Let me get back to you" when a user has a data-related question that requires extra ad hoc analysis time. More instances of needing follow ups means the dashboard is missing the mark; lower means the dashboard is serving user needs and moving the data closer to the decision-makers.
- **Accessing analytics and saving technology costs.** Dashboards often centralize analytics from across various spreadsheets or tools. Identifying where the dashboard enabled decisions that saved the company money on other business intelligence tools or product optimizations, for example, allows them to quickly identify and fix underperforming products.

Discovery Checklist

We've been comprehensive in this chapter, which comes at the expense of simplicity. The reality is that many dashboards fail not because they aren't well designed, but because they don't address user needs.

Without spending enough time in discovery, teams can find themselves reworking dashboards very late in the process or, even worse, failing to see adoption of the dashboard you invested your time in.

Focusing on the key outcomes, discovery should offer a clear understanding of your stakeholder needs and the purpose the new dashboard will serve. This will include:

User insights clearly defining who will use the dashboard and their needs and preferences:

- User interview notes and summaries
- Personas and mindsets
- Journey maps

Requirements for what the dashboard needs to deliver:

- Use cases for when the dashboard will be used
- Defined requirements and user stories for the metrics to be included
- A shared understanding of success

In the next chapter, we'll dive deeper into these discovery techniques.

Chapter 6

Discovery Techniques

Amanda Makulec and Andy Cotgreave

What Discovery Techniques Do I *Have* to Use?

Most data visualization teachers, including us, will tell you to start with your audience, and that's certainly what discovery focuses on. But that's where sometimes we get stuck. *How am I supposed to make sense of what my audience needs?*

Each technique outlined in this chapter is designed to add to your toolbox of ways to facilitate conversations, gather information, and codify what you hear into concrete, specific outcomes that you can sit down and review as a team.

The best way to define requirements and get feedback comes from working with end users, not delivering a product in isolation. Conversations at the start of the design process help build the relationship and trust between the development team and end users that lead to better adoption later.

So, where to start? At a minimum, try to conduct a few interviews with representatives from different segments of your users.

Even short interviews do two key things. First, they give you insights about user needs, which sometimes validate your own assumptions. Second, they help you build a relationship with your users by making them feel heard. This makes it easier to go back to them and ask for feedback throughout the design process.

Also, remember that you don't need to talk to *every* potential user, just a representative sample. If after interviewing six different people you're hearing the same needs, you've likely hit on the priority requirements for your dashboard.

A Use Case to Illustrate the Discovery Phase

HERE'S the scenario: Let's imagine we're working on a new vaccine supply chain dashboard for a national department of health.

As a member of a health informatics team, you've been tasked with developing a new logistics dashboard that integrates population, health outcome, and supply chain data to improve the allocation and distribution of key health commodities. These include family planning supplies and vaccines, which have specific cold chain requirements for transport and storage.

The primary user group for the dashboard is the department's regional leadership. They will use it to address stockouts (when vaccines are needed but not available) and ensure uninterrupted care at their clinics. Secondary users include national leadership and community health workers. They also access the dashboard for monitoring and identifying where services are currently available when referring to a clinic.

The timeline for releasing the dashboard is two months, with the goal to release before the next quarterly distribution of vaccines, so you're kicking off the process of understanding the end users through a series of short interviews and mapping key needs and requirements.

Even if you're not a health logistics enthusiast, this example has some common elements of dashboards: stakeholders looking for different levels of data granularity; different levels of data literacy; and varying amounts of subject-matter expertise.

Let's walk through the five discovery techniques we outlined in the previous chapter. Each of these will help you understand your users more but is not *required* to build a great dashboard. Work within the time constraints you have, and use these techniques as a starting place to build open communication between you and your users.

Supplemental Materials and Facilitation Guides

You can find more detailed materials, such as sample lists of discovery interview questions, on the supplemental materials available on DashboardsThatDeliver.com.

Why Include Infrequent Dashboard Users in Our Research? (Amanda)

Does it seem odd to include our infrequent users on that list? Hearing from people who sit on the extremes of how a tool gets used can yield great insights! Maybe the current data tools just don't serve their needs, so they just ignore them entirely.

This focus on extremes is borrowed from an ah-ha moment I had visiting IDEO, a design consultancy, in San Francisco. A former colleague worked there and gave us a tour, showing different examples of products the team had helped develop. On one shelf was a set of kitchen implements with novel hand grips. As an enthusiastic cook, I asked a bit more about the design process. She asked me to guess what groups of people they did their user testing with.

"Chefs?" I said. That one was correct. But I would never have guessed the other group: very young children who had never used a whisk before. This mix gave them insights about how someone with deep experience handled the tool but also how someone who was just learning would handle it, as the goal was to create broadly inclusive kitchen implements.

Just because a kid doesn't know how to use a whisk right now, doesn't mean they can't learn. And just because some of your potential users don't use the existing data analysis tools now doesn't mean they won't use yours.

Discovery Method #1: Interviews

This is perhaps the most obvious. Set up dedicated time to talk to users about what they want from the dashboard. You can do this through one-on-one interviews or in small focus groups.

When selecting users to include, consider:

- Which roles or groups need to be represented?
- Who are the current users who you hope will use the dashboard frequently?
- Who are people we expect to use the data, but don't?

For our vaccine supply chain dashboard, we would first identify the different user groups who represent different needs, such as:

- **Regional leadership**, who need to make decisions around where to allocate vaccine supplies from the regional warehouse or between clinics within the area
- **National supply chain leadership**, who need data to inform budgeting and allocation decisions on a national scale
- **Health workers**, who need to know what supplies they have on hand at their health facility, expected demand, and when they need to request any supplemental resupply for periods with high demand like outreach campaigns

During the interviews, ask broad, open-ended questions to give your users space to talk about their needs and preferences. Take notes, synthesize themes from across different users, and use these insights to inform development of user personas and user stories (more on each of these follows).

Discovery Technique #2: User Stories

User stories help you plan what your dashboard will do. They define the fundamental goal of the dashboard and help with more detailed requirements later.

Recall from Chapter 5, our user story structure is adapted from software development and is as follows:

As a <user/role/stakeholder >
I need <some kind of information >
In order to <do something >.

Great user stories also:

- **Stay focused.** The user story should be succinct enough to be met with one feature (chart, filter, etc.) that could be delivered within a couple of days. Think at the unit of charts not dashboards.
- **Stay brief enough to fit on an index card.** Well-written user stories should be short; think of something that could fit on an index card. This size constraint encourages the development team to be specific and focused when writing user stories, instead of trying to pack in 20 functions in a single story.

At a high level, this approach helps us gain insights into our user's most pressing needs, which not only inform what charts and metrics to include but also how to prioritize the placement and size of various elements on the dashboard. Critical information may be prioritized in the layout by positioning it near the top of the page, while charts that address key questions can be allocated more visual space to ensure they stand out.

For our regional manager Alexis, a priority user story can give us some design clues (Figure 6.1)

The hardest part of writing a user story often lies in clearly defining the "in order to...." component. Users list metrics they want to see but are often vague when describing how they will actually use those numbers.

For a dashboard to offer value beyond merely providing reporting numbers for a slide deck, you must understand the decisions and actions the data will drive.

In the example in Figure 6.1, the "I need" highlights a snapshot of a region to understand stockouts. However, the "in order to" reveals a deeper requirement for the dashboard: the regional manager needs to see their data in the context of how other regions are performing. The data must also be granular enough to pinpoint opportunities, such as identifying regions with overstock that

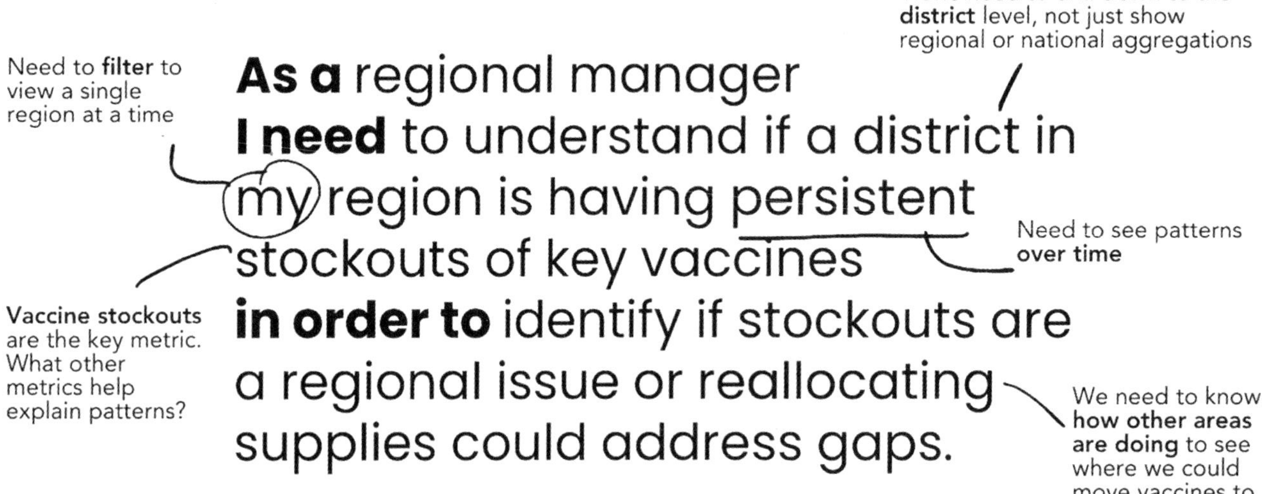

FIGURE 6.1 Sample user story for Alexis as a regional supply chain manager and how the story components give us design clues.

could potentially supply vaccines to areas experiencing stockouts.

User stories can also be helpful if you're using GenAI tools for brainstorming chart types. The user story has a defined role, need, and goal, which usefully is also a good prompt style for chat-based GenAI tools. Once you get to your prototyping phase, consider adapting user stories into prompts to brainstorm chart suggestions if GenAI tools are part of your workflow.

Discovery Method #3: User Personas

User personas help to clarify who your users are, beyond job descriptions and titles. Typically, they include a fictitious name (not someone on the team!), the stakeholder group they belong to, and information about likes, needs, pain points, and frustrations. Sometimes personas also include a demographic profile that is illustrative of a group of people.

Personas are one of those concepts best illustrated with a practical example. Let's go back to our new vaccine supply chain dashboard use case.

You work through a series of interviews and focus on each user group's responsibilities:

- **Regional leadership** responsible for the distribution of the vaccines according to population size and need
- **National health leadership** who are looking at the whole system and the progress toward national vaccination coverage targets
- **Community health workers** who play a critical role in last-mile vaccine distribution and need to know when vaccines are available for mobile distribution

For each group, we synthesize insights from our interviews into general persona.

Figure 6.2 shows an example.

Why assign each persona a name? Referring to a person instead of a job title can make it easier for your team to empathize with users. For example, saying "What would Alexis think?" can be more relatable and effective than asking "What do our regional leaders think?"

One challenge with personas is that they can reinforce biased perceptions of our users. When we build a persona from scratch, we often rely on our own assumptions about the audience's wants and needs. Insights from interviews are key. Without them, we are likely to document what we *think* we know, rather than verifying those insights directly with the actual users.

You can avoid these issues by validating your personas with your users. That can include sharing the actual personas with users for feedback and asking if they identify with one (or more) of them.

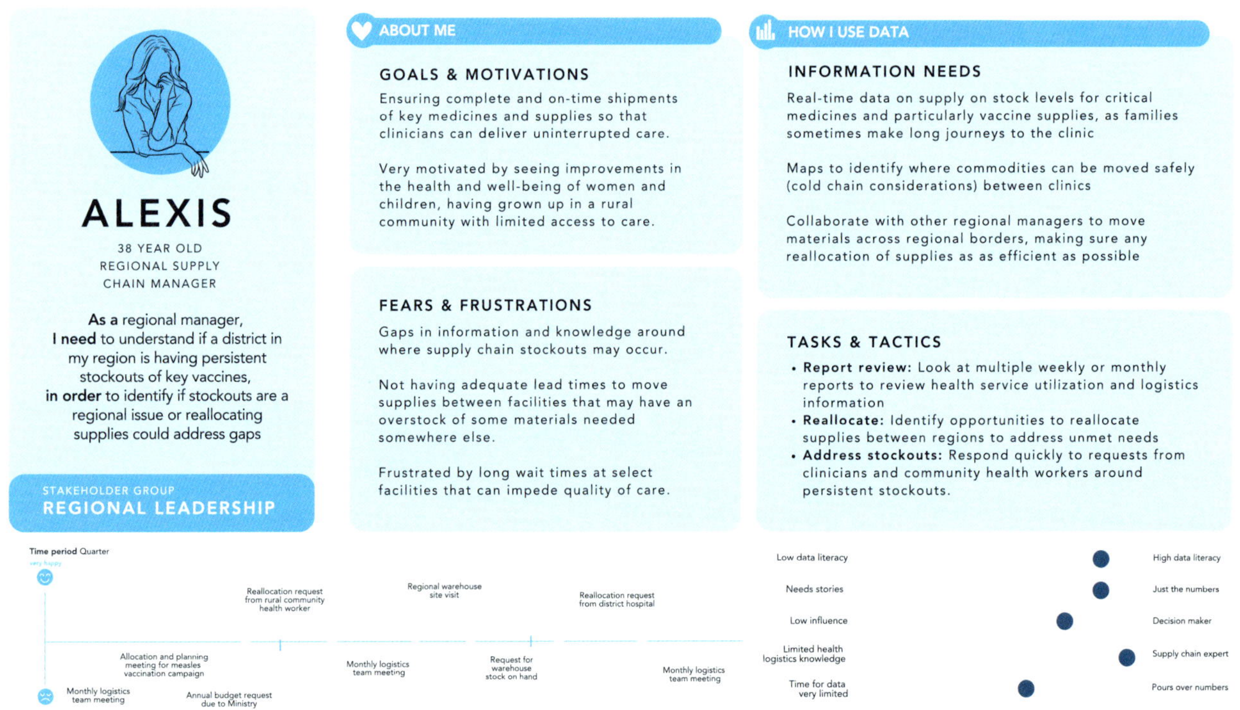

FIGURE 6.2 Illustrative persona for a regional leadership within a department of health (shared in Chapter 5).

Discovery Technique #4: Journey Maps

We also need to think about *when* our audience will use the dashboard. And to think about when they'll use this new analytical tool, we need to understand how they're currently accessing data and how they feel about the tools they have available.

What are the specific meetings or moments throughout a month or quarter when our user needs the data in this new dashboard? What resources do they currently use for this information, or is there nothing available? Do they particularly like any of these tools?

Journey maps are timelines of key touchpoints for a stakeholder to access information (Figure 6.3). They

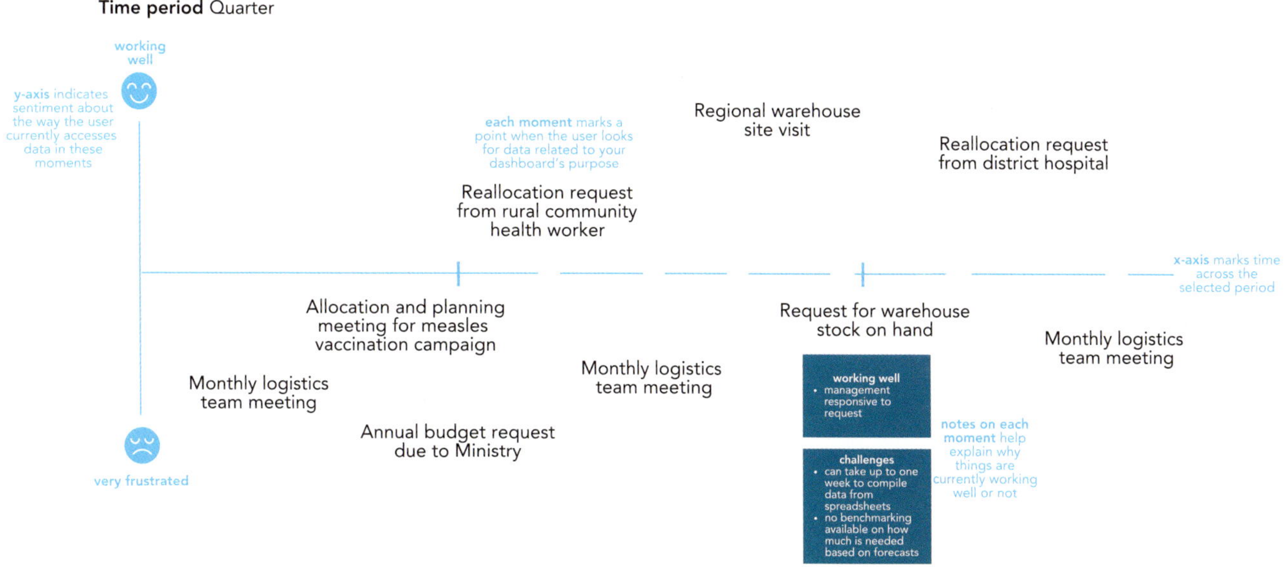

FIGURE 6.3 Journey map components showing high points and pain points for accessing data.

can be crafted during your discovery interviews, asking users to physically add moments along the blank map, or compiled from across your interviews to represent the perspectives of different users. Each of the points on the map may also show times when a user *wants* access to information but does not currently have an easy way to find it.

In addition to the linear aspect of the map, journey maps add a y-axis to capture *sentiment:* how do you *feel* about the current way you access information at a given time? For moments going well, users share what they like and for moments going poorly, identify the specific pain points. In Figure 6.3 we see that Alexis is happy with her access to information during the quarterly regional warehouse site visit and reallocation requests from different stakeholders, but frustrated with the monthly stockout reviews and other planning tasks that require access to information.

Mapping out these moments over a specific period gives you contextual clues about where the dashboard will be used. In addition, you'll surface insights into the current tools your audience uses to meet their data needs. If your users love a current slide deck or report, ask to see what it looks like and probe on what they like about it. Those ideas can inform some of your design choices on the new dashboard.

These insights inform the frequency with which the data needs to be refreshed, the sizing (e.g., viewing on a tablet during health center site visits brings different design constraints than viewing on a laptop), and the organization of information.

Journey maps are best curated in real time with a whiteboard (in-person) or a virtual whiteboarding tool (like Mural or Miro). You can even use a simple layout on a PowerPoint slide.

Discovery Technique #5: Continuum Mapping

Continuum mapping uses visualization to compare user groups across key categories, such as subject-matter expertise and data literacy. This helps identify differences and similarities, specifically relating to how they interact with the dashboard and the domain knowledge they have.

Let's look at an example in Figure 6.4. Here, we map our three user groups (regional leadership, community health workers, and national supply chain leaders) to five categories.

Each row represents a category we need to take into consideration when designing a new dashboard.

Choose categories that impact the success of your dashboard. Some are general (such as data literacy, subject-matter expertise, and time available). Others might be more specific to your domain. For example, health logistics knowledge is a key category for determining how much detail users need.

FIGURE 6.4 Continuum map of key user features and the approximated position of three different stakeholder groups.

The positioning of the dots doesn't have to be precise; the goal is to get a general picture of the position of each group. It's the relative positions of the dots that are most important.

Interpreting a Continuum Map

Let's look at how to read and act on a continuum map.

Looking Across the Individual Categories

Take a look at the first two rows in Figure 6.4. They show us that community health workers have a lower data literacy level than the other groups. They also prefer narrative insights over too many numbers. This tells us we might need to keep our chart types simpler and add some dynamic text regions in order to accommodate everyone.

Comparing the Groups

Continuum maps let you compare all your groups and assess if one dashboard design can feasibly meet the needs of all your groups. It might be that, through this process, you realize you cannot meet the needs of all user groups in a single dashboard.

Figure 6.5 shows three hypothetical situations you might see when mapping your users.

If all groups are similar (A), you'll likely require less customization to meet individual group needs. If two user groups cluster together but a third is distinct (B), or the groups all have contrasting profiles (C), you will need to customize the dashboard to address each groups' differences. You might also need to provide additional support during publication and user adoption, ensuring that each group gets the most value from the dashboard. You might even need a different dashboard for each group.

Thinking more specifically about our healthcare example in Figure 6.5, the skills, needs, and

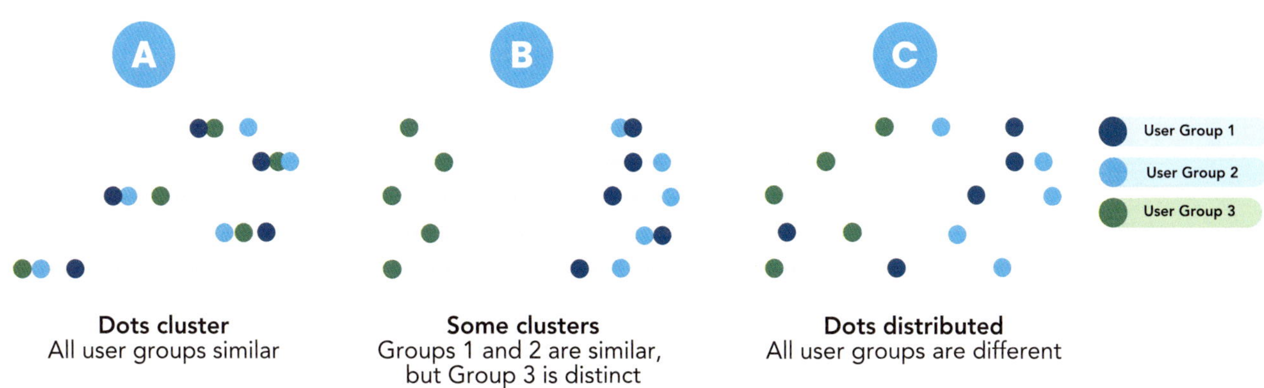

FIGURE 6.5 Three different examples comparing user groups, where A has three similar groups, B has two similar groups, and C has three very different groups.

preferences of the regional and national leaders look distinctly different from the information needs of the community health workers.

This big difference should make the team pause: *Can we meet the needs of all three groups at once? Or do we need to build distinctly different dashboards?*

In this case, we may need to create a separate dashboard for our community health workers, who need a simpler representation of the data and have much lower levels of data literacy and subject-matter expertise than our other stakeholders. The use cases for the dashboard would also be different, focused on providing real-time availability of services, creating quarterly reports, and identifying areas for increased community engagement.

Summary

In this chapter, we've gone into more detail on how to use five different techniques to better understand your dashboard users:

- Interviews
- User stories
- User personas
- Journey maps
- Continuum maps

Each approach gives you new insights as a designer, creates materials to reference as a team, and can be shared with users to validate that your understanding of their needs is accurate.

Chapter 7

Prototyping

Amanda Makulec and Andy Cotgreave

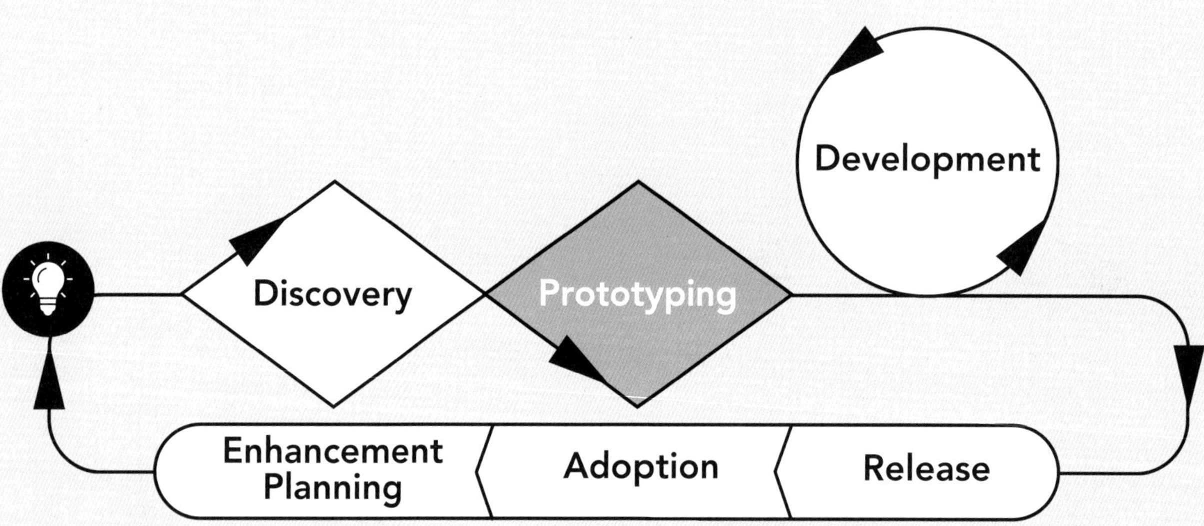

"Plan slow. Act fast."
—Bent Flyvbjerg and Dan Gardner,
How Big Things Get Done

From Discovery you have an idea of who your users are and why they need a dashboard. Now it's time for prototyping, where you will explore charts, layouts, and interactivity. In this phase, you will collaborate with your users and experiment with different dashboard designs.

We divide prototyping into two parts within the "double diamond" framework introduced in discovery (Figure 7.1). As you move through the second phase, you'll design increasingly higher-fidelity representations of what your dashboard will look like. In the first part, ideation, you and your users will generate (and throw away!) many dashboard concepts. Then, you move toward a final prototype that responds to your users' needs. This is similar to the Agile principle of getting to a minimum viable product.

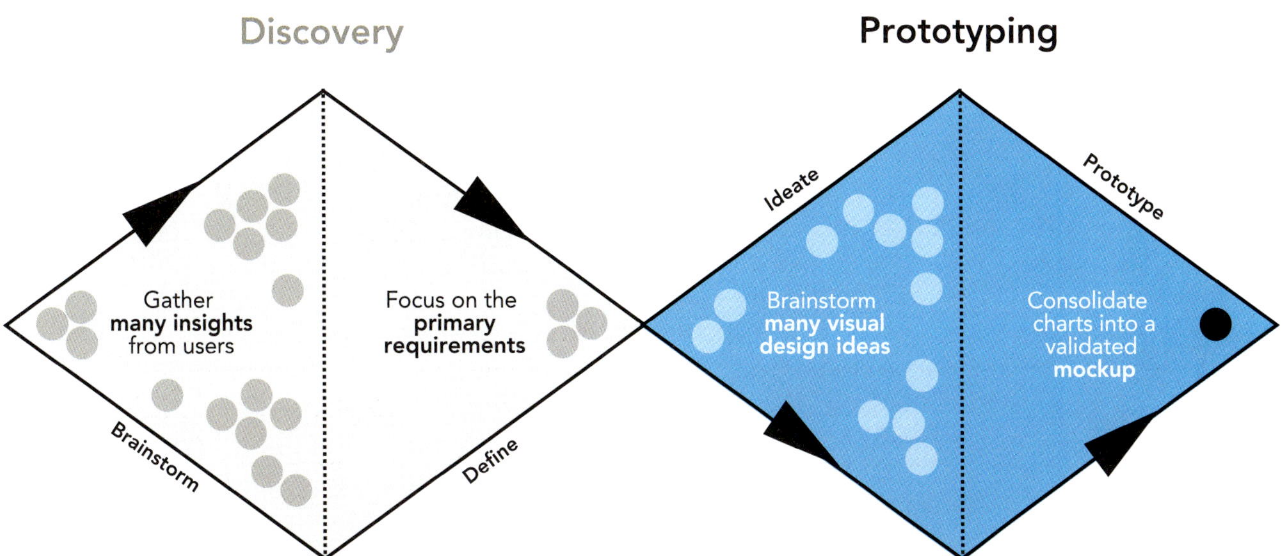

FIGURE 7.1 Design double diamond framework for discovery and prototyping illustrating how prototyping goes broad and then narrows in on a specific design concept.

What Is a Minimum Viable Product?

IMAGINE a user who wants to travel from A to B. The first mode of transport you build might be a skateboard. It does the job, but they might complain it's unstable and too slow. So next you build a bicycle. It's still slow, but they're getting to their destination, and they tell you they enjoy the feeling of wind in their hair. Finally, you build a car with an open top. It's fast and lets the wind flow through their hair. They're delighted! They've been involved in the process and seen their feedback incorporated. Now imagine instead you start off by building the car piece by piece. You give them a wheel. They have no clue what to do with that. Then you give them all the wheels on a chassis. Again, you'll be met with confusion. Finally, you show them a finished car: a luxury SUV. Since they've provided no feedback along the way, it's not the car they wanted at all. You built them an SUV, but they wanted a zippy little convertible. Building the skateboard first is the Agile principle of building the earliest, or minimum viable product.

Gathering Feedback

During prototyping, we create quick concepts with sketches and lightweight designs. Then we gather feedback on each new version. These feedback loops are quick! Changes based on user feedback at this stage are much quicker and cheaper than during development. These quick feedback loops also increase engagement, as your users weigh in on different design ideas.

Your Users' Likely First Response

Over years of working on dashboards, we've seen that even when users can articulate their needs very well, your first designs will not be perfect. When you present your first mockup your end users might exclaim, "Noooo, that's not what I meant at all! What I meant was x, y, z." It can feel disheartening, but this is a positive moment: the movement toward clarity. It's *why* we prototype.

Feedback Expectations

When requesting feedback, be specific about the phase of development you're in and what kind of feedback you're looking for. During prototyping, you should be working with smaller groups of people. Since you'll be using low-fidelity tools, you can make extensive changes quickly and cheaply. Later, in the development phase, you'll be doing more nuanced usability testing, possibly with larger groups. Changes at that point are expensive, so you are likely only to be able to respond to small changes to your dashboard.

Who Is the Expert?

When you work with your users, always keep in mind who the expert is. Is it your *users*, who know the business and what they need? Is it *you*, who understands the underlying data and how to build dashboards? It's *both* groups. Your job is to listen to feedback, find the root reason behind their notes, and then work with your users to build the best visual path to the insight they need.

Feedback loops between designer and user start in prototyping, continue into development, and move through the maintenance and enhancement phase. These loops give you valuable feedback and allow users to see progress. Sometimes, your user will disagree with your design concepts. While it can be a challenge to receive tough feedback, remember that honesty shows you're building trust with your users.

The Five Whys Technique

A good way to dig deeper into user feedback is to use the "Five Whys" technique, a problem-solving method to uncover the root cause of an issue. Imagine you've built a bar chart showing monthly sales for a clothing company. The Five Whys conversation might go like this:

User: "I don't like this bar chart."

You: "Why?"

User: "Because it's confusing to me."

You: "Why is it confusing?"

User: "Because I need more granular information about different sites. This just aggregates everything together."

You: "Why do you need granular information about different sites?"

User: "Because I need to understand trends in weekly sales volume at each store."

You: "Why?"

User: "Because sales volume helps us allocate product across stores in the future, making sure we don't run out of stock where people are going to buy the most."

Ah-ha! Now you have some insights – not just that they don't like the bar chart, but that they need the data disaggregated. Your skill is to translate that into dashboard design. Perhaps you need to add trend lines so they can track volume patterns. By probing for more *whys*, you'll discover more insights around your user needs and preferences.

Prototyping Stages

A three-stage prototyping process allows you to work nimbly with users without getting bogged down in designing the "perfect" dashboard. Working with your requirements, you'll first design a simple wireframe, then a more detailed mockup, and finally an interactive prototype. These are often called *product increments* in Agile, referencing the incremental approach to delivering something users can engage with for feedback.

Let's unpack what each of these increments looks like.

	Phase	What it is	Feedback required	Example
Low Fidelity	**Wireframe**	A static sketch using lines and shapes.	Gain consensus on structure of the dashboard design	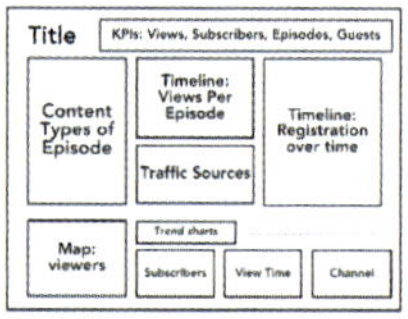
	Mockup	A visual representation of the final dashboard, including specific BANs, chart types, and filters.	Gather detailed critique on visual elements (charts, filters, etc.) and the flow of information	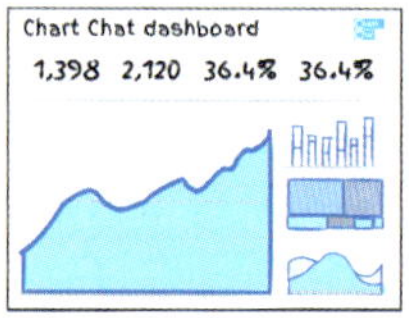
High Fidelity	**Prototype**	A working version that demonstrates aesthetics, functionality, and interactivity. Think of it as the "first draft" of the final dashboard.	Detailed usability feedback on all components, including interactivity.	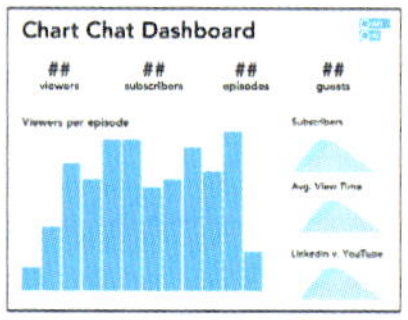

What do you actually put in these increments? What are the components of your dashboard going to be? It's time to get creative: let's take a user story and use it to consider what objects the dashboard needs to deliver an actionable insight.

Here's Alexis' user story from the previous chapter.

> "**As a** regional manager, **I need to** understand if a district in my region is having persistent stockouts of key vaccines **in order** to identify if stockouts are a regional issue or reallocating supplies could address gaps."

Here are the questions we would ask to translate the user story into dashboard components:

- **"As a regional manager..."** Should the dashboard show only Alexis' region's data? If the dashboard shows data for multiple managers, should the dashboard be pre-filtered for each manager? Or should they choose themselves from a list? Should the dashboard also be able to show all managers' data or just one at a time?

- **"...understand if a district in my region..."** "Region" is geographical data: do I need a map? Experimenting will allow me to understand if the users want to see district's spatial relationships (in which case they probably need a map) or if they want to rank them by specific measures (in which case sorted bar charts might be better). What do the words "understand if" mean in this context? Does the user need detail on why insights exist, or just yes/no indicators that they do exist?
- **"...is having persistent stockouts of key vaccines..."** What is a "persistent stockout"? Do I need to display the trend of stockouts over time (in which case I'll need a timeline) and how do I display "key vaccines"? Should I show one line per vaccine? Or stack them? How should I encode each vaccine? Should the user be able to choose from a set of vaccines or is it fixed?
- **"... to identify if stockouts are a regional issue..."** As with the previous regional requirement, do I need a map here, or can I compare them in a chart?
- **"...or reallocating supplies could address gaps."** Do I need to build scenario planning into the dashboard? If so, will the user use a parameter or other selection tool to change underlying values? Where will that be on the dashboard? How will the user know how to use it?

On top of all those specific phrases in the user story, also consider if there are any headline numbers, that should be on the dashboard.

That's a lot, right? We didn't even list specific considerations around filters, navigation, and other interactivity, which we'll get to later. Some questions require your expertise as a data designer to answer. Other questions will need more clarity from your users. Don't assume to know the answer; go ask them.

As you raise questions for clarification with your users, use this opportunity to narrow into the *priority* needs. Conversations with users often raise new ideas that are "nice to have," which can result in scope creep for the dashboard. While you can revisit and add requirements, some may need to be on the backlog but prioritized for future enhancements – not the first release.

Wireframes

Wireframes are conversation starters. They are an easy way to iterate quickly when changes are cheap and easy. They help you and your users explore functionality without the complexity of incorporating data. Your goal is not to create something perfect, but to generate multiple ideas, quickly.

Any of the following are useful methods for prototyping, listed in order by complexity:

1. Whiteboards or pen and paper.
2. Low-fidelity wireframe tools such as Figma, Miro/Mural, PowerPoint, or Excalidraw.
3. Higher-fidelity tools such as Figma (which can be used in more than one way) or Balsamiq. Some of these tools even have community-built libraries that can export finished wireframes to Tableau (for example, ladataviz.com) and PowerBI (nudgebi.com).
4. Your actual dashboarding tool (for example, PowerBI, Tableau, etc.).

Remember that at this stage you are at a very low level of fidelity. Your wireframe should consist of simple boxes breaking down the parts of the dashboard to indicate where all the information will go, as illustrated in sketches in Figure 7.2. These could include basic UX blocks indicating buttons, text, and charts.

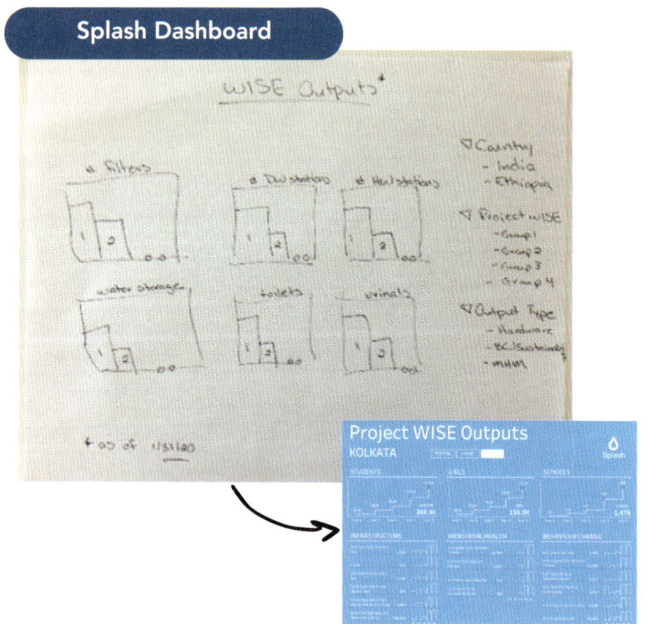

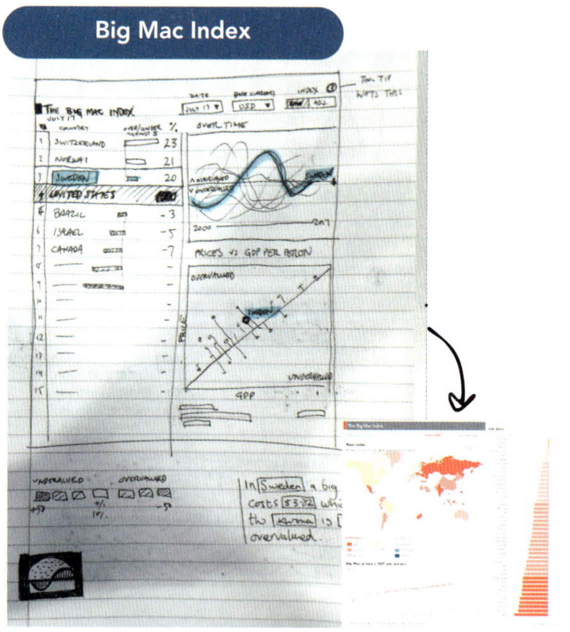

FIGURE 7.2 Two wireframe examples from scenarios in this book. On the left is a very low-fidelity dashboard "vision" for the Splash dashboard in Chapter 16. On the right is a higher-fidelity wireframe for the Big Mac index (Chapter 17).

Mockups

Low-fidelity wireframes focus on structure and flow but contain little to no actual charts. The mockup moves to medium-fidelity and shows sketches of charts, filters, colors, and early design aesthetics; it's a static representation of the final dashboard.

This is the time for you to be thinking about actual chart types and BANs for each part of the dashboard.

Where to Find More Details on Chart Types and Dashboard Design

In the next chapter, we'll walk through data visualization and design principles you can use to ensure you have the right charts, layouts, and flow to your dashboards.

As you consider your chart choices, think about the following:

- Will your audience be familiar with the charts you use? Are your users new to interactive dashboards? Or will they value complex graphics that enable more advanced analysis.
- How many components do you need to include to meet your users' needs?
- Will it be interactive or static? Will your users be routinely taking screenshots or making PDFs of your dashboard, losing the interactive insights? Interactivity allows you to put some information into tooltips and minimize clutter on the display but that only works if your audience will interact with the live version.

Design Your Own Path

In our research, we found that individuals and teams define their own design phases. Nelson Davis, founder of Analytic Vizion, begins with a sticky note phase *before* the wireframes. They give users a blank dashboard grid template and ask users to put sticky notes in each place to clarify their requirements. Their dashboard template frames the users' flow around KPIs and first-, second-, and third-level questions (see Figure 7.3).

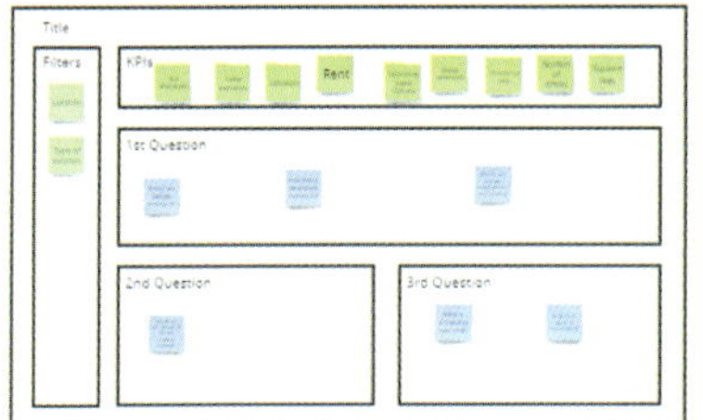

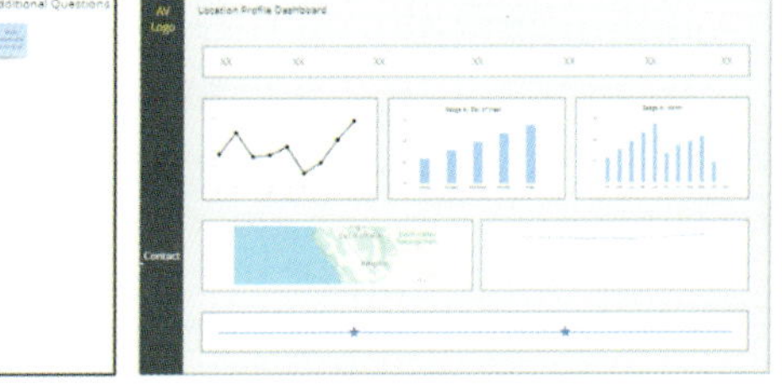

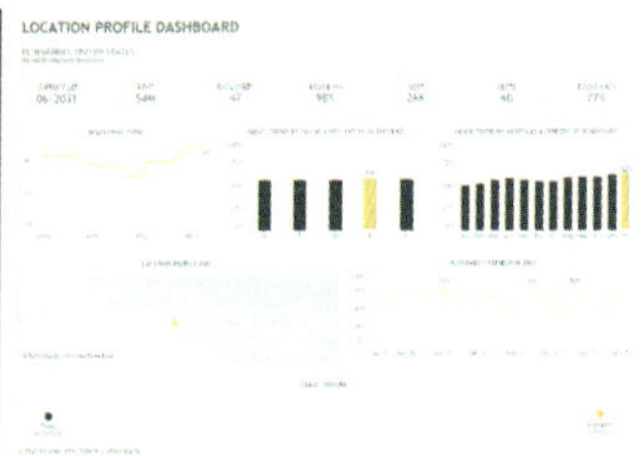

FIGURE 7.3 Analytic Vizion's progression from sticky note requirements through wireframe to mockup.

You should expect to prepare multiple mockups, continually iterating on ideas based on user feedback. When you're considering different chart types for the same analytical need, present options side-by-side to users for their input (often called A/B testing).

How to Make Your Dashboards Irresistible (Steve)

In the discovery phase you determined which metrics your target audience cares about. While the metrics that matter to different users across different organizations will vary widely, there is one dashboard technique that is practically guaranteed to attract and engage your audience:

Make your users the focus of the dashboard.

There are several scenarios in Part II that showcase this. In "The Team Coaching Dashboard" chapter, a student can easily answer questions such as "How am *I doing* compared with the top bowlers? How has *my performance* improved or gotten worse over the past six matches?"

In the Children's Hospital Association Dashboard (Chapter 19), administrators can see what percentile they are in across various metrics when compared with other hospitals. They can answer questions such as "*are we outperforming* our peers or *are we struggling* in some areas and should seek help from hospitals that are doing better?"

You may already be familiar with the JHU Coronavirus Resource Center (Chapter 25) and used it to see how *your country/state/city/neighborhood* was faring during the the pandemic.

You can explore this approach by interacting with a dashboard that allows you to see how much older or younger you are than people who live in the United States. To give it a try, visit bigpic.me/age.

Let's take a simple example. Your users want to see a trend over time across two categories. They're used to seeing the data presented in paired columns and *insist* the dashboard should do the same, but you see an opportunity for a way to improve their speed to insight.

Instead of telling them that you'll use a different chart type because *you know best*, show the user a few examples and talk through the pros and cons of each (Figure 7.4). Then, decide together on what chart to use. Engaging users in these decisions helps build a sense of shared ownership and understanding of the design decisions.

Prototypes

Finally, it's time to move to the highest-fidelity design: the prototype.

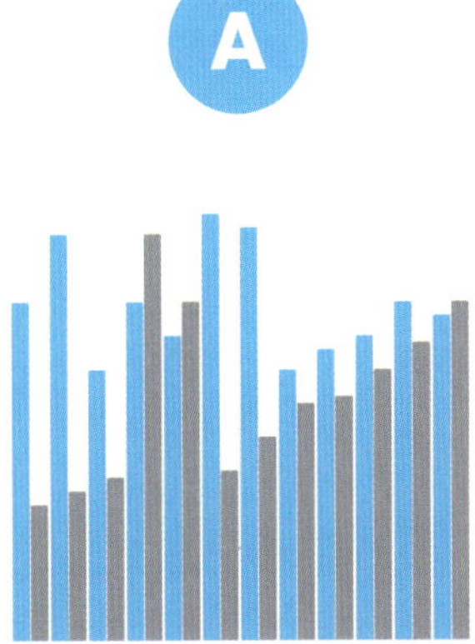

Paired Column Chart
Familiar to the user, but makes comparing what's happening within one category challenging

Clustered Column Chart
Allows user to analyze patterns within a category and a shared scale enables comparison across categories, but separate groups make it hard to compare values for a specific point in time

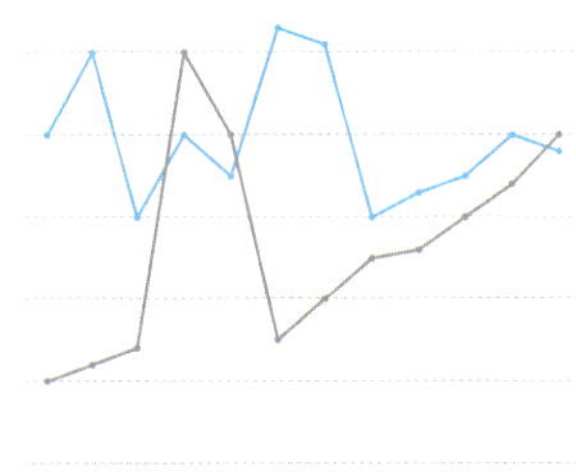

Line Chart
Shows trend for both categories and overlapping lines mean user can quickly see where one category exceeds or falls below another

FIGURE 7.4 Three sample charts to display change over time across two categories.

When your users look at and interact with the prototype, it should behave as if it is a finished dashboard, with interactivity and filters working. At this point, you're likely moving into your dashboarding tool of choice using sample data, a data extract from your actual dataset, or even the full data source if it's available to you.

When you've invested time in rounds of feedback with your users to refine your wireframes and mockups, crafting the prototype becomes more straightforward. Your mockup is the model you work from, and it's been informed by the various needs and constraints you've already defined with the users. The questions move from "What chart should I build" to "How do I build this chart?"

Share the first prototype with users and again get their feedback, iterate, and share again. Don't get stuck in a prototyping loop though. At some point, you must decide on the design and begin developing the dashboard with real data.

For some dashboard teams or consultants, prototyping is the point we're brought into the process, though: someone else has decided they need a dashboard and even drawn up a picture of what they want. Dashboard tools and datasets can present unexpected challenges turning those mockups into working dashboards though.

Take a simple example: you're brought in to build out a dashboard for a client who already has a concept that includes a set of dumbbell charts to show the difference between two points in time. The rough sketch looks great, but the chart type isn't easy to build in the client's chosen dashboarding software. When you look at some of the sample data provided the scale across different categories are very different, making the chart less useful in practice.

When Wireframing Fails (Andy Cotgreave)

EARLY in my job at Tableau, I was sent to a customer in Rotterdam. Our sales guy told me, "They've worked with a leader in the data visualization field to design their dashboard. Now they need you to go and build it in Tableau."

This seemed like a straightforward task.

I arrived and was given a beautiful hand-drawn mockup of a dashboard.

It had a lovely grid layout. There was a narrow row of KPIs at the top. Below that, the second row had a line chart. On the bottom row was a bar chart and a scatterplot. Filters and other details were in a column on the left.

It looked gorgeous (Figure 7.5, on the left). Clearly the consultant hired was worth the money.

Eight hours later, I'd rebuilt the dashboard to the template and the dashboard looked...awful (Figure 7.5, right-hand side). The client was not impressed. How come I had not built their expensively wireframed work of art?

To explain why, I first recommend you do this exercise. Grab a pen and paper, then sketch a line chart, a bar chart, and a scatterplot.

You've done that? Let me guess what they look like.

Your line chart will likely have a gentle upward curve, possibly with some teeny peaks and troughs. Your bar chart (I bet you drew a vertical one) is quite likely to be sorted, and there'll be an easy-to-see distribution. And your scatterplot? I bet it has a strong positive correlation.

My customer's data? They had huge volatility in their timeline data; instead of a gentle curve. The line chart mostly sat close to the x-axis, except for one monster spike. The same was true of the bar chart: one category was a massive outlier. Thus, it's bar was so long all the others essentially looked as if they had zero value. And the scatterplot looked more like a screen of white noise, dots randomly distributed.

The problem was the idealistic nature of wireframing. **Had they worked with the data earlier in the process, they would have seen these challenges sooner.**

They may even have realized the very questions they'd thought they needed to ask were not ones they should have been asking. The scatterplot should have triggered this. They'd expected two key metrics to show a close correlation, but they were completely out of sync. That was an opportunity, found during the prototyping phase, not only to rethink chart choices but to start again with a different question that explored the root cause of their insight.

This episode taught me that while wireframing with data can be very valuable, it does not work the same way it does in application design. Application interfaces are fixed by the designer. Data interfaces, by contrast, are at the mercy of data as well as designers. Thus, when prototyping, I always try to bring in the real data at the earliest possible moment.

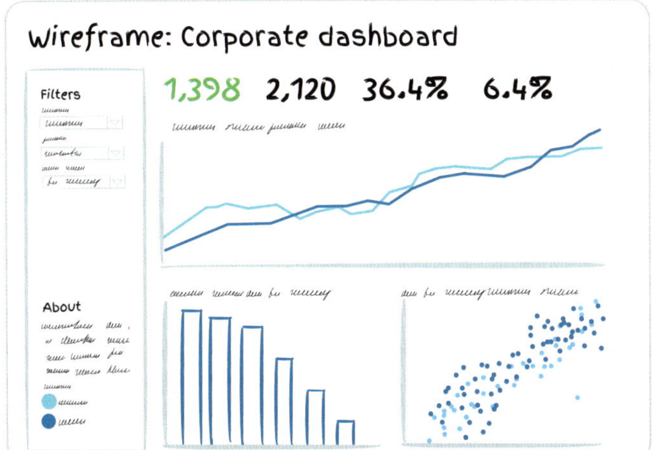

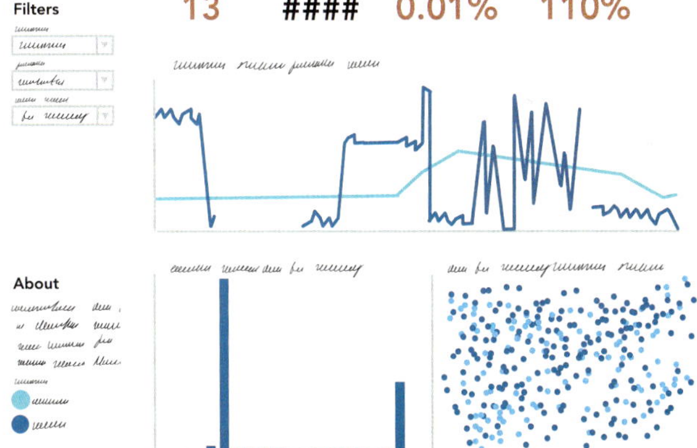

FIGURE 7.5 An illustration of how the client's wireframe used idealized charts, compared to an end result that looked disappointing.

If you find yourself in this situation, you may need to take a step back and discuss alternate chart types or other changes to the mockups. In those conversations, be specific about why you're recommending alternate displays and how they address the same analytical need.

Remember, dashboard design is an iterative process. Don't let striving for perfection hinder progress toward a live dashboard. If users have feedback left unresolved in the prototyping phase that's worth future consideration, write it on the backlog and agree to revisit when it's time to update the dashboard.

When Should You Bring in Your Real Data?

As the vignette from Andy demonstrates, there are perils to relying on sketches of idealized charts (line charts that trend up, scatterplots that correlate, etc.). There is much debate among experts as to when you should start playing with real data.

Simon Beaumont, BI director at JLL, likes to start with sketching. "Data limits your scope and vision," he says, "You risk being limited by the data you currently have. Wireframes help focus on the flow and address the business question."

In contrast, Rob Radburn, BI development leader at Leicestershire County Council in England, always starts with the actual data. "People relate to seeing their data," he says. "Using real data at the first stage quickly reveals if the data actually answers the users' needs."

In practice, this can mean using a sample from a larger dataset or the full dataset to be used on the dashboard. If you decide to work with real data, you'll likely spend more of your time prototyping in your dashboard tool of choice. Even working with real data, remember that the goal is *quick increments for feedback* – don't spend time doing all of the formatting fine-tuning that goes into a final dashboard at this stage, even though it can be tempting particularly for seasoned dashboard designers. Remember that people can see the shape of the data on the charts even with all of the design defaults still in place.

Whichever route you choose, we recommend exploring your real data as early as possible – preferably in parallel with your discovery work where you're mapping out the user needs. Exploring the source data early on will highlight data quality issues, identify where new sources or tables might be needed, and reveal any assumptions you've made about trends or insights that do not exist in your data.

If you don't have any real data yet, you should be considering how the proposed data structure (field names, data types, etc.) will map to the final dashboard. This will make the transition from prototype to development seamless.

Summary

In this chapter, we've explained the main principles and stages of prototyping. During this phase, you'll learn a lot about your users' needs through feedback on incrementally more complex versions of your dashboard, including your wireframe, mockup, and working prototype.

As you follow along in the framework, you'll have completed the following:

- Multiple static wireframes for dashboard structure
- Mockups to show visual elements
- Prototypes that mimic the proposed final behavior of the dashboard
- Requesting and incorporating feedback from users at each stage of the process.

Throughout this process, keep going back to the insights from discovery: your personas, user stories, and requirements. Remaining focused on those user needs and what you've prioritized for the first release of the dashboard can help you minimize scope creep as new "nice to haves" emerge from your user feedback.

Before we dive into the next step – dashboard development – we'll use the next chapter to walk through specific design considerations to inform the design of your mockup and prototype.

Chapter 8

Key Considerations for Dashboard Design

Amanda Makulec and Andy Cotgreave

> *"Everything should be made as simple as possible, but not simpler."*
>
> *—Albert Einstein*[1]

This chapter describes our recommendations for designing your dashboards, from the first wireframe to final development.

As you'll see, most decisions depend on your users' needs, and there are many decisions you will have to make. It might even feel like you're descending a rabbit hole as you try to solve for every possible user need. Heather Lewis, director of Institutional Analytics at Augusta University, told us how she manages this challenge. "We keep things as simple as we can," she said. "We're building data literacy as well as dashboards. We're also trying to release things as quickly as we can. You can end up being in design mode forever."

Components of a Dashboard

What goes on a dashboard? Figure 8.1 shows Kevin Flerlage's team coaching dashboard (Chapter 12) with the main components labeled. Most dashboards should have these elements, which we'll explain each in this chapter. We'll also consider the "invisible" features such as interactivity and tooltips.

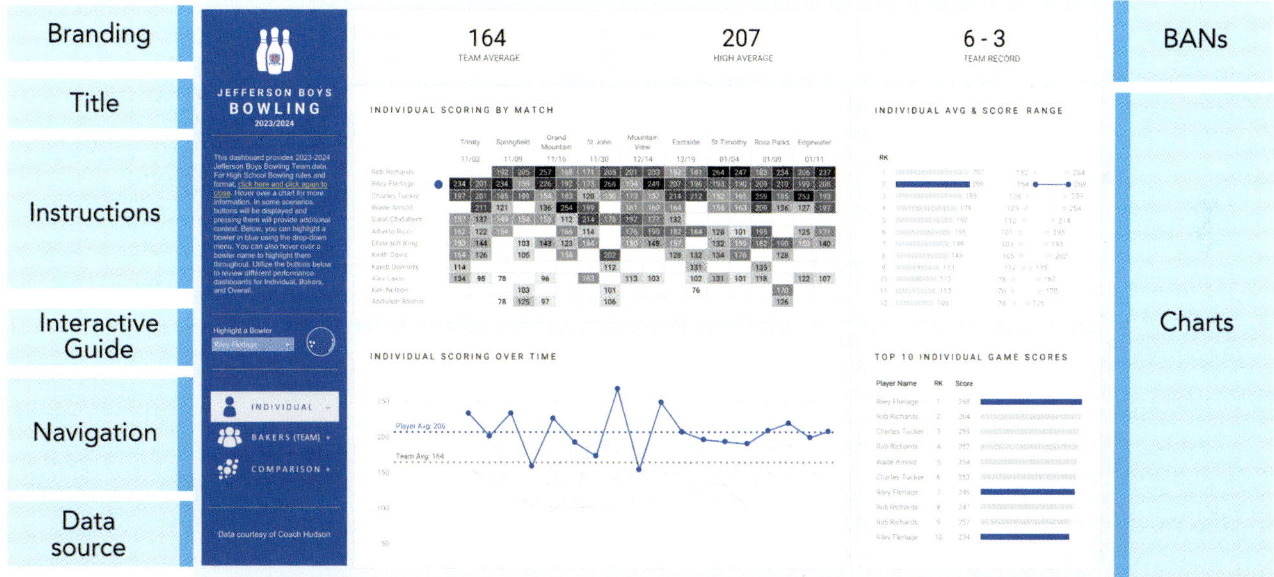

FIGURE 8.1 The main visible components of a dashboard.

[1]Did Einstein really say that? This famous quote is a simplified version of the original from a 1933 lecture: "It can scarcely be denied that the supreme goal of all theory is to make the irreducible basic elements as simple and as few as possible without having to surrender the adequate representation of a single datum of experience." You could say the simplified quote is an example of a minimum viable quote. 😊 For more info, see dtdbook.com/link7.

Key Considerations

BANs (Big-Ass Numbers)

Or Big Aggregated Numbers. Or Big Annotated Numbers. Or Big Angry Numbers.

A BAN is just a big number on a dashboard. That number is usually related to some metric the organization cares about, like annual sales, profit margin, attrition rate, and so on. When employed with care and context, BANs can answer important questions while using up only a small portion of a dashboard (for much more on BANs, see chapter 27).

Chart Choices

The main element of every dashboard will be your charts. So…what's the right chart for your data and your use case? Put simply, it depends.

Every chart choice you make will be a compromise. Consider these three challenges:

1. An aggregated bar chart makes it easy to see totals but hides granular details from the users who need them.
2. Adding a filter for just one or two metrics will keep your dashboard tidy but frustrate the user who wants to drill into a metric you didn't provide.
3. Highly complex interaction methods will please your power users but may confuse your casual users.

Let's look at the following examples, which explores how to explore data about international tourism revenue.

As you can see, whichever insight you surface, you hide another one. To find the best route through this challenge, we encourage you to work closely with your users to provide the combination of charts that works best for them. One piece of guidance is to keep things as simple as possible: don't get carried away showing off that you can build complex charts; your users want to see the insights as quickly as they can.

Rather than packing too many chart choice guidelines into this book, we encourage you to explore other books that focus on this. We recommend:

- *The Big Book of Dashboards* (Steve Wexler, Jeffrey Shaffer, and Andy Cotgreave) for examples in the context of dashboards, including a glossary of common chart types
- *Better Data Visualizations* (Jonathan Schwabish) for a primer on broad data visualization principles and chart recommendations
- *Practical Charts and More Practical Charts* (Nick Desbarats) for a decision-tree approach to choosing the right chart

Scale and Orientation

During discovery, you identified which devices people will use to access the dashboard, and the screen sizes associated with those devices. Design your wireframes and mockups to fit those sizes.

If you are designing for mobile, tools such as Tableau and PowerBI allow you to build specific versions of the dashboard for different sizes of mobile screens. These are some general guidelines for mobile views:

The aggregated view shows total tourism revenue by region. We can clearly see Europe has the highest revenue.

But…what if the users want also to see each individual country? We could try a dot plot…

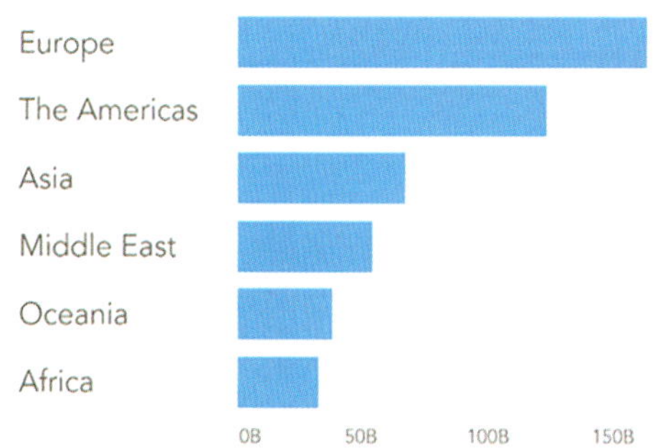

Now we see something that was hidden in the first chart: there's an obvious outlier in the Americas. It's the United States, and the chart shows that it has the highest tourism income in the world.

But…we have introduced new issues. We can no longer see the total for each region. If our users need to see that, what do we do? Also. lots of the dots overlap each other. To solve that, we could try a jitterplot…

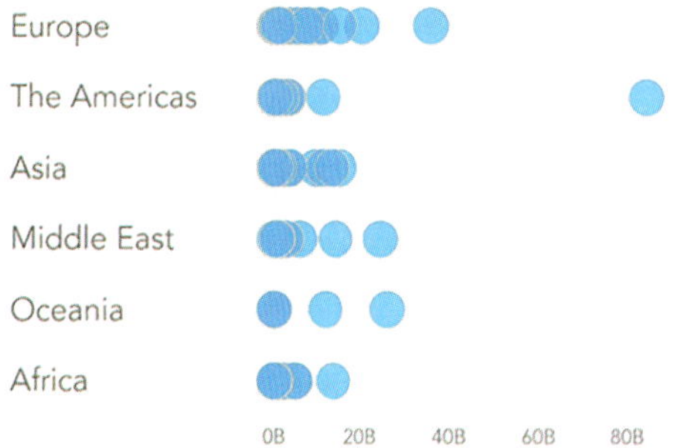

Now the data is jittered, you can see each country more clearly.

But…do your users know how to read jitterplots? A jitterplot randomly distributes each dot vertically inside the row of the chart. If you've seen them before, jitterplots are easy to understand. If your users have never seen them, might they be confused?

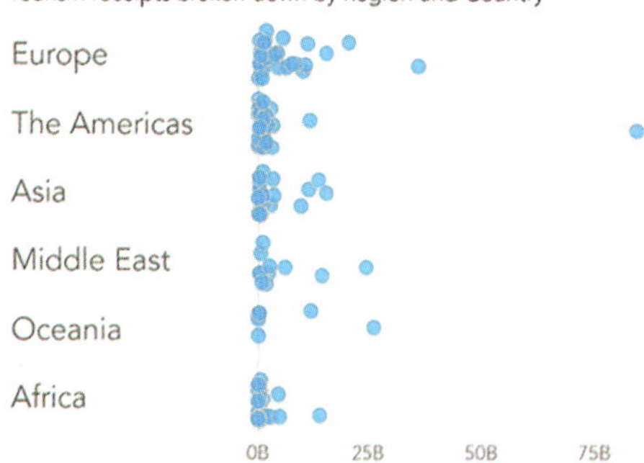

- Use fewer charts for the mobile version. Users typically want quicker, briefer insights on mobile.
- Scrolling vertically through sets of charts on a dashboard is a natural interaction for mobile. A single, tall column of components will work fine. (See Figure 8.2.)
- Simplify interactivity. A complex application with multiple filters works well when your users have a big screen and a mouse. On a mobile with their thumbs? Interactivity is harder: use fewer filters and, if you need them, avoid drop-down lists that require multiple clicks to use.

Figure 8.2 has a simple example comparing a desktop and a mobile view of the same dashboard.

Check out the Strava exercise tracking dashboard in Chapter 13 for a mobile-only dashboard.

Design to a Grid

A clear grid layout of columns and rows creates visual order and groups charts or features that are

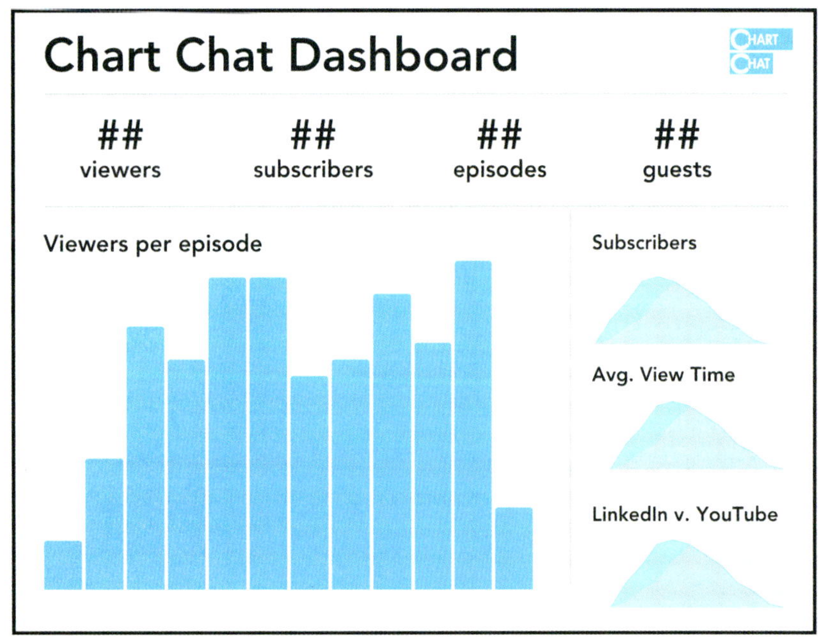

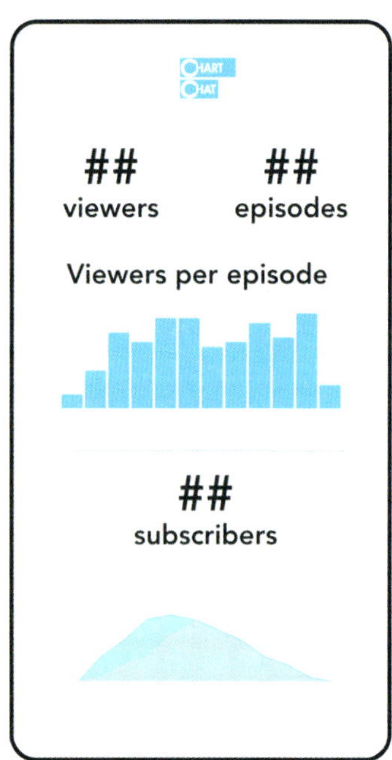

FIGURE 8.2 Comparison of a dashboard organized for viewing on a desktop or laptop screen compared to mobile viewing.

meant to be read together. A few examples of grid layouts are in Figure 8.3. The Bowling dashboard in Figure 8.1 is a good case study of using a grid to add clarity.

To choose the right grid layout, refer to your user requirements. Is there a set of main KPIs they need to track? Those could be a set of BANs across the top. Maybe you recognize a need for one main chart and three more detailed charts. The first grid (left) in Figure 8.3 would work for that.

Common design principles can help you choose the right positioning. People typically read screens in Z or F patterns (Figure 8.4).

Users scan across the top first, then drop down a level, and then scan across again. This means the top left of your dashboard is where you should put the most important information. You'll see lots of dashboards with KPIs in a row along the top of the screen, because our eyes are most likely to scan across that part of the screen first.

Eye-Tracking on Dashboards

After *The Big Book of Dashboards* was published, we did eye-tracking research with Tableau, looking at what drew people's attention on a dashboard. We found that BANs and alert colors were compelling and that the eye follows the flow built into the dashboard. You can find more details at dtdbook.com/link8.

Going back to your user stories and requirements, can you discern a flow through the insights they need to explore? List the order of insights and re-create that flow in your grid.

Create Visual Groupings

Gestalt principles of perception describe how people group similar features in our surroundings, looking for patterns or relationships that may, or may

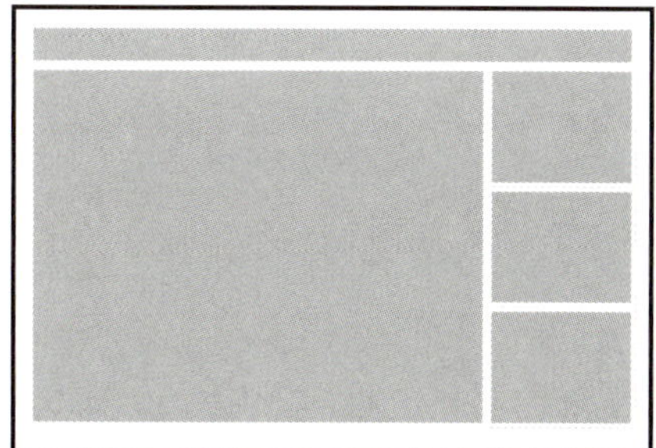

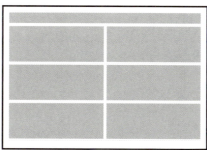

FIGURE 8.3 Illustrative grid layouts that could be used to organize dashboard components, including (from left to right) 3:1, two column, and three column layouts.

Users typically start reading in the **upper left corner,** where we often start listing our BANs.

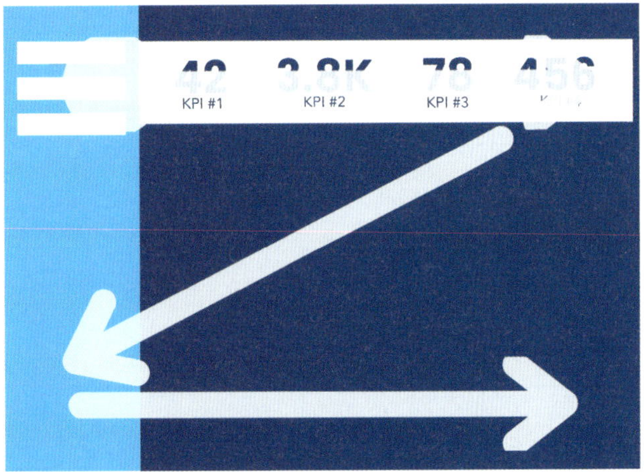

Then, they read down in a Z pattern particularly when BANs are placed along the top row to focus users' attention there first.

Or align BANs in a column along the left side of the dashboard. Users will often read down the first column or in an F pattern which has become a more common reading order in digital spaces.

FIGURE 8.4 Wireframe schematics illustrating key principles for organizing information.

not, exist. In UX design, we can use features such as proximity, similarity, enclosure, and continuity to order information, as illustrated in Figure 8.5.

Figure 8.6 shows a progression of ideas. Your first idea might be to have no gridlines. That looks tidy, but the white space in this case doesn't create strong enough visual grouping. You could add some divider lines, but you need to get the balance right. Too dark (chart 2) and the lines dominate the view. The light lines are nice (chart 3), but a gray background (chart 4) achieves the same grouping more cleanly.

In this book you'll see examples using gridlines (Chapter 21), shaded backgrounds (Chapter 12), and a hybrid approach (Chapter 16).

Color

One of the most important decisions in dashboard development is how we use color. For communicating information, there are five ways to use color (Figure 8.7).

Your users will be scanning across a swathe of charts and components. The following are three things to consider.

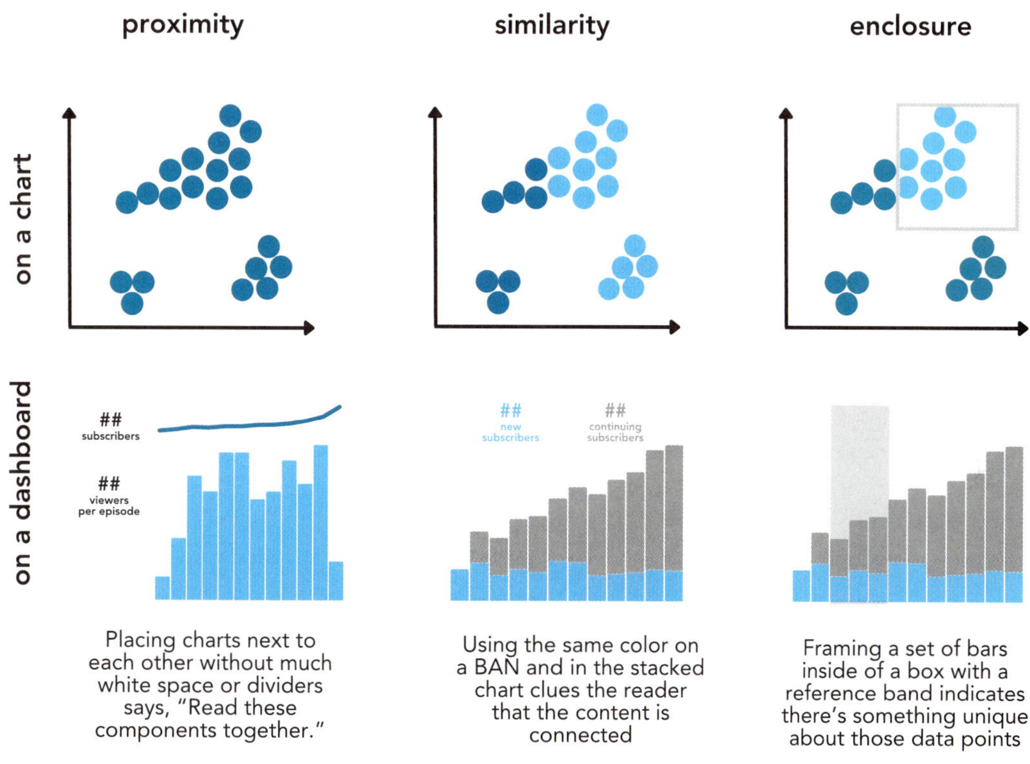

FIGURE 8.5 Illustration of select Gestalt principles of perception in action on charts and dashboards.

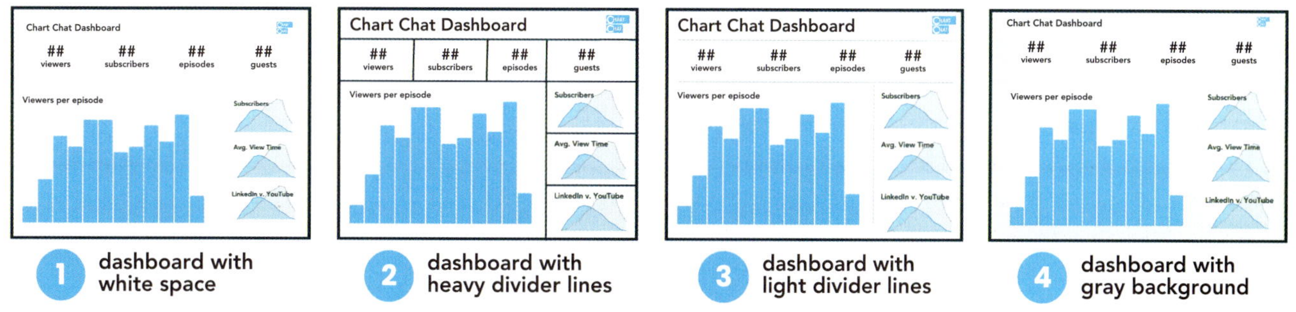

FIGURE 8.6 Four versions of a sample dashboard mockup showing different ways to divide the charts into sections using (left to right) lines, gray background shading, and white space.

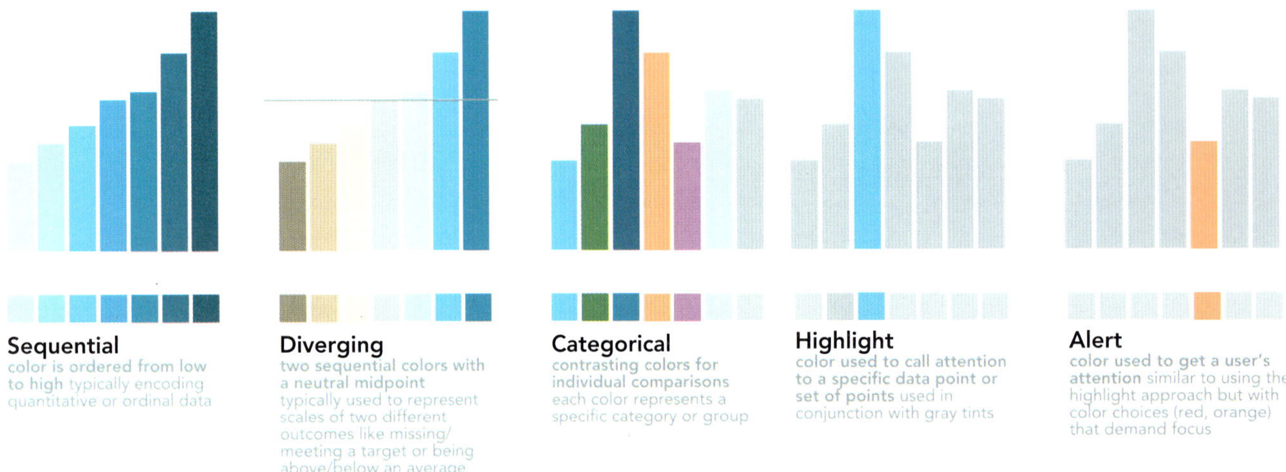

Sequential
color is ordered from low to high typically encoding quantitative or ordinal data
Diverging
two sequential colors with a neutral midpoint typically used to represent scales of two different outcomes like missing/meeting a target or being above/below an average
Categorical
contrasting colors for individual comparisons each color represents a specific category or group
Highlight
color used to call attention to a specific data point or set of points used in conjunction with gray tints
Alert
color used to get a user's attention similar to using the highlight approach but with color choices (red, orange) that demand focus

FIGURE 8.7 Five ways to use color in data visualization: sequential, diverging, categorical, highlight, and alert.

Focus

The simplest advice we can provide is use the fewest colors possible. Can you use just one primary color and a set of grays to deliver your dashboard? Don't underestimate the power of gray!

Look back to the bowling dashboard in Figure 8.1. There is one primary color, blue, used to highlight one bowler in the team. Everything else is gray. The side bar, containing instructions and navigation details, is also blue. The simplicity of color choice reduces the cognitive load required to interpret the dashboard.

Take a moment to scan through the scenarios in the book: notice how most examples use very few colors.

Consistency

Consistency is critical, particularly if you design multiple dashboards for your organization. Your users benefit if they have a consistent mental model where they learn what a given color means.

Consider the example from the data visualization style guide from the Office of HIV/AIDS (OHA) in the United States Agency for International Development (USAID). They create multiple dashboards that analyze program performance across different agencies, demographics, and more. Their style guide defines which colors to use in all dashboards; they have specific colors for their different agencies, genders, targets, and more (Figure 8.8).

This means that when their audience looks at multiple dashboards made by their team, they are already familiar with what each color stands for.

Brand

Sometimes you might be working for a client or a team that demands you use brand colors for the

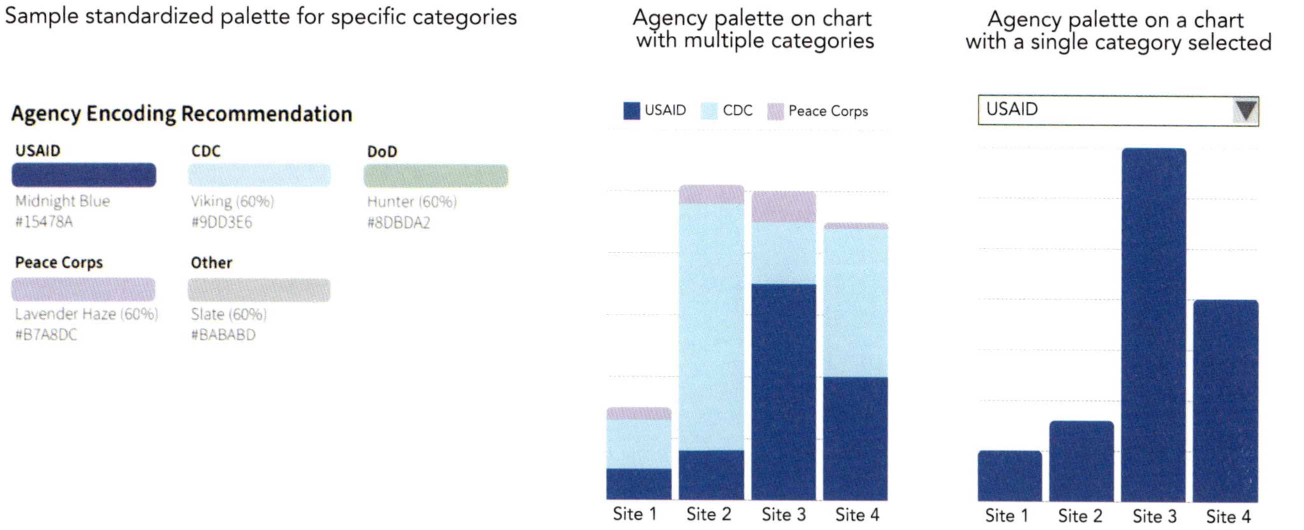

Sample standardized palette for specific categories

Agency Encoding Recommendation

USAID
Midnight Blue
#15478A

CDC
Viking (60%)
#9DD3E6

DoD
Hunter (60%)
#8DBDA2

Peace Corps
Lavender Haze (60%)
#B7A8DC

Other
Slate (60%)
#BABABD

Agency palette on chart with multiple categories

USAID CDC Peace Corps

Site 1 Site 2 Site 3 Site 4

Agency palette on a chart with a single category selected

USAID

Site 1 Site 2 Site 3 Site 4

FIGURE 8.8 OHA color definitions for identifying which agency funded the results for a particular program or funding flow.

dashboard. This can present challenges. Some brand colors create accessibility problems if the color is low contrast against a white background. Other colors carry some implied meaning that you should consider; red, for example, is often used to mark data points of concern, but is also a common brand color.

Amy Cesal, data visualization designer and accessibility advocate, says, "Most people don't understand that colors that work for your brand often don't work for charts. You need more colors and a larger spectrum of tints and shades to properly make graphs and maps. You need to be conscious of how these colors will affect chart readability and accessibility."[2]

[2]Cesal, A. *How to Create Brand Colors for Data Visualization.* Nightingale, 2020.

Filters, Slicers, and Interactivity

"Overview first, zoom and filter, then details on demand" is Ben Shneiderman's famous data visualization mantra, defined in 1996.[3]

The principle is that you should provide users with a way to start with high-level metrics and then drill down to different segments of data. You can achieve this through filters (Tableau), slicers (PowerBI), buttons or interactive charts, or reports with multiple pages and clear navigation.

Filters and Buttons

Do you want your users to take in the dashboard first and then filter, or do you want them to filter first and then take in the views based on the filter settings?

[3]Shneiderman, B. "The eyes have it: a task by data type taxonomy for information visualizations." Proceedings 1996 IEEE Symposium on Visual Languages, Boulder, CO, USA, 1996.

How you answer will drive your decision on where to place your filters (or the icon that when clicked will display the filters). Figure 8.9 shows some examples.

Which position is correct? There is no consensus; each dashboard will have its own user requirements.

In the scenarios in the book, you'll see examples with filters on the top row (see Chapter 24, "Racing Team Strategy Dashboard") and top right (Chapter 15, "Recency, Frequency, Monetary (RFM) Analysis").

On a single screen dashboard, a left-side column of filters has the advantage of being where your users' eyes land first. It's also easier to add more filters within a single vertical than along a top row as your dashboard changes with time. However, the contents of your dashboard, including the number of pages, might lead you to positioning filters along the top. For example, if you have a map view that's best viewed with more horizontal space or a mobile layout where filters across the top better match the reading order.

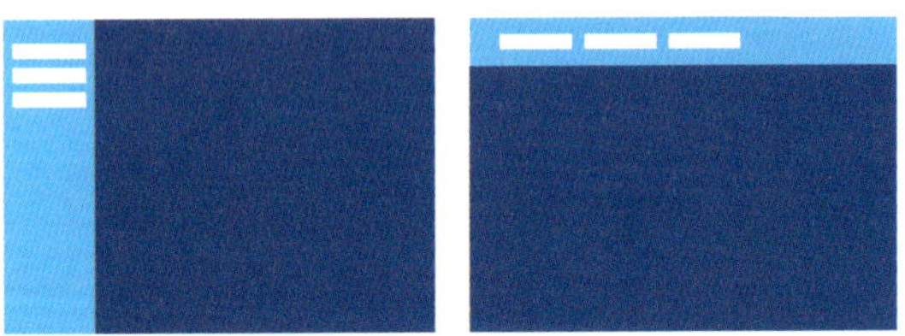

Filters in a menu that start in the upper left say **filter first, then read the charts on the dashboard.**

Filters in a menu that span the right or the bottom say **read the charts on the dashboard first and then filter.**

FIGURE 8.9 Examples of the ways filter placement can create a different order of actions for the user.

If you find the number of filters for your user seems overwhelming, remember to return to those original user needs to determine if the filters are adding value or asking too much of the user. Wherever you put your filters, make sure it's clear somewhere on your display what filters have been selected. You could do this with dynamic text in chart subtitles, with breadcrumbs at the top, or in tooltips.

On the Children's Hospital Association dashboard (Chapter 19), the team had to balance user demands for many filter options but also having limited space. You can see one example in Figure 8.10 and read Chapter 19 for a more detailed discussion on breadcrumbs and creating collapsible groups of filters that the user can opt to open and close.

Interactivity

When done well, interactivity can reveal insights as it invites users to explore. When done poorly, it can easily overwhelm or confuse users. Or worse, interactivity may be invisible because users do not discover the interactive features.

It's your job to know your users' data fluency skills and show them how interactivity works either on the dashboard itself or through training during the dashboard launch and adoption phases.

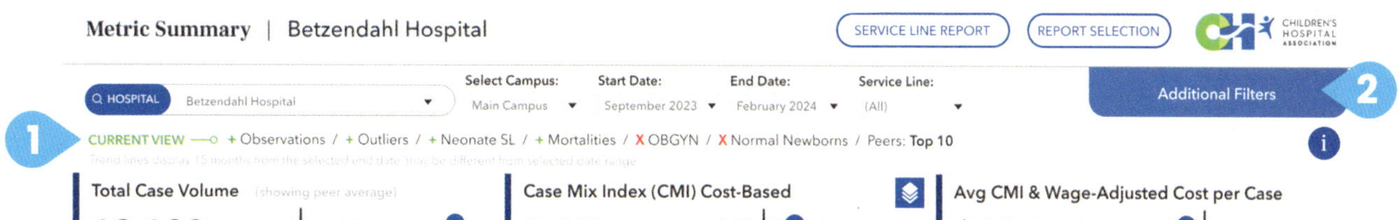

FIGURE 8.10 Example from the Children's Hospital Association dashboard (Chapter 19), showing an example of using dynamic text to show what filters are selected and a hidden tab where the user can click to view a filter menu, saving space on the screen.

Here are some considerations on interactivity to think about as you mockup your dashboard:

- Which charts should be interactive? Should all charts affect all other charts, or should the main chart be the driver of others?
- Filtering or proportional brushing? Filtering via a chart interaction is the same as using a filter object: it reduces what is shown in the chart. Proportional brushing is a technique that shows the relative proportion of selected items compared to all others (see Figure 8.11).
- How do your users know they can filter? You could add instructions to the chart title (Figure 8.11, again); put all instructions in a panel to one side, as Kevin did in the bowling dashboard; create an instructional overlay; run a training session; or share an instructional video.
- Should interactivity be driven by menus, by buttons, or by clicking the charts? Find out what your audience prefers.

Other Dashboard Items

These are other components you will likely include on your dashboard:

- **Dashboard Title.** Keep it short and descriptive. As you browse through the scenarios in the book, you'll see that most are short and nonintrusive.
- **Chart Titles.** Keep these short and descriptive as well. It can be useful to include details of any filters that have been applied in the title.
- **Logo placement.** The temptation to include a logo will feel strong. We don't object to adding a logo, but before you do, ask these questions: Should you have a logo at all? If your users are all colleagues in your organization, don't they already know where they're working? Would the logo be necessary to allow the dashboard to be used with external stakeholders too? Do you need to take up valuable screen real estate with a logo?
- **Navigation buttons.** Ensure these have a visually distinct appearance for people to discover them. See the Children's Hospital Association dashboard (Chapter 19) for an example.
- **Tooltips.** Tooltips enable you to add context to any piece of data on your dashboard. They could be as simple as a simple textual description of the data values, or mini-dashboards with more charts inside.

Bar chart Total sales by country

Stacked bar Shows sales for selected country (UK) as a proportion of each products' sales

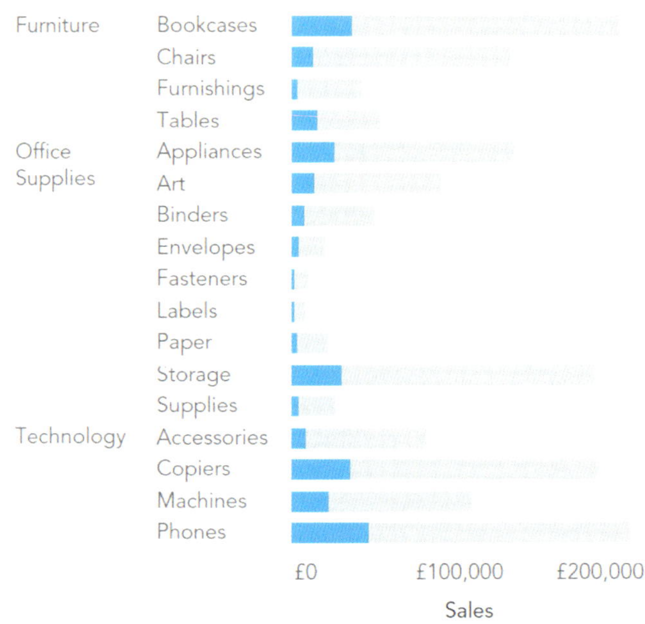

FIGURE 8.11 Proportional brushing: the user has selected the UK on the left. The right-hand chart shows all sales in gray, with the UK's proportion of those sales highlighted blue.

- **Instructions.** How do your users know how to use your dashboard? You'll know through working with users how data fluent they are, and how familiar they are with other dashboards you've built. That will help inform how much instructional detail you'll need to include. Adding instructions could be achieved in various ways:
  - Information buttons that can be clicked or hovered over that describe the dashboard functionality, and other things such as contact details or data sources
  - On-demand overlays that explain each component of the dashboard
  - A link to a short video that explains what the dashboard does and how it works
  - A permanently visible panel explaining how to use the dashboard

Declutter and Focus

If you use a tool like Excel, PowerBI, or Tableau to turn your mockup into a dashboard, you'll be at the mercy of that tool's defaults. Things will not look the way you want them to. Figure 8.12 shows how Kevin's bowling dashboard would look if you built the dashboard in Tableau and did not change a single formatting setting.

It's not *bad*, but it's not great, is it? Don Norman, in *The Design of Everyday Things*, says that all products should aim to generate a positive "visceral" response, specifically, how do we feel about something's appearance in the first few milliseconds we see it. You should always strive to make that first impression count.

To go from the defaults to the finished version, Kevin had to change colors, borders, padding, backgrounds, dividers, fonts, and more. Jeff goes into more detail about the risks of software defaults in Chapter 29.

Research shows that adding focus as well as decluttering can make insights more memorable. In one study[4] participants were given a short scenario and then presented one of three versions of a chart that solved the scenario (Figure 8.13).

On the left: a poorly designed stacked bar chart. In the middle, a decluttered version that has no focus. On the right, a decluttered version that also uses highlight color and a clear title to focus on the insight needed to solve the scenario.

After the charts were removed from view, participants were asked to redraw what they remembered about the chart.

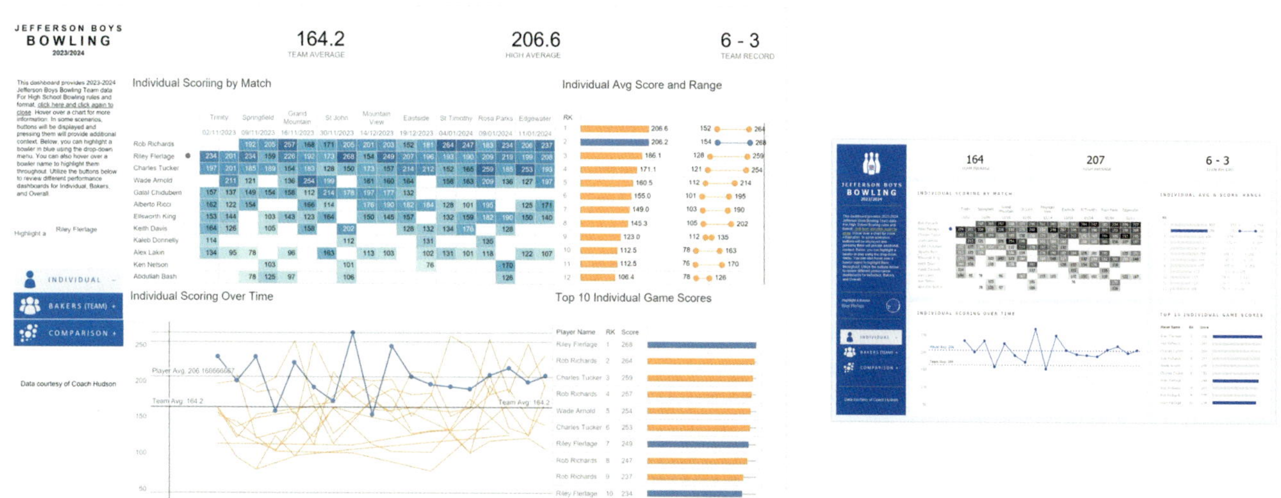

FIGURE 8.12 Kevin's bowling dashboard with Tableau's default formatting (left) compared to the finished, polished, version (right).

[4]Ajani, Kiran & Lee, Elsie & Xiong, Cindy & Knaflic, Cole & Kemper, William & Franconeri, Steven. (2021). Declutter and Focus: Empirically Evaluating Design Guidelines for Effective Data Communication. IEEE Transactions on Visualization and Computer Graphics, PP. 1–1. 10.1109/TVCG.2021.3068337.

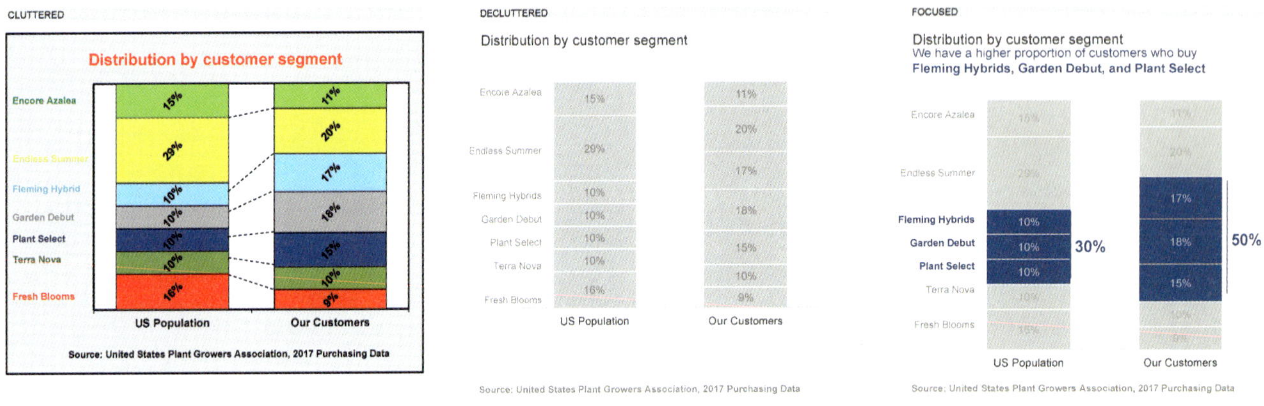

FIGURE 8.13 Three stacked bar charts: cluttered, decluttered, decluttered, *and* focused.

The results? The decluttered *and* focused versions of the charts helped people internalize the insight they needed to solve the scenario. Decluttering, *in conjunction with focusing attention with color and text*, helps your users see and then recall insights.

Using Dashboard Templates

TEMPLATES can provide a speedy starting point for a new dashboard. For example, most businesses want to track sales, marketing campaign success, and customer satisfaction. Why not let someone else do the mockup process for you and use a prebuilt template? Be warned that while you will save time in dashboard design, you might lose time fitting your data to the template's model, or tweaking things to fit your corporate style. See Chapter 15 for an example.

Branding

Creating consistency across dashboards is more than aesthetics. When dashboards across an organization are built with a similar look and feel, we create a consistent user experience across dashboards within one organization, increase opportunities for repurposing proven design concepts in new dashboards, and reduce the mental load on dashboard designers with clear guidance on fonts, colors, and chart components.

Data visualization style guides expand beyond the components in a standard corporate branding guide. A data visualization style guide is a set of documented standards for formatting and designing dashboard components such as charts, tables, layouts, etc. Style guides explain *what* you should do and *why*. The USAID Office of HIV/AIDS (OHA) style guide provides useful examples for chart choices and styles (Figure 8.14).

What to do

All graphics are two dimensions (no-3D)

Three-dimensional (3-D) graphs should be avoided. A 3-d graphic distorts the representation or encoding of the data, making it more challenging to interpret or even misleading (Cleveland and McGill 1984, Skau and Kosara 2016). If additional dimensions are need, size (e.g. size of a dot on a scatter plot) and/or color can be used to encode the data.

Why to make those design decisions

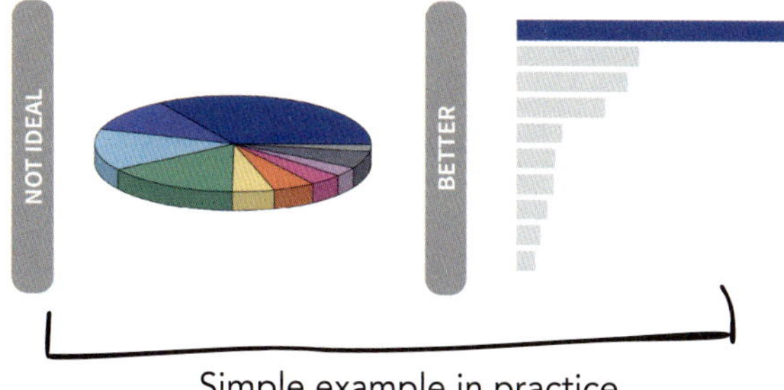

FIGURE 8.14 An example of a style guide in practice from USAID.

Typically, they include an organization's branding information (fonts, colors, icon styles), and directions on how to compose charts. Figure 8.15 shows a guide on avoiding dual axis chart problems, taken from the OHA style guide.

In our research, people repeatedly touted the value of style guides. Simon Beaumont, BI director at JLL, uses style guides for these reasons:

- **Credibility.** A consistent look and feel shows that the team takes the work seriously.
- **Attention to Detail**. Small details such as positioning, margin sizes, and filter styles make a big difference to how a dashboard is perceived. Defining these in a style guide prevents you needing to reinvent the wheel every time you start a new project.
- **Reducing barriers to adoption**. The consistency provided by a style guide creates a "dashboard muscle memory." As people become familiar with your dashboards, it becomes easier and faster for them to understand them.
- **Reducing mental load on dashboard developers.** While simplifying some of the design choices (font, colors, logo placement, etc.) can feel like constraints, a well-designed style guide can give you more time to hone your charts and interactivity

You can find many style guides online at dataviz styleguide.com, curated by Amy Cesal, Max Graze, Jon Schwabish, and Alan Wilson.

Accessibility

Building accessible dashboards is inclusive design. Accessibility improves your work for everyone, not just those who need accommodations. It's *fundamental* to the framework and should never be seen as a box-ticking exercise. When you design for accessibility, you acknowledge that some accommodations may not be visible, or declared by, your users. Your design should anticipate any accommodation.

Here we will describe three key considerations specific to dashboards. For more detail, see the Data

Style guide example for reformatting a dual axis chart

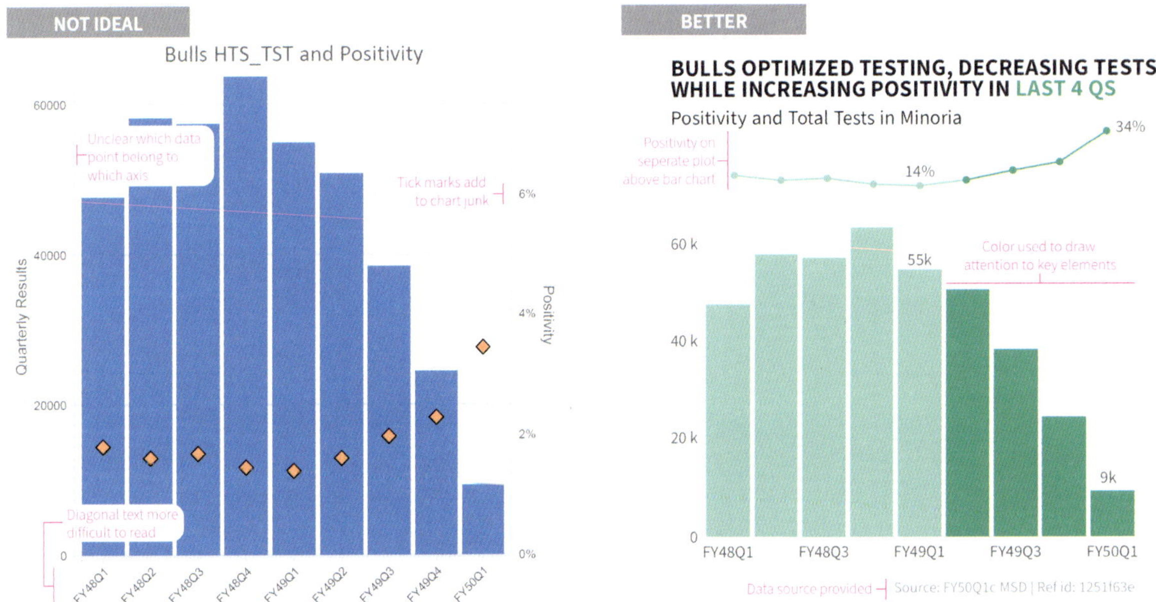

FIGURE 8.15 An excerpt from the OHA style guide.

Visualization Society's repository of accessibility resources at dtdbook.com/link9.

Navigation

Your dashboard should be navigable by someone using a keyboard. This means allowing users to tab between filters and components rather than relying entirely on navigation with a mouse.

Designing with a simple, clear grid structure also helps users follow a dashboard's flow. For those using screen readers, use a logical reading order for your BANs and charts. The grid layout we discussed earlier also helps improve accessibility.

Readability

Text should be simple and clear. Chart titles should include the metric being measured and contain detail about the filters that have been applied. Also consider how captions, tooltips, and annotations can aid your user as they navigate the dashboard. Using plain language helps all users, whatever their data literacy levels. Figure 8.16 shows an example, which also includes some redundant information deliberately to provide clear labeling of the topic in both the chart title and the axis title. Consider your audience's needs and familiarity with your dashboard when determining where duplicating text aids in interpretation or simply creates more visual clutter.

Alternative (alt) text is a written description of a visual element on a screen. In dashboards, this applies to all your charts, images, and icons. Alt text makes your visual content accessible to people who are visually impaired or who use screen readers. Alt tagging is required for public-facing government documents in the United States (section 508) and the United Kingdom.

To write alt text, think about what it is that someone who cannot see the chart would need to know. Amy Cesal suggests this format for charts with a clear analytical insight:

> "<Chart Type> of <type of data> where <reason for including the chart>."

Using this framework, the chart in Figure 8.16 would have the following alt text:

> Bar chart of course attendance by week where the chart shows attrition in the course, with half as many attendees at the last session compared to the first.

Now what about that last part, where we cite half as many attendees in the last session as the first? What happens if there is a resurgence of attendance in the sixth week? The alt text needs to change to reflect that. It may not be possible to add the "reason for including the chart / insight" text to the dashboard if the data that drives the insight changes (although this would make a great use case for AI).

Kent Eisenhuth and the Material Design team at Google have explored more nuanced approaches to alt text for interactive charts, informed by feedback from trusted testers who themselves have disabilities. The spirit of their guidelines is rooted in making charts accessible without introducing bias.

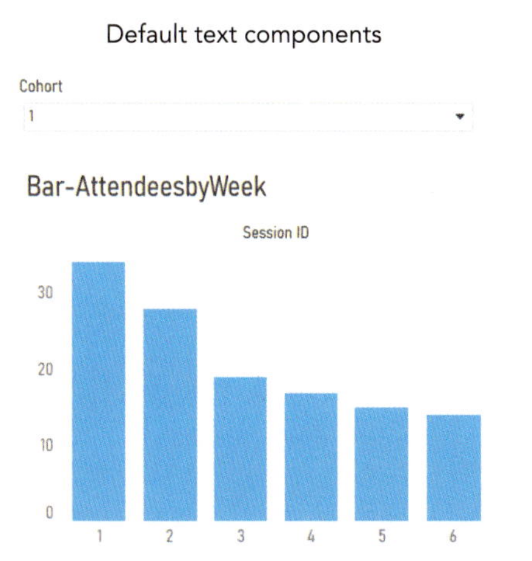

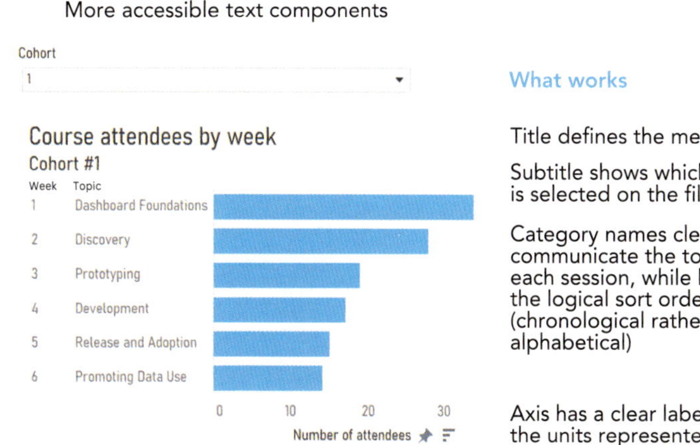

FIGURE 8.16 Before and after text revisions for readability and accessibility.

For charts where a user can find many different takeaways, they consider if a chart is designed to answer a specific analytical question. Take a stock chart, which has a very routine set of analysis questions to answer: What's the current value? Is it higher or lower than a previous period? Are there unexpected spikes and dips? Where there's confidence that the designer *knows* what questions the chart will answer, the team recommends more prescriptive alt text like the framework we shared.

If the chart is more complex with varied use cases, the alt text is more descriptive, stating the chart type and metrics displayed with a clear link to the data source. In their user feedback sessions, the team found that those who use assistive technology were even more proficient at navigating a data table than expected, reinforcing the importance of those linked resources.

But ultimately, the hero is the interactivity of the dashboard. This goes beyond alt text and ventures into other components like screen reader announcements, keyboard navigation, paths to linked materials, and more. The larger the user community for a dashboard becomes, the more likely it is that someone in your user group needs those added tools.

While a deep dive into these accessibility considerations is beyond the scope of this book, we encourage you to explore the resources on the topics from the Material Design group and other community resources (dtdbook.com/link59).

Inclusive Design Is a Community Effort

Designing more accessible dashboards can feel intimidating and requires more than a centralized checklist. Consider building a community around adopting these practices.

Kent Eisenhuth, a product designer at Google, co-founded an effort to improve the accessibility of various data visualizations within the team's cloud products. The product design accessibility recommendations he was familiar with didn't have the nuances needed for data visualization design, so he brought together a group of like-minded people across the entire company to make the team's work more inclusive.

The team published a suite of public resources on data viz accessibility, informed by their experiences and established practices in the field. Getting to share guidelines took time though, starting with mapping existing knowledge and efforts, identifying how to engage team members, and anchoring recommendations in the ways accessibility also serves the business needs, like ensuring compliance with the European Accessibility Act.

The size of the group also changed with time, interest, and availability, ranging from four to thirty people. The team worked with trusted testers with disabilities who provided recommendations for what level of detail to include in the alt text on a chart. Feedback was key to identifying recommendations that worked in practice, not just in theory.

Kent emphasized that as a leader for this kind of long-term effort, team productivity would vary. He had to be comfortable with navigating ambiguity and different levels of engagement over time. The goal was incremental progress toward better, more inclusive practices both internally and externally. The work has resulted in more sustainable organizational change toward more accessible and useful data visualization.

Accessible Color

Color is not only vital to a successful dashboard; it's a risky component because it is easy to create accessibility challenges with incorrect color usage.

Color Vision Deficiency

Approximately 8 percent of men and 0.5 percent of woman of people have color vision deficiency.[5] Ensure your color palettes are readable for those people. The most common type is a red/green deficiency, rendering most spotlight (red/amber/green) dashboards unreadable. Tools such as Adobe Color, COBLIS, and the Chromatic Vision Simulator can help you design appropriate palettes and validate your prototypes.

Color Contrast

Ensure there is sufficient contrast between foreground and background colors.

- **Text elements**. Color choices such as light gray on a white background are hard to read: ensure there is a high contrast for your text.
- **Data labels**. If your chart marks (dots, bars, lines, etc.) have labels, ensure that if there is an overlap, the text remains readable.

Let's look at three data labels in practice, testing labeling with gray text, blue text color-matched to the bar, and darker blue (Figure 8.17). Both the gray and bright blue text fails to hit the target of at least a 3:1 contrast ratio between the text and the background.

Similar to the ways AI can assist with drafting alt text for charts, there are tools to automatically check contrast levels in browser extensions (dtdbook.com/link10), within dashboard software, and using external tools such as WebAIM Contrast Checker (dtdbook.com/link11).

[5]Diagnosis of Defective Colour Vision. (1993). Oxford Medical Publication (2nd edition 2001).

Checking accessibility of data labels

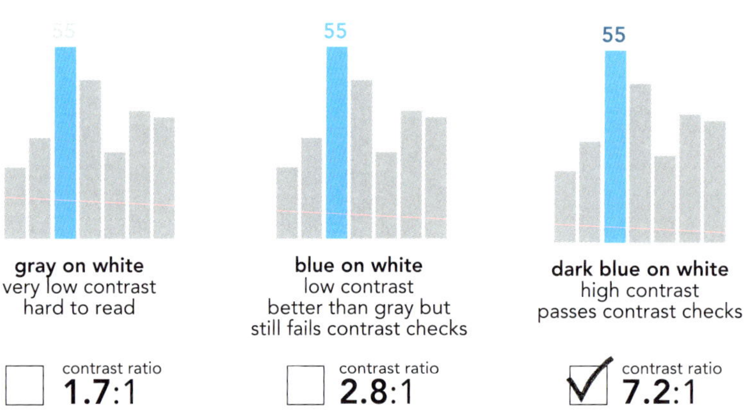

3:1 contrast ratio target to pass accessibility checks

FIGURE 8.17 Illustrating different contrast levels between text and background colors with data labels.

Summary

In this chapter, we've taken a deep dive into design recommendations to consider in your prototyping process. We've looked at multiple design considerations you should use while creating your wireframe, mockup, and prototype:

- Components of a dashboard, including BANs, charts, scale, orientation, and Gestalt principles, and interactive components
- Designing to a grid in order to create meaningful groupings and visual order on your dashboard
- Using color effectively through deliberate decisions that support different analytical insights

Each seemingly small design decision we make on a dashboard shapes the user experience in different ways. Make sure to take charge of those decisions, rather than assuming the design defaults in a tool are "good enough." You can read more about the dangers of defaults in the dedicated essay on the topic in Chapter 29.

Now, with your prototype in hand, let's move on to development.

Chapter 9

Development and User Testing

Amanda Makulec and Andy Cotgreave

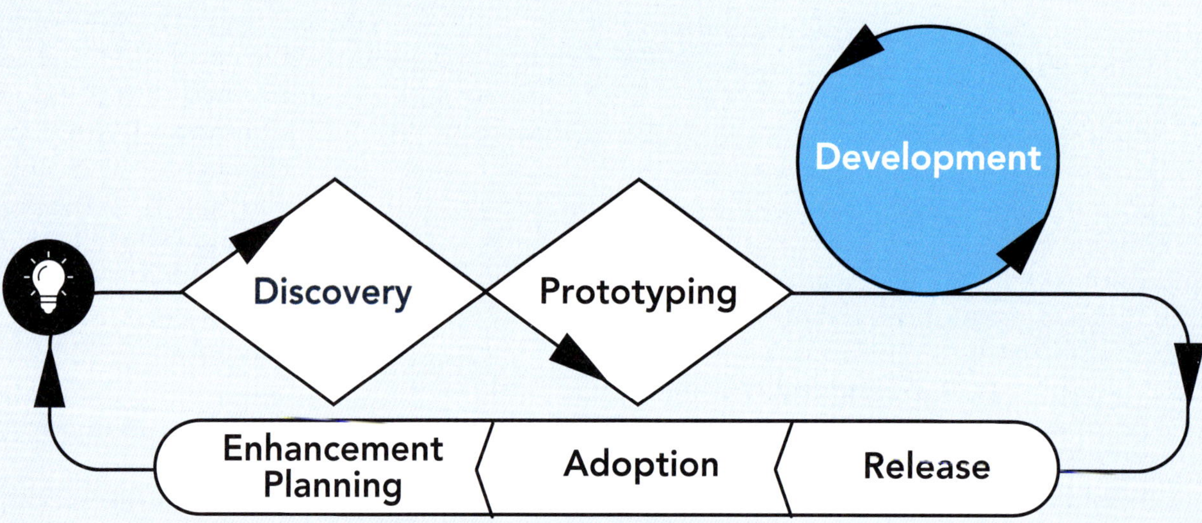

Development

While this may be one of the shortest chapters about our framework, it can be one of the longest phases in real time. During this part of the process, you're translating your design concept into a working dashboard.

In this chapter, we'll highlight process recommendations, considerations when developing as part of a team, and structures for gathering feedback. Much of the development will be shaped by the tools you use. Following our aim to write a book relevant across tech stacks, it is beyond the scope of this book to teach you the details of how to build dashboards in different tools.

Whether you're using Tableau, PowerBI, Looker, or any other tool, you'll find plenty of books and online resources for each. You should also use the knowledge base and community many tools have. If you're struggling with something in Tableau or PowerBI, it's likely that someone else has hit a similar challenge and found a path forward. Community leaders, such as Tableau Visionaries and Ambassadors or Microsoft MVPs, have excellent content (videos, blogs, etc.) that are a great place to start if you're feeling a bit lost as a new dashboard designer.

Start with Your Prototype

If you've followed the process so far, you have a defined list of requirements and a prototype. Review what you've designed so far and check for any unresolved feedback or requests: if they won't make it to this release, ensure you document the items in your backlog and clearly communicate *why* they're not being included with your users.

Development in Practice

Scenarios in Part II explore how teams translate mockups into working dashboards, with insights from the process of gathering and incorporating feedback from users. For deeper dives into this part of the process within different tools, take a look at Chapters 17 and 19.

Build Your Working Dashboard

Working within dashboarding tools with your real data, you may also realize some of the concepts that seemed like a great idea in a mockup don't translate as well to a real dashboard. When you hit those moments, go back to what business need you were trying to address with the chart and consider if there's a different way to meet that need – more interactivity? An additional filter? A different chart type? Come up with a new approach that meets the need and test it with your audience.

If you're working on a team to develop a dashboard, remember to break down the development work into pieces so the process doesn't rely on a single developer.

The following can enable better team collaboration when sharing the development workload:

- **Always designate a clear point person** so you do not end up overlapping effort. This could mean rotating responsibility and handing off files or working in a dedicated shared environment.

Creating Your Data Model

YOUR dashboard's data model is a fundamental part of the process. You might be lucky and the data already exists. More likely, you will need to do some data engineering: find the data; get permission to use it; extract it; create a data model; test and publish the data model; and finally create an updated schedule. It'd be lovely to have the model in place before you put a single chart onto your dashboard, but realistically you'll be building both in parallel.

Data engineering might not be in your job title, but the boundaries between data engineering and analysis are often blurred. If your organization has data engineers, then you'll likely be working with them to do these tasks. If not, it's a role you (and your team if you have one) will need to work on.

The engineering side of your dashboard is, alas, outside of the scope of this book. Good resources are *Fundamentals of Data Engineering* by Joe Reis and Matt Housley (O'Reilly 2022) and *Designing Data-Intensive Applications* by Maring Kleppmann (O'Reilly, 2017).

- **Have a defined backlog of development tasks** that team members can work from. Either ask team members to volunteer for different parts of the development up front or work sequentially through the prioritized list of needs. Make sure the list of tasks is specific enough that anything can be completed in a day or two, not two weeks – for example, developing one page within a dashboard with multiple pages instead of a task being "create dashboard."
- **Communicate routinely** through daily or weekly stand-up meetings where team members can share impediments to progress. Keep your meetings short and focused. Stand-up comes from the concept of a meeting where you're literally standing the whole time instead of settling into a meeting room. Use the backlog for a shared understanding on progress; focus the conversation on topics that merit conversation to move them forward. Ensure team members share if their bandwidth changes.
- **Document within the dashboard as you go,** including clear organization and labeling of calculations, annotating or using captions to explain to collaborators how and why components are set up in particular ways, and building some of the documentation of the dashboard as you go. You'll find more details about documentation in Chapter 10.

Your workflow will vary depending on whether you're developing the dashboard solo or with a team, as well as the software you're using. There are so many collaboration and development features, and they're constantly evolving, so we recommend consulting resources specific to your situation.

Address Performance Requirements

The development and testing process is about creating a dashboard that brings to life the concepts in your mockups and prototypes. As you build the working dashboard, it's important to consider how it will work with real data.

A performant dashboard not only has the charts and filters the user needs; it also responds quickly. A slow dashboard is frustrating at best and, at worst, makes people unwilling to use it.

Common metrics for performance focus on responsiveness. When a user selects a filter or takes an action on a dashboard, how quickly does the tool update the display accordingly? How long is too long will depend on your users' expectations, data complexity, and other factors. However, Ryan Sleeper, founder and principal at Playfair Data, sets a 5–10 second maximum as his benchmark.

User Testing

Once you have your working dashboard, it's time to run usability sessions to test how well the dashboard works for your users.

You can bring in larger groups of users than you did during the design phase, prioritizing users who represent different stakeholder groups and use cases. If your testing sessions are the first time your users are seeing the dashboard, take a few minutes to review its purpose, priorities, and goals so everyone has a common understanding of the work completed and the type of feedback you're looking for in a clear checklist. Otherwise, users can come in with new big ideas that are out of scope. While you can take note of these for a future dashboard, now is not the time to make large, expensive changes.

You can gather feedback in live meetings, or through collaboration apps like Slack, Teams, or even email.

During your usability sessions, use a defined structure to gather focused feedback. For example: create a short demo to walk through the dashboard and three to five scenarios that ask users to complete specific tasks. Without guidance or intervention, observe the users and ask them to think out loud so you can see where they get stuck in the exploration process. If you're gathering feedback asynchronously, ask them to make a recording of their process. Allow people to provide feedback in a shared document or repository.

Implementing Feedback

Coming out of your user feedback sessions, you'll have a list of notes from users. What do you do when the list is *long*?

Start by identifying features requested by multiple users or by high-priority user groups: these are your change requests. Estimate the effort and impact of each one and prioritize the changes according to what time you have available. Not every issue needs to be fixed. You will have a finite amount of time, and some issues can be addressed through training rather than changes.

Scaling Feedback to Include More Users Over Time (Amanda)

When you include users in your dashboard design process, who is engaged at what point may change.

I was working with a large healthcare company to develop a set of public health dashboards. The dashboards had three distinct stakeholder groups: a small leadership team and two larger groups that included the main users of the dashboard. During discovery, we interviewed users from all groups to identify the shared requirements.

Armed with our discovery outcomes, I worked with the client team who would eventually own the dashboard to develop user flows, wireframes, and mockups that could be adapted to different public health topics – a process that took weeks of iteration and back and forth. Only after we had a well-designed mockup did we go back to the wider group of users from our discovery interviews for input and feedback.

For this project, the client team were also users of the dashboards and understood the bigger picture around why the company was investing in these new tools. That knowledge enabled them to give feedback throughout the design process and helped us move faster through our wireframes and mockups.

During our usability sessions, we asked for specific feedback on the organization, flow, metrics, chart types, and text components of the dashboard; we also set some boundaries on what changes they could expect. The overall architecture with specific views would not change, for example, but we would consider adding filters or adjusting text for clarity.

We keep reiterating the importance of engaging your users but don't feel that you must to get feedback from everyone at every stage in the design and development process. Engaging different groups of users at different points gives you fresh perspectives and helps keep the flow of feedback feasible, even if you have a short development timeline.

Don't Tell Your Users How The Dashboard Works (Steve)

HERE'S an alternative way to get feedback from users the first time they see a dashboard: watch them use the dashboard without any verbal instruction. Show them the dashboard and, before *you tell them what it does*, get them to describe what they think it does.

Two years after launching the *Big Book of Dashboards* workshop, I realized I needed a capstone exercise for attendees. Jeff suggested an exercise he used in his classes where teams of four or five people would sketch a dashboard based on a written list of requirements.

These teams would have 45 minutes to sketch the dashboard, and then a representative of each team would present their work.

I called for a volunteer and the first presenter went into every detail of how the dashboard would work, what justified the team's decisions, and so on.

Uh-oh. That wasn't what I'd intended.

Three minutes into their presentation, I realized it would take the teams two hours to go through all the examples instead of the 30 minutes I had allocated. I politely stopped the talk and said something along these lines, "I'm not sure we'll have time to get into all these details, but I have an idea that might work well. Instead of you showing me the ins and outs of what you and your team crafted, I'll pretend to be your stakeholder. I'll tell you what I see and understand, and more importantly, what I don't understand."

Not only did this streamline my workshop, it became a technique that I use in my own work and that I encourage other people to do, too. Show the dashboard to your stakeholders and say as little as possible. Ask them to tell you what they understand – and don't understand. If your dashboard has an Achilles's heel (or heels), this approach will expose the flaws quickly.

Keep a central list of change requests in your shared backlog so that your other team members can see them. Changes you determine aren't feasible now are good ideas to address in future enhancements.

If you have the time, plan for an additional round of review and feedback with users after implementing the changes. Communicate clearly with users about: what changed since the last review; what changes are still planned but not completed; and which changes you will not be implementing.

Peer Review

Users aren't the only source of great feedback. Peer review from fellow dashboard developers always makes for a better final product. In our interviews, many people spoke about the benefits of peer review, particularly when dashboards were developed by a solo developer.

Peer review has three key benefits:

- Peers have data visualization knowledge. They can recommend alternate chart choices or identify where a dashboard isn't aligned with best practices, such as the use of color, missed opportunities for decluttering, or areas to improve alignment to the style guide.
- Peers can identify optimization opportunities, based on your analytics stack and data architecture.
- The skills of the entire group grow through seeing and reviewing everyone's work.

Peers who become great collaborators challenge you, celebrate you, and ultimately help you make better dashboards – and become a better designer. You can read more about our own experiences collaborating in Chapter 34.

Summary

Remember, there will *always* be something you can update and change. Often, those decisions are driven not just by what you want to deliver but by constraints like time, bandwidth, and even data availability.

At the end of the development, you should be approaching launch. Congratulations! During this phase, you should have completed:

- Data modeling and preparation to load into your dashboarding platform
- Prepared your dashboard for user testing
- Gathered feedback from user testing
- Made changes to your dashboard based on user feedback, bringing it to the point where your first release is developed and ready for quality assurance testing

Finding Dashboard Inspiration

You can also find inspiration on the Tableau's Viz of the Day and PowerBI's Data Stories Gallery. You can search each for business dashboards:
dtdbook.com/link12
dtdbook.com/link13

Chapter 10

Release and Adoption

Amanda Makulec and Andy Cotgreave

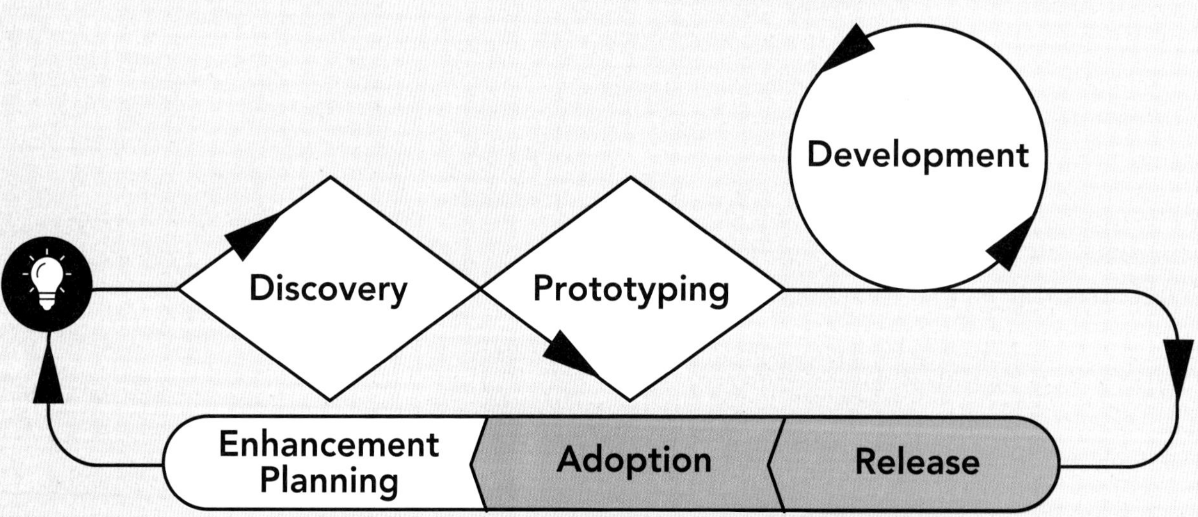

You've created your dashboard, tested with users, and iterated a few times, and you are approaching your release day. That's both nerve-racking and exciting! You might be tempted to tinker and make changes endlessly, but *don't let perfect be the enemy of launched*. Yes, the data quality needs to be rock-solid, but the front-end design can evolve with time. You can plan for future enhancements and releases, so this first release is only the start.

As you plan for your first release (or a new release, if you're making enhancements), make sure to allocate time for quality assurance checks, launch communications, and the change management work that gets users engaged with your new dashboard.

Quality Assurance

Don't let your dashboard go live without making sure the data you're presenting is accurate and the interactive components work as intended. You want to be the one catching an error before a user makes a poor decision based on bad data.

Plan time with the team to complete a dedicated quality assurance check when you're setting your development schedule and go-live date. The most beautiful dashboard in the world is useless if it's populated with poor quality data: garbage in, garbage out.

Consider: Are calculations running correctly? Does data in the dashboard match source data? When you click a filter, do the intended target charts refresh to show a different slice of the data – and do the numbers check out?

Quality assurance goes beyond double-checking the charts and features within the dashboard. Test how your users will log in to the system and navigate to the dashboard. Consider what dependencies with other IT processes could create challenges, including noting who within the organization to reach out to if issues emerge.

How apparently good choices have unintended consequences (Andy)

I was working with a large UK government department on their dashboards. They had been working on improving their data culture across the department. Things had been going well, and they were developing their second generation of dashboards, following a growth of usage on their analytics platform.

Everything worked great until the day the IT security team decided to add two-factor authentication (2FA) to their analytics platform.

In one day, visits to the site almost entirely disappeared. Their line chart tracking users' site logins was depressing: a steadily increasing line since the first dashboards were implemented, then a vertical cliff when 2FA was introduced. That piece of added friction killed the flourishing use of their dashboards.

Data security is, of course, a vital consideration, but this example showed how a seemingly small piece of friction – looking at your phone to get a password – can be enough to turn people away from a platform.

You can go a step further and define metrics for data quality. This is especially important with large scale dashboards with complex data preparation processes.

Consider an ACT framework for setting data quality metrics:

Accuracy: Challenge your team to think through how you might measure if the data in your dashboard is accurate compared with source systems. Sometimes, we're working with primary sources that *are* the system of record, so we focus more on monitoring for anomalies or inconsistencies. But what if you're consistently underreporting a number by 20%? How would you know? For priority measures, consider spot checking numbers in your dashboard against an additional data source where available.

Completeness: Check to ensure the data is complete across all metrics. For example, are there unexpected zero or low values that could indicate missing data?

Timeliness: Check to ensure the data in the dashboard spans the expected date range. If you expect to see data through the end of December but see data only through the end of November, there may be a lag or gap in your source tables.

The specific checks you make will vary from project to project. Use the ACT framework as a starting point to build a dedicated quality assurance checklist with your team. Filter the dashboard multiple times and conduct the same checks to ensure calculations, filters, and other types of interactivity operate as expected.

Documentation

If you win the lottery and don't show up to work the next day, how would anyone know how to manage your dashboard?

What if you moved on to different projects and had to come back to this current dashboard 12 months later? Would you be able to remember how the dashboard works?

Documentation is too often seen as a tedious afterthought, but it's vital to the maintenance of a dashboard.

At a minimum, for each dashboard you should have the following documentation:

- **A data dictionary** with a list of the field names, data types, sources, definitions, and additional notes someone would need to build new charts within your dashboard.
- **Business logic** used to define the calculations, data logic in the underlying tables, filters, and other components of the dashboard.
- **Data governance and security considerations,** including who should have access to the dashboard and where any additional safeguards, such as row level security constraints, should be applied.
- **A data quality log** including known open and resolved issues. A record of resolved issues will help you answer users' questions in the future and track recurring issues.

You are responsible for writing and maintaining documentation in a source system that works for you and your organization. For a small personal project, that may mean some notes in a personal document. For dashboards within a large corporation, you may use centralized knowledge management software like Confluence or Notion.

Written documentation plays a key role in building that knowledge base, but short videos can also be helpful – particularly when documenting how a feature works or the details a developer needs to maintain a complex chart. When using videos for documentation, keep them short with clear descriptions, rather than long videos that try to capture *everything*. While someone can skim a document or browse a table of contents, finding just where a particular detail is in a long video can feel frustrating.

You can also leverage the transcription capability many video recording tools have to create a starting draft for written documentation. Many recording tools also have auto-captioning capabilities; while these tools can be a bit imperfect, they remove one of the barriers to having more accessible videos. Discuss with your team what standards you'll follow around making any documentation or demo videos accessible.

Certain parts of documentation can work best in the dashboard itself. For example, adding explanations of calculation logic as comments in your calculated fields (Figure 10.1). Choose the best approach for you, be consistent, and share the decision with your team and your users.

You can also make information about the underlying data more accessible to users directly on the dashboard. Add an information button with answers to common data quality or data refresh questions, often placed in the upper-right corner of a dashboard. Refer to Chapter 19 to see the Children's Hospital Association metrics for an example of how to do this.

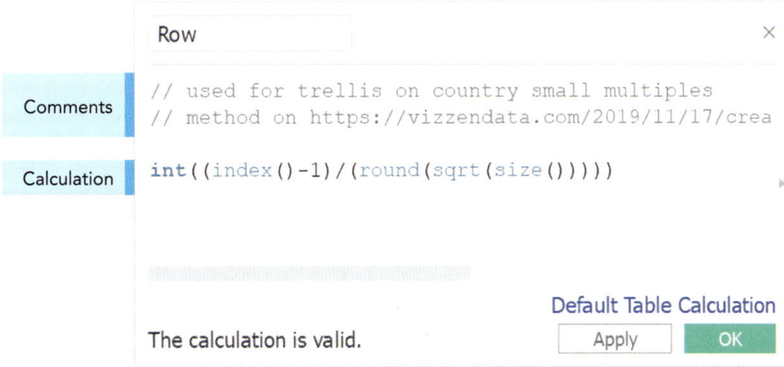

FIGURE 10.1 Example calculated field in Tableau with comments indicating what type of view the "row" calculation is used for and where a developer can review the method for setting up the trellis chart.

After working through a long development process, writing documentation may feel like an afterthought, but don't put it off. Write down your notes while the work on the dashboard is fresh in your mind.

Do Yourself a Favor and Write Good Documentation (Steve)

You will likely thank yourself later by writing good documentation as you go.

My first gig as a solo practitioner was for a major cable provider. I was tasked with visualizing survey data. What the stakeholders wanted was hard. Many of the calculations were spaghetti-like loops of nested statements. Just thinking about the challenges makes me shudder.

I was determined to crush the gig. In addition to delivering a collection of what were then cutting-edge dashboards, I provided meticulously crafted documentation. I covered everything from how the dashboards worked, explained all the thorny calculations that drove the charts, and provided a complete data dictionary. I thought, "Won't they be impressed!"

I did this so that *they* would be able to maintain and update the dashboards on their own.

Silly me.

I received a call six months later asking me to make some modifications to what I had delivered. They didn't want to make the changes themselves. They wanted *me* to make the changes.

At this point I had moved on to other projects and didn't have a clue how the dashboards worked, and I certainly didn't remember the logic behind the thorny calculations.

But I had great documentation, and I got back up to speed in about 15 minutes.

There's an interesting bonus to having written thorough documentation. From time to time, I'll need to use some of those thorny calculations in other projects. I've probably consulted that documentation a dozen times for unrelated projects.

As you mutter and grumble documenting your own dashboards, realize your future self will likely thank your present self for your endeavors.

Revisiting How You Measure Success

In discovery, you defined how to measure success for your launch; now it's time to revisit the definition. What does a successful release look like? How might the definition of success change over time? How will you collect the data you need for those measurements?

What matters most is that you have a plan to track success with your team and to *actually look at the data*. It's easy to launch a dashboard, breathe a big sigh of relief that the project is wrapped, and then let things simmer for a while without paying much attention. Don't fall into the trap of doing all this work to build and launch something without the last bit of follow-through to measure impact.

At least quarterly, assess the adoption and success of your dashboard, going back to our little "s" (things we can count) and big "S" (impact) measures of success.

Launch Communications

"If you build it, they will come!" is an ineffective way to launch a dashboard. A one-off effort, like pushing a new dashboard to your reporting portal and posting an "It's here!" on Slack, is also insufficient.

When you're ready to release your dashboard, consider the following:

- **Record a short training video:** Demonstrate how the dashboard works, working through all the main charts and interaction methods.
- **Launch meeting:** Host a demo meeting to showcase the analytical capabilities of the dashboard; don't assume that if you build it, users will immediately know how to use it! Focus on the priority users and decision-makers. Record the meeting and make it available asynchronously to those who cannot attend.
- **Launch email/communications:** Write a clear communication to distribute over email, Teams, Slack, or a dedicated portal/page including references to the purpose of the dashboard, priority requirements/features, how frequently the data will be refreshed, and who/where users can share feedback including any bugs they find and new feature requests.
- **Host office hours:** Maintain a drumbeat of opportunities for users to engage with your dashboard. Office hours can be informal meetings in the users' calendars where you can be available to respond to any ad hoc questions or training needs.
- **Enhancement request form:** Streamline requests with a feedback form and clear timelines for how often the team plans on prioritizing and accommodating those requests.
- **Enlist the support of power users:** If you have a large team with many dashboard users, consider having a smaller group of "power users" who can support others. Encourage them to be vocal advocates for the dashboard and share how they use the new tool in their work.
- **Make your champion visible:** If you have a product owner or other champion for the dashboard in leadership, make their voice heard in the launch meeting and communications. Sometimes, an influential figure on a team can give the friendly nudge for folks to shift behaviors.

Watch a Training Video Example

Recovery Data Science has excellent examples of short training videos for their dashboards. You can see one here: dtdbook.com/link14.

Release notes should include:

- **Changes to the data sources,** including any new or retired data sources
- **Any data quality issues** identified in the period from the last release (e.g., if one area of the organization is missing information from the most recent period)
- **Notable UX improvements** including new charts, buttons, or views

Communication doesn't stop after launch. Each time you make significant enhancements, let users know. If there's a noteworthy refresh of the data, let users know. If you discover bugs that won't be immediately fixed, let users know.

Change Management

In our interviews with dashboard developers, two signals that a dashboard is doomed to failure included: having no tie to a broader data culture strategy (the dashboards created for the sake of *having a dashboard* and not any other clear purpose); and a lack of organizational support, like a clear champion in a leadership seat or other influential role.

Change management practices can help teams support adoption and use. As a dashboard designer, focus on two key enablers when encouraging people to change how they use data in their work:

- Cultivate champions who can inspire others to use data more often.
- Make each dashboard project part of a larger effort to create a culture that values data.

Let's expand on how we accomplish both.

Cultivate Champions

In our interviews, developers raved about the importance of champions as a critical piece of the adoption puzzle.

Having champions engaged at the start of a project gives them visibility into what is being built and helps them better advocate – which is why they could be a great product owner or team member (as outlined in Chapter 3). Your product owner is part of defining requirements, validating wireframes and mockups, and driving prioritization decisions, so they'll have the background on why decisions were made and be bought into the final product.

Heather Lewis, from Augusta University, told us that "having senior champions like a university provost use and promote dashboards drives adoption. When dashboards are launched at large scale team meetings, having a senior leader speak to how and why the dashboard supports the organization's goals inspires others to explore the data too."

On an even larger scale, the team behind the Johns Hopkins University (JHU) COVID-19 dashboard had people out in the world advocating for using their display (read more about their design process in Chapter 25). Champions, from journalists to public health experts, initially emerged organically. Seeing the tool in use, the general public learned it was available and started referencing the dashboard on a daily basis. Over the three years the dashboard was in production, it had more than 2.5 billion views.

Champions also play a key role in fostering trust between the dashboard developer and its users. In our interviews, Andy Moore, Chief Data Officer at Bentley, describes two key aspects of trust:

The trust journey and familiarity with new formats: Moore shared about the "trust journey" in transitioning from traditional formats (like PowerPoint) to more dynamic dashboard formats like Tableau. If people are familiar with existing processes, he moves them to a new system step-by-step. If it means re-creating an existing static PowerPoint report in Tableau, he'll do it, because it makes the users' transition easier.

Trust in data accuracy and relevance: He emphasized the importance of presenting senior leaders with dashboards that they feel comfortable looking at. "These leaders often have very limited time to process the information presented to them," he said. "Therefore, it's crucial for them to quickly discern whether they can trust the dashboard, understand it, and decide on the actions needed based on the data presented."

Moore's goal is to get the leaders to trust that the dashboard is providing them with the necessary information and that the underlying data is accurate, complete, and timely.

How Do I Find Champions?

As you work on your next dashboard, ask your team at the start who your champions can be. Ideally, your product owner who is representing the user perspectives, and helping to prioritize work can be one of those champions, but a champion doesn't have to be part of the core development team.

Who is it that influences how decisions get made? Could that person use the dashboard as a new tool in their workflow? How could they showcase the tool beyond "See, it's here" and move toward demonstrating "look how I use this to help make decisions"?

If you're feeling stuck on identifying champions who are in leadership positions, consider looking at your list of users who you interviewed or were involved in the design process. Who has a lot of enthusiasm for the new dashboard? Or look at usage statistics and identify the high-volume power users who may be well positioned to explain how they're using the dashboard in their work.

Be mindful that champions or sponsors can come with challenges if *advocacy* turns into *design by committee*. If you're actively recruiting champions for your dashboard, be clear on what influence they can (or cannot) expect in return on updates and changes. Set clear boundaries on how change requests are made, prioritized, and implemented. If you have specific areas where you need feedback, ask very specific questions for feedback rather than very broad or open-ended questions. For example, "Does the color make sense?" or "Do you understand this chart?" rather than "What do you think about the dashboard?"

Build a Culture of Data Use

Changing how data is used across an organization, rather than by one individual, is challenging and does not happen overnight. The most elegant, thoughtful dashboard with the most influential champion isn't enough to support *sustained use*. Organizations and teams that have cultivated a culture of demand for, and use of, data will have a continued appetite for tools and resources that provide easy access to data that will inform decision-making.

In our interviews with dashboard developers, we heard that a thriving culture of data use was key to the success of their dashboards. Culture change and winning over people's hearts and minds takes time, though.

Based on these interviews, here are three lessons organizations at any size can adopt to improve use of dashboards in decision-making:

- **Setting a tone with leadership:** Senior leadership must be advocates. They need to support the dashboard projects and use the dashboards in their decision-making. The data leader at a major entertainment corporation told us that whenever new senior leadership joins the team, they are expected to back their assertions with the existing data assets.
- **Reduce the clicks to access:** Reducing friction in how users access the dashboards is critical to building that culture of data use; the more you can meet them in the spaces they are and serve up the data they need, the more likely they are to use those dashboards in their work. For example, no extra site logins or additional navigation required.

Where Can I Learn More About the Organizational Change Part of Dashboard Success?

Our book focuses on a process for, and examples of, dashboards that deliver – each a slice of the broader analytics ecosystem at an organization. The themes in this specific chapter hit on larger organizational needs that are the topics of whole books and bodies of work.

If you're on a data team, you may be tempted to focus all your skill building on your technical chops. But you also need to see the big picture to make sure what you create gets used and to enable analytics at scale.

Consider also exploring the following resources:

- *Leading Change* by John P. Kotter (dtdbook.com/link15) to learn more about the 8 Steps for Leading Change
- *Radical Candor* by Kim Scott to learn more about managing teams and giving effective feedback
- The Data Lodge (https://www.thedatalodge.com/) founded by Valerie Logan to explore resources on data literacy at an organizational scale, including data governance

- **Personalize:** Even a well-designed dashboard can feel overwhelming to someone unaccustomed to working with data tools. Consider ways to allow each stakeholder to only see data relevant to them, either through flexible configuration options where the data is pre-filtered based on users' roles or location or with filters placed on the left or top of the dashboard to encourage users to filter first.

At an organizational level, investing in data governance is necessary to make sure that when there's demand for data, teams have access to *quality* data. Dedicated resources and structures for data governance can help create a unified language of data and standards for data management. These standards can reduce issues with data access for developers when they're building new dashboards. Good governance can also address the challenge of "reinventing the wheel" that often plagues large organizations. Imagine how galling it would be to build a dashboard only to discover another team within the organization has built one that's nearly the same!

The Importance of Change Management in Building Successful Dashboards (Jeff)

I am a big fan of John Kotter. His book *Leading Change* has been one of the most influential books I've read. My signed copy of his book is one of the few I still keep in my office. I had the opportunity to study with Professor Kotter at an Executive Education program on Leadership at the Harvard Business School in 2006. Professor Kotter was a laidback professor, and very entertaining with a wonderful dry sense of humor. His classes were by far my favorite of the program.

When I returned to my office, I immediately printed "The 8 Steps for Leading Change" onto a small piece of paper and taped it to the bottom of my monitor in my office. It was the only piece of paper attached to my monitor, and it meant that every day I could just glance down and see those steps as a quick reminder.

I found these steps to be critical to the success of moving projects forward in that organization. It was a fast-moving environment, where things changed quickly, and the organization needed to be adaptable.

That type of environment can often lead to people feeling that the priorities and projects are always changing. "Form a Strategic Vision" and communicating it clearly was helpful to ground folks and to prioritize and focus efforts on a common goal. "Enable Action by Removing Barriers" was a helpful reminder of my purpose as the chief operating officer. Folks didn't need me to help them with the easy problems. They could figure those out on their own.

It was the harder problems that created the roadblocks. "Creating a Sense of Urgency" is important, but following up by helping to remove barriers is even more important. Would you rather have a boss that says, "Why isn't this done yet? This should be your top priority." Or one that says, "This is really important. What can I do to help you get this done?"

I found the easiest step to implement is "Generating Short-Term Wins," and celebrating these wins is great for morale and keeping momentum moving. The hardest to implement was "Institute Change" or as I had it on my list, "Make it Stick." This is where the rubber meets the road. Building something new and then implementing it as a new process at scale has always been the hardest part, but it's also where the biggest wins come from.

If you've not read *Leading Change*, then I would highly recommend doing so and trying to implement these steps into your work.

Summary

At the end of the release and adoption phase, you'll have a live dashboard out in the world, or at least out within your organization. When completing the release of your new dashboard, you should have:

- **Tested usability and performance** before release to ensure the dashboard is rendering at a reasonable pace
- **Completed quality assurance checks**
- **Confirmed clear measures of success** and how you will track dashboard usage
- **Pushed your dashboard to production** so your users can access the new tool, with any governance requirements in place
- **Created a communication and launch plan** that includes champions for promoting adoption
- **Designed a dedicated feedback form** for change requests after launch
- **Written dashboard documentation** that is usable for team members and any new collaborators on the dashboard

The launch of your dashboard isn't the end – it's a beginning, where you've created a new way for your users to access information.

Our framework is cyclical, rather than linear: you'll continue to collect feedback and implement change requests as part of a process of continuous improvement that we'll unpack in the last chapter on the framework.

Chapter 11

Maintenance and Enhancements

Amanda Makulec and Andy Cotgreave

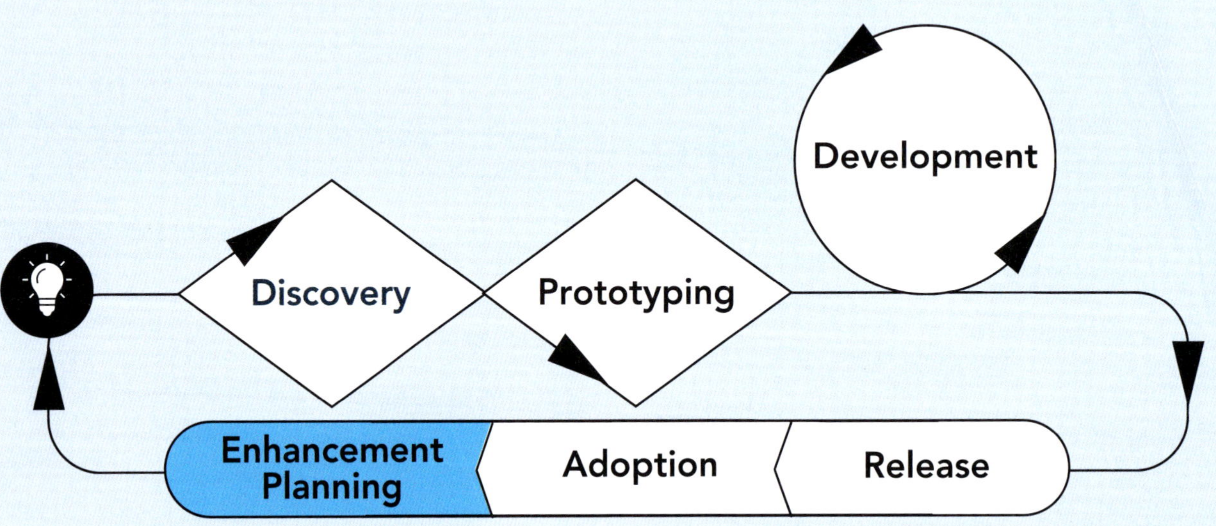

Planning for Change

Dashboards that deliver are also dashboards that evolve. That's a good thing; user needs and the metrics that matter evolve too.

Peter Tillotson, analytics lead and data scientist working as a contractor at Riot Games, told us about their main daily KPI dashboard: it has been in production for *more than a decade*. The dashboard looks very different from when it was first launched as a monthly report. While some key metrics have remained the same, the analytics, design, and release frequency have all evolved in response to user feedback.

None of this happens by accident: Riot Games developed a system for prioritizing enhancements to their dashboards. They nurtured a culture that values access to information and found ways to optimize how developers and users spend their time. This sets them up for success not just in launching *new* dashboards but in maintaining and enhancing the ones they have.

What goes into managing a dashboard once it's gone live? You need to plan how to maintain and refresh data sources and how to manage change requests. This means gathering ongoing user feedback, tracking data to inform future design decisions, and making changes to the dashboard over time.

Let's unpack *how* we can make those changes in a manageable way.

Define Who Is Responsible

In the maintenance phase, you'll be collecting and prioritizing enhancement requests. As you plan this process, consider the following:

- Who will be responsible for implementing changes, and how will time be allocated for them?
- How will you collect and store enhancement requests in a backlog of requests?
- Who will be responsible for deciding the importance and impact of change requests?

Take the time to define a process for capturing enhancement requests, which will allow you to set expectations with users. Adam Mico, data analytics and strategy leader at Moderna, told us how they made their feedback process manageable as a large organization. At first, change requests were coming in unsustainably fast. Users sent messages almost daily to various members of the analytics team. That was a positive signal indicating that users were engaging with the dashboard, but it was chaotic and caused a lot of disruption among the analytics team.

To address the pace of change requests, Adam created a weekly working session to gather input and feedback, with one person assigned as the single point of contact. This shift made everyone more efficient: the team consolidated one list of ideas and set better boundaries and expectations with the dashboard users.

Dashboard Maintenance

Data Quality

The quality assurance checks you did during release aren't a one-time assessment; you need to plan how to monitor for any ongoing data quality issues.

The charts on the dashboards themselves are a tool for monitoring data problems. Look for clues like:

- Is the value outside of the expected or allowable range of values?
- Does the data diverge notably from historic trends for the same metric?
- Are two metrics that we expect to move together instead diverging?

For example, if your dashboard tracks the average number of patients a doctor sees in a day and the patient volume more than triples in a given day, it will show up as a huge spike (Figure 11.1). That level of variance might be larger than expected and needs investigation.

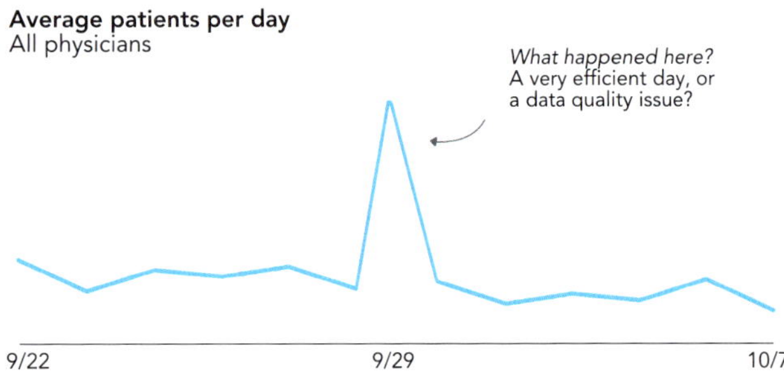

FIGURE 11.1 Sample line chart showing a big daily spike, which could prompt us to investigate if we have a data quality issue or just an abnormally high patient volume.

There could be many reasons for the spike. Perhaps there was a flu shot clinic where each patient visit was unusually quick. In that case, that data isn't an issue. But if there isn't a clear explanation for the variance, maybe a data error needs to be found and fixed. Your role is to play data detective when you see issues like these on your own dashboards: are they genuine outliers, or data errors?

Some analytics tools have functionality to set up automated alerts when values are outside of an expected range or show wide variance compared to a reference point. Use these to create an automatic monitoring system.

Bug Fixes

Things break. Your dashboard's bugs might include filters not operating as expected, missing tooltips, or instructional overlays that users can't turn off easily. While we all do our best to catch issues during quality assurance checks before the dashboard goes live, there will always be *something* your users will find after release that's wrong!

Make sure your dashboard includes information on who to contact if a user finds a bug. Then, if you receive an alert about an issue:

- Identify if it's a critical issue that requires an immediate fix or something to add to your backlog for your next round of changes (more on that shortly).
- Replicate the issue to make sure you can see what the problem is. If the feedback is unclear, ask the user to show you the problem.

- Thank the user for flagging the issue and communicating expectations around any upcoming fix. Clear communication builds trust and ensures your users feel heard.

Implementing Dashboard Enhancements

Build an Enhancement Backlog

Give users a way to provide feedback so that you can log, prioritize, and implement enhancements. You could do this in meetings, as the team at Moderna did, or through forms and collaboration software.

You could create a form for capturing users' requests. This should be accessible from your dashboard. Specific details for actionable feedback include:

- **Dashboard Name:** Identify which dashboard the feedback is about.
- **Page title:** If the dashboard has multiple pages or views, identify which page the problem was on.
- **Type of feedback:** Classify the feedback requests based on type. These can include data, design, functionality, or data quality/bug.
- **Feedback description:** Free text field for writing feedback.
- **Related images:** It's very useful when trying to re-create an issue to have pictures to refer to.
- **Name and email:** As optional fields for following up to clarify the request.

Implementing Change Requests

How frequently a dashboard is updated depends on how often the dashboard is used, how often the data updates, and whether any significant showstopping bugs get discovered. What matters is setting expectations for how frequently you'll prioritize your list of requests and make changes.

When it's time to make a round of changes, start with prioritizing your list of bugs and change requests. You can borrow ideas from Agile here, such as using a prioritization matrix (Figure 11.2). Classify every request according to its impact and the effort to implement it. This groups changes into high, medium, and low priority. Prioritize high-impact changes, including identifying ways to address those changes that are also high effort; if you always prioritize high-impact, *low-effort* changes, you'll miss the opportunity to tackle the bigger change requests. You may choose not to implement every request, and *that is okay* if you communicate those decisions clearly with your users.

As you did in earlier phases, engage your users as you make updates. Considering a few different chart tweaks to accommodate a request? Show suggested changes to the person who submitted the item and get their feedback. While enhancement sprints are typically speedier than completing a whole new dashboard, you don't want to abandon our user-centered mindset.

Once you've implemented your changes, do a quality assurance check, compile additions to your documentation (for your developers), write your

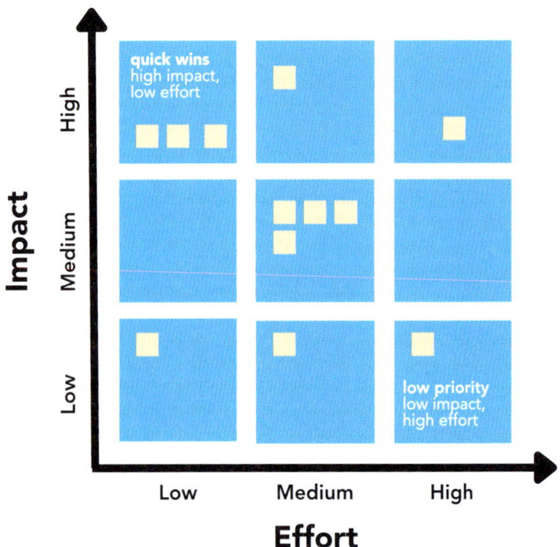

FIGURE 11.2 A prioritization matrix can help you decide which changes to implement.

release notes (for your users), and publish. You can follow many of the same recommendations outlined around quality assurance checks and user communication in the previous chapter.

Remember, users are often quick to complain about what they *don't* like. The same feature one user can't stand might delight someone else, who won't always itemize what you did right. A colleague of Andy's at Salesforce told us about multiple complaints they were getting about the behavior of date filters on their main dashboard. The team implemented a change, only to receive howls of pain from a previously quiet group who *loved* the original date filters and the change in the filters impacted the performance for some users. On reflection, they had been careful to listen to the issues being raised, but did not do enough user research before implementing the enhancements. Test your changes not only with users who made the request (ensuring you've addressed their need) but also with other users who may bring a different perspective.

When I Didn't Know How to Say No (Andy)

EARLY in my days as a dashboard developer at the University of Oxford, I did my best to accommodate all my users' change requests. I remember releasing one of my first dashboards where I'd deliberately tried to keep things simple. I got lots of requests from users for new filters and charts.

I took this as a good sign. They were using the dashboard, and I'd clearly not given them enough ways to answer all their questions. Aiming to please my audience, I'd add the features they requested. More requests came in. More features got added.

It went on for months until a new user told me they couldn't make any sense of the dashboard. "How could that be?" I thought. "I've literally implemented everything their colleagues wanted."

I showed my dashboard to a more senior developer, and they pointed out that I'd been too accommodating. What had once been a pleasing dashboard with a limited scope had turned into a sprawling, confusing mess. I no longer have access to that dashboard to share with you, but Figure 11.3 shows the kind of outcome I remember: the clean, original, dashboard on the left, and the result of me adding all the requests on the right.

The episode taught me that it's vital that we, the dashboard designers, do not say yes to everything. That doesn't mean you aren't helping your users. There are many ways you can implement requests without sacrificing the integrity of your design. You can build in features that expand and collapse on demand to reveal more advanced features. You could build new dashboard pages containing new sections of analysis. Sometimes you might even need a whole new dashboard.

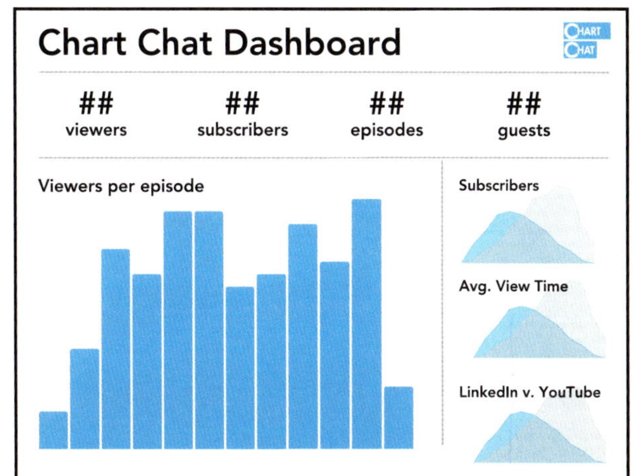

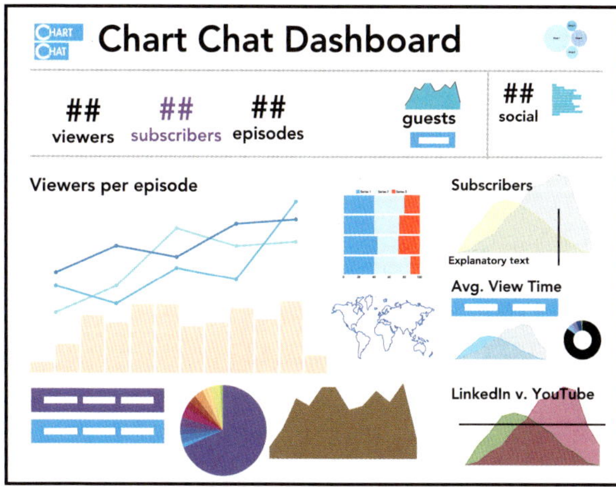

FIGURE 11.3 The possible outcome of accommodating every request from your users.

Decommissioning a Dashboard

You may need to decide if a dashboard will be *decommissioned*, no longer refreshed with new data or actively managed by a team member. This decision is often made for one of three reasons:

- **No longer needed.** This can happen if the business question the original dashboard was designed to answer is no longer relevant. This could be because it had a finite life span (e.g., tracking a specific marketing campaign) or the overall strategy has fundamentally changed.
- **No longer used.** This will be evident in usage statistics, signaling that the dashboard no longer serves your users' needs. If it's unclear *why* the dashboard isn't being used, consult with some of the users or the product owner for insights before moving forward with decommissioning.
- **Not successful enough to be worth the effort.** This becomes an important consideration when the manual data refresh and maintenance tasks start taking longer and longer. Go back to your measures of success and consider if the time and energy to manage the dashboard is still worthwhile.

If you decommission a dashboard, don't just throw it in the trash folder on your computer. Keep a copy for reference if someone requests to revisit the same analysis in the future.

Maintain and Enhance Checklist

Maintenance is an ongoing process that matches users' evolving needs and really ends only when you decommission your dashboard.

During maintenance, you should have:

- A clear process for users to share their feedback and requests for new features.
- A central backlog of change requests, gathered through a form or another means of user communication.
- A prioritized list of changes to implement for your enhancement sprint, including a clear estimate of the level of effort changes will take.
- Release notes for your users communicating changes and new features. If there have been big changes, revisit some of the recommendations around launch communications in the previous chapter such as hosting a demo meeting.

Centering People

As we close out the first part of this book, let's take a step back and look at the big picture. We've covered a detailed process for designing dashboards that may have you feeling a bit overwhelmed. Our aim isn't to create an impossibly deep set of expectations – instead, we want you to have an adaptable roadmap to design and build a dashboard that delivers.

Dashboards by Committee (Steve)

DASHBOARDS by committee can work.

Shortly before embarking on writing *The Big Book of Dashboards*, I received a call from Troy Magennis, the president of Focused Objective, LLC. Troy is an expert in software development, modeling, and forecasting. Software firms hire him to help them bring in solid products on time. Troy was working with a company that developed kanban software and thought that I would be a good fit for the firm.

The engagement would consist of embedding Tableau dashboards inside the company's product. They needed top-notch stuff as the dashboards would all be customer-facing and would reflect the company itself.

Troy called me in because the dashboards were anything but top-notch, consisting of impossible-to-decipher "cumulative flow diagrams." You can look up what they are or just take my word that they are not helpful.

This all sounded fun and challenging until Troy described how our two-day onsite engagement would work. I would come in and help people on the team build prototype dashboards, using nonstop feedback from the marketing team, sales team, and senior management, who would all take part in designing the dashboards.

This was not how I built dashboards. I thought this would be "dashboard by committee," and people would insist on 3D pie charts and lots of colors. I would have to spend many hours as people got into shouting matches. I was convinced this would end horribly.

Boy, was I wrong.

Troy's approach soon became the way I would build dashboards. He was a superb facilitator and led us through a process that incorporated many of the elements in our framework, including

Spark. Troy and senior management realized that the embedded dashboards were neither polished nor providing insights. They had to have something better if their offering was going to be competitive.

Discovery. We had the heads of sales and marketing present, and they acted as proxies for end users. They had already done their persona mapping and user journeys. Indeed, they had virtually all the right people in the room for important discussions. And don't worry, they got real end users involved before the product was released.

Prototyping (and Development). Working with a data engineer and a dashboard-designer-in-training, we iterated quickly. When we had something to show we would reassemble all the interested parties in the conference room and present our work. We'd have lively discussions, listen to feedback, and then ask folks to go back to their offices for 60 minutes or so while we tinkered. Yes, it would only take 60 minutes as the engineer knew the data and we had a tool that would allow us to iterate – fast! The ping-ponging of ideas led to some great stuff, much better than what I would have built without fast feedback.

Important: we weren't asking senior management to commit to two full days while we built working dashboards. We certainly needed people onsite so we could meet when needed, but all told, the teams and senior management only spent three hours out of the two days in the conference room.

Adoption. The stakeholders, now co-authors, took pride in the new dashboards. They would later become ardent promoters when the new dashboards were rolled out. Now champions for the cause, these dashboards were no longer glossed over in product demos but something that was promoted with pride.

This was an enthralling experience for all involved. For me, it was helpful to see things, in real time, through fresh eyes and better understand the pain points for users. For the stakeholders, they got to see how what we were building led to better and faster insights.

Ryan Gensel, principal strategist at Thinking Interface Design, says processes and frameworks shouldn't be rigid, and we agree. We hope you'll adopt the same mindset when adapting this framework to your work.

Following a standard process to the letter to build your dashboard is not the ultimate goal. People matter more than process. Engaging with your users throughout the process helps you create a dashboard they'll delight in using. Through that partnership with your users, you also build trust. That trust can change the shape of your conversations as you collaborate with users on enhancements and new analytical products.

Across our experiences and in our interviews with developers across industries, the most important enabling factors that set up a team for dashboard design success include:

- Having a clear purpose
- Engaging with users throughout the process
- Defining success early on
- Having champions who support a culture of data use
- Building trust in the data and the tools

Supporting your users with adoption of new dashboards is critical; it isn't as simple as "build it and they will use it." Instead, teams and organizations that succeed are investing in data literacy programs to support the use of data for decision-making at all levels.

Adam Mico, at Moderna, shared how the organization supports data culture across the organization starting with seeing *everyone* as a data person. Everyone in the organization is given the opportunity to attend a two-day, in-person data literacy training developed in partnership with an Ivy League university. That's a significant investment, particularly when considering time away from daily responsibilities and travel for more than 5,000 staff a year. But the cost of not investing in data knowledge across the firm is higher. Giving all employees the skills to analyze and understand data empowers them to use data in every decision. This in turn encourages more people, from C-suite to entry-level logistics staff, to bring data to their conversations and decisions.

No matter how you choose to apply our design framework, we hope it empowers you to build *dashboards that deliver*.

PART II

SCENARIOS

In this part, we include more than a dozen real-world scenarios. We describe why their design works and share key stories about how the developers applied elements in our design framework as part of their projects.

We envision you browsing through the scenario section looking for an example that most closely matches what it is you are tasked with visualizing and sharing via a dashboard. This internal conversation should be at play:

> *"Although my data isn't exactly the same as what's in the scenario, it's close enough, and this dashboard really does a great job of helping me see and understand it."*

Don't skip over scenarios that at first appear to have little or no relevance to the work you are doing. We wouldn't be writing about it if we didn't think there was wisdom you could apply to your own work.

Consider the bowling dashboard in Chapter 12. It would be ridiculous for us to write about something that *only* benefits high school bowling coaches; they're not exactly our primary target audience. But there are so many things in that scenario that you can apply outside of the bowling context (e.g., customer support monitoring or restaurant franchise comparisons). We can guarantee that the process discussions will be worth reading as the debates among the book authors and dashboard designer are eye-opening.

The same applies to the NASA hyperwall scenario in Chapter 26. We suspect there aren't too many people reading this book that are building 20-foot-wide displays to be consumed by the public in an exhibit setting. But as with the bowling dashboard, it uses techniques you can apply to your own work.

Chapter 12

Team Coaching Dashboard

Kevin Flerlage

Dashboard Designer: Kevin Flerlage

Organization: High school bowling team

How This Dashboard Delivers: The key stakeholder, a coach of a high school bowling team, can now determine which players should play when and in so doing win more matches. Parents can now appreciate the coach's decisions, and players can see what they need to do to improve.

Audience: High school coach, students on the team, and parents of students on the team.

Team: A single developer/subject-matter expert (SME) with input from primary stakeholder (the coach).

Tools: Excel spreadsheets to create and maintain the data and Tableau for the dashboard. The interactive dashboard is viewed using a desktop or laptop browser.

Timeline: Inception to release was one month. The data is updated manually as matches are played. Improvements are made on an ad hoc basis. The audience views the dashboard once or twice a week.

Chapter Author: Steve Wexler

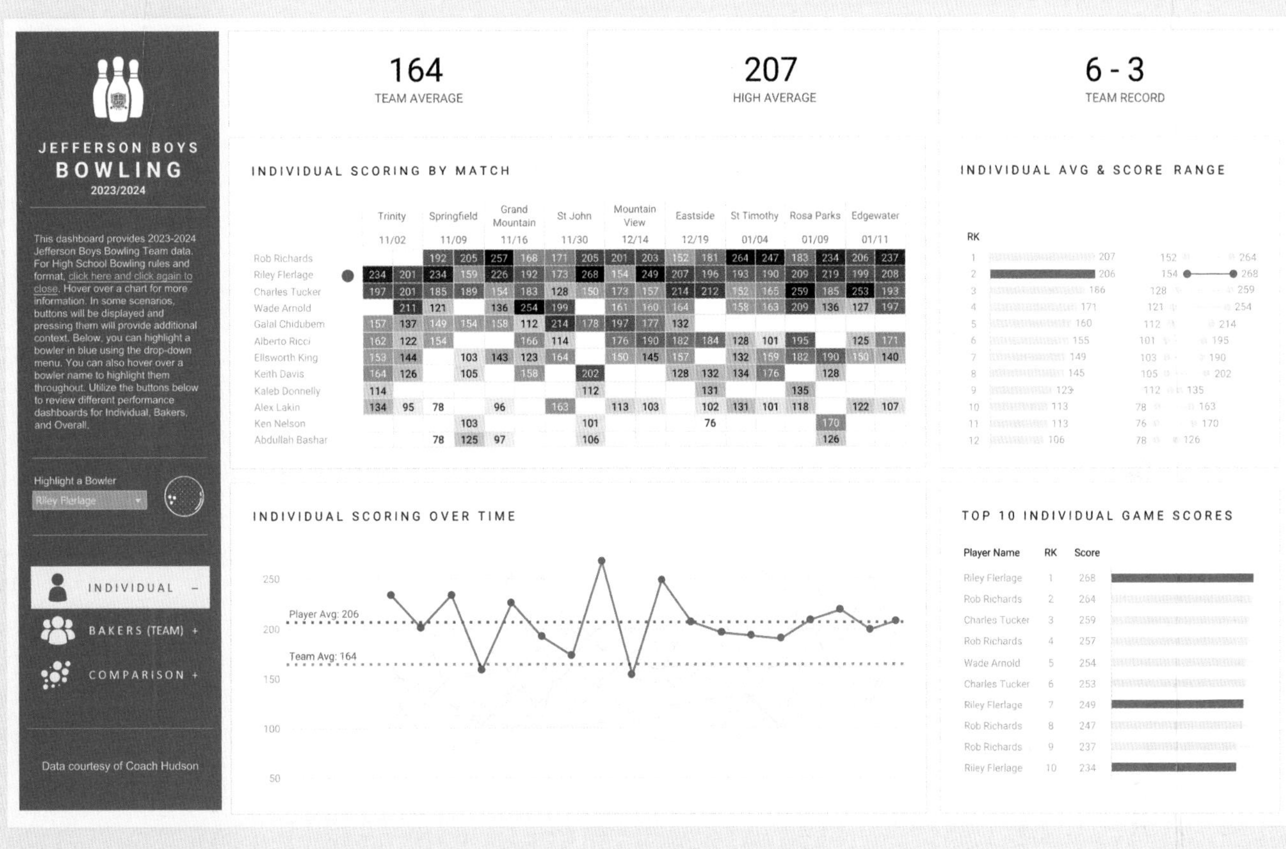
JEFFERSON BOYS
BOWLING
2023/2024
This dashboard provides 2023-2024 Jefferson Boys Bowling Team data. For High School Bowling rules and format, click here and click again to close. Hover over a chart for more information. In some scenarios, buttons will be displayed and pressing them will provide additional context. Below, you can highlight a bowler in blue using the drop-down menu. You can also hover over a bowler name to highlight them throughout. Utilize the buttons below to review different performance dashboards for Individual, Bakers, and Overall.
Highlight a Bowler
Riley Flerlage
INDIVIDUAL –
BAKERS (TEAM) +
COMPARISON +
Data courtesy of Coach Hudson
164
TEAM AVERAGE
207
HIGH AVERAGE
6 - 3
TEAM RECORD
INDIVIDUAL SCORING BY MATCH
Trinity 11/02
Springfield 11/09
Grand Mountain 11/16
St John 11/30
Mountain View 12/14
Eastside 12/19
St Timothy 01/04
Rosa Parks 01/09
Edgewater 01/11
Rob Richards
Riley Flerlage
Charles Tucker
Wade Arnold
Galal Chidubem
Alberto Ricci
Ellsworth King
Keith Davis
Kaleb Donnelly
Alex Lakin
Ken Nelson
Abdullah Bashar
INDIVIDUAL AVG & SCORE RANGE
RK
INDIVIDUAL SCORING OVER TIME
Player Avg: 206
Team Avg: 164
TOP 10 INDIVIDUAL GAME SCORES
Player Name RK Score
Riley Flerlage 1 268
Rob Richards 2 264
Charles Tucker 3 259
Rob Richards 4 257
Wade Arnold 5 254
Charles Tucker 6 253
Riley Flerlage 7 249
Rob Richards 8 247
Rob Richards 9 237
Riley Flerlage 10 234

Big Picture

You are the coach of a high school bowling team, and you want to figure out who should be playing so you have the best chance of winning a match. You need to determine the best bowlers (or which ones are on a hot streak) to play in individual head-to-head matches. You also need to assemble the best players for team participation (called "Bakers") where each student plays two frames, and the total score is assembled from individual and team play.

But there is more to this than your expert opinion as the coach. Over-zealous parents may demand that their child play more often, and you want to be able to justify your decisions with easy-to-understand visualizations.

Finally, you want the students to understand how you are making decisions, see where they stand with respect to their teammates, and recognize what they need to do to improve.

Specifics

You need to be able to

- See which players have the highest averages.
- See which players have a high average but have "cooled off" over the past several matches.
- See which players have a low average but have become "hot" over the past several matches.
- See which players mark (meaning they get a strike or spare) consistently. This is particularly useful in team play (Bakers) when there are many players playing one or two frames each.

Related Scenarios

- You are the director of customer support for a tech product and need to monitor for each representative the number of support tickets closed, time spent on phone calls/chat sessions, and customer satisfaction ratings.
- You own several franchise restaurants and need to compare sales, patron turnover, employee turnover, and a variety of other metrics across all the restaurants. Your goal is to see which locations are performing well and apply their approaches to help the other restaurants perform better.

How People Use the Dashboard

The Individual Dashboard

The coach (and interested parents and students) have access to three separate dashboards that provide insights into the performance and trends of individual players. In Figure 12.1 we see the Individual dashboard (1) that highlights a single player's performance. In this case, Riley Flerlage is selected (2), and his scores are highlighted using a dot (3). Accessing the other dashboards is a matter of clicking the Bakers or Comparison buttons along the left side, directly below Individual (1).

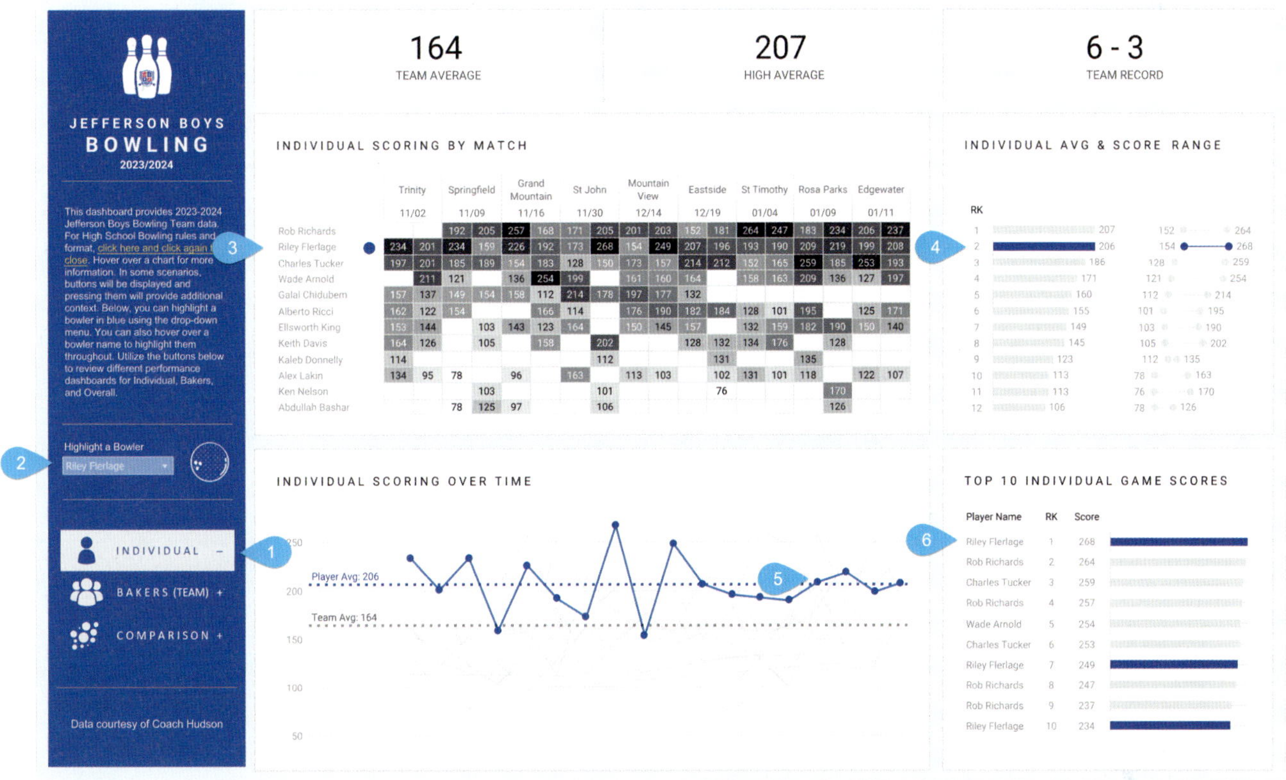

FIGURE 12.1 Various components of the individual dashboard. Note that in the Individual Scoring Over Time line chart (bottom left), we can see the selected player's average score and compare it to the team average score.

> ## The Power of the Little Dot
>
> **The** blue dot next to Riley Flerlage's name is one of the smallest elements on the dashboard, but it instantly identifies which player is the focus of our exploration.

We can see that Riley has played in every match (there are no gaps in the highlight table that occupies the upper left of the dashboard), is the second-ranked player with an average of 206, has a range of scores from 154 to 268 (4), has been playing consistently at or near his average the last four matches (5), and has three of the top 10 individual game scores (6).

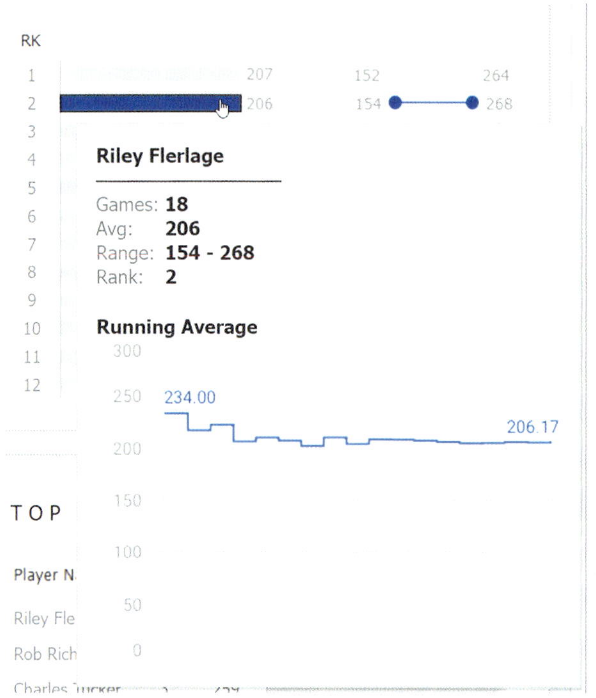

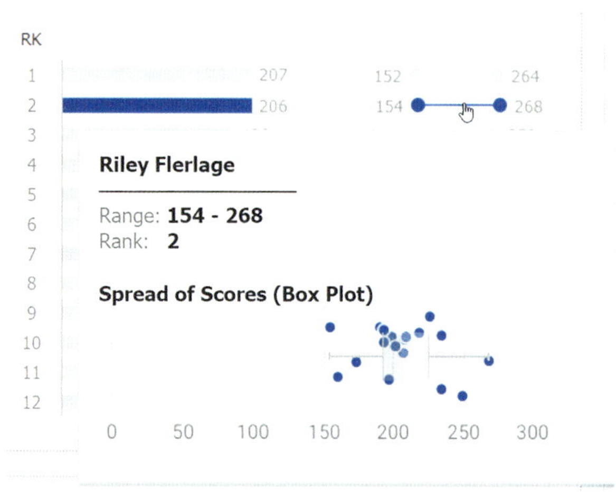

FIGURE 12.2 Tooltips display the running average and a jittered box plot of all scores for the selected player.

In the Individual Avg & Score Range chart, hovering over the bar (4) displays a running average of the selected player's scores over time, and hovering over the score range shows a jittered box plot of all the player's scores. See Figure 12.2.

The Comparison Dashboard

Viewers can navigate to other dashboards, and return to the main one, using the buttons along the left side. See Figure 12.3.

FIGURE 12.3 Navigation buttons make it easy to move among the three dashboards. Note that we will not explore the Bakers dashboard, which is bowling specific.

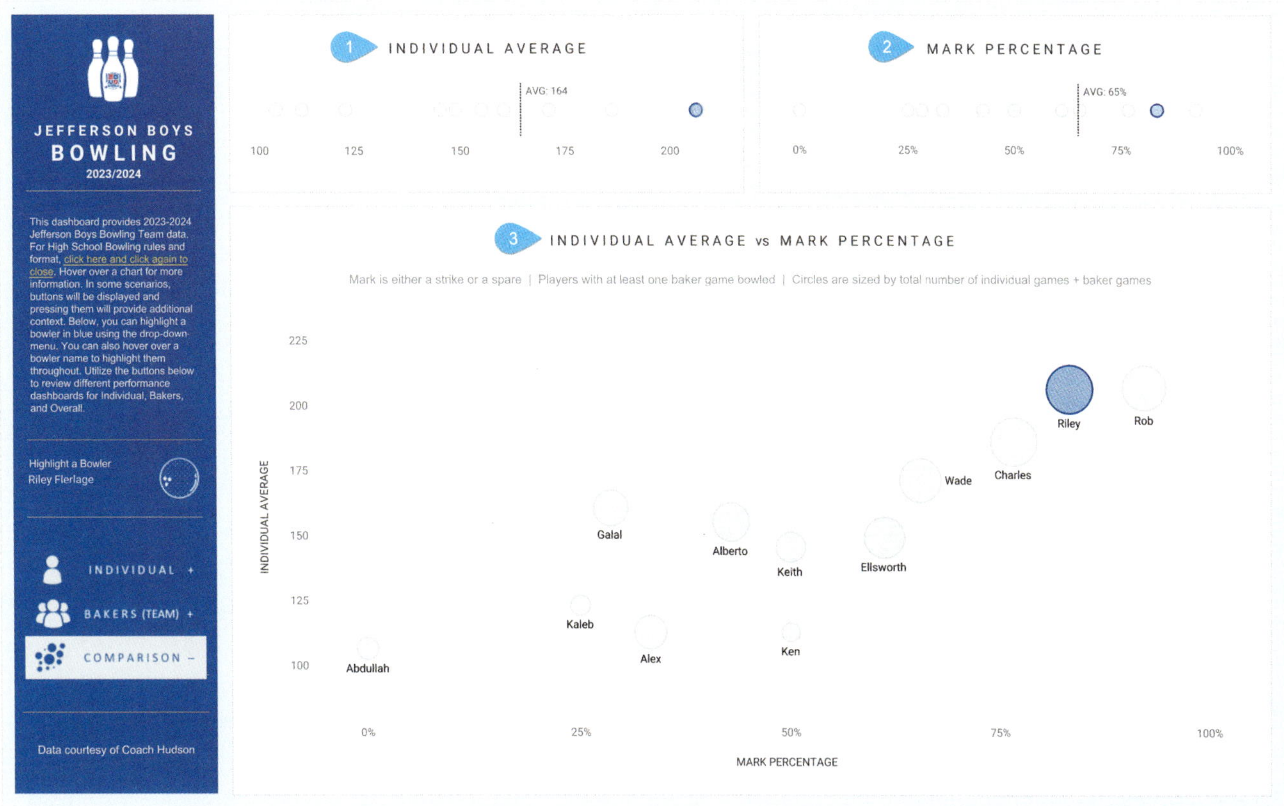

FIGURE 12.4 Strip plots and a scatterplot make it easy to see how an individual player is performing compared to his peers.

The Comparison dashboard in Figure 12.4 shows strip plots for Individual Average (1) and Mark Percentage (2), where mark percentage refers to the percentage of times the selected player gets a strike or a spare. We also see a scatterplot that shows the relationship between these two measures (3).

Why This Works

BANs Highlight Key Metrics and Make Good Conversation Starters

In Figure 12.5 we see what Kevin Flerlage (dashboard designer, knowledgeable bowler, and parent)

FIGURE 12.5 BANs showing key measures.

thought would be useful for the coach and other interested parties. While there isn't a context for each metric (i.e., we don't know if the team average is above or below goal or is trending up or down), they are good conversation starters.

Do These BANs Give You Bang for Your Buck?

My fellow authors and I disagree about the usefulness of the BANs in Figure 12.5. Are they worthy headlines that provide a context for the details below them? Do they help decipher the dashboard components that follow them? Are they good conversations starters, as I think they are? Or are they taking up a lot of precious screen real estate without providing much value?

We'll explore BANS in Chapter 27.

It's Easy to Change the Highlighted Player and See Related Stats

Changing which player is highlighted is simply a matter of clicking that player's name (or the drop-down selection along the left side, or the line, bar, or dot associated with that player.) In Figure 12.6 we see that Charles Tucker is now the focus of the dashboard (1) and that in the previous four games he performed at or well above his average (2).

We also see a reference line showing team average and selected player average (5).

The highlight table in Figure 12.6 also shows when a player (and not just the selected player) performed particularly well (3) and when a player did not compete (4).

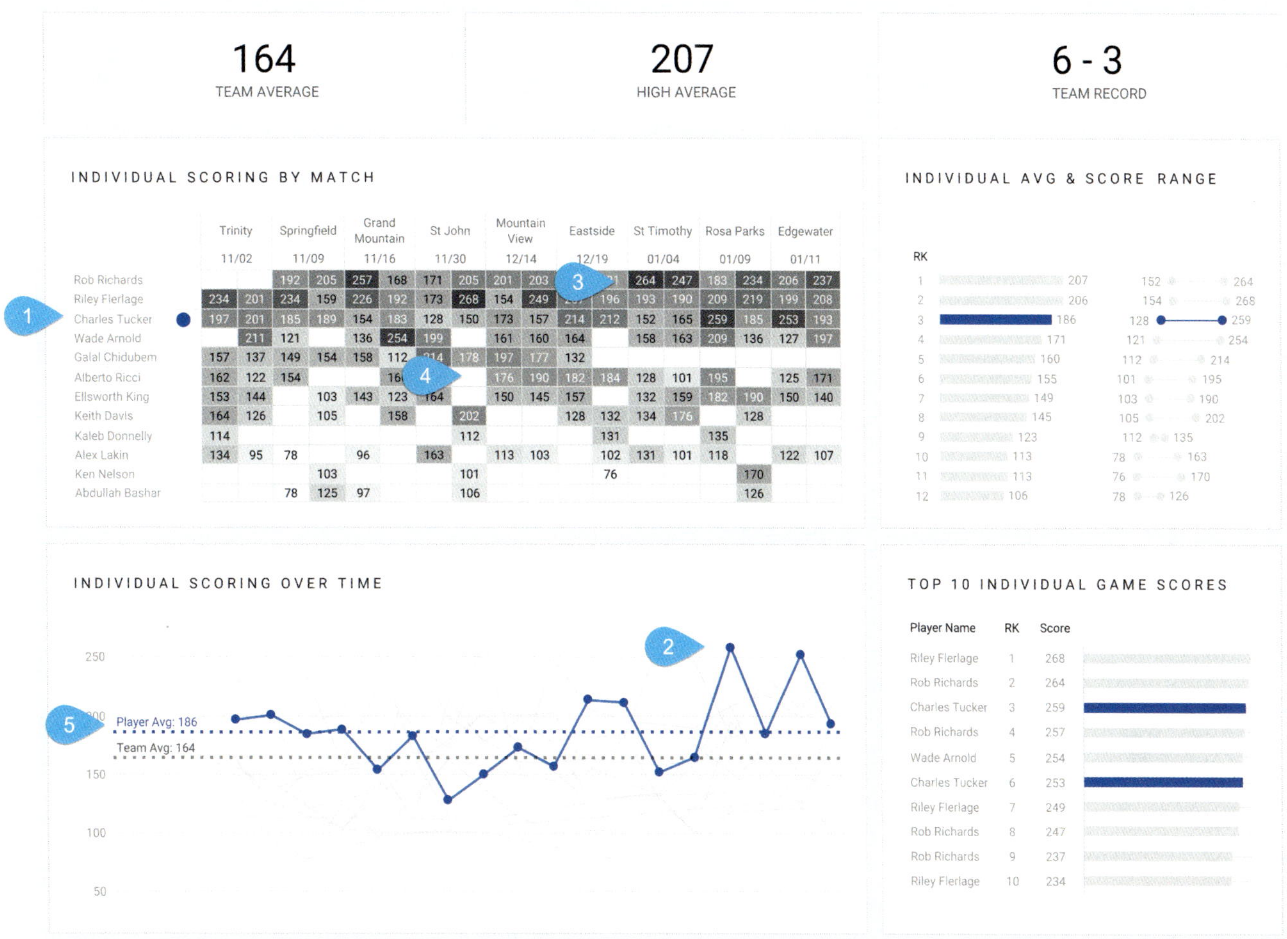

FIGURE 12.6 New player focus, trends, which players are hot or not for each match, and where a player did not compete. A darker shading indicates a higher score.

Comparison Dashboard Makes It Easy to Compare Performance for Multiple Measures

In Figure 12.7 we see how an individual is performing with respect to his peers in average score and mark percentage. There are strip plots at the top, marked (1) and (2), and a single scatterplot at the bottom (3).

There is some redundancy in that the bottom visualization combines the two major measures into one

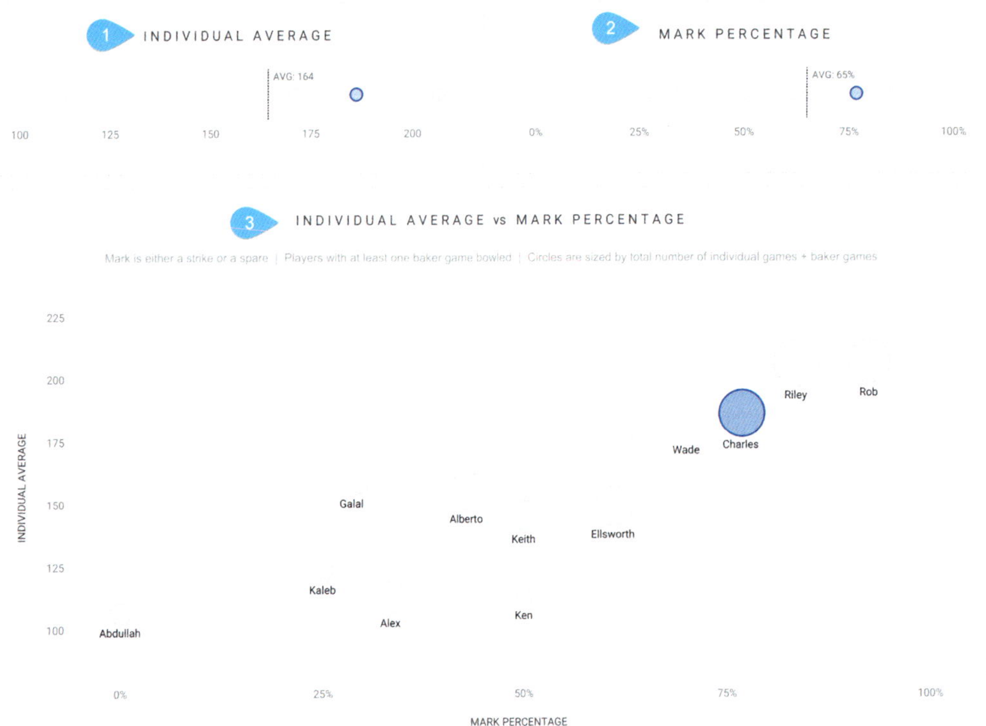

FIGURE 12.7 Strip plots and a combined scatterplot showing how players compare to one another for average score and mark percentage.

chart (and makes it easy to see the names of each player), but the strip plots will prove very useful if the dashboard evolves and the coach wants to see more than two measures (e.g., number of matches played, frames bowled, etc.). It will also prove invaluable in other use cases, such as tech-support monitoring, where there are many measures that stakeholders will want to compare. For certain, if we add more measures, this dashboard will need to be modified as it will be difficult to cram strip plots along the top, plus we would want to allow users to specify which measures to display in the scatterplot.

Process

Two Versions of the Dashboards

What we've been looking at is the *second* version of the dashboard. There were two distinct processes for the two iterations, and both warrant exploration.

But before we go into understanding either of the two associated processes, we want to show you Bowling Dashboard, Version One.

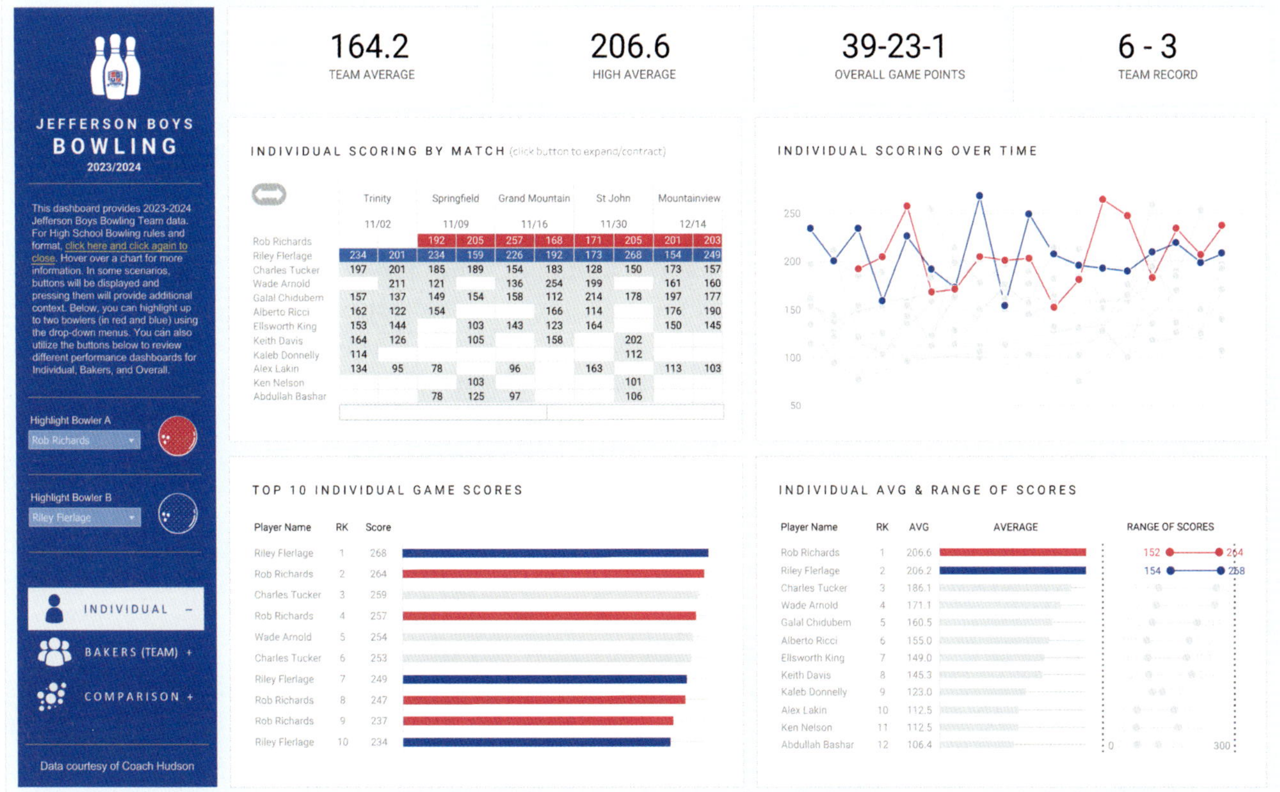

FIGURE 12.8 First version of the dashboard.

Meet the First Dashboard

In Figure 12.8 we see the first version of the dashboard. This version made it to the shortlist of the 2023 Information is Beautiful awards in the business analytics category.[1]

While not radically different from what we explored previously, you may be wondering what's up with the red and blue. Is blue good and red bad? Is this a comparison of Republicans versus Democrats? Why are *two* players highlighted?

The colors are simply the school colors, and while I may think they relate to politics, the coach and other interested parties did not.

As for why two players are highlighted, Kevin thought it would be valuable to be able to compare two players and see how they stood out from the rest of the team.

[1] See dtdbook.com/link16.

Process for Version One

Unlike many of the dashboards that have a formal process that works through discovery, prototyping, developing, testing, and so on, this is a great example of a bottom-up dashboard. Instead of a senior executive (or in this case, the coach) proclaiming "I need a dashboard," the spark was a parent stepping forward and saying to the coach, "I'm not sure you are playing the best players. I can help you make better decisions about who to play by analyzing and visualizing the player data."

Indeed, the coach was a soccer coach with little or no bowling experience and was using handwritten sheets like the one shown in Figure 12.9.

Yikes! This is data for *one* match. Imagine having 10 of these handwritten sheets. How would you be able to make sense of the information?

What Are *You* Waiting for?

Many dashboard designers and data analysts, especially those working in large organizations, wait for others to provide directives. But I've seen many great dashboards come from people asserting themselves, as Kevin did, and showing others that there are better ways to do things. Yes, politics and protocols may make this difficult if not impossible in some organizations, but there are a lot of open-minded people who would love to see what you have to offer.

The open-minded coach was delighted to get whatever assistance Kevin had to offer, and Kevin took it upon himself to build an easily updateable spreadsheet that contained the game and match data, and a Tableau dashboard based upon the data.

There are some key things here that must not be overlooked. The first is that the coach was thrilled to get something more useful than handwritten sheets. I've known lots of practitioners who have tried this "bottom up/I can show you a better way" approach and failed because the potential stakeholders weren't open to new approaches. Those of you who are out there with better ideas, please don't give up but be prepared for failure – or at least some strong-willed resistance.

The second thing that made development almost frictionless is that Kevin was also a bowler and his son was one of the stars on the team. Both the discovery and prototyping phases were greatly accelerated as nobody had to bring Kevin up to speed with what measures the dashboard should show, and Kevin could collaborate with the coach easily on what would be the most helpful assemblage of charts. In many respects, Kevin was the subject-matter expert (SME) as well as the dashboard designer.

Measuring Success

Even the first draft of the first version of the dashboard was an unmitigated success as it allowed the coach,

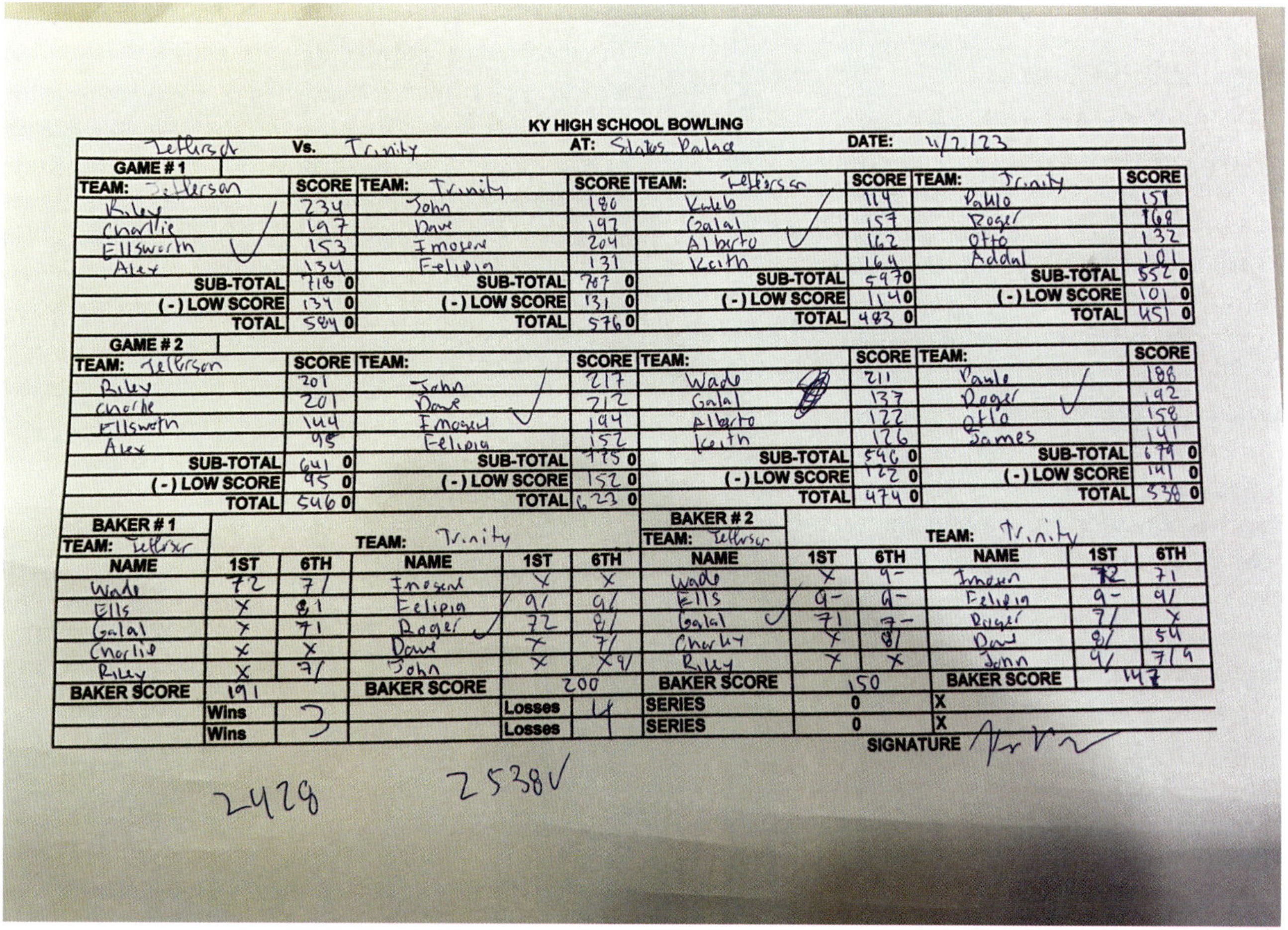
KY HIGH SCHOOL BOWLING

Jefferson	Vs.	Trinity		AT: Strikes Palace		DATE: 4/7/23	
GAME # 1							
TEAM: Jefferson	SCORE	TEAM: Trinity	SCORE	TEAM: Jefferson	SCORE	TEAM: Trinity	SCORE
Riley	234	John	180	Kaleb	114	Pablo	151
Charlie	197	Dave	192	Galal	157	Roger	168
Ellsworth	153	Imogen	204	Alberto	162	Otto	132
Alex	134	Felipe	131	Keith	164	Addal	101
SUB-TOTAL	718 0	SUB-TOTAL	707 0	SUB-TOTAL	597 0	SUB-TOTAL	552 0
(-) LOW SCORE	134 0	(-) LOW SCORE	131 0	(-) LOW SCORE	114 0	(-) LOW SCORE	101 0
TOTAL	584 0	TOTAL	576 0	TOTAL	483 0	TOTAL	451 0
GAME # 2							
TEAM: Jefferson	SCORE	TEAM:	SCORE	TEAM:	SCORE	TEAM:	SCORE
Riley	201	John	217	Wade	211	Paulo	188
Charlie	201	Dave	212	Galal	137	Roger	192
Ellsworth	144	Imogen	194	Alberto	122	Otto	158
Alex	95	Felipe	152	Keith	126	James	141
SUB-TOTAL	641 0	SUB-TOTAL	775 0	SUB-TOTAL	596 0	SUB-TOTAL	679 0
(-) LOW SCORE	95 0	(-) LOW SCORE	152 0	(-) LOW SCORE	122 0	(-) LOW SCORE	141 0
TOTAL	546 0	TOTAL	623 0	TOTAL	474 0	TOTAL	538 0

BAKER # 1 TEAM: Jefferson NAME	1ST	6TH	TEAM: Trinity NAME	1ST	6TH	BAKER # 2 TEAM: Jefferson NAME	1ST	6TH	TEAM: Trinity NAME	1ST	6TH
Wade	72	7/	Imogen	X	X	Wade	X	9-	Imogen	72	71
Ells	X	81	Felipe	9/	9/	Ells	9-	9-	Felipe	9-	9/
Galal	X	71	Roger	72	8/	Galal	71	7-	Roger	7/	X
Charlie	X	X	Dave	X	7/	Charlie	X	8/	Dave	8/	54
Riley	X	7/	John	X	X9/	Riley	X	X	John	9/	7/9
BAKER SCORE	191		BAKER SCORE	200		BAKER SCORE	150		BAKER SCORE	147	
	Wins	3		Losses	4	SERIES	0	X			
	Wins			Losses		SERIES	0	X			

SIGNATURE

2429 2538✓

FIGURE 12.9 Keeping track of player performance with handwritten sheets.

who had been flying blind, to see scores, trends, and, most importantly, which players he should be playing.

Choosing players is always difficult for a coach. Most parents are understanding, but we all know the potentially pesky parents who might loudly ask why their child isn't being played. A dashboard like this allows the coach to show that his choices are based on insights about performance. That level of transparency was not available when scores existed only on multiple handwritten sheets of paper.

The bottom line is that the coach made better decisions, and the team won more matches.

(Mic drop.)

Process for Version Two

Given the undisputed success of Version One, why is there a Version Two?

The audience changed.

As we considered the audience for this book, we discovered it was no longer just a high school bowling coach and interested parents and students.

It was now the thousands of readers of this book and potentially tens of thousands of end users who would be using a dashboard like this to monitor franchise restaurant sales, manage tech support centers, and so on.

The discussion among the book authors and Kevin centered around the question of whether the data displays were as good as they could be. That is, could we get people to "ah-ha" faster? This "provide the greatest degree of understanding with the least amount of effort" is one of the central themes of this book and *The Big Book of Dashboards*.

> **Provide the Greatest Degree of Understanding with the Least Amount of Effort**
>
> Of course, when we say "least amount of effort," we're referring to our stakeholders. The dashboard designers will probably have to work hard to make things as easy as possible for the stakeholders.

The conversations with Kevin and my fellow authors in prototyping, designing, and testing Version Two of the dashboard were exhilarating, exactly what you would hope to find with strong collaborators who were aligned in best serving the audience (our readers). In fact, it inspired me to write Chapter 34, "Find Good Sparring Partners," in Part III of this book.

What follows are the highlights of our debates and experiments. I fervently believe that the collaboration led to a better dashboard, and I encourage readers to find good collaborators who will provide pushback.

Each of the following sections represents stages of debate and discussion among us all.

So, Just What Do We Have Here?

What was it that we thought warranted change?

Let's again look at the first version of the main dashboard.

Dropping the Ability to Highlight Two Players

The original dashboard allowed users to highlight two players using drop-down menus (Item 1 in Figure 12.10). This is a novel and useful feature. Why was it abandoned?

We considered how people would use the dashboard, and being able to click any name, line, dot, or bar to change which player received the focus

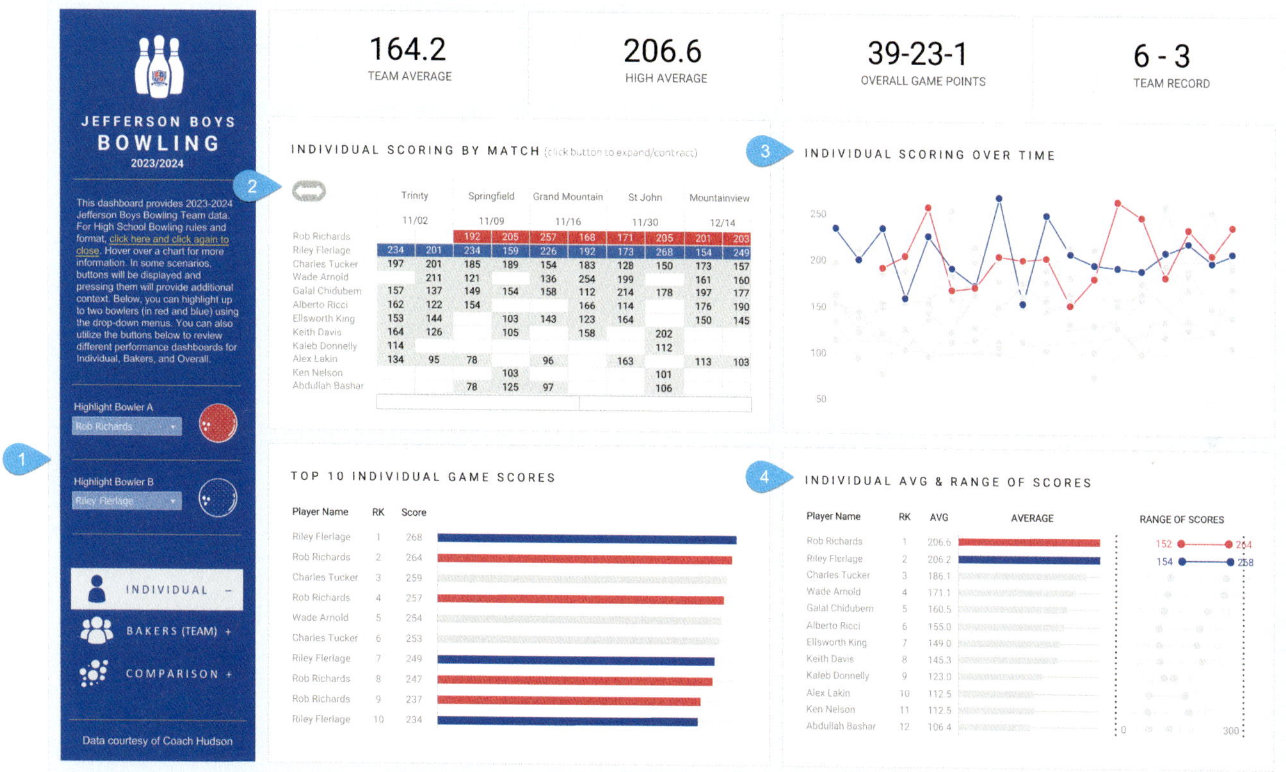

FIGURE 12.10 The components of the original dashboard.

was very alluring. We thought that would be more useful than being able to highlight two players.

Why Is a Text Table Getting Prime Dashboard Real Estate?

I had qualms about The Individual Scoring by Match text table (2). That is not the most important element of the dashboard, so why is it in the upper left?

Kevin admits that the dashboard presents a sequential story and doesn't prioritize the placement of elements based on their importance. Indeed, the most important element is (4), which shows the individual averages and score ranges. This is beautifully rendered, but why put this gem in the bottom-right corner?

Also, why are we only seeing half of the text table? Yes, there's a toggle button to expand the text table and replace the line chart, but as we'll see later, we'll see better insights if we present both elements at the same time, albeit rearranged.

Use a Highlight Table Instead of the Text Table

Like many of my colleagues, I have a major bugaboo about spreadsheets and text tables. While the text table is cosmetically appealing, the coach must go through each number sequentially and try to remember high scores and low scores. Humans are not good at this.

Why not have a highlight table, like the one shown in Figure 12.11?

I thought this was dandy, but Amanda and Andy thought a highlight table formatted in this way added noise to the dashboard and conflicted with the dashboard's blue theme. I then proposed a simplified version that used only two colors (relatively high score and relatively low score) (Figure 12.12).

What About a Marginal Histogram?

Readers of my blogs or LinkedIn posts know that any time I see a highlight table or scatterplot, I wonder if a marginal histogram might be a good addition. (I discuss this in length in "Dynamic Duos" in Part III of the book.) It turns out that that chart in the bottom-right corner will assume the duties of a marginal histogram when we change its placement. Stay tuned.

I'll admit I like this, but Jeff and Kevin preferred the version with the continuous color ramp (Figure 12.11), and as Kevin is the designer, we went with his wishes.

INDIVIDUAL SCORING BY MATCH

	Trinity 11/02		Springfield 11/09		Grand Mountain 11/16		St John 11/30		Mountain View 12/14		Eastside 12/19		St Timothy 01/04		Rosa Parks 01/09		Edgewater 01/11	
Rob Richards			192	205	257	168	171	205	201	203	152	181	264	247	183	234	206	237
Riley Flerlage	234	201	234	159	226	192	173	268	154	249	207	196	193	190	209	219	199	208
Charles Tucker	197	201	185	189	154	183	128	150	173	157	214	212	152	165	259	185	253	193
Wade Arnold		211	121		136	254	199		161	160	164		158	163	209	136	127	197
Galal Chidubem	157	137	149	154	158	112	214	178	197	177	132							
Alberto Ricci	162	122	154			166	114		176	190	182	184	128	101	195		125	171
Ellsworth King	153	144		103	143	123	164		150	145	157		132	159	182	190	150	140
Keith Davis	164	126		105		158		202			128	132	134	176		128		
Kaleb Donnelly	114							112				131			135			
Alex Lakin	134	95	78		96		163		113	103		102	131	101	118		122	107
Ken Nelson				103				101				76				170		
Abdullah Bashar			78	125	97			106								126		

FIGURE 12.11 The highlight table uses color to identify high scores (dark) and low scores (light).

INDIVIDUAL SCORING BY MATCH

	Trinity		Springfield		Grand Mountain		St John		Mountain View		Eastside		St Timothy		Rosa Parks		Edgewater	
	11/02		11/09		11/16		11/30		12/14		12/19		01/04		01/09		01/11	
Rob Richards			192	205	257	168	171	205	201	203	152	181	264	247	183	234	206	237
Riley Flerlage	234	201	234	159	226	192	173	268	154	249	207	196	193	190	209	219	199	208
Charles Tucker	197	201	185	189	154	183	128	150	173	157	214	212	152	165	259	185	253	193
Wade Arnold		211	121		136	254	199		161	160	164		158	163	209	136	127	197
Galal Chidubem	157	137	149	154	158	112	214	178	197	177	132							
Alberto Ricci	162	122	154			166	114		176	190	182	184	128	101	195		125	171
Ellsworth King	153	144		103	143	123	164		150	145	157		132	159	182	190	150	140
Keith Davis	164	126		105		158		202			128	132	134	176		128		
Kaleb Donnelly	114							112				131			135			
Alex Lakin	134	95	78		96		163		113	103		102	131	101	118		122	107
Ken Nelson				103				101				76				170		
Abdullah Bashar			78	125	97			106								126		

FIGURE 12.12 A binary highlight table, with scores greater than or equal to 176 highlighted in a dark gray.

I was not going to fight for the simplified highlight table as it was not that important to me. What's important here is that these conversations are vital: there are always compromises and subjective decisions to make when designing dashboards. The goal isn't to be "perfect" because you never will be. The goal is to make informed decisions, and those are best made by working with collaborators.

Rearrange the Elements

Consider how the elements have been rearranged in Figure 12.13.

The highlight table (1) makes it easy to see which players are hot or not for a particular game and which players did not compete at all. It's not as good as a line chart for showing trends accurately, and it's hard to make the individual we're interested in stand out.

The line chart (2) is great for showing trends for individuals but not for seeing the performance of all players simultaneously. If all the lines were thick and dark, it would look like spaghetti. We also can't see when players did not compete.

By pairing these two charts, one below the other, we see the complete picture.

Perhaps most important is that Individual Average (Avg) & Score Range (3) has been paired with the

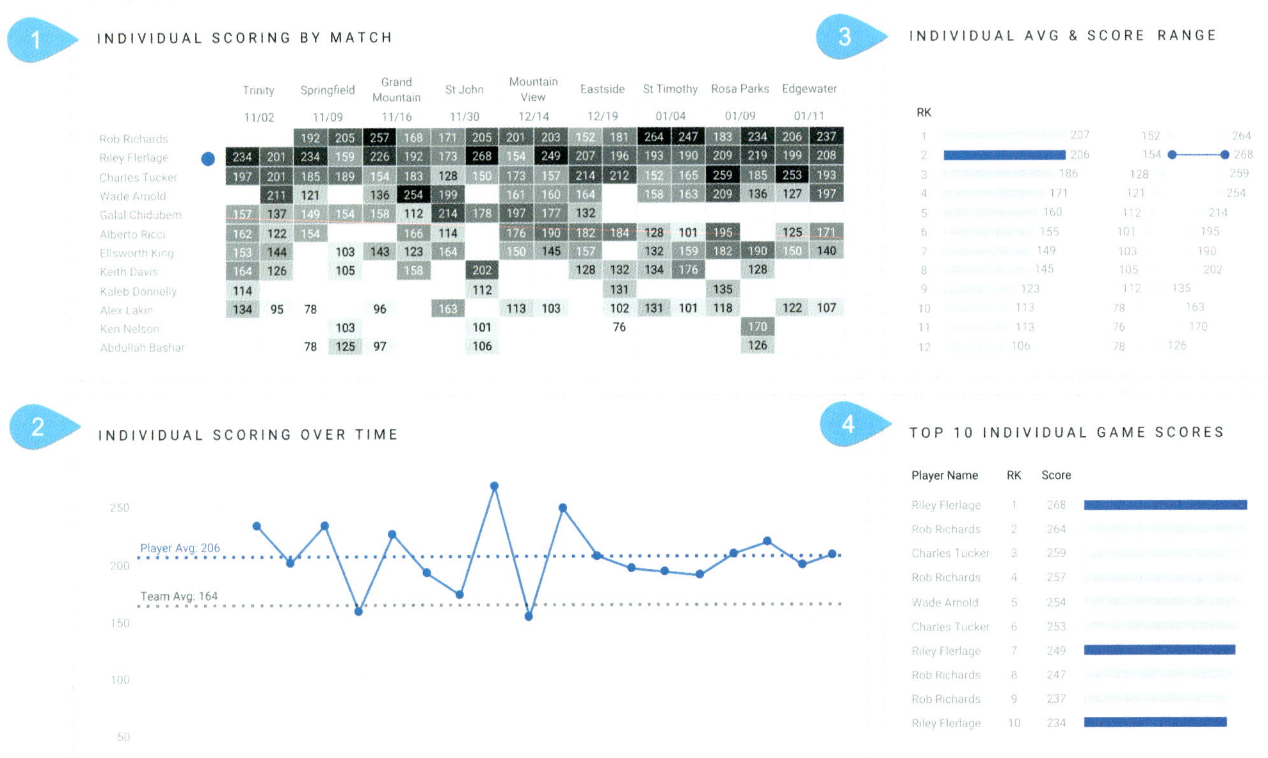

FIGURE 12.13 Elements rearranged.

highlight table (1). It serves as a marginal histogram in that it summarizes the performance of each player.

Finally, the least important element, Top 10 Individual Games Scores (4), has been moved to the bottom right.

I will confess, reluctantly, that I find the warm blue highlight table more inviting than the gray version, which I think is harsher. But will the use of blue cause confusion because we use blue to highlight the selected player? Kevin thought that the blue version is "prettier" but that it might confuse users.

But Wait. There's More!

As you'll see when you read about Andy's Strava dashboard, Andy is a big fan of Don Norman's book *The Design of Everyday Things* and considers the visceral reaction people have when first seeing a dashboard.

He finds the dark grays in the highlight table somewhat uninviting and suggests using subtle blues, as shown in Figure 12.14.

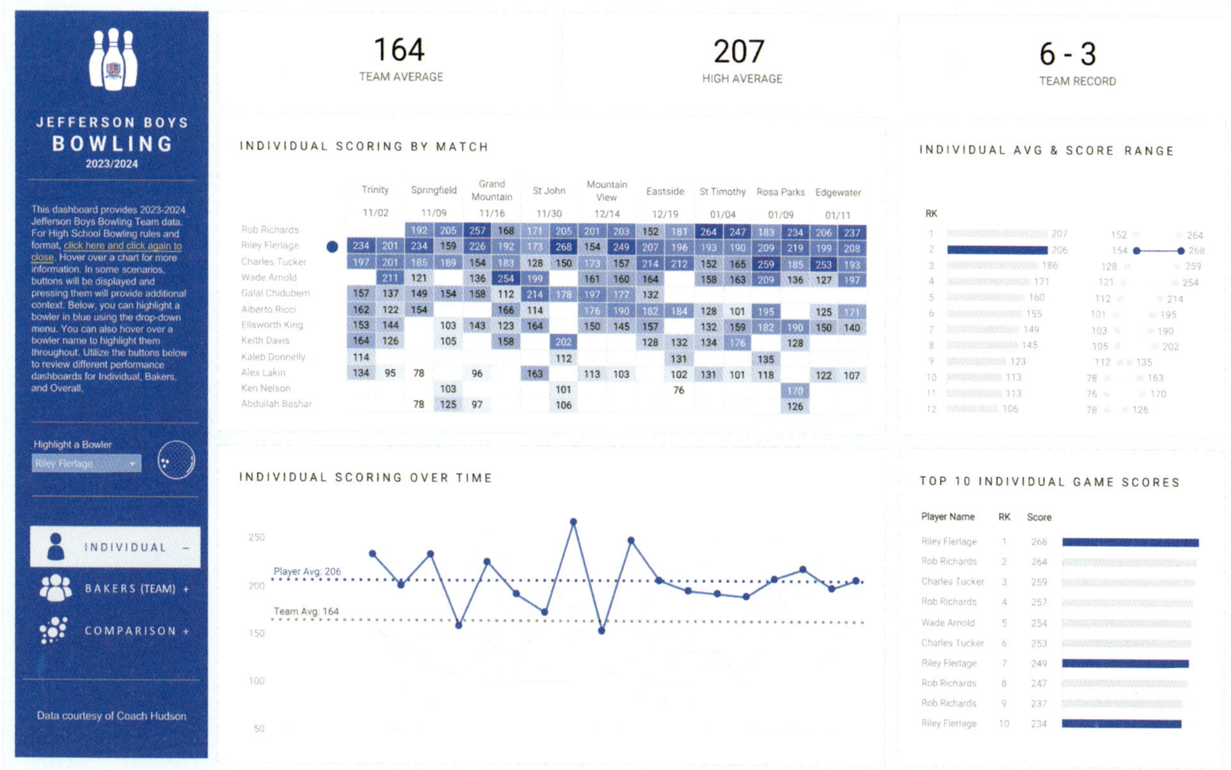

FIGURE 12.14 Making the dashboard "warmer" using blues instead of grays.

I think it's time to bring in the stakeholders and get their thoughts.

Author Commentary

STEVE: There are so many subtle things that I did not address, but that makes this a very inviting dashboard. Consider the effective use of color (in both versions of the dashboard), balanced layout, typography, iconography, and instructions along the left side (the overlay that appears when you click is terrific). But these are mostly cosmetic elements. The critical thing is that Kevin created a dashboard that really helps stakeholders understand their data.

There is one addition I'd like to see and that would be the ability to focus on the most recent matches. Right now, I see the average for all games, but it takes some effort to see who is heating up and who is cooling down. I'd love some mechanism to see just stats about the most recent matches.

I'd also love to see the BANs do some heavier lifting. Is the 164 team average good or bad?

Can we combine the team average and player high average into some type of combined BAN?

Do I hear Version Three of the dashboard calling?

AMANDA: One of the most notable parts of the story of this dashboard, for me, goes back to knowing the subject matter for the dataset you're working with. Being a soccer coach, the coach probably had deep knowledge of soccer measures, but Kevin had much deeper knowledge of bowling metrics that matter and the analytical questions a coach could answer.

When designing dashboards, one of the most frustrating moments for me is when a client knows they need better access to actionable data but can't define key metrics or questions. In those circumstances, it's hugely helpful to engage a subject-matter expert or to *be* a subject-matter expert who can provide some direction on standard indicators or analyses. Chapter 5 about discovery in Part I recommends how to work with stakeholders to define requirements, which is particularly helpful when a client isn't very prescriptive about their needs.

ANDY: I confess when we first considered this dashboard, I thought it would be an easy chapter for Steve to write. Kevin is a world-class dashboard designer, and bowling is a "light" topic. I was wrong. We went down so many rabbit holes. We made steps forward, sidewards, and backwards as we tweaked the dashboard. Every iteration was about considering how the audience could get to the right insights as fast as possible. Even as I write this commentary, there are more things I think we could change. However, we have a deadline to meet for this book, and the dashboard is more than good enough. This collaboration and iteration were exhilarating and resulted in better work. Every dashboard you design should go through these iterations.

Chapter 13

Fitness Goal Tracker

Team: Andy Cotgreave

My Strava tracking dashboard

Team: Andy Cotgreave, Dashboard Designer

Organization: Andy Cotgreave

How This Dashboard Delivers: I aim to record 1,000 miles (1,609 km) of walking in Strava each year. This dashboard shows me how close I am to a daily target of 2.7 m (4.4 km), and my progress against the goal, through the whole year.

Audience: Me. 🙂

Team: Just me.

Tools: The data comes from Strava, a fitness tracking app. The data is added to a Google Sheet via ifttt.com (a web service that lets you connect apps and devices). The data is made ready in Tableau Prep and the dashboard is built in Tableau.

Timeline: The first version was built in a day but has been tinkered with and improved over six years.

URL: dtdbook.com/link17

Chapter Author: Andy Cotgreave

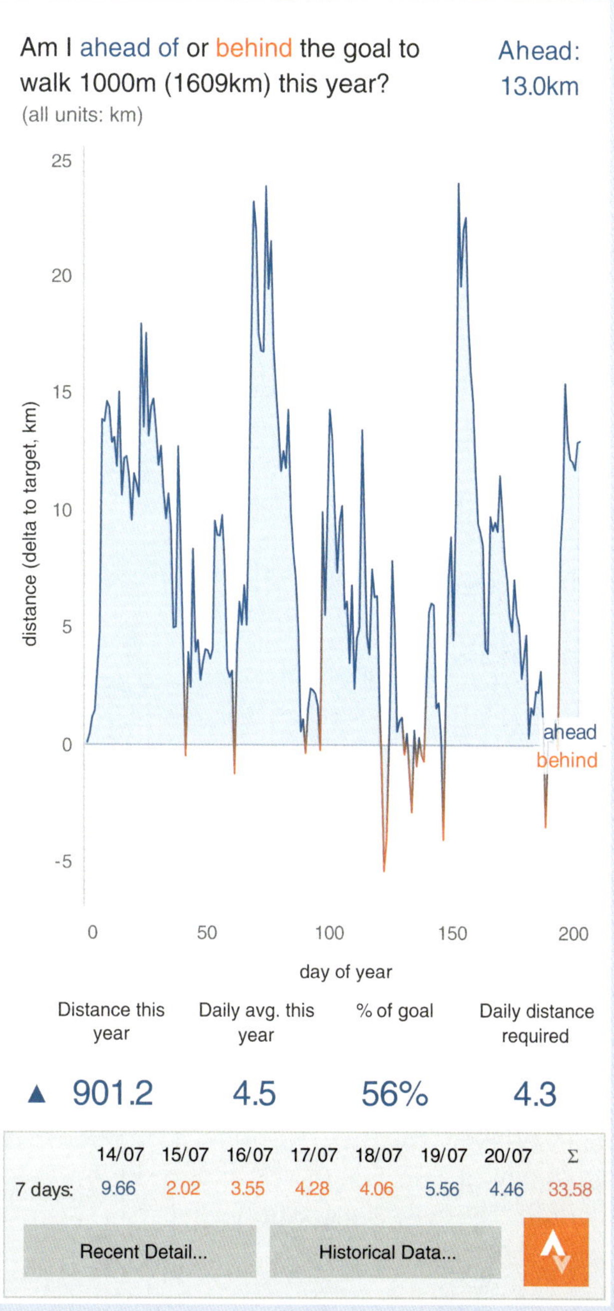
Am I ahead of or behind the goal to walk 1000m (1609km) this year?
(all units: km)
Ahead:
13.0km
distance (delta to target, km)
25
20
15
10
5
0
-5
ahead
behind
0
50
100
150
200
day of year
Distance this year
Daily avg. this year
% of goal
Daily distance required
▲ 901.2
4.5
56%
4.3
14/07 15/07 16/07 17/07 18/07 19/07 20/07 Σ
7 days: 9.66 2.02 3.55 4.28 4.06 5.56 4.46 33.58
Recent Detail...
Historical Data...

Big Picture

You track your walks using Strava and have a goal to walk 1,000 miles (1,609 km) a year. That requires a daily average of 2.7 miles (4.4 km). Your primary need isn't to see the total miles you've walked so far; it's to see how close you are tracking to the goal: how far ahead or behind the goal are you? Knowing how your current distance walked compares to the distance expected allows you to tailor your activity plans.

Specifics

This dashboard has an audience of one (me, Andy).

After a long injury to my Achilles tendon, it turned out I could no longer run, but I did love walking. I did, however, find it hard to motivate myself to get out as regularly as when I was running.

A hiking magazine I read posed a challenge to people: can you walk 1,000 miles in a year (1,609 km, about the distance from Florida to New York City)? The magazine was intentionally vague about how that should be measured. Some people would measure step counts. Others would count only those walks done in walking boots. The magazine's intent was not to create some sort of race, or league; it was to get people into active habits.

For me, I defined "a walk" as any walk I was doing for the sake of walking. Thus, walks to the shops didn't count, nor did picking up my kids from school. But a lunchtime stroll would count, as would choosing to walk to the office instead of catching the train. Also, of course, short or long hikes in the hills counted.

I first did the annual challenge in 2019 and continue it to this day. It has truly become a habit.

Note: I use kilometers in the rest of this chapter, not miles, because that's the default unit I am most used to. I acknowledge that it's a little strange to measure a 1,000-mile goal in kilometers, but that is the confusion of being a British person in the generation that switched from imperial to metric measurements.

Related Scenarios

- You organize events and track ticket sales in the run-up to an event. You want to know if sales are on or off-target.
- You are a charity and track donations. You need to check fundraising goals over time as they relate to specific goals.
- You track personal financial goals and want to have saved a particular amount by the end of the year.

How I Use the Dashboard

This dashboard exists only for viewing on a smartphone. I only look at this dashboard on the go (or sitting on my sofa!), so the desktop version is irrelevant.

I check on this dashboard every few days to make sure that I'm on target. In periods where I have built up a lot of slack, it is nice to look at the dashboard and feel a sense of achievement. It also means I can relax my pace a little.

Why This Works

The dashboard has evolved over time to address one specific question: am I on target to hit my goal? Seeing my progress against my annual goal helps me determine what remedial action I need to take if I am falling behind.

The dashboard has gone through many iterations, as I'll show in the process section. Initially I tracked daily distance walked and then cumulative distance walked for the year. Cumulative distance showed progress toward the annual goal, but I still had to do mental gymnastics to work out where I was compared to where I should be on that day. The dashboard evolved to answer just that specific question: **Am I ahead of or behind the goal to walk 1,609 km (1000 miles) this year?**

There are four dashboard sections (Figure 13.1):

1. A title section with a single summary KPI.
2. A line chart showing the difference between distance walked and expected distance for the current day of the year.

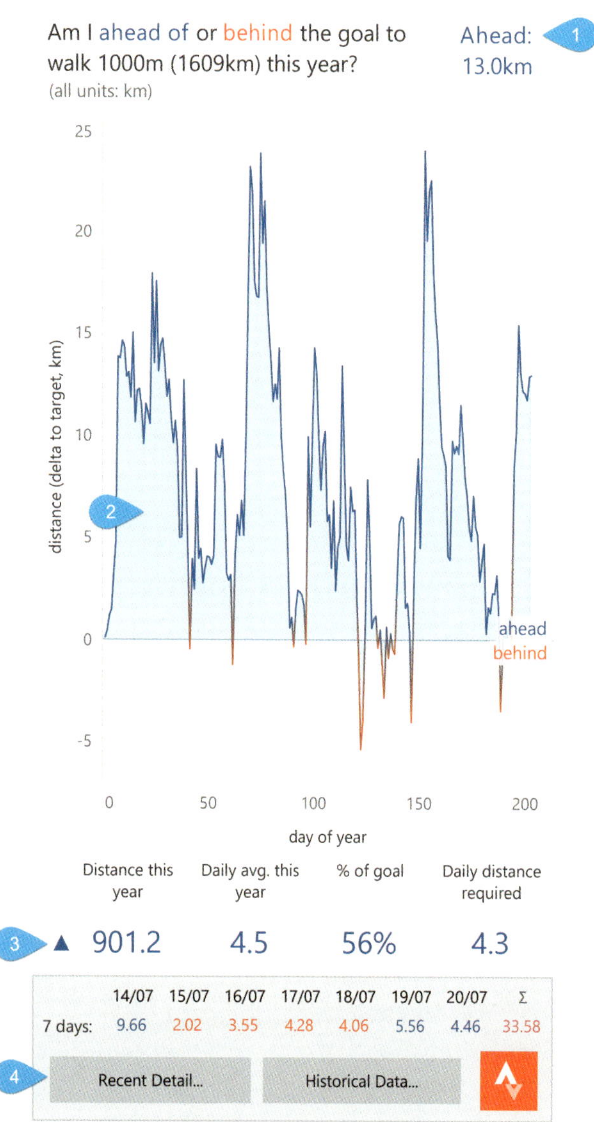

FIGURE 13.1 The sections of the dashboard.

3. A set of BANs providing context (see Chapter 27 for more on BANs).
4. A weekly detail summary above two buttons to access historical data. One button reveals data for the current year; the other shows data for all my Strava activity since 2012.

One Summary BAN

The BAN at the top right is all I need to answer my specific question. At the top of the dashboard (see Figure 13.1) you can see I was comfortably ahead of the goal: 13 km. If I fall behind the goal, the BAN also changes color to orange.

Line Chart Showing Delta Against the Target

The chart shows my progress against the expected distance I should have walked on each day of the year. In this scenario, that's 1,609 km/365 days (or 366 in a leap year), which is 4.41 km (2.74mi) per day. The higher the line is above the x-axis, the further I am ahead of my goal; if the line is below the x-axis, I'm behind my goal.

Figure 13.1 was created on July 20, 2024, day 202 of the year. You can see two significant peaks where I was over 20 km ahead of goal. Following the second peak, I slowed down, but by July 20, I was back to 13 km above target.

Actual, Not Moving Average (Accuracy Over Aesthetics)

When I design a dashboard, I know aesthetics are vital. Don Norman, in his book *The Design of Everyday Things*, describes three levels of processing when we meet a designed object: visceral, behavioral, and reflective. Each level must be a success for the user to have a harmonious experience they would want to repeat.

The visceral level describes the split-second, subconscious decision we make based purely on appearance. "This has nothing to do with how usable, effective, or understandable the product is," says Norman. "It is about attraction or repulsion. Great designers use their aesthetic sensibilities to drive those visceral responses." I apply this to thinking to all dashboards I build.

This dashboard needs to impress only one person: me. It could, in theory, be ugly, but if it works for me, it succeeds.

When writing this chapter, though, I got worried about your reactions. I'm aware that the main line chart is spiky, volatile, jarring. For me, the sole viewer, it doesn't matter.

I feared that you, the reader, might see the spiky blue line and think, "Ugh, that line is spikey. In fact, it's ugly."

I even went as far as building a new version of the line chart, replacing the spiky line with a different version that has a thick moving average line plotted above a thin, faint line showing actual value. Figure 13.2 shows both versions.

The moving average version is, I think, more pleasing to the eye, but it comes at the cost of accuracy. It's too easy to look at the thick blue line as a representation of the actual state.

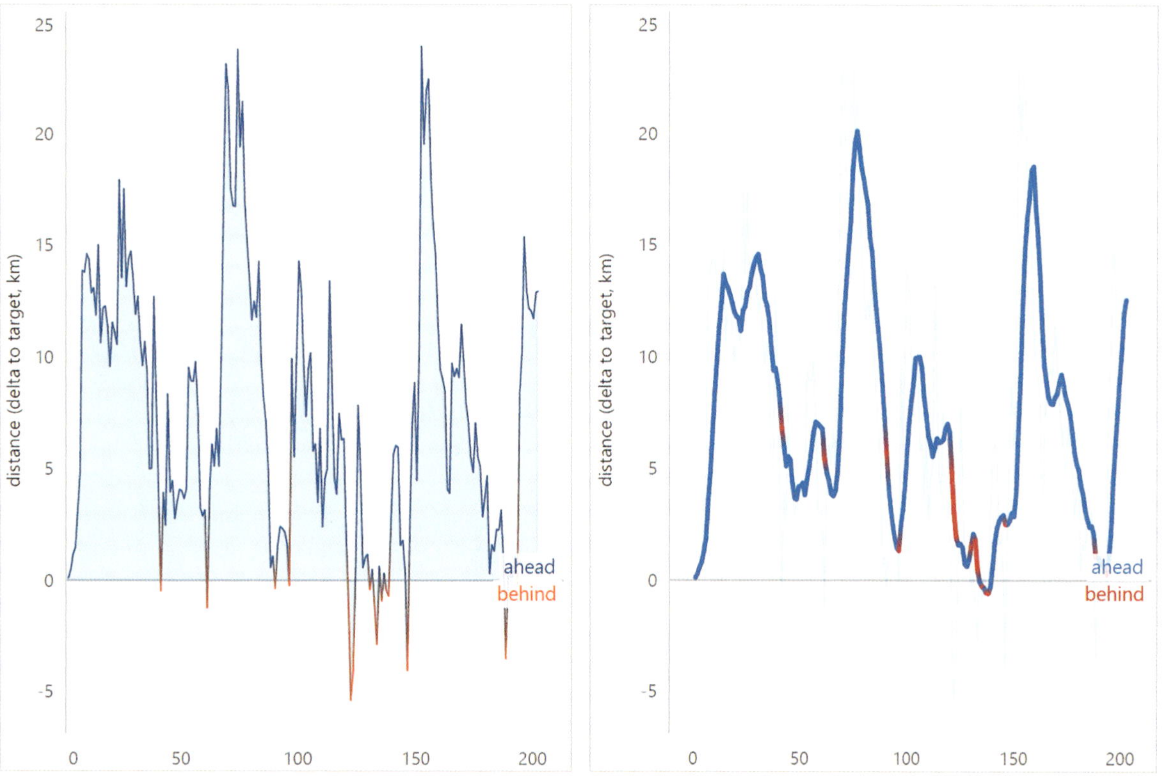

FIGURE 13.2 Two ways to visualize time: the "spiky" actuals (left) alongside a moving average (with the actuals shown in a faint line in the background).

I showed the different versions to multiple people. Non–data people tended to prefer the calming moving average chart. Data people preferred the actuals. There was a vibrant debate on a LinkedIn post.[1] Referring to the moving average, one colleague said "Andy, what would happen if you got to the penultimate day of the year to find that your smoothing had hidden that your last day needed to be a big one?"

In the end, I got over my worries about the spikiness of the actuals. Accuracy is more important in this situation.

Scaling x-Axis

At the end of every year, the target resets and I'm back to January 1, with 365 (or 366!) days ahead of me. So how many days should be represented on the chart's x-axis?

[1]"Which do you prefer?" dtdbook.com/link18

- If I fix the x-axis at 365 days, the line barely registers for the first 2 months; it's barely visible at the left of an expanse of white.
- If I fix the end to be the current day, the line looks really goofy for the first 2 months: there aren't enough marks to fit the space.

To solve this, I set the x-axis length to extend dynamically depending on the number of days completed in the year. At the start of the year, it's fixed at 50 days. Then it's fixed at 100, then 200, then 366 (to account for leap years). It creates an aesthetically pleasing line regardless of what day of the year it is. Figure 13.3 shows the x-axes at three different parts of 2023.

Use of Color

There's no separate color legend on this dashboard. Instead, the color encoding is in the dashboard title. Doing this is a great way to save real estate on your own dashboards. Also, did you notice that the color for "behind goal" is the same orange hue of the Strava logo?

Why Aren't all the KPIs at the Top?

Look again at Figure 13.1. Why is there one KPI at the top (teardrop 1) and four near the bottom (teardrop 4)? Originally, all 5 KPIs were at the top, but as I used the dashboard more and more, the only vital KPI is the one that's still there: am I ahead or behind, and by how much?

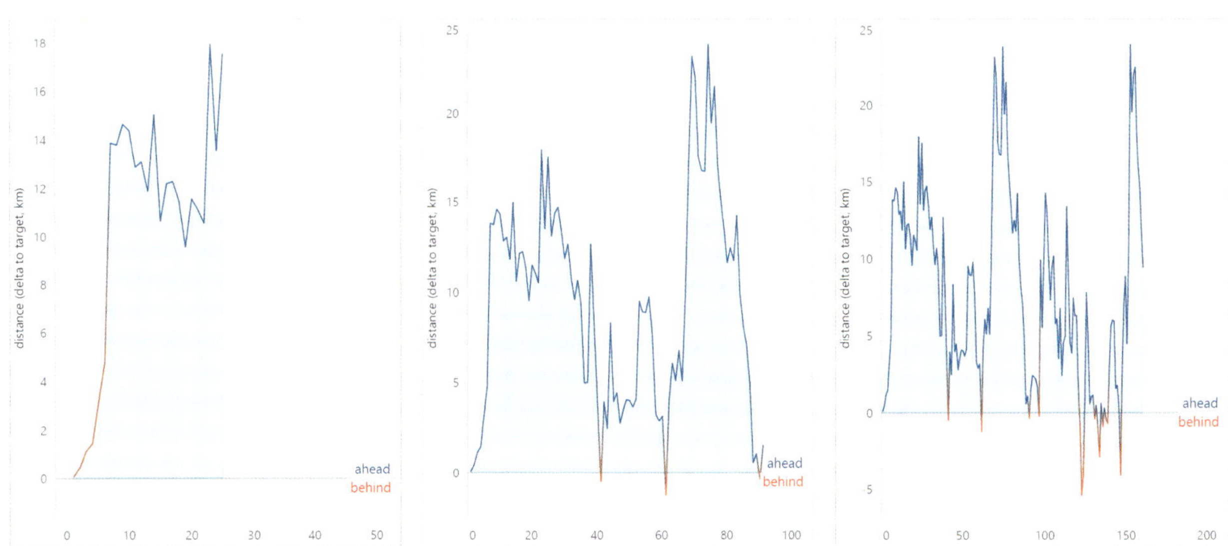

FIGURE 13.3 Three snapshots from 2023, taken on days 25, 90 and 160.

The other four are of secondary importance. From left to right, these are:

- How far have I walked this year? (Note that we'd normally advocate adding "km" after the number, but in this case, because it's my personal dashboard, I know what the values are.)
- What's my daily average distance this year (it should be at least 4.41 km)?
- What percentage of total distance have I walked this year?
- What should my daily distance be to hit the target?

If my daily distance has fallen behind 4.41 km, the arrow at the left points down, and all the KPIs are shown in orange, not blue. The KPIs are intentionally "no frills." The audience is me, and I know what each number should be, so they don't need extra context.

Summary and History Pane on Demand

Two buttons at the bottom reveal overlay pages, one of which is recent detail (see Figure 13.4).

First, a table of the previous 7 weeks. It's useful to validate data flow is working correctly.

Second, the bar chart shows the distance walked for each week in the current year. The historical views don't help me achieve my goal, but are useful when reviewing my year so far.

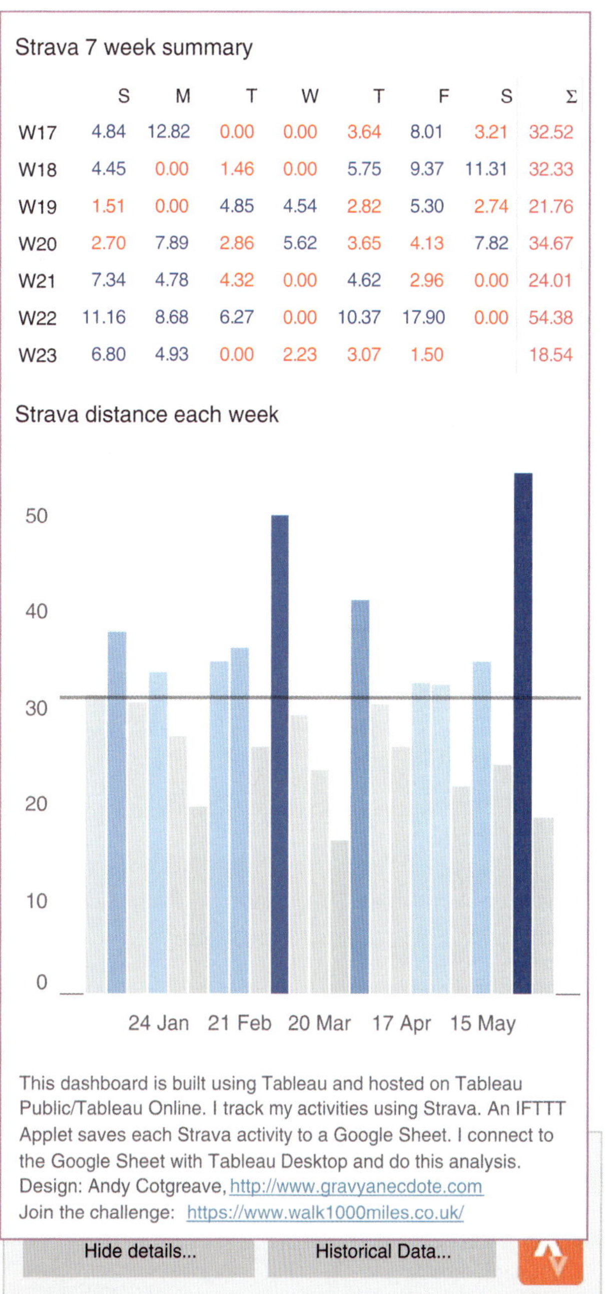

Strava 7 week summary

	S	M	T	W	T	F	S	Σ
W17	4.84	12.82	0.00	0.00	3.64	8.01	3.21	32.52
W18	4.45	0.00	1.46	0.00	5.75	9.37	11.31	32.33
W19	1.51	0.00	4.85	4.54	2.82	5.30	2.74	21.76
W20	2.70	7.89	2.86	5.62	3.65	4.13	7.82	34.67
W21	7.34	4.78	4.32	0.00	4.62	2.96	0.00	24.01
W22	11.16	8.68	6.27	0.00	10.37	17.90	0.00	54.38
W23	6.80	4.93	0.00	2.23	3.07	1.50		18.54

Strava distance each week
50
40
30
20
10
0
24 Jan
21 Feb
20 Mar
17 Apr
15 May
This dashboard is built using Tableau and hosted on Tableau Public/Tableau Online. I track my activities using Strava. An IFTTT Applet saves each Strava activity to a Google Sheet. I connect to the Google Sheet with Tableau Desktop and do this analysis.
Design: Andy Cotgreave, http://www.gravyanecdote.com
Join the challenge: https://www.walk1000miles.co.uk/
Hide details...
Historical Data...

FIGURE 13.4 The "Recent Detail" button reveals more granular recent details.

Process

I refer to this as my "comfort dashboard." It is something personal I can use to experiment with, to iterate at speed, to give myself a feeling of security in my own skills.

What are the benefits of a personal dashboard like this?

- It's regular exercise for a data analyst. Enhancing the dashboard keeps my Tableau and data design "muscles" strong.
- I can incorporate new features to test them. There are lots of very specific Tableau features in here that were incorporated to test them when they were released.
- There is freedom in being able to update a dashboard without any pressure from external stakeholders or deadlines. It allows you to be creative, while still solving your specific dashboard goal.

Visualize the Actionable Insight (or Iterate, Then Iterate, Then Iterate Again)

The biggest success of this dashboard is its evolution to show the purest representation of the question being asked.

My first iteration (Figure 13.5) showed the running total for the year: was I heading toward my annual goal? The orange/red running total chart in Figure 13.8 tells me I've walked and run 668 km this year (via the label at the end of the line). That's interesting but not helpful: 668 km run this year does not help me adjust my behavior *today*.

Figure 13.6 shows my first evolution, into a large dashboard. Looking back, it feels very cluttered!

However, there is progress toward my goal: a BAN toward the top shows average daily distance (4.36 km at the time of this snapshot), and the line chart (marked 1 in Figure 13.9) shows how the average

FIGURE 13.5 My very first Strava tracker.

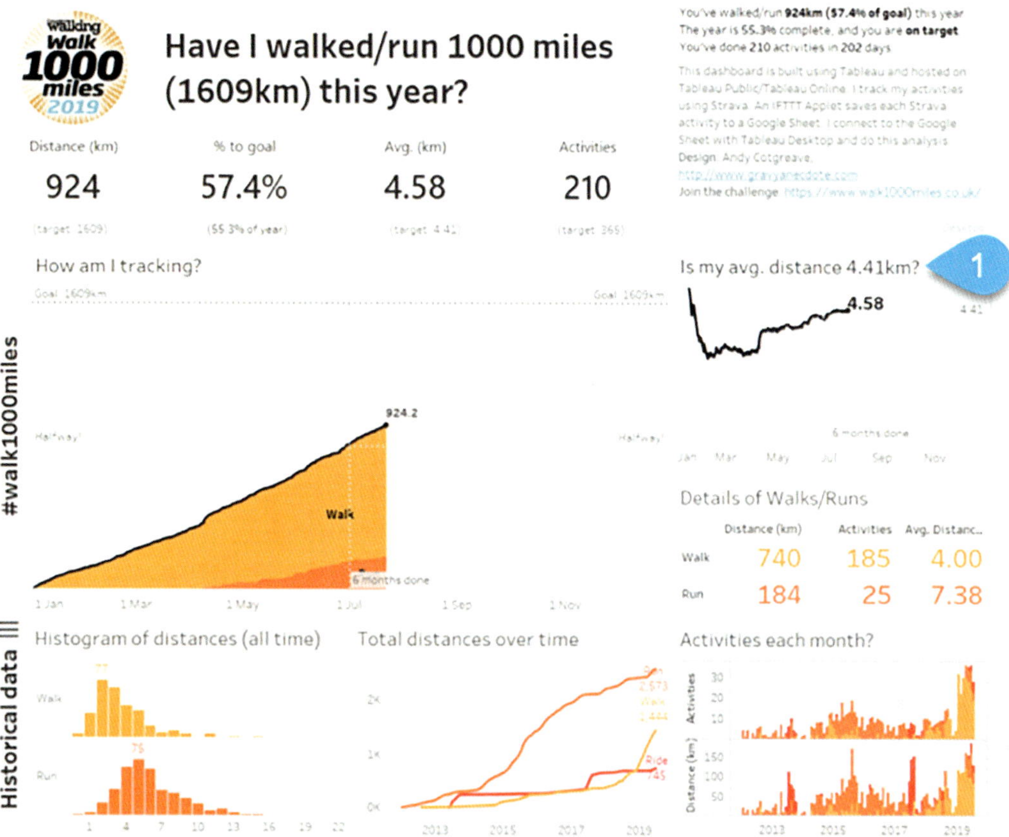

FIGURE 13.6 The first desktop dashboard: note the black line chart on the right: the first time I started tracking average daily distance.

daily distance for the year has changed. This was an improvement since I could now see if I was on target.

But it still wasn't good enough: I needed to iterate the design so I could see *exactly* how far ahead or behind I am. I switched the focus from running total, or yearly average, to focus on the delta, which is the metric you see in the latest version of this dashboard, which opens this scenario.

In this case, as sole user, there's no bottleneck for iterating. I am both the designer and the user. It's a lot easier to design for the actionable insights I want.

Mobile Only

There was a desktop version for a long while, but that was jettisoned when I realized the only place I checked the dashboard was on my phone. I never looked at this dashboard during the day but did when I walked or when I sat on my sofa.

I had no need for a full screen with an elaborate design. Instead, I could focus just on the insights that helped me hit my goal, so I created a mobile-only version.

Beware the KPI Becoming the Goal

Goodhart's law is best summarized by anthropologist Marilyn Strathern, who explains that "When a measure becomes a target, it ceases to be a good measure."[2] Figure 13.7 shows my progress to goal for every year I have attempted this walking project. In 2019, I started halfway through the year, with lots of enthusiasm, and I smashed the goal by walking 1,772 km. The following year was also successful, but after that? You can see that I barely hit my goal. In fact, in 2022 and 2023 I only made the goal on the last couple of days of the year. The total distance I've walked has declined year by year, and now barely scrapes above the target.

Is measuring things with increasing accuracy causing me to exercise differently? With this dashboard I always know how much I need to walk to hit the goal. Does that mean I walk to hit the target, rather than simply for exercise and pleasure? Possibly.

Certainly, an average daily walking distance of 4.41 km is healthy, but if I turned off this dashboard,

FIGURE 13.7 How has my walking evolved since starting tracking to a goal?

[2]Strathern, M. "Improving ratings": audit in the British University system. *Eur Rev.* 1997; 5(3):305–321. doi: 10.1017/s1062798700002660.

what would happen? Would I walk more for pleasure, freed from a target? Or would I stop walking?

I don't have answers to these questions, but it does show that any well-visualized goal risks becoming a goal to hit, not exceed.

Author Commentary

AMANDA: I love the evolution toward simplicity in this dashboard. Often, when we're making enhancements on our dashboards, we add more views, charts, or whole pages to address evolving analysis questions, rather than revisiting if there are charts or pages we can retire or fully redesign. With a dashboard with an audience of more than one person, spending a bit more time validating that you're not removing information someone else relies on is necessary but worthwhile to avoid a bloated and cumbersome analytical product. (For example, if someone else used this dashboard and *did* care about the cumulative number of miles as a KPI, you'd have to weigh that in your design decisions.)

JEFF: I too loved the simplicity of this dashboard. I had the opportunity to work with Andy on this chapter, so I had the benefit of seeing some of his iterations and the thought process behind them. As you saw in the chapter, he considered what "a reader" of this book might think even though he was the only user of this dashboard. Even so, the same thought process and design decisions were made thoughtfully. For example, knowing whether your users will be "in the field" when they use your dashboard on mobile is critical knowledge in the design process.

Also, don't gloss over the end of this chapter. I've seen organizations run into the trap of performing to the average, or landing on a target that was originally just a placeholder. Setting goals/targets can be very challenging. If it's too high or not based in reality then it will discourage people, making them feel like nothing they do will make a difference. On the other hand, if it's the same goal they've always had, then people can be routine about hitting it, or even complacent. So then we have to ask, if Andy didn't have a dashboard monitoring his steps, would he have walked more?

STEVE: Andy and Jeff make good points about what happens when a measure becomes a target. I wonder if it's reasonable to increase the target, or do you move on to another challenge altogether? I also think about how the question "how am I doing compared with peers" might serve as a motivator. If Andy were doing this challenge with a small group of friends, would he want to track his performance against others, and would he be motivated to walk more?

Tracking if you are on pace to meet your goals is a common challenge in many businesses. For another take on how to do this, see Chapter 7 in *The Big Book of Dashboards*.

Chapter 14

eCommerce Dashboard

Dorian Banutoiu

Organization: Canonicalized, for CIMALP

Dashboard Designer: Dorian Banutoiu

How This Dashboard Delivers: This dashboard allows senior management at a company to see product performance over time and identify the best- and worst-performing products. This allows them to better manage inventory and optimize marketing resources.

Audience: CEO, CMO, COO, and people who report directly to these senior executives.

Team: A single developer with input from primary stakeholders.

Tools: Google Analytics to maintain the data and Tableau for the dashboard.

Timeline: Spark to release for the first version was one week. The data is updated automatically. Improvements were made on an ad hoc basis but stabilized after a month. A PDF of the dashboard is emailed to stakeholders every morning.

Chapter Author: Steve Wexler

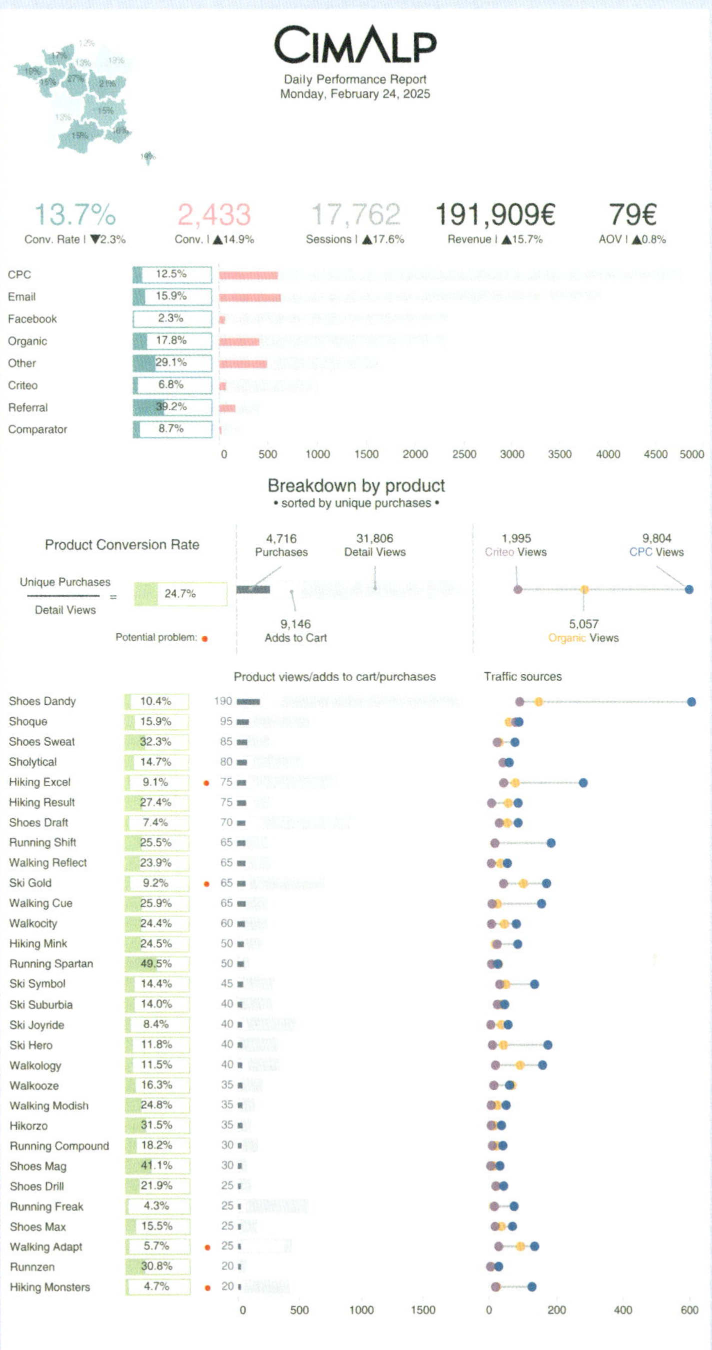
CIMALP
Daily Performance Report
Monday, February 24, 2025
13.7%
Conv. Rate I ▼2.3%
2,433
Conv. I ▲14.9%
17,762
Sessions I ▲17.6%
191,909€
Revenue I ▲15.7%
79€
AOV I ▲0.8%
CPC 12.5%
Email 15.9%
Facebook 2.3%
Organic 17.8%
Other 29.1%
Criteo 6.8%
Referral 39.2%
Comparator 8.7%
0 500 1000 1500 2000 2500 3000 3500 4000 4500 5000
Breakdown by product
• sorted by unique purchases •
Product Conversion Rate
Unique Purchases
Detail Views
= 24.7%
Potential problem:
4,716 Purchases
31,806 Detail Views
9,146 Adds to Cart
1,995 Criteo Views
9,804 CPC Views
5,057 Organic Views
Product views/adds to cart/purchases
Traffic sources
Shoes Dandy 10.4% 190
Shoque 15.9% 95
Shoes Sweat 32.3% 85
Sholytical 14.7% 80
Hiking Excel 9.1% 75
Hiking Result 27.4% 75
Shoes Draft 7.4% 70
Running Shift 25.5% 65
Walking Reflect 23.9% 65
Ski Gold 9.2% 65
Walking Cue 25.9% 65
Walkocity 24.4% 60
Hiking Mink 24.5% 50
Running Spartan 49.5% 50
Ski Symbol 14.4% 45
Ski Suburbia 14.0% 40
Ski Joyride 8.4% 40
Ski Hero 11.8% 40
Walkology 11.5% 40
Walkooze 16.3% 35
Walking Modish 24.8% 35
Hikorzo 31.5% 35
Running Compound 18.2% 30
Shoes Mag 41.1% 30
Shoes Drill 21.9% 25
Running Freak 4.3% 25
Shoes Max 15.5% 25
Walking Adapt 5.7% 25
Runnzen 30.8% 20
Hiking Monsters 4.7% 20
0 500 1000 1500
0 200 400 600

Big Picture

You are a C-level officer at an outdoor clothing and equipment company. You need to monitor click-to-purchase activity for multiple products across multiple channels. You want to make sure you are not wasting funds on products and channels that are underperforming and that you are adequately funding products and channels that are in demand.

You also need to see if there are any products that are getting a lot of interest, but, for whatever reason, people are not buying (conversion rate is low).

Specifics

You need to be able to see:

- Which channels and individual products generate the most interest and conversions, and which are less popular.
- "Problem" products, with problem being defined as a product that has a high cost-per-click (CPC) and a low conversion rate. In this example, any product with a CPC greater than 200 views and a conversion rate less than 10% is marked with a red dot.

Related Scenarios

- You are a sales director and need to track sales across different regions. Each region has a different goal, so you want to be able to compare actual sales and percentage of goal for each region.
- You are a health administrator for a state/region, and you need to track vaccinations and vaccination rates across multiple counties.
- You are promoting a free workshop and launch a social media campaign across different platforms to drive registrations for the event. You need to see the number of people who viewed the campaign, the number of people who registered, and the percentage of people who viewed and registered on the different platforms.

How People Use the Dashboard

While envisioned as an interactive dashboard, the C-level audience of this dashboard receives a static report in their respective email inboxes every morning. They also receive weekly and monthly summary reports.

These reports allow leadership to see which channels are producing the best results but, more importantly, which products need the most attention.

Why This Works

BANs as Color Legend

The key performance indicators (i.e., BANs) at the top of Figure 14.1 show both key metrics and serve as a color legend. Teal represents conversion rate (1), pink represents conversions, and gray represents the total number of sessions (3).

CiMALP uses the term *sessions* to describe interactions with a potential customer. Customers initiate sessions by visiting CiMALP's retail website, which can happen by clicking an ad (CPC) or promotional message, shopping via social media, or navigating to the site directly. The conversion rate measures the percentage of customers who made a purchase during their session.

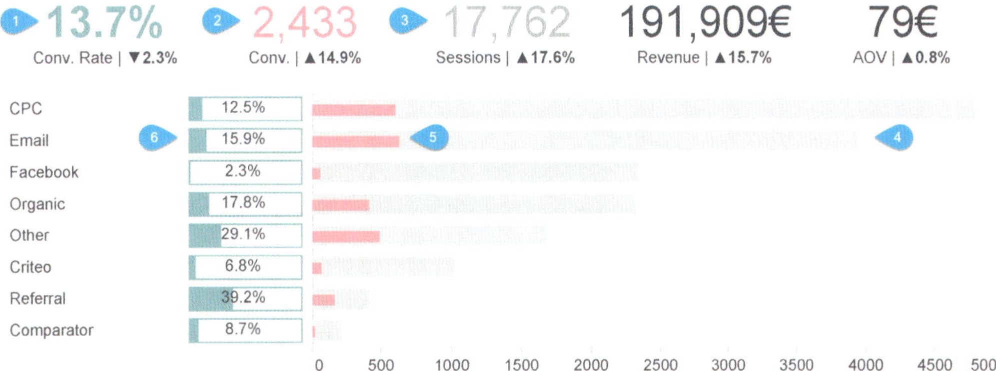

FIGURE 14.1 The top portion of the dashboard makes it easy to compare sessions with conversions, and the key performance indicators also serve as a color legend.

Beneath the BANs there are two charts: a bar-in-bar chart (4 and 5, above) and a progress bar chart (also called a "thermometer" chart, 6). These make it easy to see how many sessions and conversions there were for a particular product. In this example, we see that for email there were around 4,000 sessions (4) and approximately 600 conversions (5), resulting in conversion rate of 15.9% (6).

Bars Allow for Easy Comparisons

In Figure 14.2 we see that the bars make it easy to see that there were roughly twice as many CPC *sessions* (1) as there were Facebook sessions (2), but a small amount more email *conversions* (3) than CPC conversions (4).

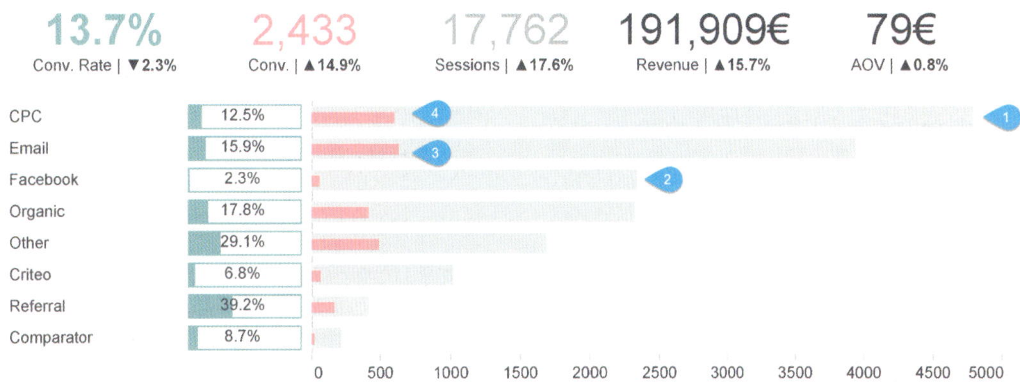

FIGURE 14.2 Comparing sessions and conversions across different channels.

Notice the bar-in-bar chart (the pink bars inside the gray bars) allows the dashboard developer to pack a lot of information into a small area.

Progress Bar Makes It Easy to Compare Conversion Rates

In addition to the number of sessions and number of conversions, we need to be able to compare the conversion rates, and the teal progress bars make this easy to do (item 5 in Figure 14.1).

"How to Read" Legend Explains How to Read the Chart Triptych

There are three charts for each product and a very well-designed graphic legend that explains how to read each chart. See the top of Figure 14.3.

We first see product conversation rate as a progress bar (1), which makes it easy to compare conversion rates across products. Indeed, we can see some standout products have a high number of conversions and a very high conversion rate (5).

The bar-in-bar-in-bar chart (2) allows us to see views (gray), items placed in cart (white), and purchases (black). Notice that Walking Adapt near the bottom has a very high "adds to cart" bar but very few purchases. That's something the CEO may want to look into.

The third chart (3) shows traffic sources (organic views, internet ad platform Criteo, and CPC).

Do We Need the "How to Read" Legend?

GIVEN that the stakeholders look at this report daily, why show a legend when they already know how to use the dashboard?

This is a case where a live interactive dashboard would solve the problem with collapsable components that can be turned on and turned off. "First time here and not sure how to read the charts? Click this button to see an overlay that explains the different components."

The indicator dots (4) draw attention to products that have a high CPC cost (anything over 200) but relatively low conversion rate.

Process

The spark for this dashboard was when the company's CEO asked to see product performance over time so he could easily identify the best- and worst-performing products. He needed both greater detail and better insights than what Google Analytics was showing (Figure 14.4).

Dorian Banutoiu, the dashboard designer, first made an interactive dashboard with maps and filters, but

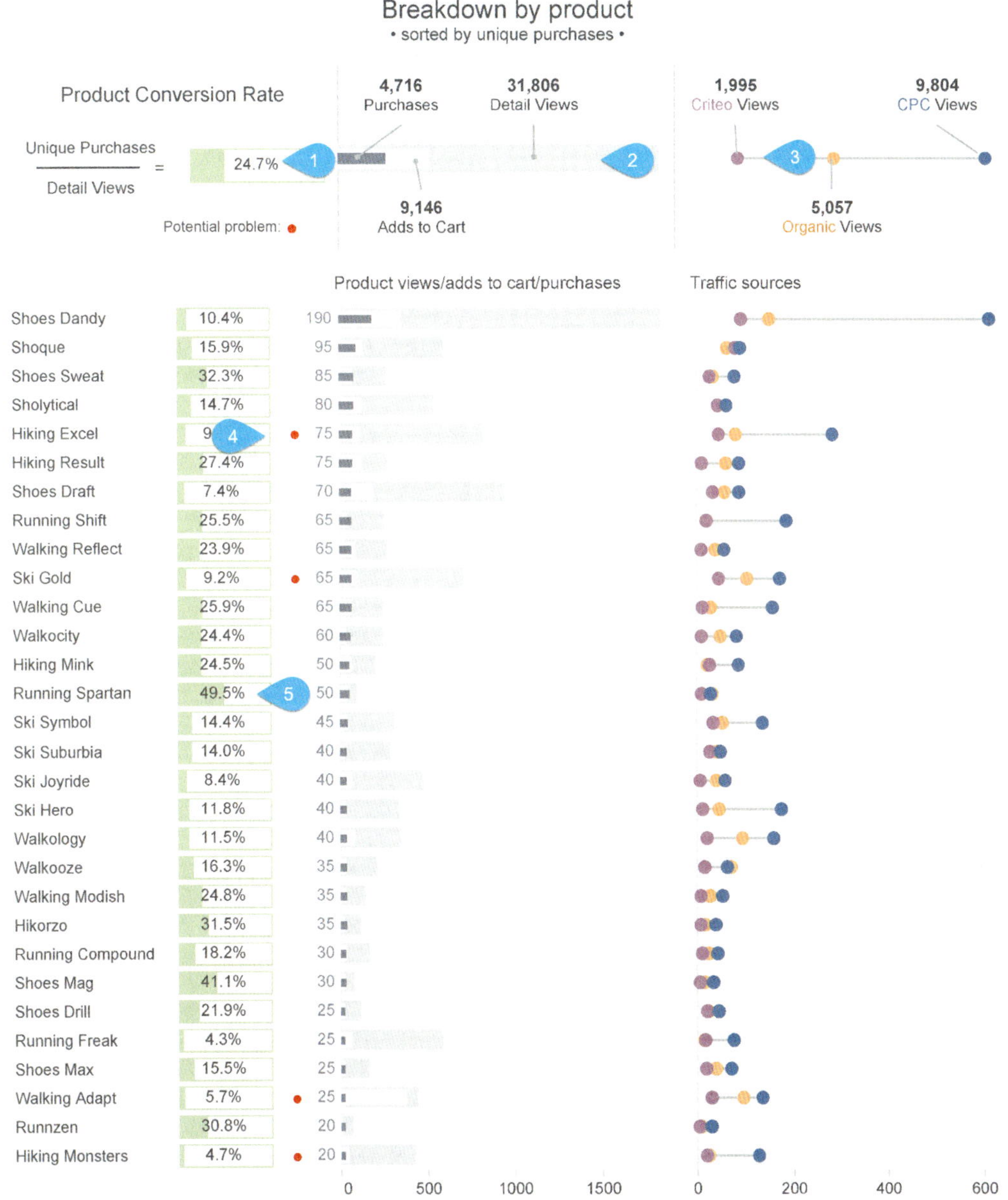

FIGURE 14.3 Conversion rates, conversion activity, and traffic source costs for each product.

Total Revenue

€12,298.39

% of Total: 100.00% (€12,298.39)

Average order value

€99.99

Avg for View: €99.99 (0.00%)

Visits

4,755

% of Total: 100.00% (4,755)

Ecommerce conversion rate

2.59%

Avg for View: 2.59% (0.00%)

Transactions

123

% of Total: 100.00% (123)

Top 10 products

Product	Product Revenue	Unique Purchases
Shoes Dandy	€2,158.20	18
Shoque	€999.00	10
Shoes Sweat	€996.00	4
Sholytical	€838.60	12
Hiking Excel	€715.36	8
Hiking Result	€679.60	4
Shoes Draft	€679.60	4
Running Shift	€599.00	10
Walking Reflect	€566.20	21
Ski Gold	€559.50	5

Visits and Product Revenue by Source / Medium

Source / Medium	Sessions	Revenue per User
google / cpc	1,618	€2.57
Newsletter_promo / email	502	€4.25
google / organic	456	€4.17
(direct) / (none)	326	€7.20
facebook / Shoes Sweat	278	€0.36
criteo / retargeting	252	€0.24
criteo / display	185	€0.46
bing / cpc	159	€3.26
facebook / Sholytical	143	€0.59
facebook / ppl	143	€0.25

CA par région

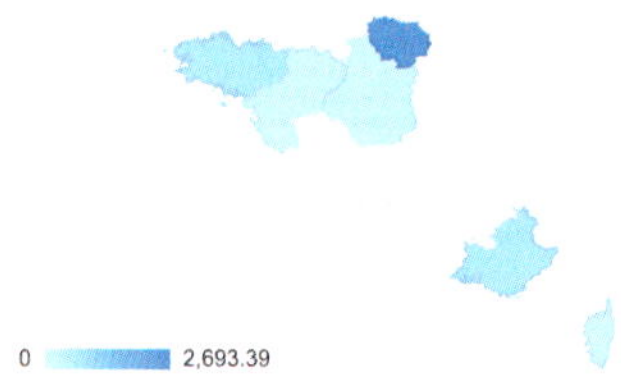

0 2,693.39

FIGURE 14.4 The original attempt using a Google Analytics dashboard to show conversion rates and advertising costs per product.

the CEO found it too much work to log into the system and asked that a static dashboard be emailed to him daily. He also requested weekly and monthly summaries.

As Banutoiu recounts, "I created a draft dashboard and the CEO said it was difficult to use as he had to log in. More important, what I had built wasn't close to what he wanted. He needed something basic for each product so he could see sessions, views, and all that.

"I went back and created a couple of more views including a heat map and bar chart, and then he started warming up to it.

"Initially I had only the top part, and as good as it is he felt he could get that information from Google analytics. It was the individual product information – the sessions and the conversion rates and the ease of comparison – that made the dashboard so valuable."

Clearly Defined Audience with Clearly Defined Needs

The major reason for such a fast design and implementation was that discovery was easy. There was no need to determine the audience and canvass their needs. The audience was the CEO, and he was able to articulate what he needed and *why he needed it*.

And that "why" bit undoubtedly influenced Banutoiu's chart choices and design decisions. He understood what things the CEO needed to see, quickly.

Multiple Iterations and Feedback

The CEO was clearly engaged in the project as evidenced by the feverish back-and-forth communication during development and user testing as Banutoiu iterated and the CEO provided feedback. Many projects don't enjoy the luxury of a single articulate stakeholder and a single uncommonly gifted dashboard designer. Having both the designer and stakeholder focused allowed them to produce a fully functional dashboard in one week.

Noteworthy Challenges

The biggest hurdle to success was getting all the data from Google Analytics. The connector used was not terribly robust and limited the amount of data that could be accessed at one time. Banutoiu had to create three different data connections and combine them into a single harmonized source. Fortunately, his workaround was relatively straightforward, but "getting the data just so" sometimes takes weeks if not months.

Measuring Success

While they did not conduct a formal ROI analysis, the consensus among the stakeholders is that the dashboard is saving the organization money in that it allows them to identify and fix underperforming products, quickly. Release and successful adoption were buoyed by the CEOs insistence that the CMO, COO, and senior managers use the dashboard daily.

Author Commentary

STEVE: This dashboard has been a favorite of mine since I featured it in the book *The Big Picture*. Banutoiu has crafted a clear and elegant way to show actuals and percentages at the same time in a compact space, something we'll explore more in "Dynamic Duos" later in the book.

I wonder if Banutoiu's approach to showing actuals and percentages at the same time would have come about had he not been in direct communication with the stakeholder. A requirements document might simply have stated "show the conversion rates, product view, and cart additions for all products" and Banutoiu might have shown a table full of numbers, fulfilling those requirements, but making insight more difficult.

But in really understanding the needs of his stakeholder (and because of the dashboard's success, now *stakeholders*) Banutoiu crafted a dashboard that makes it easy to focus on product problems and product opportunities.

We did give Banutoiu some pushback on use of screen real estate, with the company logo and "how to read" legend taking up so much space. We've already addressed the legend, but the stakeholders really like the logo as it indicates this is a customized dashboard, specific to their company and not just generic Google Analytics.

As the dashboard is delivered by email versus a mobile app where every pixel is precious, we see little downside in having a legend and a logo.

ANDY: As a newbie looking at this dashboard for the first time, I see BANs saying "Conv. Rate" and "Conv." That's not helpful to me because I don't know what those terms mean. Does that mean the dashboard is wrong? No. Sometimes it might be tempting to call on the designer to fix this, using terms that are immediately obvious to all. However, a dashboard designer needs to consider the domain expertise of the users. Will everyone using this dashboard know what "Conv." means? If not, how hard is it to tell them once what the term means, and then be comfortable that the abbreviation is fine. In this case, it's fine: the CEO and other stakeholders know these terms intimately.

AMANDA: One of the questions I ask anytime I'm reviewing a dashboard is "Why these colors?" since color is such a powerful way to encode information and organize a dashboard. In this case, my gut instinct on the use of the teal and pink is to assume meaning; teal (green) for conversion rate being "good" and pink (red) for conversion performing poorly. Sometimes, that outside perspective on how a person viewing the dashboard with new eyes can be helpful, since we can identify where there are conventions or mental models we have for colors and other encodings. Here's where the connection between the designer and the audience adds necessary insight. If the color palette works for the audience, great! If the user group expands, though, take the time to get feedback from the new users and ensure they're not projecting the same meaning on the color choices.

Chapter 15

Recency, Frequency, Monetary (RFM) Analysis

Tableau

Dashboard Designer: Tableau

Organization: This is a template dashboard that any organization can use.

How This Dashboard Delivers: Using just three fields of data (Customer Name, Sales Order Dates, and Sales Value), this dashboard visualizes customer segments. Using this as a template dashboard, an analyst can get to a released dashboard quicker than starting from scratch.

Audience: Recency, frequency, and monetary (RFM) analysis can be used by people in marketing to create different types of campaigns.

Tools: Tableau.

URL: dtdbook.com/link19scenario

Chapter Author: Andy Cotgreave

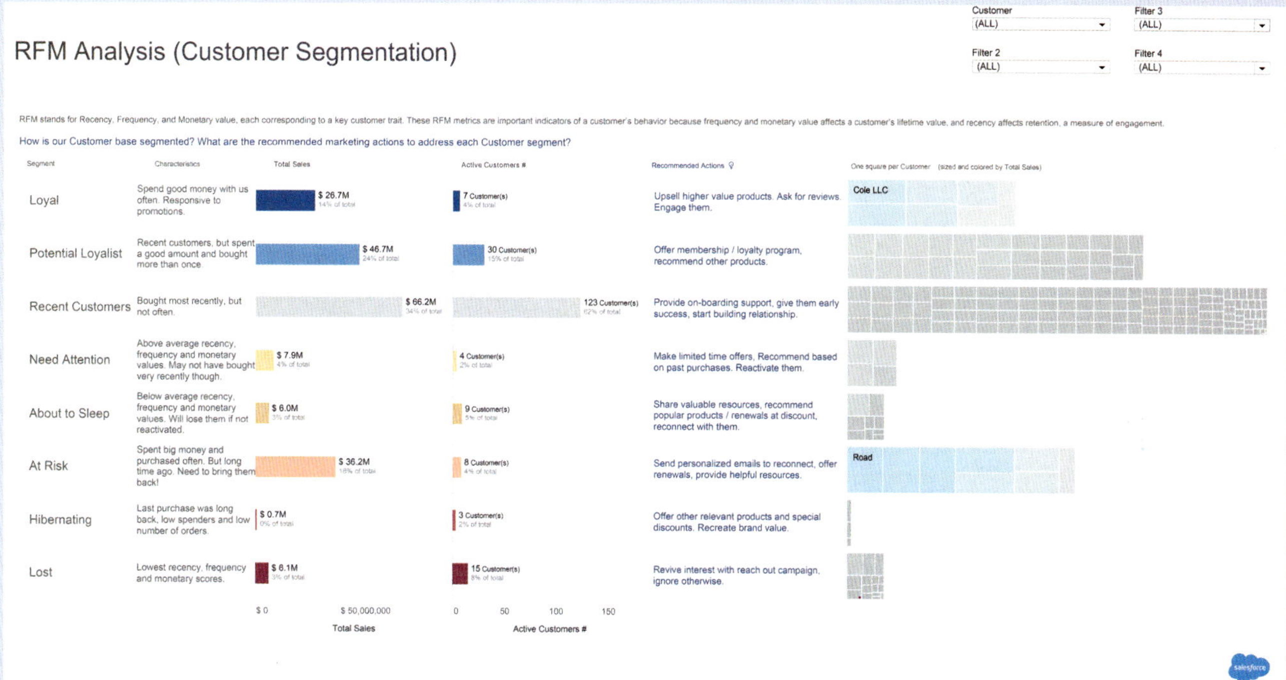
RFM Analysis (Customer Segmentation)
Customer
(ALL)
Filter 3
(ALL)
Filter 2
(ALL)
Filter 4
(ALL)
RFM stands for Recency, Frequency, and Monetary value, each corresponding to a key customer trait. These RFM metrics are important indicators of a customer's behavior because frequency and monetary value affects a customer's lifetime value, and recency affects retention, a measure of engagement.
How is our Customer base segmented? What are the recommended marketing actions to address each Customer segment?
Segment
Characteristics
Total Sales
Active Customers #
Recommended Actions
One square per Customer (sized and colored by Total Sales)
Loyal
Spend good money with us often. Responsive to promotions.
$ 26.7M
7 Customer(s)
Upsell higher value products. Ask for reviews. Engage them.
Cole LLC
Potential Loyalist
Recent customers, but spent a good amount and bought more than once.
$ 46.7M
30 Customer(s)
Offer membership / loyalty program, recommend other products.
Recent Customers
Bought most recently, but not often.
$ 66.2M
123 Customer(s)
Provide on-boarding support, give them early success, start building relationship.
Need Attention
Above average recency, frequency and monetary values. May not have bought very recently though.
$ 7.9M
4 Customer(s)
Make limited time offers, Recommend based on past purchases. Reactivate them.
About to Sleep
Below average recency, frequency and monetary values. Will lose them if not reactivated.
$ 6.0M
9 Customer(s)
Share valuable resources, recommend popular products / renewals at discount, reconnect with them.
At Risk
Spent big money and purchased often. But long time ago. Need to bring them back!
$ 36.2M
8 Customer(s)
Send personalized emails to reconnect, offer renewals, provide helpful resources.
Road
Hibernating
Last purchase was long back, low spenders and low number of orders.
$ 0.7M
3 Customer(s)
Offer other relevant products and special discounts. Recreate brand value.
Lost
Lowest recency, frequency and monetary scores.
$ 6.1M
15 Customer(s)
Revive interest with reach out campaign, ignore otherwise.
$ 0
$ 50,000,000
Total Sales
0
50
100
150
Active Customers #
salesforce

Big Picture

You work in marketing and want to create campaigns that appeal to different types of customers, according to their purchase history: how recently did they purchase, how frequently do they purchase, and how much do they spend when they purchase?

Your dashboard's data model automatically divides customers into different segments according to those criteria. You use insights from this dashboard to create specific marketing campaigns tailored to each segment.

How This Chapter Works

THIS scenario is a little different from others in the book. This dashboard is a template that can be used by any team creating marketing campaigns. In this specific scenario, you open the template in Tableau, map it to your data, and you're (in theory) ready to go. In this chapter's "Process" section, rather than describing how the original template was built, we'll discuss how to use templates, along with the pros and cons of doing so.

If you choose to use a template, you will still need to follow most elements from our framework. Who are your users? Will the template work for them? How will you do user testing?

It is possible that the complications of fitting your data and process into a template is worse than starting from scratch. Ensure you test templates diligently.

Specifics

Recency, frequency, monetary (RFM) analysis places customers into different segments according to their purchase history. For each category, customers are scored on a 1–5 scale. For example, someone making large orders regularly and recently would be a 5-5-5. A customer who once made a very large order, a long time ago, and has never repurchased would be a 5-1-1.

The score profiles (from 5-5-5 down to 1-1-1) are grouped into segments that predict future purchasing probability. Different RFM models define different numbers of segments. In this scenario, there are nine:

1. **Loyal:** Active spenders and responsive to promotions
2. **Potential Loyalist:** Recent customers who spent a large amount and have bought more than once
3. **Recent Customer:** Made a recent purchase but are not regular customers
4. **Need Attention:** Above average on frequency and order size, but not bought recently
5. **About to Sleep:** Below average on all metrics
6. **At Risk:** Has spent large amounts but not recently
7. **Cannot Lose Them:** Has spent the most of all customers, but not recently
8. **Hibernating:** Low on all counts, but was somewhat active in the past
9. **Lost:** Lowest scores across all measures

Marketing experts can tailor unique marketing campaigns for each segment. For example, loyal customers could be upsold to, asked for reviews, and be responsive to exclusive product offers. Customers in the Need Attention segment could be targeted with time-limited special offers for products like their earlier purchases.

Related Scenarios

- You track retention rates in HR. Using metrics such as engagement, attendance, and performance, you can categorize employees by level of flight risk and then take different actions for each group.
- You are a project manager overseeing multiple projects. You want to group them according to how on or off schedule they are and then take steps for each category.

How People Use the Dashboard

The main view (Figure 15.1) assigns one row to each customer segment. Each row has the following sections:

1. On the left is the name of the segment, along with a description of what that segment means.
2. A bar chart shows the total amount of lifetime sales for each segment.
3. A second bar chart shows the number of customers in each segment.
4. A tree bar shows all customers, sized and colored according to lifetime sales.
5. Filters allow you to drill into specific customers or other categories.

The user can click any segment to drill into another view showing all the customers in that segment. For example, if the user clicks the Recent Customer segment in the main dashboard, they'd get to a second view, shown in Figure 15.2.

There are three sections to this view:

1. An overview describes the segment and the recommended action.
2. A dot plot shows *all* customers according to the three RFM metrics.
3. A scrollable list showing detail for all customers in this segment. There is a bar chart for each measure and a dot plot showing sales history (sized by transaction amount).

Using this data, action can be taken. For Recent Customers, the best recommended action is to provide onboarding support, reward early success, and start building a relationship. Each segment has a specific marketing action that can be taken.

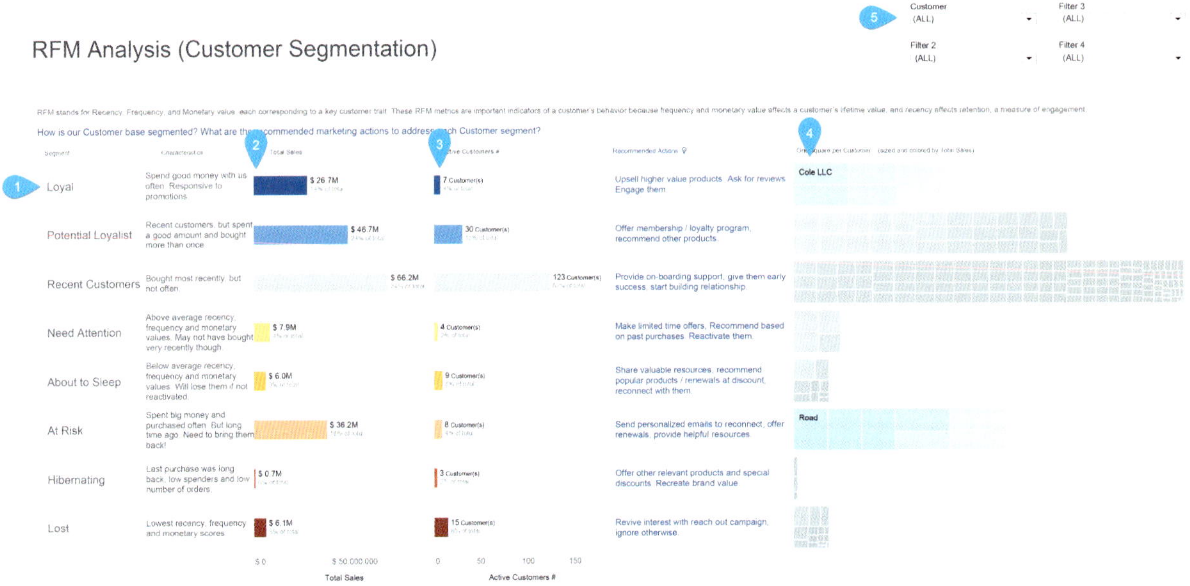

FIGURE 15.1 Annotated dashboard.

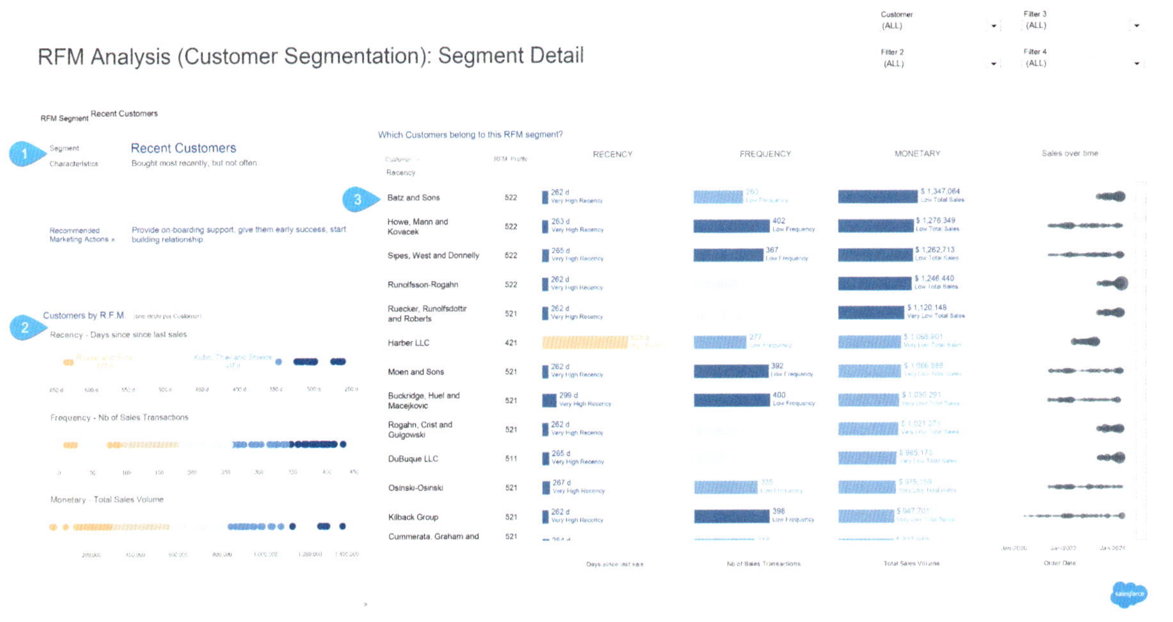

FIGURE 15.2 The second dashboard showing customers in the "About to Sleep" segment.

Why This Works

Effective Design: White Space, Grid Layouts, and Color

This dashboard displays three successful design choices:

1. A simple layout. The layout is very simple: it's a grid where each segment has a single row.
2. Row-shading. The alternate row shades make it easy to keep your eye following each segment from left to right.
3. Sparing use of color. The blue-to-yellow-to-red palette of the Total Sales and Active Customers bars is aesthetically pleasing and creates a visual clue on how to interpret the rows ("best" customers at the top, "lost" customers at the bottom).

Labels Instead of Axes

See Figure 15.3. The bars showing Total Sales and Active Customers each have a two-line label on them: total and percentage of total. The bar charts don't have x-axes. Is this the right choice? Is it not better to show the axis to keep your dashboard as clean as possible?

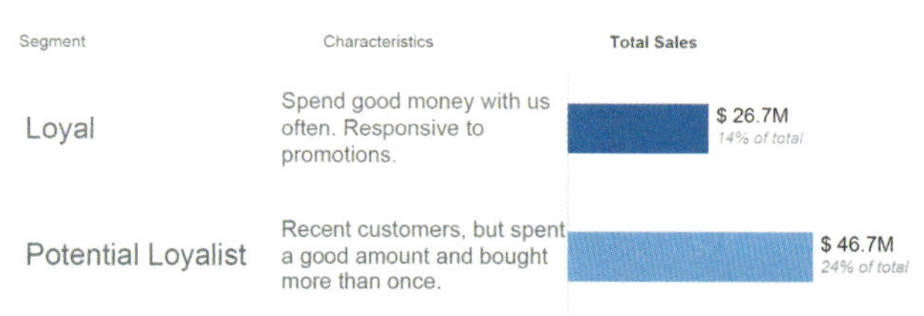

FIGURE 15.3 Each bar has a two-row label showing value and percentage of total.

Let's take a look.

I created a version that removes the labels and adds an x-axis. Compare that to the original in Figure 15.4.

Is labeling a bar *better* than showing an axis?

This is an example of the tensions of dashboard design, and I don't think there is a definitive answer. On the one hand, you want to reduce clutter (i.e., *no* labels, *show* the x-axis). On the other hand, we want to put the information where people's eyes are (labels, no axis). A third option, not shown, is to include both the axis and the label. This would emphasize the 0-starting point on the x-axis *and* give specific values for each data point.

What's the right choice? Every data design choice is a compromise, and you'll have to use your experience and design skills to choose what's right for you.

In this case, I think the labels are the right choice. Since each segment has a whole row dedicated to it, the labels mean your eye can make one scan, left to right, to glean all the necessary information. With an axis instead of labels, the left-to-right scan would be interrupted by an up-and-down movement to discern the values, shown in Figure 15.5.

Actionable Insights from Three Fields

Do you need a complex dataset with dozens of fields to create a dashboard that delivers actionable

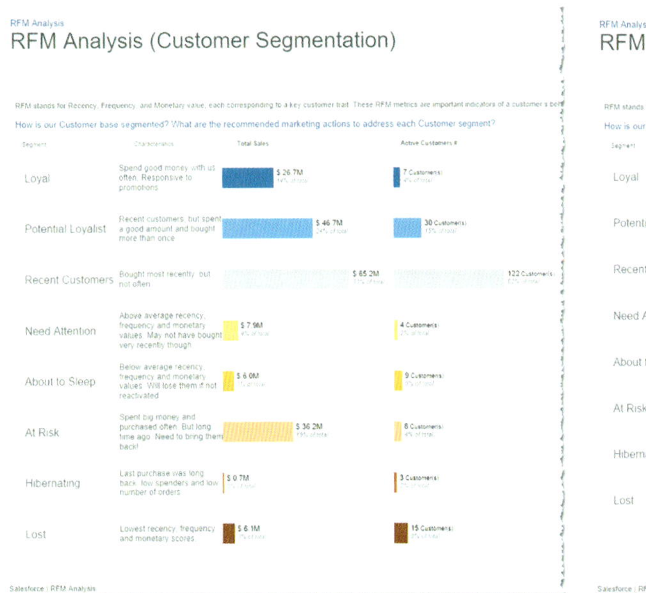

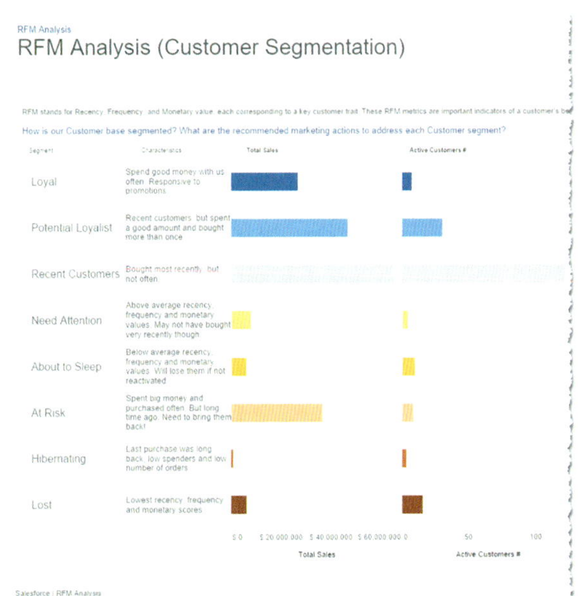

FIGURE 15.4 Two versions of the bar chart with and without labels and axes.

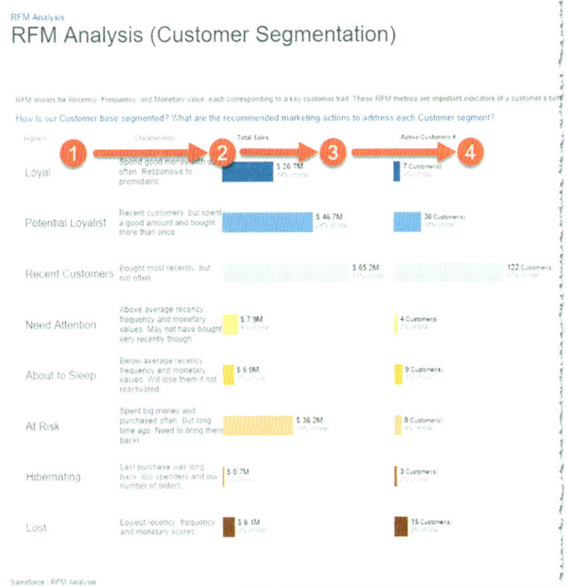

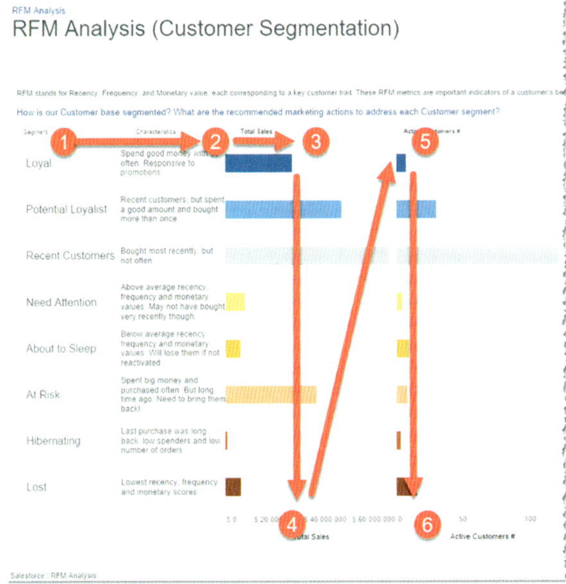

FIGURE 15.5 The red arrows and steps show the eye flow one takes when reading the chart with labels (on the left) or with an axis (on the right).

insight? No. This scenario creates actionable insight from just these fields:

- Customer Name
- Order Date
- Order Amount

That's all you need to segment your customers via RFM analysis. You can then tailor unique marketing campaigns to each segment.

Process

Templates as a Starting Point

You've had a spark: you, your manager, or your team, want to group your customers into segments so you can do targeted campaigning.

You move onto discovery. At this point you discover that your spark is something that thousands of companies have done before. In this case your goal to create campaigns based on customer behavior is a common strategy: recency, frequency, monetary analysis.

At this point you can ask yourself, do I need to start every dashboard from scratch? Is it feasible to get a head start and use a template dashboard?

That's the promise of templates. The goal is to reduce the time you spend in discovery and prototype. Why bother with countless design cycles if a good template could provide you with a ready-built solution?

From Template to Development

Using a template is not a way to sidestep the steps in our framework; although you're probably going to save time overall, you still need to ensure it matches your users' requirements. Let's consider some of the items you'll have to follow to determine whether the template will save time over building something from scratch.

Does Your Data Map Easily?

First, you'll need to compare the template's data structure to your own data. Carefully read the template's documentation to understand the logic and any dependencies of the data.

This RFM template has a built-in data mapper (Figure 15.6). In this case it shows that, indeed, you

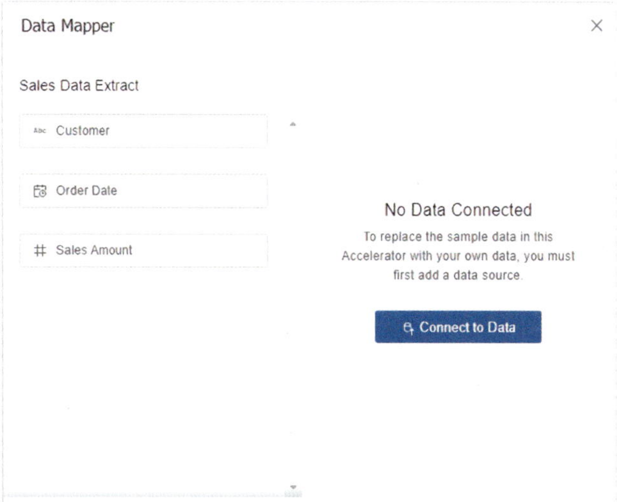

FIGURE 15.6 The data mapping tool for the RFM dashboard showing just three fields are needed.

do need just three data fields. Other templates might be much more complicated.

Can You Maintain the Dashboard Logic?

Closely examine the logic used to build the dashboard. In this scenario, even though there are just three data fields, the dashboard requires 30 parameters to work (Figure 15.7) and more than 30 calculated fields.

This is not atypical for a dashboard, but your role in assessing the use of a template is to consider what happens if you want to change the logic. For example, this RFM template is designed to bucket your customers into eight categories. What if you want only six categories? What calculations would you have to change? What if you wanted to make the number of categories dynamic? Is that possible in the template?

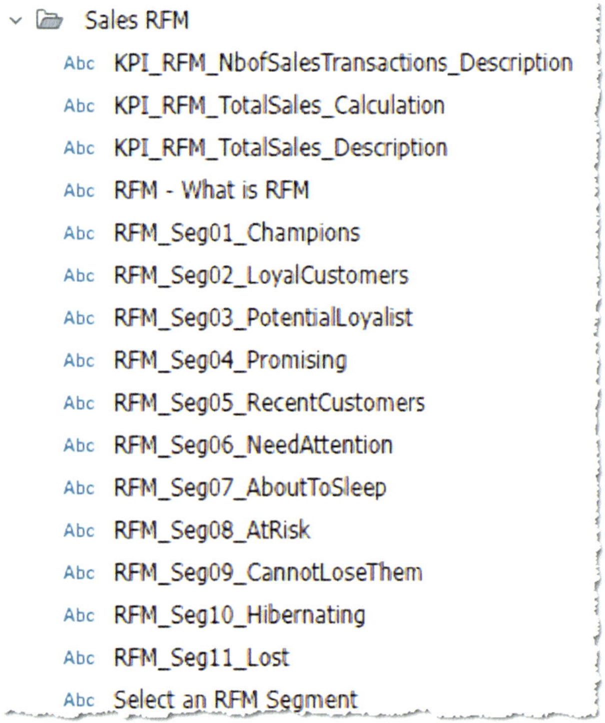

Sales RFM
Abc KPI_RFM_NbofSalesTransactions_Description
Abc KPI_RFM_TotalSales_Calculation
Abc KPI_RFM_TotalSales_Description
Abc RFM - What is RFM
Abc RFM_Seg01_Champions
Abc RFM_Seg02_LoyalCustomers
Abc RFM_Seg03_PotentialLoyalist
Abc RFM_Seg04_Promising
Abc RFM_Seg05_RecentCustomers
Abc RFM_Seg06_NeedAttention
Abc RFM_Seg07_AboutToSleep
Abc RFM_Seg08_AtRisk
Abc RFM_Seg09_CannotLoseThem
Abc RFM_Seg10_Hibernating
Abc RFM_Seg11_Lost
Abc Select an RFM Segment

FIGURE 15.7 Some of the 30 parameters used to create the RFM categories.

You might ultimately want to move the logic for calculating the RFM categories out of the dashboard and into your data warehouse itself. That would be useful to allow you to use the analysis elsewhere in your organization. In that case, you would need to estimate how much effort it would be to rework the logic in the template.

Does It Fit Your Style Guide?

If your organization has a defined style guide, how easy will it be to edit the template to fit your style guide? You should look carefully at every design element (fonts, colors, layouts, tooltips, etc.) to ensure they be changed with minimal effort.

Will It Work in All Destinations?

If you plan on using the dashboard on mobile devices, or embedded, or in email, does the dashboard fit or adapt to those form factors? If not, consider the effort needed to fit the dashboard to those formats.

In this scenario, for example, the design leans heavily on using rows to represent all details of each segment. Each row contains segment name, sales, active customers, actions, and customer detail. On a mobile device, it would be hard to fit that information in a narrower portrait orientation. If mobile usage is a requirement, you'd need to consider how to change the display to fit.

Does It Fit Your Users' Needs?

Even if the technical hurdles listed are small, the template still needs to fit your user's needs. It is just as important to go through a discovery process, including thinking about personas and user stories, to be sure the template matches your needs. The users need to be involved in testing the functionality and logic of the dashboard, too.

Author Commentary

ANDY: Should you use templates?

Will a template be a *perfect* match for your needs? It's unlikely, but it might get you close.

You could start with a blank page every time. But are your requirements truly unique and novel? Almost definitely not: it's almost guaranteed that other organizations have already faced the same dashboard challenge, and solved them.

Bent Flyvbjerg and Dan Gardner, authors of *How Big Things Get Done*, agree. They describe how perceptions of uniqueness can lead project teams to ignore lessons from other, similar projects. Treating every project as unique leads to longer development times. Dashboard templates are the same. They can greatly reduce time in your prototyping and user testing phases. However, there are important conditions you need to check first, which I discussed earlier.

AMANDA: Thinking beyond the design of this template for marketing analytics, I love the concept of dashboard templates and have seen it work in some of my own projects. Years ago, I worked with community organizations across a few different countries, all collecting and analyzing the same community scorecard data on a quarterly basis. Each organization had limited capacity and time for data visualization design work and wouldn't set up their own bespoke dashboard. We created a shared dashboard template to connect to their data tables and create a quick prototype dashboard they could use internally, reducing the time to insight.

If you create your own templates to use across teams, locations, or even clients, consider two key challenges in setting up and maintaining those dashboards.

First, a template works *if* you structure your data to match the structure of the sample dataset. Take time to understand, define, and document the data transformation steps to match your data to the template. Small changes, like different field names, can result in a page of errors and a lot of frustration.

Second, templates can feel hugely empowering for newer dashboard creators but can come with frustrations if someone wants to make changes and doesn't know the tool well. Make sure the team managing the dashboard has the necessary technical knowledge to make design changes and monitor data quality issues. With the right technical skills, the template can work like an instant prototype to interact with, and then you can identify what changes are necessary to customize the display to your analytics needs.

STEVE: This scenario celebrates the power of a good template and may make you want to craft templates for your own organization. Before you do, think of applying elements from our framework. Who is going to use the template? How will the template help them? Who will give you feedback as you create the template? How will you test the template to make sure it maps easily to your target users' data? Once it's built, how will you ensure people use the template?

As much work goes into making a dashboard template as goes into making a dashboard. Do what you can to make sure that effort is rewarded.

JEFF: I think templates can be really useful to help people get started. One of the frequently overlooked resources in the Tableau community is the Accelerators that are available on the main splash screen of Tableau. There are countless dashboards available, many from excellent designers and groups, including the Information Lab, and the insurance dashboard by Ellen Blackburn and featured in Chapter 21. This allows anyone with a related scenario to gather their data, immediately connect it, and visualize it. Even if your data is not identical, these can provide wonderful mini-scenarios just like our book, to help inspire you and give you ideas to use in your own work.

I would be a bad professor if I didn't mention the bar chart treemap in this dashboard. In general, I don't find these useful charts for making comparisons. That said, have a listen to our podcast Chart Chat, episode 27, where we did a chart makeover.

In my makeover, I used a pie chart and a bar chart with a treemap, two charts I rarely use (dtdbook.com/link20). In this case, showing individual bars for a precise comparison of customers would take 198 bars, requiring scrolling to even find most of the bars, thus making comparisons very difficult. A stacked bar chart might be an alternative, but it offers the same challenges as the treemap bar chart, and in this case, it's worse (Figure 15.8). With so many small slices, it introduces another challenge, the borders. Borders of any color (or white or black) make it impossible to see the smallest segments.

While this treemap bar chart has its issues, it does offer the ability to easily highlight even the smallest segments. Also, if I were using this template, I would drop the alternating row banding colors and use a white background.

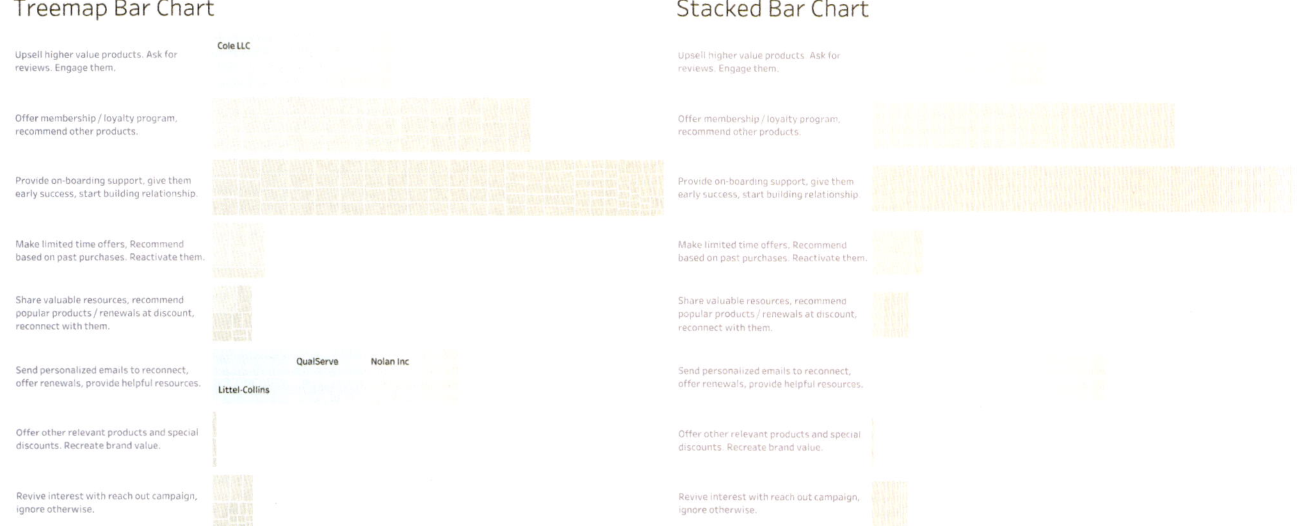

FIGURE 15.8 A comparison of a treemap bar chart and a stacked bar chart without row banding colors.

Chapter 16

Splash Project WISE Dashboard

Jeffrey A. Shaffer and Christopher DeMartini

Project WISE Outputs Dashboard

Dashboard Designers: Jeffrey A. Shaffer and Christopher DeMartini.

Organization: Splash's Project WISE (WASH-in-Schools for Everyone).

How This Dashboard Delivers: The dashboard allows the CEO to show current and potential donors how the project is improving the lives of underserved people.

Audience: Dozens of current and potential donors who need to be convinced of the project's impact.

Team: The original dashboard designers and multiple people to maintain and improve the dashboard including Eric Stowe, Maria Lugovets, Simon Beaumont, and Elaine Yuan.

Tools: Tableau, Excel, Mapbox, and Snowflake.

Timeline: The time from spark to initial release was four weeks.

Chapter Author: Jeffrey A. Shaffer

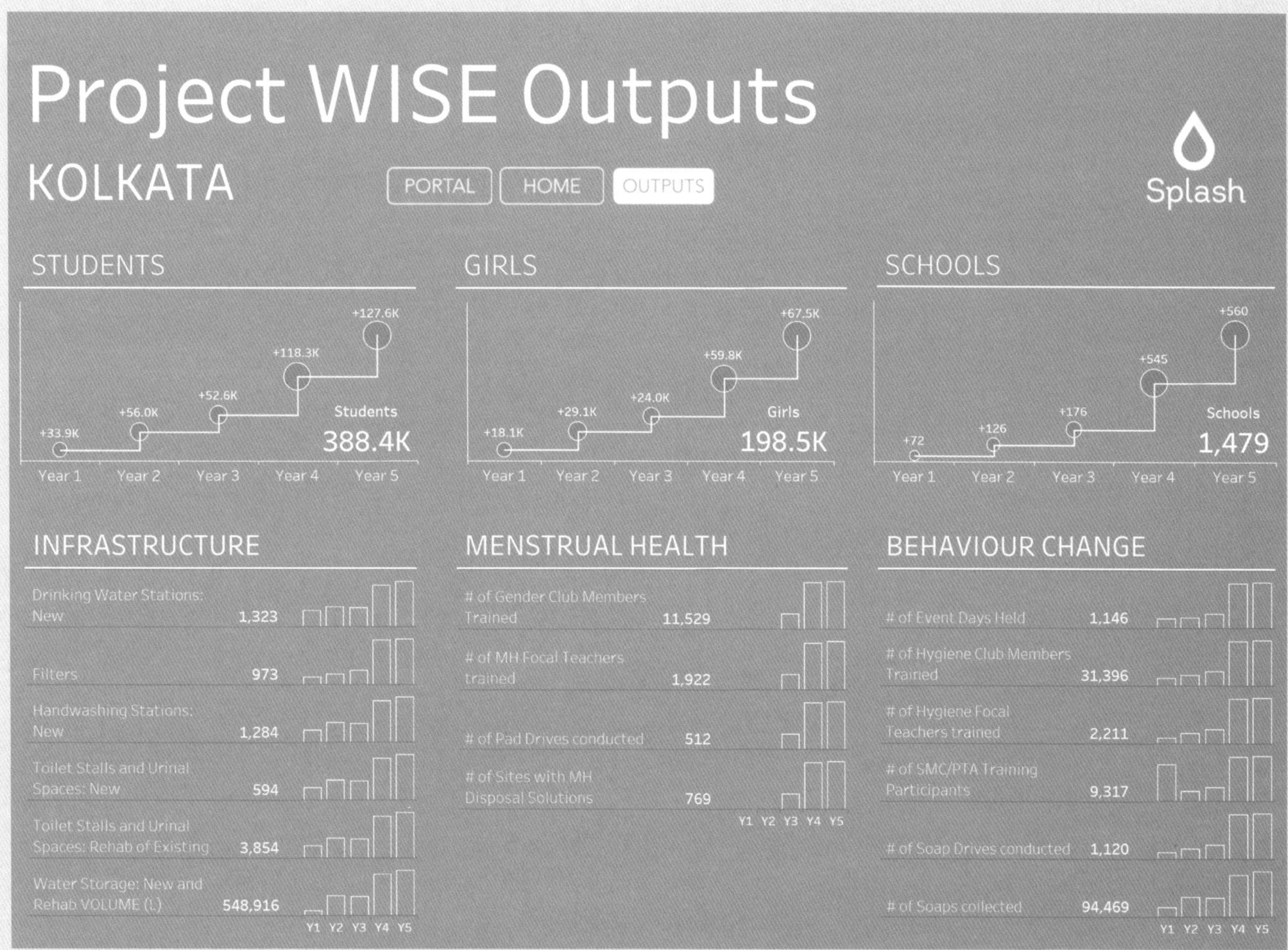
Project WISE Outputs
KOLKATA
PORTAL
HOME
OUTPUTS
Splash
STUDENTS
+33.9K
+56.0K
+52.6K
+118.3K
+127.6K
Students
388.4K
Year 1
Year 2
Year 3
Year 4
Year 5
GIRLS
+18.1K
+29.1K
+24.0K
+59.8K
+67.5K
Girls
198.5K
Year 1
Year 2
Year 3
Year 4
Year 5
SCHOOLS
+72
+126
+176
+545
+560
Schools
1,479
Year 1
Year 2
Year 3
Year 4
Year 5
INFRASTRUCTURE
Drinking Water Stations: New 1,323
Filters 973
Handwashing Stations: New 1,284
Toilet Stalls and Urinal Spaces: New 594
Toilet Stalls and Urinal Spaces: Rehab of Existing 3,854
Water Storage: New and Rehab VOLUME (L) 548,916
Y1 Y2 Y3 Y4 Y5
MENSTRUAL HEALTH
# of Gender Club Members Trained 11,529
# of MH Focal Teachers trained 1,922
# of Pad Drives conducted 512
# of Sites with MH Disposal Solutions 769
Y1 Y2 Y3 Y4 Y5
BEHAVIOUR CHANGE
# of Event Days Held 1,146
# of Hygiene Club Members Trained 31,396
# of Hygiene Focal Teachers trained 2,211
# of SMC/PTA Training Participants 9,317
# of Soap Drives conducted 1,120
# of Soaps collected 94,469
Y1 Y2 Y3 Y4 Y5

Big Picture

You are a C-level officer of a nonprofit organization that operates programs to improve children's access to clean water and sanitation facilities in public or institutional spaces. You need to demonstrate to donors, potential donors, and board members the impact the project has had and will have. The aim is not merely to raise money but to demonstrate the scale and potential impact of a project. You want to highlight the organization's impact on an entire city and be able to drill down into a single location around a school to provide context and detail.

The dashboard needs to embody the organization's brand identity.

Specifics

You need to be able to:

- Select a city from the portal page.
- From each city selection, navigate to a home page, which will show a map of the location for each water purification system installed and the total children served by year.
- For each year, see the total number of students served as well as the projections for future years of the project, and the total number of children served.
- For each city's home page, navigate to an outputs dashboard that will give various statistics about the actual and forecasted outputs in addition to water filtration systems (water storage tanks, sanitation facilities, hygiene trainings for students and teachers, etc.).

Related Scenarios

You are a:

- Healthcare administrator and need to see a high-level map view along with a drill-down to a lower-level view (country to city, city to neighborhood, or neighborhood to school)
- Fundraiser for a university or nonprofit and need to see the progress of an initiative over time, showing separate periods and the overall total
- Marketing director and need a branded dashboard or analytical application that has very specific design needs to match your website, branding material, and brand message

What Is Splash?

SPLASH is a nonprofit organization dedicated to improving water, sanitation, hygiene (WASH), and menstrual health conditions for children living in urban poverty. Founded in 2007 and headquartered in Seattle, Washington, Splash focuses on ensuring that children in schools, orphanages, hospitals, and shelters have access to clean water and proper sanitation facilities.

The organization operates in countries across Asia and Africa. Through its initiatives, Splash has reached more than one million children, providing them with safe drinking water, handwashing stations, and child-friendly toilets.

One of Splash's major projects is Project WISE, which aims to provide clean water and child-friendly toilets, change behavior regarding hygiene practices, and strengthen menstrual health services. This project is particularly focused on urban areas with high concentrations of underserved young people.

For more information, see dtdbook .com/link21.

How People Use the Dashboard

This dashboard works as both an interactive dashboard and as a static image in a PowerPoint presentation. From the beginning, Eric Stowe, CEO for Splash, explained that he would use the dashboard "out in the field" giving live demos to donors, potential donors, and board members in all sorts of locations, including a presentation on a bus (Figure 16.1).

Why This Works

Three-Part Dashboard with Overview, Filter, and Details on Demand

There are three main views to this dashboard, a portal page, a home page, and the outputs dashboard (Figure 16.2).

FIGURE 16.1 Eric Stowe, the founder of Splash, presenting the dashboard to donors and board members on a bus in Ethiopia.

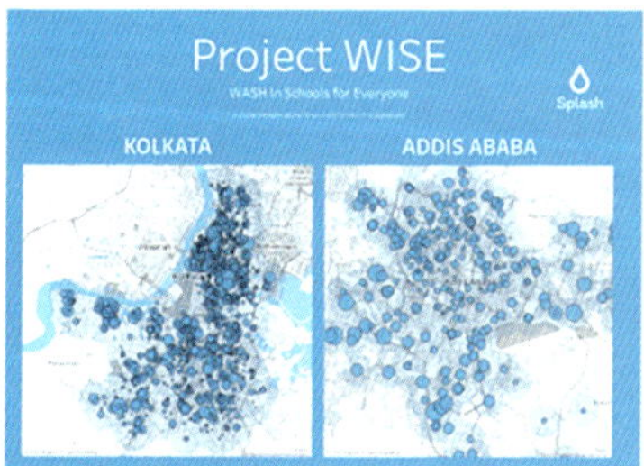

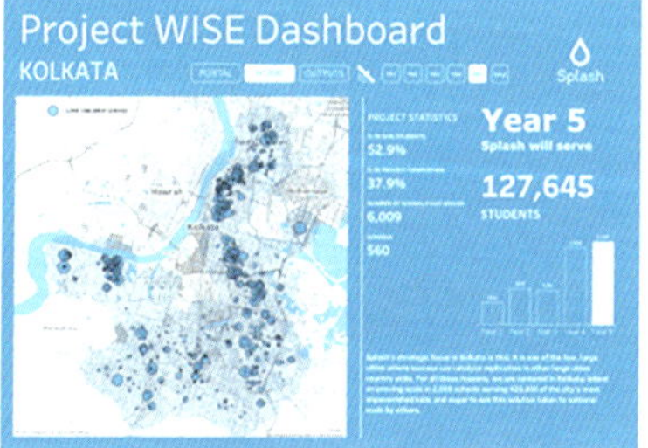

FIGURE 16.2 Thumbnail images of the three main views of this dashboard: a portal page, a home page, and the outputs dashboard.

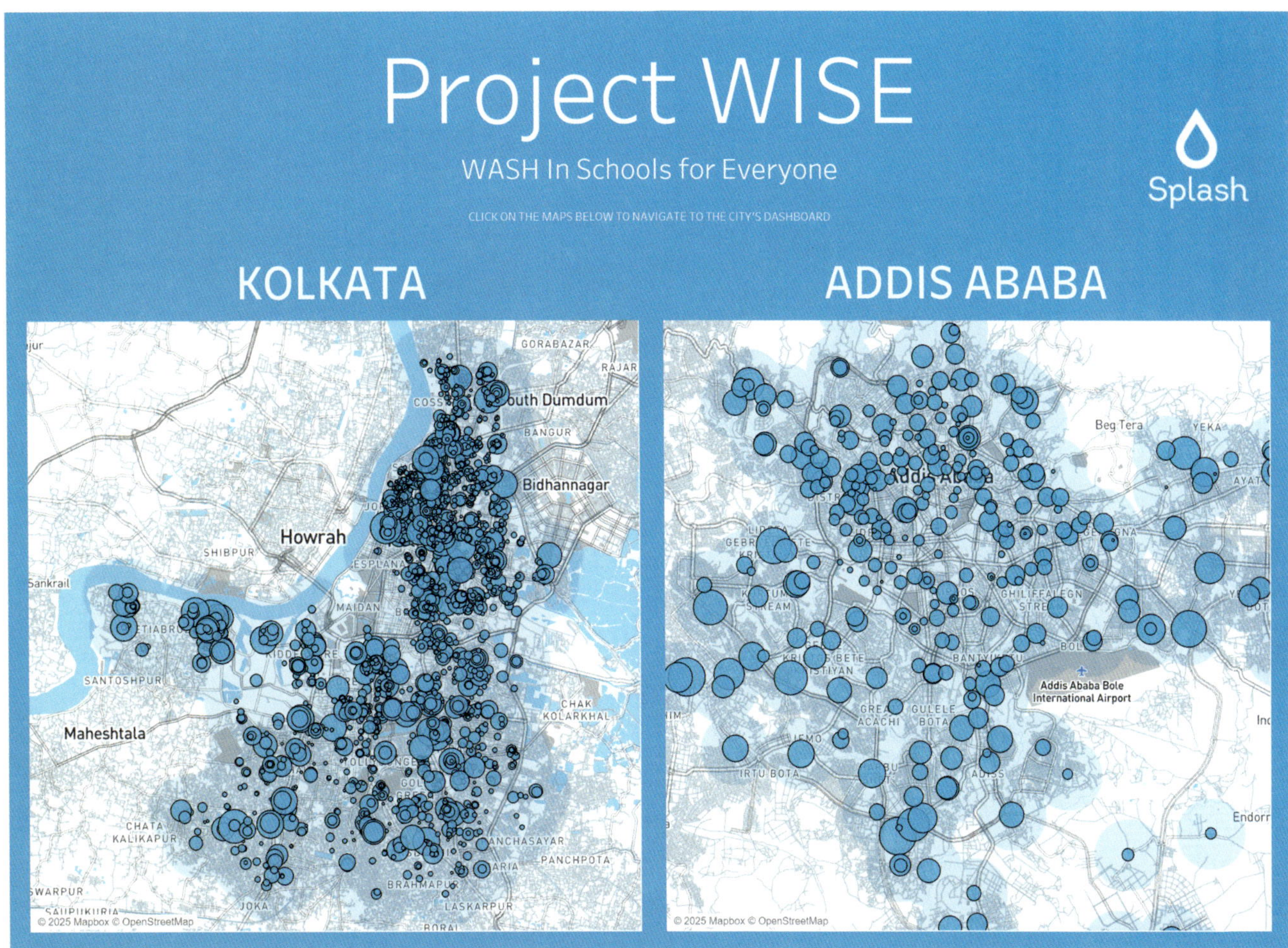

FIGURE 16.3 Portal page where user can select between two cities, Kolkata or Addis Ababa.

Ben Shneiderman's Mantra

Consider Ben Shneiderman's mantra when designing dashboards: overview first, followed by zoom and filter, and then details on-demand. This example clearly follows this recommendation.

The portal page starts as an overview of each city and provides navigation to both cities' home page (Figure 16.3).

The user selects a city and then navigates to that city's home page (Figure 16.4).

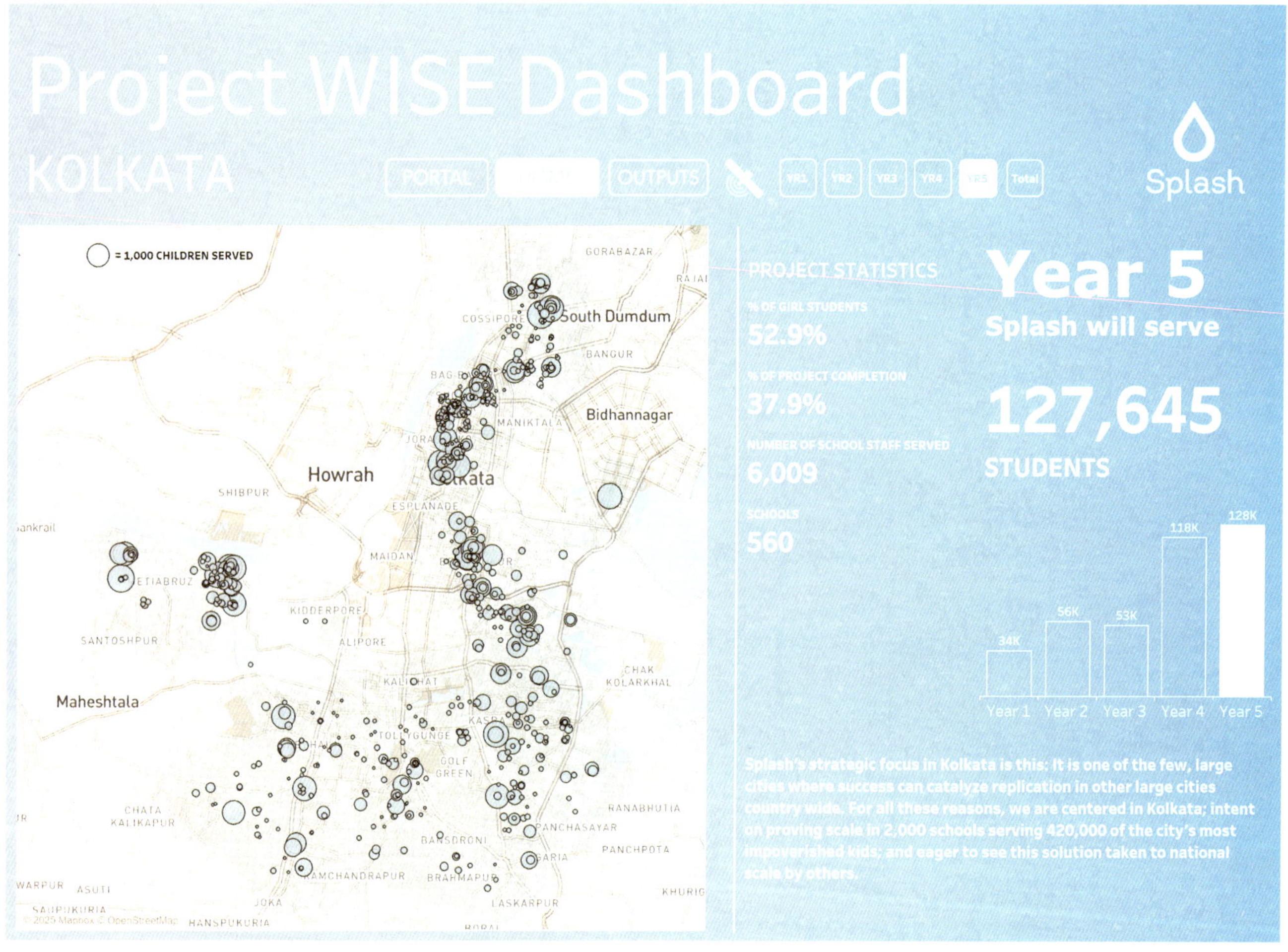

FIGURE 16.4 Home page dashboard for Kolkata.

On each city home page there are:

- Navigation buttons at the top to navigate to the Portal, Home, and Outputs dashboard.
- Filter buttons to show each year of the project and the totals for the project.
- BANs showing the year of the project or the total, and the number of students served.
- Additional measures showing the percentage of girl students, percentage of project completion, number of school staff served, and number of schools.
- A custom note that is dynamic for the year and city selected provides the user with a short description of the project in the selected city.

- A satellite button to change from a map view to a satellite view. In a future iteration, I combined the Map and Satellite views into a single interactive map using Mapbox (see the "Map and Satellite View" section).

BANs Show Key Statistics

In Figure 16.5, BANs show the year of the project and the total students served in that year (noncumulative). These are the largest numbers on the dashboard. The bar chart below these BANs provide context for the number of students over time. For example, in this view of Kolkata for Year 5, we see 127,645 students served.

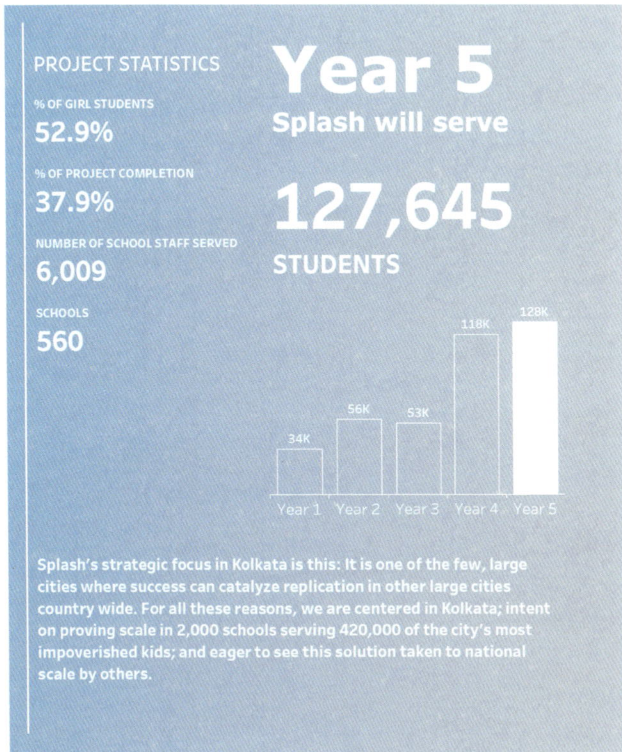

FIGURE 16.5 Elements of home page dashboard for Kolkata.

The chart shows that the biggest impact is in year 4 and 5, which reflects, at a high level, the normal life cycle of these projects.

Additional statistics are also captured and displayed including the percentage of female students, the percentage of the project that is completed, the number of school staff served, and the number of schools involved in the project. All these numbers update when the user selects a year or total from the filter, and the bar chart highlights the year selected by turning the bar white compared with the outline bars.

A custom note was added at the bottom of the view. The note is dynamic text that changes based on the city and year selected and provides the user with a short description of the project in the selected city and year. This allows the organization to customize the text, tailoring the message to each city and each stage of the project.

Map and Satellite View

The map was a key element to the dashboard. Eric wanted a high-level city map showing the school locations, but he also wanted a satellite view of the map that would be interactive, drilling down into an area of the city or an individual school, and the area surrounding a school.

Each dot represents a school, and the size of the dot represents the number of students at that school

(Figure 16.6). When selecting a year on the top menu, the map shows the schools that are part of that year's plan. There is also a tooltip on the map so when Eric hovers over a dot, it shows the year, the name of the school, and how many students are served.

The goal was to illustrate the differences in school concentrations and infrastructure challenges between cities and to highlight the project's potential impact on the children. In Kolkata, for example, there could be five schools on the same block, making it difficult to build new infrastructure (so focus is on upgrading existing infrastructure). In contrast, Addis Ababa is much less concentrated. Again, the aim was not merely to raise money but to demonstrate the scale and potential impact of the project. This is why the map was crucial, as it was a way for Eric to demonstrate visually the unique challenges and required strategies for each city.

In a future iteration, I replaced this with a single map, incorporating a custom Mapbox map that had the same functionality but built into a single map view. In this new version, the map would change views as the viewer zooms in on the map view, morphing from a map view to a satellite view as the viewer zoomed in. This eliminated the need for separate maps and the satellite icon and made for a seamless transition from the overview map of the city to the satellite view of the neighborhood.

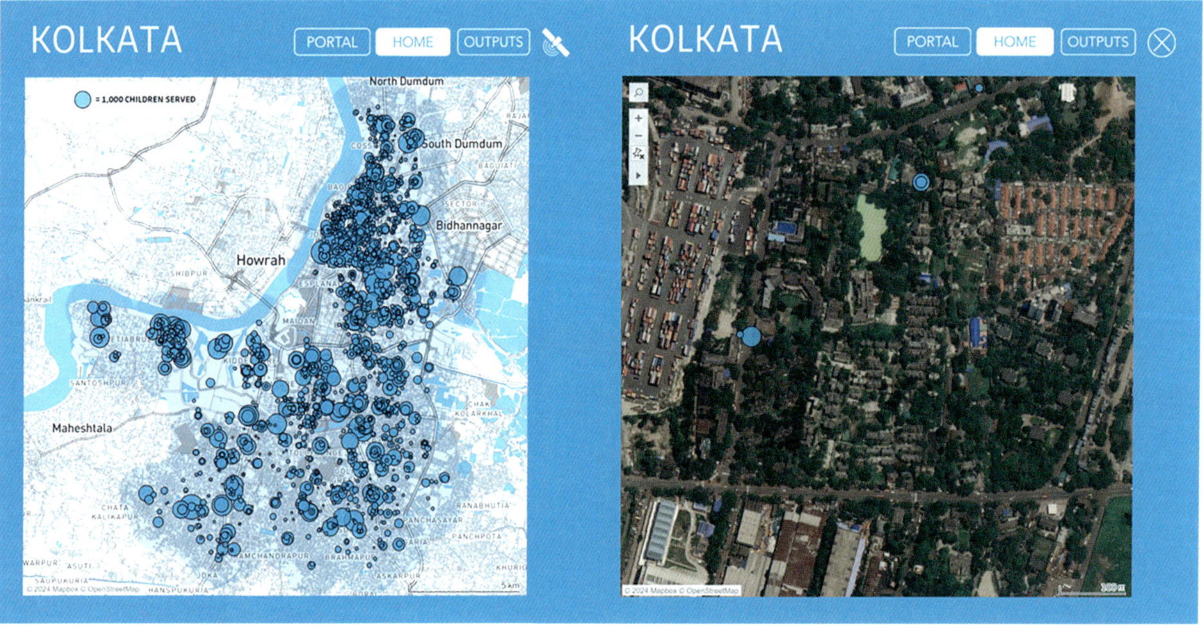

FIGURE 16.6 Map on home page dashboard of Kolkata showing city-level map and an interactive satellite view zoomed in to a few schools.

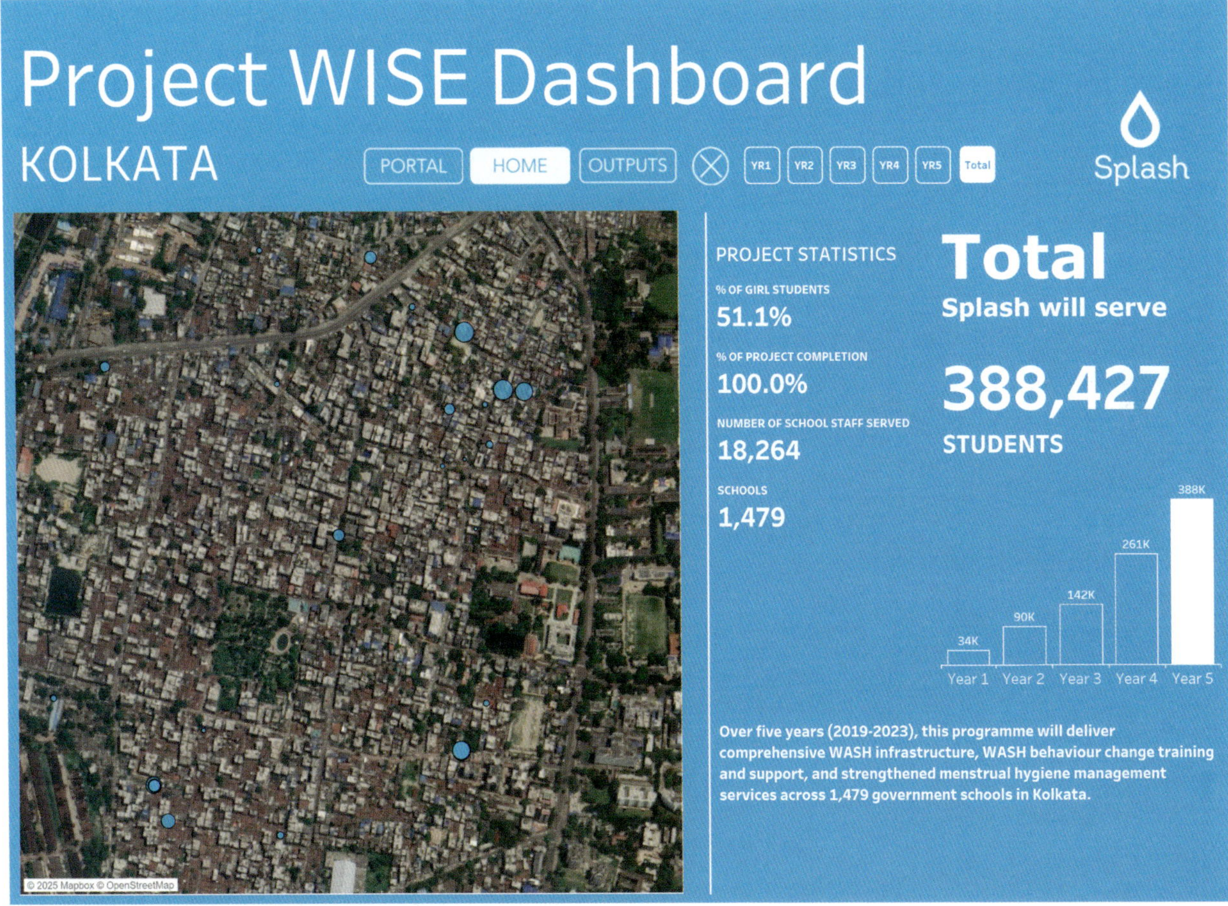

FIGURE 16.7 Updated Mapbox map with zoom-in to satellite view showing the seamless transition from a city map to a satellite map as the user zooms in.

> **How to Build This Mapbox Map**
>
> THIS dashboard was built using Tableau, and this map was built using Mapbox. See my blog post at DataPlusScience.com called "How to Create a Custom Mapbox Map with Zoom in to Satellite View for Tableau":
>
> dtdbook.com/link22

This mapping functionality may seem simple, especially once you see how it's built in the dashboard, but it was a key component to the success of this dashboard.

Monochromatic Design

In addition to the functionality of the dashboard, Eric and Maria Lugovets (project lead) were particular about the design aspects of the dashboard. They provided a folder of design material as inspiration, including logos, website, marketing material, and even sketches and sample charts.

> "If we are going to convince folks to aspire to these products, this needs to be high quality aesthetically. Clean, positive, vibrant, bright, colorful, splash as a verb / noun – all of the branding decisions align to those sentiments. People leave lofty and inspired, rather than weighed down."
>
> —*Eric Stowe, CEO*

This dashboard utilizes a *monochromatic design*. We are big fans! In Chapter 8 we discuss color and the importance of using it purposefully.

Monochromatic design refers to a color scheme that is based on variations of a single color hue. This design approach focuses on using different shades, tints, and tones of one color to create a cohesive and harmonious look. Here are some key aspects of monochromatic design:

- **Single hue:** The design centers on one primary color.
- **Shades, tints, and tones:** Variations are created by adding black (shades), white (tints), or gray (tones) to the base color, or by using a single color on a single background (e.g., white on blue). This adds depth.
- **Simplicity and elegance:** Monochromatic designs are simple and elegant, creating a clean, sophisticated aesthetic, important in this dashboard.
- **Focus on details and data:** With color less dominant, other design elements like position, texture, pattern, and form become prominent.
- **Mood and atmosphere:** Color choice influences design mood. Blues can be calming, reds can evoke urgency or passion. Similar design considerations apply to websites and dashboards (e.g., Chase.com versus OkCupid.com).
- **Versatility:** Monochromatic designs can match style guides and branding easily, as seen with Splash.org's use of white and blue.

By using different values and intensities of a single color, or a single color on a background color, monochromatic design achieves visual interest while maintaining a unified and balanced look. In this dashboard, the blue color was picked to symbolize water, which is the core idea of Splash: provide clean water to students. All the text, maps, charts, and graphs are done in white. This creates a clean and crisp look.

Process

The spark for the dashboard is articulated in the project vision from 2019:

Over the next five years, we are focused on reaching 100% of government schools in two major growth cities: Addis Ababa, Ethiopia and Kolkata, India.

This initiative, Project WISE (WASH-in-Schools for Everyone), will bring improved water, sanitation, and hygiene infrastructure; behavior change programs for kids and adults; and strengthened menstrual health services for girls aged 10 and above.

Working in kindergarten, primary, and secondary schools, this project will reach large concentrations of underserved young people, typically living in the poorest urban communities.

Our goal is to demonstrate a scalable, durable, and cost-efficient WASH-in-Schools (WINS) model that can be effectively replicated beyond the initial two

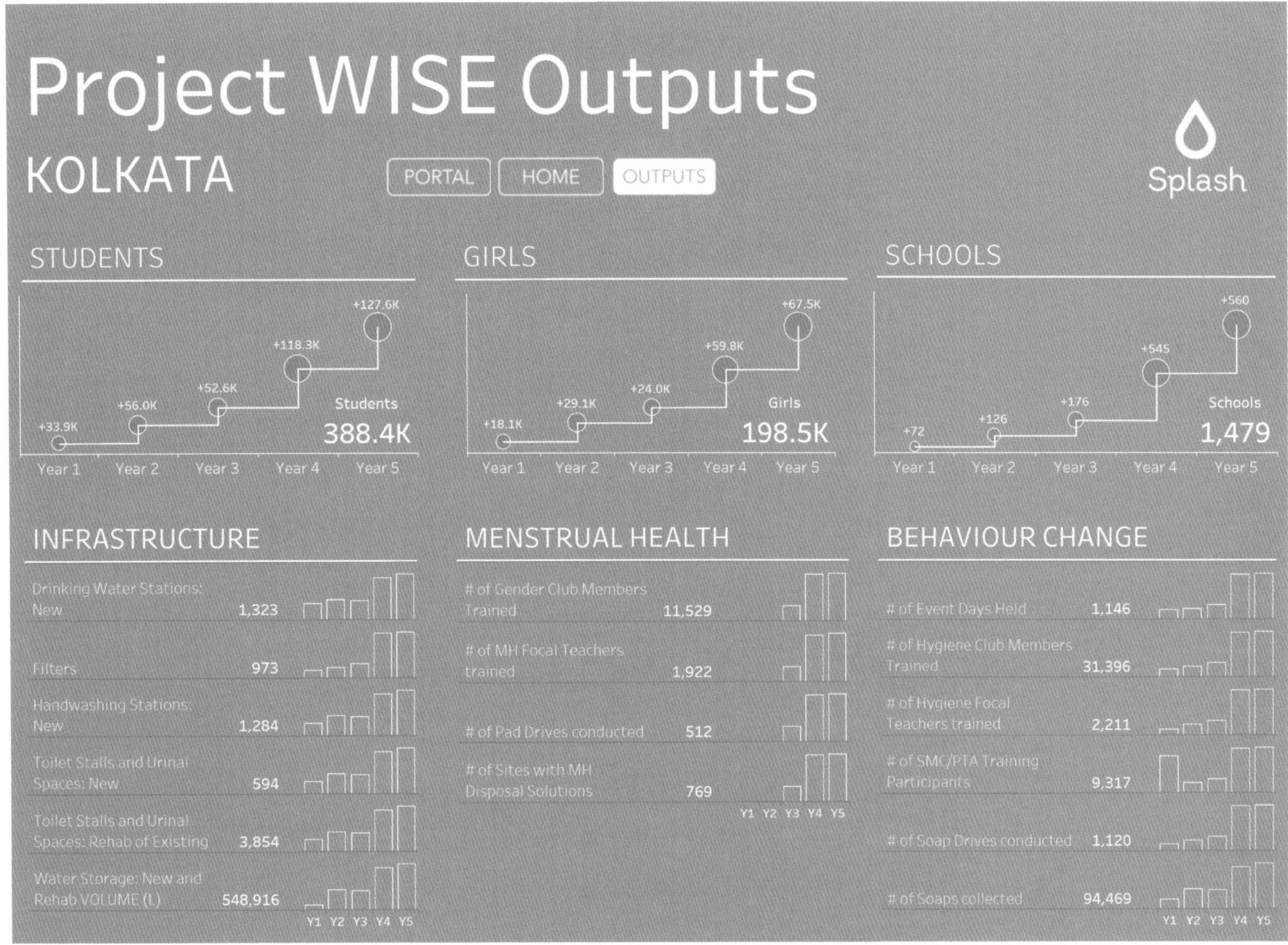

FIGURE 16.8 The outputs Dashboard as an example of monochromatic design.

target cities and countries. For the first time, all government schools in Addis Ababa and Kolkata will have clean drinking water, handwashing stations, and child-friendly toilets that are cost-effective and sustainable.The impact will be healthier students and improved school attendance, especially for girls.

In Q4 2019, the Tableau Foundation asked for volunteers for various community projects. Chris DeMartini and I responded and joined the Splash project shortly thereafter. In January 2020 we started discovery with a team kick-off meeting. Maria immediately shared a Dropbox folder of materials. She provided viz mockups, Splash branding materials, and data sources. Eric and Maria had a good handle on how the dashboard would be used so we focused on prototyping.

They had spent a lot of time on the Splash's brand and identity, and it was important that the dashboard reflect "how we speak about ourselves and portray ourselves externally" (see Figure 16.9).

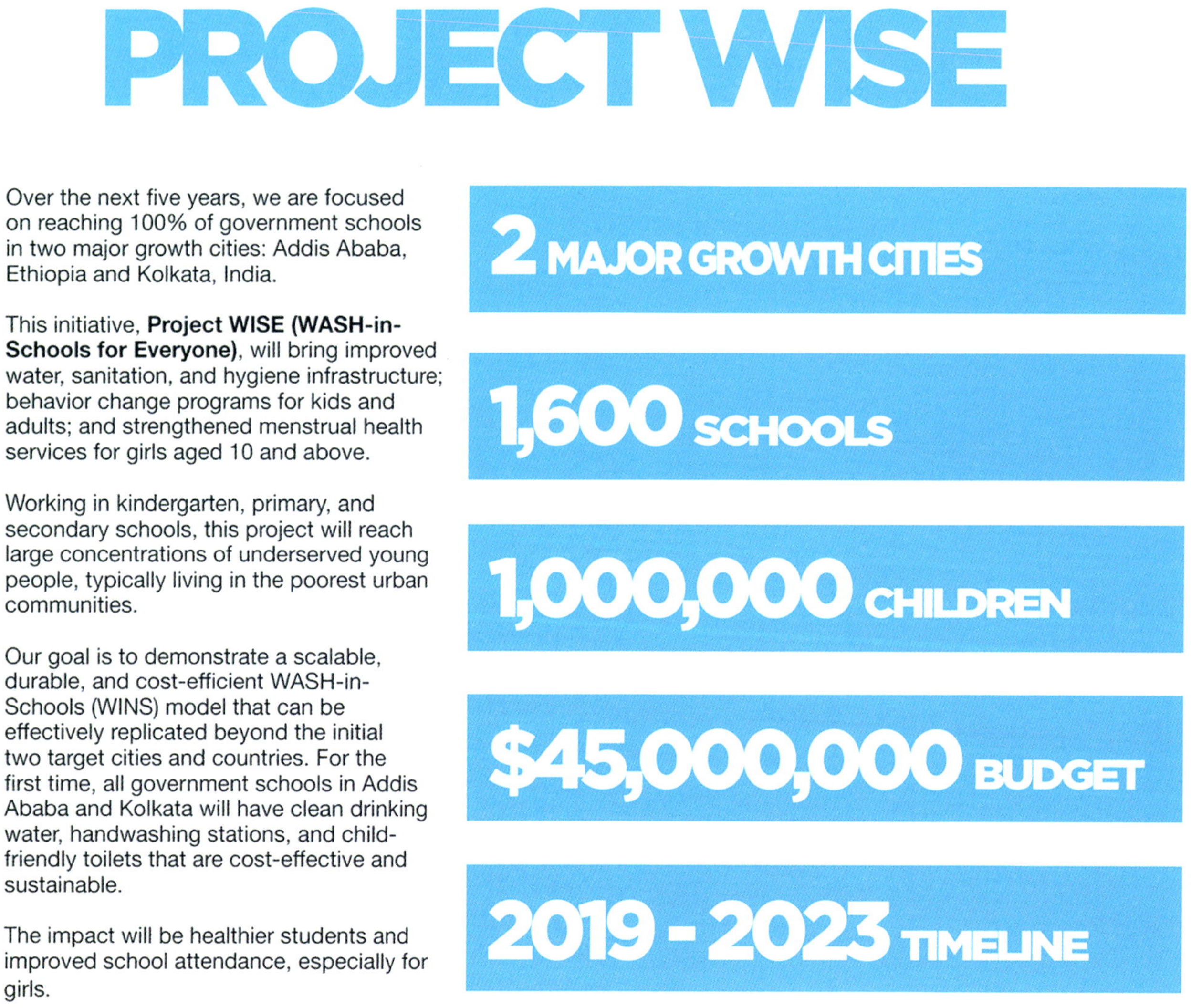

PROJECT WISE

Over the next five years, we are focused on reaching 100% of government schools in two major growth cities: Addis Ababa, Ethiopia and Kolkata, India.

This initiative, **Project WISE (WASH-in-Schools for Everyone)**, will bring improved water, sanitation, and hygiene infrastructure; behavior change programs for kids and adults; and strengthened menstrual health services for girls aged 10 and above.

Working in kindergarten, primary, and secondary schools, this project will reach large concentrations of underserved young people, typically living in the poorest urban communities.

Our goal is to demonstrate a scalable, durable, and cost-efficient WASH-in-Schools (WINS) model that can be effectively replicated beyond the initial two target cities and countries. For the first time, all government schools in Addis Ababa and Kolkata will have clean drinking water, handwashing stations, and child-friendly toilets that are cost-effective and sustainable.

The impact will be healthier students and improved school attendance, especially for girls.

2 MAJOR GROWTH CITIES

1,600 SCHOOLS

1,000,000 CHILDREN

$45,000,000 BUDGET

2019 - 2023 TIMELINE

FIGURE 16.9 Branding documents supplied by Splash for Project WISE.

The Splash data team created visualization mock-ups that included three sketches, a site map, WISE targets, and WISE outputs. These were the starting points for what became the three dashboard views (Figure 16.10).

The team communicated through email and periodic update calls and shared files through a Dropbox folder, which also handled the versioning.

The goal was to have a draft of the dashboard in time for an upcoming presentation. Over a four-week period we developed 14 different iterations of the dashboard. Eric gave the first presentation using this dashboard to a major donor on February 21, 2020.

Multiple Iterations and Additional Enhancements

This dashboard wasn't the finish line. After deployment, Splash worked with others to iterate and expand its use, as well as expand day-to-day analytics. Maria took over the maintenance and continued handling that through 2023. Simon Beaumont joined the project as part of the work with the Tableau Foundation. Simon worked with Maria to develop Tableau templates for Splash, creating an organizational branding for analytics centered around users and user journeys. They took several of the key Splash operational projects and developed analytics in Tableau that enabled them to better manage progress toward the outcomes of these projects across the various schemes, teams, and locations.

> "Having seen the amazing engagement that can be achieved through the impactful work completed by Jeff and Chris, the Splash team had a growing appetite to scale their approach and leverage production organizational analytics for day-to-day operations and project delivery."
>
> —*Simon Beaumont*

In 2023, Elaine Yuan worked on the project as part of her course work at the Data School in the United Kingdom. Her primary focus was on the Portal dashboard. The original portal page displayed only two cities, but the portal page needed to reflect Splash's expansion into more cities. Elaine modified the portal page so that a list of cities could be shown and then selected for the map view. Her redesign of the layout avoided overcrowding by positioning the list of cities on the left-hand side of the view and maps on the right, ensuring the corresponding map appears when a city is selected. She also created a lookup table for current and future cities, and a default Project WISE map displays when no current or future city is selected (Figure 16.11).

The other major enhancement Elaine worked on was the map zoom-in to satellite view that was discussed earlier. She refined the main dashboard's map using my Mapbox map and adjusted the zoom level so that the transition to satellite view would happen earlier.

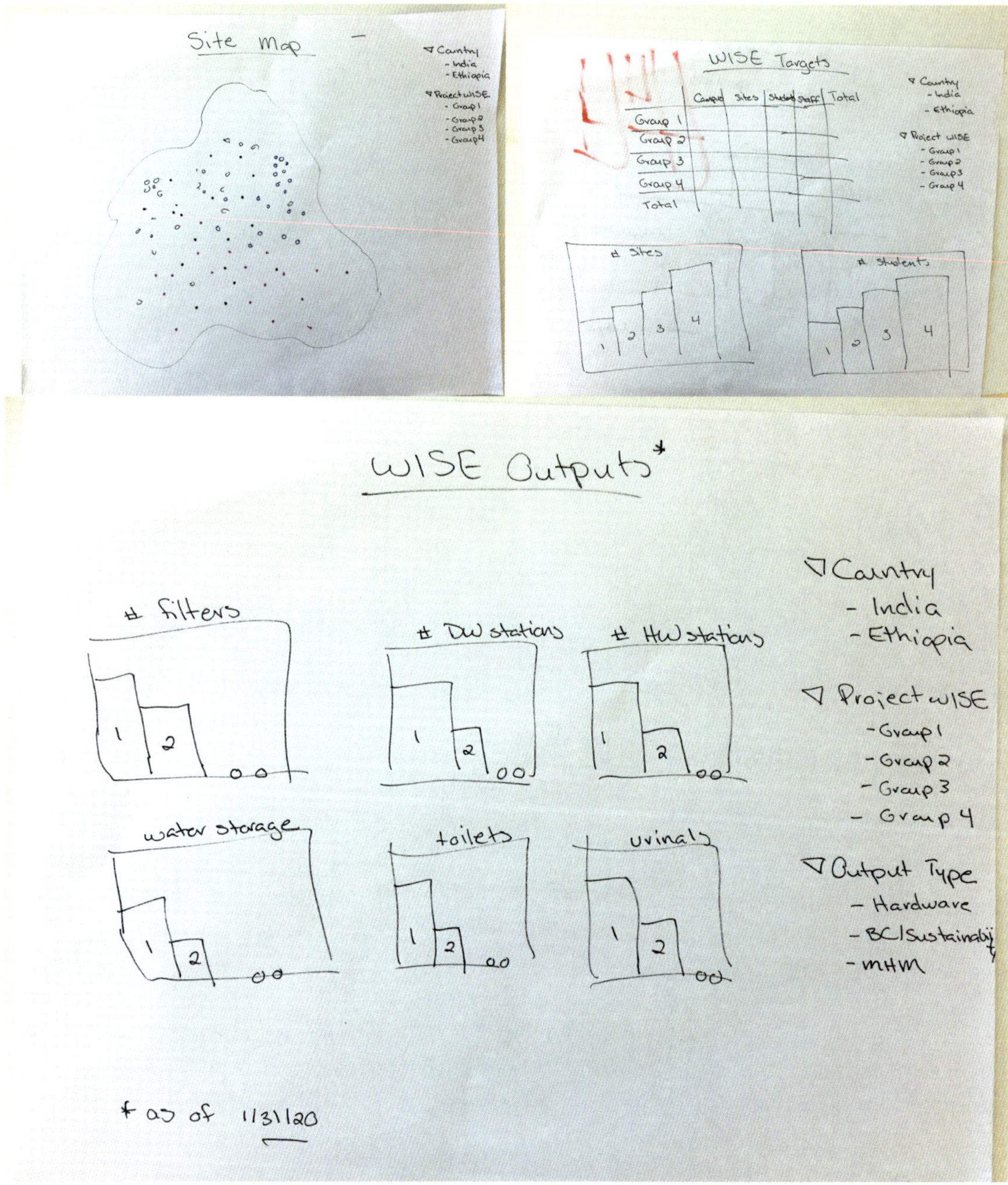

FIGURE 16.10 Three sketches provided by Splash as the vision for their dashboard.

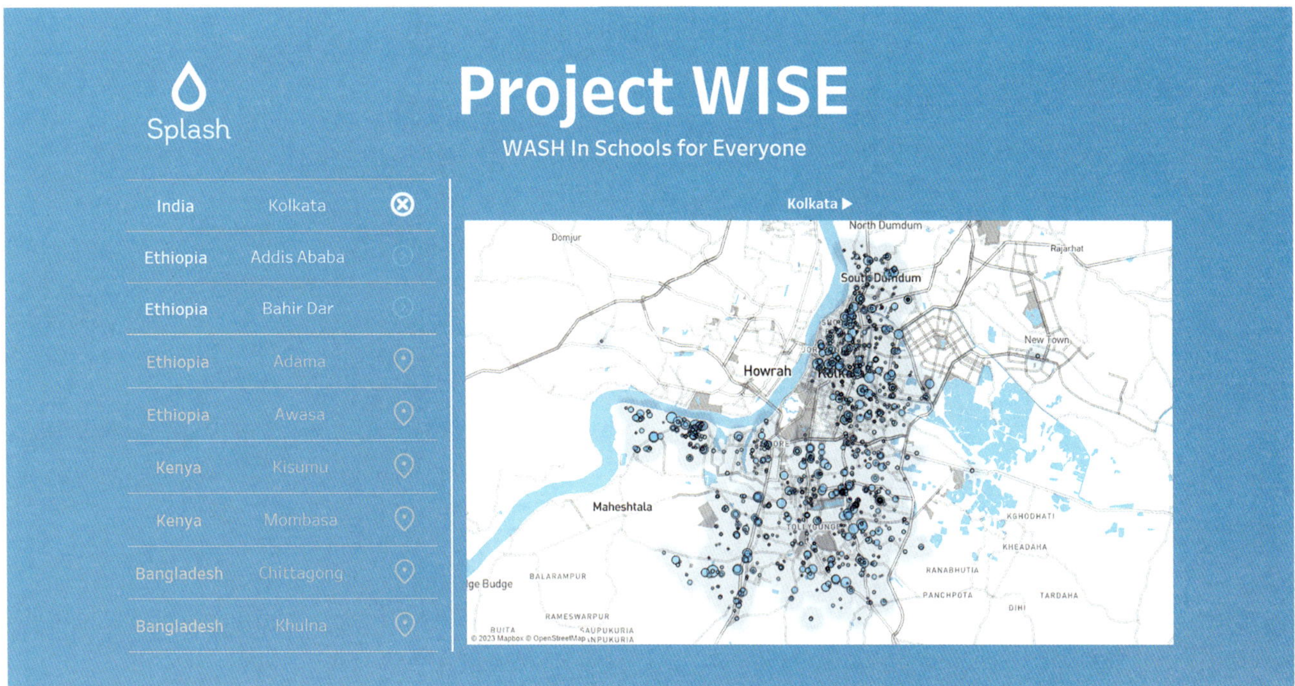

FIGURE 16.11 New portal page for dashboard developed by Elaine Yuan in 2023.

Noteworthy Challenges

Eric gave the first presentation of the dashboard on February 21, 2020, less than two weeks after we delivered the final version. Just a few weeks later, Seattle went into lockdown with the start of the COVID pandemic. This made travel impossible and stopped Eric from being able to give in-person presentations.

Many dashboards would have failed if they encountered such a significant challenge at the time of deployment. The inability to travel and present the dashboard in person could have rendered it ineffective or delayed its implementation indefinitely. While its use was indeed delayed, the dashboard proved resilient. The organization successfully utilized the dashboard once travel restrictions were lifted and normal operations resumed. This highlights the dashboard's robust design and its value to the organization, as well as the organizational commitment to the project, even in the face of unforeseen global disruptions.

Measuring Success

Eric reflected on five years of using the tool:

> "This is the single most used thing I've ever deployed for fundraising since 2019. I can walk you through the specifics of our projects at a school level, but when I try to tell you about what this looks like across an entire city, it's near impossible to get people's heads to wrap around that. With the dashboard, I can show you, and it resonates immediately."
>
> —*Eric Stowe, CEO of Splash*

Eric adds:

> "At a recent fundraising event, over two days, I used the dashboard 15 times in conversations."
>
> —*Eric Stowe, CEO*

This dashboard had an immediate impact within the organization. Eric was able to more easily explain the impact Splash was having and was able to keep and attract more donors to Splash's cause.

Author Commentary

STEVE: This is one of the few cases I've seen where the use of brand colors works well. I certainly understand the need as this is a public facing dashboard. I've seen so many cases where a company has a red or orange brand color and their *internal* facing dashboards are a sea of red or orange bars. It's impossible to tell where the organization is performing well and where it's performing poorly. Even worse are organizations that have two or three brand colors that they insist on inflicting on their dashboards. It becomes a kaleidoscope of color making it difficult to glean insight.

As for the BANs in this dashboard, I usually push for BANs with context. Consider Figure 16.4 where we see 560 schools served. Is that above or below goal? But maybe there isn't a goal yet, and these numbers serve as terrific conversation starters.

ANDY: I confessed to Jeff while writing this book that I'd never really liked this dashboard. Sure, it looked pretty, but where was the actionable insight? What did all the blue dots mean? And why was it all so blue? It was only by fully digesting the motivation and process of the dashboard that I finally got it.

I'd missed several key points. First, the dashboard was a tool to explain the value of Splash. Therefore, the color scheme is needed to fit their brand.

Second, the dashboard worked best when presented by Eric, Maria, or other Splash employees. The human being was a fundamental part of design. Does that requirement stop it being a dashboard? No: it's still a visual display of data used to facilitate understanding.

AMANDA: The design, usability, and clear use case for this dashboard showcase the best of what a dashboard can be for a nonprofit. Unique to this being a tool built for a nonprofit is the engagement with an external group of developers – in this case, through Tableau Foundation, but there are other organizations today that offer similar services like DataKind and Viz for Social Good.

The (necessary) reliance on external support to get dashboards like this spun up reflects the common gap in data skills/team members within many nonprofits, who often get caught in the "unicorn trap" where one or two people are expected to deliver on and maintain all data products (see Dashboard Teams and Roles in Part I).

If you're collaborating with external volunteer support to get a data dashboard spun up, Splash showcases how successful that work can be but also carries the cautionary tale of planning for maintenance. As staff change and time continues to be allocated to mission-centered work, organizations can lose sight of the value of investing in enhancements and refreshes of a dashboard. Splash solves for this issue with an executive champion for the tool, but, like many nonprofits, has also had to manage the challenges of maintaining the tool and updating the underlying data sources particularly as new cities join their portfolio.

Chapter 17

Big Mac Index

Matt McLean and The Economist Data Team

Dashboard Designer: Matt McLean and *The Economist* data team.

Company: *The Economist.*

How This Dashboard Delivers: Anyone with a passing interest in global economics can use the index to compare currencies against each other.

Audience: Any visitor to The Economist website, be they students, teachers, economists, or otherwise interested people.

Tools: Design done in Figma, Adobe Illustrator, and R.Development in D3, Svelte, and Layercake

Team: One designer, two developers, and one researcher.

Timeline: The index has evolved since 1986. The first interactive version appeared in 2012. The data is updated twice a year in January and July.

Chapter Author: Andy Cotgreave

Our Big Mac index shows how burger prices differ across borders

Last updated on January 28th 2025

CURRENCY		% UNDER/OVER VALUED
Switzerland	Franc	38.0
Argentina	Peso	20.1
Uruguay	Peso	19.3
Norway	Krone	15.3
Euro area	Euro	2.8
Costa Rica	Colón	1.9
United States	US$	**BASE**
Britain	Pound	-1.1
Sweden	Krona	-2.1
Denmark	Krone	-5.2
Canada	C$	-6.2
Lebanon	Pound	-7.4
Turkey	Lira	-8.2
Poland	Zloty	-10.0
Colombia	Peso	-10.6

Jan 2025 | The Norwegian krone is 15.3% overvalued against the US dollar

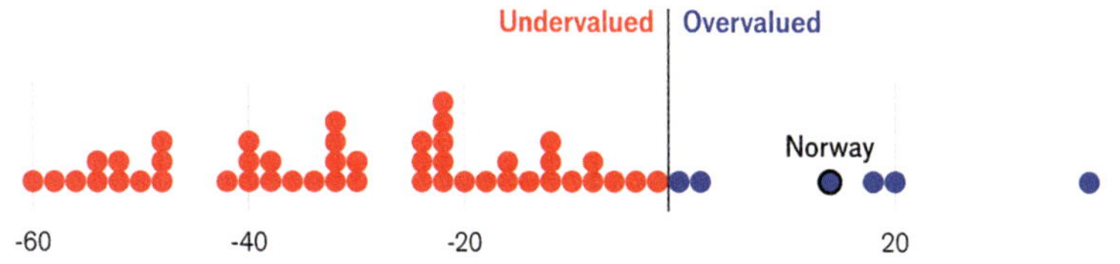

A Big Mac costs **NKr75** in Norway and **US$5.79** in **the United States**. The implied exchange rate is **12.95**. The difference between this and the actual exchange rate, **11.24**, suggests the Norwegian krone is **15.3% overvalued**.

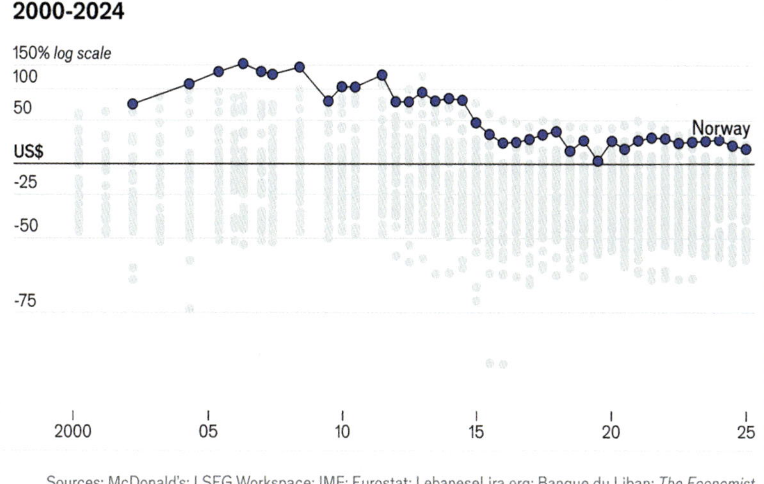

Note: All prices include tax

Sources: McDonald's; LSEG Workspace; IMF; Eurostat; LebaneseLira.org; Banque du Liban; *The Economist*

Scenario

Big Picture

You are an economist, or someone with an interest in economics, and want to compare the strength of one currency against another (known as purchasing-power parity). You could do this using complex models based on large shopping baskets of diverse goods. Or you could compare the price of one globally standardized product: a McDonald's Big Mac. How much does one cost in countries around the world, compared to the major currencies? For example, is a Big Mac more expensive in America or China and therefore is the Chinese yuan over- or under-valued compared to the U.S. dollar?

Specifics

You want to:

- See the worldwide variation in currency valuations.
- Compare GDP per person to Big Mac prices.
- See how the index has changed over time.
- Rank all currencies balanced against one base currency (the dollar, pound, euro, yen, or yuan).

Related Scenarios

This is a dashboard that uses a benchmark to enable comparisons across different categories. Examples might include:

- You are an education administrator and want to track performance of different schools in your district using measures such as student attainment.
- You are a coach monitoring fitness levels of players and want to compare them over time.
- You measure environmental sustainability of facilities in a region or industry and want to compare them against an expected level of performance.

How People Use the Dashboard

> WE featured the 2012 version of the Big Mac index in *The Big Book of Dashboards*. The dashboard had a full refresh in 2018 and an incremental refresh in 2025.

In 1986, *The Economist* developed the index as a fun currency valuation tool. Since then, it has become popular with economists, academics, and students of exchange-rate theory. The purpose of the index is to understand currency misalignment, and it's based on the concept of purchasing-power parity (PPP).

PPP implies that exchange rates are decided by the value of goods that currencies can buy. Differences in local prices – Big Macs in this case – can suggest what the exchange rate should be. Using "burgernomics," the dashboard gives an estimate of how much one currency is under- or over-valued relative to another.

For example, in January 2025, a Big Mac cost NKr75 in Norway and US$5.79 in the United States. The implied exchange rate is 12.95. The difference between this and the actual exchange rate, 11.24, suggests the Norwegian Krone is 15.3% overvalued (as shown in Figure 17.1).

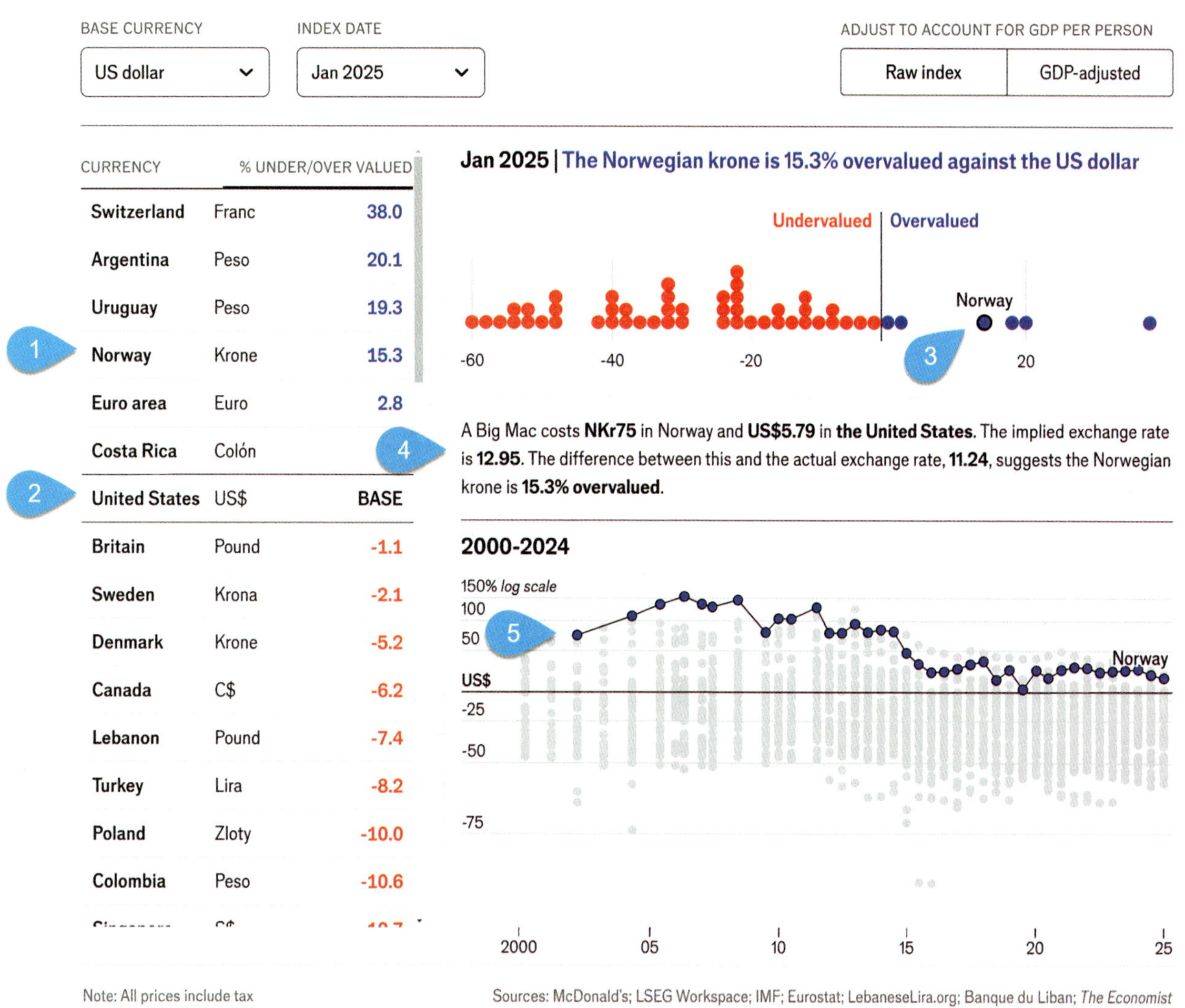

FIGURE 17.1 The components of the Big Mac index dashboard.

Figure 17.1 shows the main dashboard components across three different charts. In the example, the selected baseline country is the United States, and Norway has been selected as a highlight country to compare against the United States:

1. The scrollable list on the left shows all currencies in the Big Mac index. The three columns are country name, currency name, and finally current value against the United States.
2. The selected baseline country (the United States) is highlighted between black row dividers. The user can change baseline country, and time, in the filters. The light-gray shading is the currently highlighted country (Norway).
3. The sorted dot plot shows all countries' Big Mac prices compared to the United States. The x-axis shows how over- or under-valued it is, along with color (red for under-valued, blue for over-valued).
4. A narrative sentence describing the PPP of the Big Mac for the selected time, comparing Norway against the United States.
5. The combo chart shows a timeline of Norway compared to the United States over time. A gray dot plot behind the line shows all other countries over time.

The user can download the data from a link at the bottom of the page hosting the Big Mac index.

Why This Works

Layout Emphasizes Rankings

Based on user research (see the Process section later in this chapter), *The Economist* prioritized the ability to see ranking of currencies. The vertical list is sorted by the value against the baseline. In our example, here, it makes it easy to see that Switzerland is the most over-valued currency against the United States (38%). The dot plot's x-axis positions currencies left to right according to the same level.

A Consistent Color Scheme

The design employs a simple and consistent color palette (blue and red) to stand for over-valued and under-valued currencies, respectively. This helps users quickly grasp the concepts behind the Big Mac index.

Responsive Design

For mobile, the dashboard is shown as a vertical series of charts rather than on a grid. The list is moved to the bottom, ensuring the charts and filters are visible when opened (Figure 17.2). The 2018 version showed different charts in the mobile and desktop versions; see the "Process" section for more details.

Explanatory Text

A key user request was for explanations of what the comparisons mean. This is an important context-specific addition. Many people viewing this dashboard are not domain experts; they are likely not fluent in the language of economics or purchasing-power parity. The text (#4 in Figure 17.1) provides them with a clear, plain language description of what they are seeing.

This intelligent dashboard design recognizes one of the key aspects we always suggest you consider: who is your audience and what do they know?

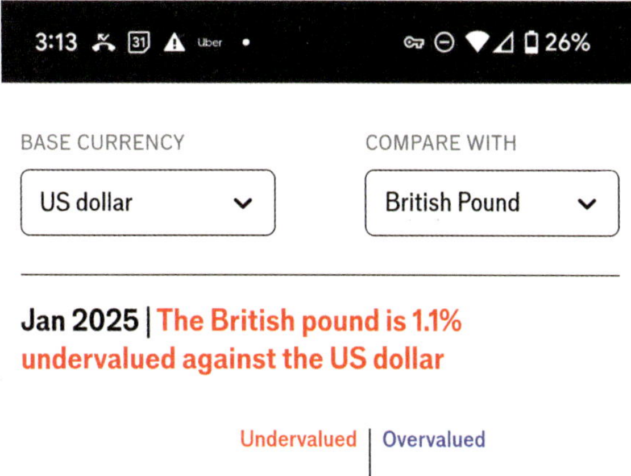

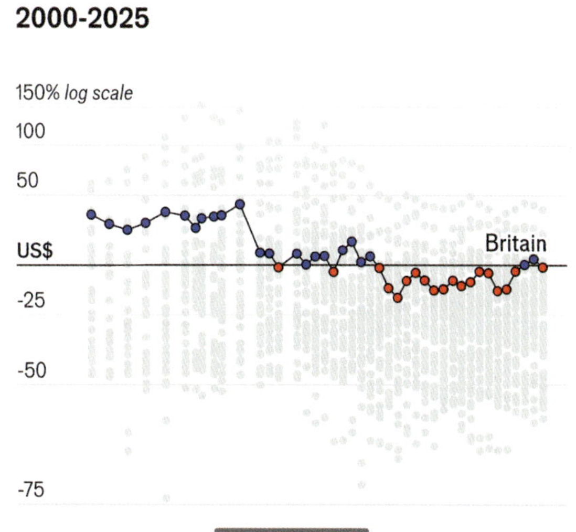

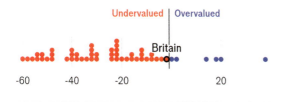

FIGURE 17.2 The mobile version of the Big Mac index.

If you know your audience is all experts in the data behind your dashboards, you probably don't need so much explanatory text. But what if your audience isn't experts? How can you build in the contextual descriptions they need? *The Economist* chose to put the detail on the dashboard itself. If screen real estate is tight, this information could also go in a tooltip. *The Economist* chose not to use tooltips on this dashboard because the number of visitors who interact with the data (beyond changing filters) is very small.

Geospatial Data Doesn't Always Need a Map

The earlier version of the Big Mac index had a map. Why remove it?

- Choropleth maps create a selection bias: larger countries like Russia are easier to see and select than smaller ones such as Singapore.
- A world map shows *all* countries, but many countries are not included in the index: there's a lot of empty space.
- There is no meaningful geographic pattern to the data.

That said, the maps can be useful for people interacting with a dashboard. Maps provide a valuable shortcut to orient the user and, in this case, convey the global scope of the dataset. In the end the team decided to remove the map, concluding that the benefits did not outweigh the costs.

Dashboard design always features compromise. In the case of geospatial data, a map is not always the best choice.

Process

Changing Tastes and Design Modes

The Big Mac Index was first printed as a text table in 1986. The first interactive version was released in 2012 and featured in *The Big Book of Dashboards*. By 2018, it was beginning to creak: old code, poor color choices, no mobile versions. *The Economist* had their spark: one of the most popular pages on their site was outdated. The Big Mac index underwent a major redesign. In January 2025 the team refreshed the dashboard. You can see all the versions in Figure 17.3.

This most recent refresh was seen as an iterative update rather than a complete overhaul. It had three goals:

- Adhere to *The Economist* web graphics style guides.
- Unify the mobile and desktop versions.
- Simplify the user experience.

This process section looks at the decisions behind the 2018 overhaul and the 2025 refresh.

Ask the Users, Then Iterate

The index is one of the most popular pages on *The Economist*'s website and has a lot of return visitors. This created a challenge for the 2018 major redesign: the 2012 version was dated, but they didn't want to break a tool people already knew. This is something all dashboards need to consider: people can react badly to unexpected change.

They knew they needed to revisit user needs with a new *discovery* phase. The team sought feedback from users in two main ways. First, they added Hotjar to the code running the application. Hotjar is a plugin that lets you see how users interact with your website (in this case, a dashboard). This let *The Economist* see users' click paths, what sections receive the most focus, and even mouse movements.

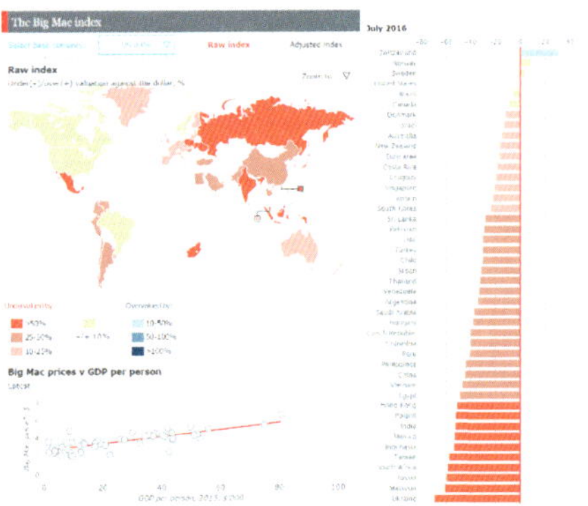
The Big Mac index
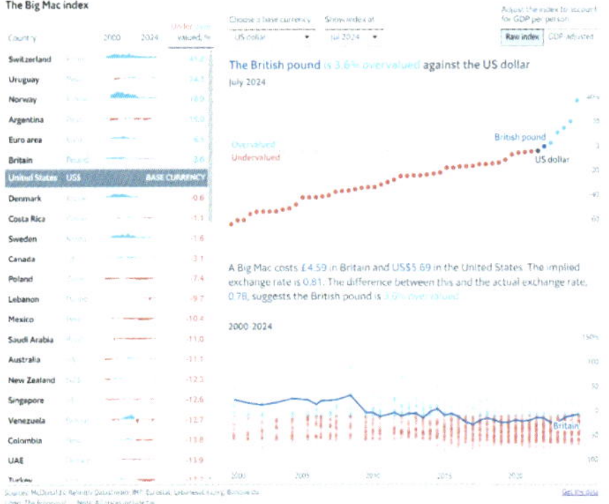
The Big Mac index
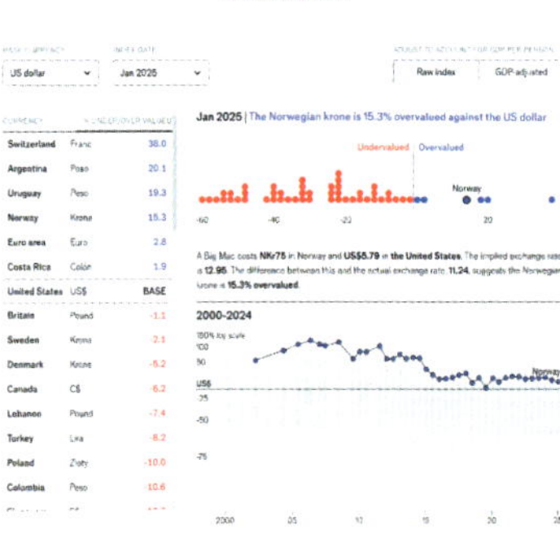
Our Big Mac index shows how burger prices differ across borders

FIGURE 17.3 The 2012, 2018, and 2025 versions of the Big Mac index.

As part of their development and user testing phase, they also added a popup survey to the dashboard, asking for qualitative feedback. The team categorized this feedback to provide the broad, prioritized categories for the redesign (Figure 17.4).

This feedback led them to focus on three main principles for the redesign:

- Add more explanations.
- Allow viewers to see the whole timeline of the index.
- Create a responsive design that worked on mobile and desktop.

Prototype Pitfalls: Sketching and Big Screens

In this book's dashboard framework, we explain how sketching can be an important part of the *prototype* phase. It's an inexpensive and fast way to explore ideas. Figure 17.5 shows one example, and you can see how ideas at this stage informed the final dashboard.

As the team moved to digital prototypes, they had the luxury of designing on large monitors. An early design had one large chart at the top and the details below. Matt discovered that "while that main chart worked well on our 27-inch screens at the

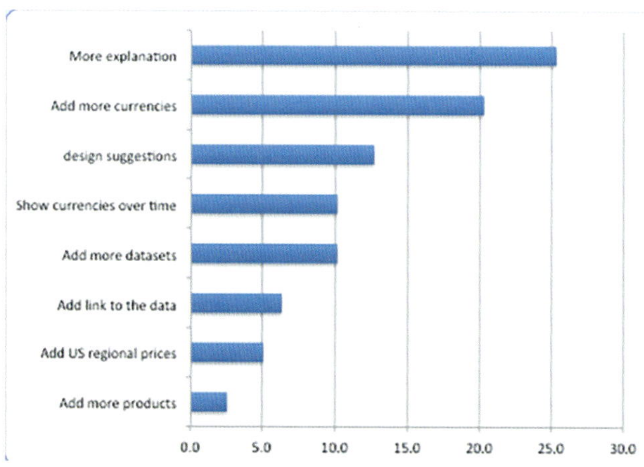

FIGURE 17.4 Categorized results of the feedback survey (the x-axis is percentage of respondents who ticked a category).

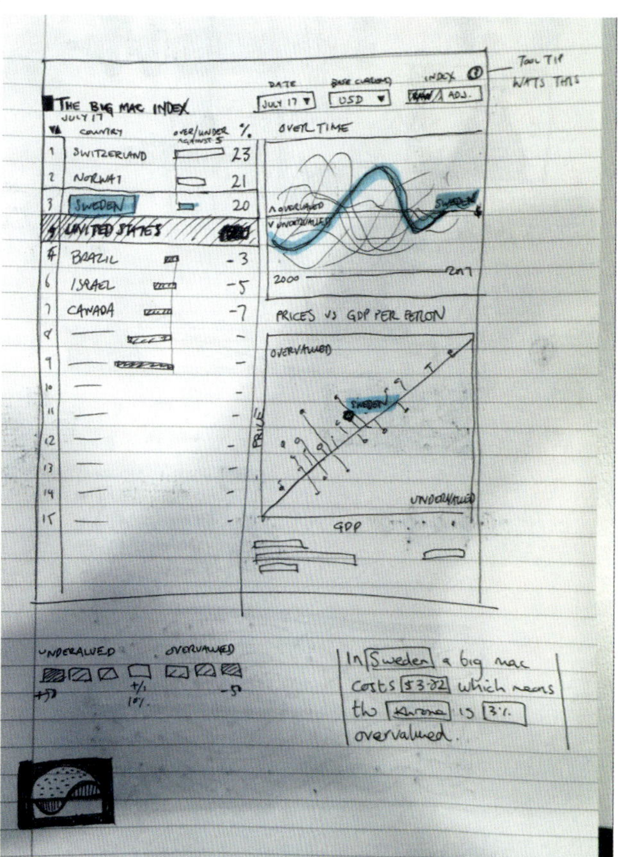

FIGURE 17.5 One of the sketch prototypes for the 2018 redesign.

office, it was simply too tall on laptop and mobile screens, and users got lost." This is a pitfall I've fallen into many times. You must evaluate your prototype across different devices. Just because you're working on a large monitor doesn't mean your viewers are.

Matt describes one of the other challenges they had with their sketches: "Sketching is useful for composition, but there's always the problem that you're probably drawing an idealized chart, and your real data might actually be quite dull."

Sketching is great, but always get your real data into early digital prototypes as quickly as possible. The patterns in your data should inform your design. Later, in the 2025 refresh, this was even more important as some outlier currencies were so extreme, they made the design appear broken when plotted on the dashboard.

Color and Accessibility

"In 2018 we wanted to limit the palette as much as possible and use color to aid explanation," says Matt. "To achieve this, we used a binary blue/red combination to highlight over/under valuations, and that color is consistent across all the charts and the explanatory text."

Following the 2018 refresh they realized their color choices were not good from an accessibility perspective. One place that could be seen was in the color-encoding on the explanatory text, which mixed blue, red, and gray text (you can compare the 2018 and 2025 versions in Figure 17.6).

For the 2025 refresh, color was reduced across the dashboard. Not only did the team reduce color in the text, they also changed how color was used in the dot plot (Figure 17.7).

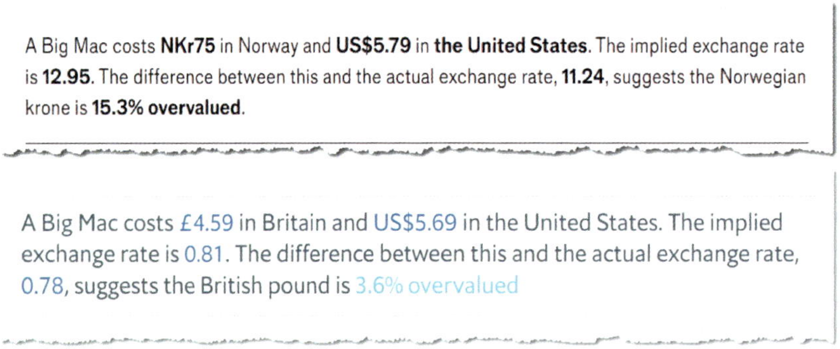

A Big Mac costs **NKr75** in Norway and **US$5.79** in **the United States**. The implied exchange rate is **12.95**. The difference between this and the actual exchange rate, **11.24**, suggests the Norwegian krone is **15.3% overvalued**.

A Big Mac costs £4.59 in Britain and US$5.69 in the United States. The implied exchange rate is 0.81. The difference between this and the actual exchange rate, 0.78, suggests the British pound is 3.6% overvalued

FIGURE 17.6 The 2025 (top) and 2018 (bottom) explanation text.

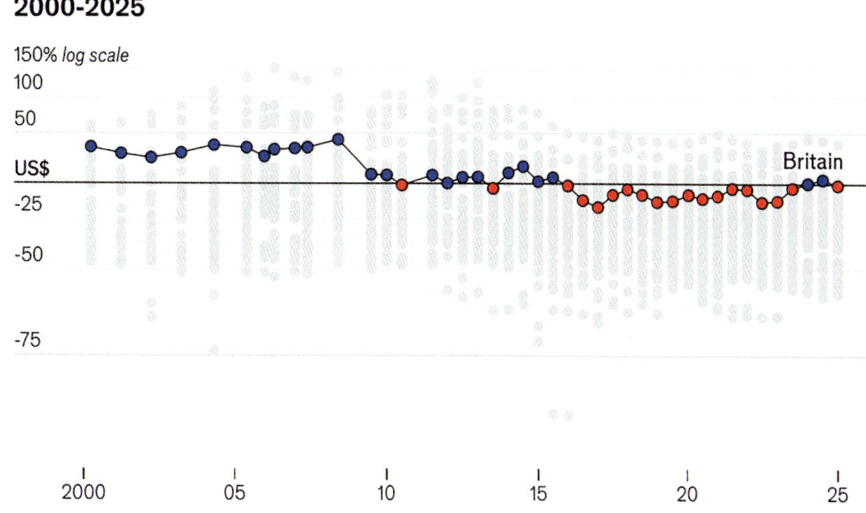

FIGURE 17.7 The dot plots from 2018 and 2025.

The 2025 Refresh: A Shorter Timeline, a Quicker Process

For the 2025 refresh, the team were under much more time pressure. The new data would release in January and the team did not start the rework until quite late. In this update, they did not do extensive user testing. Instead, they relied on the feedback they'd had over the years since the last update and experience they had using the dashboard.

The main changes, which you can see in Figure 17.3, are as follows:

1. Removed the sparkline from the list. The team felt they created too much information in one place. He wanted the viewer to focus more on the key takeaway and to provide more space for the main charts.
2. Simplified colors, as explained in the previous section.
3. Unify styles and chart types. In the 2018 version, the desktop and mobile versions had different chart types (a dot plot showing currencies in order on desktop became a bee swarm chart on mobile). For 2025, they wanted consistency; now both mobile and desktop have the same dot plot in the top right. Also, the dashboard was updated to use the same font (Economist Sans) that is used for all graphics across the site and in print.

Author Commentary

AMANDA: The change from the chart types (bar chart, map) used in the 2012 release to the more complex chart types (dot plot, a log scale) in the 2025 release parallels the increasing levels of complexity we see in data journalism and other spaces, including the work of *The Economist's* data visualization team through Graphic Detail and their other work. Informed audiences now have more exposure to chart types beyond the basics, which can open up possibilities for dashboard designers too. When we're accustomed to seeing dot strip plots and lollipops in news articles, we also become more comfortable with using them for other analytical purposes.

The evolution of this dashboard also showcases the long tail that a continuous feedback loop can have on a dashboard, years later coming back to gather user inputs and assess how to make one of the most visited data assets of the publication have more value. Just because you're getting a lot of page views on a dashboard doesn't mean there aren't opportunities for improvement. While some improvements (enhancements) might happen through short, regular sprint cycles, sometimes opening up the possibility for a full redesign is necessary to meet the moment.

STEVE: I love when I get to see how the pros think about things, and you're not going to get more "pro" than *The Economist*. A lot of things struck a chord with me, including ditching the map (I tell all my workshop attendees just because you have geographic data doesn't mean you have to make a map), the possible pitfalls of sketching (idealized versus real data), and how they surveyed users during the redesign to get feedback.

I also look at what small design decisions they make. What color do they use for gridlines and for the background? How do they demark a chart title, besides the font? The next time you see a chart from them, look at how they approach these things and think about applying elements of their aesthetic to your own work.

Chapter 18

Guided Pathways Dashboard

Kimberly Coutts, Dashboard Designer

Team: Kimberly Coutts, Dashboard Designer.

Organization: MiraCosta College.

How This Dashboard Delivers: The dashboard enables college administrators and support staff to see the flow of a cohort of students through their first seven semesters of college.

Audience: College administrators and support staff.

Tools & Data: Tableau connected to structured data from the college database systems. The interactive dashboard is viewed using a desktop or laptop browser. The data is updated twice a year. The audience views the dashboard periodically throughout the year while evaluating the effectiveness of support programs.

Timeline: This dashboard was developed, on and off, over the course of nearly two years.

Chapter Author: Jeffrey A. Shaffer

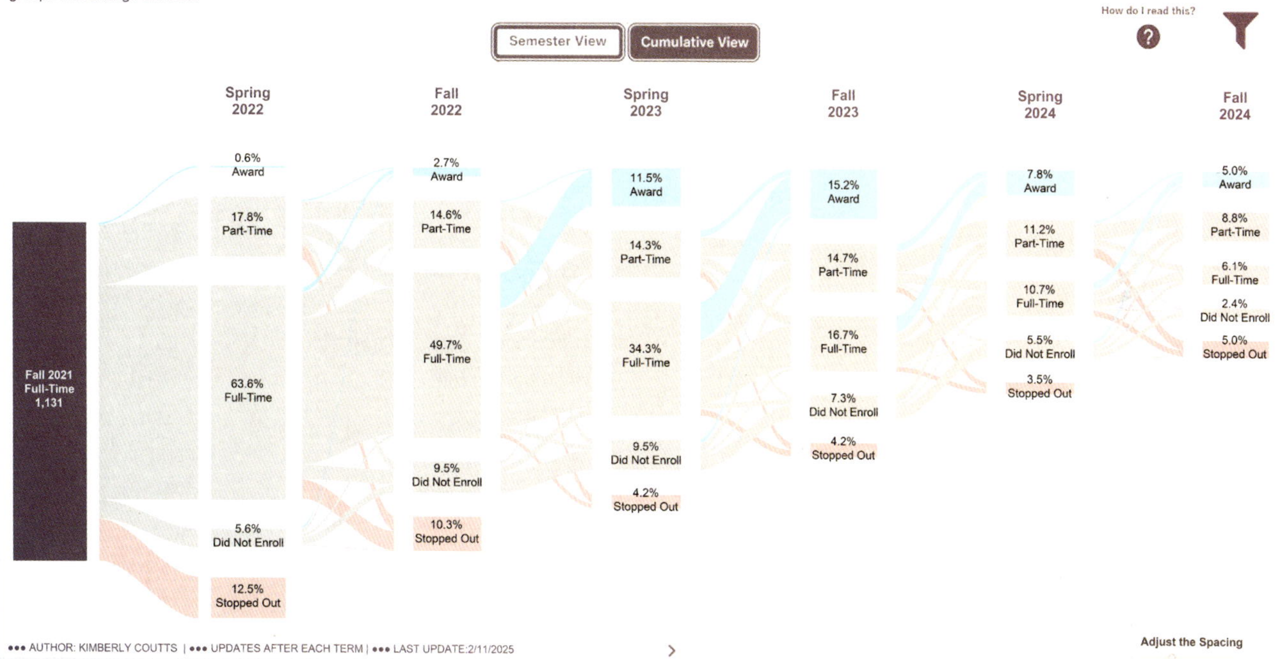
MiraCosta College
GUIDED PATHWAYS
Semester by Semester Sankey Flow Chart - Fall 2021
Follow a cohort of Guided Pathways students over the course of their first seven primary semesters. Click the filter button on the right to select specific student groups and change cohorts.
How do I read this?
Semester View
Cumulative View
Spring 2022
Fall 2022
Spring 2023
Fall 2023
Spring 2024
Fall 2024
Fall 2021 Full-Time 1,131
0.6% Award
17.8% Part-Time
63.6% Full-Time
5.6% Did Not Enroll
12.5% Stopped Out
2.7% Award
14.6% Part-Time
49.7% Full-Time
9.5% Did Not Enroll
10.3% Stopped Out
11.5% Award
14.3% Part-Time
34.3% Full-Time
9.5% Did Not Enroll
4.2% Stopped Out
15.2% Award
14.7% Part-Time
16.7% Full-Time
7.3% Did Not Enroll
4.2% Stopped Out
7.8% Award
11.2% Part-Time
10.7% Full-Time
5.5% Did Not Enroll
3.5% Stopped Out
5.0% Award
8.8% Part-Time
6.1% Full-Time
2.4% Did Not Enroll
5.0% Stopped Out
••• AUTHOR: KIMBERLY COUTTS | ••• UPDATES AFTER EACH TERM | ••• LAST UPDATE:2/11/2025
Adjust the Spacing

Big Picture

You are a college administrator, and you want to know how the students in your college progress through their program over numerous semesters. Starting with a full-time or part-time cohort, you want to see how students progress semester by semester as they complete the program, move or remain part-time/full-time, stop out, or simply don't enroll in the following semester.

Specifics

You need to see:

- A cohort of full-time or part-time students in a starting semester
- Each subsequent semester, going out seven semesters, which is a three-and-a-half-year time period
- For each semester, the percentage of students who:
  - Were awarded a degree or certificate or transfer to a four-year institution
  - Remained full time
  - Switched to part time
  - Did not enroll in that semester but returned at a later point in time
  - Stopped out

Related Scenarios

- You are a hospital administrator watching the patient flow over time, or through stages or phases of procedures and recovery.
- You are a web marketing manager tracking the flow of users on your website, from the home page, through all of the other pages on the website.
- You are a production/inventory manager monitoring the flow of production or the inventory as it moves.

How People Use the Dashboard

Colleges often face major challenges in serving diverse student populations, ranging from degree-seekers to lifelong learners pursuing certifications or personal development. For example, at the University of Cincinnati, I teach courses and workshops in three categories: graduate and undergraduate courses that are part of several degree programs (for example, a master's in business analytics), courses within certificate programs (such as, a certificate in artificial intelligence), and noncredit two-day workshops through the Center for Business Analytics.

Similarly, the Guided Pathways dashboard was developed to visualize the complex educational journey of students at MiraCosta College. It provides actionable insights into how students progress through their programs, with a long-term goal of improving retention and success rates. The dashboard focuses on tracking a cohort of students who start as full-time or part-time students over seven semesters, analyzing their transitions between full-time, part-time, and nonenrollment categories.

The dashboard developer, Kimberly Coutts, told us, "We had a tendency to assume that full-time and part-time students were these unchanging groups, meaning that if a student started part-time, they stayed that way through their entire experience. Seeing the amount of flow between the different enrollment statuses was the first big eye-opener for many."

Serving multiple stakeholders, including deans, administrators, and trustees, the dashboard is primarily accessed through MiraCosta's Tableau environment. It offers a combination of interactive and static views, with its centerpiece being a horizontal Sankey diagram that maps the flow of students over time. Users can apply interactive filters to drill down into specific demographics or student attributes, making it an interactive tool for understanding student dynamics and finding insight.

Why This Works

Great Use of a Sankey Diagram

Sankey diagrams can be very useful to illustrate flow through a system, but they can appear complicated, especially if you have never seen one before. When teaching students, I always point to higher education as the perfect use case of a Sankey diagram (i.e., students moving from one semester to the next and switching degrees, transferring, dropping out, etc.). So when I saw the Sankey diagram used in this case, my first thought was, "Of course."

The Sankey diagram is an ideal choice for visualizing student pathways because it captures the complexity of their transitions in an intuitive and engaging way. By showcasing the flow of students across categories, such as full-time, part-time, stopped out, or not enrolled, the Sankey provides a clear picture of where students succeed and where they encounter challenges.

This visualization emphasizes the dynamics of student movement semester by semester, making areas of attrition immediately evident. For example, the thinning of the bands from one semester to the next clearly illustrates where students are dropping out or switching enrollment statuses. For example, in Figure 18.1, we can quickly see 12.5% of full-time students from the fall 2021 cohort stopped out after the semester and didn't return for spring 2022 or any other semester.

This visualization transforms abstract data about thousands of students each with their own journey, into a single overall view, allowing stakeholders to quickly identify problem areas and allocate resources effectively.

Interactive Features

One of the most powerful aspects of the Guided Pathways dashboard is its interactive features, particularly the ability to customize views.

Users can filter the data by various demographic attributes (Figure 18.2).

These filters allow the user to drill down into specific student populations. This level of flexibility ensures that the dashboard is not a one-size-fits-all tool but an interactive tool tailored to the needs of diverse stakeholders.

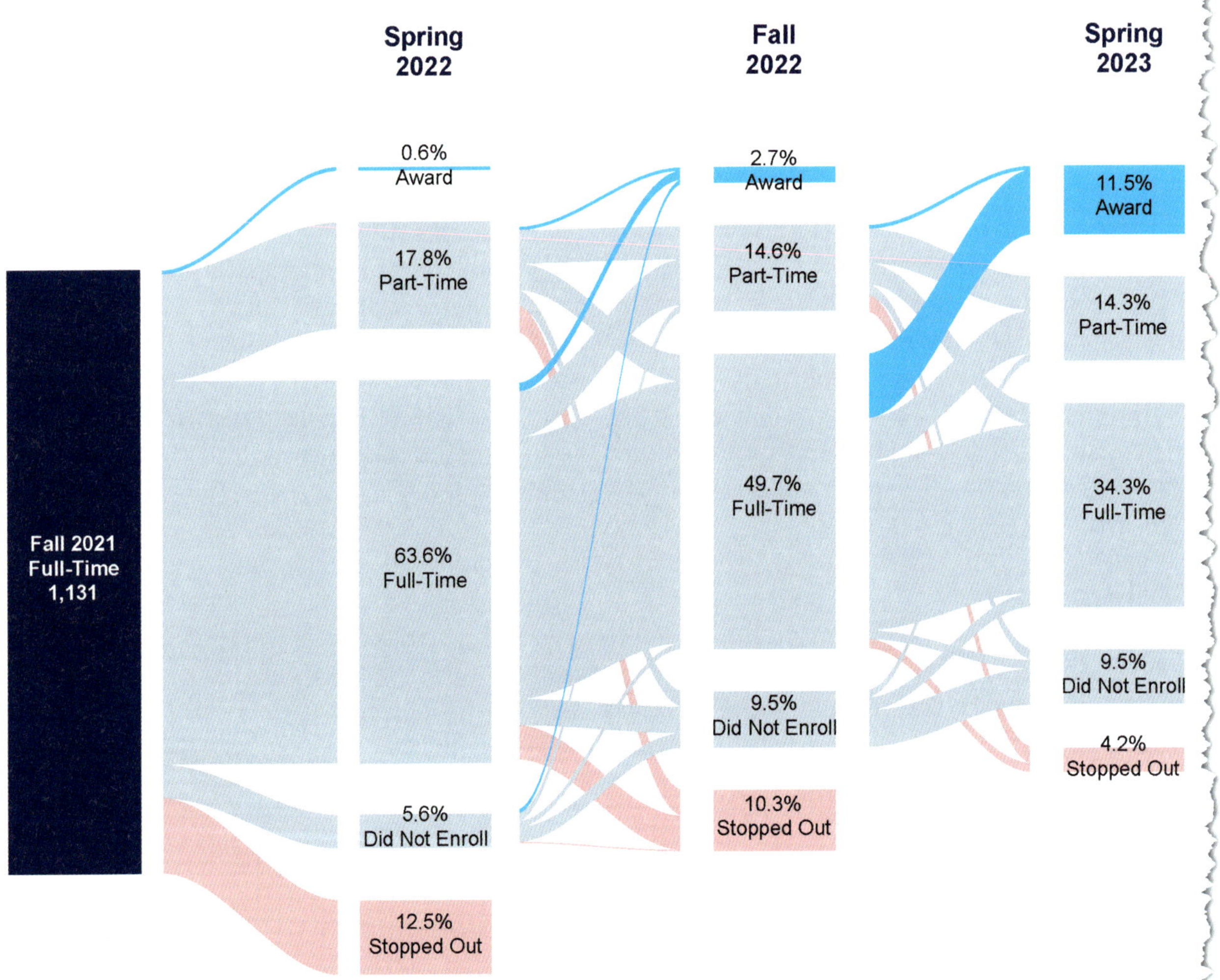

FIGURE 18.1 The first few semesters of the fall 2021 semester cohort of students.

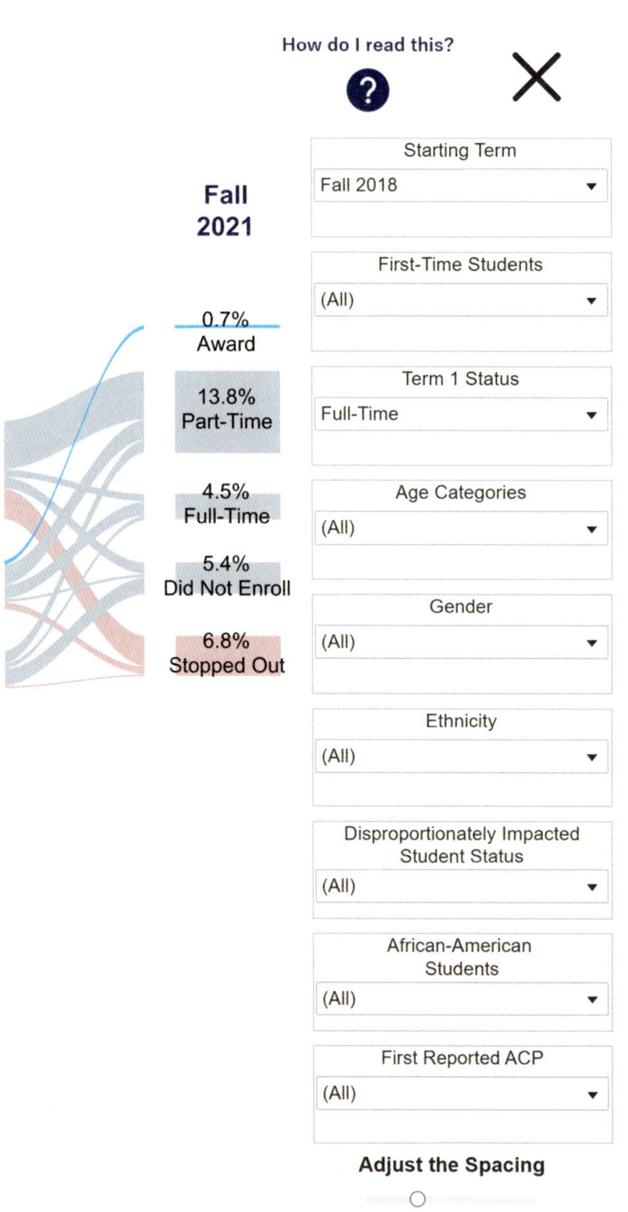

FIGURE 18.2 Nine filters expand by pressing the filter button on the dashboard.

For instance, administrators focusing on equity initiatives can filter the dashboard to view the experiences of specific demographic groups, such as first-generation college students or part-time students, to identify patterns of attrition and success. Similarly, program leaders can use these filters to evaluate the outcomes of targeted support programs for underserved populations.

This ability to customize and segment data also fosters more meaningful discussions.

As Kimberly explained, "Frequently, someone will share a link to this dashboard with a specific team or leadership group. They may be interested in not just the overall student body but in understanding how specific populations, such as African American students, are navigating their pathways."

These tailored insights make it possible to align institutional strategies with the unique challenges and goals of different student groups.

Hidden Filters

As we've now seen, nine filters creates a rich interactive experience, but placing nine filter options on a dashboard would quickly clutter the view Kimberly provides a simple filter button (the funnel icon in the upper-right corner in Figure 18.3) that can expand or collapse to show the nine filters and change them.

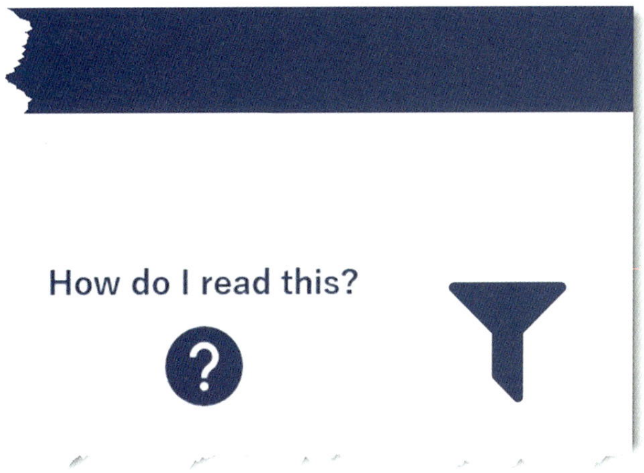

FIGURE 18.3 The dashboard filter button (the funnel icon) allows for the maximum amount of space without cluttering the view with nine filters.

Instruction Overlay

The Guided Pathways dashboard includes a thoughtfully designed "How do I read this?" (Figure 18.4) overlay feature, ensuring that even nontechnical audiences can easily understand and navigate the visualization. With just a click of a button, users can access a detailed guide that explains each component of the dashboard (Figure 18.4).

The overlay shown in Figure 18.4 provides a breakdown of the key elements of the Sankey diagram.

This overlay design anticipates common user questions and makes a chart type that can feel complex more accessible. Even if a user hasn't read data from a Sankey chart, the overlay puts the functions and content into plain language.

> *"For someone who gets a link to our dashboard and may not have the benefit of one of us sitting next to them explaining what to do, this 'How do I read this?' feature ensures they can still navigate and explore the data effectively."*
>
> *—Kimberly Coutts*

This ensures the dashboard remains a self-service tool that users can understand and leverage, regardless of their technical expertise.

Alternate View

The semester-based view we've seen simplifies the flow for non-data-savvy users by focusing on changes between individual terms. In addition to the semester-based view, an alternate cumulative view is also available. This cumulative view provides a holistic understanding of attrition and retention trends across the three-year timeline.

Figure 18.5 shows the cumulative view for the fall 2021 cohort. In this view, every student at the start of the cohort is represented throughout the entire visualization.

Let's compare the two views side-by-side (Figure 18.6). Notice how these two views answer different questions. In the noncumulative view on the left, you can see that 12.5% of students stopped out by the spring 2022 semester, and another 10.3% stopped out by fall 2022. The semester view makes it easy to see the remaining students after each semester, but what if you wanted to know the total percentage of students that have stopped out from the fall 2021 cohort?

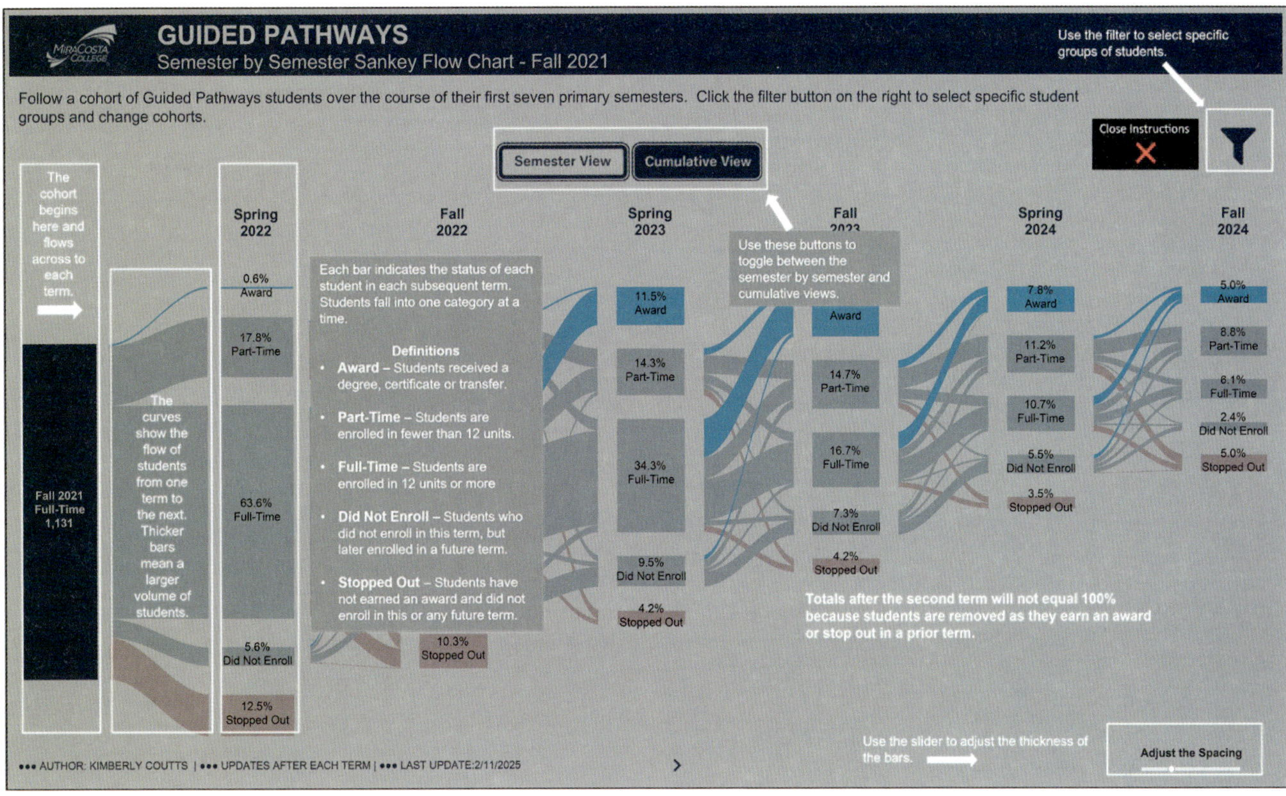

FIGURE 18.4 An instructional overlay that guides the reader in how to read it.

The view on the right provides an easy way to see those cumulative numbers without the mental math necessary to keep a tally. We can easily see the breakout of the entire cohort, total awards, total remaining, total stopped out, and all of them at any point in time.

Process

The spark for this dashboard came from conversations with the dean of Research Planning and Institutional Effectiveness, Dr. Chris Hill, who envisioned a tool to track student attrition visually. The dean told Kimberly that she thought it would be helpful to see how a cohort of full-time students progress semester by semester.

Kimberly initially explored a vertical funnel diagram but quickly pivoted to a horizontal Sankey diagram.

Kimberly told us, "A vertical view limits the available real estate, forcing people to scroll down. Downward scrolling conceptually felt off to me, as our other success charts are typically displayed in an upward trajectory. I tried to display it from bottom

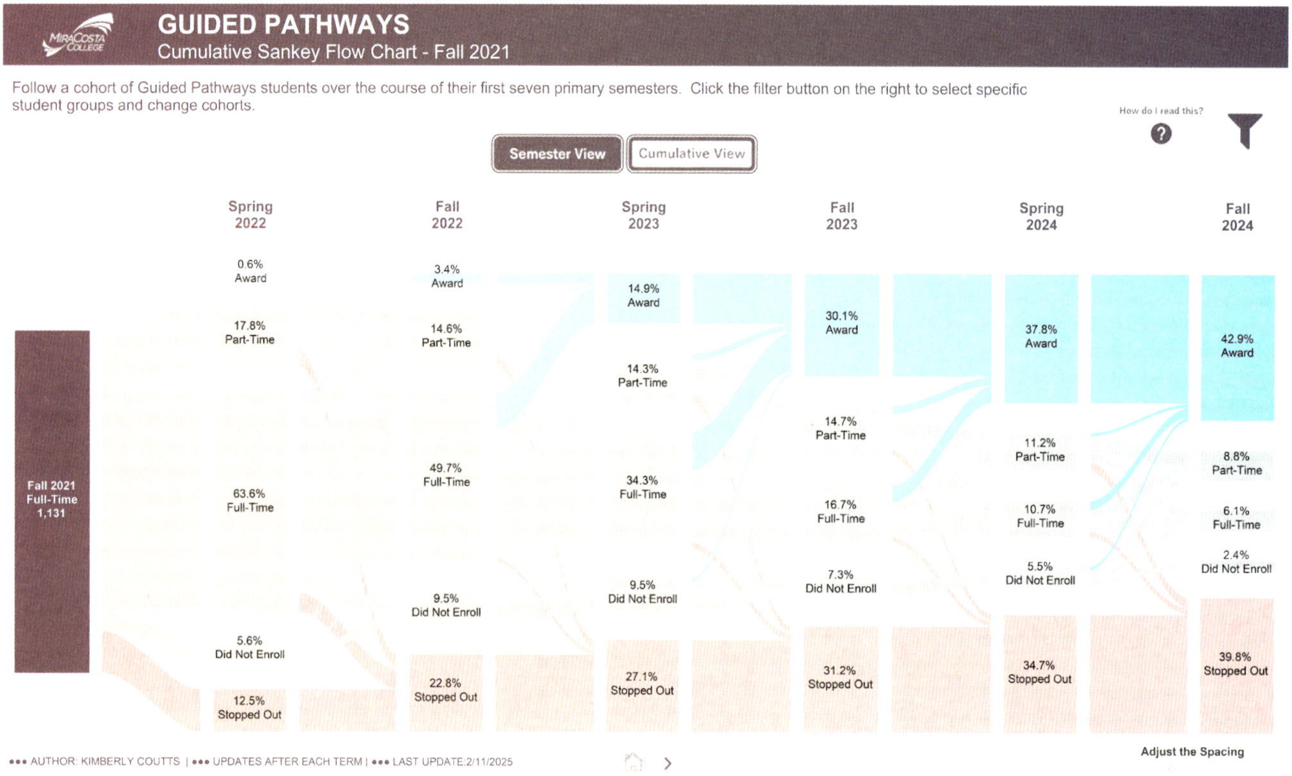

GUIDED PATHWAYS
Cumulative Sankey Flow Chart - Fall 2021

Follow a cohort of Guided Pathways students over the course of their first seven primary semesters. Click the filter button on the right to select specific student groups and change cohorts.

How do I read this?

Semester View | Cumulative View

Fall 2021 Full-Time 1,131

Spring 2022: 0.6% Award; 17.8% Part-Time; 63.6% Full-Time; 5.6% Did Not Enroll; 12.5% Stopped Out

Fall 2022: 3.4% Award; 14.6% Part-Time; 49.7% Full-Time; 9.5% Did Not Enroll; 22.8% Stopped Out

Spring 2023: 14.9% Award; 14.3% Part-Time; 34.3% Full-Time; 9.5% Did Not Enroll; 27.1% Stopped Out

Fall 2023: 30.1% Award; 14.7% Part-Time; 16.7% Full-Time; 7.3% Did Not Enroll; 31.2% Stopped Out

Spring 2024: 37.8% Award; 11.2% Part-Time; 10.7% Full-Time; 5.5% Did Not Enroll; 34.7% Stopped Out

Fall 2024: 42.9% Award; 8.8% Part-Time; 6.1% Full-Time; 2.4% Did Not Enroll; 39.8% Stopped Out

••• AUTHOR: KIMBERLY COUTTS | ••• UPDATES AFTER EACH TERM | ••• LAST UPDATE:2/11/2025

Adjust the Spacing

FIGURE 18.5 Cumulative view of the fall 2021 cohort.

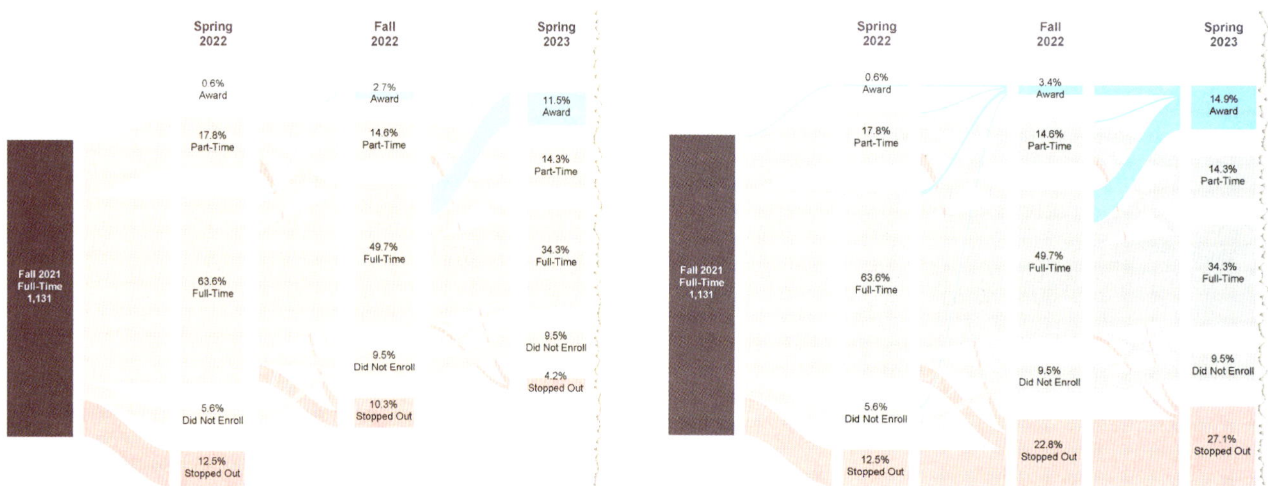

FIGURE 18.6 Noncumulative view and cumulative view, side-by-side.

to top, but thought that would be too challenging for our audience and would require too much scrolling. Ultimately having everything on a single page with success at the top and stop-outs at the bottom made the most sense."

She recalls thinking that a Sankey diagram would be a great way to visualize the student flow over time on a single page. Specifically, because the dean wanted to be able to see the percentage of students remaining full-time or in other various categories semester by semester.

A Sankey diagram wasn't easy to implement since it wasn't a default chart type within Tableau. These types of visualizations in Tableau required complex calculations and data structures. She encountered many early challenges, including complex data transformations and iterative design revisions. Early attempts involved complex Excel calculations, which made data processing very slow. Tableau's table calculations were another hurdle, with minor configuration errors often causing major issues.

The dashboard took nearly two years to develop, with periods of trial, failure, and revision. Like most developers, Kimberly worked on the dashboard as one project in a larger portfolio. Eventually, she leveraged templates built by Ken Flerlage, which streamlined development and helped get the first release out the door.

Tools and Methods Change and Advance Over Time

Having built the first Sankey diagrams in Tableau leveraging the sigmoid function and complicated data structures, I am all too familiar with the process that Kimberly went through. However, the Tableau community is terrific, and they stepped up (see Chapter 35).

Over the years, people in the community have continued to develop different methods for making Sankeys in Tableau with each improving on the last. Early on, Olivier Catherine improved on my approach to Sankeys by using a polygon technique. Then, a few years later, Ken Flerlage developed templates Tableau developers could use with their own datasets to create almost-instant Sankeys. This template is what Kimberly ended up using as her solution.

Even with a streamlined solution like Ken's, the community kept pushing to reduce *any* barriers to building these more complex chart types. Tristan Guillevin developed a web-based tool called AdvViz that assists users in creating all sorts of bespoke visualization. Fast-forward to the latest version of Tableau at the time of writing (2025) and there is a newer feature called Viz Extensions that allows users to create these more complex visualizations directly in Tableau, all with a few clicks.

Read more about Ken Flerlage's Tableau templates: dtdbook.com/link23

Tristan Guillevin's web-based tool AdvViz, a free advanced visualization generator for Tableau:

https://www.ladataviz.com/

Overall, the development of this dashboard was an iterative, trial-and-error process that required deep engagement with data structuring, various visualization techniques, and working with stakeholders. The initial requesting dean was very involved in the early development stages but retired about a year into the process. Kimberly was the interim dean for a while, and once she had a working prototype she worked with the new incoming dean of research planning and institutional effectiveness as well as the primary users, the dean of instructional services and her staff.

Also, it's important to note the very long life cycle of a cohort of students (5–7 years). While it's too early to measure the direct impact of this visualization, it has already improved transparency and decision-making as it relates to student retention strategies.

About three years ago, the college implemented the Caring Campus initiative. Instead of offering students services and hoping they would take advantage of them, college staff reached out directly to these first-time students. Students were encouraged to develop a long-term educational plan, offered peer mentors and other support services that are tailored to each student's specific needs.

They measure several leading/lagging indicators as a part of each student's experience. The users of this dashboard track the cohorts in this Sankey and compare them with their metric achievement (i.e., completing their educational plan, persisting to the second semester and completing college math and English) to ensure that the college is doing everything they can to prepare students for each stage of their education.

Kimberly said, "For us, 'success' will mean that larger portions of these cohorts transition to the Award group within the first three years, and fewer will stop out."

The response from the deans: "Using those charts, our ACP Success Teams saw when the most pain points are for students and when most drop off. The two things that come to mind are changes to 1) our onboarding efforts for our new students so they are more prepared to start classes and stay to complete their goal, and 2) our changes in proactive year-round case management (phone campaigns) even during the intersessions (winter and summer) to support retention since we lose so many students between semesters. We have also started to track and contact students beyond year 1 since many students still need support and encouragement to make it past year 2 and 3, especially part-time students. The dashboards emphasized the need to continue to include part-time students in our outreach and case management efforts."

Author Commentary

STEVE: What a wonderful story of how a dashboard came to life. From the spark (the dean's recognition that visualizing students' progress would help the college better serve its students) to the actual dashboard that allows the dean, administrators, and support staff to see which students were succeeding and which needed more help. A big reason this succeeded was Kimberly's experience and data visualization literacy. She knew that a Sankey diagram would be the best way to understand the flow of students over time. It's also a wonderful example of leveraging the expertise and generosity of the data visualization community. Kimberly didn't have to build this solution from scratch as Ken Flerlage had made his solution readily available.

You can see more examples of leaning on the community in "Ask the Community for Help" in Chapter 35.

AMANDA: Often when we think about dashboards, we imagine a mix of different charts and numbers mapped onto some kind of gridded interface. What I love about this dashboard is its simplicity: one anchor visualization that you can customize to narrow in on specific time periods, student cohorts, and more. The initial nudge from the dean to create the dashboard speaks to the importance of champions, whether at the spark or through to the adoption of a dashboard. When someone in a position of influence speaks to the importance of using data in decision-making or models pulling up a dashboard during a meeting, they nudge others to do the same.

ANDY: I often wonder how you, the reader, react to seeing the dashboards we include. When you see a complicated one like this, I worry you'll have a quick reaction and think "Ugh, that dashboard's not for me." I am prone to having those visceral reactions.

When I first saw this, my thoughts were that a Sankey-based dashboard was going to turn people off. As we worked with Kimberly, I came to realize just how good it is at revealing extensive insights. I now know it's an exceptional way to show cohort data.

If you make complex dashboards, it makes user engagement all the more important. Some of your users might have the same initial reaction as me to your work. A big part of our framework describes the importance of early and continued engagement with users, followed by training and support. That stage is vital to win them over to the value of complex visuals like this one.

Chapter 19

Children's Hospital Association Dashboard

Lindsay Betzendahl with Kathy Rowell and Dan Benevento from HealthDataViz, a Sellers Dorsey solution

Organization: NACHRI, known as the Children's Hospital Association (CHA).

How This Dashboard Delivers: Leaders can monitor their KPIs over time and compare their performance with other hospitals, allowing them to quickly identify areas where they need to take action, consolidating information from across departments into one consolidated suite of dashboards.

Audience: Executives and analysts at children's hospitals across the United States and Children's Hospital Association staff.

Team: Lindsay Betzendahl with Kathy Rowell and Dan Benevento from HealthDataViz, a Sellers Dorsey solution.

Tools: Tableau and Figma.

Timeline: 15 months.

Note: All values in the dashboard are anonymized and do not represent real values.

Chapter Author: Amanda Makulec

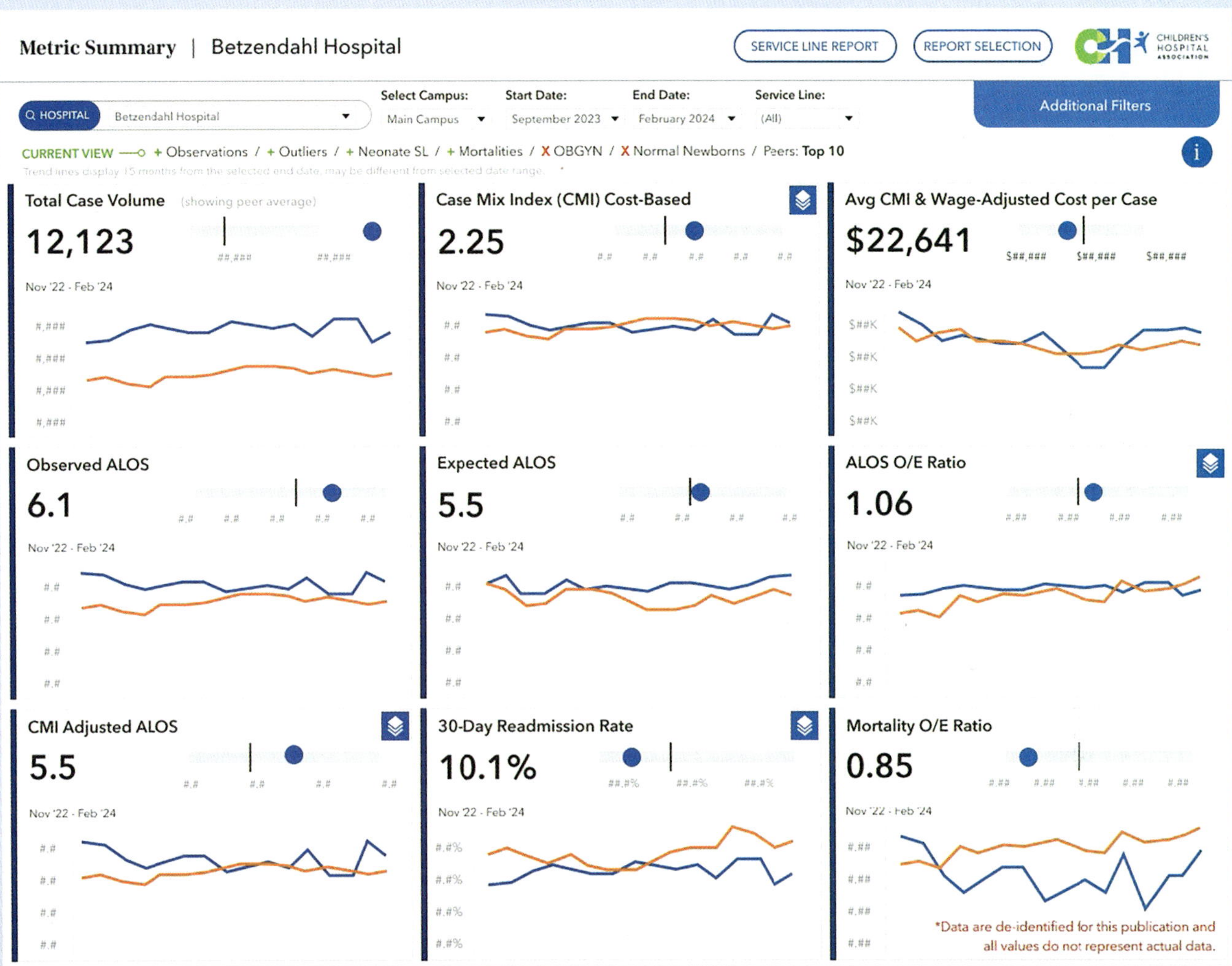

Children's Hospital Association summary metrics dashboard (image property of CHA with sample data for demonstration only).

Big Picture

You are an administrator at a hospital that is a member of the Children's Hospital Association (CHA), which includes 200 children's hospitals, health systems, and related organizations that care for children in their communities and beyond. One of the services provided by the CHA is analytics, including benchmarking performance compared to peer institutions.

While many analytic tools lump together general (adult) and pediatric facilities, the CHA's offering only includes data for children's hospitals. This means administrators can better assess performance relative to peer institutions and focus solely on data specific to children's care and medical treatment. The suite of dashboards includes 21 different reports, providing a comprehensive snapshot of hospital performance.

Specifics

You need to:

- Quickly access KPIs from across departments
- Compare how one hospital system is performing relative to peers of similar size or with other similar characteristics
- Analyze performance by specific disease area to assess what areas may be most impacting overall performance on health system KPIs

Related Scenarios

- You are a national sales manager for a large retail chain and need to compare store performance across a group of key performance indicators.
- You are a school district administrator monitoring KPIs across the elementary schools in your district with the aim of identifying high-performing schools, which may have model programs for other schools to adopt.

How People Use the Dashboard

The suite of dashboards includes 21 separate views addressing a wide range of user needs. Let's walk through the two summary views that users encounter first: the Key Opportunities dashboard and the Metric Summary dashboard.

Key Opportunities Dashboard

The Key Opportunities view for executives gives a snapshot of four key performance indicators. For each, we see the most recent value, trends over time, and a comparison with peer hospitals (Figure 19.1).

This quick reference dashboard also orients the user with:

1. *Filters* at the top of the page prompt users to narrow the view to their hospital system, campus, and date range.
2. *Text components* provide breadcrumbs highlighting what has been included/excluded in the current display, along with summary context about the number and type of patients in the report based on selections.
3. *Four cards* with the same repeating structure, which provide KPI values, comparisons to peer median and percentile range (gray bar, showing

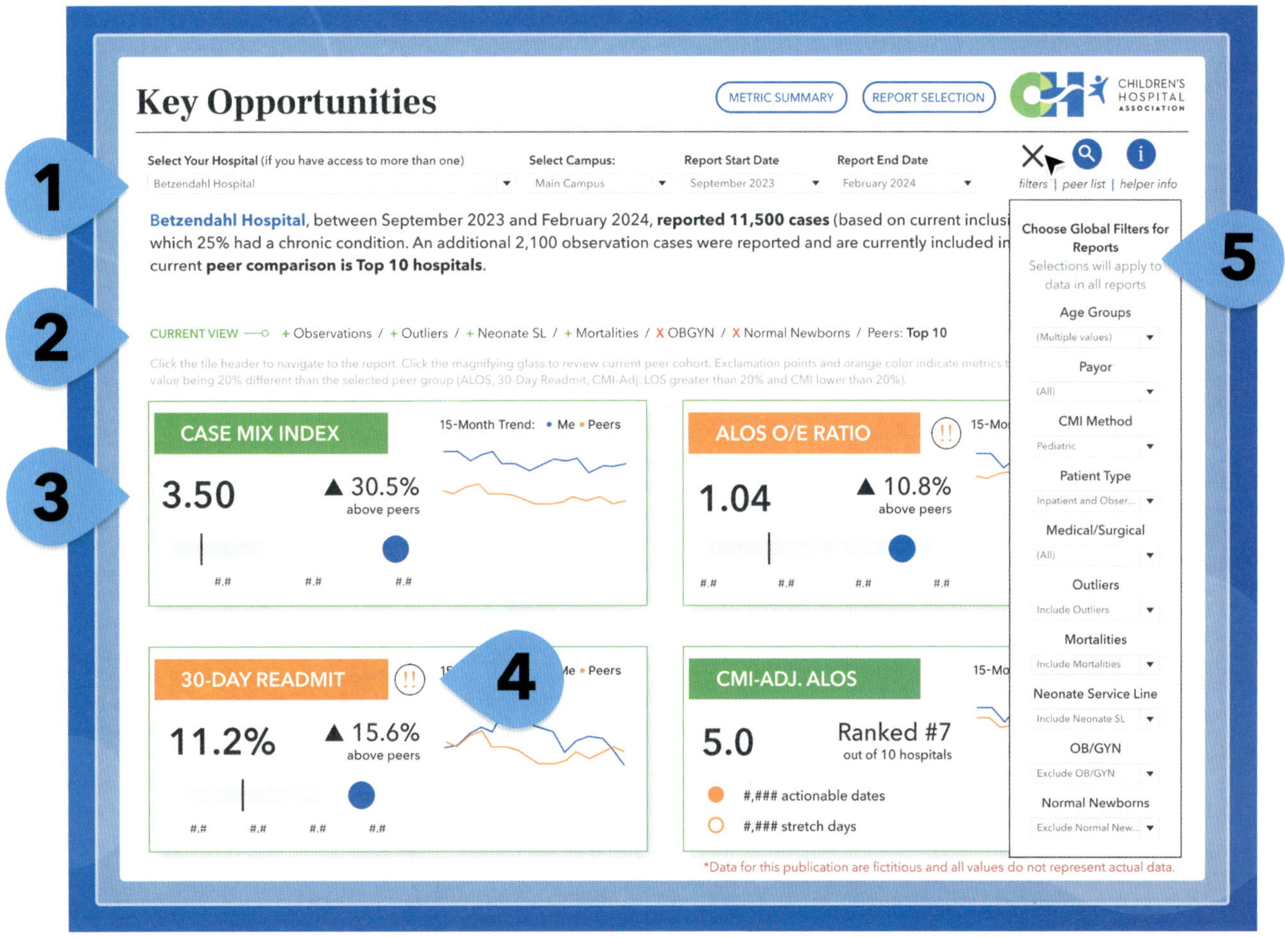

FIGURE 19.1 Key Opportunities dashboard (image property of CHA with sample data for demonstration only).

a percentile range (e.g., 10th–90th), vertical line showing the median, and blue dot, showing the selected hospital's data), and trends.

4. *Color-coded metric names and an alert icon* to focus the user's attention, alerting them to where there may be cause for concern.
5. *A collapsible filter menu* to apply across all views in the dashboard minimizes visual clutter while still maintaining the availability of the global filters.

In addition, the dashboard has buttons that let the user navigate to other pages, such as the Metric Summary dashboard (discussed next).

The page also serves as the entry to the suite of reports where hospital users can initially set important global filters and define peer comparisons.

Metric Summary Dashboard

The Metric Summary dashboard expands on the first view with metrics pediatric hospitals commonly monitor (Figure 19.2).

The display includes summary values compared with peers (the floating bar chart) and 15-month trends. The design mirrors the setup on the Key Opportunities dashboard; users learn how to read a "card" for a metric once and use that mental model throughout the dashboard (Figure 19.3).

The cards on the Metrics Summary include multiple features to aid the user:

1. *Filters* placed in the same location across the top as on the previous screen.

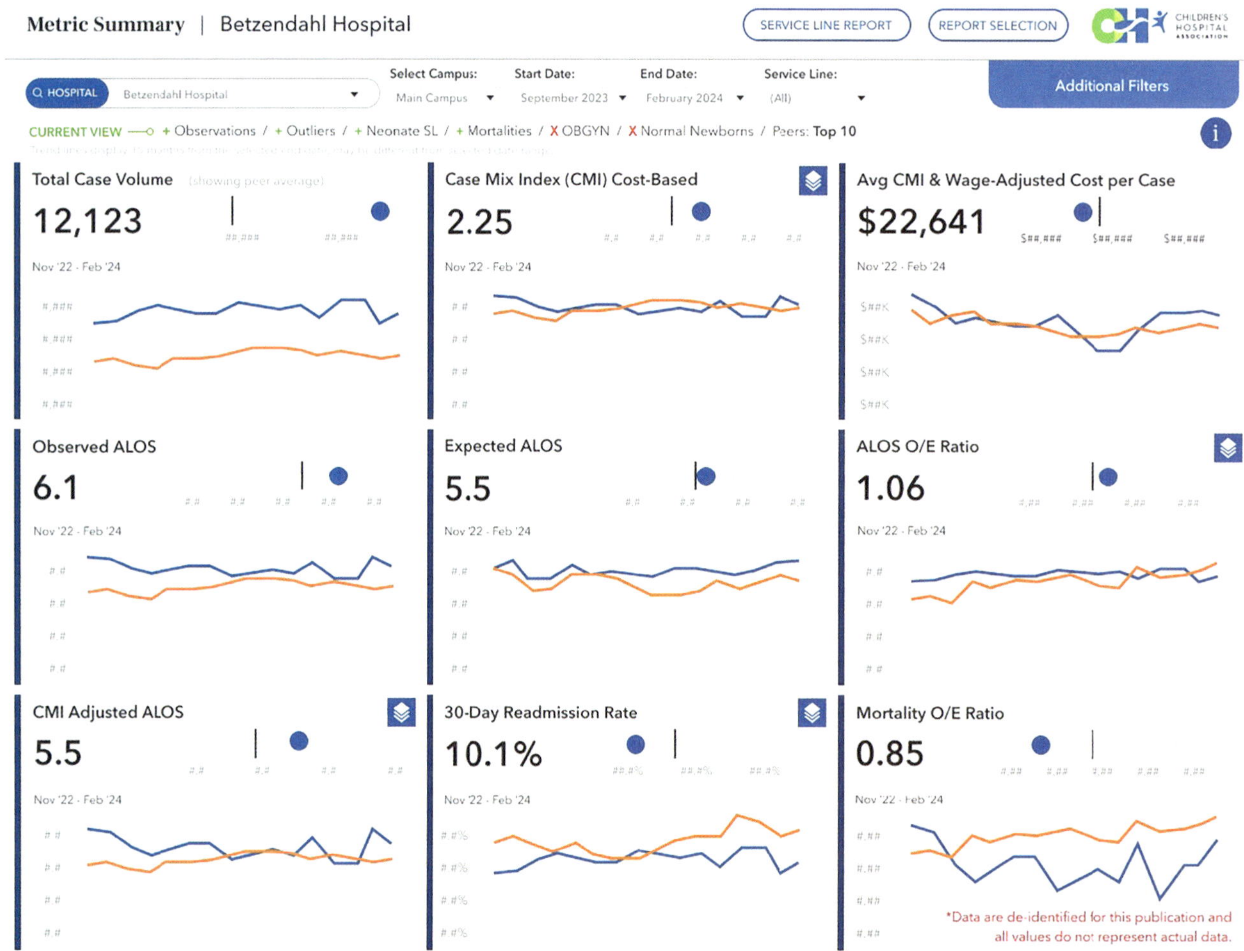

FIGURE 19.2 Metric Summary dashboard (image property of CHA with sample data for demonstration only).

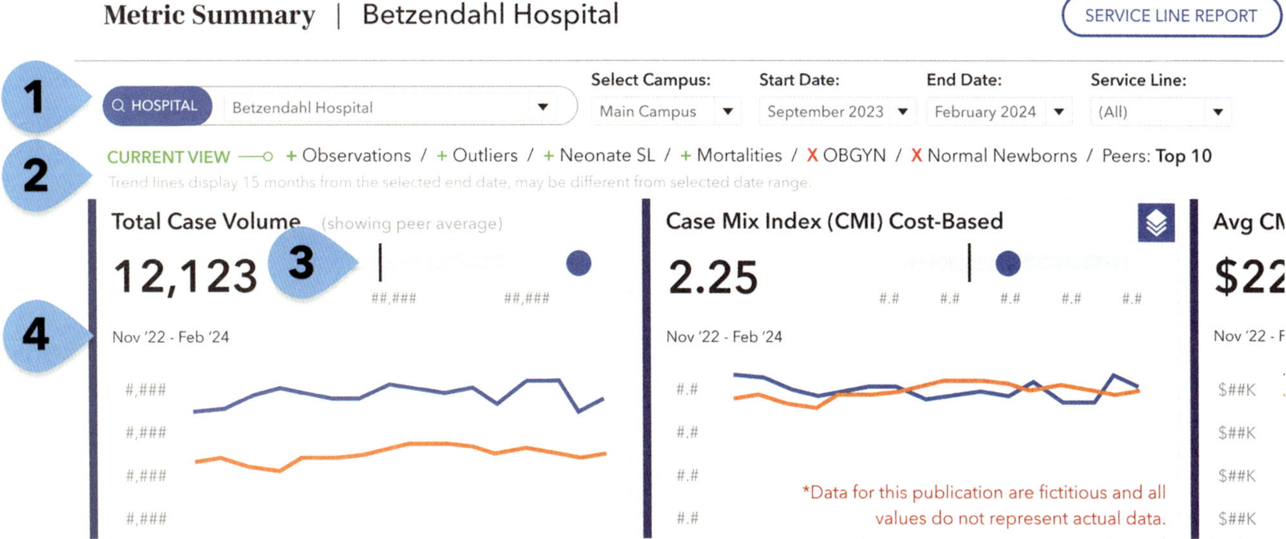

FIGURE 19.3 Snip from the Metric Summary dashboard highlighting specific components (image property of CHA with sample data for demonstration only).

2. *Breadcrumbs* reminding users of the filter selections applied to the view, including double-encoded icons that show both what is included (green plus sign) and what was excluded (red X).
3. *Benchmarking chart* with clearly labeled value for peer average to compare against as a reference line and against a percentile range (gray bar) for peer hospitals (e.g., 10th–90th)
4. *Time period* showing the selected start and end dates noted in the filters and the rolling 15-month period for the trends above the line chart, as the period for the trend chart is fixed.

Each of these seemingly small interactive elements ensures users are clear on what data is being included in the view. These clues are particularly important since global filters that are applied on the Key Opportunities page persist throughout the dashboard.

Detailed Views

From the overview dashboards, users can drill into specific metrics across 19 additional dashboards. The service line selection comparison dashboard is one example that drills into data to answer: "How am I doing compared to another group?"

The source data is based on individual patient encounters each mapped to a primary service line like respiratory care. Using the dashboard, administrators can identify service lines with the greatest opportunity to improve hospital performance.

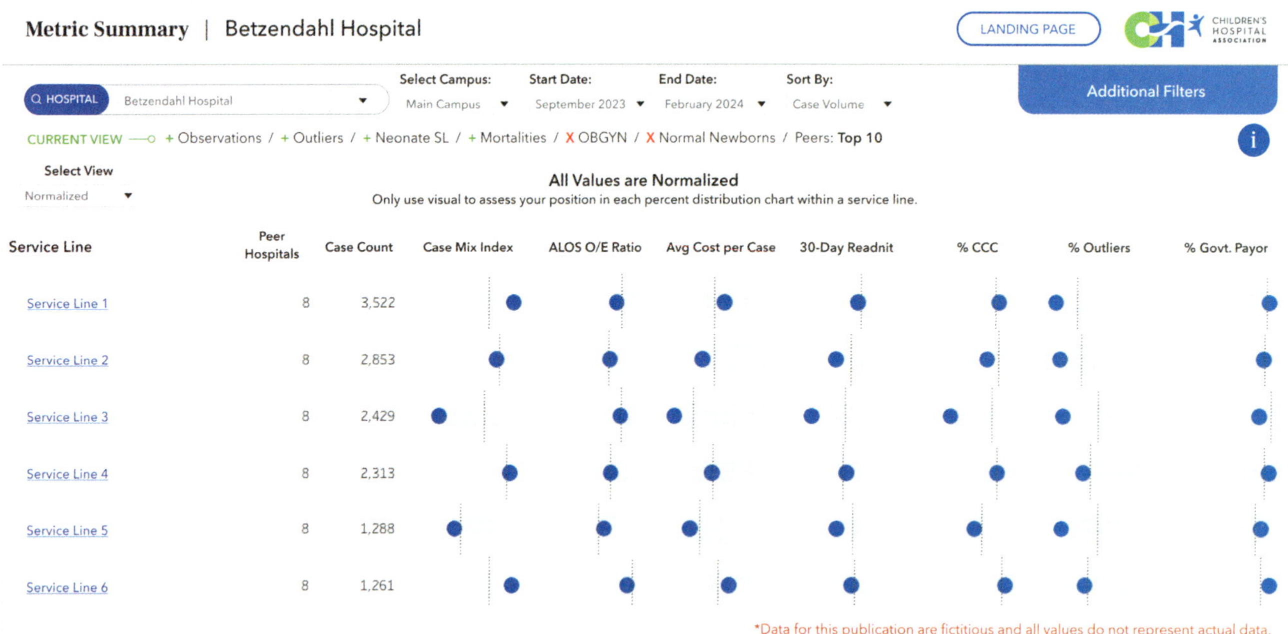

FIGURE 19.4 Service Line comparison view (image property of CHA with sample data and service lines for demonstration only).

These data dense displays provide the details needed for actionable insights. The service line comparison (Figure 19.4) uses the structure from the KPI cards with gray bars showing a comparison range and a blue dot for the selected hospital, scaled across multiple metrics and service lines. In addition, the matrix includes the number of peer hospitals analyzed for that service line, represented in the gray bar, and the total case count for the service line for context.

A toggle allows users to view the data either normalized or as a numeric view. Some of the metrics have much larger ranges than the others, so plotting them all on a common axis would obscure the view. Normalizing the metrics ensures comparisons can be made across all metrics simultaneously.

While we don't showcase all the views within the dashboard, the other detailed pages come back to the same question as the service line view: How are you doing compared with your peers?

Why This Works

Big Picture First, Zoom and Filter, Details on Demand

One of the design team's key goals was not to overwhelm the user when they first open the dashboard. Instead, they used HealthDataViz's Guided Analytic

Framework to create layers of detail and enable exploration.

Navigational flow and drill-down capabilities ensure users can continue to ask questions of the data and easily move into deeper analyses after reviewing the KPI cards. This follows Ben Shneiderman's mantra for dashboard design: big picture first, then zoom and filter, then details on demand. While the KPI cards in the primary views may seem simple on the surface, they act as a meaningful entry point into the analysis.

Always Centering the User

Across the dashboard, the selected hospital is often compared with peers or a custom comparison group.

Let's look back at the Service Line comparison, which the users love (Figure 19.4). Each of the design decisions was rooted in a specific user need or preference—even one that might run counter to our instincts as designers.

A data viz developer would likely ask why there aren't alerts for being outside of the expected range or peer comparison. Is this a missed opportunity for data-driven alerts for quicker speed to insight?

The decision to keep the colors simple was deliberate. There isn't a clear indication if individual points are cause for celebration or concern because across the different measures, a low number can be good, bad, or neutral, depending on expected values. For example, a low case mix index (which represents the complexity and severity of a hospital's patient mix) could be due to issues like coding incorrectly. Alternately, a smaller share of children with medically complex conditions could be driven by population or social determinants of health that aren't good or bad—they just *are*.

Meaningful Benchmarks

The question of "how are we doing compared with..." is a more complex question than it appears on the surface. Creating benchmarks for comparison turned out to be one of the biggest challenges, as everyone had different ideas for how to set meaningful points of comparison.

Creating Meaningful Units of Analysis

Getting the right data structure was key to enable benchmarking within the dashboard.

Consider the wide range of expected values for a metric like length of stay (how long a pediatric patient is a patient within the facility). More complex conditions or those requiring ongoing care, like pediatric cancer, may expect to have longer lengths of stay. Then, when creating comparison groups of other hospitals, consider that patient mix may vary between hospitals. Hospital A could have many more long-term care conditions compared with Hospital B, which primarily provides outpatient services may have very different lengths of stay even if both hospitals are performing well.

Some ideas considered included:

- Your hospital versus other hospitals as an industry, without considering more nuanced slices of different types of systems or patient load
- Your hospital compared with a section of peer hospitals that have specific shared characteristics, like geographic location or facility level
- Your hospital compared with peers based on an analytical model to identify other facilities "like me" based on attributes and characteristics like patient volume, patient demographics, and location

Letting hospitals choose their peer group while also respecting the privacy and security of health information can be a challenge that requires creativity to balance performance of the dashboard against the ability to offer the user a customized experience.

Right Tool for the Job

"We've figured out the right tools for the audience and for each task," said a member of the CHA team, reflecting on how the Tableau workbook was being used in practice. The dashboards are accessible for verified members and are ideal for rapid analysis of hospital performance.

Sometimes users still want access to the underlying data. That could have been implemented in Tableau, but it would have been extremely complex and would have raised security and privacy concerns. The team developed the Tableau UX to pass the correct parameters to CHA's legacy reporting tool, allowing users to extract the data they needed.

Process

Discovery

The spark for the CHA dashboard was a recognition that the existing reports had become outdated and could be dramatically improved, not just aesthetically, but in the layers of analysis they could offer to member hospitals.

While users loved having access to the quality and performance metrics produced by CHA over nearly 10 years, the legacy reports were cumbersome to access and navigate. CHA hired HealthDataViz, a Sellers Dorsey solution, to collaborate with its data analytics team to design and develop a new suite of dashboards.

The team focused on reimagining how to display the data valued by users while much improving navigation, comparison analysis opportunities, and custom analytical capabilities. The HealthDataViz team focused on thoroughly understanding users' needs: what questions they were likely to ask, what their role was, what their priority data needs were, and other user preferences.

The team interviewed 12 people who represented different user perspectives. Then, they synthesized insights from the interviews into personas and core requirements for the new dashboard. See Figure 19.5 for two examples.

CHA PERSONAS

TARGETED BULLET POINT DESCRIPTIONS

Member Children's Hospital **CEO**

- Requires **single page summaries** of high-level key opportunities that can be printed and quickly understood with narrative and explanations
- Needs to easy access to plain language metric definitions and clearly understand and agree with CHA peer grouping methodologies
- Metrics should **highlight areas** that help him ensure the financial viability of the hospital (cost data, payor mix), understand the quality of care (ALOS/readmissions/mortality) **where to focus resources, and opportunities** for new programs through peer comparisons
- If interacting with the report, the **interactivity needs to be easy** and simple to flow through, with clear and logical drill paths that do not get complicated, though likely won't drill to granular data
- Insights need to be **comprehended within 90 seconds**

Member Children's Hospital **CQO, CMO, CNO**

- Frequently needs **data to monitor performance (trends)** on key quality indicators that she can **compare to other similar hospitals** across various specific programs/service lines
- Needs to **identify opportunities for improvement** and be able to **identify drivers** of the performance (payor, APR-DRG, service line, age group, outliers, etc) in order to develop plans to improve
- While she more likely gets reports from her staff, staff need the ability to uncover the answers to her questions and **identify the "why"** behind the data (contributing factors) in the key metrics, which often requires **focused reports**
- Insights need to be **comprehended within 5-8 minutes**

Persona descriptions condensed by Lindsay Betzendahl, HealthDataViz

FIGURE 19.5 Persona examples created during discovery, summarized by designer Lindsay Betzendahl.

The five personas represent the range of user needs, including both CHA internal stakeholders and users at member facilities. Two of the personas are shown in Figure 19.5, including:

- **CHA:** Senior Executive, Subject-Matter Expert/Client Liaison.
- **Member hospital:** CEO (single page summaries, highlights), C-suite (CQO, CMO, CNO), analyst (gets to a more focused, detailed need for information.

In addition to mapping illustrative personas, the team mapped how users accessed data with the legacy tools, allowing them to identify existing features that worked well, and specific pain points the users were experiencing with the legacy reports.

Prototyping, Design, and Development

The team moved into iterative prototyping, starting with simple wireframes and working toward more polished mockups. Throughout prototyping, the five personas served as touch points to check that the designs matched user needs.

As a starting point for a new way to organize the information, the team mapped a very high-level wireframe. The schematic started with a series of connected boxes (Figure 19.6), each of which eventually

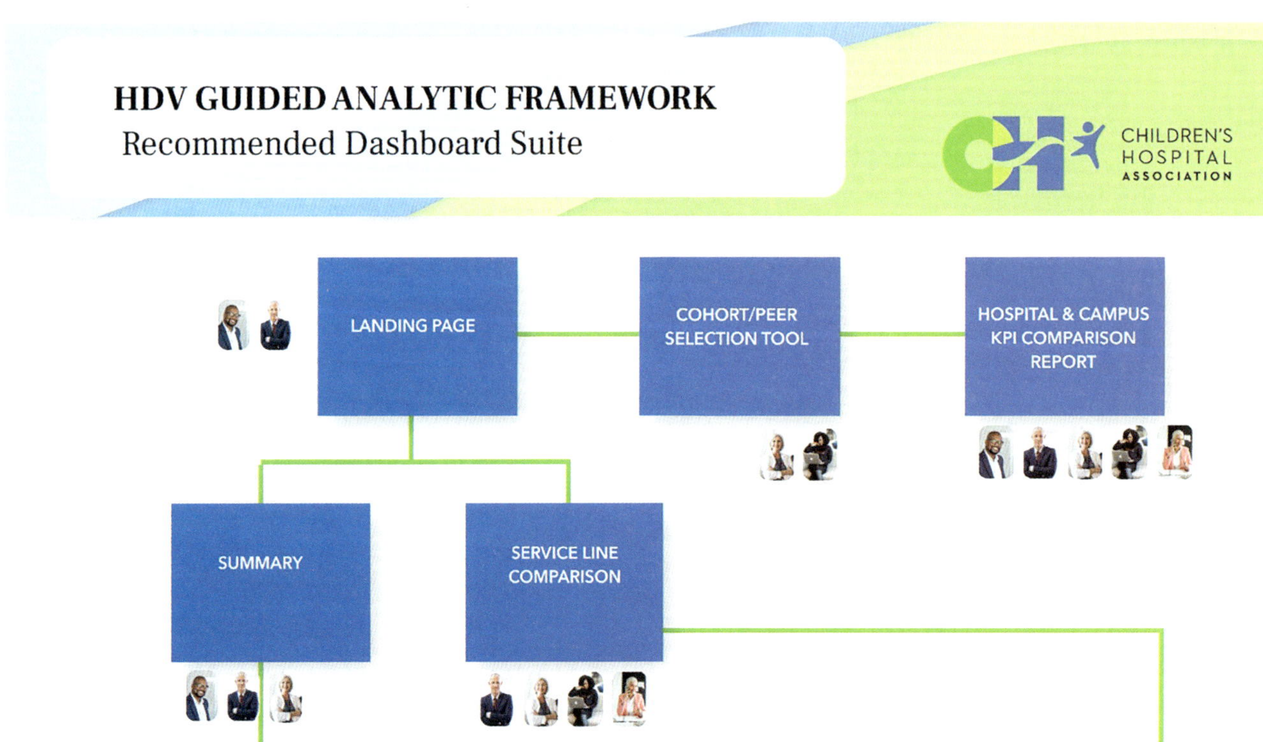

FIGURE 19.6 Section of early wireframe showcasing the hierarchy of views and which personas are served by each one.

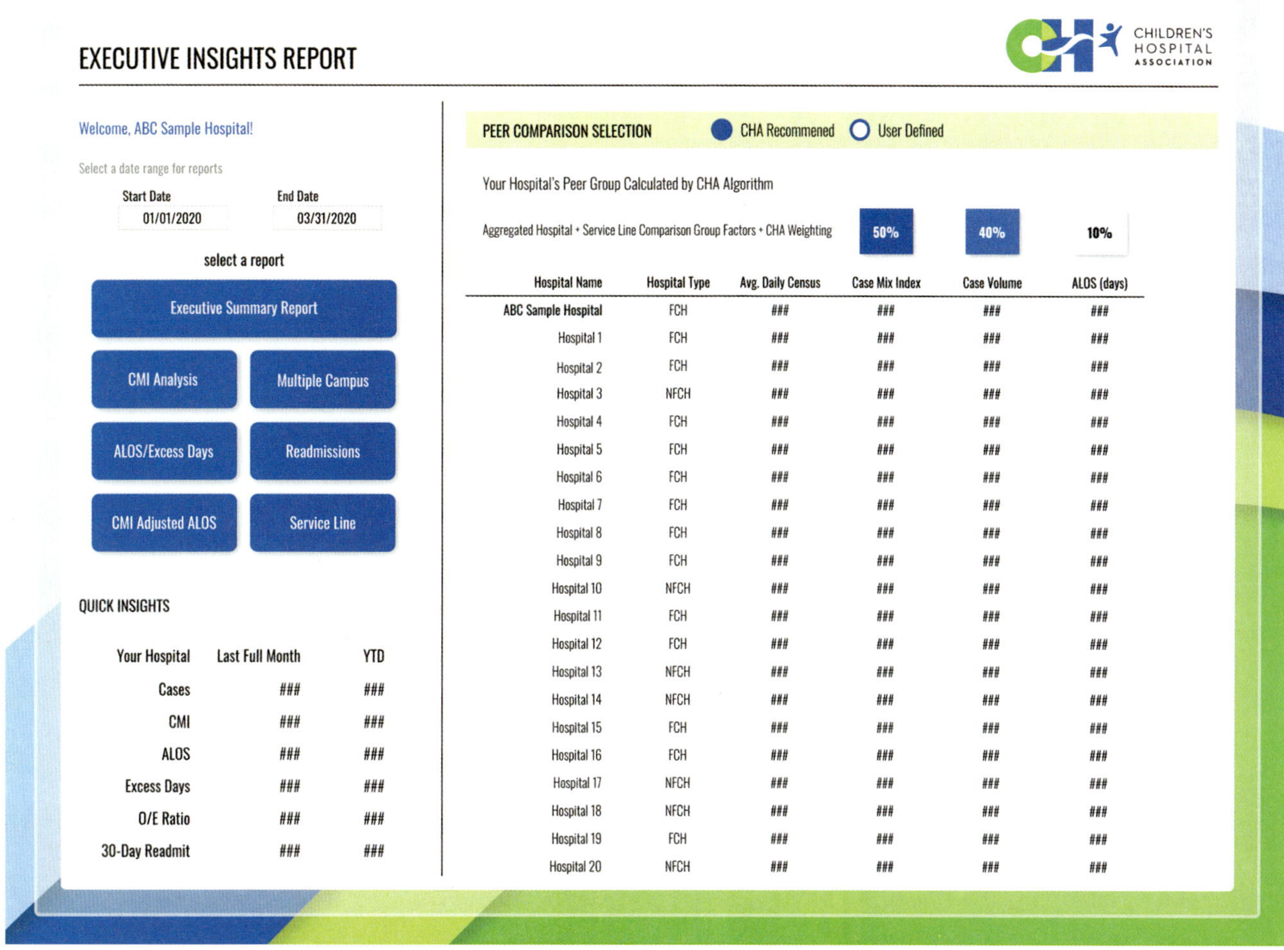

FIGURE 19.7 An early prototype design in Figma.

became one of the dashboards in the larger suite. Starting with the wireframe allowed the team to map where different user personas would find value in the suite of different views without getting into the weeds of chart choice and color palettes.

Early concepts mocked up in Figma started the user journey on the metric summary page. The initial data-dense designs included detailed tables to maximize the volume of information, along with a panel of navigation buttons (Figure 19.7).

In the next iteration of the mockup, the design team evolved the comparison concepts to be more visual with fewer metrics than were in the original table view (Figure 19.8).

In this iteration, we see the shape of the first dashboard release start to take shape. The additional bar charts didn't make the final cut; they show a more specific comparison of the selected hospital to peers.

Equipped with a clear wireframe and a set of mockups that had gone through multiple rounds of revisions, the team was ready to move over into Tableau to build the dashboards with real data.

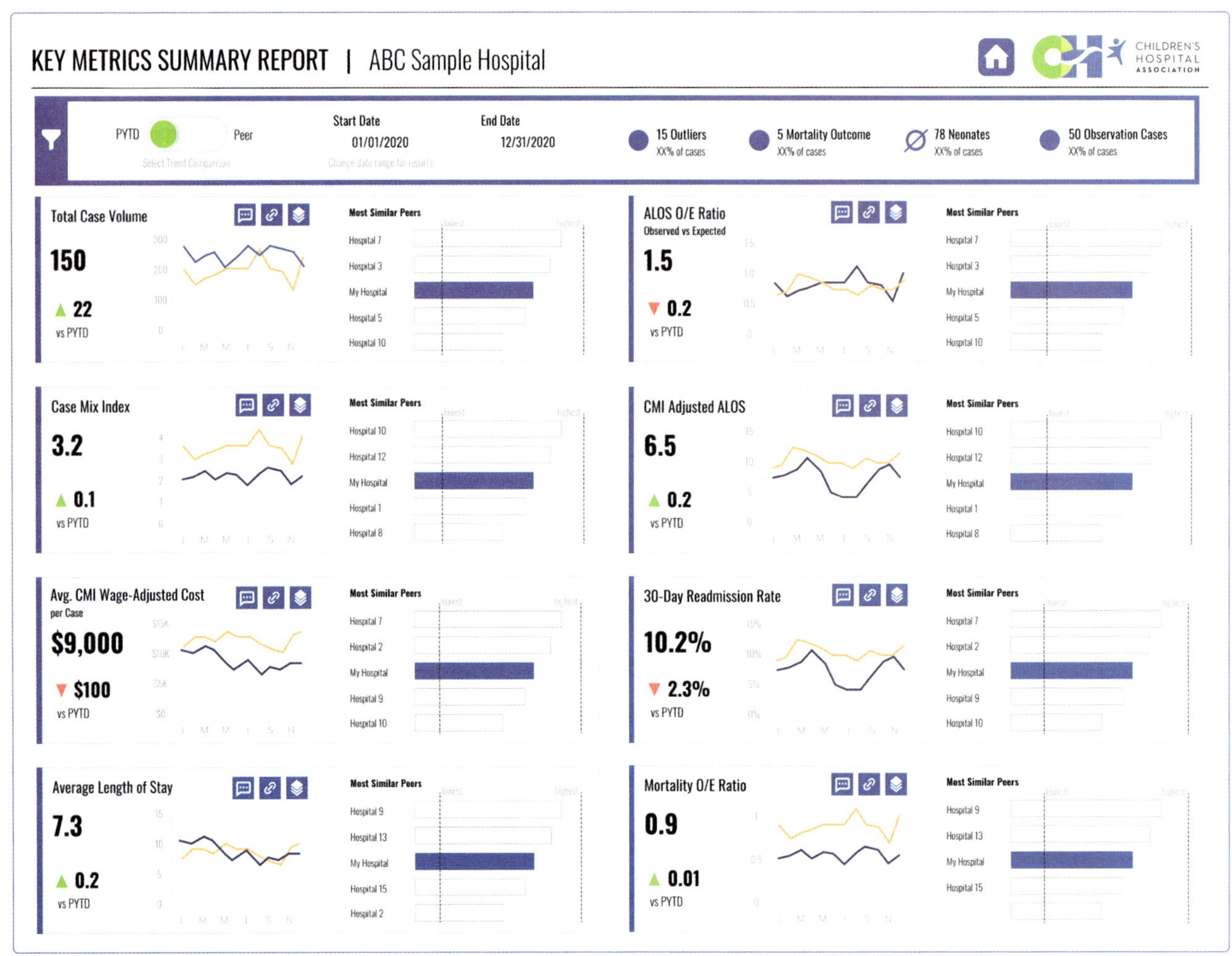

FIGURE 19.8 Mockup of Key Metrics Summary Report (image property of CHA with sample data for demonstration only).

User Testing

While designing the dashboard, each of the final views went through user testing for feedback on chart choice, design, and navigation.

Sometimes user testing identified disparate opinions, leaving it to the designer to decide whether to include or exclude a feature. For the CHA dashboard, the collapsible filter panel on the overview pages had mixed reviews. Some people didn't like the added clicks required to open and close the panel, but having it visible all the time meant the team couldn't display as many charts as they would like. This was the case for all the dashboards. Considering the benefits and the gripes, the team decided the collapsible menus would stay, as illustrated in Figure 19.9.

Sometimes user testing also identifies unmet needs at a larger scale. With a working dashboard in hand, CHA and HealthDataViz realized that the dashboards didn't meet the needs of the Executive persona defined in discovery, who may be overwhelmed with the nine KPI card view as a starting place for analysis.

Instead, the team needed to build something even simpler as the start for busy executives, which is where the Key Opportunities view explored at the start of this chapter was born (Figure 19.1). What that means: just four KPIs and the breadcrumbs to navigate to more details if needed.

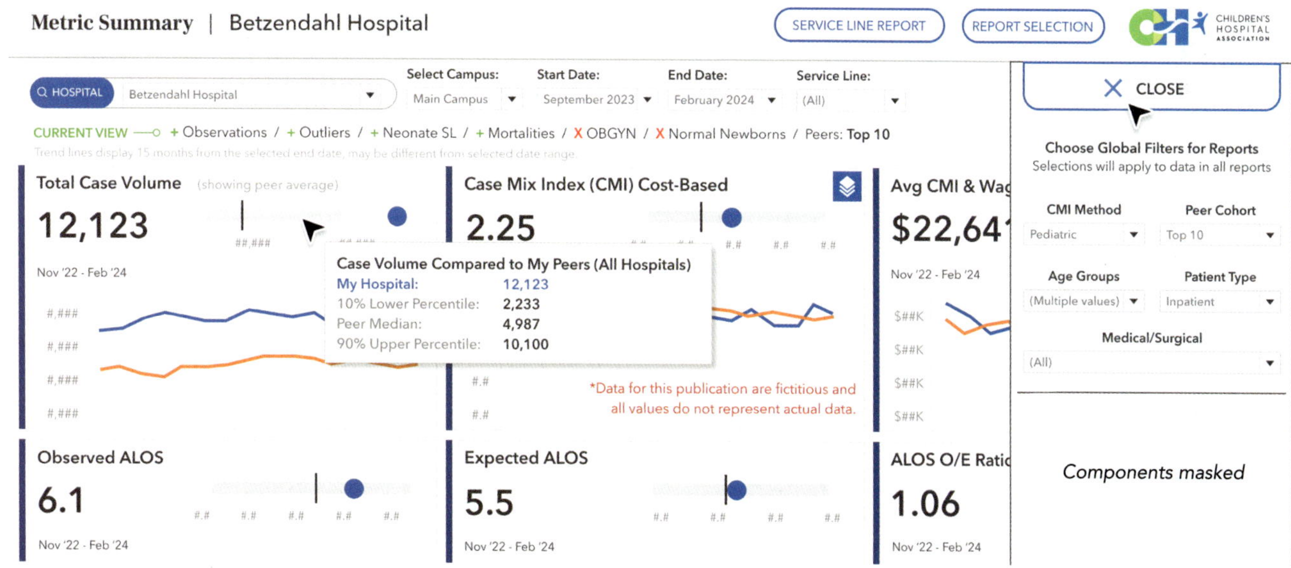

FIGURE 19.9 Example from the Metric Summary showing the user navigation for closing the menu (Image property of CHA with sample data for demonstration only).

Performance Considerations

Sometimes user testing isn't just about design; it's also about performance. On the CHA dashboard, some pages would take 30 seconds or longer to load. This is where the team had to assess if that load time was acceptable and what effort would be required for even incremental improvements.

The dashboard has a massive volume of data with complex security, and the workbook itself is well designed but remarkably complex. Looking at the dashboard stats, the Tableau workbook has:

- 3 data sources
- 21 dashboards
- 311 worksheets
- 340 fields
- 623 calculated fields
- 34 parameters

Key features that feel simple and seamless are technically complex. These included data-driven colored headers to alert users of metrics that aren't performing well, dynamic narratives, breadcrumbs showing current filter selections, and complicated user security requirements. Blend the functionality with a clean, welcoming, and aesthetically pleasing design and you have one very challenging project.

Ultimately, the team recognized that while performance and responsiveness could improve slightly, any changes would be high-effort. The rendering times weren't so slow that they would put people off from using the dashboard, but maybe longer than some users would expect due to the load time for rendering data from across all hospitals for comparison statistics.

Measuring Success

Measuring the success of this suite of dashboards started with usage statistics and monitoring per user views – with some reservations. While the detailed tracking data on usage allows for mapping out current paths through the dashboard (which is helpful for identifying points where individuals get stuck), the team didn't want to fall into the trap of assuming that *lots of views* were all that mattered.

CHA recognized that occasional but important moments for accessing these tools matter more than usage stats. For example, when a hospital needs to plan for next year's budget and needs quick access to KPIs, *one use* would be a success.

Some of the best testaments to the dashboard's success aren't the quantitative measures, but instead in how often leaders at children's hospitals actively use the dashboard in meetings and related spaces.

For example, a CHA hospital wanted to have a strategic conversation with counterparts primarily serving adult patients. During the meeting, the leader of the children's hospital accessed the system, found the metric they needed, and had a meaningful conversation about the different challenges the hospitals and their patient populations face.

As analytics folks, their team was accustomed to looking at a lot of numbers. While the usage data is helpful there, "making sure people have the right information to have the right conversations" is the greatest measure of success for the team.

Managing Enhancements

After launch, the team held monthly meetings to identify problems with the dashboard and review issues and enhancement logs. When talking through what to do next on the dashboard, prioritization is a constant challenge that requires balancing "big lifts" with "easy fixes."

Since the dashboard went into production, the team has had at least four major releases and has added new views and data sources.

Over the series of releases, the HealthDataViz team provided mentorship support as the in-house team took ownership of releases and updates, hosted internal Tableau trainings, oversaw quality assurance checks, and wrote updated documentation. As a result, this information-rich dashboard has had a successful handoff to the team, allowing them to manage improvements on their own.

Author Commentary

STEVE: There are three things that jumped out when reviewing this scenario. The first is that there are so many techniques and approaches here that can be applied to virtually any organization and industry. How can you read this scenario and not think, "Ooh, I could use *that.*"

The second is how HealthDataViz's process mirrors so much of our recommended framework: spark, discovery, personas, user journeys, rapid prototyping, thoughtful testing, and managing enhancements.

The third is how the designers made the organization using the dashboard the focus of the dashboard. I can practically guarantee that people will use this dashboard and use it repeatedly.

ANDY: This chapter challenged our vocabulary. Lindsay and her team built 21 different views of data for Children's Hospital Association. What should we call each one? Is that 21 pages? 21 dashboards? And what do we call the collection of all of them together? Is the whole thing a dashboard? Or a report? Or even a suite of dashboards? In our experience, if we asked 10 people to answer these questions, we'd get 10 different answers. I address this in more detail in the essay "What the Heck Is a Dashboard?" in Part III.

In a nutshell, even after decades of business intelligence, nobody has created a definitive answer. I doubt they ever will. I encourage you to find a common language in your organization, but don't get stressed by what others might call the objects you build.

Chapter 20

Metric Tree

Klaus Schulte, Merlijn Buit

Dashboard Designer: Klaus Schulte, Merlijn Buit.

Company: The dashboard was built by AppsForTableau for Kramp, a European agricultural spare parts provider.

How This Dashboard Delivers: Viewers can analyze Kramp's overall operating profit, identifying strengths and weaknesses. Interactivity lets viewers start at the highest level and drill into the details that need further exploration.

Audience: People making strategic and operational decisions, at all levels of the company.

Team: Three to five developers built the dashboard, following many working sessions with Kramp to define the organization structure.

Tools: Tableau, JavaScript, and a lot of whiteboarding. The final dashboard is interactive, in a browser, and can be viewed on large meeting room screens as well as laptops.

Timeline: The initial design took four months. Data is updated daily, and the design is reviewed as and when needed.

URL: dtdbook.com/link24

Chapter Author: Andy Cotgreave

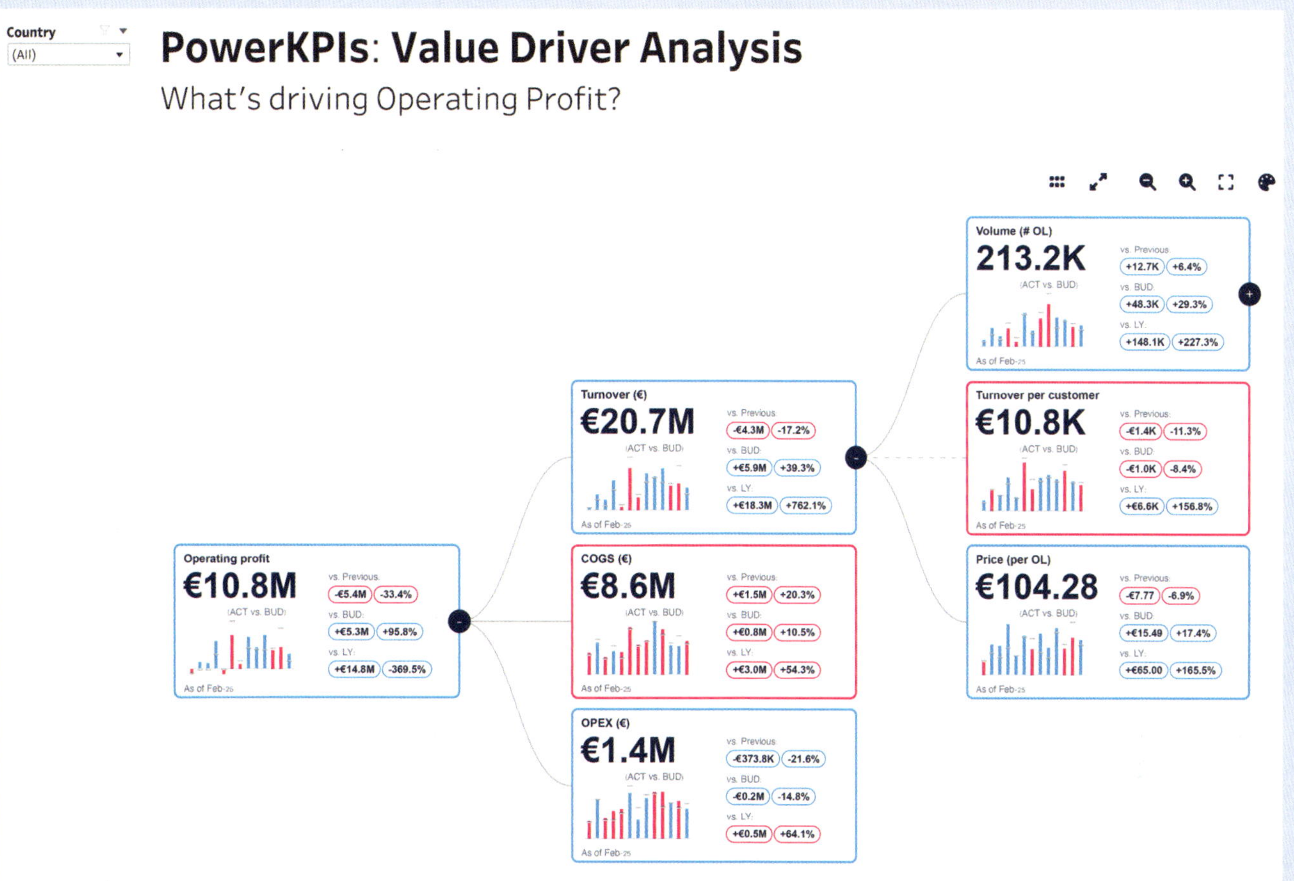

Country
(All)
PowerKPIs: Value Driver Analysis
What's driving Operating Profit?
Operating profit
€10.8M
vs. Previous: -€5.4M -33.4%
vs. BUD: +€5.3M +95.8%
vs. LY: +€14.8M -369.5%
As of Feb-25
Turnover (€)
€20.7M
vs. Previous: -€4.3M -17.2%
vs. BUD: +€5.9M +39.3%
vs. LY: +€18.3M +762.1%
COGS (€)
€8.6M
vs. Previous: +€1.5M +20.3%
vs. BUD: +€0.8M +10.5%
vs. LY: +€3.0M +54.3%
OPEX (€)
€1.4M
vs. Previous: -€373.8K -21.6%
vs. BUD: -€0.2M -14.8%
vs. LY: +€0.5M +64.1%
Volume (# OL)
213.2K
vs. Previous: +12.7K +6.4%
vs. BUD: +48.3K +29.3%
vs. LY: +148.1K +227.3%
Turnover per customer
€10.8K
vs. Previous: -€1.4K -11.3%
vs. BUD: -€1.0K -8.4%
vs. LY: +€6.6K +156.8%
Price (per OL)
€104.28
vs. Previous: -€7.77 -6.9%
vs. BUD: +€15.49 +17.4%
vs. LY: +€65.00 +165.5%
(ACT vs. BUD)

Big Picture

You want to understand how each key performance indicator (KPI) in your organization is affected by others. You want an interface that shows your top-level KPI and allows you to drill down to see how lower-level KPIs contribute to the higher-level ones.

By exploring the drivers at different levels of a hierarchy, you gain an understanding of how variations in one driver impacts overall outcomes.

For example, you want to understand operating profit. That KPI sits at the top of the tree. You can drill down to see how turnover, operating expenditure, and cost of goods contribute. You can then drill further into each metric to see how all KPIs contribute to the highest level.

Specifics

You need to be able to:

- Understand the composition of key metrics in your organization
- Discover the value chain in your organization
- Identify bottlenecks in your organization or find opportunities to increase value by building strategies to change contributing metrics

Related Scenarios

- You are a sales director and need to track how different product categories contribute to sales and profit in your organization.
- You lead an engineering team and want to improve software development efficiency. You create a structured performance model to pinpoint areas for process optimization.
- You run a mining company and want to increase efficiency of truckloads. By analyzing truck usage, loading times, and loading efficiencies, you build an explorable model of your organization.

How People Use the Dashboard

The dashboard can be set so that it opens on the root node, or any number of levels within the tree, including the entire tree, if wanted. Figure 20.1 shows how the view expands.

The user can click to expand the card to see the KPIs that contribute to that value. In this example,

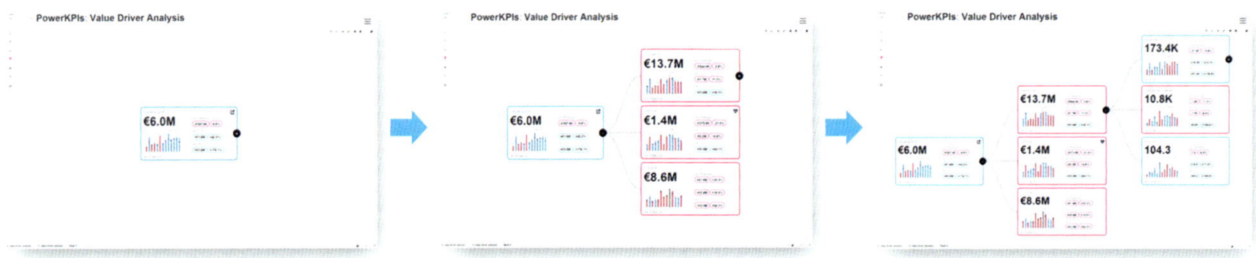

FIGURE 20.1 Three images showing the click cascade. From left to right, there are three different levels visible.

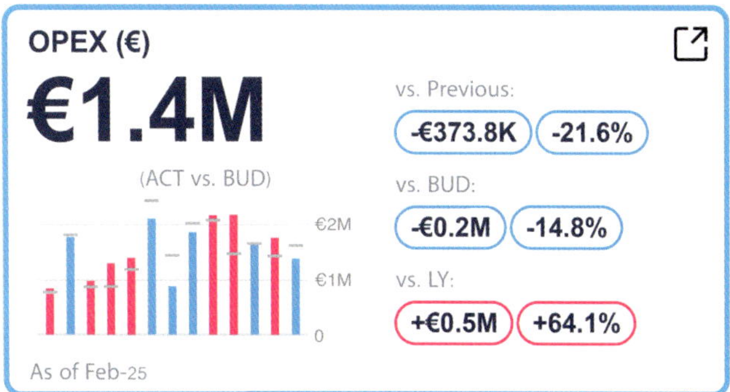

FIGURE 20.2 A close-up of a single KPI card. Here we are tracking operating expenses, so exceeding budget (the small horizontal lines) is a bad thing.

Operating Profit is the sum of Turnover, Operating Expenses (OPEX), and Cost of Goods Sold (COGS). The user may continue to click deeper into the KPI tree to understand how all metrics roll up and contribute to the highest level.

Each card shows the current value, trends, and comparisons to targets and previous periods (Figure 20.2 shows a KPI card in detail). Colors, lines, and shapes all indicate whether KPIs are on target or not.

Each KPI card might also have links to external dashboards that show more detail. So the dashboard is not only a high-level overview but a "front page" to the rest of the organization's dashboards. These links are indicated by an icon in the top right of the KPI card.

Why This Works

A Dense Display of Data

Imagine the KPI cards were as vanilla and plain as possible (Figure 20.3).

Turnover per customer
€10.8K

FIGURE 20.3 The plainest possible turnover per customer KPI.

What can you see? Turnover per customer is €10.8K; that's it. This number generates more questions than it answers: is that on target? Is it trending up? How does it compare to this time last year? A plain KPI, without context, is needlessly hobbling your users' ability to gain insights.

Now compare that number to the cards in this scenario (Figure 20.4).

This card has many extra layers of detail:

- It shows our main KPI number (€10.8K).
- The card has a red border: we're off target.
- The number is compared against multiple other measures: previous, budget (BUD), and last year

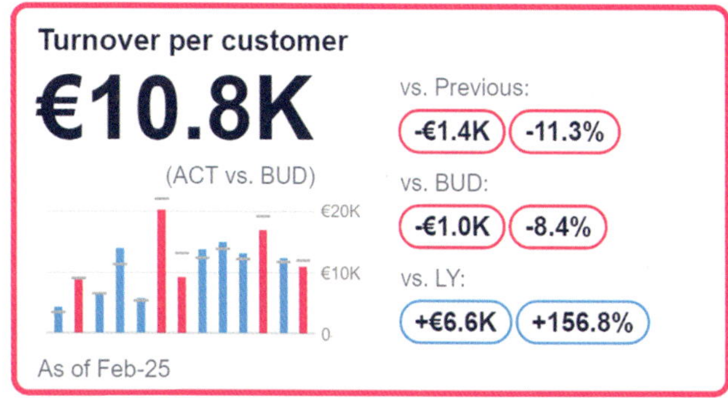

FIGURE 20.4 The same number with extensive extra context.

(LY). The red and blue also shows us where the current value is above or below each one.

- A bar chart shows the values for the last 12 months. Each bar is colored red or blue. There is also a small reference line showing target. The bars are also colored red or blue according to whether they are on target.

It is an information-dense card; it requires time to glean all insights from it. In this case, the dashboard is designed for group conversations and for thoughtful exploration. As such, the designers have packed as much information as possible into each tile. This allows many questions to be answered in the moment without reaching a data dead-end.

More Info on BANs and Context:

For more on KPI cards and BANs, see Steve's Chapter 27. For more on adding context, see Jeff's Chapter 31.

A Drillable Hierarchy: "Active Learning"

Dashboard designers generally try to put as much information onto a single screen as possible. In the racing strategy scenario (Chapter 24), Michael Gethers explicitly tries to pack as much as possible into the default view so casual viewers can get the most from the dashboard. In Michael's design, clicks are for advanced users who want to explore and find out more. In general, this is a rule we suggest you adhere to.

Ever the one to find exceptions to a rule, I believe this KPI tree dashboard works *because* it requires interaction to reveal more data. In education, there is a principle of active learning, a method where students are experientially involved in the learning process.[1] Engagement leads to mastery of content. This dashboard takes a similar approach by requiring the user to click to reveal deeper levels of the KPI hierarchy. I believe the user is actively thinking while asking, "What is the driver of this KPI?"

Another reason to like this approach is that you see only the KPIs you want to see. If your task involves drilling into Turnover, for example, there's no need to see all the KPIs that are related to Cost of Goods Sold. The KPI tree provides details on demand. The tree, with its color encoding showing where things are behind target, makes it easy to see which parts of an organization or process are underperforming. You can immediately identify where you need to act.

Full Configurability

The end user has a large amount of control over the layout and color schemes. For example, Figure 20.5 shows the same information configured with red/green colors and in a grid layout, rather than a tree (I discuss the choice of red and green later in the chapter).

[1] Bonwell, C. C., & Eison, J. A. (1991). *Active Learning: Creating Excitement in the Classroom*. School of Education and Human Development, George Washington University. Available at: dtdbook.com/link25

FIGURE 20.5 The KPI tree configured as a grid, with red/green KPI cards.

Multiple UX "Small Features"

It's so important to put every effort into making a dashboard a pleasant and simple experience. "We are on the Internet all day, and we know what a good website looks like. If we can implement something of this in our analytics products, that can only help," says Klaus Schulte, the dashboard designer.

The KPI cards are packed full of useful user experience and data visualization good practice components that get Klaus to reach his goal. Looking back at Figure 20.2, you can see the following:

- Color encoding immediately indicates whether a value is ahead of or behind a goal.
- Horizontal reference lines in the bar charts show the target for that period.
- Even the lines connecting KPI cards convey information (see Figure 20.6). Solid lines indicate where the parent metric is calculated based on the child KPIs; dotted lines represent a non-mathematical relationship, where the cards deeper in the hierarchy can add useful context.
- Gestalt principles make it easy to identify the elements of each KPI card. In this case, closure and proximity make us see the KPI card as its own distinct entity.

Process

A hierarchical KPI tree, or value tree, is not a new concept. The DuPont Analysis, a tool used in financial analysis, was originally defined in 1902[2] and is

[2]Phillips, Matt. (9 December 2015). "The DuPont invention that changed how things work in the corporate world." Quartz (publication). dtdbook.com/link26

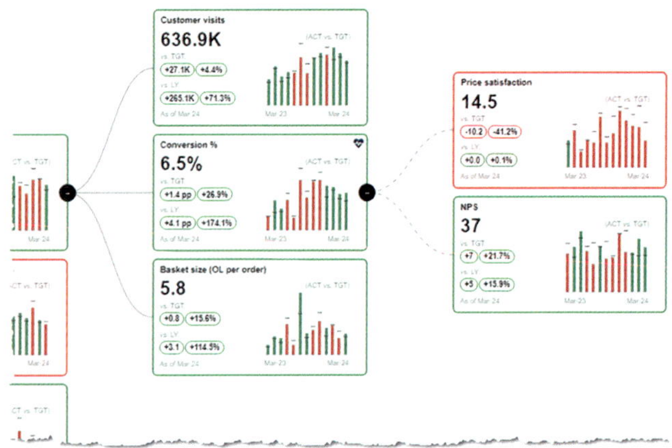

FIGURE 20.6 Solid and dotted connecting lines convey different information.

still widely used today. It allows investors to understand the drivers of return on equity, a measure of a company's financial performance.

For the development of this scenario's version, the regular process we define in Section I was turned on its head: prototyping came before discovery. This is like the E3CI scenario, which began as a hackathon (see Chapter 23).

Experimentation: Prototype *before* Discovery

Klaus is a lecturer at Münster School of Business in Germany. He is an expert in business management and data visualization. He has a long history of experimenting with new ways to visualize business processes. He has spent years thinking of new ways to show financial data, such as a reimagined profit and loss statement shown in Figure 20.7. Will the world adopt this new method? Probably not soon, but experimentation is important because it inspires new thinking and new methodologies.

This was the same approach with the KPI trees. In 2023, he published a proof-of-concept value driver tree, built in Tableau (Figure 20.8). This was the spark, not a specific request, but instead an idea, an experiment.

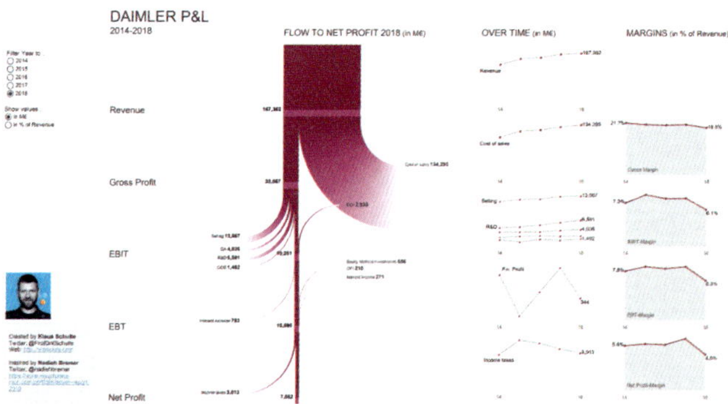

FIGURE 20.7 A reimagined profit-and-loss statement.

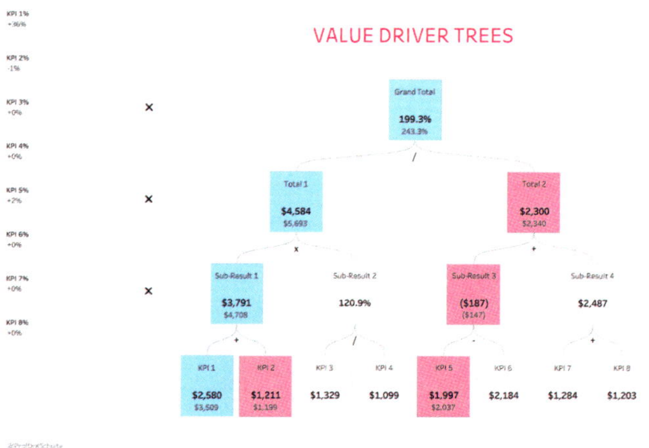

FIGURE 20.8 A proof-of-concept value driver tree.

On LinkedIn, Klaus asked people to consider if this was a useful approach. Schulte said that building this proof of concept required major hacking of Tableau to achieve. His goal was to spark conversation, and it did. People reached out with ideas, and one person had a genuine use case for Kramp.

His speculative experiment led to a real use case. Prototyping led to the spark, which led to discovery (and then *a lot more* prototyping).

Kramp had 3,000 dashboards across their organization; it was overwhelming. They did, however, have a well-defined, high-level KPI structure and wanted a KPI tree to show those. They also wanted the tree to be an entry point, via hyperlinks, to the detailed dashboards they already had.

"Mandatory" Whiteboard Prototyping

"If you can't sketch out how you define your business, you're just going to flounder," said Daan Vloedgraven, business consultant at Kramp.

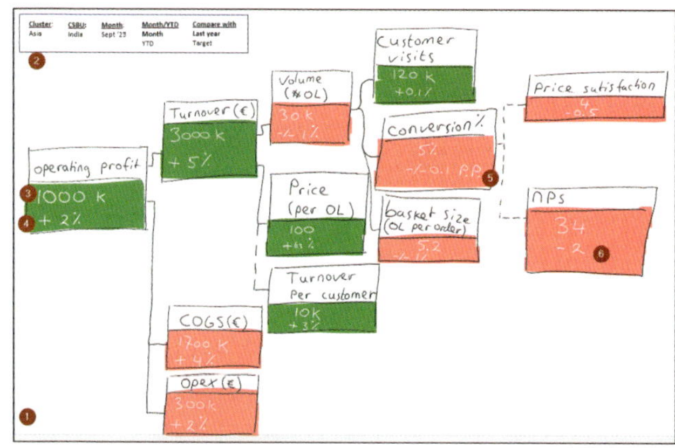

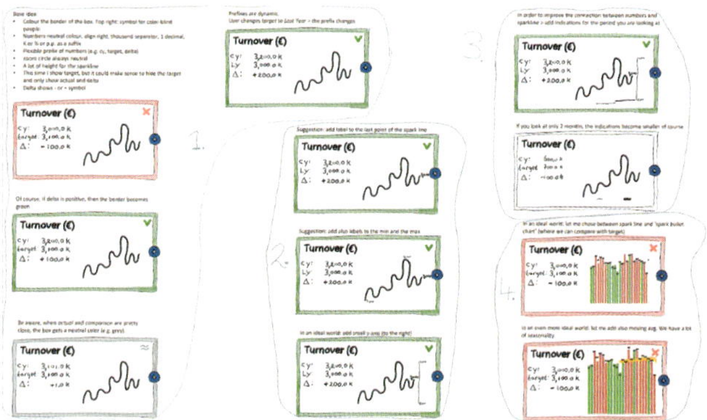

FIGURE 20.9 On the top is an early wireframe. The figure below shows a more developed prototype.

For KPI trees, or any other dashboard with a strict relationship among metrics, those relationships must be clearly defined before you can start. Schulte and Vloedgraven recommend that, for this type of dashboard, "Start with a whiteboard, or PowerPoint; draw your tree; really think about those metrics."

From there, the team sketched out multiple ideas, shown in Figure 20.9. You can see the progression of the design between the two images.

Data ownership is another vital part of the early sketching and definition phase. A dashboard like this encompasses the whole business. Who is responsible for defining and maintaining each KPI? Do you give responsibility for the metric's data to the department who influences it, or control the data centrally in your IT department? Each option has its pitfalls. However, if you don't attempt to capture this information at the start of the process, it will lead to bigger problems later. Figure 20.10 shows how the team sketched this out.

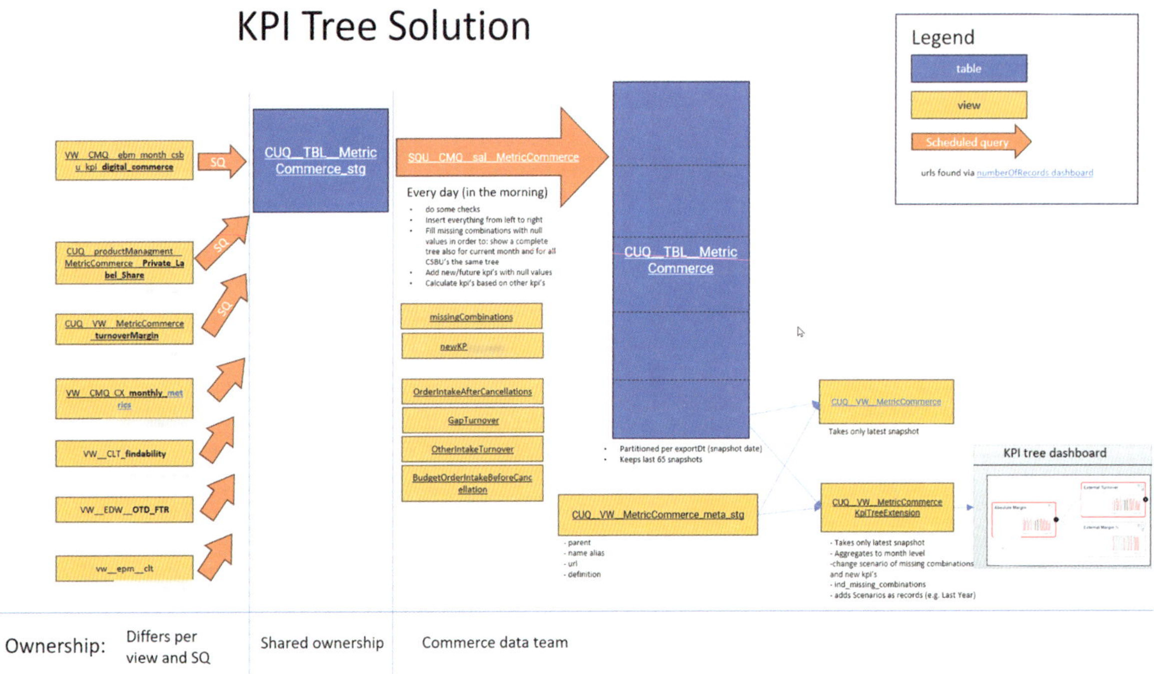

FIGURE 20.10 Data ownership sketches during the prototype phase.

Design for Reuse

Klaus worked with Merlijn Buit from AppsForTableau, a consultancy that creates Tableau extensions for clients. As they developed the dashboard, they also considered ways to reuse it for different applications. Could they make a usable template that would work with any kind of KPI hierarchy? Could they design it so it worked for a grid of KPIs, with no hierarchy? Could they design a template that anyone could install and apply to their own business?

To all of these questions, the answer was yes; this application can be downloaded as a Tableau extension and mapped to any kind of data structure, including an option to "build your own tree" from the measures in the dataset.

Many readers will not be working for consultancies, but the concept of reusability is still important. Wherever you are building multiple dashboards, reusing components has advantages. At a minimum, this could be a style guide, defining color schemes, font hierarchies, and so on. Reusing components saves development time and makes it easier for your end user to understand any new application you build.

Color Choice

For this chapter, I chose blue/red as the main good/bad color choices. In the first versions of the KPI Tree, Klaus and the team used the blue/red as the default. Best practice rules in data graphics tell us we should avoid red/green because people with color vision deficiency cannot distinguish them.

However, Klaus ultimately decided to make the default color choice green/red, despite the issue. Figure 20.5 shows a grid layout with colored backgrounds in green/red and Figure 20.11 shows a close up of the KPI cards. How come Klaus, such a diligent and professional data communicator, would release something he knows flouts what some people call the "rules" of data visualization?

With almost every client they have worked with, their first question had been "Can we change the blue/red to green/red?" Ultimately, they changed the settings to *start* from green/red and from there they encourage clients to move to blue/red.

There is a point in all dashboard designer's lives where they must decide whether to give a client, or colleague, what they ask for; even when the client is asking for things you might not think are correct (see also: pie charts, gauges, etc.). There is no fundamental right or wrong answer to this challenge; it is down to you to assess each situation as it arises.

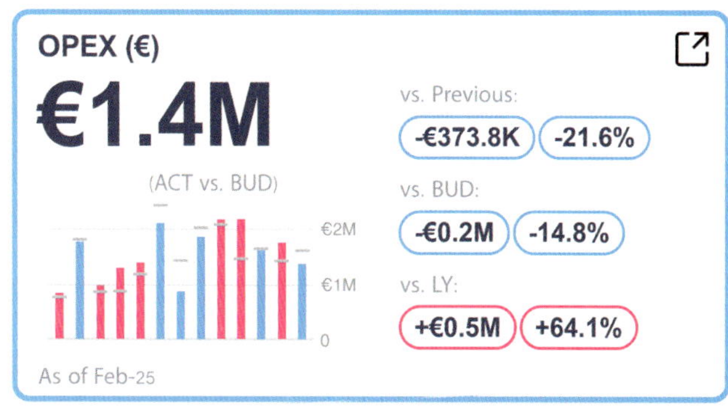

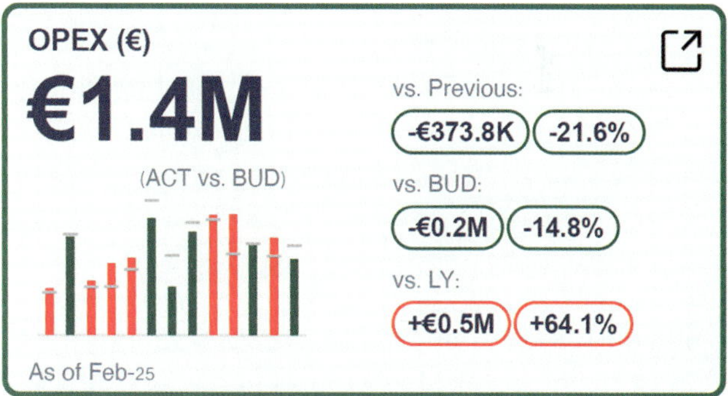

FIGURE 20.11 Two KPI card color choices: blue/red and green/red.

Author Commentary

ANDY: Is this KPI tree a dashboard? There are several reasons a traditionalist would say no:

- Not all the data is visible. You must click to open a path and see more data.
- When fully expanded, the cards can be small.

My response is to consider these questions:

- Does this KPI tree let you monitor a set of metrics?
- Does it let you see what contributes to those metrics?
- Are the individual tiles designed with rapid insight in mind?

The answer to all of those is surely yes. This scenario blurs the line between an application and a dashboard. Trying to define where the boundary between those two concepts is difficult. I explore it further in Chapter 30, "What Is a Dashboard?" As data dashboards become more complicated, the difference will surely become more blurred.

AMANDA: Reading this KPI tree didn't have me questioning if it was a dashboard – instead, my instinct was that each *card* felt like its own dashboard. The tree makes the case for the value of drilling down and exploring underlying patterns, since we know that aggregate measures can mask more nuanced analytics but also showcases the analytical power of simple displays.

Starting with a single card also addresses the sense of information overload that users can face when faced with a dense screen of numbers, and the branching approach follows a mental model that may feel familiar to those who have used decision trees in the past.

STEVE: I particularly like how many components are presented on the cards. Yes, the overall color of the card may be blue (or green), but there will be some item on the card that is red. That may encourage a dashboard user to do a little more exploring and find that while overall the KPI is good, there are things that if addressed would make it even better.

Klaus is always thinking "is there a better way to show this?" and there often is...because he came up with the better way! The KPI tree is an example of his ongoing quest.

Chapter 21

Insurance Broker Portfolio Dashboard

Ellen Blackburn

Dashboard Designer: Ellen Blackburn.

Organization: UK-based insurance company.

How This Dashboard Delivers: The insurance dashboard enables underwriters to quickly assess broker performance, optimize their decision-making, and reduce risk.

Audience: Tens to hundreds of underwriters at the insurance company.

Team: A single developer/SME with input from primary stakeholder (the coach).

Tools: Tableau for the dashboard. The interactive dashboard is viewed using a desktop or laptop browser.

Timeline: Inception to release was one month.

Note: The data for this dashboard is proprietary and the insurance company is confidential. The names and data on this dashboard have been replaced with data from Mockaroo.[1]

Chapter Author: Jeffrey Shaffer

[1]Mockaroo.com is a web-based tool that allows users to generate customizable and realistic test data for software development and testing purposes.

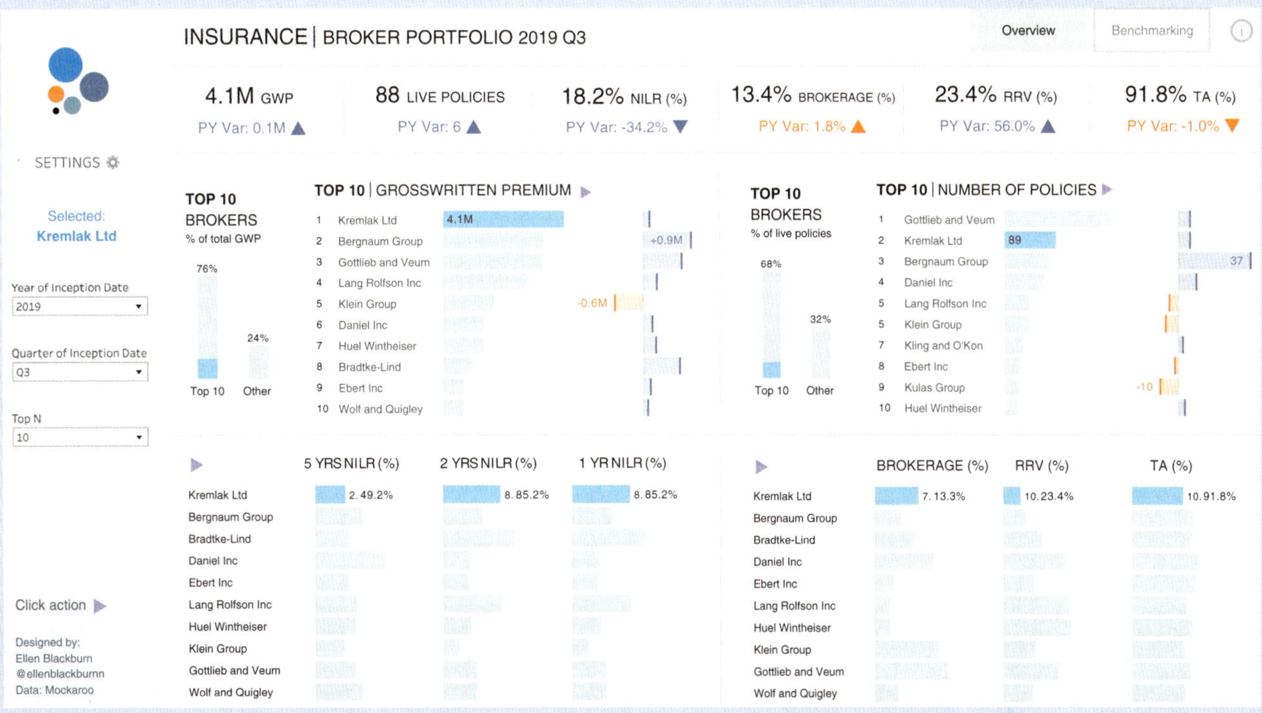
INSURANCE | BROKER PORTFOLIO 2019 Q3
Overview
Benchmarking
4.1M GWP
PY Var: 0.1M
88 LIVE POLICIES
PY Var: 6
18.2% NILR (%)
PY Var: -34.2%
13.4% BROKERAGE (%)
PY Var: 1.8%
23.4% RRV (%)
PY Var: 56.0%
91.8% TA (%)
PY Var: -1.0%
SETTINGS
Selected:
Kremlak Ltd
Year of Inception Date
2019
Quarter of Inception Date
Q3
Top N
10
Click action
Designed by:
Ellen Blackburn
@ellenblackburnn
Data: Mockaroo
TOP 10 BROKERS
% of total GWP
76%
24%
Top 10
Other
TOP 10 | GROSSWRITTEN PREMIUM
1 Kremlak Ltd 4.1M
2 Bergnaum Group +0.9M
3 Gottlieb and Veum
4 Lang Rolfson Inc
5 Klein Group -0.6M
6 Daniel Inc
7 Huel Wintheiser
8 Bradtke-Lind
9 Ebert Inc
10 Wolf and Quigley
TOP 10 BROKERS
% of live policies
68%
32%
Top 10
Other
TOP 10 | NUMBER OF POLICIES
1 Gottlieb and Veum
2 Kremlak Ltd 89
3 Bergnaum Group 37
4 Daniel Inc
5 Lang Rolfson Inc
5 Klein Group
7 Kling and O'Kon
8 Ebert Inc
9 Kulas Group -10
10 Huel Wintheiser
5 YRS NILR (%)
2 YRS NILR (%)
1 YR NILR (%)
Kremlak Ltd 2. 49.2% 8. 85.2% 8. 85.2%
Bergnaum Group
Bradtke-Lind
Daniel Inc
Ebert Inc
Lang Rolfson Inc
Huel Wintheiser
Klein Group
Gottlieb and Veum
Wolf and Quigley
BROKERAGE (%)
RRV (%)
TA (%)
Kremlak Ltd 7. 13.3% 10. 23.4% 10. 91.8%
Bergnaum Group
Bradtke-Lind
Daniel Inc
Ebert Inc
Lang Rolfson Inc
Huel Wintheiser
Klein Group
Gottlieb and Veum
Wolf and Quigley

Big Picture

You manage an insurance brokerage company and need a dashboard to track both broker and portfolio performance. It would also provide underwriters with a powerful tool for analyzing broker results and risk levels, helping them make quick, informed decisions. By offering insights into which brokers deliver the highest profitability or present the lowest risk, the dashboard supports strategic, optimized underwriting.

In addition to its high-level overview, the dashboard allows for deeper analysis, adapting to the varied needs of its users, whether that's spotting portfolio trends or evaluating individual broker performance. Trends can be viewed over multiple time frames (1 year, 2 years, 5 years), enabling users to anticipate future outcomes based on historical data. This comprehensive yet flexible approach ensures that both management and underwriters can effectively guide their strategies and maximize overall portfolio performance.

Specifics

This dashboard includes several terms commonly understood by professionals in the insurance industry. While their definitions are provided here, a detailed understanding of these terms is not essential for following this chapter.

Definitions

NILR % (Net Incurred Loss Ratio): Represents the ratio of net written premiums to incurred claims, measuring underwriting profitability. In simpler terms, it shows how much of the premiums collected are being used to cover claims.

BROKERAGE %: Indicates the percentage of gross written premiums spent on acquisition costs. Basically, it reveals how much is spent to acquire new policies, such as broker commissions or marketing costs.

RRV % (Renewal Rate Variation): Reflects the variation in renewal rates based on net written premiums as a share of the policy premium. This shows how renewal pricing changes compared to the expected premium share.

TA % (Technical Adequacy): Measures the adequacy of net written premiums compared with the benchmark net premium. Put simply, it checks if the premiums collected are enough to meet industry standards or benchmarks.

LIVE POLICIES: Counts the distinct policies that are both bound and active. This is the total number of policies currently in effect and actively providing coverage.

GWP (Gross Written Premium): The total amount of premium written by an insurer before deductions like reinsurance or expenses. In simple terms, it's the total income from all policies sold before any costs or adjustments.

You need to be able to:

- **Identify top brokers**: See which brokers contribute the most to GWP and prioritize high-value relationships.
- **Monitor performance trends**: Track brokers with high NILR to spot issues and assess risks.
- **Spot improving brokers**: Identify brokers with a low NILR that have shown improvement over different periods (1 year, 2 years, 5 years).
- **Evaluate cost-effectiveness**: Analyze brokers with consistently high brokerage percentages to determine the most cost-effective partnerships.
- **Support strategic decision-making**: Use interactive features to drill down into broker details and adjust underwriting strategies based on real-time data.

Related Scenarios

- You are a retail manager tracking sales, inventory turnover, and customer satisfaction across multiple stores.
- You are a hospital administrator monitoring patient flow, wait times, and treatment outcomes to enhance care quality.
- You are a supply chain manager analyzing supplier delivery times, defect rates, and order fulfillment.
- You are a sales director measuring team performance metrics such as deal closures, response times, and customer retention.

How People Use the Dashboard

The Dashboard Components

Underwriters use this insurance dashboard extensively to gain insight into broker performance, specifically higher profit and/or lower risk, and make informed decisions. The dashboard provides a comprehensive view of various key metrics and offers multiple interactive features that allow underwriters to drill down into the data for deeper analysis. There are BANs across the top of the dashboard (Figure 21.1), giving the reader the headline, with the key performance indicators.

FIGURE 21.1 BANs with context, showing the key performance indicators along with an up or down arrow to indicate performance of the KPI against the prior year.

The BANs provide not only the key information at a glance but also additional context for the numbers. The slate blue text and up or down arrows indicate performance that improved from the prior year. For example, GWP, Live Policies, and NILR are all up over the prior year. Orange text and up or down arrows indicate worse performance. Notice that the color is consistent with better or worse performance, with slate blue indicating improvement and orange flagging worse performance. This is important because in some cases "better" (slate blue) is a lower value, and in other cases "worse" (orange) is a higher value. This use of color is key to helping the audience quickly understand the BANs in context.

Note that all of the important metrics from each of these charts make up the BANs at the top of the dashboard (Figure 21.2).

Interactive Features

The dashboard has several interactive features that allow the user to explore the data. For example,

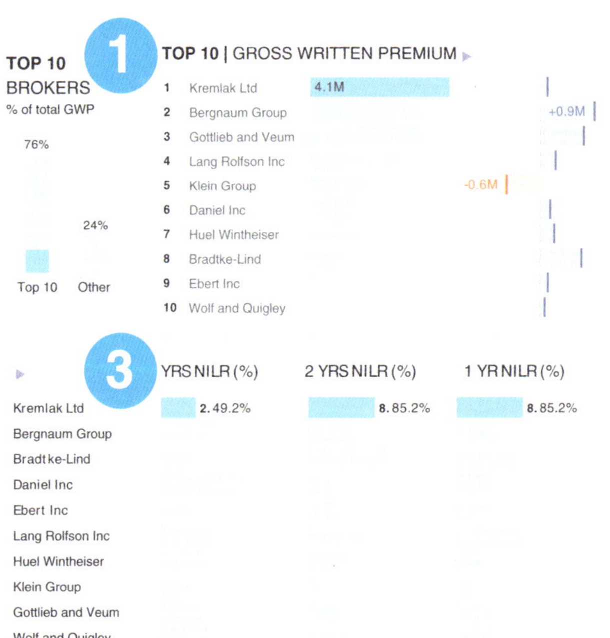

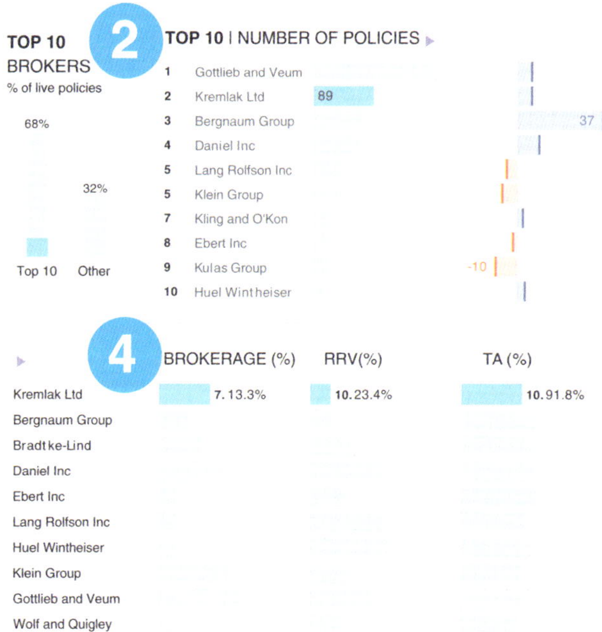

FIGURE 21.2 Four main charts of the dashboard.

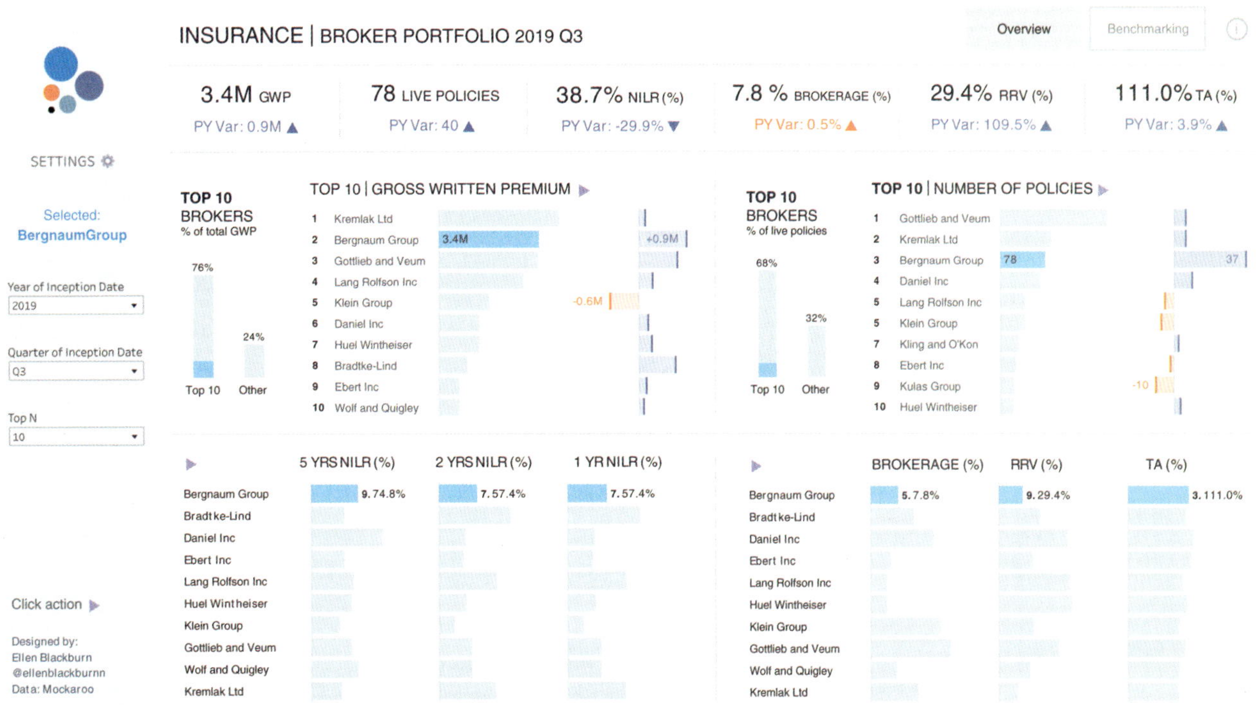

FIGURE 21.3 Dashboard with the Bergnaum Group selected and highlighted.

the user can select any company listed in any of the four charts, and that selection will change the selected company and the highlight color throughout the visualization. Selecting the Bergnaum Group changes the dashboard from the original Kremlak Ltd selection and highlight to the Bergnaum Group (Figure 21.3).

The dashboard also has a left pane that gives the user several options for changing the time period of the dashboard view. There is a drop-down menu for the year and quarter of the inception date and a drop-down menu for the Top N, allowing the reader to change to the Top 10, 20, or 30 in two main bar charts (Figure 21.4). This is a nice feature, as the

FIGURE 21.4 Navigation pane on the left side of the dashboard allowing the user to change the time period of the dashboard and the Top N.

Top 10 bars fit on the dashboard without scroll bars, which makes it very clean and clear. If the user needs to see the Top 20 or Top 30, then they can change that option as needed and scroll to the additional companies in the list.

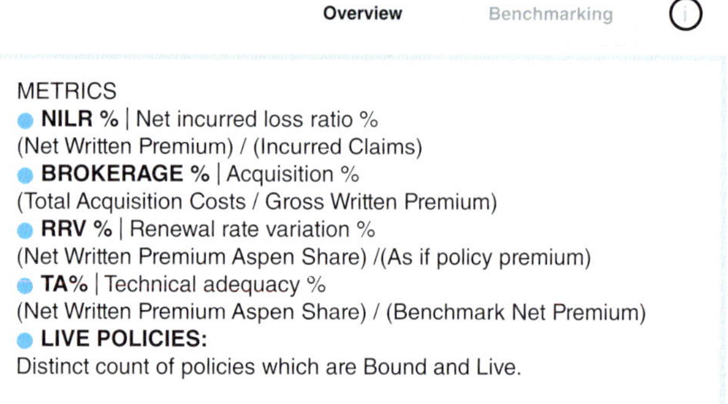

FIGURE 21.5 Information icon providing details for the definitions and formulas for the key metrics used on the dashboard.

Information Icon

The information icon in the top-right corner of the dashboard provides a great description of the terms used in the dashboard, as well as the actual formulas for how they are calculated (Figure 21.5).

Why This Works

Well Organized and Designed to a Grid

The dashboard is organized well, with the settings menu on the left side and navigation in the top-right corner. In addition, the placement of the elements on the dashboard is **designed to a grid**. It is a basic four-quadrant dashboard with BANs across the top with all elements aligned both vertically and horizontally. The horizontal and vertical lines add to this very clear grid design (Figure 21.6).

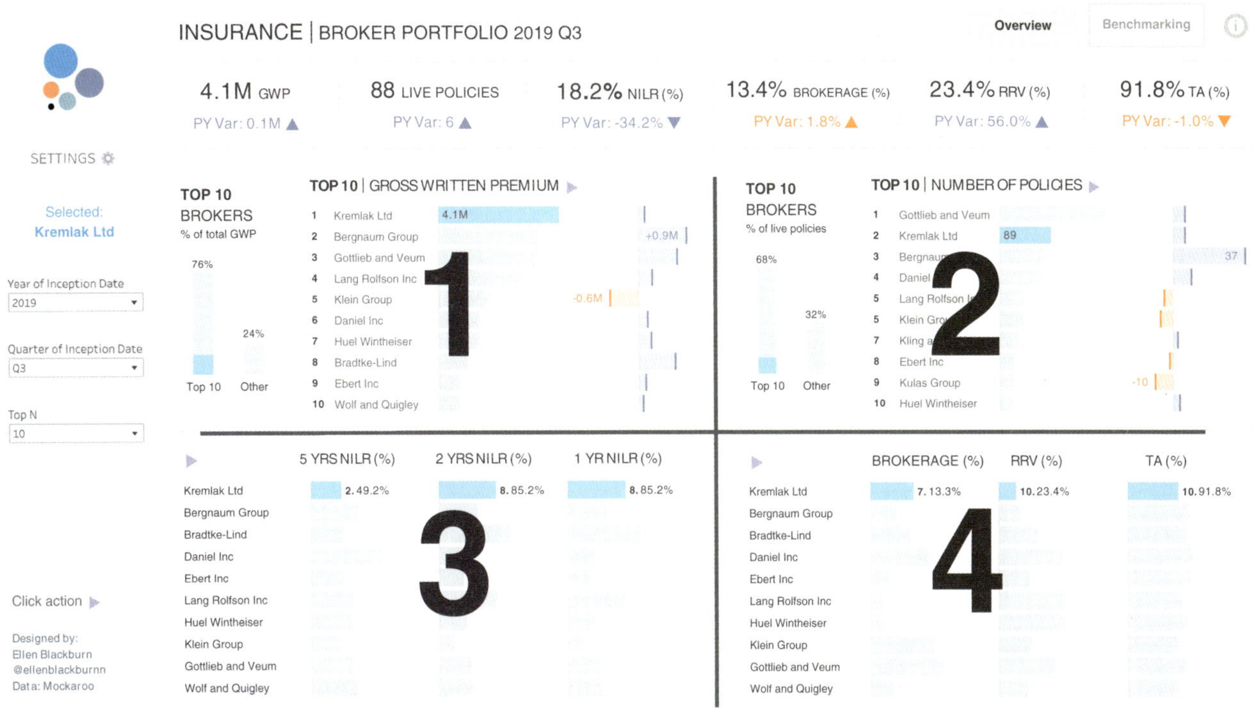

FIGURE 21.6 A traditional four-quadrant dashboard that is designed to a grid.

I generally prefer not to use divider lines on my dashboards. You can design dashboards to a grid without any additional elements added, so the additional divider lines here aren't really necessary. However, Ellen took great care to ensure that the divider lines aren't dominating the visual design of the dashboard. Notice in Figure 21.6 how these divider lines are very thin, use a muted gray, and are not fully connected. By leveraging the Gestalt principles of closure and proximity to visually organize the dashboard elements, the dashboard is clean and uncluttered and avoids having every element "boxed in."

BANs with Context Highlight the Key Metrics

The use of BANs provides a summary or "headline" for the dashboard (Figure 21.7). This makes it easy to see the key metrics for the selected broker, scanning across the top of the dashboard, right where readers will typically start reading.

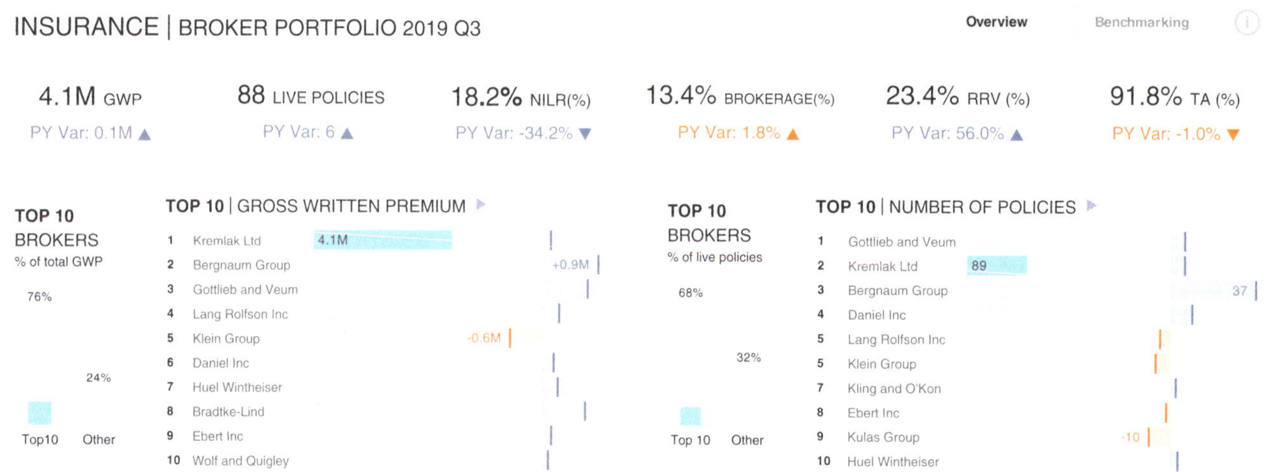

FIGURE 21.7 BANs with context, showing the key performance indicators along with an up or down arrow to indicate performance of the KPI against the prior year with Kremlak Ltd selected.

Simple Use of Color and Good Font Contrast

The dashboard effectively balances complexity and simplicity in its use of color. Despite color encoding multiple variables, the design remains clean and cohesive. For instance, blue highlights brokers on the bar charts and stacked bar charts. As mentioned previously, the color remains consistent with performance, even when "better" (slate blue) corresponds to a lower value in some cases, and "worse" (orange) represents a lower value in others. This double encoding, using color along with the up/down triangles, enhances clarity. Additionally, the same color scheme is applied consistently across all dashboard elements, like the diverging bar charts that visualize variance by broker, ensuring a seamless user experience (Figure 21.8).

The dashboard's effective use of font contrast enhances readability and hierarchy. The main title, "Insurance," is presented in bold, all-caps, commanding attention. In contrast, the dashboard name, "Broker Portfolio 2019 Q3," uses a different font size, subtly differentiating its importance (Figure 21.9). This thoughtful typography extends seamlessly into the BANs and chart titles, while the lower-level font is a more subdued font style and is reserved for labels and supporting text, maintaining a clear visual structure throughout.

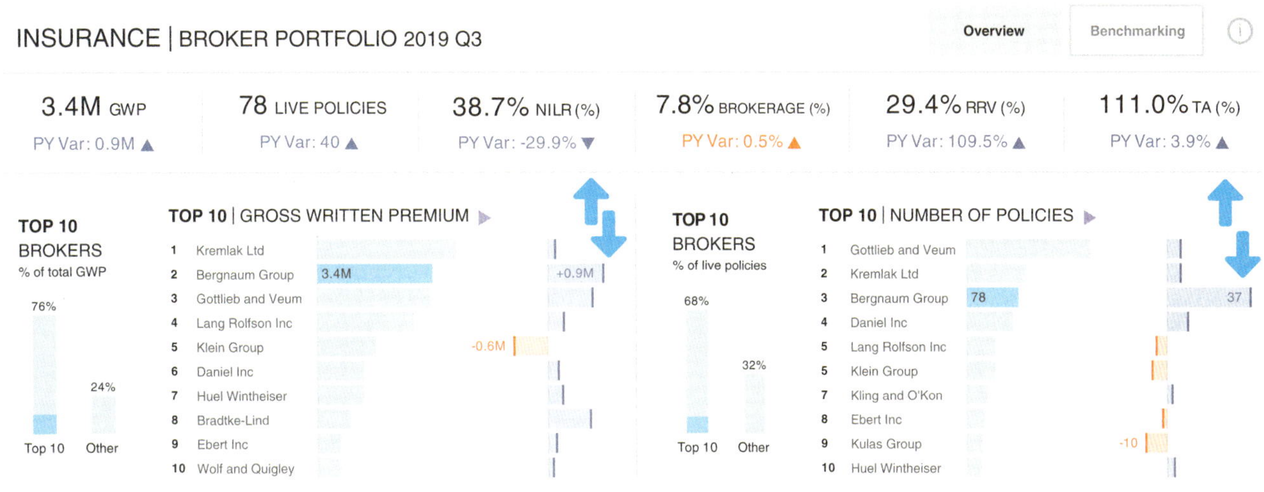

FIGURE 21.8 Top 10 brokers as a bar chart and diverging bar charts showing the prior year variance for each broker with Bergnaum Group selected.

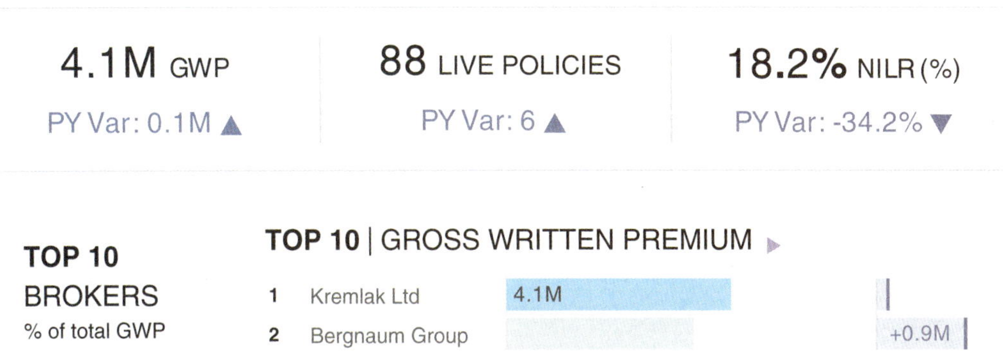

FIGURE 21.9 The use of font contrast in various parts of the dashboard.

The design of the bar charts emphasizes clarity and consistency. The standard bar charts use a single color with clear labeling for the selected broker, maintaining a clean and focused look. The diverging bar charts introduces a subtle variation with more opaque bars and line caps at the ends, adhering to the slate blue and orange color scheme for positive and negative movements, independent of broker selection. The stacked bar chart further enhances understanding by showing the selected broker's share as a percentage of the top 10 brokers, juxtaposed against another chart displaying the remaining brokers outside the top 10, offering a comprehensive comparison.

Deeper Analysis through Broker Benchmarking

The dashboard navigation enhances user experience by enabling drill-downs into a Benchmarking section, leading to a detailed time-series view of the selected broker. Consistency is maintained by carrying over the original color scheme.

To emphasize the selected quarter, Ellen cleverly introduced a dark gray highlight, contrasting it against the light gray of the other quarters (Figure 21.10). This subtle yet effective design choice ensures the selected data point stands out, guiding the user's

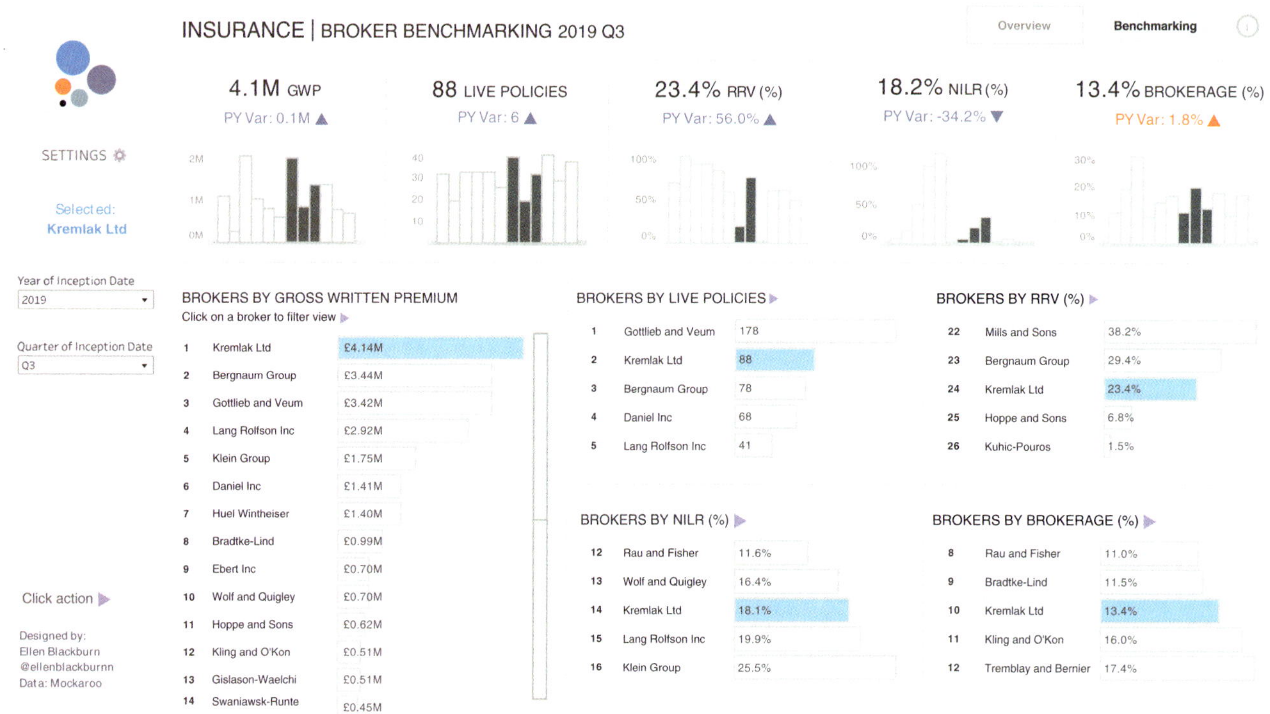

FIGURE 21.10 Broker Benchmarking dashboard view showing the selected broker with 12-month time-series data and the selected quarter highlighted in dark gray.

focus without conflicting with the overall color scheme or disrupting the overall visual harmony.

Process

The spark of this dashboard was dual purpose. First, it was to meet an immediate business need, that, is for underwriters at the insurance company to gain insight into the performance of the insurance brokers. Second, the dashboard would showcase Tableau's capabilities within the company. Originating from a departmental initiative, the project was aimed to demonstrate its potential value and to encourage broader adoption across the organization.

Internal presentations and training sessions were the initial methods for promoting awareness and usage. Developed by a single technical contributor (Ellen) over the course of four weeks, the dashboard was refined through feedback from a very small group of stakeholders and user tests. As is common in consulting work, Ellen was brought in for this specific project, and once that project was completed, she moved on to other projects at other companies. The long-term impact of this dashboard is unknown, but the project successfully demonstrated how tools like Tableau could enhance business processes and inspire similar initiatives in other departments, and she received positive feedback at the end of the project.

Top-Down vs. Bottom-Up Deployments

Deciding between a top-down or bottom-up approach for deploying new software in the enterprise has long been a topic of debate. There are pros and cons with each approach, so it's not as simple as one is always better than the other. However, I have had good success with the bottom-up approach.

Starting small with a focused project in one department is a great way to build momentum for a new dashboard or tool. By tackling a specific business problem and showing clear value to a group, for example, the underwriters, you can create a solid proof of concept. This approach makes it easier to refine the dashboard as you gather feedback, ensuring it truly meets users' needs (see Chapters 5 and 6).

For a tool deployment, Tableau in this case, this approach proves its value and gets users on board. It can naturally grow to reach more people in the department and eventually other parts of the organization. This kind of bottom-up approach works very well because people see the benefits firsthand, making them more likely to embrace it and support it. In addition, it avoids the pushback that sometimes comes with top-down rollouts, leading to smoother implementation and a higher likelihood of adoption.

A Bottom-Up Tableau Deployment (Jeffrey Shaffer)

I had a similar experience with an enterprise deployment in 2011. I was leading a team of data analytics professionals, and we used a tool (Tableau) in this small group. We built out a few dashboards for the operations group in the company. The number of dashboards and usage grew over a short period. The following year, when it came time to present and discuss an enterprise deployment across the entire company, the vice president of sales saw what we had built for the vice president of operations, and together they fully supported and helped push for enterprise adoption of Tableau across the entire organization. I was also involved in an enterprise-wide Slack deployment, which followed a very different path. It was implemented with a top-down approach, and it was never fully adopted. Over time, the number of licenses was reduced based on the lack of usage, and eventually the tool was dropped entirely.

If deploying with a top-down approach, be aware that different departments may have different goals and/or requirements for tools and applications (reference personas in Part I), so achieving a focused vision at the enterprise can be a major challenge.

According to the International Data Corporation (IDC)[2], the major barrier to a top-down approach is "getting senior executives to choose a strategy and stick to it." They found the barriers of the bottom-up approach to be, "lack of support from IT, lack of centralized budget, multiple systems to manage and sources of truth, and training and adoption."

Notice that many of these barriers are things we discussed about dashboard adoption in Part I.

Author Commentary

STEVE: If Apple sold business dashboards, I think they would look something like this. In addition to the superb functionality there are subtle things that make for a delightful experience.

Here are two examples. Consider the vertical lines that accentuate the end points for the performance over/under the previous year. You could certainly just have the bars pointing left and right,

[2]Transforming Enterprise Work Execution: An IDC InfoBrief, Sponsored by Smartsheet, October 2018. dtdbook.com/link27

but the lines draw your attention to these bars. Also consider how Ellen uses lines to group and separate items on the dashboards. I've worked with Jeff for over a decade, and he tends to be "team white space only" and I'm "team lines and rules." I think Ellen's thin, divider lines present a terrific middle ground that leverages Gestalt techniques without weighing down the dashboard with heavy borders.

Chapter 22

Banking Executive Financial Dashboard

Will Perkins

Original Dashboard designer: Will Perkins.

Organization: Large bank in the United States.

How This Dashboard Delivers: The dashboard is a decision-making tool designed to provide the flexibility needed to show tailored displays of the data on demand.

Audience: C-level executives and business leaders within a large bank.

Tools: Tableau.

Timeline: The time from spark to initial release was six weeks.

Note: This dashboard has been re-created using fake data to anonymize.

URL: dtdbook.com/link28

Chapter Author: Jeffrey Shaffer

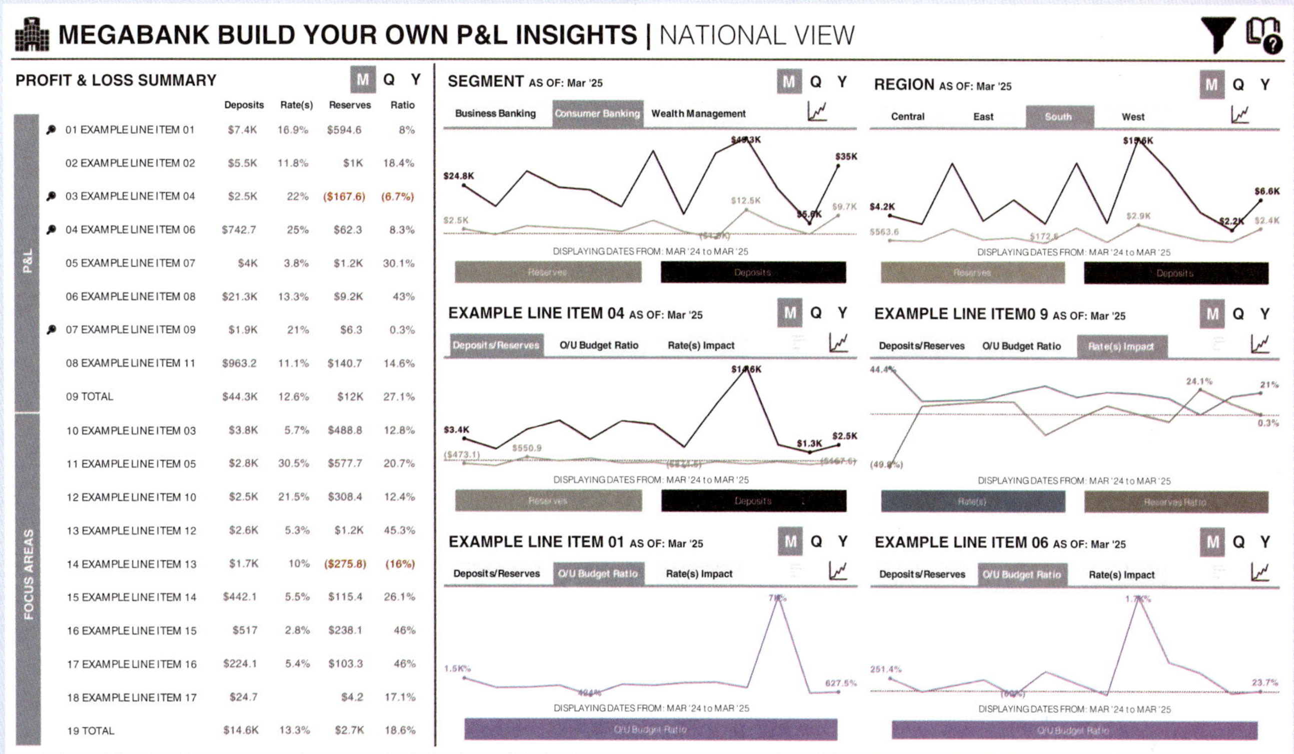

		Deposits	Rate(s)	Reserves	Ratio
P&L	01 EXAMPLE LINE ITEM 01	$7.4K	16.9%	$594.6	8%
	02 EXAMPLE LINE ITEM 02	$5.5K	11.8%	$1K	18.4%
	03 EXAMPLE LINE ITEM 04	$2.5K	22%	($167.6)	(6.7%)
	04 EXAMPLE LINE ITEM 06	$742.7	25%	$62.3	8.3%
	05 EXAMPLE LINE ITEM 07	$4K	3.8%	$1.2K	30.1%
	06 EXAMPLE LINE ITEM 08	$21.3K	13.3%	$9.2K	43%
	07 EXAMPLE LINE ITEM 09	$1.9K	21%	$6.3	0.3%
	08 EXAMPLE LINE ITEM 11	$963.2	11.1%	$140.7	14.6%
	09 TOTAL	$44.3K	12.6%	$12K	27.1%
FOCUS AREAS	10 EXAMPLE LINE ITEM 03	$3.8K	5.7%	$488.8	12.8%
	11 EXAMPLE LINE ITEM 05	$2.8K	30.5%	$577.7	20.7%
	12 EXAMPLE LINE ITEM 10	$2.5K	21.5%	$308.4	12.4%
	13 EXAMPLE LINE ITEM 12	$2.6K	5.3%	$1.2K	45.3%
	14 EXAMPLE LINE ITEM 13	$1.7K	10%	($275.8)	(16%)
	15 EXAMPLE LINE ITEM 14	$442.1	5.5%	$115.4	26.1%
	16 EXAMPLE LINE ITEM 15	$517	2.8%	$238.1	46%
	17 EXAMPLE LINE ITEM 16	$224.1	5.4%	$103.3	46%
	18 EXAMPLE LINE ITEM 17	$24.7		$4.2	17.1%
	19 TOTAL	$14.6K	13.3%	$2.7K	18.6%

Big Picture

You are a C-level executive at a major financial institution. Your role involves making high-stakes decisions based on complex financial data such as deposits, reserves, ratios, and rates that ultimately tie to the P&L. You need a tool that not only provides you with the necessary data but also allows you to customize and drill down into specific details such as business segment or geographic region whenever required. The goal is to have a dashboard that is as dynamic as the decisions you make.

This dashboard is designed to give you the power to interact with financial data in real time. Whether you need to analyze profit and loss, track key performance indicators (KPIs), or compare current performance against historical data, this tool is built to adapt to your needs. You can easily switch between different views, update parameters, and customize the charts to focus on the data points that matter most to you.

Specifics

As a user, you need the ability to:

- **Select time intervals:** Easily switch between monthly, quarterly, and yearly views.
- **Customize charts:** Dynamically change the type of charts displayed based on your current focus.
- **Apply filters to refine the data:** Focus on specific regions, business lines, or product categories.
- **Adapt views:** The dashboard adjusts automatically based on the data you select, allowing you to see the most relevant information.

Related Scenarios

- You are an operations manager needing a customizable dashboard to oversee inventory levels, sales performance by region or store, and customer foot traffic data, but you also need the ability to drill down into specifics such as sales trends or product performance.
- You are a hospital administrator needing a dashboard for real-time, customized views of department-specific metrics like patient wait times and operating room utilization.
- You are a sales director and need a dashboard showing an overview of total revenue but with specifics like regional and team performance and client-specific revenue.

How People Use This Dashboard

Executives use this dashboard to ensure alignment with organizational objectives, reviewing metrics to gauge progress. The customizable viewing options allow them to tailor the display of data to their specific needs, focusing on the most relevant metrics or adjusting the scope of information for different strategic views, including time periods, business segments, and even chart types. This flexibility empowers leaders to make informed, data-driven decisions efficiently.

The dashboard is embedded within other applications. This encourages adoption, minimizes friction, and enhances the user experience.

Why This Works

Impact

This dashboard was a major innovation within the bank, providing executives with a tool that was both powerful and user-friendly. Will Perkins and his team designed the dashboard to ensure that it met the rigorous demands of financial reporting. The dashboard's dynamic capabilities have made it a vital tool for executives because it allows them to make data-informed decisions quickly and efficiently.

> This dashboard has opened up a lot of doors for us, allowing our team to present complex financial data in a way that's both understandable and actionable. It's been a game-changer in how we interact with our data.
>
> —*Will Perkins*

Before implementing this dashboard solution, the CFO faced a challenge: she received multiple P&L reports from seven sub-lines of business (LOB) CFOs, all in slightly different formats. This inconsistency made it difficult to read the financials quickly, and she often struggled to determine which metrics needed focus based on the report alone. One day, she asked, "Is there a way I could just have certain standard drill-downs but click on the P&L items to make one of the charts change dynamically?" That question sparked an idea – how could they solve her frustration while driving consistency? Also, Will knew if he could design one drill-down chart like that, he could design all of them the same way.

Will developed a standardized dashboard and data model structure that streamlined P&L reporting while allowing flexibility to adapt to changing business priorities. The system dynamically updates six key financial focus areas with the feedback of the LOB leaders, enabling end users to drill down into relevant metrics as conditions shift. One month, the focus might be deposit growth and declining loan originations due to a Fed rate cut; the next, it could shift to hiring trends or ATM usage.

What makes this system powerful is its adaptability. While it provides default views based on current business needs, users can swap metrics with a single mouse click and explore trends. By prioritizing a data-first approach, Will gave leadership a tool that simplifies reporting and enhances decision-making.

Build Your Own Adventure

When we think of an interactive dashboard, we typically talk about interacting with the data in a dashboard such as clicking something to filter or highlight. This dashboard includes those elements of interactivity but goes deeper than most interactive dashboards. It offers the ability to build your own adventure. The user can control filters, add/remove metrics from the charts, change the time frame displayed, slice the data by different segments, and even change the chart types. This gives users the ability to see what they want to see, how they want to see it, and drill down as needed to explore different aspects of the data in different ways. It's important to note that these dashboard users must have a high level of data literacy.

> "The real success of this dashboard comes from its ability to let the end-user dictate what they see and interact with. It's not just about presenting data; it's about giving users the tools to explore and understand that data in a way that makes sense to them."
>
> —*Will Perkins*

Select a line item from the P&L. Want to see the trend over time? Click the line chart icon and toggle between the different time frames. Need to see the detailed numbers for more precision or explore a region? Click the table icon and see the data in a table for the East region (Figure 22.1).

Alternatively, you can see deposits and reserves by year as a line chart or dive deeper into the analysis and see a year-over-year comparison as a bar chart (Figure 22.2).

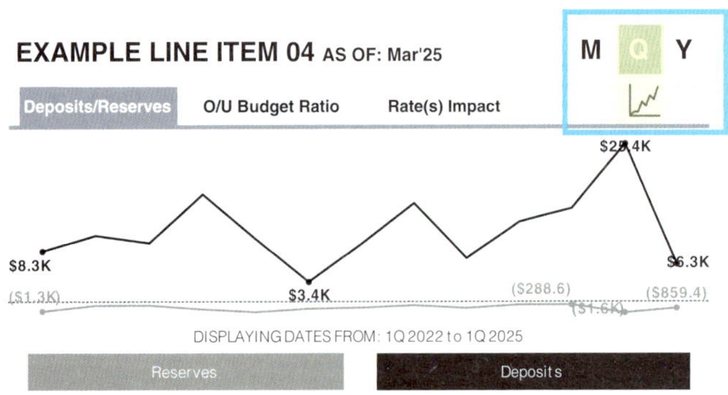

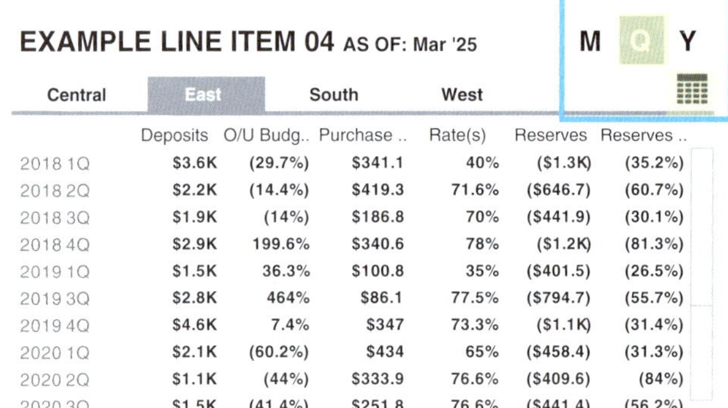

EXAMPLE LINE ITEM 04 AS OF: Mar '25

M Q Y

Central | East | South | West

	Deposits	O/U Budg..	Purchase ..	Rate(s)	Reserves	Reserves ..
2018 1Q	$3.6K	(29.7%)	$341.1	40%	($1.3K)	(35.2%)
2018 2Q	$2.2K	(14.4%)	$419.3	71.6%	($646.7)	(60.7%)
2018 3Q	$1.9K	(14%)	$186.8	70%	($441.9)	(30.1%)
2018 4Q	$2.9K	199.6%	$340.6	78%	($1.2K)	(81.3%)
2019 1Q	$1.5K	36.3%	$100.8	35%	($401.5)	(26.5%)
2019 3Q	$2.8K	464%	$86.1	77.5%	($794.7)	(55.7%)
2019 4Q	$4.6K	7.4%	$347	73.3%	($1.1K)	(31.4%)
2020 1Q	$2.1K	(60.2%)	$434	65%	($458.4)	(31.3%)
2020 2Q	$1.1K	(44%)	$333.9	76.6%	($409.6)	(84%)
2020 3Q	$1.5K	(41.4%)	$251.8	76.6%	($441.4)	(56.2%)

FIGURE 22.1 P&L line item 4 selected with a quarterly view of deposits and then drilling down to see the East region in a detailed table.

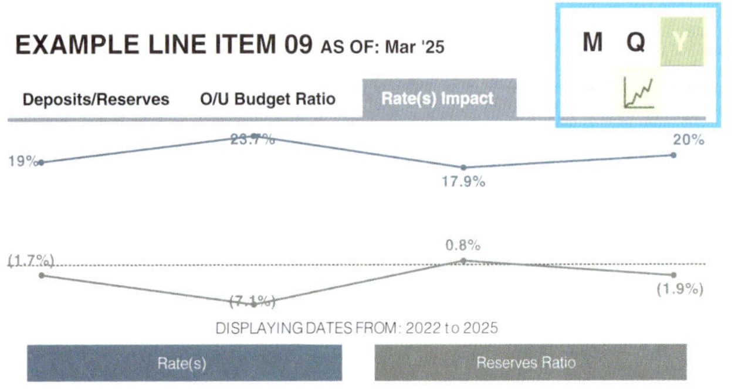

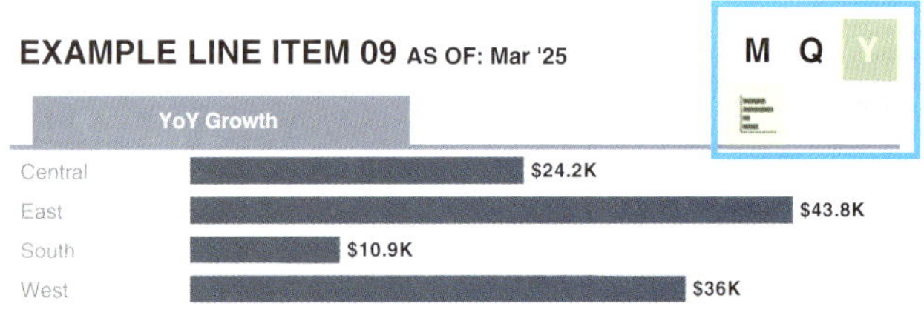

FIGURE 22.2 P&L line item 9 showing deposits by year in a line chart and year-over-year growth by region in a bar chart.

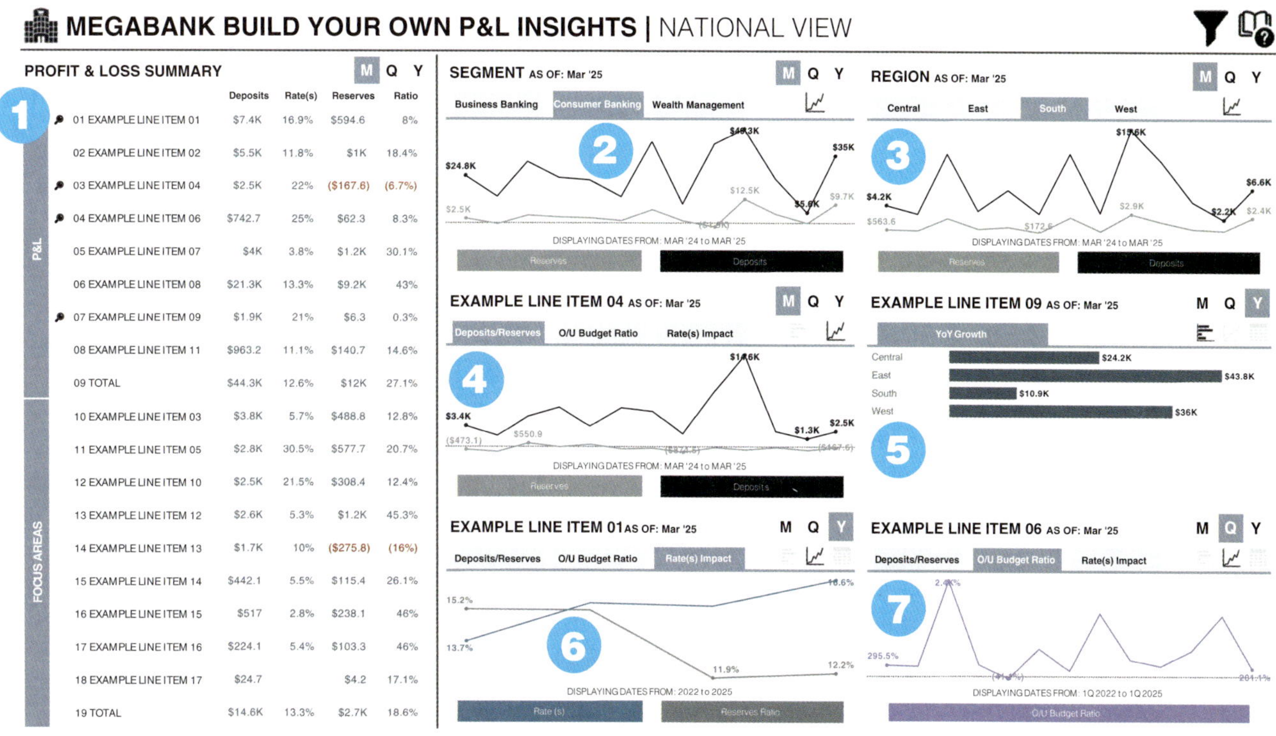

FIGURE 22.3 Dashboard example of the different views that are possible.

Observe the various combinations of views in Figure 22.3, showcasing just one example of the countless possibilities available to the user.

Everything in **bold** is a selection by the user.

1. **P&L Summary** displays **monthly** data in **a table** with **Line Items 1, 4, 6, and 9** selected (magnifier glass indicator)
2. **Segment** displays **monthly** data as a **line chart** for **Consumer Banking**.
3. **Region** displays **monthly** data as a **line chart** for the **South**.
4. **Line Item 4** (selected from P&L Summary) displays **monthly** data as a **line chart** for **Deposits/Returns**.
5. **Line Item 9** (selected from P&L Summary) displays **yearly** data as a **bar chart** as **Year over Year Growth**
6. **Line Item 1** (selected from P&L Summary) displays **yearly** data as a **line chart** for **Rate(s) Impact**.

7. **Line Item 6** (selected from P&L Summary) displays **quarterly** data as a **line chart** for **O/U Budget Ratio**.

The colored boxes at the bottom of each chart act as a color legend: black for deposits, gray for reserves, and purple for the budget ratio. They also act as a highlight feature; click Deposits, and any view that is showing deposits will highlight (Figure 22.4).

Clear Direction on How to Use

This dashboard is rich with interactive features that allow the user to slice and filter the data and change the view. Will provides a creative solution to help guide the user. An overlay provides detailed instructions to the reader on how to use the visualization, while at the same time keeping the dashboard uncluttered and free from additional instructional text (Figure 22.5). This is a great solution because new users can see exactly where to click, but seasoned users aren't burdened with additional text that is always on the dashboard.

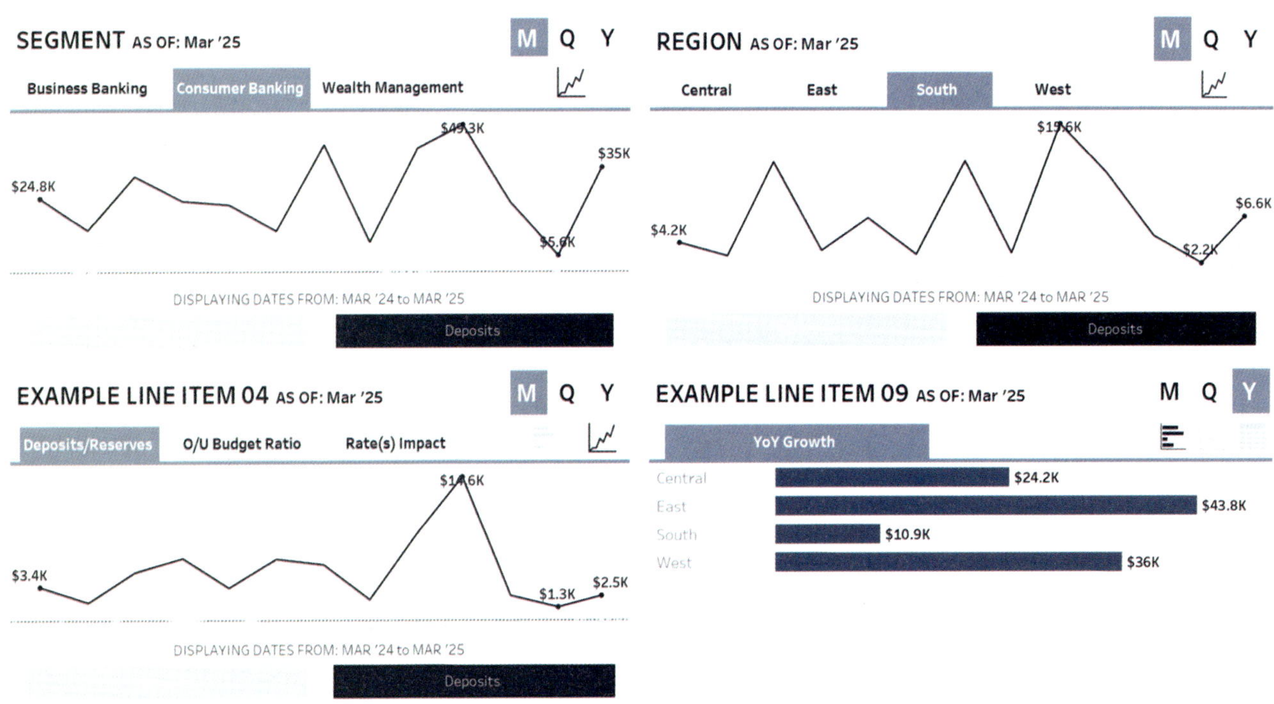

FIGURE 22.4 Deposits selected on the dashboard that highlights any view where Deposits is being used.

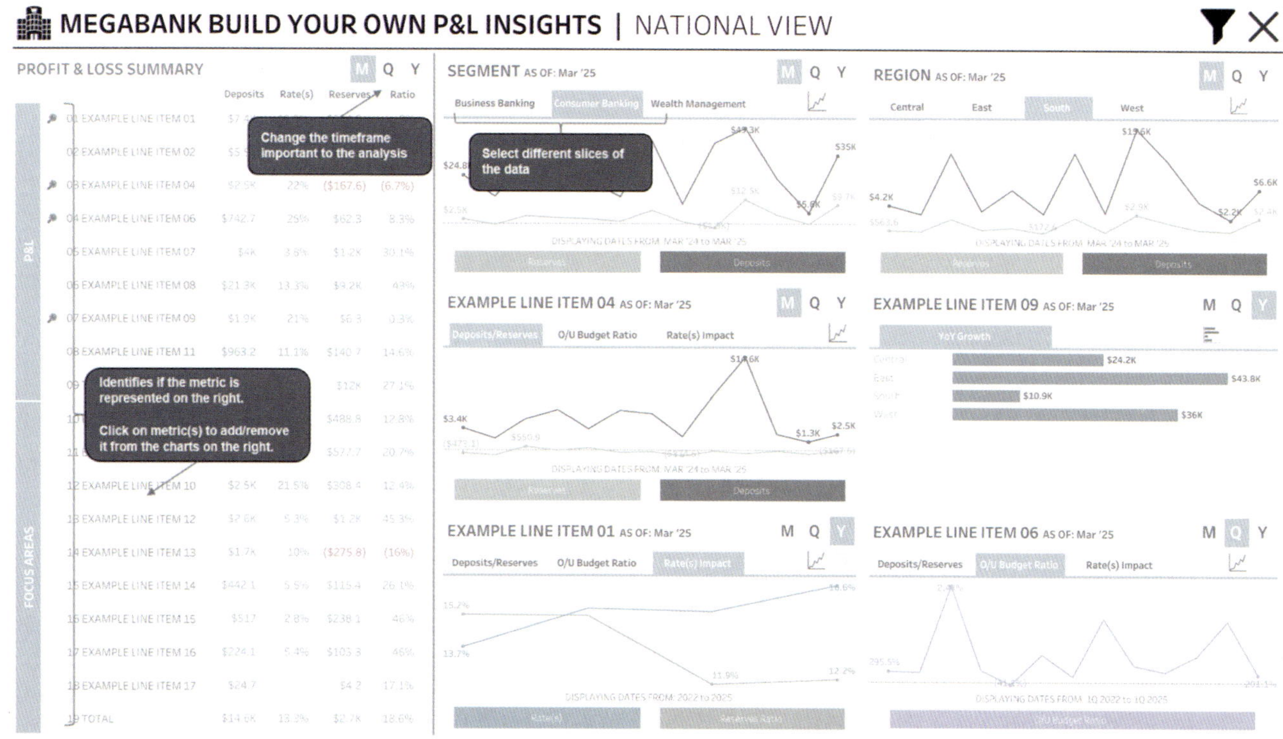

FIGURE 22.5 Overlay of instructions on dashboard showing user how to use the dashboard.

Process

Background

The development of this dashboard began with a clear directive from the CFO:

> "I want to have a P&L with 6 charts next to it. I want 5 of those charts to focus on my key metrics. The 6th chart should be dynamic, and change based on whatever metric is selected from the P&L. I also need it to have monthly, quarterly, and yearly views."
>
> —*request from CFO*

In a nutshell, the CFO wanted a profit-and-loss tool that was flexible and powerful.

The project kicked off with a thorough analysis of the existing reporting tools and identified key areas where improvements could be made.

User-Centric Design

The design process was highly collaborative, involving a close partnership with end users to ensure the final product was aligned with their needs. By focusing on flexibility and usability, the team succeeded in creating a tool that not only meets current needs but is also adaptable for future requirements.

The dashboard and the supporting data structure offer flexible configuration in several key areas:

- **Default settings:** The initial parameters for the dashboard are controlled by a secondary data source. So if anyone needs to modify these default settings, such as the starting filters or metrics, the dashboard designer can simply update the corresponding entries in the data source.
- **Interactive exploration:** Beyond the default setup, users can explore elements from a sidebar. This feature allows the user to drill down into any item number of the P&L to uncover deeper correlations or patterns, tailoring the display to show exactly what they find most relevant.
- **Data visualization options:** There are data structure definitions to support various visualization formats like line charts for time-series data, bars for categorical comparisons, and tables for detailed views. The dashboard designer can add or remove these elements from the data structure to enable or disable their views. This eliminates the need for additional dashboard design if a user asks to see a new metric over time or by category.

Will emphasized the critical importance of understanding the end user's needs through a "What, So What, and Now What" framework during requirements gathering.

"What? So What? Now What?"

The "What? So What? Now What?" framework is a tool that provides a structured approach to delivering information and engaging an audience. Here's a breakdown of the three elements:

1. **What:**
   - This is the core information or the facts.
   - It answers the question, "What happened?" or "What is this about?"
   - Example: "Our sales of this product increased by 20% last quarter."
2. **So What:**
   - This part explains the significance of the information.
   - It answers the question, "Why should the audience care?" or "How does this impact them?"
   - Example: "This growth indicates that our new marketing strategy is effective."
3. **Now What:**
   - This element focuses on the future, the next steps.
   - It answers, "What should we do differently?" or "What lessons can we apply moving forward?"
   - Example: "If we apply this same marketing strategy across all of our products, we could increase all product sales."

The framework ensures the message is clear, meaningful, and connected to the audience's interests, making it a powerful tool for communication in various contexts.

> "Focus on the user; understand their needs, and design with them in mind. That's how you build something truly useful."
>
> —*Will Perkins*

Prototyping and Iterative and Flexible Design Process

Prototyping was done using Tableau, where initial designs were tested and refined. Iterative development involved regular feedback sessions with the executive team, ensuring that each new feature added value.

The iterative design process played a crucial role in the success of the project, allowing for continuous refinement based on real-time feedback from stakeholders. This approach ensured that the final product was both aligned with the initial goals and adaptable to evolving needs. Depending on data availability, access, and other technical roadblocks, they were able to get changes into production very quickly after validation, sometimes in just a few hours. By embracing flexibility throughout the development cycle, the team was able to make necessary adjustments, leading to a dashboard that truly met the end-user's needs.

At the same time, the team struck a careful balance between flexibility and structure in gathering initial requirements. They worked with a spectrum of inputs, from very detailed requests to more open-ended problem statements, which allowed them to explore various solutions and identify the most effective approach. This balance ensured that the dashboard could accommodate both specific user needs and broader, evolving business goals, making it a versatile tool in the organization's toolkit.

Avoiding the "Burger King" Mentality

WILL Perkins highlighted the dangers of the "Burger King" mentality when gathering requirements, where users often expect to "have it their way" by specifying exactly what they think they need. However, his team takes a more collaborative approach, engaging in conversations to dig deeper into the true challenges the users face. Instead of just delivering on surface-level requests, they focus on uncovering and addressing the underlying issues, or root causes, behind those requests. This allows them to create dashboards that solve the core problems, leading to more effective and impactful solutions.

Noteworthy Challenges

One of the main challenges was ensuring that the dashboard could handle the complex and varied data requirements without becoming too cumbersome or difficult to use. The solution was to create a highly modular design, where each component of the dashboard could be independently configured and updated. This modular design also allowed for easy updates and maintenance, ensuring that the dashboard could evolve alongside the business.

Delivery

The first version of the dashboard was delivered in six weeks, and it was met with widespread acclaim from the executive team. The dashboard's success has led to ongoing development, with additional features and capabilities being added based on user feedback.

Author Commentary

STEVE: This is a case study on how to engage with stakeholders. It sounds like Will and his team did a lot of listening and a lot of probing. There are also some clever techniques that had not occurred to me, particularly around default settings and allowing new metrics to be added easily. Instead of hard coding these things into the dashboard Will built an editable configuration file that can turn on and off chart types, drill down functionality, etc. Brilliant.

AMANDA: As someone not accustomed to looking at financial reports daily, this dashboard feels like a lot of information. But the grid structure, interactivity, and simplicity in the chart types keep the display organized and are packed with user-enablement functions for customizing the views. The customization and ways Will has responded to specific user needs makes this dashboard an exceptional example of user-centered design, including probing for root cause challenges that move beyond the surface level data needs from his users. He found creative solutions to address many different requests through his modular approach and crafted something that *works for his users*. And to have gotten to a first release in six weeks? Remarkable.

Chapter 23

E3CI Data Station

Team: Cinzia Bongino (dashboard designer), Federica Guerrini (climate scientist), Alberto Arlandi (developer)

Team: Cinzia Bongino (dashboard designer), Federica Guerrini (climate scientist), Alberto Arlandi (developer).

Organization: The European Extreme Events Climate Index (E3CI), a project by the International Foundation Big Data and Artificial Intelligence for Human Development (IFAB). Implemented by Euro-Mediterranean Center on Climate Change (CMCC), Leithà Gruppo Unipol. Distributed by Hypermeteo, and Radarmeteo. Design and development by Tracce.

URL: https://datastation.climateindex.eu/

How This Dashboard Delivers: Viewers can explore and understand the frequency and distribution of extreme climate events across Europe.

Audience: Anyone interested in understanding climate change could use the dashboard to understand the data. More granular data is available for institutions such as banks and agriculture and research organizations who need the data for advanced modeling.

Team: A cross-discipline team of climate scientists, data analysts, and web developers.

Tools: Initial ideas were developed in a hackathon. For the published dashboard, Figma was used for wireframing and JavaScript for the end result.

Timeline: The hackathon was two days. Turning ideas to the published results took four months.

Chapter Author: Andy Cotgreave

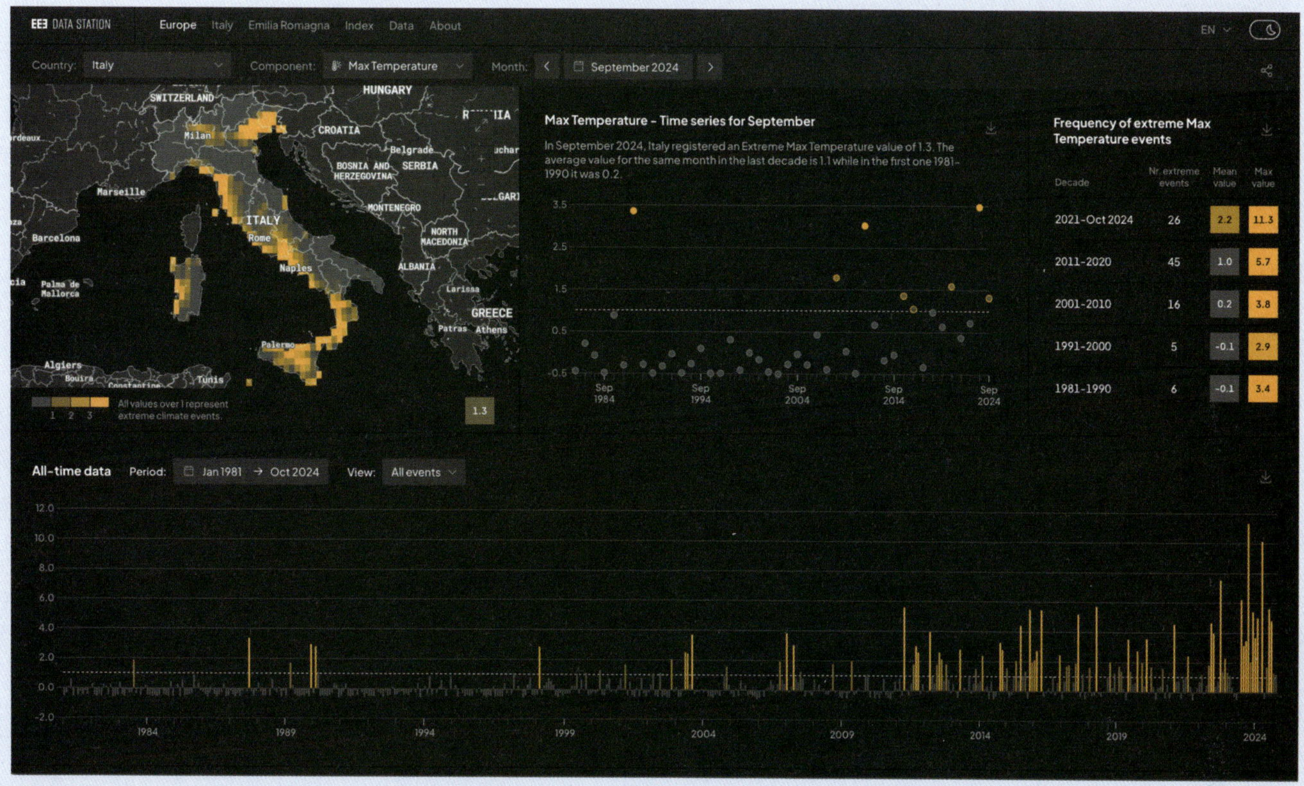
DATA STATION
Europe
Italy
Emilia Romagna
Index
Data
About
EN
Country: Italy
Component: Max Temperature
Month: September 2024
SWITZERLAND
HUNGARY
Milan
CROATIA
Belgrade
BOSNIA AND HERZEGOVINA
SERBIA
Marseille
MONTENEGRO
ITALY
Rome
Barcelona
NORTH MACEDONIA
ALBANIA
Naples
Palma de Mallorca
Larissa
GREECE
Patras
Athens
Palermo
Algiers
Tunis
All values over 1 represent extreme climate events.
1.3
Max Temperature – Time series for September
In September 2024, Italy registered an Extreme Max Temperature value of 1.3. The average value for the same month in the last decade is 1.1 while in the first one 1981–1990 it was 0.2.
Sep 1984
Sep 1994
Sep 2004
Sep 2014
Sep 2024
Frequency of extreme Max Temperature events
Decade
Nr. extreme events
Mean value
Max value
2021–Oct 2024 26 2.2 11.3
2011–2020 45 1.0 5.7
2001–2010 16 0.2 3.8
1991–2000 5 -0.1 2.9
1981–1990 6 -0.1 3.4
All-time data
Period: Jan 1981 → Oct 2024
View: All events
1984
1989
1994
1999
2004
2009
2014
2019
2024

Big Picture

The European Extreme Events Climatic Index (E3CI) enables the analysis and monitoring of extreme meteorological events to allow for the management of the impact of these events.

The E3CI data can be used to understand trends and estimate the climatic changes across Europe. The data covers several types of weather-related hazards, like extreme maximum and minimum temperatures, drought, fire, wind, precipitation, and hail. E3CI creates a monthly snapshot of what has happened in Europe. This dashboard provides an overview of recent and historical trends in these categories at various geographic levels.

Specifics

The E3CI index presents up-to-date climate information organized into three levels: country (all European nations), region (for the 20 Italian regions), and province (only available for the Emilia-Romagna region). The geo-referenced data points, spanning seven components, are updated monthly. The dashboard lets users explore each measure over time and geographically. More granular data is available for purchase for customers who want to have more detail.

Related Scenarios

- You look at demographic distributions across geographies, such as population, political affiliations, religions, or age groups.
- You track disease prevalence in different regions.
- You want to analyze web traffic by region.

How People Use the Dashboard

This dashboard presents the latest data for various administrative units (nation/region/province). There are filters for the specific nation/region/province, the seven components, and month (from 1981 to the present).

When a user chooses a single weather component, the data is displayed four different ways: a map, dot plot, table, and timeline (Figure 23.1 shows the Max Temperature component for Italy in February 2024). Each component is represented as an index, not an actual value. The index ranges from −3 to 3, with a bell curve distribution. This means that the higher (or lower) the value, the more extreme the weather event is; anything over 1 is considered extreme.

The map is divided into grid segments and shows the spatial variation of the index. A dot chart facilitates the comparison of values for the same month over time, and a table lists the frequency of extreme events over all decades since 1980 related to the selected component.

In the lower section, a bar chart shows full historical data for the selected measure.

Users can download data snapshots, save individual charts as images, or embed the dashboard into other sites. The dashboard is fully responsive and

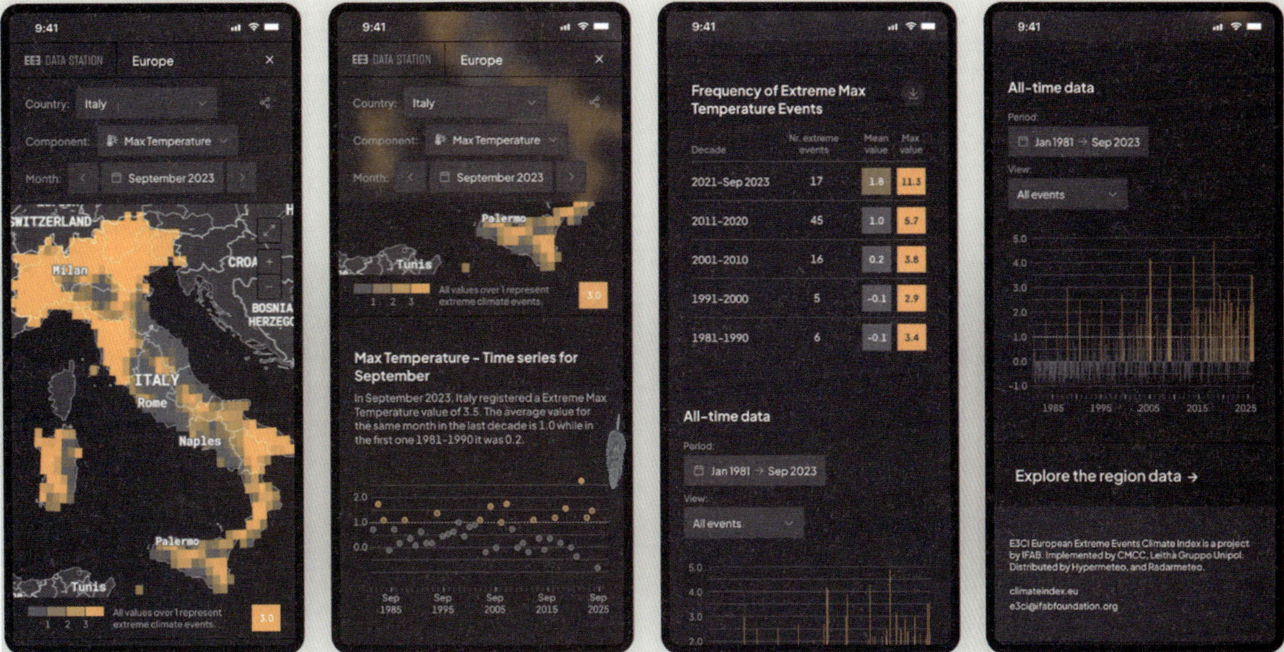

FIGURE 23.1 The mobile view of the E3CI dashboard.

switches to a long-form view on mobile devices, as shown in Figure 23.1.

Why This Works

Accessibility in Mind

To ensure optimal readability in all lighting conditions, there is a dark and light mode on the dashboard (Figure 23.2). The color palettes were chosen to ensure they were effective in both modes.

Gist Over Accuracy: Circles and Squares

If the user selects All from the components list, the view switches to a seven-row beeswarm plot. It shows a full timeline of all events for the selected region (Figure 23.3).

The top row shows Max Temperature extreme events. Circles are sized by the intensity of that event. You can see how the density has increased: Max Temperature events are more frequent, but are not becoming much more intense

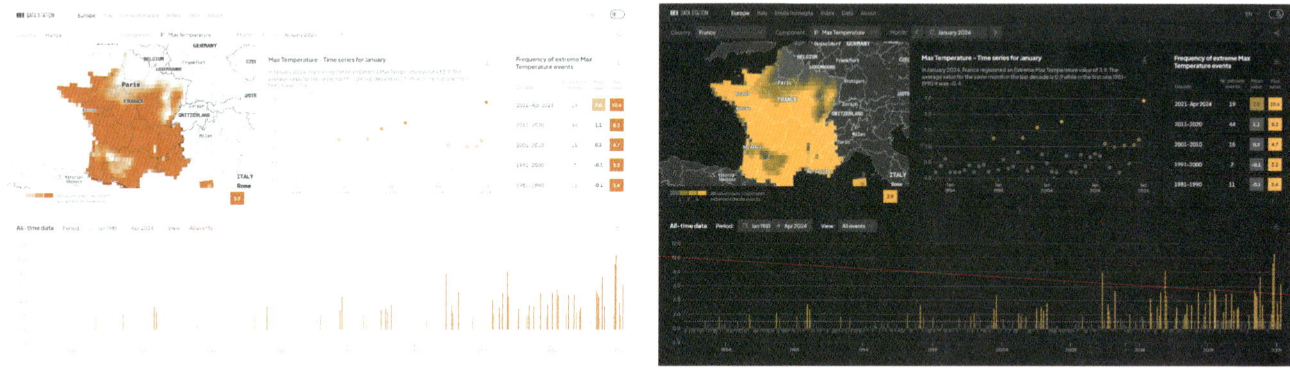

FIGURE 23.2 Light and dark versions of France's max temperature index in January 2024.

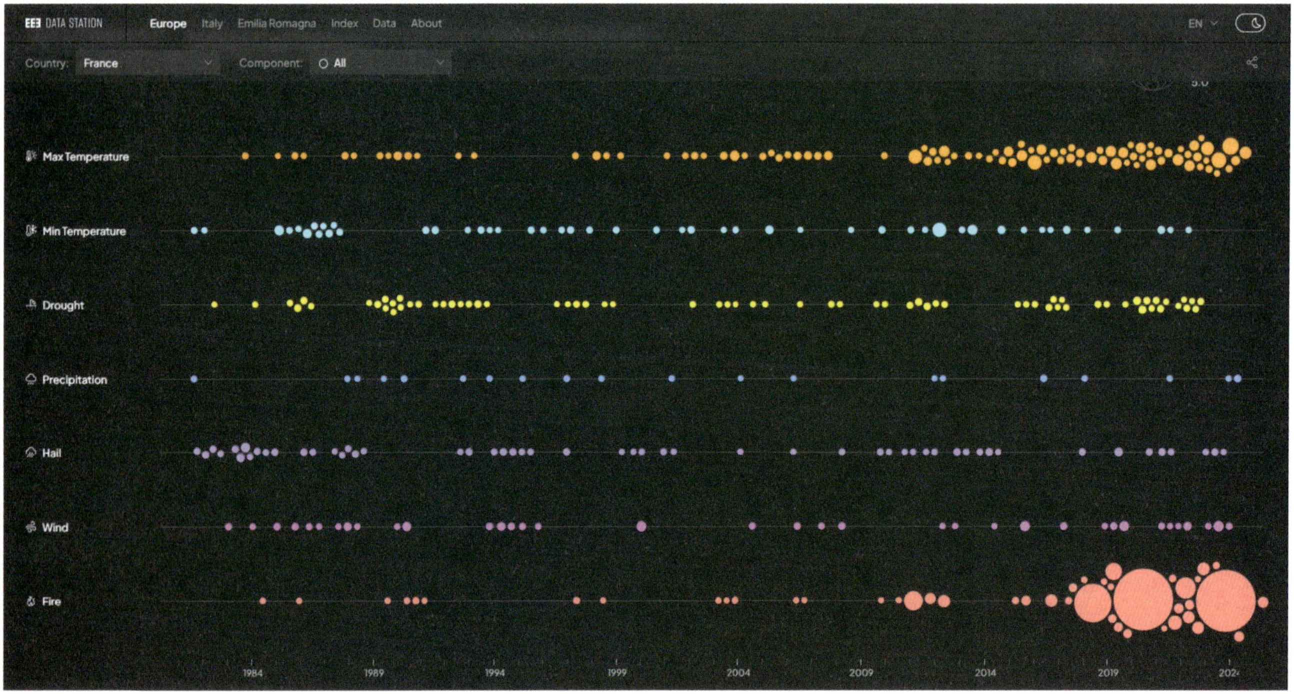

FIGURE 23.3 A bee swarm chart showing all index components for France.

(they're all a similar size). The bottom row, showing the extent of Fire, is also interesting: fires are more frequent and they are also more intense, as shown by the bigger circles.

Data encoded as circles sized by value are hard to decode accurately; we can all see if any circle is *much bigger*, or *much smaller*, than any other, but we cannot accurately define *how* much bigger one circle is compared to another. Look at the three big circles in the bottom right of the Figure 23.3: how much bigger are the larger ones than the smaller ones? It's hard to say.

Bar charts, by contrast, use length to encode data. Research shows that we can very accurately compare different lengths.

So should we always use bars, not bubbles? Did Cinzia make a bad design choice?

Not at all.

First, some of the values are hugely disproportionate to others in the chart. If she had encoded them using bars, they would have totally dominated the display: the extreme bars would be so big, all other bars would be tiny. The bee swarm allows all values to be seen.

Second, she intentionally set out to provide the gist of the individual marks' values. The *primary* goal of this view is to see trends, ebbs, and flows of the indicators over time; this is accurately encoded using position along the x-axis. The *secondary* goal is to add the context about intensity, in this case using a less-accurate encoding. This is a perfectly reasonable choice for any chart you may build.

Every Chart Is a Compromise

ANY choice you make emphasizes one thing at the expense of another. While accuracy is important, it's not always best to prioritize it over the general trends.

A similar design decision was encoding the extreme event frequency section in the top right of the dashboard (Figure 23.4).

Could the value have been a bar chart instead? Cinzia's initial sketches were for a bar chart in this section. Encoding data using length is a good way to allow users to make precise comparisons. The values for France shown on the left of Figure 23.4 certainly would look good in a bar chart, but it's not that simple.

In France, the Fire component maximum values range from 3.3 to 10.6. Check out the values for Cyprus's maximum precipitation on the right of Figure 23.4. The values range from 3.1 to 155.3 mm! In those cases, the outliers would be so long, all the other bars would essentially be invisible; Cinzia felt this would create visual confusion among viewers who aren't familiar with data visualization. She chose to encode the data in a simple table to mitigate this outlier challenge. Tables negate the effects of

Frequency of extreme Precipitation events

Decade	Nr. extreme events	Mean value	Max value
2021-Apr 2024	2	-0.1	3.4
2011-2020	19	2.1	155.3
2001-2010	9	0.0	4.0
1991-2000	13	0.0	3.0
1981-1990	9	-0.0	3.1

Frequency of extreme Max Temperature events

Decade	Nr. extreme events	Mean value	Max value
2021-Apr 2024	19	2.0	10.6
2011-2020	44	1.1	8.3
2001-2010	15	0.2	4.7
1991-2000	7	-0.1	3.3
1981-1990	11	-0.1	3.4

FIGURE 23.4 Could these have been bar charts? The left panel shows max temperature events in France up to April 2024; the right shows extreme precipitation events in Cyprus for the same time period.

outliers (at the expense of visualizing relationships); this was a compromise Cinzia deemed necessary.

When Wireframes Meet Reality

THIS is one reason why being too rigid with wireframes can be problematic: the idealized line or bar chart you sketch and design may not adapt to the actual shape of your data.

Process

An Unusual Beginning: A Hackathon Brings Ideas from Anywhere

The spark for most dashboards comes from an initial set of questions, followed by prototyping. Dashboard designers work closely with stakeholders to develop ideas. This dashboard's spark, however, came from a hackathon.

iFab, the owners of the E3CI data, sought new ways to track extreme events and promote their data. They invited data and climate professionals to come up with new ideas, based on their data for the Italian territory. Participants formed teams of complementary skills. For example, Cinzia, a graphic designer, was partnered with Federica Guerrini, a climate data scientist.

Federica was able to extract the data with Python and immediately visualize the grid-based visualization that characterizes the E3CI index. Together, they looked at how reputable sources present climate data (from forecasts to reports) and quickly realized there were so many "standard" ways to represent weather that it was not easy to choose one. Prioritizing web accessibility over fancy dashboard design, most of the visual models now implemented in the Data Station were already outlined during the 24-hour hackathon.

Following the hackathon, Cinzia was approached to turn the prototype (Figure 23.5) into the final working version we feature in this scenario.

Ideas can come from anywhere, and hackathons are excellent ways to let people with different types of domain expertise bring creative and new ideas to life. Instead of starting with a specific question, curious people can explore data to surface new opportunities.

One word of warning: If a hackathon is designed to discover and launch new ideas, there must be a plan, budget, and resources to follow up and support any chosen ideas.

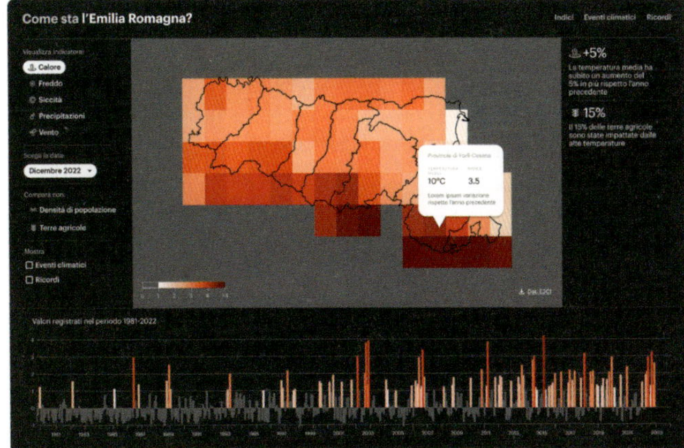

FIGURE 23.5 The hackathon prototype dashboard.

Wireframe? Site Map? Data? Which First

Should you design your dashboard on paper before you get to your data, or should exploring the data be the starting point? We discuss this debate in our process section.

Cinzia's prototyping started by creating a sitemap defining the full path through the various dashboard views. From there, she created ideas and wireframes using Figma. Figma allowed Cinzia to present her ideas to stakeholders so they could approve the early concepts; it is better to discover issues at this stage than later.

One early idea, rejected at this stage, was to use the timeline as a film strip (Figure 23.6). Users could scroll the bar chart in a way similar to the functionality of video editing software, quickly moving from the start to the end of the all-time data. This idea seemed interesting but was quickly discarded because it would not translate well to mobile devices.

When the wireframe was signed off by the client, it was time to design the user interface (UI). Early sketches depicted a "boxed" layout, closing each data visualization with white frames on a gray background. This solution didn't feel quite right: it is quite a common style for dashboards, but it cut out space for the visualization.

Deciding a Color Scheme

An original version of the E3CI index used a red-green diverging palette. People with color

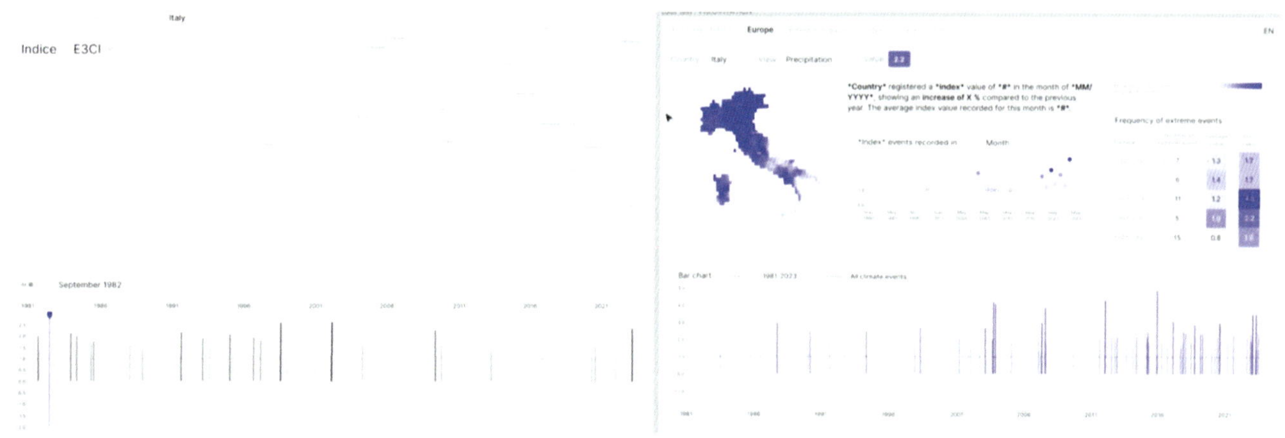

FIGURE 23.6 Rejected early ideas: film strips and boxed layouts.

vision deficiency couldn't distinguish the hues, and it had an arbitrary center point. In short, it didn't work.

As already sketched in the hackathon project, each index component was assigned a specific color that could help identify it. Given that the index is an abstract representation of climate (the values are expressed in numbers, not with degrees, millimeters of rain, hectares or wind speed), a single-hue sequential color bar seemed the best way to represent it. The initial hues for the Data Station were, according to Cinzia, "just out of my heart." This is a valid starting point. Sometimes there are brand or other constraints on your colors, but at other times you can go with what your experience tells you will work.

From her starting point, Cinzia used the Leonardo[1] color tool to iterate on workable palettes that worked in light and dark settings. You can see in Figure 23.7 that the palettes for light and dark backgrounds have different saturation levels. She also did full accessibility tests, again using Leonardo, on the color palettes (Figure 23.8).

FIGURE 23.7 The color palettes for E3CI dashboard.

[1]Leonardo: https://leonardocolor.io/

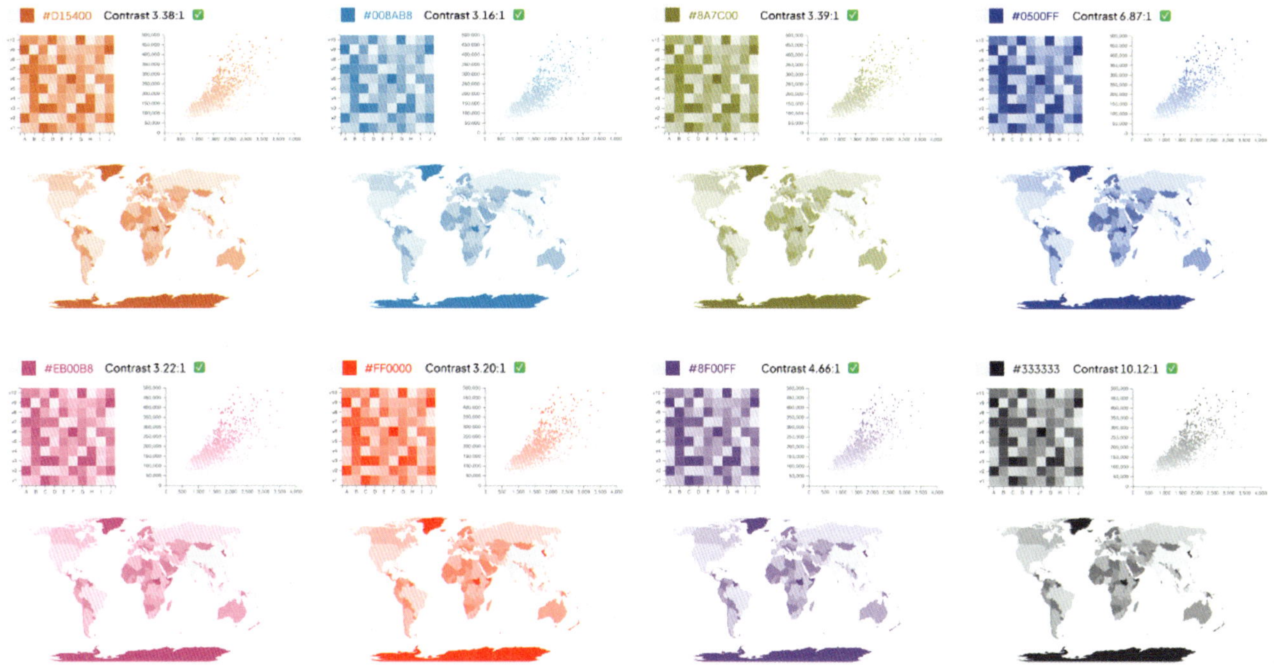

FIGURE 23.8 Testing the color palettes for accessibility in Leonardo.

Author Commentary

STEVE: I'm very impressed with this dashboard and the process that got them to something so polished (engagement with stakeholders, the hackathon, etc.) I also appreciate the thoughtfulness that went into choosing the color palettes and the modifications to work with light and dark colored backgrounds. The linchpin for me is the ability to look at different countries in Europe. I would imagine someone living in Croatia (or thinking of moving there) would use the dashboard to get insights into climate issues for that country.

Here's a feature request if they are thinking of adding new features: I'd love to see a way to compare one country with all of Europe or compare several countries at the same time, but I recognize this is not a trivial undertaking.

AMANDA: Seeing a product evolve from a hackathon concept reinforces two things for me: first, that a spark and a great dashboard concept can come together quickly; second, that what we build in hackathons on tight time scales often needs lots of fine-tuning. We love stories about the dashboard built in a day as much as the next person, but the added care that went into color selection, design decisions, and iterations on the original ideas are what really make this dashboard effective.

Moving into a longer development timeline after a hackathon also creates space for more user testing. Often in rapid prototyping environments, the time we have for feedback loops with users is extremely limited or nonexistent. Making decisions about trade-offs of precision – like the decision to use shaded boxes instead of bars – is best done through feedback with potential users for the dashboard, who can give you insights around where they want to make very detailed comparisons and where relative scales are just as useful (and perhaps a bit less overwhelming visually, depending on the space available).

Chapter 24

Professional Racing Team Race Strategy Dashboard

Michael Gethers

Organization: A professional motorsports team.

How This Dashboard Delivers: Team engineers can see in real time during a race event how well their drivers are performing on any sector of a lap and compare them to other drivers.

Audience: Race team engineers, performance engineers, and drivers look at this dashboard throughout, and after, a race event.

Team: One developer worked with 10 stakeholders to create the dashboard, which was then used by up to 50 team members.

Tools: Wireframing and prototyping with Figma and pen/paper. The dashboard is developed in d3.js. It is designed for interactive viewing on a desktop display.

Timeline: Three months from "spark" to release. Updates are added when needed.

Chapter Author: Andy Cotgreave

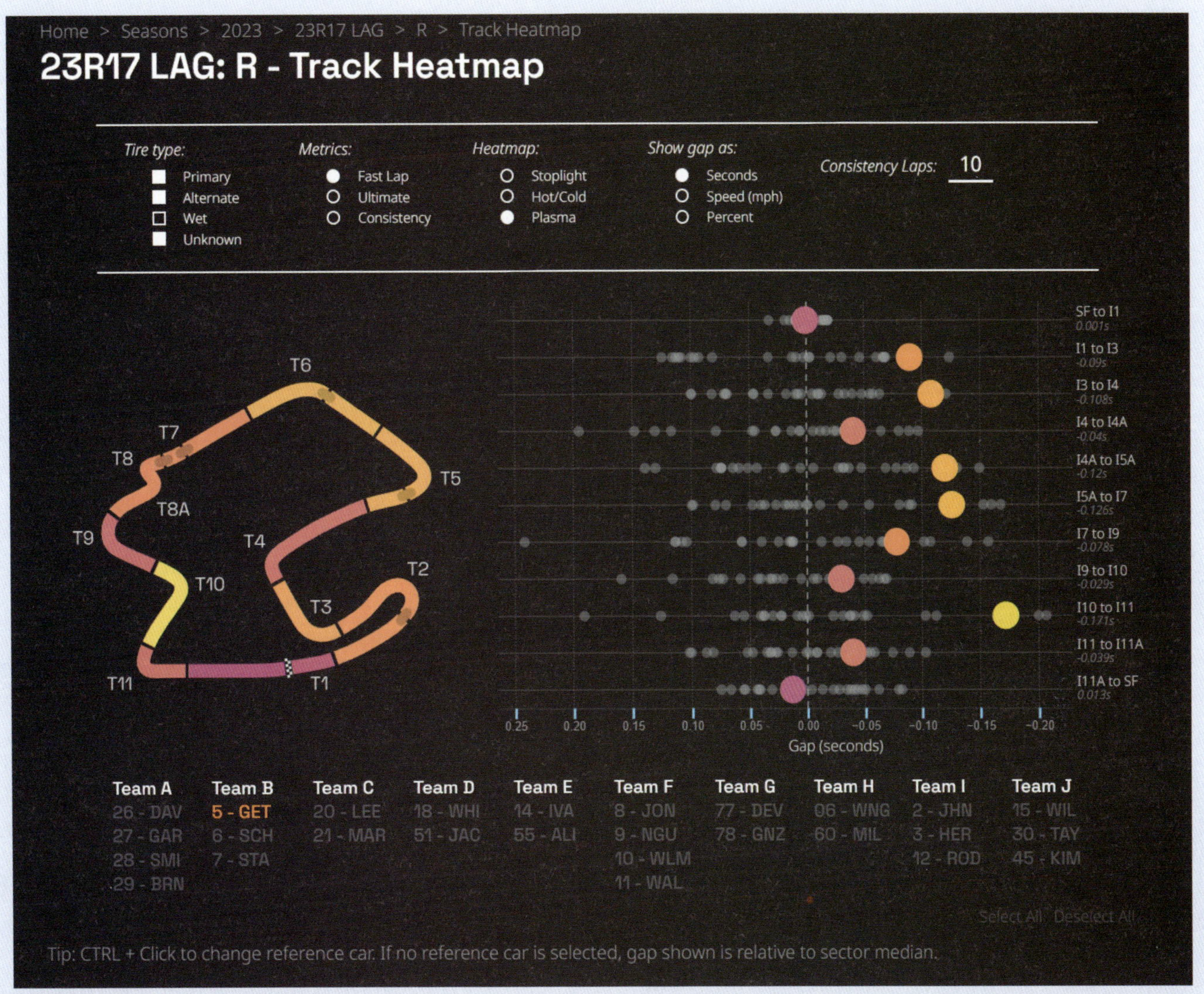

Home > Seasons > 2023 > 23R17 LAG > R > Track Heatmap
23R17 LAG: R - Track Heatmap
Tire type:
Primary
Alternate
Wet
Unknown
Metrics:
Fast Lap
Ultimate
Consistency
Heatmap:
Stoplight
Hot/Cold
Plasma
Show gap as:
Seconds
Speed (mph)
Percent
Consistency Laps: 10
T6
T7
T8
T8A
T5
T9
T4
T2
T10
T3
T11
T1
SF to I1 0.001s
I1 to I3 -0.09s
I3 to I4 -0.108s
I4 to I4A -0.04s
I4A to I5A -0.12s
I5A to I7 -0.126s
I7 to I9 -0.078s
I9 to I10 -0.029s
I10 to I11 -0.171s
I11 to I11A -0.039s
I11A to SF 0.013s
0.25 0.20 0.15 0.10 0.05 0.00 −0.05 −0.10 −0.15 −0.20
Gap (seconds)
Team A
26 - DAV
27 - GAR
28 - SMI
29 - BRN
Team B
5 - GET
6 - SCH
7 - STA
Team C
20 - LEE
21 - MAR
Team D
18 - WHI
51 - JAC
Team E
14 - IVA
55 - ALI
Team F
8 - JON
9 - NGU
10 - WLM
11 - WAL
Team G
77 - DEV
78 - GNZ
Team H
06 - WNG
60 - MIL
Team I
2 - JHN
3 - HER
12 - ROD
Team J
15 - WIL
30 - TAY
45 - KIM
Select All Deselect All
Tip: CTRL + Click to change reference car. If no reference car is selected, gap shown is relative to sector median.

Big Picture

You are an engineer at an IndyCar race team. You use this interactive application to explore drivers' time through different sectors in each lap during and after an IndyCar race. With these insights, you can take immediate action during a race or make strategic engineering decisions after a race.

Specifics

The lap map shows an overall picture of the race. Engineers can click one or more sectors to compare their drivers against others. They can filter to individual laps and different tire types and use this dashboard to navigate to other views of the data.

Related Scenarios

- You are a project manager tracking the progress of different teams working on various phases of a large project, including comparing each team's performance and highlighting bottlenecks or delays across milestones.
- You are a healthcare provider and track different treatment plans. Healthcare providers could use this approach to check different treatment plans according to different phases of treatment. The sector map could be replaced with different stages of treatment, and the dot plot would compare patients at each stage.
- You are a team leader tracking a team's progress across multiple areas of skill development and training. A similar dashboard would help find star performers and areas where some team members need help.

How People Use the Dashboard

The dashboard provides four areas of display and interactivity, labeled in Figure 24.1:

1. The map of the track is divided into color-coded sections. The colors show how a selected driver's sector times compare to a baseline of either all other drivers or one specific driver (depending on selections made elsewhere).
2. Each sector is also represented in a dot plot. The large dot represents the selected driver, the small dots represent all other drivers. The x-axis shows the gap between the driver and the baseline.
3. Clicking a driver changes the dashboard to focus on that driver. Ctrl-clicking a driver changes the *baseline* from comparing all drivers to comparing against that specifically clicked driver.
4. There are a set of filters and display choices the user can set.
    a. Tire type lets the user see timings on one specific tire type
    b. The Metrics filter compares against different definitions of "fast":
        i. Fast Lap compares drivers' fastest laps.
        ii. Ultimate compares drivers based on a lap consisting of the drivers' fastest sector times, whichever lap they happened in.
        iii. Consistent compares the fastest *n* laps, as specified in the text field on the right of the filter section.

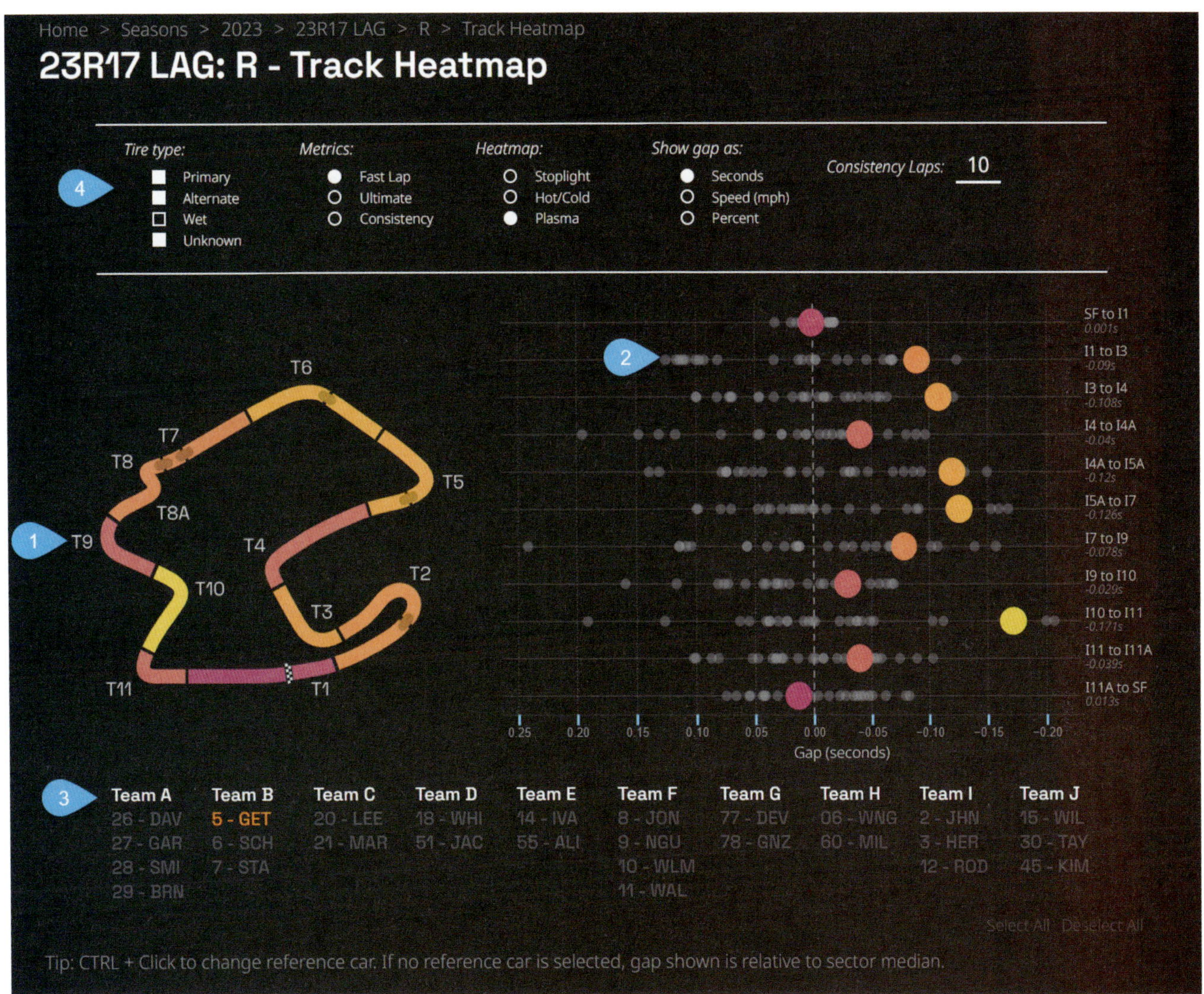

FIGURE 24.1 The four areas of interaction in the dashboard.

c. Heatmap changes the color palette.

d. Show Gap As changes the way the comparison is made. Users can look at the gap in raw time (seconds), speed, or percentage difference.

Why This Works

Aesthetics

"Aesthetic appeal is a vital part of dashboard success," says Michael Gethers, the dashboard designer, "A clean, uncluttered design eliminates distractions, enabling the viewer to grasp the data's message effortlessly."

This echoes what Don Norman says in *The Design of Everyday Things*. "Designers produce pleasurable experiences. Experience is critical, for it determines how fondly people remember their interactions."

Norman describes three levels of processing people have when they use our work: visceral, behavioral and reflective. Each is key to success. The visceral response is subconscious and instant; it is the immediate response to seeing the dashboard. "It has nothing to do with how effective or understandable the product is; it is about how attractive it is," says Norman.

Gethers' design focuses strongly on this visual, visceral appeal. The colors, the grid layout, the standout familiarity of the lap layout: all are visually appealing, creating an important positive first reaction.

Color Is Relative, Not Absolute

The color does not encode raw speed; it encodes the drivers' speed *relative to* the median of all other drivers. This is a subtle but powerful choice. To win a race, you only need to be faster than others; the points for victory (i.e., the main KPI for a racing team!) are the same whether you win by one-tenth of a second or 10 seconds.

Luminosity-Based Color Palette

The default color is a d3 palette called Plasma. This is specifically designed to satisfy vital aspects of visual design:

1. **Colorful:** the palette contains a wide palette of colors.
2. **Perceptually uniform:** values that are close to each other have similar colors, but those that are far apart appear more different.
3. **Color vision deficiency:** it works for people with color vision deficiency and in grayscale printing.
4. **Visually appealing.**

Some on Gethers' team prefer to use a red-green palette, which they associate with good and bad performance. They can choose this in the Heatmap option at the top of the dashboard, but Gethers defaults to the Plasma palette for better dashboard accessibility.

Hierarchical Feature Implementation

Gethers builds dashboards to work for both advanced and casual users by layering levels of complexity inside different levels of interactivity. His first assumption is that casual users are less likely to click around or explore settings. He is diligent in making the default view display the most useful representation of the data *for the most users.*

The most common interactions are implemented by hovering (tooltips or highlighting) or with just a single click (for example, changing the driver). For power users, the more complex functions, such as changing the baseline reference, require a Ctrl-click to work.

Gethers says, "The people who are interested enough in data investigation tend not to mind learning these more complex actions to do what they want, but the casual user generally doesn't even need to know or care that they exist."

Process

Is It a Dashboard?

Gethers calls this an analytical app rather than a dashboard. We discuss the challenges of defining and naming dashboards in "What Is a Dashboard?" (Chapter 30). For consistency in this book, I refer to it as a dashboard.

The Spark

IndyCar teams do not suffer from a lack of data. For any given race, they collect data from: hundreds of sensors on the car, up to 2,000 times a second; car location in real time; weather details; and track temperature.

The problem Gethers was solving wasn't data capture: it was the lack of data infrastructure. Data was stored in log files on servers, not searchable or queryable. Before the dashboard, analysis was done in an ad hoc way in large, cumbersome, error-prone Excel files. Insights were shared in silos, often ineffectively. Gethers says, "While motor sport is a niche domain, these are not niche problems." A lifelong motorsport enthusiast, he was brought into the team to take the opportunity to build a solution from the ground up.

The spark occurred when Gethers was hired into the team to provide fresh ideas for data displays and analysis.

Development and User Testing

Before joining the racing team, Gethers was a well-known data storyteller in the IndyCar fan community. He would see stories unfold during races and then find the data and tell the story of the race with that data. This is an effective approach in a community setting: people want to see insights (and then debate them!). After joining the team, Gethers' first task was to transform the original sector timing report, the top part of which is shown in Figure 24.2.

23R01 STP Practice 1

Fast Lap ONLY

Fast Lap								
Pos	Car	TLA	Time	Diff	%	Engine	Tire	Lap
1	9	NGU	61.615	0.000	0.00%	HON	P	6
2	26	DAV	61.648	0.033	0.05%	HON	P	4
3	10	WLM	61.679	0.065	0.10%	HON	P	4
4	27	GAR	61.685	0.071	0.11%	HON	P	2
5	60	MIL	61.696	0.082	0.13%	HON	P	5
6	21	MAR	61.851	0.237	0.38%	CHE	P	7
7	18	WHI	61.861	0.247	0.40%	HON	P	3
8	12	ROD	61.892	0.277	0.45%	CHE	P	5
9	11	WAL	61.944	0.330	0.53%	HON	P	6
10	3	HER	61.988	0.374	0.60%	CHE	P	6
11	5	GET	62.018	0.403	0.65%	CHE	P	4
12	77	DEV	62.036	0.422	0.68%	CHE	P	1
13	8	JON	62.073	0.459	0.74%	HON	P	3
14	28	SMI	62.106	0.492	0.79%	HON	P	6
15	6	SCH	62.109	0.495	0.80%	CHE	P	7
16	29	BRN	62.251	0.636	1.02%	HON	P	5
17	30	TAY	62.324	0.709	1.14%	HON	P	5
18	06	WNG	62.329	0.715	1.15%	HON	P	3
19	78	GNZ	62.363	0.748	1.20%	CHE	P	1
20	14	IVA	62.403	0.789	1.26%	CHE	P	8
21	7	STA	62.462	0.847	1.36%	CHE	P	3
22	2	JHN	62.515	0.901	1.44%	CHE	P	3
23	20	LEE	62.548	0.934	1.49%	CHE	P	1
24	51	JAC	62.816	1.201	1.91%	HON	P	5
25	45	KIM	63.041	1.427	2.26%	HON	P	1
26	15	WIL	63.139	1.524	2.41%	HON	P	3
27	55	ALI	63.513	1.899	2.99%	CHE	P	3

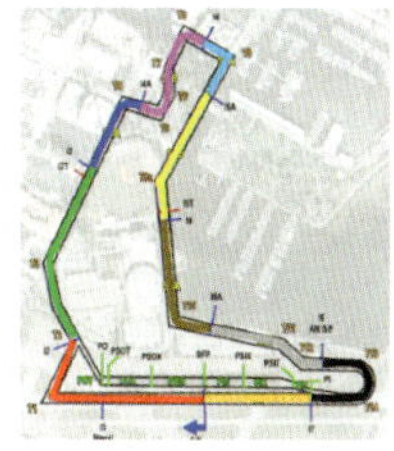

S1								
Pos	Car	TLA	Time	Diff	%	Engine	Tire	Lap
1	28	SMI	8.932	0.000	0.00%	HON	P	6
2	10	WLM	8.973	0.041	0.45%	HON	P	4
3	9	NGU	8.988	0.056	0.62%	HON	P	6
4	5	GET	8.992	0.060	0.67%	CHE	P	4
5	18	WHI	8.997	0.065	0.72%	HON	P	3
6	60	MIL	9.003	0.071	0.78%	HON	P	5
7	26	DAV	9.012	0.080	0.89%	HON	P	4
8	3	HER	9.016	0.084	0.93%	CHE	P	6
9	12	ROD	9.022	0.090	1.00%	CHE	P	5
10	21	MAR	9.025	0.093	1.03%	CHE	P	7
11	77	DEV	9.025	0.093	1.03%	CHE	P	1
12	8	JON	9.028	0.096	1.06%	HON	P	3
13	20	LEE	9.035	0.103	1.14%	CHE	P	1
14	27	GAR	9.043	0.111	1.23%	HON	P	2
15	6	SCH	9.046	0.114	1.26%	CHE	P	7
16	29	BRN	9.051	0.119	1.32%	HON	P	5
17	14	IVA	9.068	0.136	1.49%	CHE	P	8
18	51	JAC	9.070	0.138	1.52%	HON	P	5
19	06	WNG	9.089	0.157	1.73%	HON	P	3
20	78	GNZ	9.098	0.166	1.82%	CHE	P	1
21	45	KIM	9.104	0.172	1.89%	HON	P	1

S2								
Pos	Car	TLA	Time	Diff	%	Engine	Tire	Lap
1	9	NGU	6.537	0.000	0.00%	HON	P	6
2	77	DEV	6.554	0.017	0.26%	CHE	P	1
3	60	MIL	6.590	0.053	0.81%	HON	P	5
4	8	JON	6.600	0.063	0.95%	HON	P	3
5	26	DAV	6.605	0.068	1.03%	HON	P	4
6	7	STA	6.619	0.082	1.23%	CHE	P	3
7	10	WLM	6.629	0.092	1.39%	HON	P	4
8	78	GNZ	6.651	0.114	1.71%	CHE	P	1
9	21	MAR	6.660	0.123	1.85%	CHE	P	7
10	12	ROD	6.666	0.129	1.94%	CHE	P	5
11	6	SCH	6.669	0.132	1.98%	CHE	P	7
12	27	GAR	6.670	0.133	1.99%	HON	P	2
13	18	WHI	6.671	0.133	2.00%	HON	P	3
14	5	GET	6.675	0.138	2.07%	CHE	P	4
15	3	HER	6.680	0.143	2.15%	CHE	P	6
16	29	BRN	6.684	0.147	2.20%	HON	P	5
17	30	TAY	6.690	0.153	2.29%	HON	P	5
18	28	SMI	6.693	0.156	2.33%	HON	P	6
19	11	WAL	6.705	0.168	2.50%	HON	P	6
20	14	IVA	6.724	0.187	2.78%	CHE	P	8
21	51	JAC	6.753	0.215	3.19%	HON	P	5

FIGURE 24.2 The original sector timing report and Michael's first remake.

To understand any given sector, viewers of this report had to look at the small map to see which color the sector stands for. Then they must find that table among all the others and then scan through the text table to get the details.

While the report does have all the information, it's a cumbersome, unpleasant experience to try to glean any insight. Even when you find the value you want, it's not possible to make any kind of rapid comparison to another data point.

Figure 24.3 shows Gethers' first attempted solution for the team; it shows the details for one driver. The main visual is a *raincloud plot* for each sector, allowing people to see the variation of that driver's times in each sector and compare it to other drivers' times.

While Gethers was proud of this and his ability to tell the story this way, it did not engage his engineers. It didn't show the differences between drivers; it didn't show actual sector times accurately; and it didn't show driver's ranks. Those factors are all vital for the engineers, but Gethers had made editorial decisions to favor other insights. In many ways, the engineers preferred the original tabular report over Gethers' story dashboard.

The error Gethers had made was to focus on his passion for story*telling* instead of the team's need for story*finding*. His users wanted something versatile enough to explore the data based on whatever possible questions arose during a race. "It's a cliché of the industry," says Gethers, "but the fundamental first step is to know your audience."

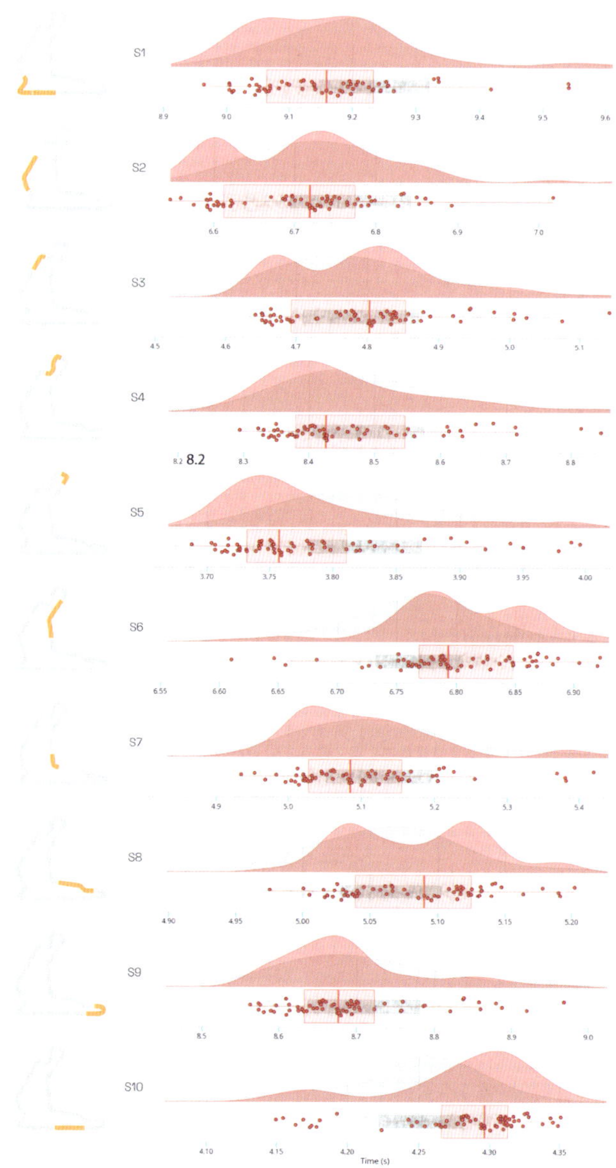

FIGURE 24.3 Michael's first driver analysis dashboard.

Recognizing the mistake, Gethers created an interactive version of the original table (Figure 24.4). Its goal was simpler: re-create the original tabular report with interactive color highlighting to show drivers within each sector.

Gethers also added extra functionality. First, the ability to select multiple sectors simultaneously. Second, as well as showing rank, the scope to show the distance between each position. These were significant additions analytically welcomed by the team.

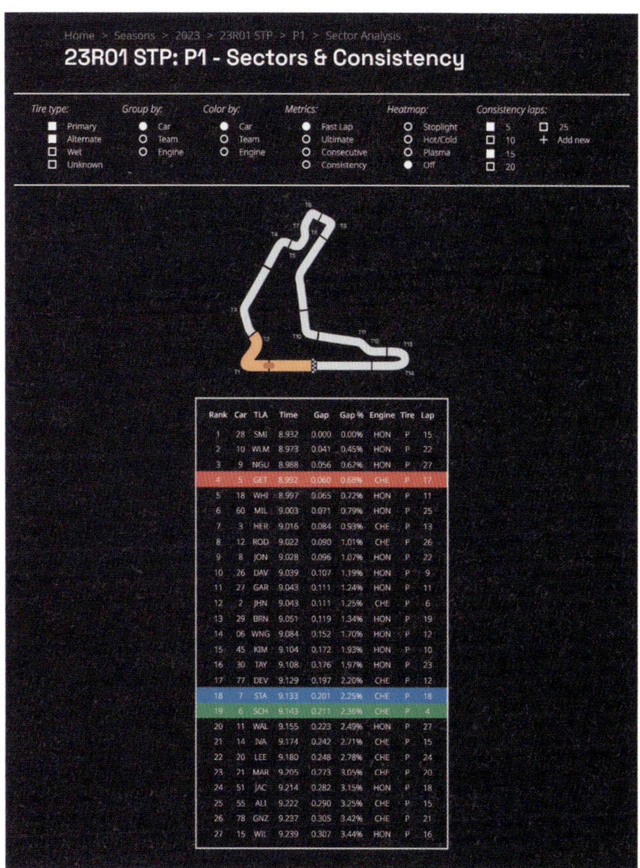

Rank	Car	TLA	Time	Gap	Gap %	Engine	Tire	Lap
1	28	SMI	8.932	0.000	0.00%	HON	P	15
2	10	WLM	8.973	0.041	0.45%	HON	P	22
3	9	NGU	8.988	0.056	0.62%	HON	P	27
4	5	GET	8.992	0.060	0.68%	CHE	P	17
5	18	WHI	8.997	0.065	0.72%	HON	P	11
6	60	MIL	9.003	0.071	0.79%	HON	P	25
7	3	HER	9.016	0.084	0.93%	CHE	P	13
8	12	ROD	9.022	0.090	1.01%	CHE	P	26
9	8	JON	9.028	0.096	1.07%	HON	P	22
10	26	DAV	9.039	0.107	1.19%	HON	P	9
11	27	GAR	9.043	0.111	1.24%	HON	P	11
12	2	JHN	9.043	0.111	1.25%	CHE	P	6
13	29	BRN	9.051	0.119	1.34%	HON	P	19
14	06	WNG	9.084	0.152	1.70%	HON	P	12
15	45	KIM	9.104	0.172	1.93%	HON	P	10
16	30	TAY	9.108	0.176	1.97%	HON	P	23
17	77	DEV	9.129	0.197	2.20%	CHE	P	12
18	7	STA	9.133	0.201	2.25%	CHE	P	18
19	6	SCH	9.143	0.211	2.36%	CHE	P	4
20	11	WAL	9.155	0.223	2.49%	HON	P	27
21	14	IVA	9.174	0.242	2.71%	CHE	P	15
22	20	LEE	9.180	0.248	2.78%	CHE	P	24
23	21	MAR	9.205	0.273	3.05%	CHE	P	20
24	51	JAC	9.214	0.282	3.15%	HON	P	18
25	55	ALI	9.222	0.290	3.25%	CHE	P	15
26	78	GNZ	9.237	0.305	3.42%	CHE	P	21
27	15	WIL	9.239	0.307	3.44%	HON	P	16

FIGURE 24.4 An interactive version of the original.

Even though all Gethers had done was essentially rebuild the table in an interactive view, these additions were transformational. By adding simple, intuitive interactions and impactful visual cues, he'd begun the process of showing his audience a path that goes from simple tables to dynamic highlight tables and from there to complex charts. "We met people where they were," says Gethers, "and began building bigger and better from there."

Having proven the value of the interactive table, Gethers was able to iterate one step further and bring more interactivity and more visualization to the team. This led to the version of the dashboard featured in this scenario.

How Much Is Too Much?

A common tension with dashboards is around how many features and interactivity pieces should you add. Gethers says, "Additional features can be very powerful, but they can also be very confusing." He's seen people get so distracted by the apps he and his team build that they stop using them. His approach is to understand the question, and answer that. "If a feature is not making the data easier to understand," he says, "then it can safely be assumed that it is making it harder to understand."

Gethers works hard to create a clean design. Clutter damages dashboard effectiveness. Instead of trying to cram as many answerable questions into the fewest dashboards, he's happy to make multiple dashboards that each answer just a couple of questions.

If new features are requested that would add clutter to a dashboard, he will build a new one for those specific requests.

Watch People Use Your Dashboard

It's important to sit and watch people use your dashboard. Give them a task but no instructions. This will highlight areas in which people struggle to understand your design. Gethers says one of the most powerful "light bulb moments" was when they were able to watch someone using the dashboard when they were not aware he was watching them.

The exercise of watching others shows the difference between how power users and casual users will use your dashboard. "Power users will try every feature, click through every option, and offer feedback on how to improve," says Gethers. "Casual users, on the other hand, may never change a single default parameter and only use the hover functionality." As we discuss in our framework, you should have defined your user segments already. This exercise helps discover if those segments are being accounted for.

Both types of users are valid, and you need to design for both. As discussed previously, interactivity is built so that the simplest features are the easiest to access.

Adoption

Measuring Dashboard Success

Once you have released your dashboard, measuring success is something we have found many teams struggle with. Gethers tries to be thoughtful and diligent when choosing his own dashboard's success criteria. For this dashboard, he measured its success by the number of change requests he received. More change requests equal more success.

It might feel counterintuitive. Surely, if a user is asking for a new feature, it means you missed something out? On the contrary, Gethers sees a feature request as a measure of engagement. If people want new features, it means they are using what you built.

Find Key Stakeholders Early

Gethers believes a key reason for his success was getting buy-in from influential people in the team. Gethers recommends three key aspects of this:

1. Who are your power users going to be?
2. How do they currently answer the questions your product will answer?
3. What would keep them from using your product?

"If you can answer these questions," he says, "you can foresee the hurdles to adoption you might get from the broader team."

Get these people on board, as partners in the project. "They will help you do the work of getting others to use the dashboard," says Gethers. "It's been a game-changing approach for me."

Having key stakeholders evangelize small steps in the project leads to other teams wanting their data in the dashboards.

Author Commentary

AMANDA: The simplicity and thoughtfulness in avoiding dashboard bloat is a big takeaway from Michael's work, though that can be harder in practice than in principle. Often, dashboard requirements list feels ever-expanding. Prioritization matters, but even mapping a list of five needs out of 15 can create a cluttered display. Instead, Michael shows an approach that builds an ever-expanding ecosystem of connected or linked dashboards to explore as you seek more depth. Given the ways modern dashboards are deployed, thinking about an *analytical ecosystem* is both practical and more user friendly in many cases.

STEVE: I'll confess, I'm a huge fan...of this dashboard and its author.

There is a lot of functionality in this dashboard, but it doesn't feel at all cluttered. There are so many different metrics you can explore (Fast Laps vs. Ultimate vs. Consistent) so many ways you can make comparisons (seconds, speed, percent) and three color combinations for displaying the findings (Stoplight, HotCold, Plasma).

But it's Michael's working with and identifying stakeholder needs that is for me the most noteworthy facet of this scenario.

Let's start with the default settings. Michael wanted to present what is most useful to the most users. As someone whose mantra is "for the largest number of people, provide the greatest degree of understanding, with the least amount of effort," I just want to stand up and cheer. But also look at how Michael at first failed, how he got his stakeholders involved, and how he found the stakeholders who would champion the work. Finally, look at his metric for success: people asking for improvements. He's right, that's a clear indication that people are using the dashboard and want more ways that they can benefit from it.

JEFF: I am a big fan of dot plots/strip plots and dot plots with jitter. It's so easy to see "how am I doing versus everyone else?" And you can make that comparison with or without divulging the details of everyone else. For example, you can show salary or ratings or other sensitive and confidential data, and you can show the comparisons without giving up the names. Combine the individual versus group comparison, along with the view of the distribution of the dots, and the race track, and it becomes a really powerful tool.

Chapter 25

Coronavirus Resource Center

Johns Hopkins University

Team: At any given time during the project, 10 core team members and 20 support team members supported the Coronavirus Resource Center, which hosted the dashboard and additional resources.

Organization: The Coronavirus Resource Center drew on the expertise and collaboration of researchers and faculty from across Johns Hopkins, including the Applied Physics Laboratory, the Bloomberg School of Public Health, the Center for Systems Science and Engineering in the Whiting School of Engineering, the School of Medicine, Sheridan Libraries, and the Bloomberg Center for Government Excellence (GovEx).

Audience: General public, with a focus on creating a reference tool and dataset for use by journalists, policymakers, and public health professionals.

Timeline: Design and launch of the first dashboard took weeks. The scope of the project grew from a data source into a dashboard and eventually into the full Coronavirus Resource Center (CRC), which remained in production for three years with updates sunsetting March 2023.

How This Dashboard Delivers: Over three years, the COVID dashboard within the Coronavirus Resource Center was the go-to place to check for updates on COVID case data. The underlying data integrated information from thousands of data sources on a daily basis and was made publicly available from inception, functioning as a system of record and data source for other data communicators throughout the COVID-19 pandemic.

- **Tools:** GitHub.
  - CSSE COVID-19 GitHub Repository (dtdbook.com/link29).
  - GovEx COVID-19 GitHub Repository (dtdbook.com/link30).
- ArcGIS.
- D3/JavaScript (for more bespoke data visualizations).

Chapter Author: Amanda Makulec

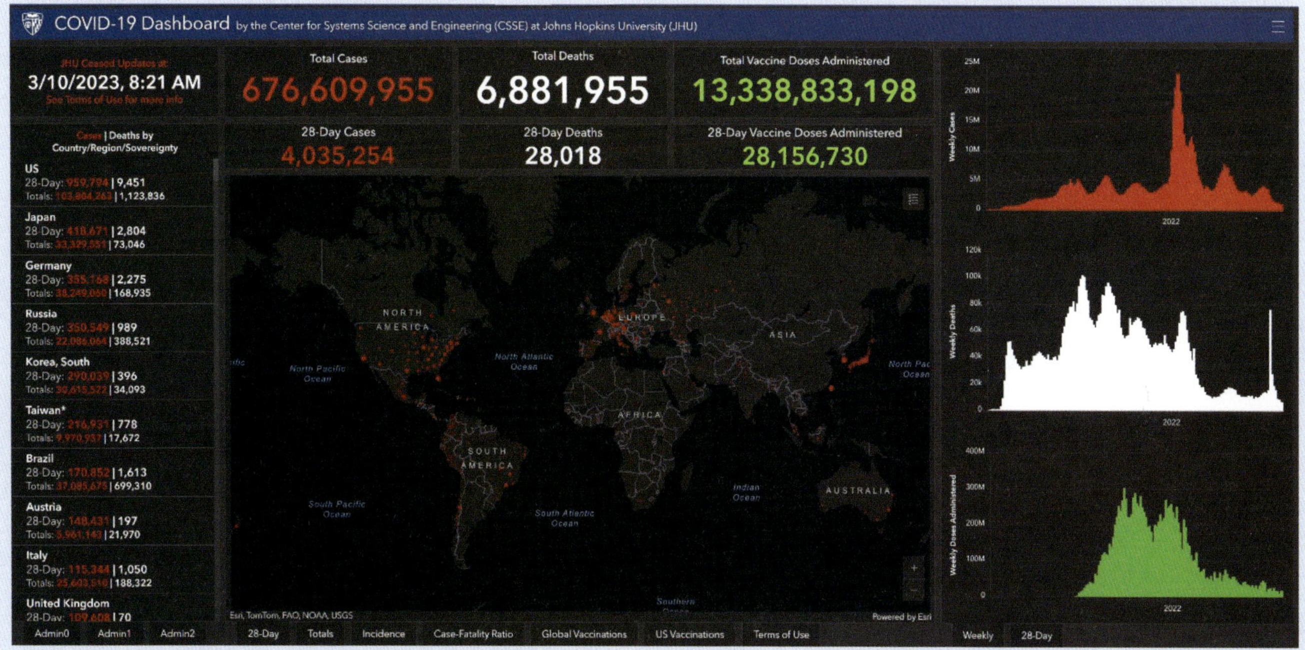
COVID-19 Dashboard by the Center for Systems Science and Engineering (CSSE) at Johns Hopkins University (JHU)
JHU Ceased Updates at
3/10/2023, 8:21 AM
See Terms of Use for more info
Total Cases
676,609,955
Total Deaths
6,881,955
Total Vaccine Doses Administered
13,338,833,198
28-Day Cases
4,035,254
28-Day Deaths
28,018
28-Day Vaccine Doses Administered
28,156,730
Cases | Deaths by Country/Region/Sovereignty
US
28-Day: 959,794 | 9,451
Totals: 103,804,263 | 1,123,836
Japan
28-Day: 418,671 | 2,804
Totals: 33,329,551 | 73,046
Germany
28-Day: 355,168 | 2,275
Totals: 38,249,060 | 168,935
Russia
28-Day: 350,549 | 989
Totals: 22,086,064 | 388,521
Korea, South
28-Day: 290,039 | 396
Totals: 30,615,522 | 34,093
Taiwan*
28-Day: 216,931 | 778
Totals: 9,970,937 | 17,672
Brazil
28-Day: 170,852 | 1,613
Totals: 37,085,675 | 699,310
Austria
28-Day: 148,431 | 197
Totals: 5,961,143 | 21,970
Italy
28-Day: 115,344 | 1,050
Totals: 25,603,510 | 188,322
United Kingdom
28-Day: 109,608 | 70
NORTH AMERICA
EUROPE
ASIA
AFRICA
SOUTH AMERICA
AUSTRALIA
North Pacific Ocean
North Atlantic Ocean
South Pacific Ocean
South Atlantic Ocean
Indian Ocean
Esri, TomTom, FAO, NOAA, USGS
Powered by Esri
Admin0
Admin1
Admin2
28-Day
Totals
Incidence
Case-Fatality Ratio
Global Vaccinations
US Vaccinations
Terms of Use
Weekly Cases
25M
20M
15M
10M
5M
0
2022
Weekly Deaths
120k
100k
80k
60k
40k
20k
0
2022
Weekly Doses Administered
400M
300M
200M
100M
0
2022
Weekly
28-Day

Scenario

Big Picture

In the early days of the COVID-19 pandemic, people needed a way to track the spread and impact of the disease. The Center for Systems Science and Engineering (CSSE) at Johns Hopkins University (JHU) launched a publicly available data source, one of the first and most trusted, often referenced by major newspapers and government entities reporting on COVID.

To enable people to explore, download, and collaborate around this data source, the team developed a dashboard with a few key BANs (tests, cases, deaths, and eventually vaccinations), a bubble map plotting cases by country, and charts for trends over time. That dashboard rapidly became a definitive source of information not just for data communicators but for the public, even though the data in the early stages of the pandemic was incomplete or had data quality issues.

Developing a dashboard visualizing data from tables sourced from thousands of different discrete sources daily is no small feat. The team relied on Agile methods to triage, prioritize, and implement change requests. Over three years, the project grew from a single global dashboard representing cases, deaths, and eventually vaccines to a robust site, the Coronavirus Resource Center, which contained multiple dashboards, data visualizations, articles, and briefings to better reflect evolving metrics, hanging data, and the emerging needs of the users.

Ultimately, the dashboard was viewed more than 2.5 billion times with an added 1 billion hits on the data, making it one of the most viewed dashboards of all time.

While few of us will create a dashboard with 2.5 billion views that impact lives on a global scale, there are approaches and techniques this heroic team used that you should apply to your work too.

Specifics

You need to be able to:

- Communicate rapidly updating COVID-19 data to a wide audience, including using the data visualizations as a tool to influence what data is collected and shared for analysis
- Identify pandemic hotspots at a global scale
- Update dashboards to reflect changing definitions, data collection mechanisms, and variable data quality across data collection systems (in this case, different state or national systems)
- Build a reusable data set aggregating local COVID-19 data sets from across states and countries that can be used by public health agencies, journalists, health communicators, and other stakeholders
- Be responsive to the needs and questions posed by downstream users, and factor them into iterative development to make the information as consumable as possible

Related Scenarios

- You work at a public health department or federal agency monitoring communicable disease surveillance data.
- You are responsible for maintaining a national or global dashboards with real-time data, particularly for topics where geographic data plays an

important role in the analysis, like public transportation or flight data.

How People Use the Dashboard

The Red Bubble Map

The bubble map (Figure 25.1) became a recognizable symbol of the pandemic. Bubbles representing the case counts grew rapidly and showed the global spread of the virus.

As the scale of the outbreak grew, country-level bubbles for large populations obscured smaller countries. The team evolved the map to have more geographic granularity, instead plotting bubbles for states or other municipalities.

BANs for Key Metrics

A set of BANs complement the map, summarizing cumulative case and death statistics and eventually expanded to include vaccination data. The position of these elements, the level of granularity (eventually going to US state and county levels), and metrics available evolved over time. Early on, the big numbers were in the hundreds and thousands; on the last day the dashboard was updated, the total was approaching 677 million cases, as in the last frame of Figure 25.2.

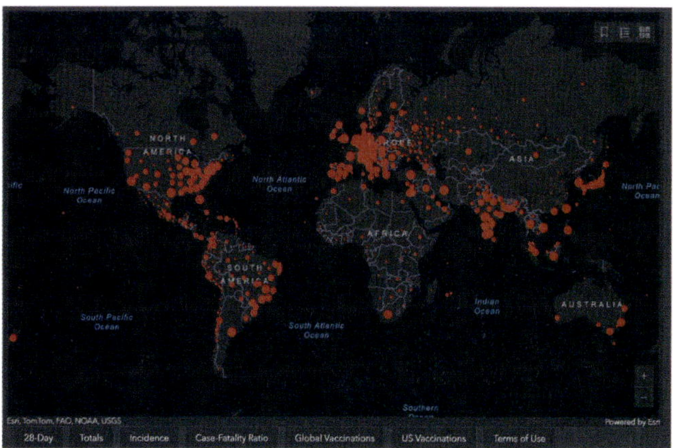

FIGURE 25.1 JHU COVID map.

Simple Interactivity

Public health professionals and laypeople alike followed the daily data updates to watch the spread of the coronavirus. As the time frame for the data expanded, interactivity allowed for both big picture and narrower views of trends over time with simple toggles to change the granularity of the views. For example, in Figure 25.3 the user can switch from an area chart by week to a bar chart by day for a 28-day window, which appears on the right side of the desktop view.

Because of the nature of how people accessed information during the COVID pandemic, the dashboard was also optimized for mobile viewing. The mobile interface allowed users to change between five views, starting with BANs of key aggregate measures over time and then disaggregating those metrics geographically. Users move between different pages within the mobile view (Figure 25.4) with navigation buttons across the bottom of the screen.

Why This Works

Keep It Simple

The simplicity of the dashboard and the accessibility of the underlying data tables were two

January 22, 2020

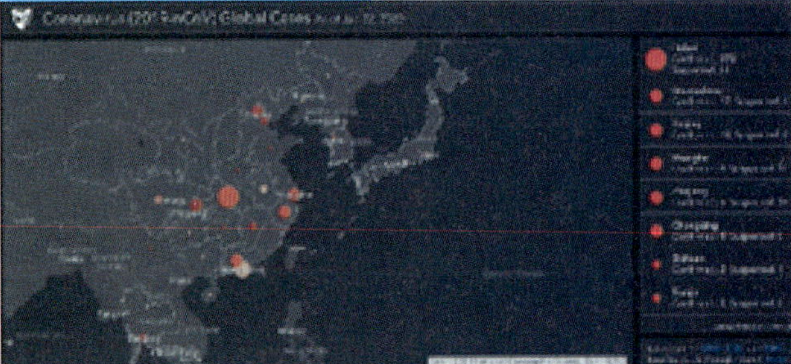

April 20, 2020

March 10, 2023

FIGURE 25.2 JHU COVID dashboard from launch to last data update, showing the evolution in the placement of different components and the addition of new metrics like vaccination data (visible in green in the March 2023 screenshot).

Source: Screenshot from 1/22/2020 courtesy of Ensheng (Frank) Dong.

primary reasons for the dashboard's wide adoption and use. Remember, the dashboard started as a data source. Then, the team developed the dashboard to make the information more available to the public.

The team also had first-mover advantage. The Johns Hopkins dashboard was one of the first aggregated trackers for COVID-19 data, built specifically to meet the immediate data needs of public health departments, journalists, and the public alike.

The JHU team had the combined expertise necessary to manage the growing data on the back end and the front-end components, including addressing design and performance considerations. When the team created their initial data governance guidelines, they agreed they were creating a public good: no proprietary tools, no gating, with an open license to adapt and use both the data and the visualizations. The team valued making everything open and accessible. As a result, over the life of the dashboard the team recorded more than 2.5 billion page views.

Constant Communication with Users

COVID-19 data was often incomplete or operating on a lag due to limited testing availability and long waits for laboratory capacity. As the website traffic volume increased and public appetite increased for understanding both the data and COVID-19, the team also worked to create materials to aid others in interpreting and using the data.

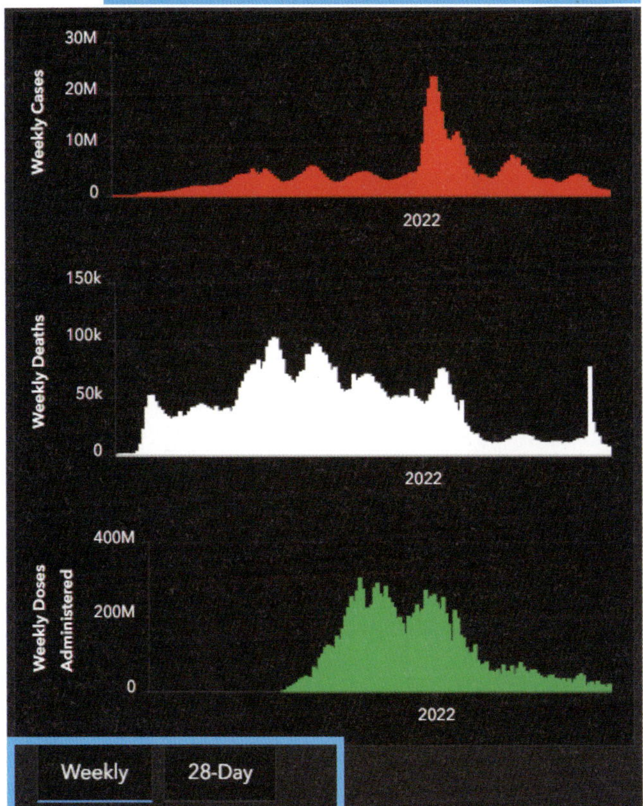

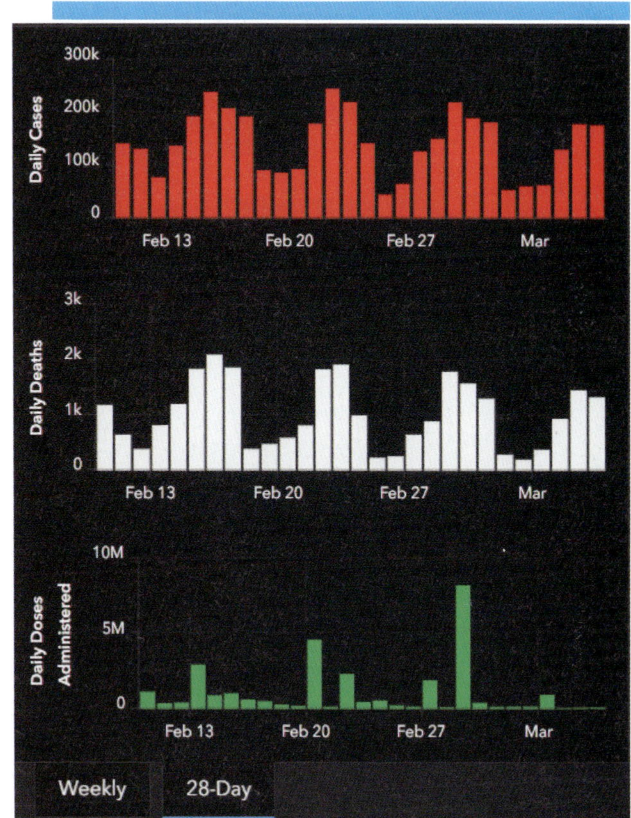

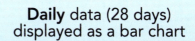

FIGURE 25.3 Changing visualizations when toggling between weekly view (area chart) and 28-day rolling daily numbers (bar chart).

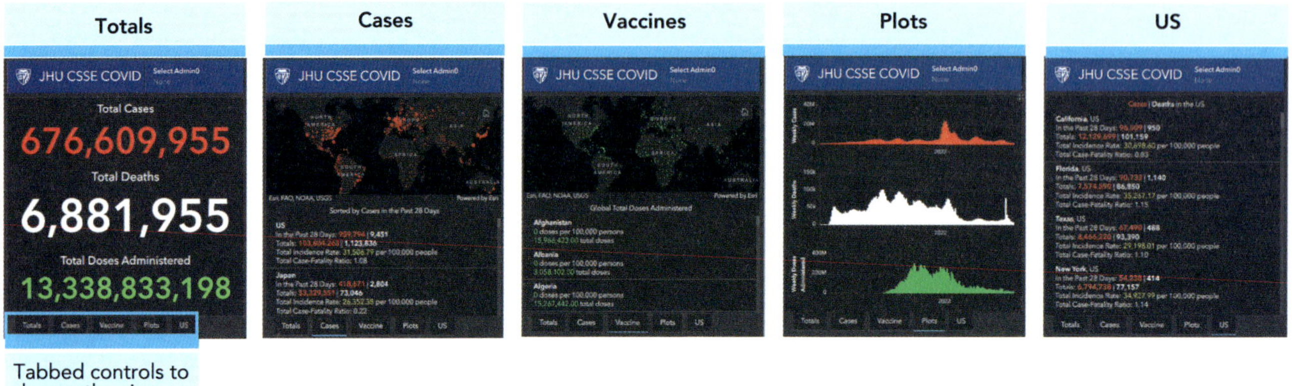

FIGURE 25.4 Mobile version of JHU CSSE dashboard.

Through the Coronavirus Resource Center, the team added analyses and data to conceptualize what was happening. These resources included blogs about the data itself, highlighting data gaps and challenges.

"We were getting tons of traffic, but the team wasn't in control of how the data was being interpreted. As part of Johns Hopkins University, the first research university in the country, we felt it was our job to contextualize data," said Beth Blauer, Johns Hopkins vice president of Public Impact Initiatives. The whole notion of activating the data to make decisions was happening in real time.

Throughout the pandemic, the team continued to host calls with experts and public briefings to review COVID-19 statistics. On the calls, the dashboard was a jumping off point for conversations. Throughout the first year of the pandemic, the team would have thousands of people joining to ask questions about the numbers.

Process

"The dashboard started off as a data source, but by the time March hit, the dashboard was embedded in the New York Times, the CDC website, and even the CNN ticker."

Spark

In January 2020, Beth Blauer and the GovEx team were going about their usual work and preparing to travel to India for a public health project. There was a "rumored pathogen" spreading in China and other parts of Asia. They looked for data but couldn't find anything that was reliable or accessible.

While they were searching for more insights, the team learned a faculty member, Dr. Lauren Gardner in Johns Hopkins' Center for Systems and Science Engineering, had published a map tracking the cases in China. They reached out and Dr. Gardner provided the underlying data on COVID-19 cases to date. It may seem odd for the spark of a public health dashboard to start in an engineering department rather than the school of public health, but this speaks to the wide interest in understanding the spread of this new disease.

While the engineering department was building an internal resource, the team realized that every public leader beyond Johns Hopkins University needed to have access to this kind of data to drive decisions as they observed the rapid spread of the virus.

That first request to share data sparked a collaboration to build a better dashboard along with efforts to fortify the back end to accommodate higher traffic volume. The CSSE team then worked with the JHU Applied Physics Lab to stabilize the back end.

Next, JHU's leadership prioritized building out the front end of the dashboard to make the information more widely accessible. "The dashboard was originally built for researchers, but then people like my parents started using it to decide if they were going to the grocery store," reflected Beth Blauer, who was one of the original product owners of the Coronavirus Resource Center.

With that foresight, the JHU Global COVID-19 dashboard and Coronavirus Resource Center emerged as *the* data partner for major research and news organizations reporting on the rapid spread of COVID-19, thanks to the work done to aggregate information from local data sources.

Want to Hear More About the Origin Story of the Coronavirus Resource Center?

If you'd like to hear more about the spark and development of the Coronavirus Resource Center and the dashboard, check out the following articles and podcast:

- Dong E, Du H, Gardner L. An interactive web-based dashboard to track COVID-19 in real time. Lancet Inf Dis. 20(5):533-534. doi: 10.1016/S1473-3099(20)30120-1
- "The Role of the Applied Physics Lab" by Justyna Surowiec (JHU News Release), dtdbook.com/link31
- GovEx Data Points Podcast #84: The Women Behind the Coronavirus Resource Center, dtdbook.com/link32

Building the Team

At its peak, the team managing the dashboard consisted of approximately 30 employees among multiple organizations within JHU; however, 10 people made up the core team. For comparison, the New York Times had up to 130 people working on tasks related to their COVID tracker during the peak of the pandemic, including up to 50 people fully dedicated to the tracker.

The core, cross-functional leadership team drove the day-to-day work of developing and maintaining the dashboard and set the vision for the dashboard as a global good.

Throughout the pandemic, and particularly in the early days, relevant experts seemed to split into two camps around access to information: those aiming to use the data for good, whether driving public decision-making or curating the data as a global good for wider use, and those with more self-serving intents, including paid experts and consultants who monetized their expertise. The team observed that it was mostly women in the public decision-making group, which was an often-discussed topic with other global-good advocates like the Kaiser Family Foundation.

Mary Conway Vaughan, deputy director for Research and Analytics in the Bloomberg Center for Government Excellence (GovEx), functioned as the project manager gathering the feedback from and representing the interests of different stakeholders. She set the agenda and managed the team in their daily work to keep the site updated and work throughout items in the backlog.

In addition to the full-time JHU staff and faculty, the team also included vendor partners responsible for piping data into the visualizations and ensuring data quality. But with such a small core team, everyone was "hands on" with the data.

Dr. Lauren Gardner and the CSSE team worked specifically on data quality issues and figuring out substitutes where data was missing or disaggregates didn't align to the dashboard standard. Vaughan tracked data integrity on the visualizations, acting as the first check, ensuring visualizations didn't fail or throw errors, and that all calculations ran correctly. Dr. Sara Bertran de Lis, director of Research and Analytics at GovEx, also worked with the team to ensure the calculations reflected best practices in public health, as epidemiologists on the team were concerned if the team used the right calculation for things like testing positivity.

An Agile Approach

The team used an Agile management approach to stay on top of tasks to keep the dashboard up to date, plan for incremental improvements, and add new features.

At the outset, each day kicked off with a scrum meeting every morning at 6 a.m. with the data engineers to ensure the latest update to the public repository was correct. The day ended with a closing meeting at 9 p.m. every night with leadership for priority setting and unblocking challenges. That meeting cadence was out of necessity; early on the team seemed to be building the plane as they were flying it and there was an open Zoom room available most of the day between meetings to address quick questions or decision points.

The Coronavirus Resource Center team quickly established four key meetings to keep the work on track. Two meetings kept the work on track (daily dev/ops scrum and daily product owners meeting) and two addressed niche data topics requiring more focus (twice weekly testing data meeting and weekly vaccinations meeting). Communication and keeping the team on the same page was key to maintaining and enhancing the dashboard and associated resources.

Vaughan led the charge on implementing an Agile approach to managing the Coronavirus Resource Center, having used Agile methods in previous workspaces. She found it aligned with the method that vendor partners used, creating a natural alignment on work structures.

In addition to the daily scrum and closing meetings, team leaders hosted a "scrum of scrums" with subteams that met and worked with each other. Delegating and owning different parts of the design and development work, while staying abreast of what other teams were doing, was critical to the pace of work. They also actively took in feedback from end users that was used to prioritize fixing bugs and implementing change requests.

The team developed a criticality rating value for change:

- **Category 1 (Critical):** Anything that was to fix an error or broken component was triaged and handled immediately
- **Category 2:** Backlog items addressing issues with visuals or data that could be misleading but not wrong
- **Category 3:** Backlog items that were nice to change (e.g., color, content) but not critical to using the data
- **Category 4:** Anything else that's a nice idea, but not a priority, primarily kept in the backlog to revisit in the future

The team didn't set prescribed go-live dates for any visualizations due to the pace of change. Instead, they set a daily release schedule and then slowed to a more reasonable pace in the months and years that followed. Because the data was changing so quickly, managing the data streams alone could take the full day: the data was updated every hour or even as quickly as every 15 minutes during some windows.

The cost of the labor and technology to build and maintain the Coronavirus Resource Center and the dashboard for three years was estimated at $13 million by the JHU GovEx team, as reported by NPR (dtdbook.com/link33).

Building Tables from Local Sources

At the end of February 2020, with a growing red bubble on the United States, the team looked for an approach to provide more granular information at the local level. But where to get that level of very granular data in a country without a strong, national health informatics infrastructure?

Go local.

Developers started building scrapers to collect data from local health departments. The data scraping process started as a wholly manual endeavor. With time, the process shifted to more automation, verification, and anomaly detection engineering in the front end and back end.

Gathering information wasn't as simple as scraping tidy tables from a county health department website. Instead, updating the data meant getting on the phone with local health departments, where you would find seemingly simple categorizations varied. Age bands and definitions of race and ethnicity varied markedly: at one point, there were over 1,000 different definitions of race and ethnicity, with no real standards for how data was captured or coded. These differences created a lot of complexity in synthesizing county data into a state or national number.

As a result, the team started creating and sharing standards. Building on their relationships with local health departments, they asked for departments to align to specific standards. To support the data users, the team also created additional resources, like data FAQs, to address data governance challenges related to aggregating data across sources.

Triaging Feedback

The team hosted a global email mailbox for gathering feedback on the dashboard, where they received practical change requests and tips about data quality issues, but also received thousands of notes and stories more personal in nature.

The inbox was originally monitored by the communications team and later monitored by Vaughan herself with some support from the team. These included useful reports on data quality issues for specific countries, since there was too much data for quality assurance checks to work on hundreds of data sources feeding into the data tables populating the dashboard. As the volume grew, systems for documenting requests changed too.

Design and Prototyping

The team was constantly iterating around how to improve the usability of the site once the data itself was stable. Early on, the primary metrics were Cases and Deaths with the bubble map representing the snapshot of the current state, without additional visualizations to show trends or a historic view.

Based on feedback from the public, the team added features like the trend charts and filter functionality.

Any demographic data was managed through a public health lens, with a high priority to avoid misrepresenting information or misleading the public regarding how to interpret demographic patterns. For example, the disease was disproportionately impacting Black communities not because of biology, but because of issues around access to care and historic issues of systemic racism within the US health system that impact health outcomes now recognized by the CDC (dtdbook.com/link34). Out of context, data disaggregated by race could be misunderstood.

Over time, the team also prioritized adding context to the individual country details. Clicking a country opened a card with additional details about that country's population, including levels of access to health insurance, demographic breakdowns, and who is being impacted by the disease, as illustrated with the New York data in Figure 25.5.

Decisions on which measures to include were driven primarily by where the team could integrate publicly available data organized in three areas: demographics, access to care, and COVID-specific data.

Being one of the most widely used dashboards of the modern era, with millions of daily users, didn't exempt the dashboard from criticism from data visualization designers. The data visualization

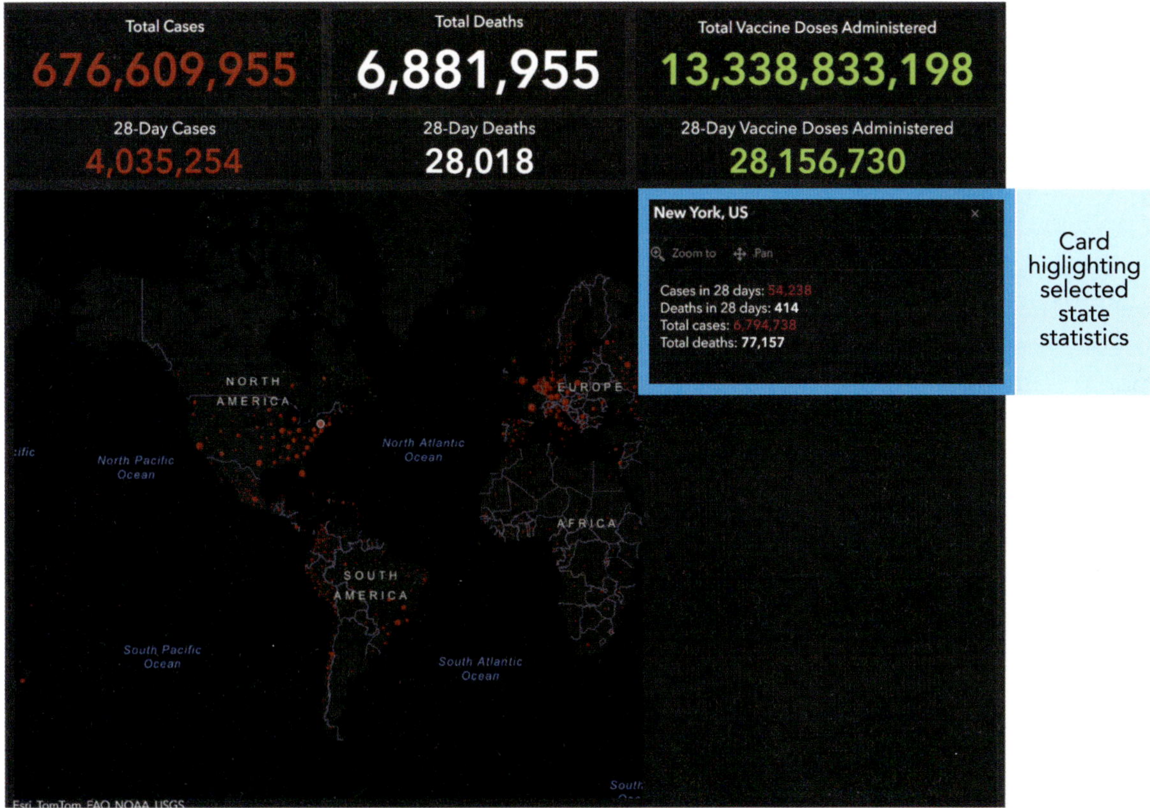

FIGURE 25.5 Bubble map with detail card open for New York state.

community had many early critiques of the bubble map, from debates over the use of red as an alarmist color to the challenges of overlapping bubbles that obscured countries and states with smaller case load as the virus spread. Most of the time, these critiques were made without much consideration of the labor necessary to maintain the dashboard with its usage and data volumes ever-increasing.

One point of frustration for the team was that the map became increasingly hard to use as the data grew, with large bubbles obscuring other countries. Instead, the team made some UX changes, including showing more granular levels of geography like displaying state level data instead of total numbers for the United States, and changed the levels of opacity on the bubbles to make it easier to see smaller circles that may be obscured.

Using the Dashboard to Influence Data Collection

The design team didn't see the dashboard as a one-way communication product for data. Instead, they used data visualization to influence the source data itself and address gaps: what was being collected, how it was being collected, and how it was prepared for analysis.

For example, public health professionals needed to tell a more complete story about which demographic groups were being disproportionately impacted by COVID-19, but that information wasn't routinely collected or available.

For example, the dashboard team heard from clinical colleagues that Black people in the United States were dying at higher rates, but they didn't have the data to segment cases, deaths, and tests by race or ethnicity. At the time, a limited number of states captured demographic data. Most states, after having this pointed out, began reporting this data out fairly quickly (even if they weren't thrilled about having it pointed out).

What to do when users are asking for data that doesn't actually exist? The team decided to add a component to the Coronavirus Resource Center (dtdbook.com/link35) showing the two states on a map where the demographics were available, leaving much of the map blank (no data). Instead of waiting for more complete information, they used that visualization as a means for raising awareness around the need for more complete demographic data. See Figure 25.6.

The team didn't simply rely on the hope that people in the know would step forward with the missing data; they also coordinated with other key actors,

State COVID-19 Data by Race

Which states have released breakdowns of Covid-19 data by race?

This map shows the U.S. states that have released Covid-19 data by race, broken down into three critical categories: confirmed cases, deaths, and testing. It is essential that policy-makers and other decision-makers have access to these data to inform their response to the pandemic. It is also important that these data are released publicly to shed light on the intersecting forces of racial disparities, underlying conditions, and poverty that affect how the virus spreads throughout the U.S.

This page was last updated on Tuesday, April 28, 2020 at 11:52 PM EDT.

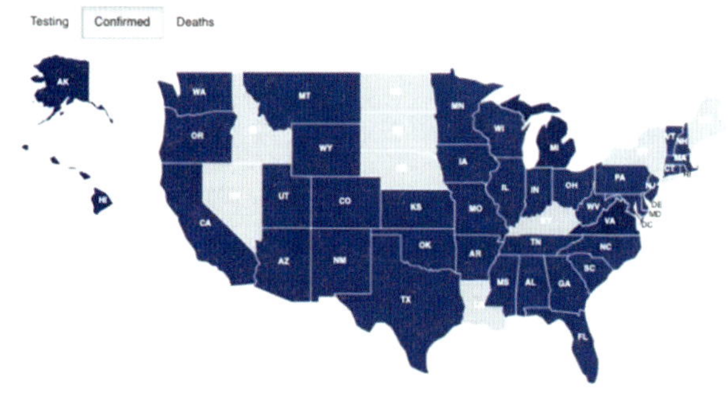

FIGURE 25.6 Map of states reporting COVID case data disaggregated by race as of April 28, 2020.

like the Kaiser Family Foundation, to amplify calls for better data.

At the end of a two-week period from the web component being added, more than 75% of states added demographic data to their COVID-19 data collection processes.

Gratitude, Not Vitriol

We now live in a world where many people disbelieve numbers in front of them, whether about a pandemic, climate change, or other global crises. As we watched COVID-19 cases and deaths climb, many of us also thought of the people represented in each of those numbers and had personal connections to people who were sick or had died from the disease.

But for some of those who didn't know friends or family impacted by COVID, the growing global cases on the dashboard seemed *unbelievable*. Thanks to the success of the dashboard, the shared inbox for feedback also became a landing zone for endless criticism.

While many appreciated and valued the insights from the dashboard, the team also received lots of "I don't agree with what you said on CNN" notes or assertions like, "You're wrong – deaths went down in Ohio," when the data told a different story. Most of these notes weren't actionable for the team but did take valuable time to sift through. And when you're already working 12+ hour days on a dashboard, that added burden is even more frustrating.

Looking through the inbox, sometimes the messages veered personal. Some heartbreaking notes looking for advice like "I want to visit my grandparents in Florida and don't think I can because of the test positivity so what should we do?" These types of "how do I act on the data" questions were often more broadly addressed in the blogs and media appearances discussing the dashboard findings. But other messages unfortunately veered into harassment, thanks to the polarized landscape of the pandemic in the United States.

Our peek behind the scenes of how one of the most viewed dashboards of all time was maintained fascinated us as data visualization designers. There were so many design decisions, so many stakeholders, and so much at stake. We ourselves used the dashboard as a reference and saw the ways the data served as a source far beyond this single interface. The team created an exceptional public good in the midst of a global pandemic, for which the developers deserve our gratitude, not vitriol.

Author Commentary

STEVE: I suspect anyone reading this book has been under pressure to present good work quickly, but I wonder how many readers have had to create a dashboard where the whole world isn't just watching you work, but *relying on* your work?

The scope of your projects won't match what the JHU team was tasked with doing, but there are many approaches they took that you can apply to your own work. Consider the section on keeping it simple. The dashboard designers presented the most important metrics as simple-to-understand BANs. They provided the ability to filter by region, then drill down into the details. Yes, this aligns perfectly with Ben Shneiderman's mantra of overview first, filter, details on demand.

With explanations and blog posts, the team also made sure to provide context for all the data. Ensuring proper understanding and use of the data was critical, as misinterpretation could be a matter of life and death.

And that draws me to the one thing that stands out more than anything else with this project: integrity.

I mean the integrity of the data itself and the integrity in how they presented the data. As you embark on your next dashboard project, think about making that your lodestar.

JEFF: Take a second and ask yourself, "What are the top 10 or top 5 data visualizations of all time?" If you've studied data visualization in a class or workshop, then famous visualizations such as Minard's depiction of Napolean's campaign into Russia, Florence Nightingale's visualization of the Scutari barracks, or Dr. John Snow's Cholera map would certainly be contenders.

The interesting thing is that every semester, in every data visualization class that I teach, and in every workshop, I always show Minard's visualization and ask the room, "How many of you have seen this before?" In a room of say 50–60 students, graduate and undergraduate classes, I will only see one or two hands that go up. When teaching public workshops, then maybe a few more. So Minard's visualization is arguably one of the most famous visualizations in history, and yet so few people outside of the data visualization community have seen it or know what it represents.

Now let's compare that with the John Hopkins dashboard. This dashboard has had more than 2.5 billion views. Consider for a minute that the entire population of the world in 1850 was around 1.2 billion. So, to put this in perspective, every single person on the planet in 1850 would have seen the COVID dashboard twice. That is remarkable.

You might counter, "Well, ask 50 students in the year 2150 what this dashboard is and see how many know." Fair enough, but even so, I can't think of another data visualization or dashboard that ever deployed at the scale at which this dashboard was deployed.

I was part of those 2.5 billion views, as were most of the people I know. We checked it frequently, sometimes daily, and it provided great insight into what was happening in the world around us, which was something we all needed at that time. And in my opinion, because of its scale and utility, this visualization is one that should now be included when we talk about the top-ranking data visualizations of all time.

Chapter 26

NASA's Earth Information Center | earth.gov

NASA Scientific Visualization Studio

Audience: NASA leadership, scientists, the general public, and policymakers.

Team: NASA's Scientific Visualization Studio oversees hyperwall content and operations. Multiple teams and programs across the agency along with Earth Information Center interagency partners contributed to the content displayed. Specific contributors included:

- EIC Program Manager: Eleanor Stokes
- EIC Project Manager: Nicole Ramberg-Pihl
- Hyperwall Lead: Mark SubbaRao
- Data Dashboard Lead: Helen-Nicole Kostis
- Hyperwall technical support and operations: Brenda Lopez Silva, Michael Chyatte, Alex Gurvich
- Data dashboard contributors:
  - NASA's Scientific Visualization Studio including: AJ Christensen, Kel Elkins, Trent Schindler, Alex Kekesi, Greg Shirah, Cindy Starr, Zoey Armstrong, former team member Michala Garrison and Horace Mitchell.
  - Global Modeling and Assimilation Office (GMAO) led by Lesley Ott and Joseph Ardizonne, NASA Worldview Team, Earth Observatory, NASA FIRMS, Eyes on Earth, climate.nasa.gov, EONET
- Eric Hackathorn from NOAA

Chapter Author: Amanda Makulec

How This Dashboard Delivers: Making climate data exciting and accessible can be challenging. At the NASA headquarters, visitors explore earth science data on dashboards, hear stories through short videos, and see "beauty pieces" all in one loop on a 21 foot-long hyperwall. The delivery on a massive screen draws you in, and the near real-time data visualizations often drawing from satellite sensors or computational models spark curiosity, while communicating about our changing planet in a way that cuts across political lines and audiences.

Tools: Visualizations produced with Maya, Houdini, Mantra, RenderMan, Python, APIs, Web portals and services; design process also used Figma, Adobe Suite.

Timeline: Nine months from project kickoff (October 2022) to hyperwall opening (June 2023), with continuous development and enhancements ongoing.

Earth Now data dashboard on the hyperwall at the NASA Earth Information Center.

Source: *Image courtesy of Helen-Nicole Kostis*

Big Picture

You work for a government agency or large corporation interested in communicating key data and information in public spaces to raise awareness about environmental issues like climate change. Your vision is to design a "mission control center" for Earth: charts, data-driven visuals, and videos that help viewers understand how our climate is changing, the impact around them, and how NASA data improves people's lives.

Specifics

You need to be able to:

- Engage viewers across different audience groups with varying degrees of data literacy, from policymakers to students, on a topic that can be politically charged, creating a space for conversation and connection
- Communicate information based on large volumes of data without overwhelming the audience, using tactics like guided highlights, animation, and clever use of visual metaphor in your charts to keep an audience engaged
- Tell clear stories that connect big-picture trends on topics like sea level rise and wildfires and their impact on people

Related Scenarios

- You are an executive at a global corporation and want to showcase key performance indicators about your company on a large-scale display in a lobby. Examples of these displays have been installed and used at companies including Norfolk Southern and Procter & Gamble.
- You are a nonprofit leader who wants to showcase metrics about your organization's impact, interwoven with footage and stories from your beneficiaries.
- You are a museum curator or exhibit designer looking for creative ways to engage your visitors on a data-driven topic or leverage the presentation surface of bigger-than-life displays with visually rich content.

How People Use This Dashboard

The Earth Information Center (EIC) hyperwall contains a series of dashboards that present a picture of our changing planet through imagery and data streams from satellites, models, and ground-based and airborne measurements. These dashboards are meant for large public displays, with the first unveiling at NASA HQ in the center of Washington, DC in 2023. The content featured on the display addresses the nine core themes of EIC on an approximately 30-minute loop.

On the hyperwall, the dashboards are spliced with videos and "beauty pieces," data-driven visualizations meant purely to create a sense of awe. Each theme is presented with a three phase approach: a video, followed by a data dashboard, which is then followed by a beauty piece. See the hyperwall in action in Figure 26.1.

FIGURE 26.1 NASA's Disasters Response Team meeting.
Source: Photo courtesy of Helen-Nicole Kostis.

The NASA Scientific Visualization Studio (SVS) led the development of the hyperwall content. SVS creates data visualizations for the purpose of science communication, including large-scale public displays and niche internal products. Data visualizations and products created by the SVS are openly and freely available to the public.

The Audience

The hyperwall audience is larger than the audiences of most scenarios in this book, with far more varied information needs than could be satisfied by most dashboards.

The team identified priority audiences during development, including:

- NASA leadership. Administrator Bill Nelson served as a champion for the project and had a very specific vision for a Mission Control–style display with the information density and scale someone might expect from a control room for a space mission.
- Scientists, who would look for more granular details within specific charts or maps of interest to their work. They could eventually use these dashboards for their outbound communication efforts to peers and the general public.
- The general public, who have limited time and can be overwhelmed by data-dense displays, particularly around climate data, but could stay engaged with added features like video and awe-inspiring beauty pieces.
- Policymakers, who could visit the hyperwall as an advocacy and learning opportunity with staff or visitors to the Capitol.

Throughout the development process, different audience needs pulled the design decisions in different directions. The dashboard designs and approaches represented a balancing act across those varied needs, with different design treatments and data visualization leveraged to meet those needs. Watch the full 30-minute loop at NASA HQ, and you'll see simple line charts but also more creative animated data stories that address the wide and varied user needs.

Online Version Available

While the team designed the dashboards and additional components with a hyperwall-first approach, select dashboards are currently available online so anyone around the world can experience them by visiting earth.gov/hyperwall. The team plans to make all data dashboards available online in the future. See Figure 26.2.

The online versions have the same dimensions and wide format as the digital display at NASA HQ, rather than being organized in a scrolly-telling format where the reader scrolls through a sequence of charts. The wide, single screen view keeps the sense of scale of the display. The dashboards have been reconfigured in layout formats for other display systems, such as 3x3 tiled hyperwall displays.

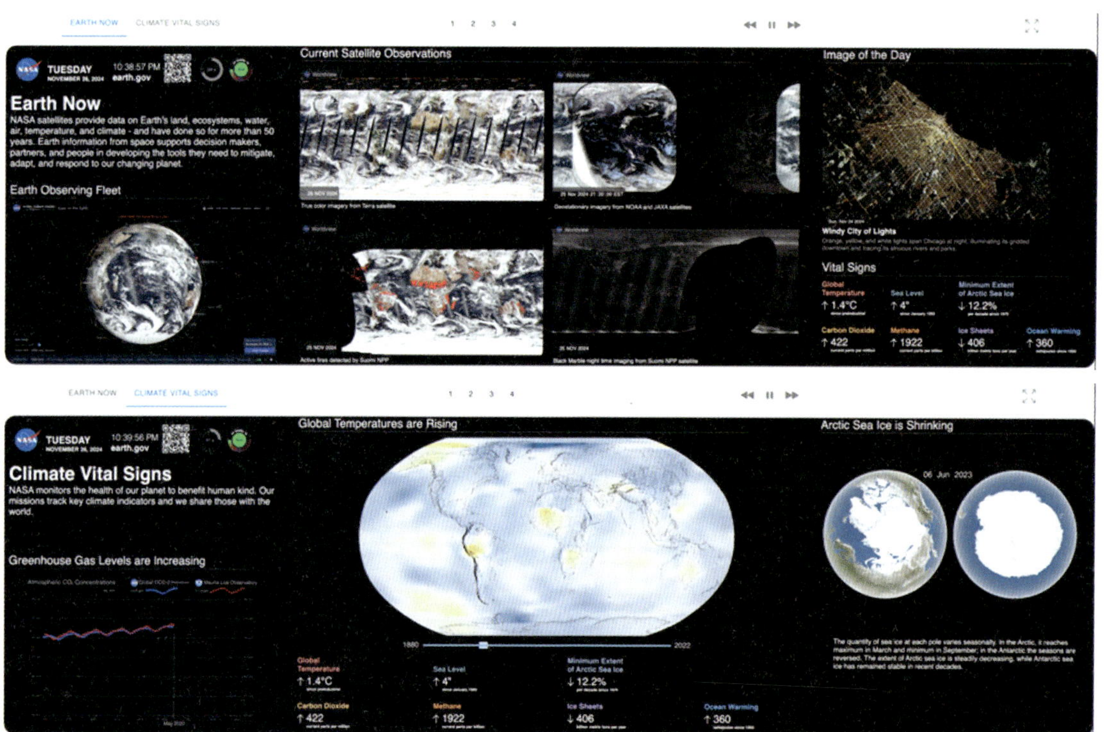

FIGURE 26.2 Screenshot of online Earth Now and Climate Vital Signs data dashboards made accessible globally.

Source: earth.gov/hyperwall.

Why This Works

Maps and BANs

On the hyperwall, the dashboards include some familiar visualizations. Maps feature prominently, given the importance of looking at geographic patterns. Big Awesome Numbers (BANs) are used to display key performance metrics, but their placement on the dashboards runs counter to the common recommendation for BANs to start in the upper left and fill the top row of the dashboard.

Look at the layouts on the Earth Now and Climate Vital Signs dashboards, which have key indicators in the lower right and lower center, respectively (Figure 26.3).

The positioning of the BANs in these dashboards reflects their priority. In the upper-left corner where someone might look first on a traditional dashboard, viewers see text summaries providing context and a short synthesis of what is presented. An additional consideration is the scale and placement of the hyperwall. When you walk into the NASA building, the center of the hyperwall is directly in front of you, placing the BANs in the position where viewers may read first.

Three Notable Graphics

Across the nine dashboards and additional data art pieces, the NASA Earth Information Center is a vault of visualizations that is far more expansive than what we can cover in a single scenario in this book. Watching the display loop at NASA headquarters, three notable visualizations illustrate the ways the team balanced audience needs to design displays that are engaging and diverge from the more typical graphics we celebrate in other scenarios.

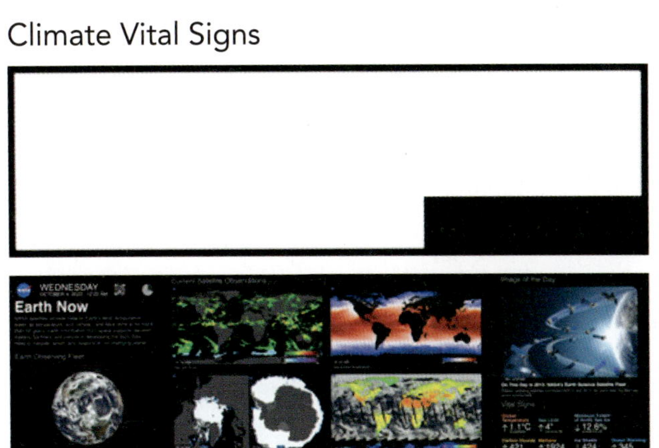

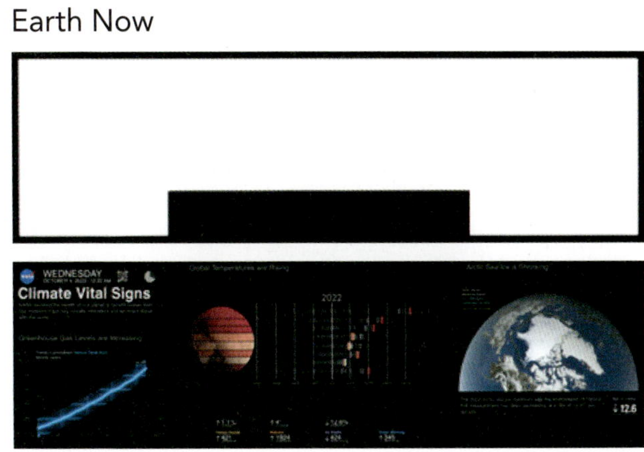

FIGURE 26.3 Positioning of BANs on two of the Earth.gov dashboards.

Climate Spiral Viz

In this chart, the display plots circles with one "ring" for each, showing monthly temperature change. Then, after all of the circles are plotted over 100+ years of data, the rings are sliced and "unrolled" into a line chart where each line represents a year. Then, the screen transitions to a more traditional line chart view animating the same data with each line representing a year and the x-axis showing months. The sequence of charts is displayed in Figure 26.4. Across the charts, the familiar red-blue diverging color scale from Ed Hawkins's climate

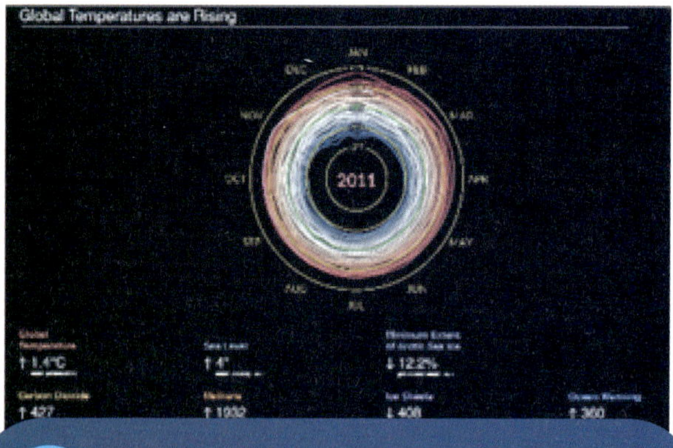

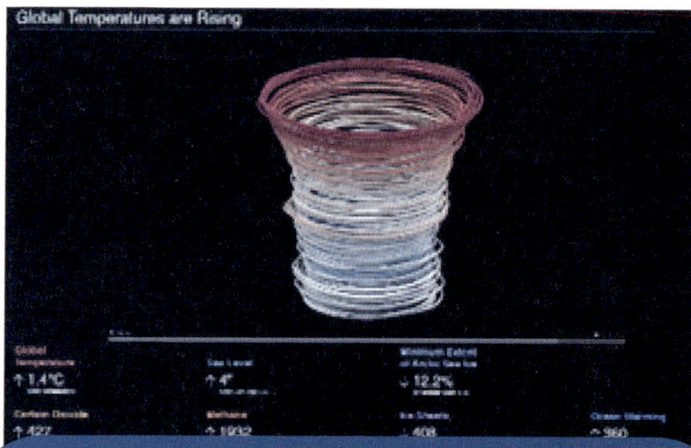

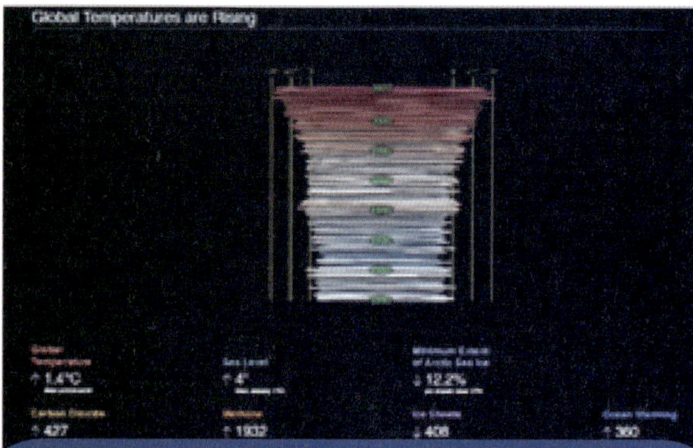

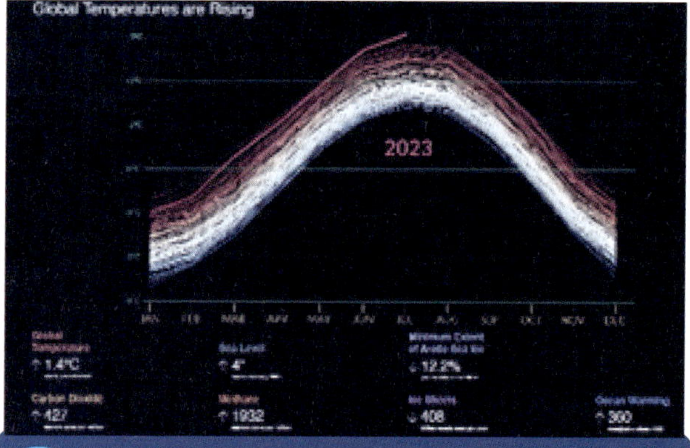

FIGURE 26.4 Sequency of displays of temperature change, simulating how the animation changes on the EIC hyperwall.
Source: Screenshots from Earth.gov.

stripes graphics reinforce where temperatures were hotter (red) or colder (blue) than baseline.

The spiral chart isn't the most precise way to display the data; as designers we know that a line chart can give us quicker speed to insight. The rings make many viz designers think of seasonality, but temperature anomalies aren't something we see over seasons as the timing of high and low temperatures across the globe balance out across hemispheres.

The decision to first plot the rings, in the face of a "better" chart was deliberate, according to the SVS team. The animated spiraling captures your attention, which is a priority in the midst of a 30-minute loop.

Globe and Strip Plot Chart

In another view of global temperature data, the display pairs a globe with a strip plot using vertical lines for individual encodings, all in an animated view.

The globe shows a set of stripes corresponding to latitude bands while the lines each represent the relative change in overall temperature at that latitude (Figure 26.5). The colored marks on the stripe plot show the value for the displayed year, and then turn white and fade to gray, creating the effect of a streak of the year-over-year temperature changes with the subtle fade.

This approach to visualizing the same data adds a dimension of geography, showing the larger relative change closer to the poles and focusing attention on the more recent changes with a whisper of the more distant periods.

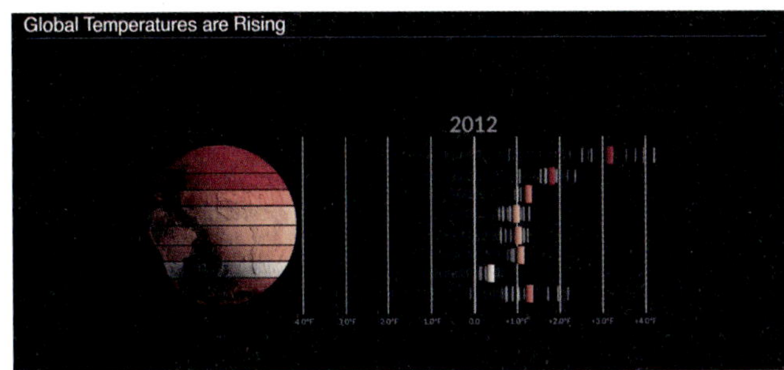

FIGURE 26.5 Strip plot and globe visualization from the animated hyperwall loop.

Porthole Visualizations

The use of visual metaphor in some of the dashboard displays creates compelling points of engagement necessary to achieve the EIC's science communication goals.

On either side of the NASA headquarters hyperwall display are two circular displays. As part of a display around the rising sea levels related to changes in our planet, one of the two circle displays takes on the appearance of a porthole with 3D rendered water rising. The animation showing sea level rising over time gives the sense of being on a sinking ship, which is more emotionally impactful than a line chart of sea level over time.

The porthole concept started as a rough sketch (Figure 26.6), taking inspiration from real-world experiences of looking out of a round window, and evolved to the final animated display next to the hyperwall (Figure 26.7).

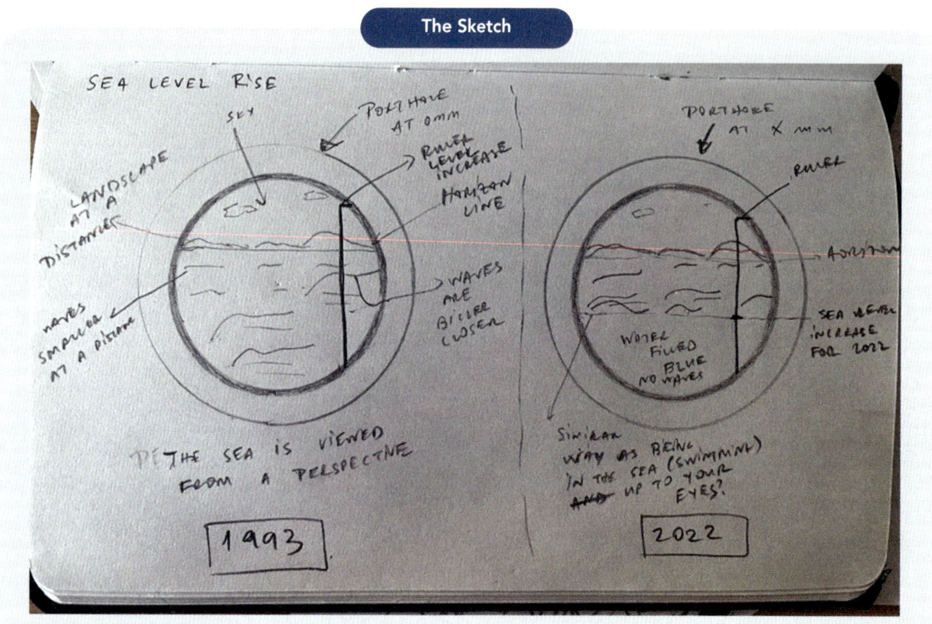

FIGURE 26.6 Sketch of porthole sea level rise visualization.

Source: Sketch courtesy of Helen-Nicole Kostis.

The Inspiration

View from ferry porthole from travels in the Aegean sea. Experiencing this view during multiple travels served as an inspiration for the sea level rise visualization.

The Installation

Sea Level Rise visualization, as it is installed at NASA Headquarters.

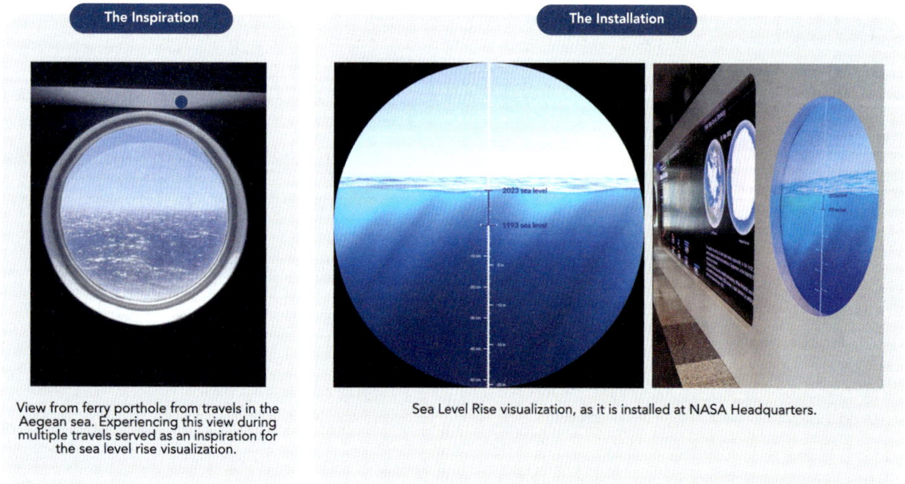

FIGURE 26.7 View from ferry porthole from travels in the Aegean sea. Experiencing this view during multiple travels served as an inspiration for the sea level rise visualization.

Source: Ferry porthole photo courtesy of Helen-Nicole Kostis.

Process

While the public communication goal is different from most use cases for dashboards in this book, many of the insights gained from the development process are relevant to any operational dashboard designer.

From designing with multiple audiences in mind to sorting out when to break the data viz rules with intention, the team made very purposeful informed decisions throughout. In addition, SVS collaborated across teams and agencies, dealing with competing interests and power dynamics that have relevance far beyond the agency responsible for sending astronauts to the moon.

A Note on Breaking the "Rules" on Purpose

THROUGHOUT the design process, the team found many creative ways to create visualizations that would engage people by deliberately breaking the data viz "rules."

On a business dashboard, where speed-to-insight can be paramount, morphing the same dataset into four different charts may not be practical and nudges toward the world of data art. But for the EIC audience, design decisions that created a sense of visual metaphor were prioritized over analytical precision in many charts, from the "tree rings" effect of the climate spiral visualization and the "sinking" sensation of watching the porthole visualization described previously.

Alberto Cairo, a leader in the data visualization field, has written about the ways the "rules" are changing, where we should prioritize ethical and justifiable design decisions rather than just blindly following a set of prescriptions for effective visualization, which is a principle the design team behind the EIC has lived out in this installation.

To understand how such a monumental project was built, is maintained, and connects people to meaningful information, we need to go back to the origin story of the project.

The Origin Story

The NASA EIC concept started at NASA headquarters, taking inspiration from a World Economic Forum white paper titled *Space for Net Zero* (dtdbook.com/link36), which dug into the ways aerospace, a domain where NASA is a global leader, could help the global community achieve net zero emissions. White papers typically lay out a key concept and then present a set of recommendations for experts and policymakers. The paper recommended two things: (1) put data viz front and center with a giant display concept modeled on the Apollo Mission Control and (2) reframe slowing climate change as a moonshot-level project governments should invest in.

One of the authors of the paper was former NASA Chief Economist Alexander MacDonald, who pitched the idea to the NASA administrator. Soon after, the NASA administrator wrote a blog post about "Climate Change Mission Control" (dtdbook.com/link37), which officially shifted the concept from "this could be interesting" to "we're going to build this!" This shows the importance of having a powerful champion behind a project.

Why Champions Matter

Having a leader within an organization championing the development of a dashboard was a frequent theme in our conversations around what makes a dashboard successful. Champions can mobilize resources, staff time, and enthusiasm for a data visualization project, and serve as a key advocate for adoption once a dashboard goes live. Across organizations, seeing a leader reference and use a dashboard can spark interest from other staff and serve as a reminder of the dashboard's capacity to support analysis and decision-making needs.

That blog post jumpstarted the discovery phase for the data dashboards. The original goal was to serve as a climate resilience and design center where city planners and others making real-world urban design decisions could go and see the data about climate change in real time. Soon after the administrator published his blog, an initial planning team met at the Goddard Space Center outside of Washington, DC to engage the Scientific Visualization Studio team who had experience with NASA's hyperwall displays.

The team iterated on the idea and the language: how to describe this *big* project? The team made sure to describe the project to reflect the vision and inspire curiosity, avoiding trigger words related to conspiracy issues that unfortunately come with climate conversations. Phrases like "Mission Control for climate" may sound overreaching to the general public and work counter to the goal to spark wide interest and adoption. During those initial meetings, the team also expanded the vision beyond climate and incorporated public health, agriculture, and other climate-adjacent topics.

Once the project kicked off, leadership pushed the team to quickly create a prototype. While the team started with early ideas to have a fully operational display at NASA headquarters by June 2023 as the concept evolved and grew, it took a bit more time to get to launch. See Figure 26.8.

FIGURE 26.8 Hyperwall display with Greenhouse Gases dashboard at NASA headquarters in Washington, DC.

The white paper, blog, and leadership discussions all paved the way to defining the nine theme areas of the EIC. The early roadmap for the display included two parts: the physical exhibit and an online portal where anyone can access the information.

The NASA team first worked on the physical exhibit (launched in June 2023) and then developed alternative versions for public access, including the online portal and adapting the data dashboards to other hyperwall systems including at the Smithsonian Natural History Museum less than a mile from NASA HQ. While it may seem a bit counterintuitive to start with the physical display with all of its complexities, starting with the big wall crystallized ideas and benefited from momentum as a high-profile project with stakeholders in senior leadership.

The Team

As the concept for the EIC crystallized in Phase 1 (discovery) of the design process, Phase 2 was when the development and design team formed. The NASA SVS team added a formal product manager to oversee the design process of data dashboards and develop a roadmap for visualizations. The team also broadened beyond the SVS data visualization developers, collaborating with senior strategists, external partners, and the NASA communications team. The SVS, at the time, included 16 data visualization developers, which might make it one of the largest public science visualization teams in the world.

The volume of visualizations in the hyperwall loop necessitated collaborating and adapting existing visualizations into unified views, rather than starting entirely from scratch. The SVS team wanted to collaborate with colleagues, but also bring in knowledge and expertise from visualization researchers and experts who could inform how to make existing content and the overall design even more engaging.

With the goal to jumpstart a closer community of practice around climate visualization, the team attended the 2022 IEEE Vis Conference, a premier annual convening of visualization experts and researchers. The SVS team hosted the Viz4Climate workshop (dtdbook.com/link38) with the goal to learn from others working on similar topics, incorporating insights from research into the hyperwall's design.

Collaborations continued beyond the workshop. A paper by Benjamin Bach on dashboard design patterns (dtdbook.com/link39), presented at the VIS 2022 conference helped define a taxonomy and vocabulary for the data dashboards. Kostis reached out to Benjamin Bach, which sparked a years-long informal collaboration.

Together with Fanny Chevalier, the SVS team and Bach have been meeting almost weekly ever since discussing challenges and sharing ongoing work.

In designing the wireframes and prototypes for the dashboard displays, the SVS team started with custom visualizations already built by the team for NASA. Then, they brought in key partners from across the agency to provide a holistic view of science efforts, including near-real time satellite data from NASA Worldview, high-resolution models updated daily on the Discover Supercomputer by the Global Modeling and Assimilation Office (GMAO), the Image of the Day from the Earth Observatory, active fires using NASA FIRMS, and the team behind the climate.nasa.gov site who curate the climate vital signs.

The list of contributing teams is evolving as new dashboards are brought to life. The Studio at JPL designed the "Earth Pulse" data sculpture and the immersive room experience which accompany the hyperwall. Together, these components make up the Earth Information Center exhibit.

Design and Development for the REALLY Big Screen

The SVS team had the advantage of knowing what other teams were doing across the NASA viz ecosystem. Instead of looking to develop visualizations for the EIC data dashboards on their own, they knew the strengths of other internal groups. The team aimed to leverage and showcase the unique capabilities of teams across the agency by identifying and customizing visualization assets for the dashboards.

The project created a great space for collaboration, with various partners contributing different charts. The dashboard aesthetics came from the idea of modeling on a "mission control" model, with a dark background. The tech stack for designing and rendering a 21 feet wide, high fidelity data display looks a *bit* more complex than most business dashboards. The final display includes a center 8K display with two 4K displays on the side. See Figure 26.9.

The data dashboards are driven by digital signage software pulling content from many sources and of various formats. The software seamlessly integrates animations, still images, web links, and applications into one central view creating the 30-minute hyperwall experience.

Any data viz designer visiting the hyperwall would likely ask the obvious question: what tools are used to make the graphics? The answer is a mix. Visualizations created by SVS are pre-rendered with a 3D rendering platform called Houdini or developed using Python or R. Visualizations from the Global Modeling Assimilation Office are rendered overnight on the Discover Supercomputer based on state-of-the art models and near-real time data are provided by NASA's Worldview and NASA's FIRMS with custom production URLs. The web applications creating the

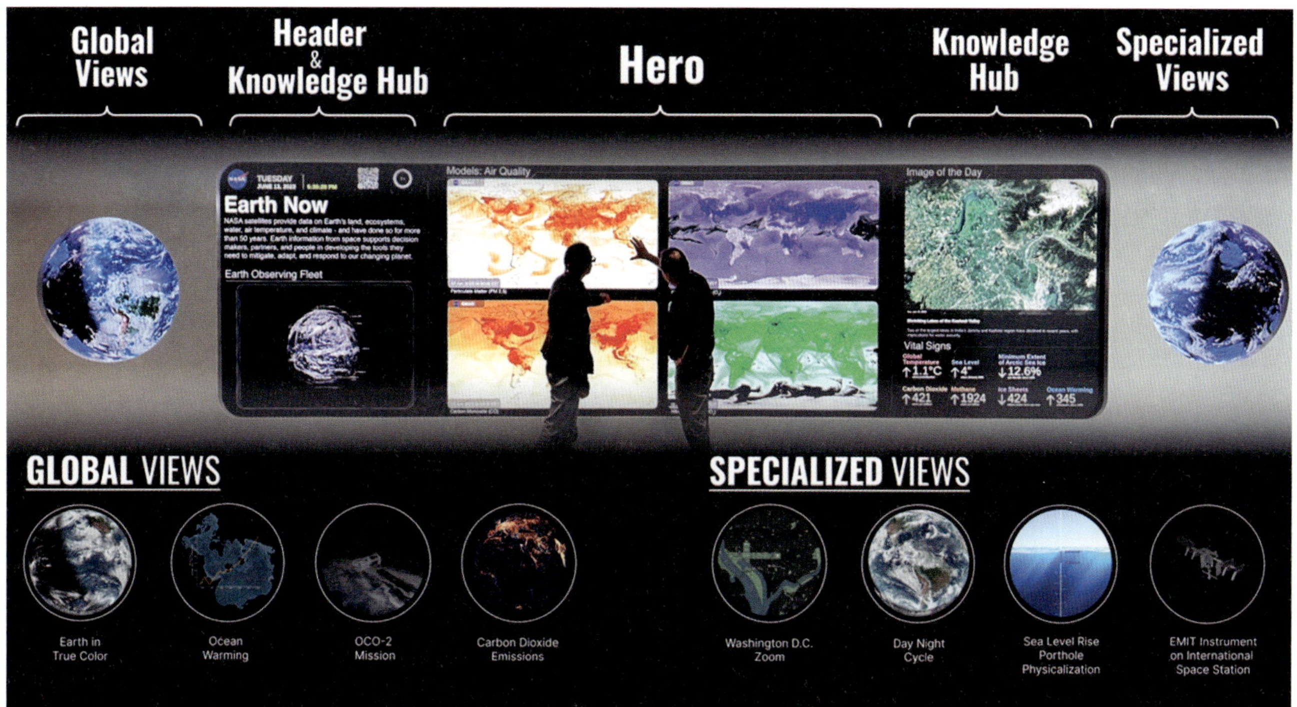

FIGURE 26.9 Content layout and design strategy for Hyperwall data dashboards.
Source: Image courtesy of Helen-Nicole Kostis.

content loop were developed with JavaScript, React, and by programming the visual signage software. Here, the team brings together different kinds of graphics including static and animated components.

With big projects also come big challenges. One of the biggest technical challenges was around the timeliness of data updates, which vary across the different chart components. Real-time updates, particularly for high-profile events like wildland fires and disasters, were high priority. To meet those needs, the team leveraged near-real time capacity from partners and upended internal infrastructure and pipelines to update visualizations automatically overnight.

Inspiring, Not Just Alarming

Viewing data about climate change can create a sense of existential crisis for certain audiences; we've seen those from younger generations feeling diagnosable "climate angst" related to what the state of the planet will be in 30 or 50 years. However, to entice someone to engage with the data more, the team recognized the need to inspire hope, rather than angst, and actively tried to ensure the hyperwall didn't become an experience that left audiences feeling a sense of doom and negativity.

But why *should* someone feel hopeful looking at some of the staggering data on the hyperwall? For the NASA-led team, hope comes from recognizing how much we now know, evident in the many data dashboards and visualizations showcasing NASA's research efforts.

For this endeavor Kostis, the dashboard lead, realized early on that hope could be woven into the design and language of the data dashboards by breaking free of some "typical rules" of data dashboards. Three specific approaches included:

- Adding plenty of breathing space between widgets to avoid a sense of being overwhelmed
- Inserting bits of explanatory text in simple language to make complex information more accessible
- Most importantly, creating a "visual feast" for the viewers by leveraging the power of data using shape, form, and color to engage and inspire with intermittent "beauty pieces" in the loop

These principles came together in the sequence of different displays in the loop. The team spliced video narrations and the dashboards together and then added "beauty pieces" – data visualizations at a scale that spanned the full display so that people could bask in the aesthetic delight. In designing the sequence of components, what the team could control was the "visual feast," said Kostis. More beautiful charts were successful by their own measures (engagement and inspiration) even if the design decisions didn't always align to "the rules."

> Mark SubbaRao (NASA SVS Lead) said bluntly, "I don't care if people can accurately pick a number off the graph and decode information. If people are scrolling on their phone, I'm trying to get their attention.
>
> —*Mark SubbaRao (Lead, NASA Scientific Visualization Studio) about the design of the hyperwall loop*

While these beauty pieces are created with data accuracy and scientific integrity, the team recognized that they functioned more as data art than driving insight. Each encodes information with color and shape in a more creative display, and less as functional visualizations. The rainbow-colored map of ocean current movement is such an example (Figure 26.10).

As a result, the final design of the hyperwall displays considered the "beauty bias": our willingness to engage with and sometimes believe prettier visualizations more than the cluttered and unpleasant ones. The user experience integrates these moments where the dashboard displays shift between pure enjoyment and focused interpretation.

FIGURE 26.10 Beauty piece at the hyperwall: a rainbow-colored map of data-driven ocean flows at NASA headquarters in Washington, DC.

Enhancements and Continued Development

The hyperwall and adjacent components are ever evolving. The tech stack and underlying framework of discrete pieces of a looping display allows the team to develop new components (like video explainers around a topic) and continue to add new visualizations to the displays thanks to the flexible architecture.

In 2024, the year after the initial release, the team started experimenting with timed overlays and annotations in an effort to add explanations for the data visualizations to the public.

An online version of these dashboards is available on Earth.gov, including additional graphics where people can personalize climate change to their community. In addition, a new EIC exhibit opened at the National Museum of Natural History (Smithsonian Institution) on October 2024 and the SVS team continues to think through ways to achieve their goals of connecting people to climate information in ways that gets them to think.

Defining Success

Designing for a physical display, meant to be viewed by a wide range of audiences for different purposes, also means a different approach to measuring success. While the team can count the number of visitors, their reflection on one of the biggest measures of success was less about numbers and more about sentiment: "Someone wants to come back, not run away."

That metric diverts away from thinking about the number of data-informed decisions made or times views. When we think about measures of success, this is a "big S" measure focused on impact and sentiment, rather than a "small S" count of visitors. Focusing on sentiment reflects the goal of the hyperwall: to inspire and engage as a piece of science communication, not to directly inform decisions despite an early aim to use the tool with city planners for more decision-making.

When you invest millions of dollars in a project though, you don't wholly ignore the visit counts. Since opening in 2023, the team has had many visitors actively engaged in viewing the display in person, from heads of state visiting from other countries to school groups. That reach will continue to scale with new installations open at the Kennedy Space Center and the Smithsonian Natural History Museum and as Earth.gov grows.

The intended takeaway from visiting the hyperwall isn't that you understand everything you see. You can watch the cycle of dashboards, videos, and beauty pieces over and over but still see something new each time. Instead, it reminds you that people are working on all of these topics, from wildland fires to issues facing agriculture and food production, in service of a brighter future for our planet and communities.

Author Commentary

ANDY: Is this a dashboard? For those who want to adhere to a strict definition, there are countless red flags. "It's on a wall! It's got videos! Data art? Circular animate charts? Heresy!"

Crying heresy reveals a misunderstanding of the diverse ways in which people might need to understand data. There is a space and a need for accurate, austere, crisp charts that optimize for specific insights that can be understood in seconds. There is, however, also a need for data monitoring displays that provide the gist of a dataset, that provide an insight that can sit and influence slowly over time. That's the goal of this large display, and it is one that's inspiringly executed.

Furthermore, large wall displays of data are ones often requested by clients. The techniques learned from the NASA dashboard are applicable to those.

STEVE: I almost always channel my inner Stephen Few and make reducing the time to insight the driving goal. I think you would get that with bar charts and line charts. But here I believe getting people to think differently about something – to *feel* something – is more important than time to insight.

You may not be able to apply the giant display and bespoke charts to your work, but the process and thinking explored here is likely applicable to any multifaceted project.

JEFF: There are so many little details that were considered when creating this project. The animations and transitions really stand out. The video is timed, so the user is not in control; they are just along for the ride. However, the animations and transitions seamlessly move the user from one part of the story to another. The animations also help to explain the information. For example, the radar chart animates and transforms into a line chart.

I also love the way they visualized the Global Temperature Rising (Figure 26.5) with the globe and bar code chart. We often see temperature represented as a global number rising (on a line chart), but it's more complicated than that. This visualization breaks down the temperature rising by latitude, alongside a spinning globe. It animates year by year, plotting the temperatures against latitude, while showing the BANs across the bottom. This animation is really fun to watch, but it is also effective in telling the story over time.

PART III

SUCCEEDING IN THE REAL WORLD

From Dashboards to Big Ideas

Our goal in writing this book was to share practical insights around how great dashboards get built. In Part I we presented and explained our design framework. In Part II we provided 15 scenarios that we hope will inspire you (and hope you will borrow from).

Now, we want to provide some broader perspectives. What is shaping the demand for and development of dashboards today? What are some design concepts we've seen that help dashboards succeed across our scenarios and in our work?

In Part III we present essays that will smooth the way as you navigate the challenges of producing effective dashboards.

We've grouped these essays into two big categories: design and perspectives. You can read them in order or hop to anything that catches your fancy.

Design

While each dashboard you create is unique, there are many common challenges we face as designers that go deeper than the grid layouts and recommendations discussed in Chapter 8.

In these essays, we explore:

- **BANs**: Here we share approaches for going beyond just displaying big numbers to add context and make the data more meaningful.
- **Dynamic duos**: These are our recommendations for chart types that pair well to address common analysis needs.
- **Beware of software defaults**: Dashboard software comes with various design defaults, including how gridlines appear, fonts, color palettes, and chart types. We make the case that you should *always* make sure that the default settings don't steer you toward creating something that is confusing and, in some cases, misleading.

Perspectives

In writing this book, we found ourselves talking about larger themes that have impacted our work over the last five years. Here we explore some of the larger trends shaping the industry and influencing the ways people engage with information.

In these essays we explore:

- **What the Heck Is a Dashboard**? A deep dive into the history of the word and how it's used today, and how managing your audience's understanding of the word will lead to better outcomes.
- **Numbers in Context and Critical Thinking in Data Analysis**. How framing the question changes the meaning and relevance of data you visualize, and how to think critically about the data you are analyzing.
- **Generative AI and Data Analytics.** How you can harness Generative AI to make better dashboards faster (but beware of the pitfalls).
- **Use Dashboards to Find Stories, Not Tell Them**. While a dashboard may not be a great place to tell a story, it's a great place to find a story worth telling.
- **Want to Make Better Dashboards? Find Good Sparring Partners**. See how feedback and pushback from peers can improve your work.

- **Ask the Community for Help**. The data visualization community is extraordinarily knowledgeable and generous with its collective expertise. If you are stuck, you should tap into that expertise.

The Screaming Cat Is Back

Most of the figures throughout these essays are good examples, but there will be some bad examples, and we mark these bad examples with a screaming-cat icon (Figure 1). We use this icon so you won't have to read the surrounding text to determine if the visualization is something you should emulate or avoid.

FIGURE 1 The screaming cat. If you see this icon, it means don't make a chart like this one (Illustration by Eric Kim).

Chapter 27

BANs (Big-Ass Numbers)

Or Big Aggregated Numbers. Or Big Assertive Numbers

Steve Wexler

Prior to working with Jeffrey Shaffer and Andy Cotgreave on *The Big Book of Dashboards*, I tended to look at BANs – large, occasionally overstuffed key performance indicators (KPIs) – as ornamental rather than informational. I thought they just took up space on a dashboard without adding much analysis.

I was totally aligned with Randy Krum, who writes in his excellent book *Cool Infographics*: "Using big fonts in an infographic to make the numbers stand out is not data visualization. This is a big pet peeve of mine, and it's done by designers in thousands of infographic designs and PowerPoint presentations. Displaying the number in a large font doesn't make it any easier for the audience to understand."

Figure 27.1 reflects Randy's point. It shows several metrics that appear on an About page for a corporate website.

What's the problem with this?

We're missing context. For example, the revenue figure on the left, is it up or down from last year? What about five years ago? How does it compare with other companies that sell similar products and services?

And what about that net promoter score on the right? First, what is a net promoter score? Once we know that, we'll probably want to know if it has gone up or down from last year. How does it compare with other companies? It's the same set of questions we have around revenue.

I agree with Randy that in most situations we'd be making things easier for our stakeholders to understand data if our BANs answered questions like the ones I've posed here, but there is a good reason to just have numbers, which I'll explain.

Hans Rosling's Thoughts on "Lonely Numbers"

In his book *Factfulness*, Hans Rosling calls numbers without context "lonely numbers" and encourages people to avoid them. He writes:

The most important things you can do to avoid misjudging something's importance is to avoid lonely numbers. Never, ever leave a number all by itself. Never believe that one number on its own can be meaningful. If you are offered one number, always ask for at least one more. Something to compare it with...

...When I see a lonely number in a news report, it always triggers an alarm: what should this lonely number be compared to? What was that number a year ago? Ten years ago? What is it in a comparable country or region? And what should it be divided by? What is the total this is a part of? What would this be per person? I compare the rates, and only then do I decide whether it really is an important number.

$27.8B

revenue

43,000

employees worldwide

3,900

customers

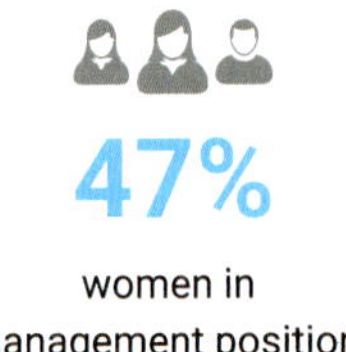

47%

women in management positions

56.2

net promoter score

FIGURE 27.1 A series of BANs displayed on a corporate website.

The History of the Term BAN

Big numbers on dashboards have been around for a long time, but the term *BAN* is relatively new.

In August 2016, I was working with Vanessa Edwards and Eric Edwards, the principals at Creative Performance Inc., and Ryan Gensel, currently the principal

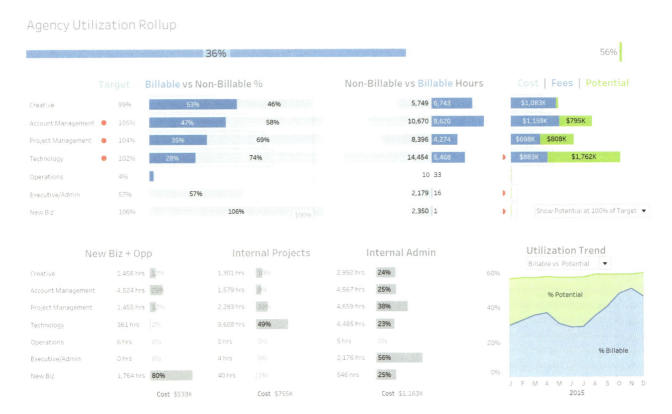

FIGURE 27.2 A not-quite-finished version of the utilization rollup dashboard.

at Thinking Interface Design. With stakeholder input, we built the dashboard shown in Figure 27.2.

I thought it was a very good dashboard, but it was missing something...something that would summarize the dashboard with a few key findings. I said to Ryan and others in a meeting, "We need to put some Big-Ass Numbers at the top," and I quickly sketched what I had in mind on a whiteboard.

Ryan and I made quick work of adding these new components to the dashboard, and the updated version, shown in Figure 27.3, is featured in Chapter 25 of *The Big Book of Dashboards*.

Soon thereafter I shortened *Big-Ass Numbers* to BANs and unintentionally became the creator of a popular acronym that's become part of the vernacular.

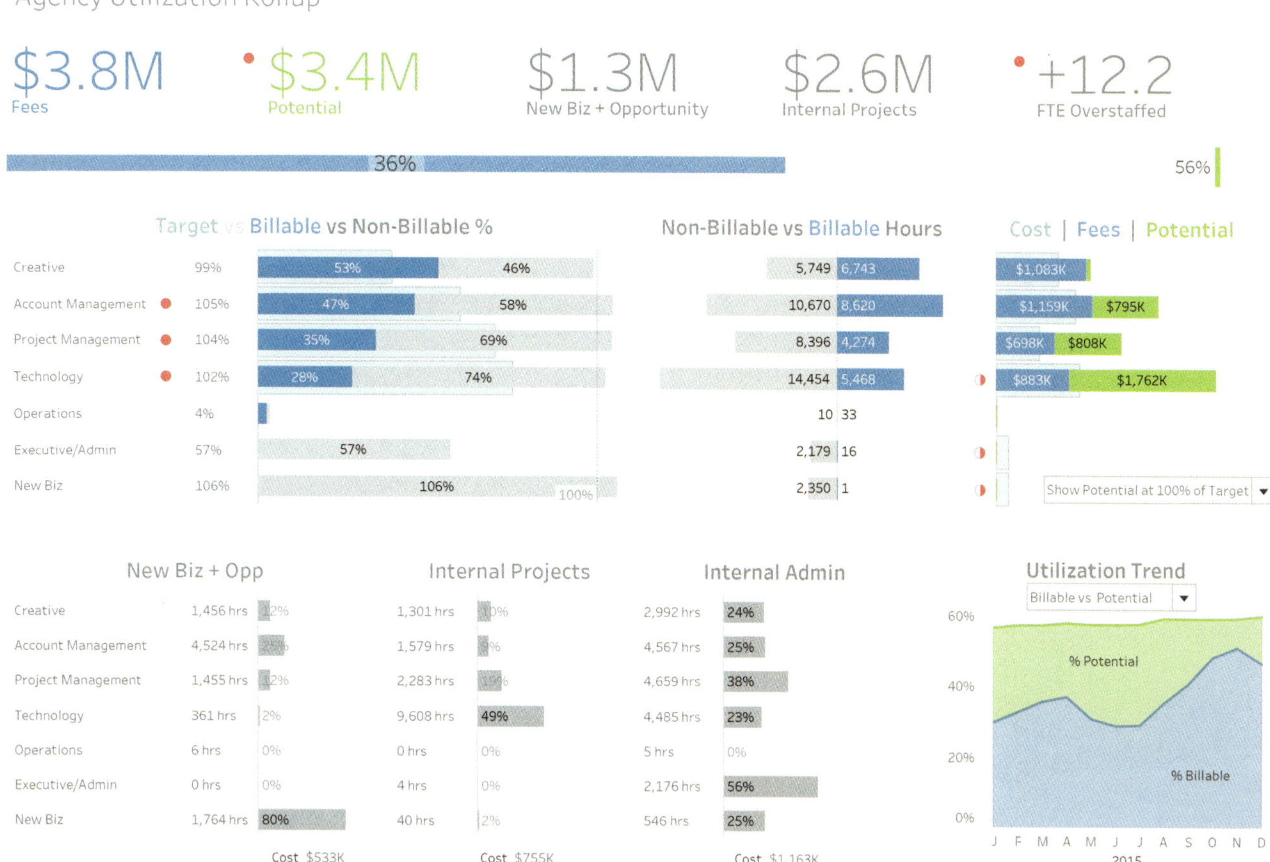

FIGURE 27.3 Utilization rollup dashboard, with BANs.

BANs as a Color Legend

Looking at the first two BANs in Figure 27.4, we can see that the agency makes $3.8 million and could make $3.4 million more if it were to meet its billable goals. That is the most important takeaway, and it's presented in big, bold numbers right at the top of the dashboard.

But the BANs do more than draw attention to key points. They inform us that blue represents fees and green represents potential, so I know exactly how to interpret bars that are those colors when I look at a chart like the one shown in Figure 27.5.

$3.8M
Fees

$3.4M
Potential

FIGURE 27.4 The first two BANs show key takeaways and serve as a color legend. If we had to distill this entire dashboard down to one key point, it would be that the current sales are $3.8M, but they could be $3.4M more (hence the red dot).

BAN Contrast Issues

The green text on a white background in Figure 27.5 fails a contrast check test and would not adhere to Web Content Accessibility Guidelines (WCAG). This means that some people may have difficulty reading the number and understanding that it refers to potential. There are several ways we can address this, including changing the foreground color or changing the background color. If you have a defined set of stakeholders and they all say they can read the text, then you don't have to change anything. But if you have a large audience and haven't polled all your users or if you need to be WCAG-compliant, we encourage you to test your BANs (and any text) using a contrast checker and, if warranted, make some changes so everyone can read the text.

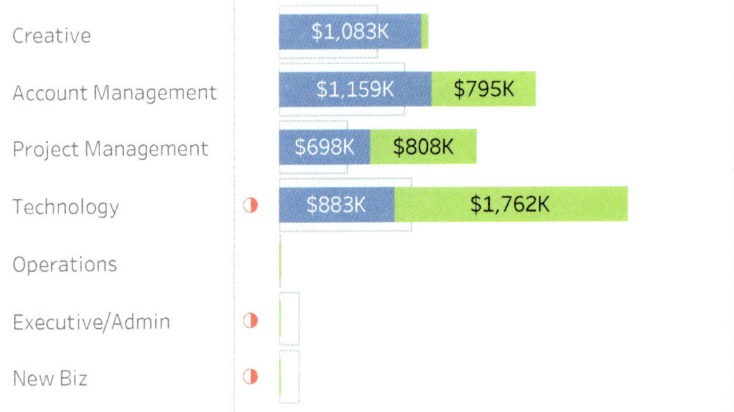

FIGURE 27.5 Because the BANs show how to interpret color, we can see that for Technology the company billed $883K but could bill an additional $1,762K if it were to hit its targets.

As someone who often needs to use every pixel, I like being able to combine the KPIs and the color legend into a single visual saving a lot of space.

BANs with Context

Retention Rate

Imagine you've been called into a meeting to discuss HR metrics in your organization. Someone has prepared a dashboard that includes this context-free BAN (Figure 27.6).

So, the entire organization's retention rate for the current quarter is 76%. Is that good or bad? If you are not steeped in the HR metrics of your organization, you'd have no idea if you should be celebrating or panicking.

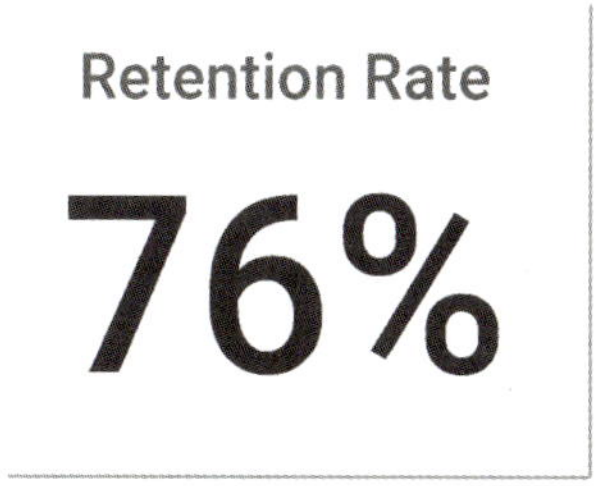

Here's a variation that lets us know that 76% is bad, which works when we've set up the mental model with our users that the orange dot means to pay closer attention (Figure 27.7).

That's certainly an improvement over just having a number, but just how bad is it? Are we under our goal by a little or a lot?

Let's answer that question by making the font a little smaller and adding a bar with a reference line (Figure 27.8). We can now see that our goal is 90%, and we are quite a bit below that goal.

At this point, we might want to know if this is a new development or if it has been going on for a while.

Figure 27.9 shows a version that shows the trends for the past three years and that the current

Retention Rate

76%

FIGURE 27.6 A BAN showing retention rate. If you were unfamiliar with the HR metrics of your organization, you'd have no idea whether this was good or bad.

Retention Rate

76%

FIGURE 27.7 The little orange dot alerts us that something is amiss.

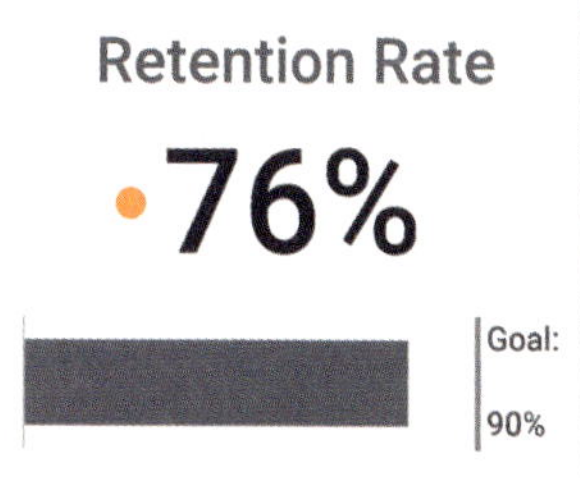

FIGURE 27.8 The bar with a reference line allows us to see just how far we are from our goal of 90%.

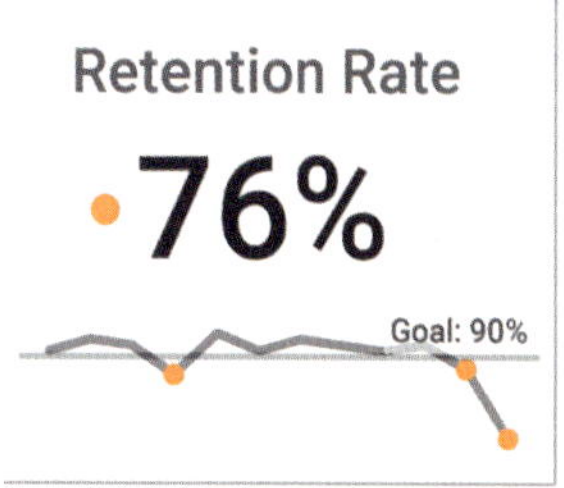

FIGURE 27.9 The sparklines allow us to see that not only are we below goal but that the latest quarter is considerably lower than any quarter over the past three years.

quarter is much lower than any of the previous quarters.

Look how many questions we can answer by adding context to the BAN! In a space no larger than the first BAN, we communicate that the 76% is bad, it's substantially below our goal of 90%, and that the current quarter is the worst value we've had in three years.

As for the obvious questions: "Is this low rate for the entire company, or is it a handful of divisions that are responsible?" and "Was there a particular event that triggered this low retention rate?" Well, that's what the rest of the dashboard should show.

Adding Context to Election Polling Displays

In 2019, Andy recalled seeing polling data presented in *The Guardian* that looked like what we see in Figure 27.10. The 2019 UK general election was particularly volatile, as Boris Johnson was installed by the Conservatives in desperation to find a solution to the Brexit challenges created by the 2016 referendum.

While colorful, we must work hard to compare the magnitude of the values. This would be easy with a bar chart or some type of graphic that compares position from a common baseline. We also can't tell how polling values have been trending over time; this was an important part of the story of the campaign, because of the volatility described. We

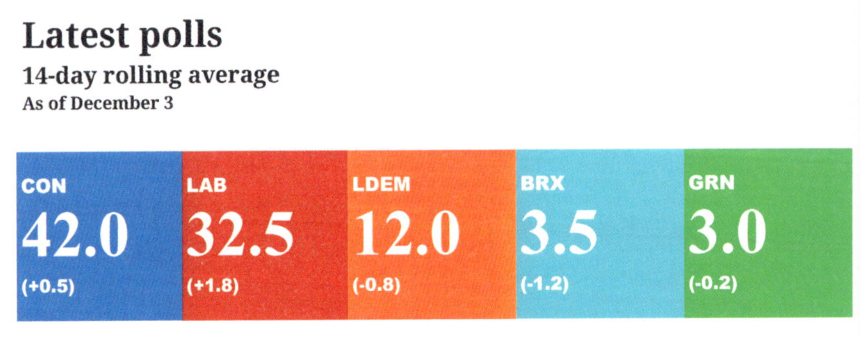

FIGURE 27.10 Colorful polling results with no context.

can see only the change (+ / –) from the previous polling period.

Compare that with the same 14-day rolling averages but with added context (Figure 27.11).

Both displays take up the same amount of space, but the second one allows us to see both trends and magnitude, as it's easy to compare the height of the lines from a common baseline. We get a lot more value for your screen real estate buck!

BANs with Context or KPI Cards?

I've argued that we can often do better than simply displaying a big number by adding some simple visualization elements (e.g., warning dots, reference lines, etc.) that provide a context to better understand the BAN.

But many developers are taking this a step further and creating fully working "mini dashboards" around a particular metric. These mini dashboards are sometimes called KPI cards and can be rendered in groupings on a desktop or sequentially on a phone. Here are some examples.

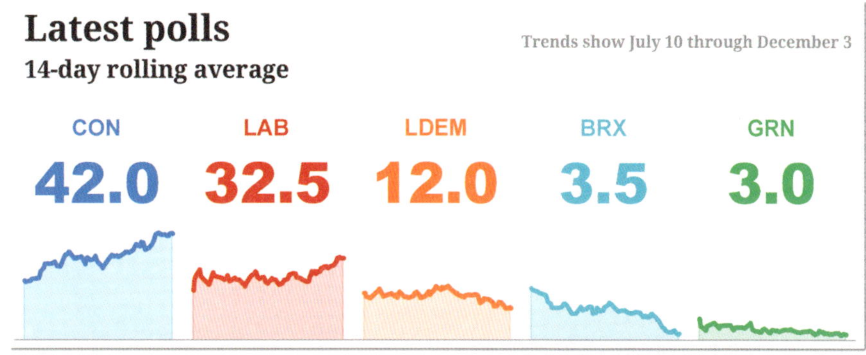

FIGURE 27.11 The same data, same BANs, but with added context.

Profit Ratio KPI Card

Consider this KPI card from Anastasiya Kuznetsova (Figure 27.12).

We see the date period, metric name, metric value, change from the previous period, and spark bars to show trends and provide context. A lot of thought went into the size and placement of each element, with the metric name and value providing the headline, and the other elements providing context.

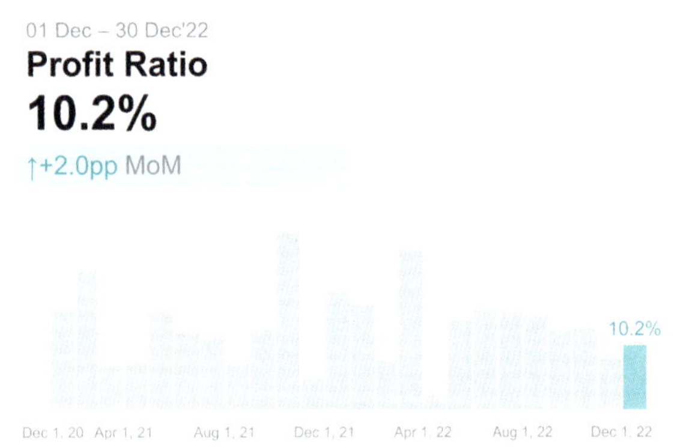

FIGURE 27.12 The Profit Radio Super BAN/KPI Card packs a lot of information into a small space.

Tableau Pulse Sales Insight

In Figure 27.13 we see a rich KPI card that provides both commentary and a line chart with projections to understand if we should be pleased or

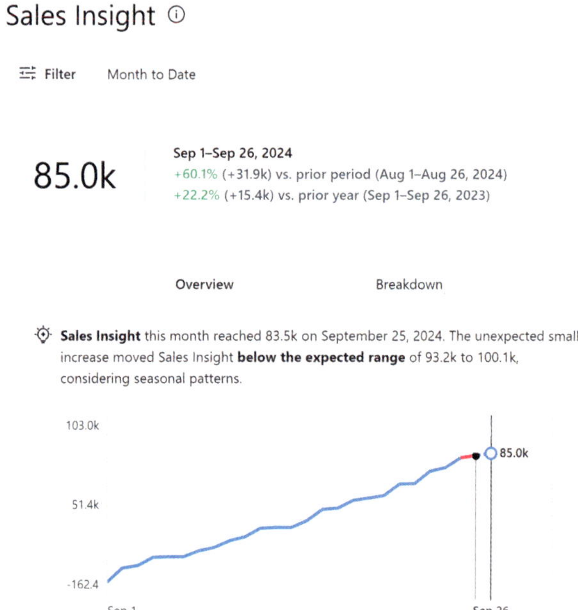

FIGURE 27.13 Tableau Pulse KPI card with automatically generated line chart and AI-generated insights.

Is it a BAN? Is it a KPI Card?

AND do we really need to draw a distinction? We could argue that the BAN with context in Figure 27.12 is really a KPI card. I'll confess I can't tell you where sophisticated BANs end and where KPI cards begin. If the BAN with context reaches some threshold of complexity, it becomes a KPI card. Let's not lose sleep over this.

Andy suggests that the moment a BAN with context becomes a KPI card is when the number is no longer the biggest thing.

disappointed with the 85.0K in sales (we should be disappointed). While sales are up from the prior period and prior year, they are below expectations for this year. There's also some AI-generated text that explains the key takeaways from the data that drives the chart.

A Multiple Metrics KPI Card

Figure 27.14 shows a versatile multiple metrics KPI card developed by dashboard and BI developer Gustaw Dudek. This mini dashboard allows users to select different metrics (Engagements, Impressions, New Followers, etc.) and time periods (last 7 days, 14 days, 30 days, etc.) The example here shows Engagements over the last 90 days, emphasizing the BAN (13.2K total engagements) but also showing actual and percentage increases from the previous period, accompanied by a bar and moving average chart. All these elements are presented in a small and easy-to-read card that works great on both large and small screens.

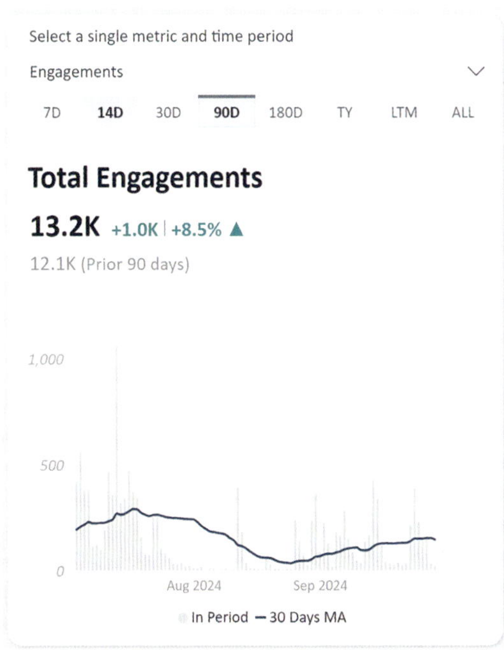

FIGURE 27.14 A multiple metrics KPI card developed in Power BI by Gustaw Dudek.

Multiple KPI Cards

All the KPI card examples provide context for just one BAN or KPI at a time, but there's no reason why you can't have multiple KPI cards on a single dashboard. That's what Lindsey Poulter did with the dashboard in Figure 27.15.

Here we see the BANs, how far above or below target they are, and monthly trends, all in a compact, easy-to-read arrangement.

Do note that the KPI tree that we explored in Chapter 20, when partially or fully expanded, is an example of multiple KPI cards playing nicely together on a single screen.

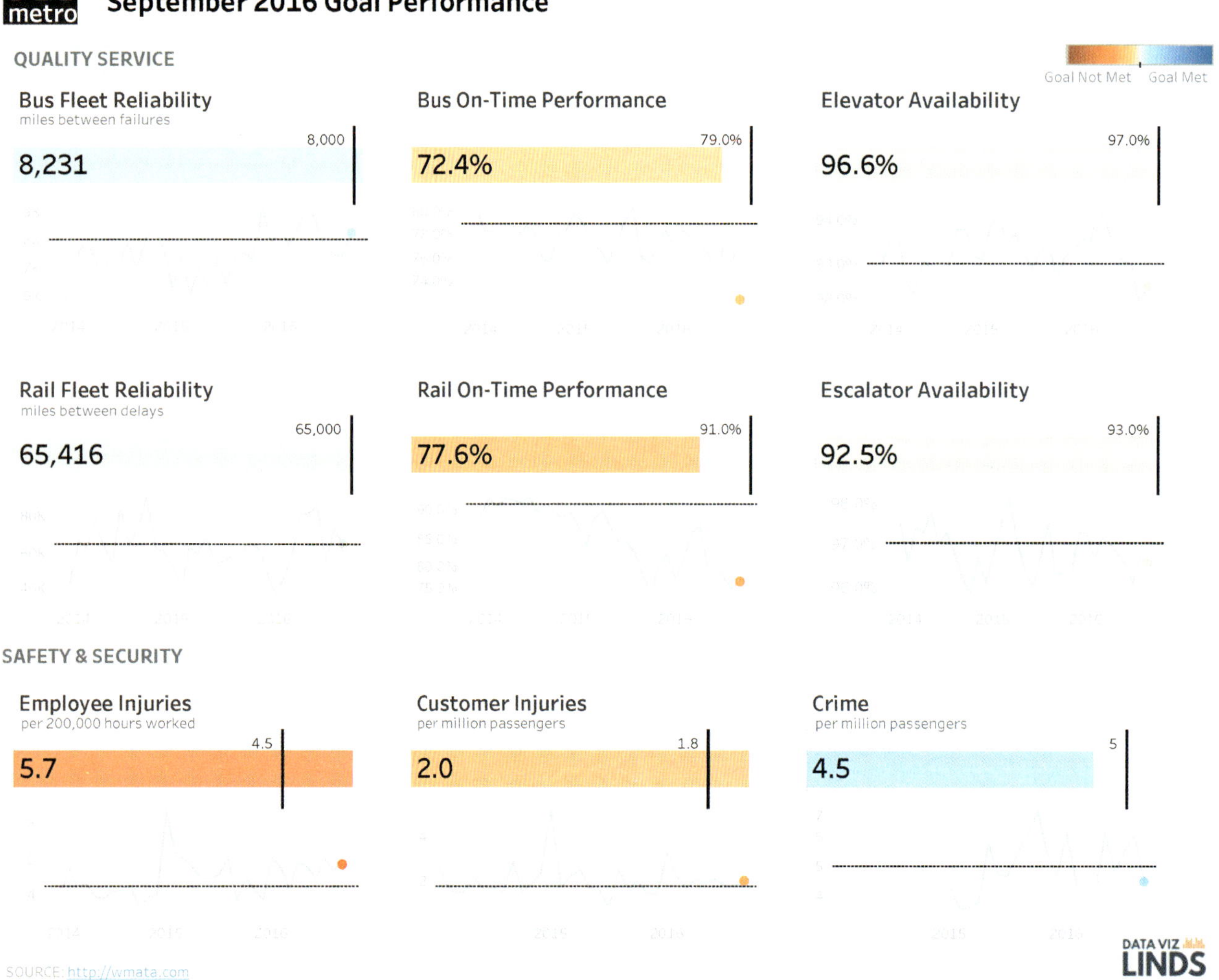

FIGURE 27.15 Nine KPI cards in one dashboard.

Mobile-Friendly BANS and KPI Cards

MULTIPLE KPI cards can work great on a mobile device. Figure 27.16 shows how Lindsey's KPI dashboard might render on a phone.

BANs as Conversation Starters

As I indicated at the beginning of this chapter, I used to pooh-pooh just having numbers on a dashboard, but I've seen them work effectively as conversation starters. For example, imagine you founded a company that, in a short period of time, has ballooned from three employees to 103. You want to gauge employee engagement, and you send out a survey. Your operations manager prepares a dashboard with several metrics, including the one shown in Figure 27.17.

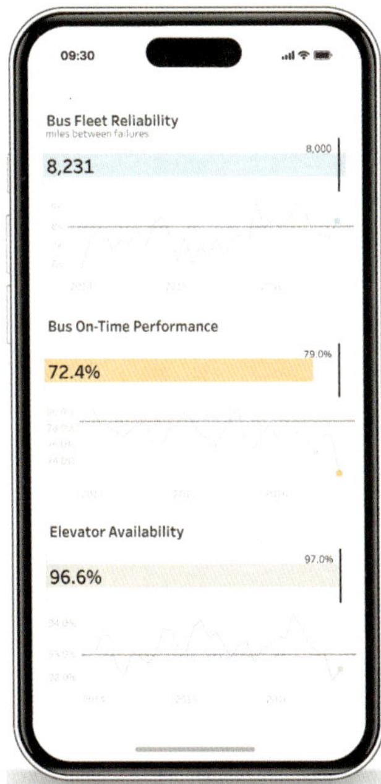

FIGURE 27.16 Multiple KPI Cards displayed on a phone.

What are you to make of this number? As a founder you probably want to know if this score is good or bad. How do you even determine if it's good or bad? How often should you conduct the survey? Is there a correlation between engagement and retention rates? Are people in certain demographic groups more likely to have higher scores?

Great questions, all of which came from a single BAN that sparked a conversation.

Sometimes there isn't a need to create goals or do comparisons. Consider a snippet of the "Music Major / Data Miner" dashboard that Jeff created in

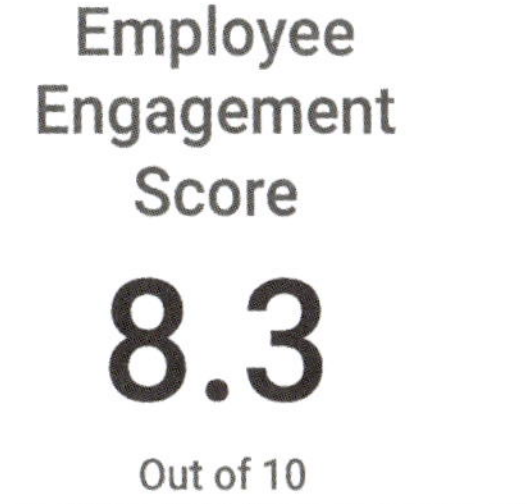

FIGURE 27.17 A BAN with no context. But it still can be useful.

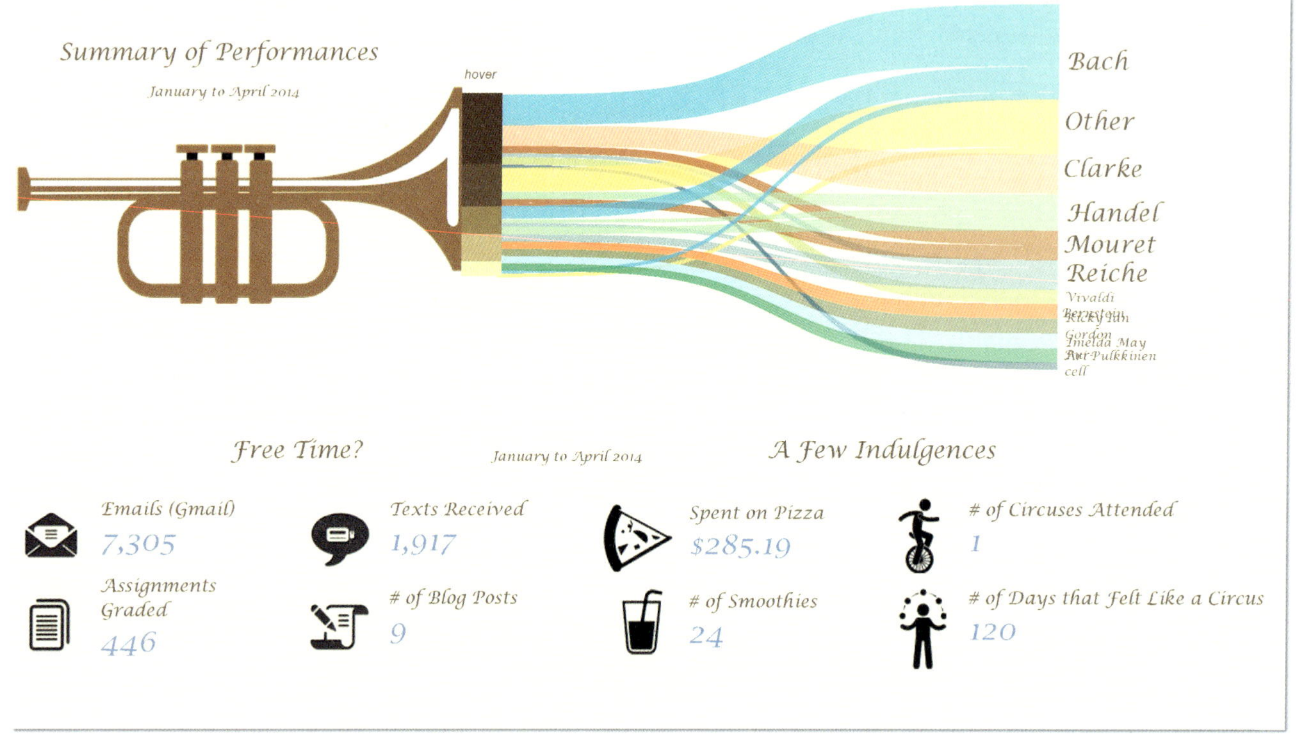

FIGURE 27.18 A snippet from Jeff's winning entry. The BANs are inspired by Nicholas Felton, famous for his quantified-self visualizations and his award-winning annual Feltron report.

2014 as part of the Tableau Iron Viz Quantified Self feeder competition (Figure 27.18).

There's nothing to compare here and no goals to be achieved. Just fun facts about Jeff.

Jeff's feeder entry was miles ahead of what people were creating with Tableau at the time. I was blown away and sent an email to Jeff telling him how much I liked his dashboard and that I wanted to chat. His work – and these BANs – led to thousands of conversations and a wonderful and ongoing collaboration.

You Have a Limited Number of Pixels, So Use Them Wisely

Eye-tracking research shows that our eyes are attracted to BANs. It's up to us as dashboard designers to take advantage of the time people spend looking at them. Color, indicator dots, bars with reference lines, and sparklines are all small additions that will add a lot of contextual punch to your BANs. As we've seen with the various examples, it's possible to add these elements in ways that don't take up more screen real estate or clutter the display.

Chapter 28

Dynamic Duos

Chart Pairings That Work Well Together

Steve Wexler

We've assembled a collection of examples that address common "How do you show this?" situations. All the examples share one thing in common: you need two charts working in tandem to tell a complete story.

Actuals and Percentages

In our dashboard design workshops, we ask attendees how they would show percentage of goal across four regions given the data shown in Figure 28.1.

Most of the attendees propose a bar chart with a reference line, like the one shown in Figure 28.2.

Percentage of goal

North	95%
South	105%
East	65%
West	135%

FIGURE 28.1 Percentage of goals for four regions.

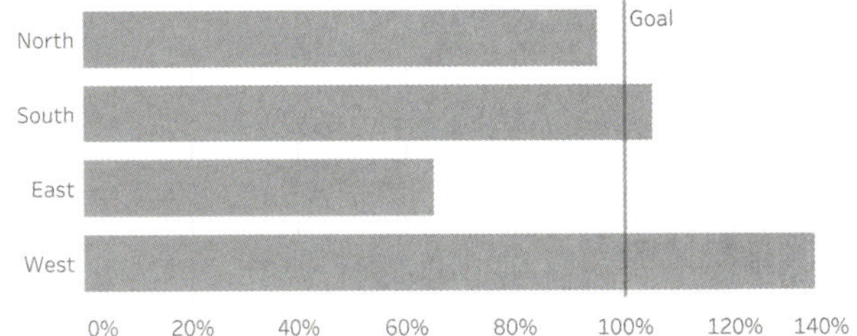

FIGURE 28.2 Percentage of goals reached using bars and a reference line.

This is certainly a good way to present the data as you can see what is ahead of the goal, what is behind, and by how much.

But maybe you can see the same shortcoming to this approach that a lot of attendees notice: We don't know what the goals are for each of the regions. For example, what if the goal for East is $500K but the goal for North is $2M (Figure 28.3)?

Both the actuals and percentages views contain useful data. Is there a way we can combine both into a compact view?

This is precisely what Dorian Banutoiu achieved in his eCommerce dashboard (Chapter 14). Let's borrow his technique and apply it to this example (Figure 28.4).

Now we have the best of both words. The progress bars show us if we are ahead or behind our goals, and the actual bars make it easy to see how much larger one region is than another.

As a similar challenge, let's suppose you are an HR leader and looking at attrition versus retention

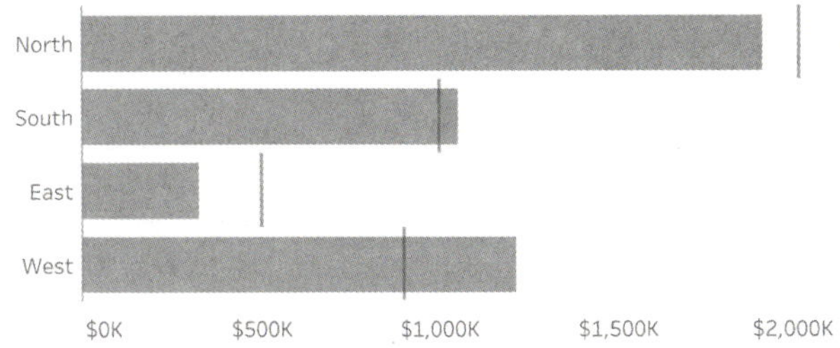

FIGURE 28.3 Showing actuals instead of percentages presents a very different story.

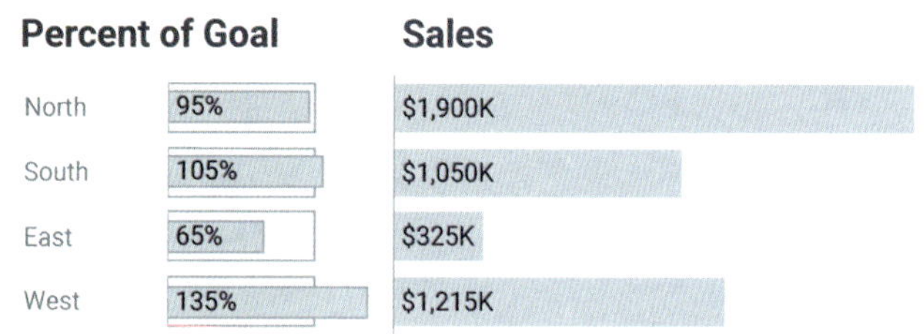

FIGURE 28.4 Showing percentages and actual side-by-side. Note that we could also show the progress bar with bars and a reference line.

across various job roles in your organization. The organization's goal is that no job role has an attrition rate greater than 20% and that you don't need to fill too many openings simultaneously.

Figure 28.5 shows the data in a table format.

Compare the tabular view with the combined percentages and actuals shown in Figure 28.6.

Rentention and attrition by role

	Retention	Attrition	Attrition rate
Research Scientist	245	47	16%
Laboratory Technician	197	62	24%
Customer Success Rep	122	9	7%
Manager	97	5	5%
Sales Representative	50	33	40%

FIGURE 28.5 Retention and attrition data in a tabular format.

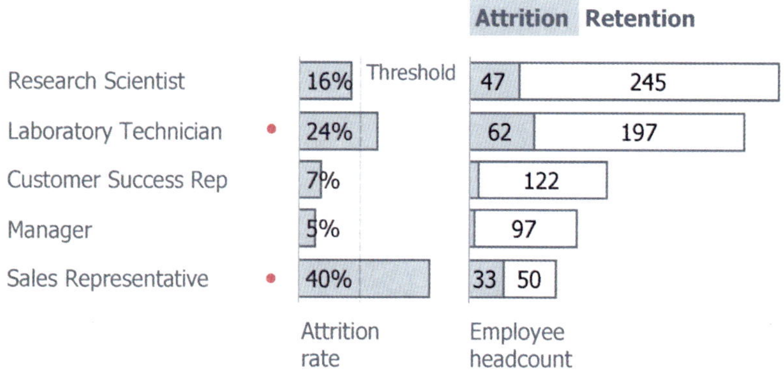

FIGURE 28.6 Percentage attrition and attrition/retention count. Red dots indicate where attrition rate is greater than 20%.

So many things that were buried in the table become clear in this visualization. For example, while there are roughly twice as many laboratory technicians who have left the company as sales representatives (62 versus 33), the attrition rate for sales reps is much higher (40% versus 24%).

Relative Size vs. Part-to-Whole

Part to Whole with Interactivity

Consider the bar chart in Figure 28.7 that shows sales for 10 different states. It's easy to see that California is the top seller with more than twice the sales of Texas (the third bar from the top).

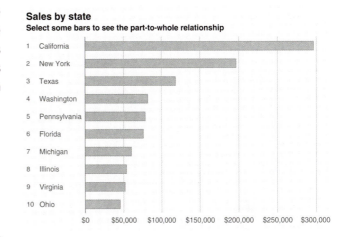

FIGURE 28.7 A sorted bar chart showing sales in 10 states.

But suppose you want to know what percentage of the total sales come from California? Clicking that state will display a pie chart where it's easy to see that California accounts for a little more than one-quarter of sales (Figure 28.8).

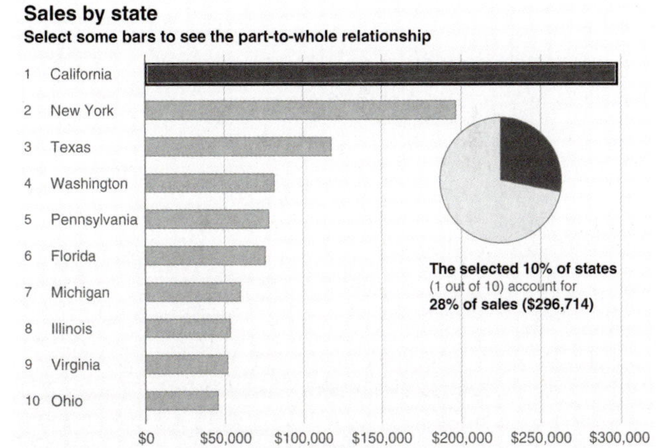

FIGURE 28.8 Selecting a state displays a pie chart showing the part-to-whole relationship.

Selecting several states will show the combined percentage of sales. In Figure 28.9 we see that the four selected states account for just under 50% of sales.

Part to Whole Without Interactivity

This on-demand part-to-whole pie chart works great...if your audience will be interacting with a dashboard that has these actions built in.

But suppose you need to show actuals and percentages in a static environment (e.g., PDF or email). How might you show the actuals and percentages?

Kevin Flerlage developed a nice technique that I emulate in Figure 28.10.

The bars allow us to answer the "How much larger is this bar than that bar?" question, and the mini pies[1] answer "What part of the whole is this segment?"

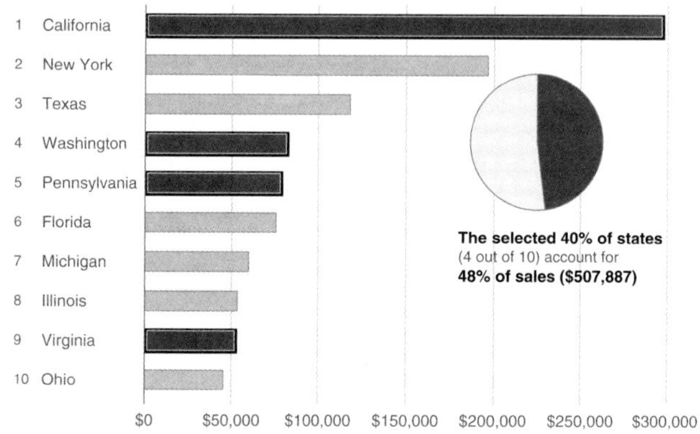

FIGURE 28.9 Selecting several states displays a pie chart showing the part-to-whole relationship for those states.

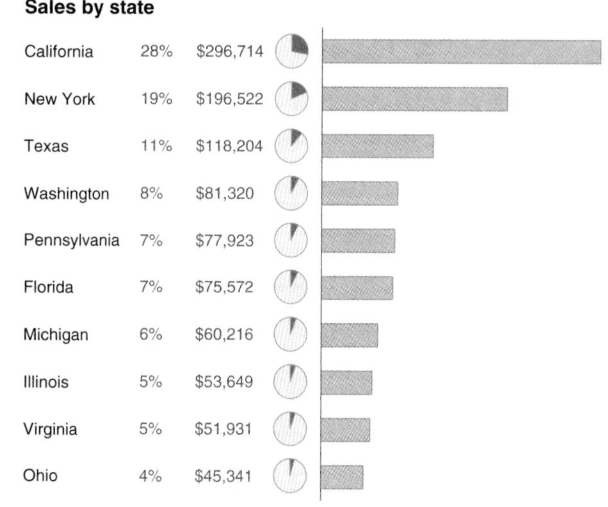

Sales by state
California 28% $296,714
New York 19% $196,522
Texas 11% $118,204
Washington 8% $81,320
Pennsylvania 7% $77,923
Florida 7% $75,572
Michigan 6% $60,216
Illinois 5% $53,649
Virginia 5% $51,931
Ohio 4% $45,341

FIGURE 28.10 Bars show sales for each state and mini pies show percentage of all sales for each state.

[1]Patrick Therriault coined the term *tart chart* for these mini pies. Steven Franconeri calls them "cutie pies."

Showing Now vs. Then

I recently read an article[2] from Nick Desbarats about the problems with slope graphs and was inspired to build on his work and show some alternative approaches.

Consider the chart in Figure 28.11, which shows the payroll changes for selected baseball teams between 2022 and 2024.

Which team appears to have the biggest change? Based on the slope, one might guess either the Arizona Diamondbacks or the Texas Rangers.

But if we instead create an arrow chart combined with a bar chart, we can see that the biggest percent age increase would be for the Baltimore Orioles (Figure 28.12).

The first chart shows the actual change, while the second shows the percentage change.

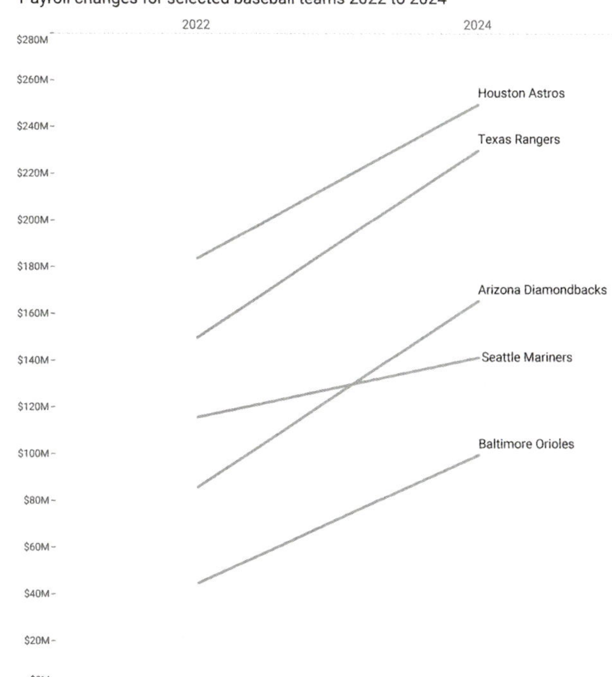

FIGURE 28.11 Slope graph showing change in payroll for selected baseball teams from 2022 to 2024.

[2]dtdbook.com/link40

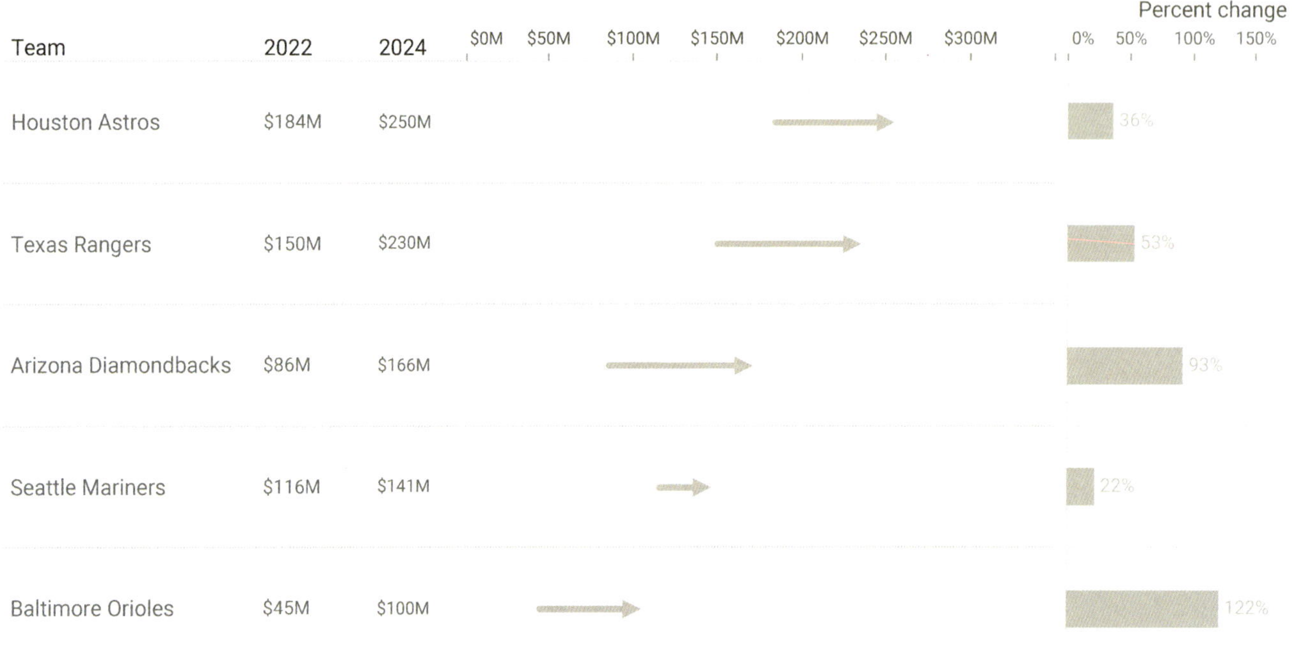

FIGURE 28.12 Arrow chart combined with a bar chart.

You need both perspectives to be able to answer the question about which team had the biggest payroll increase. Both the Texas Rangers and Arizona Diamondbacks increased their payroll by $80M, but the Baltimore Orioles, with a $55M increase, boosted their payroll by 122%!

Before we go any further, let's give that first arrow chart some love. It's compact, it's instantly understandable, and because it uses position from a common baseline, it's easy to make accurate comparisons by period and across different teams. It's no surprise that you'll see the arrow chart as a "go to" for organizations like *The Economist* (Figure 28.13).

Marginal Histograms and the Need to See with Fresh Eyes

Or, your curse of expertise, and how to defeat it.[3]

I think people who read my posts know that I'm a big fan of marginal histograms. I mean, what's not to love?

[3]From Northwestern Professor Steve Franconeri.

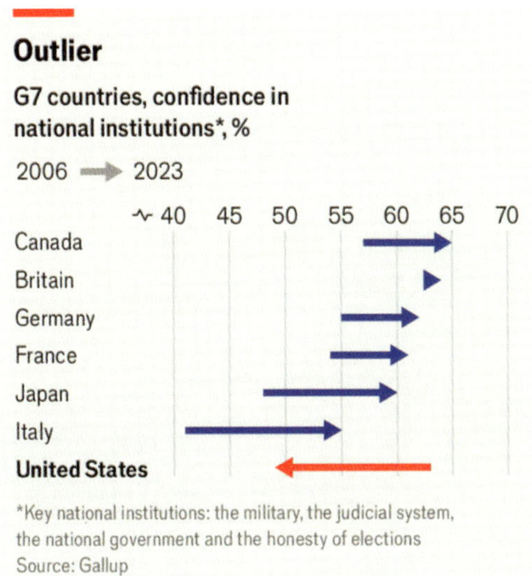

FIGURE 28.13 Arrow chart from *The Economist*.

While I wouldn't say that there's been violent disagreement, the discussions among my fellow authors have caused a bit of a kerfuffle as not everyone is sold on them. More importantly, some of the approaches I've taken, which are very clear *to me*, may not be so clear to others. Indeed, the ability to see with fresh eyes, or what Northwestern University professor Steven Franconeri calls "the curse of expertise," is something I want to explore along with the marginal histogram.

What Is a Histogram?

A histogram shows the distribution of values. Histograms plot continuous measures with ranges of the data grouped into bins, which is why the bars often touch as there aren't supposed to be any breaks.

A Nonconfrontational Example

Figure 28.14 is a heat map from a dashboard by Ellen Blackburn that shows ticketless travel by day and time. While we can see pockets of activity, we can't tell which hours and days have the most and least activity).

Now let's see what happens when we add a marginal histogram (Figure 28.15).

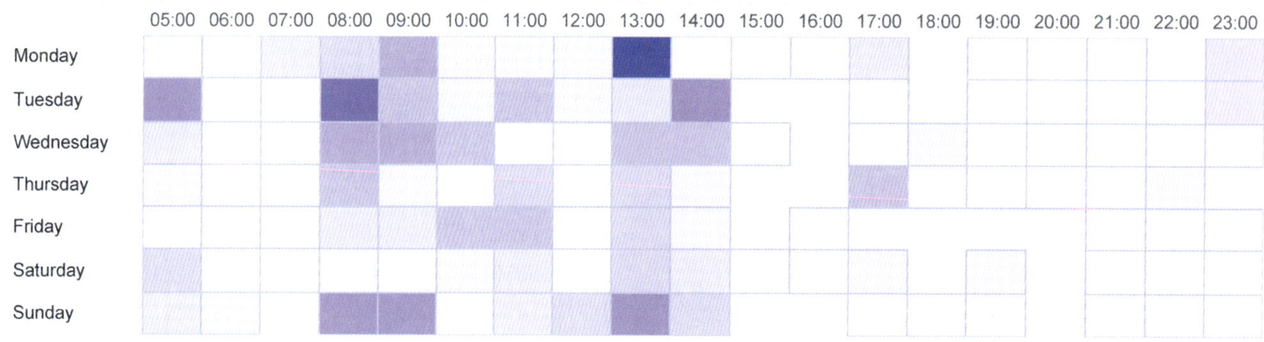

FIGURE 28.14 Heat map showing activity by hour and day.

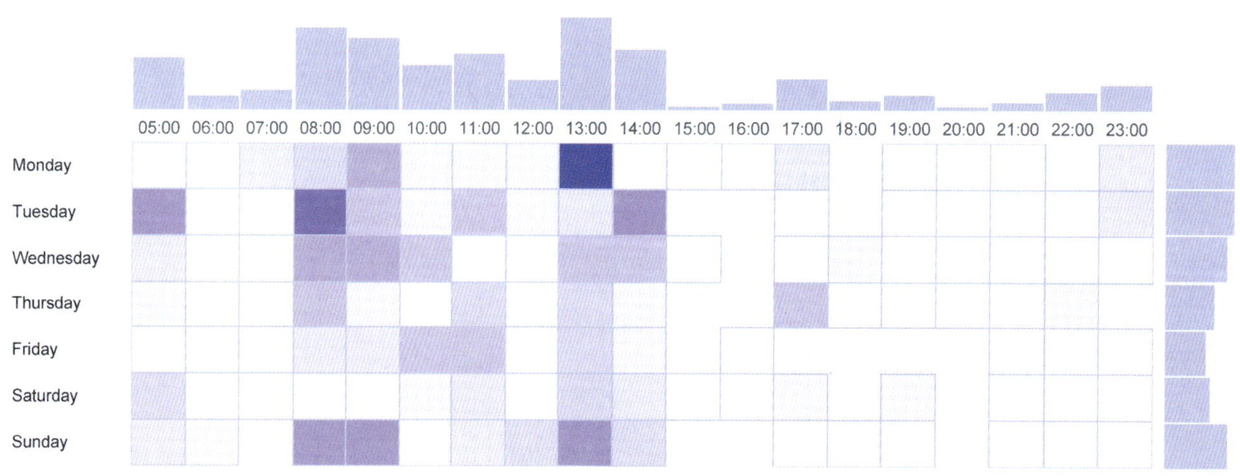

FIGURE 28.15 Heat map with marginal histogram.

A ton of insights pop out. Hour with the highest volume? 13:00. Day with the lowest? Friday.

Figure 28.16 shows another example from *The Big Picture* tracking tech support calls by day of week and hour of the day.

While there are some formatting considerations (do we need to see all the numbers in the two histograms?), I have no problem with the inverted bars along the bottom.

That is, I, a professional chart-looker-atter, have no problem with the inverted bars along the bottom.

I've seen so many of these renderings I don't have to think about what the chart is trying to tell me.

But I've seen enough people who stumble with this approach and have been convinced to move the weekly histogram to the top (Figure 28.17).

Tech Support Calls

By hour and day of week

	Mon	Tue	Wed	Thu	Fri	Sat	Sun	
12 AM	109	100	103	115	126	81	100	734
1 AM	113	79	124	86	104	103	92	701
2 AM	65	115	133	88	109	100	102	712
3 AM	66	117	125	112	147	171	81	819
4 AM	35	142	80	67	130	88	118	660
5 AM	49	19	72	17	53	6	36	252
6 AM	6	17	39	9	10	7	4	92
7 AM	6	1	13	2	9	6	2	39
8 AM	4	4	6	1	3	2	1	21
9 AM	23	17	35	4	13	9	19	120
10 AM	98	115	199	69	104	28	59	672
11 AM	183	225	226	229	220	208	85	1,376
12 PM	241	244	230	333	276	273	204	1,801
1 PM	184	210	249	234	221	200	209	1,507
2 PM	174	176	239	176	146	125	166	1,202
3 PM	116	124	119	126	166	102	117	870
4 PM	75	104	87	74	110	113	108	671
5 PM	79	72	98	93	105	77	77	601
6 PM	69	112	73	84	69	89	112	608
7 PM	103	92	133	75	82	146	143	774
8 PM	97	82	97	113	133	143	117	782
9 PM	104	103	138	83	124	175	102	829
10 PM	110	107	105	114	132	220	100	888
11 PM	109	113	108	115	111	142	128	826
	2,218	2,490	2,831	2,419	2,703	2,614	2,282	

FIGURE 28.16 Highlight table with marginal histogram along the right side and inverted histogram along the bottom.

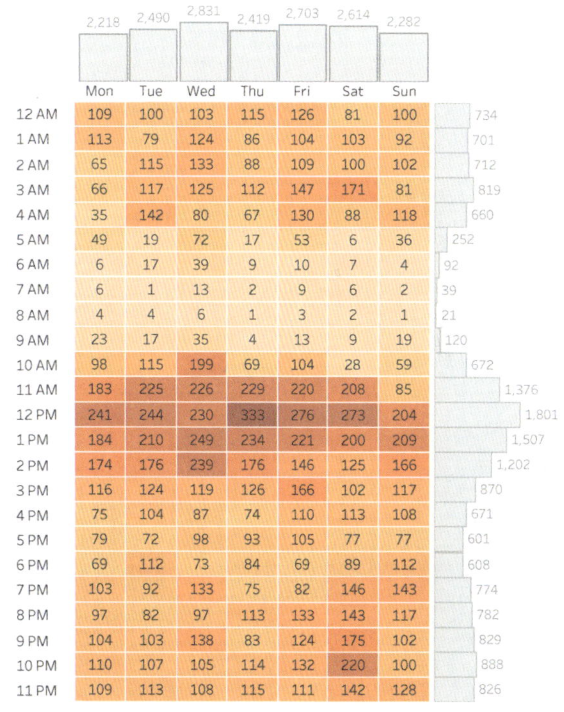

FIGURE 28.17 Highlight table with weekly marginal histogram along the top.

Marginal Histograms and Scatterplots

Consider the scatterplot showing the relationship between age and salary (Figure 28.18).

You can probably glean some insights. For example, younger people make less. Salaries peak around age 55 and then decline. And while there are some outliers, most of the salaries cluster in groups.

Now, let's see what happens when we add a marginal histogram (Figure 28.19).

What a difference! The age distributions and salary distributions are now crystal clear.

Summary

Whether showing actuals versus goals, part to whole, or this period versus a previous period, all

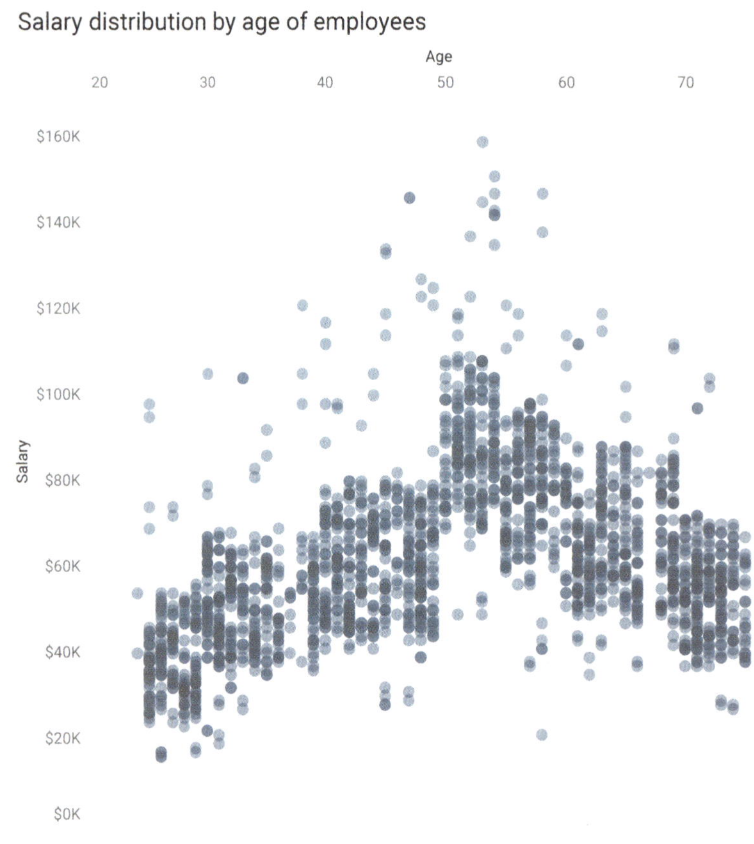

FIGURE 28.18 Scatterplot showing the relationship between age salary.

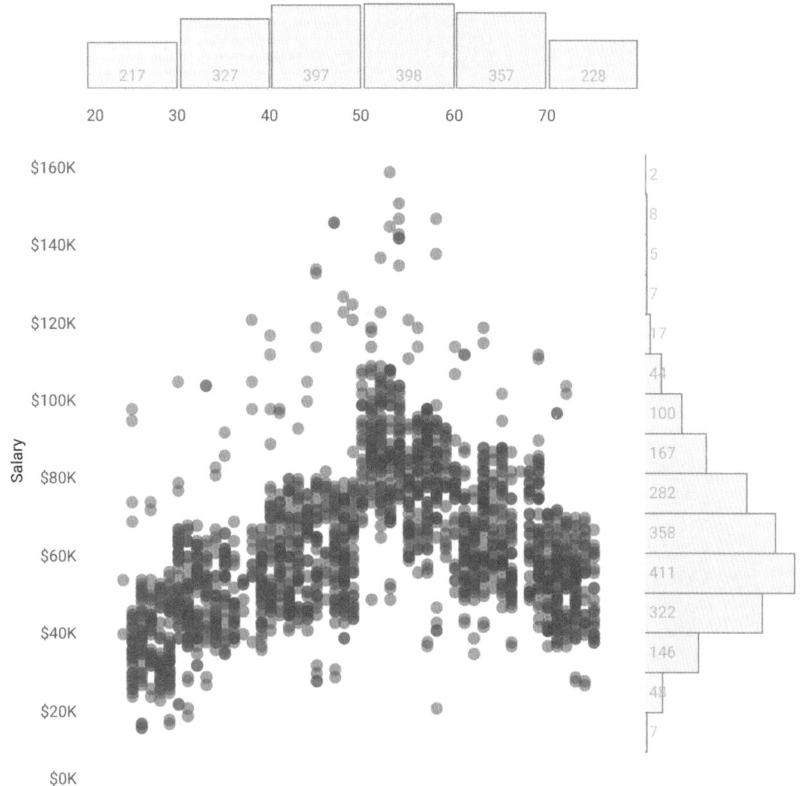

FIGURE 28.19 Scatterplot with marginal histograms.

these data visualization challenges share one thing in common: you need more than one chart to tell the full story.

With interactivity or with the intelligent juxtaposition of complementary charts, you should be able to address the nuanced challenges of showing two facets of your data.

If you want further thoughts and examples of dynamic duos, we dedicated an entire episode of Chart Chat to the subject. Check it out here: dtdbook.com/link41

Chapter 29

Defaults vs. Design: The Pitfalls of Software Defaults

Jeffrey Shaffer

Note: While some table formatting has been applied, the charts in this chapter are the default charts that are produced without any modifications.

Charts and maps are powerful tools that can transform complex datasets into comprehensible visual narratives. However, their effectiveness depends on their design and how accurately they represent the underlying data.

One aspect to consider when creating a chart is that users often rely on the software's default settings. This could be out of convenience or because they don't realize the impact that these defaults might have on the final design being automatically applied by the software instead of deliberately determined by the designer. Each tool has defaults intended to provide a quick starting point, but they can introduce pitfalls that compromise the clarity and accuracy of the visualized data.

In this chapter, we will explore some of the issues encountered when over-relying on data visualization software design defaults.

The Illusion of Simplicity and Chart Choice

Software tools like Excel, Tableau, PowerBI, and others come with built-in defaults. Defaults are necessary. Without them, setting up the basic structure of a chart would be far too cumbersome for most analysts. Defaults give us a place to start, and, as designers, we then use our data visualization knowledge to customize things to communicate more effectively.

Ideally the design defaults should serve to build effective charts. However, without a pause to evaluate what the chart is communicating, even experienced users may be drawn in by how easy it is to generate a chart with a few clicks. It seems amazing at first: "Wow, look how simple it was to create this!" However, this simplicity masks the complexities of effective data visualization and leads to homogenous design, depending on the tool you use.

Let's look at an example from my data visualization class at the University of Cincinnati. The dataset for this example is the count of my trick-or-treaters on Halloween (Figure 29.1), which I publish each year as a public dataset. Over the years, this has become a popular dataset for learning data visualization. In addition, check out the Tableau Public campaign from as far back as 2016 where people from around the world visualize this data (#HalloweenViz on dtdbook.com/link42).

Professors from around the world also use it as a class assignment, as I have done since 2012. I started tracking this data in 2008, and I update it each year after Halloween. (For more information, see https://dataplusscience.com/HalloweenData.html.)

Halloween Trick-or-Treat Data

Excel Data Structure

Year	6pm	6:30pm	7pm	7:30pm	8pm	Total (8:15pm)
2024	34	143	346	487	598	631
2023	48	164	342	462	546	570
2022	0	130	277	387	483	512
2021	8	109	259	357	449	487
2020	11	55	107	155	211	219
2019	0	117	262	406	483	523
2018	18	191	342	497	589	600
2017	41	190	357	549	710	776
2016	22	160	386	612	759	822
2015	13	148	336	523	667	747
2014	0	106	197	321	436	454
2013	33	152	233	303	371	391
2012	0	147	310	542	653	673
2011	0	172	367	619	816	869
2010	0	172	351	538	723	726
2009	0	52	229	379	522	542
2008	0	75	192	339	483	492

FIGURE 29.1 Jeff's Halloween Trick-or-Treat data collected since 2008.

Let's jump in a time machine and go back to 2012. At that point in time there were only four years of data. This was the first assignment in the first week of my data visualization class at the University of Cincinnati, and at that time, most of the students used Excel for their first assignment and then switched to Tableau for the rest of the class. Keep in mind, they had little or no training in data visualization at this point. Let's look at a few examples of what my students created in Excel with this data back then.

What do you notice about these charts in Figure 29.2? Yes, they are not very good examples of data visualization, so I'm thrilled their creators signed up for my class! But more than the quality of the visualization, do you see a pattern here? They are all the same chart, some with the same colors and styling.

Is this plagiarism? Are the students cheating off each other? No, rather, they've all walked through the same steps in Excel to set up their graphics.

The vast majority of students are highlighting the data and simply selecting Insert > Line Chart from the Excel toolbar. By default, they get a cumulative line chart that looks like everyone else's cumulative line chart. They are simply using the software defaults. Excel automatically plots this cumulative line chart and, in 2012, used these default colors (purple, green, red, blue), and the default gridlines, borders, markers, legend placement, and more. Therefore, it's easy to see how the students' charts look nearly identical, with many of the same design choices.

Load the latest Halloween data into Tableau using the Tableau version of the data file, and it's highly unlikely that a new user will make a cumulative line chart, as it takes a concerted effort to create one. You need to create a table calculation first that uses the cumulative running sum. While that added step

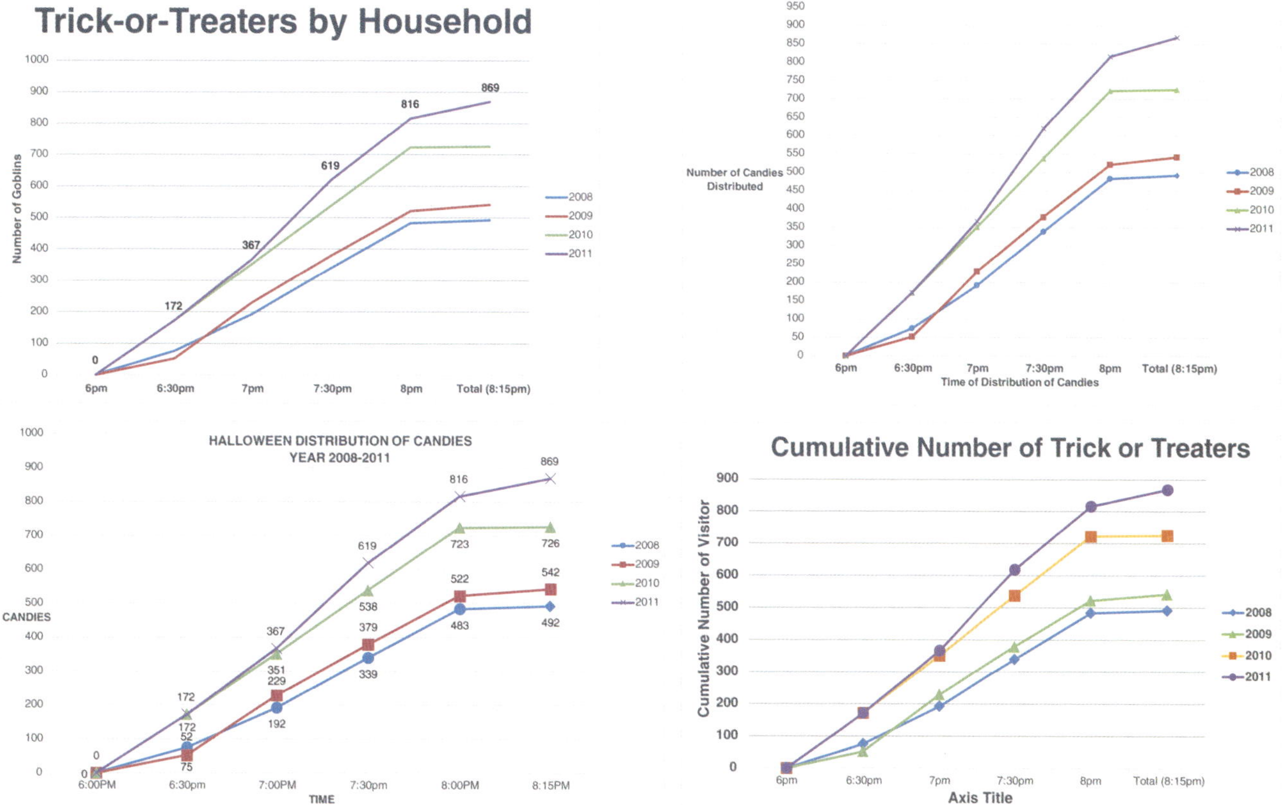

FIGURE 29.2 Default line charts using Excel.

isn't technically difficult, that option is not what shows up by default after a few clicks.

The Tableau chart that most students create with the same data is a line chart of total trick-or-treaters by year. The "default" mark type in Tableau is known as the "Automatic" mark, which when showing time-series data like this (count of trick-or-treaters by year as a date field) typically defaults to a line as the mark type (Figure 29.3).

Same data table, two very different line charts thanks to different defaults across Excel and Tableau. The examples from this class assignment highlight how default settings can lead to homogeneous design, especially when users are unaware of the nuances involved. Are these the best chart types to show the data? Possibly, but did the students think through options and settle on these specific chart types when they created them? Or did they just click a few things and create something by default?

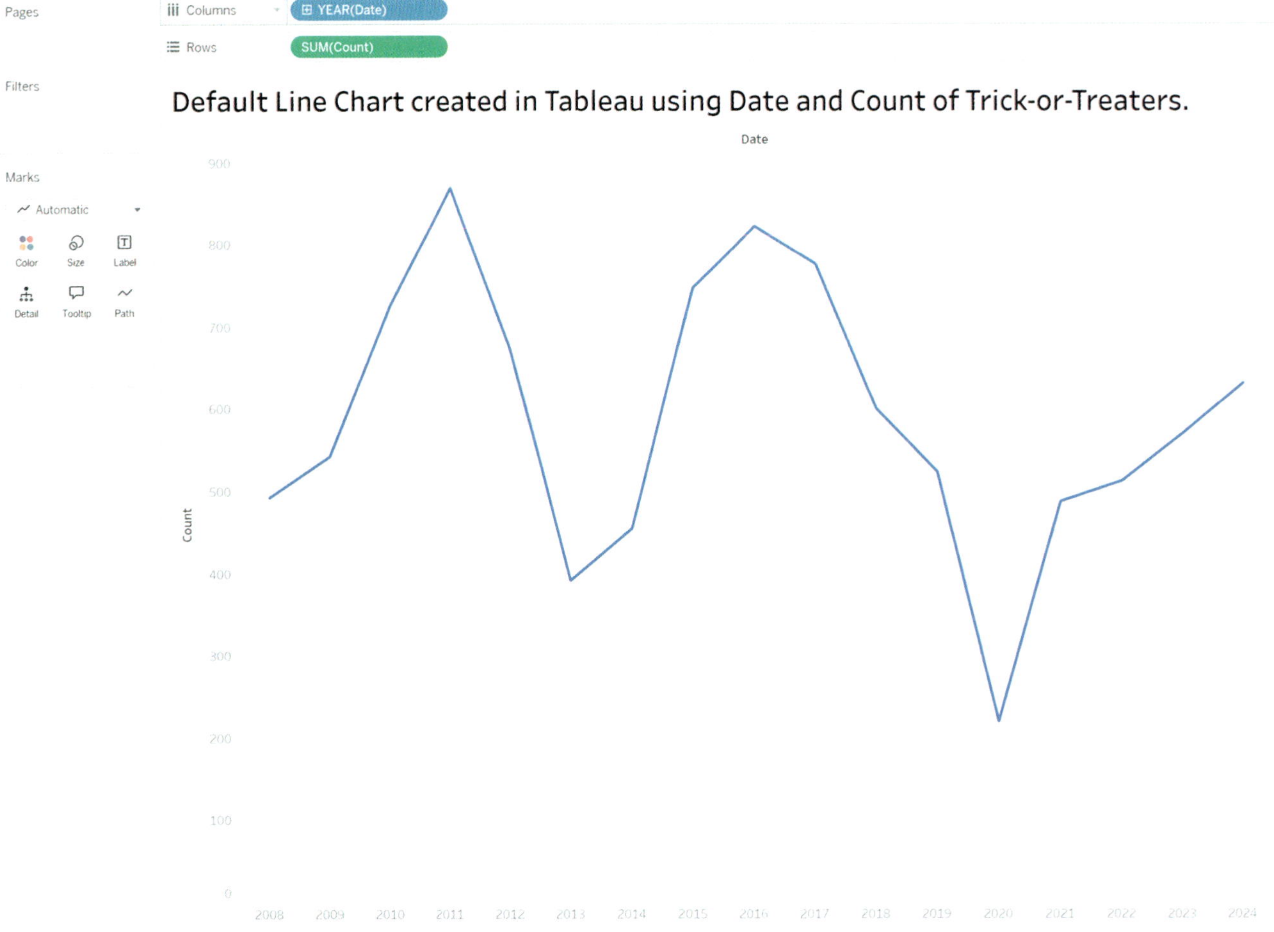

FIGURE 29.3 Default line chart created in Tableau using Date and Count of trick-or-treaters.

Not only do these two charts created from different tools appear different, they provide different analytical insights. The cumulative line chart in Excel offers a comparison between years for the trick-or-treaters from 6 p.m. to 8:15 p.m., while the Tableau line chart offers a broader view of the total trick-or-treaters by year. Both are valid and interesting views of the data if that was the intended insight to visualize.

Defaults Driven by the Data: Understanding Software's Response to Data Structure

Understanding how your data is structured for your specific tool of choice is very important as well. Because different tools require different data structures, I offer two download links for the Halloween data, one for Tableau, in a "tall" or "tidy" data structure (Figure 29.4), and one for Excel, a pivot table structure (Figure 29.1). If a user imported the data structure from Figure 29.1 directly into Tableau, then they would get a mess of fields to deal with, one field for each time slot (6 p.m., 6:30 p.m., 7 p.m., etc.). To import into Tableau, you would ideally want two columns, a Date/Time field and the count of trick-or-treaters as a noncumulative count.

Date and Time	Count
10/31/2008 18:00	0
10/31/2008 18:30	75
10/31/2008 19:00	117
10/31/2008 19:30	147
10/31/2008 20:00	144
10/31/2008 20:15	9
10/31/2009 18:00	0
10/31/2009 18:30	52
10/31/2009 19:00	177
10/31/2009 19:30	150
10/31/2009 20:00	143
10/31/2009 20:15	20
10/31/2010 18:00	0
10/31/2010 18:30	172
10/31/2010 19:00	179
10/31/2010 19:30	187

FIGURE 29.4 Halloween data for Tableau structured as a "tall" or "tidy" data set with two columns, Date/Time, and the count of trick-or-treaters as a noncumulative count.

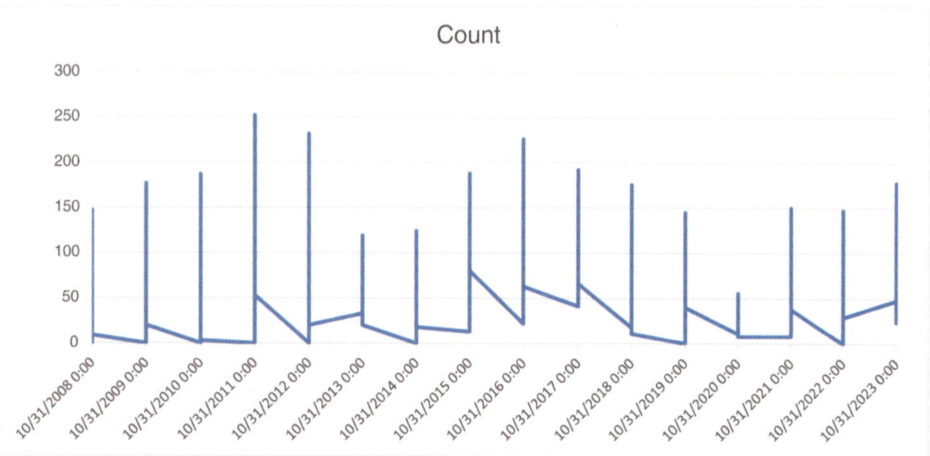

FIGURE 29.5 A default Excel chart using the Halloween data in a "tall" or "tidy" data structure that would be ideal for Tableau.

Halloween Trick-or-Treat Data

Excel Data Structure

Year	6pm	6:30pm	7pm	7:30pm	8pm	Total (8:15pm)
2011	0	172	367	619	816	869
2010	0	172	351	538	723	726
2009	0	52	229	379	522	542
2008	0	75	192	339	483	492

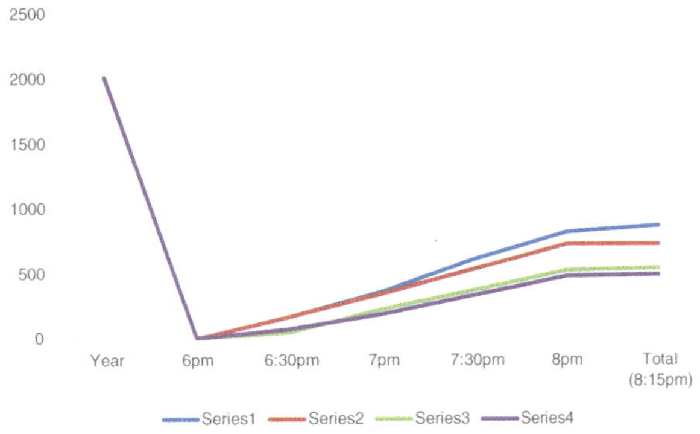

	6pm	6:30pm	7pm	7:30pm	8pm	Total (8:15pm)
2011	0	172	367	619	816	869
2010	0	172	351	538	723	726
2009	0	52	229	379	522	542
2008	0	75	192	339	483	492

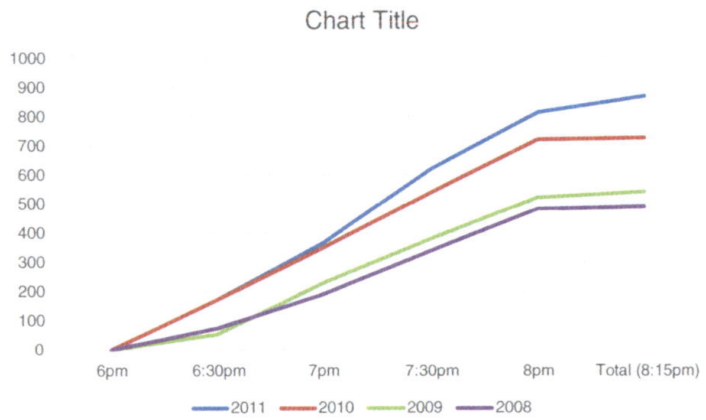

FIGURE 29.6 Comparison of default line charts in Excel based on a column header for year versus no column header for year.

Knowing how your tool handles the data is very important. If I use the data file optimized for Tableau (Figure 29.4) and followed the same steps as before in Excel, then I would get a completely useless Excel chart (Figure 29.5).

In addition to the data structure, the layout of the data matters as well. For the students to get those default cumulative line charts in Excel (Figure 29.2), they had to make a simple change to the data and remove the "Year" header on the first column; otherwise, Excel would automatically plot the year as a series along with the times (Figure 29.6). If they don't remove the "Year" column header, then it would require additional steps in Excel to change the data for the Series to create the same cumulative line chart (e.g., right-click the x-axis, select Select Data, remove Year, and adjust the Series as needed).

The examples shown so far of my Halloween data were from 2012 when there were only four years of data. What happens if there are just a few more years of data? Do we get the same default chart? Figure 29.7 shows the difference between having six years of data with six columns versus seven years of data with six columns. Notice how Excel swaps

Halloween Trick-or-Treat Data

Excel Data Structure

	6pm	6:30pm	7pm	7:30pm	8pm	Total (8:15pm)
2013	33	152	233	303	371	391
2012	0	147	310	542	653	673
2011	0	172	367	619	816	869
2010	0	172	351	538	723	726
2009	0	52	229	379	522	542
2008	0	75	192	339	483	492

	6pm	6:30pm	7pm	7:30pm	8pm	Total (8:15pm)
2014	0	106	197	321	436	454
2013	33	152	233	303	371	391
2012	0	147	310	542	653	673
2011	0	172	367	619	816	869
2010	0	172	351	538	723	726
2009	0	52	229	379	522	542
2008	0	75	192	339	483	492

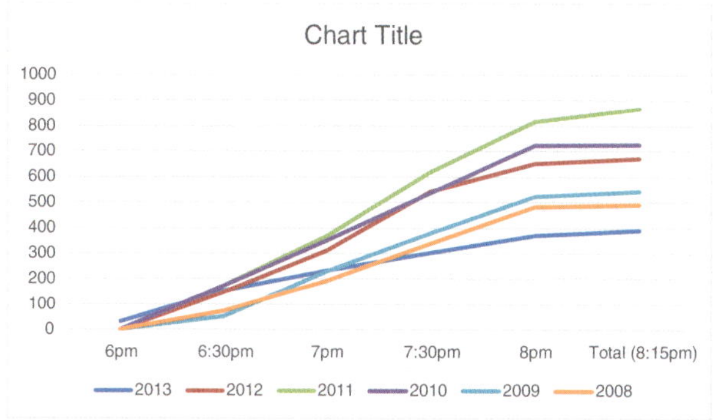

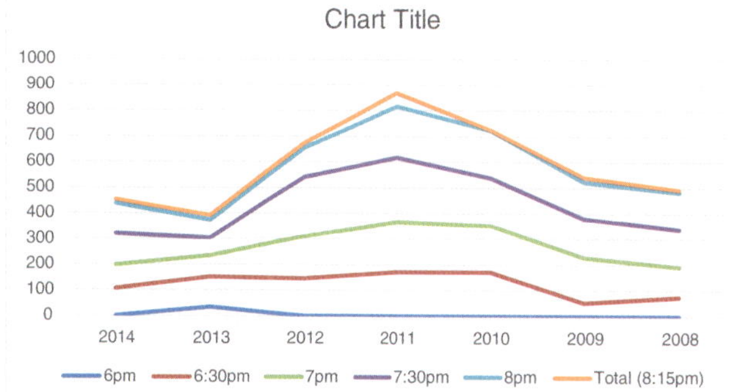

FIGURE 29.7 Default line charts in Excel with six years of data versus seven years of data plotted in reverse chronological order.

the Rows and Columns automatically, which now requires an additional step of right-clicking on the x-axis and swapping them back. Like the previous example, this is an easy change to make, but the default settings of the tool are again driving the design decisions automatically.

A Mental Checklist

Experienced data visualization practitioners often develop a mental checklist or a personal "auto-pilot" mode when creating charts. After years of experience with a visualization tool, you build this mental checklist of all the little steps needed to deal with the defaults. This often involves decluttering your visualizations, removing elements such as borders and gridlines, adjusting labels and axes, adding negative space or white space, and adjusting the colors.

For example, I use Tableau as my primary visualization tool. I know on every visualization that I will have to visit the "format pane" options over and over again to remove borders around charts and maps and to remove gridlines. I will have to select

A SPOOKY ANALYSIS OF HALLOWEEN DATA

Each year, Jeff gets hundreds of trick or treats on Halloween, so he counts them. (2008-2019)

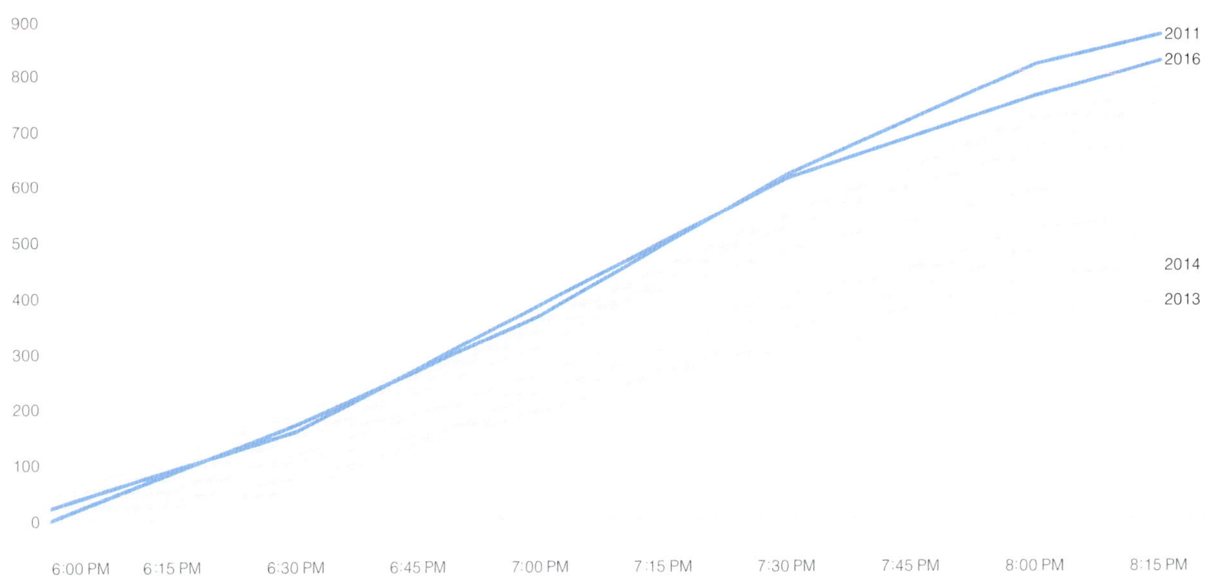

DATA: HALLOWEEN DATA FROM DATAPLUSSCIENCE.COM | CREATED BY: JEFFREY A. SHAFFER

FIGURE 29.8 A Halloween visualization with deliberate design designs instead of using software defaults.

the layout pane to add padding for white space. I will need to adjust the color, especially if using the Tableau default categorical colors. We take for granted all these little steps it takes to create a finished visualization. Depending on the visualization, the intended audience, and the purpose, a designer could spend as much time or more on the formatting of the visualization as they did on the creation of the elements going into the visualization.

Every chart that we've seen so far is the default chart. Figure 29.8 is an example of a visualization that uses the same cumulative line chart but focuses the story of the data by applying some of these things to declutter the visualization.

If you are starting out on your journey and are new to data visualization or you are using a new tool, then it might be beneficial to create a check list. For example, I created this data visualization checklist for my students at the University of Cincinnati: https://dataplusscience.com/DataVizChecklist.html.

The Pitfalls of Default Settings

Look at the chart in Figure 29.9 of my followers on X (formerly Twitter). Quickly, do I have more than twice the followers of Shirley Wu?

Most people will answer yes. They're wrong.

Since you're a data graphics professional and a reader of this book, you may have noticed the pitfall in this chart. Look at the y-axis: it's truncated and starts at 31,500. To answer my question, you would need to cross-reference the top of each bar to the axis. Only then will you see that I have 36,000 followers, and Shirley has just over 33,000 followers. We all actually have very similar audience sizes.

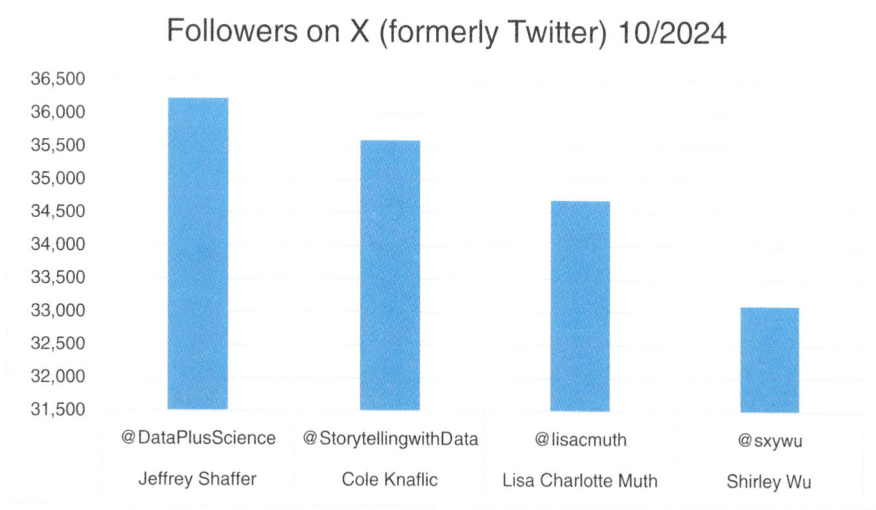

FIGURE 29.9 A default bar chart in Excel.

A truncated y-axis is one of the most universally known data pitfalls. It's considered a "graph crime" to build a chart this way because it is so deceptive.

Starting the Axis at Zero

ON graphs that use length, height, or area to encode the data for comparison (e.g., bar chart, bullet graph, lollipop chart, area chart), always start the axis at zero; otherwise, you will distort the comparison of the data. If encoding with position (e.g., dot plot, box plot, line chart), breaking the axis away from zero sometimes can be useful and will not distort the comparison of the data.

Surely charting tools' defaults wouldn't lead you down this path of deception. Alas, they do. One of the most dangerous default behaviors is Excel's 5/6th rule.

Excel's 5/6ths rule is an automatic axis scaling feature that adjusts the vertical y-axis when the ratio of the smallest value to the largest value in the dataset is greater than 5/6ths. In this case, Excel will truncate the axis to avoid showing a nearly flat line or bar, which would make small differences in the data hard to discern. However, this truncation can be problematic when encoding height or length from a common baseline, like in bar charts, because it distorts the visual comparison. The truncated axis exaggerates small

Excel's default is proper scaling

Data Difference **Beyond 5/6ths** with Proper Axis Scaling

Name	Handle	Twitter Followers
Jeffrey Shaffer	@DataPlusScience	36,229
Andy Cotgreave	@acotgreave	18,021
Steve Wexler	@DataRevelations	10,609
Amanda Makulec	@abmakulec	8,089

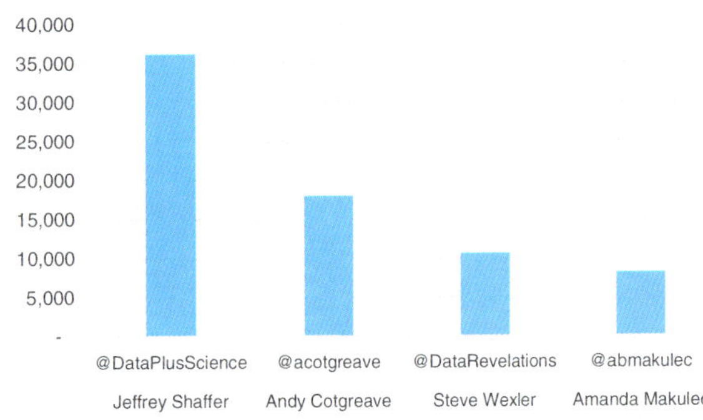

Excel's default is improper scaling

Data Difference **Within 5/6ths** and Excel's Automatic Axis Scaling

Name	Handle	Twitter Followers
Jeffrey Shaffer	@DataPlusScience	36,229
Cole Knaflic	@StorytellingwithData	35,603
Lisa Charlotte Muth	@lisacmuth	34,696
Shirley Wu	@sxywu	33,098

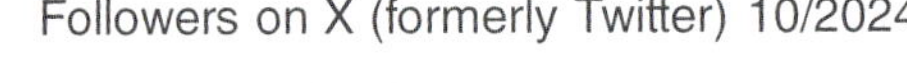

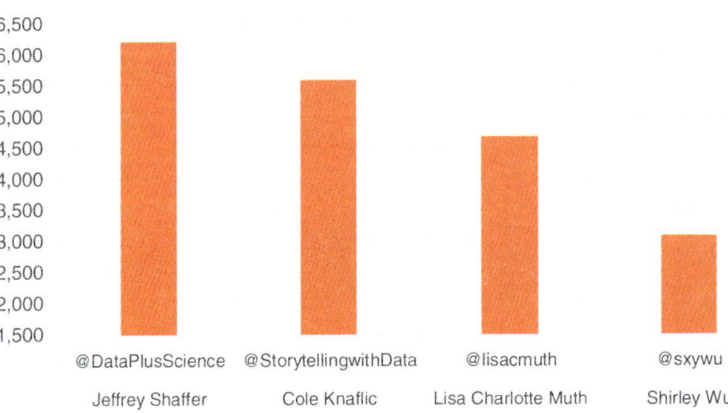

FIGURE 29.10 Default bar charts in Excel and differences in the data below and above the 5/6ths value.

differences between values, making them appear more significant than they really are. This can lead to misinterpretation, showing values that appear to be "doubling" or "tripling" when, in fact, the differences are much smaller.

Figure 29.10 shows an example of Excel applying a 5/6ths rule to a bar chart. On the left side, the data range goes from 8,089 to 36,229. On the right, nearly everyone has the same number of followers; therefore, the range is very narrow, from 33,098 to 36,229. Dividing 36,229 by 33,098 equals 91.36%, which is greater than 83.33% or 5/6ths. Because of the small difference in the data, Excel automatically truncates the y-axis and starts at 31,500. This makes the bars on the right side of Figure 29.8 appear as if Lisa Charlotte Muth has twice as many followers as Shirley Wu, which is not the case.

As with most software defaults, it's pretty easy to correct this improper scaling by setting the y-axis to start at zero. And comparing these side-by-side really shows the visual difference between the two. The improper scaling makes it seem that I have a huge number of additional followers, when in reality the audience size is nearly the same for all of us (Figure 29.11).

Examining this kind of behavior from various software tools provides some insight into the bad charting decisions we frequently see from news sources,

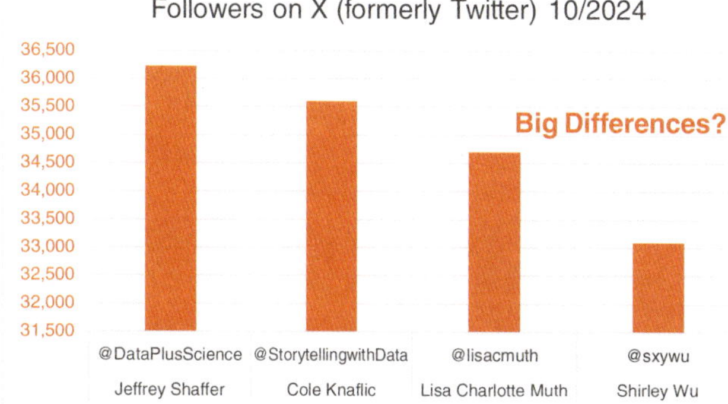

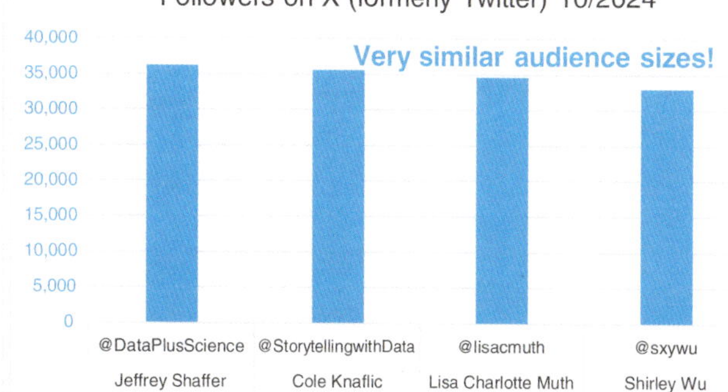

FIGURE 29.11 A comparison of the default bar chart in Excel compared to the same data, but starting the y-axis at zero.

governments, and elsewhere. For example, the UK Treasury posted a chart in February 2023 showing a drop in inflation. It had dropped from 11.1% to 10.1% (i.e., "not very much"). However, they truncated the y-axis to start at 8%. This made the smallest bar look like it was nearly half the length of the longest; at first glance, it looked like inflation had a huge drop. This was either software defaults making poor design choices or deliberate deception. Either way, it incurred a letter of reproach from the UK Office For Statistics Regulation.[1]

If creators aren't paying close attention, then it would be easy to overlook something like this. Thankfully, Tableau and PowerBI do not use this rule for bar charts, but as we've learned in this chapter, every tool has its own set of rules and behaviors.

In Summary: A List of Potential Pitfalls

Here is a short list of some of the software defaults that may trip you up when trying to craft clear and insightful visualizations:

- **Inappropriate chart types:** Users might end up with a default chart that doesn't suit their data, like using a line chart for categorical data or a colorful donut chart with way too many categories and colors. Tools like Excel make it far too easy to make terrible charts, for example 3D exploding pie charts.
- **Cluttered visuals:** Default settings often include design choices that impact the gridlines, borders, shading, labels, titles/subtitles, legends, and overuse of color.
- **Color misuse:** In addition to overuse of color, the default color schemes may not be suitable for all audiences, especially for those with color vision deficiency. Also, tools may not properly encode the data using sequential, diverging, or categorical color schemes. Starting with grayscale and adding color intentionally can make charts more accessible and effective. I am also a big fan of monochromatic design. (See the Splash dashboard from Chapter 16 as an example.)

The Importance of Intentional and Deliberate Design

Creating effective charts requires intentional design choices that go beyond default settings. This involves understanding the data, the message to be conveyed, and the audience. Building a toolbox of chart types and design techniques allows practitioners to tailor their visuals more effectively.

Recommendations for Practitioners

The following are some recommendations:

- **Start with a clean slate:** Begin with a blank canvas or a minimal template to avoid the constraints of defaults. This is where sketching on paper or a whiteboard could help.

[1] dtdbook.com/link43

- **Understand your data:** Perform exploratory data analysis to determine the most appropriate chart type and design elements.
- **Customize thoughtfully:** Adjust axes, scales, labels, and colors to enhance clarity and avoid misrepresentation.
- **Seek inspiration:** Curate examples of effective charts to expand your design vocabulary.
- **Test with your audience:** Get feedback to ensure that your charts communicate the intended message effectively.

While the defaults in software tools offer convenience, they can also lead to ineffective or misleading visualizations. Practitioners should be wary of relying too heavily on these defaults and instead engage in intentional design practices. By doing so, you can create charts that not only look aesthetically pleasing but also convey the true essence of the data, leading to better insights and decision-making.

Chapter 30

What the Heck Is a Dashboard?

Andy Cotgreave

How important are semantics in our field?

Here's our definition of a dashboard, used first in *The Big Book of Dashboards* and again in this book:

> *A dashboard is a visual display of data used to monitor conditions and/or facilitate understanding.*

Simple, right? Not so fast. It turns out people have more complex approaches to defining dashboards.

After the book's publication, Stephen Few, author of *Information Dashboard Design* (2006), wrote a 1,000-word blog post about our definition, concluding that only two of our twenty-eight scenarios qualify as "rapid-monitoring displays."[1] We "undermined our ability to teach anything that is specific to dashboard design." Ouch.

This chapter explains how we got to our broad 15-word definition and why Stephen Few's response didn't bother us. We don't think you should be too worried about what you call your data-driven monitoring displays. Call them "faceted analytics displays." Call them "data applications" or "algorithmic cockpits." Heck, call them "thingamajigs" if you want, as long as you and your users know what you're talking about.

How We Define a Dashboard

During the process of writing *The Big Book of Dashboards*, our working definition got longer and longer. With every complete scenario, we had to add more subclauses and clarifications to the definition. At one point, it was 123 words long!

As we debated and iterated, we realized our definition was absurd. More complexity implies that every scenario is accounted for, rather than casting a wide net. We shortened it to the 15-word version shown at the start of this chapter. It's broad, which reflected our research: ask 10 people what a dashboard is, and you'll get 10 different definitions.

For us, a broad definition is inclusive: it generates conversation.

When I teach dashboard courses, I invite students to challenge some examples from the first book: do they push the boundaries of their personal definitions of a dashboard?

Let's look at three ways some of the first book's dashboards challenge people's personal definitions of the term. These are real objections I've heard from students.

Objection 1: "It Doesn't Fit on a Single Screen"

Few's dashboard definitions stated that a dashboard must fit on a single screen. I adhered to that requirement for a long time. But is it still a requirement today?

My favorite way to challenge this is to show people the FT Economies At a Glance dashboard (Figure 30.1).

[1] "There's Nothing Mere About Semantics," dtdbook.com/link44

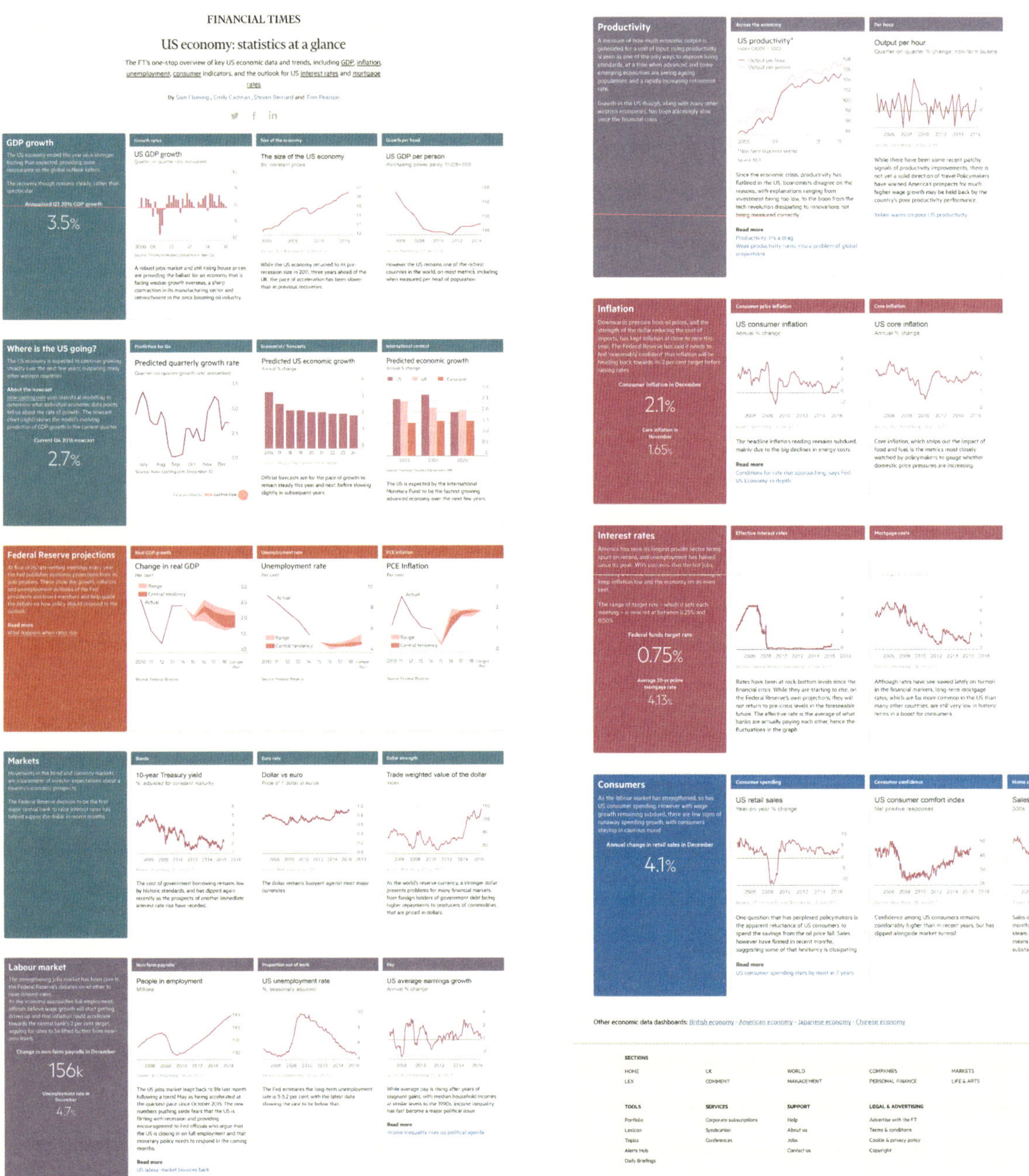

FIGURE 30.1 FT Economies At a Glance dashboard.

FIGURE 30.1 *(Continued)*

It has 29 charts, most with paragraph-length commentary, and the reader has to scroll when viewing it. Is it a dashboard? In my classes, people sometimes object to scrolling; they seem beholden to Few's mandated "single-screen" views.

I then show students the tweet[2] in Figure 30.2 from Martin Stabe, data editor at the FT.

Look at that right-hand spread: it's the *same* dashboard, printed *on a single page*: not a scroll bar in sight! This resembles the information-dense, printout style of dashboards championed by Few.

All that has changed is that it's all on one page, a single view. If I gave that printout to a CEO who

Our long-running UK economic dashboard makes its print debut
ft.com/dashboard

Emily Cadman and Alan Smith

10:37 AM · Nov 23, 2017

FIGURE 30.2 Is it a dashboard? A printed version of the FT Economy At a Glance dashboard that fits on a single page.

---

[2]dtdbook.com/link45

wanted an overview of the economy, is it now a dashboard? At this point, students who initially felt it wasn't a dashboard feel less sure.

What if I removed the annotations and there were only 12 charts, which could fit onto a single screen, as shown in Figure 30.3?

At this point, most protests fall away.

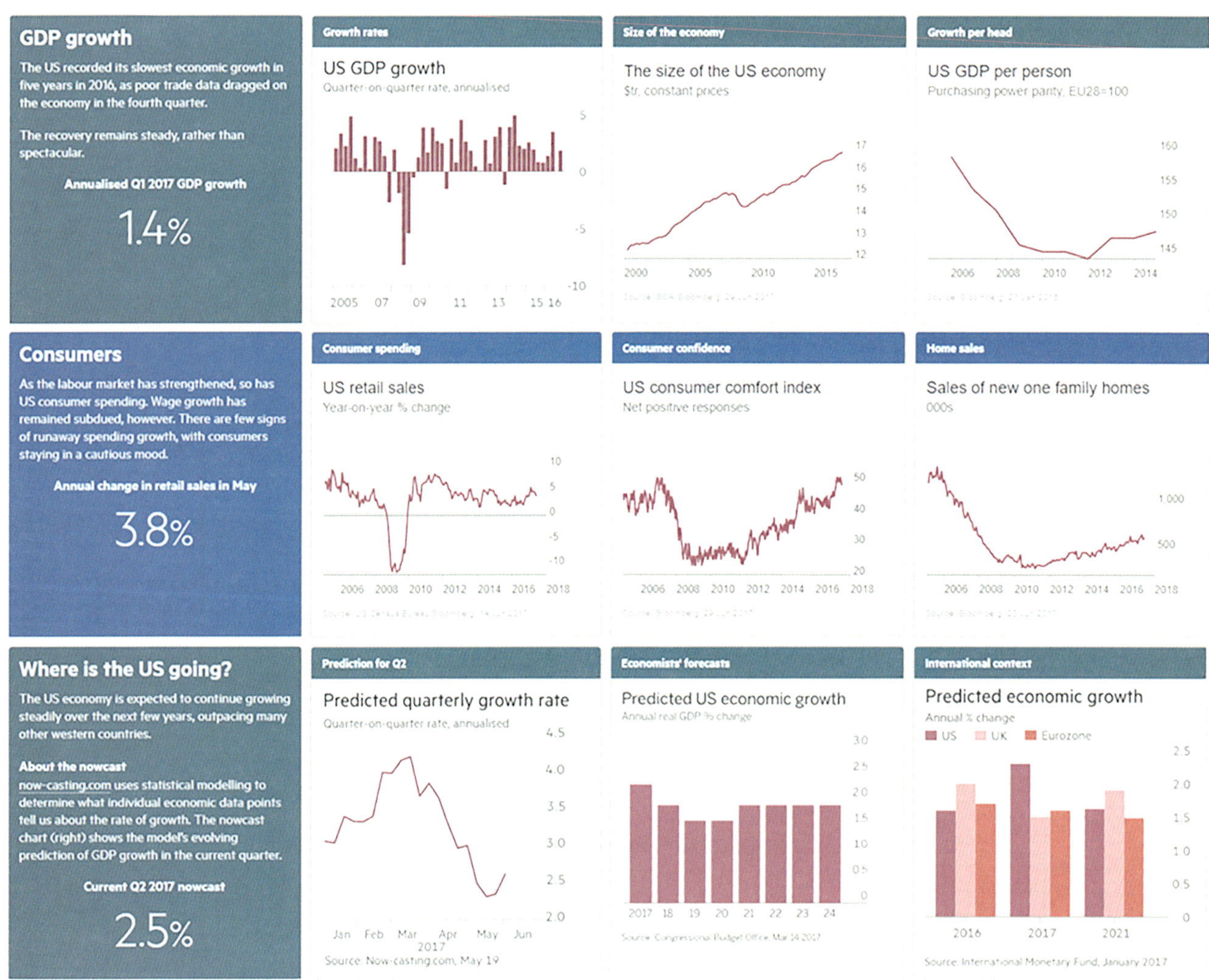

FIGURE 30.3 Is it a dashboard? An adapted version that could now fit on one screen and has only three annotations.

Objection 2: "Dashboard Data Should Be Aggregated"

How about the patient tracking dashboard shown in Figure 30.4? Each row represents a hospital patient. The top section shows patients admitted to a ward in the last 24 hours, and the lower section shows patients who have been there longer than 24 hours. The dot plot represents a timeline of interactions each patient has had outside of the hospital

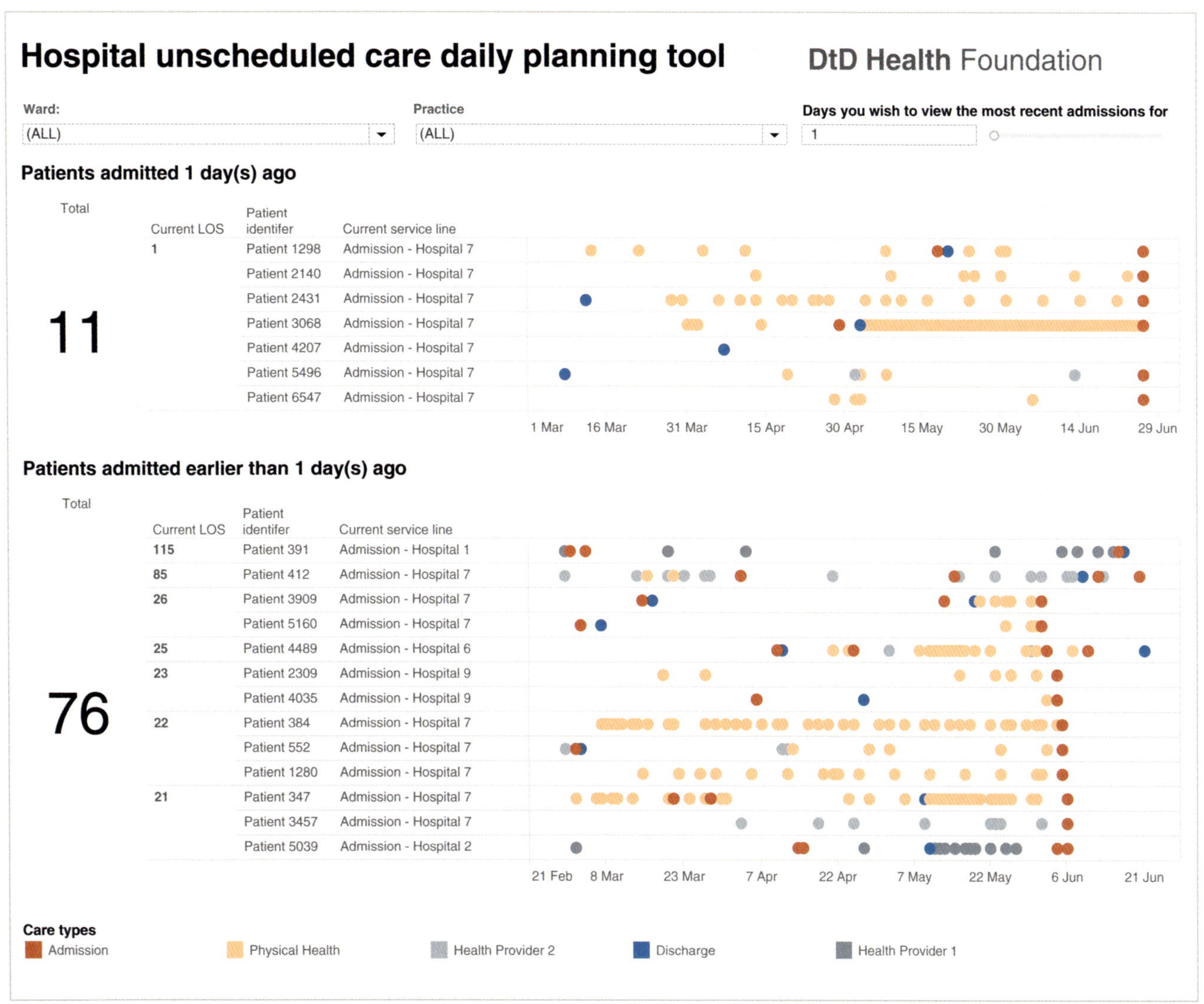

FIGURE 30.4 A hospital's patient dashboard, showing unscheduled care history for each patient on their wards.

with various care teams (represented with different colors). It's used by ward staff to quickly understand patient history and help begin a care plan to get them ready for discharge as soon as possible.

What we're seeing is disaggregated data. The number of visits is not summarized in "total visits." Many students I've taught object to this by saying "A dashboard should show summary KPIs, not this level of detail."

If I were *running* a hospital, I'd want to see a high-level, highly aggregated dashboard showing the macro-level movement of patients in and out of wards. However, if I'm a ward nurse, the overall hospital performance is of little relevance to my day job. As a ward nurse, I'd need to understand *each patient's health history* and help them get back out of hospital. For a nurse, a disaggregated overview is very important, and this example provides that. It's a single view of the visit details of all patients in the ward. Sure, you can't *run* a hospital on this data, but you can run a ward.

Dashboards only need to be aggregated to the level needed by the person using them.

Objection 3: "There Aren't Enough Charts"

One chapter I wrote for *The Big Book of Dashboards* was rejected by Steve and Jeff and not published. It described a dashboard used by a nonprofit organization that provides emergency mental health support via text messages. An organization such as that needs to be sure it is running a good service. A slow reply could be the difference between life and death. They need to know if they have counselors and texters available to meet demand at any given time, if the quality of response is high enough, and if the wait times are low.

As you can see in Figure 30.5, the dashboard is a bot in Slack. It's text-only. Is it a dashboard? Steve, Jeff, and I had robust debates around this one.

My defense of this being a dashboard is that it is still a display of data used to monitor conditions. That's literally our definition of a dashboard, right?

"Andy, there are no charts; it's just text!" Steve exclaimed, vehemently, in our debates about this chapter, "We can do better at reducing time to insights *with charts*." (Note: these debates are the best part of my collaboration with my co-authors; we all get better when we challenge each other.)

stats BOT7:01AM

--KPI (1 day / 28 days) --

Counselors: 267 / 1516

Texters: 1068 / 23500

Quality: 90% / 87%

Wait Time (<5min): 71% / 76%

FIGURE 30.5 A slack-based dashboard showing counsellor availability.

Find Out More

FOR more on finding collaborators, see Steve's "sparring partners" (Chapter 34).

In our editorial meetings, I pushed back: my argument was that expert users, familiar with the data, would know what each of the numbers should be and thus could quickly see if there were any problems.

My arguments didn't sway Steve and Jeff. Since we already had plenty of powerful scenarios for the first book, we dropped this one.

I have continued to hold a soft spot for this example since our first book came out. I love its simplicity. The method of delivery, Slack, gets the data to viewers on-demand, in the flow of work (the same approach could be used in Microsoft Teams, Notion, or any team collaboration platform). The text-only design fits the medium and the audience. It gets the right info to the right people in the format they need to reach insights fast.

As I look back, I wonder if there are small changes that could appease Steve's objections. Could it be as easy as adding some contextual arrows to the output? This could be done with ASCII characters or, in Slack, using custom arrow emojis. One possible solution is shown in Figure 30.6.

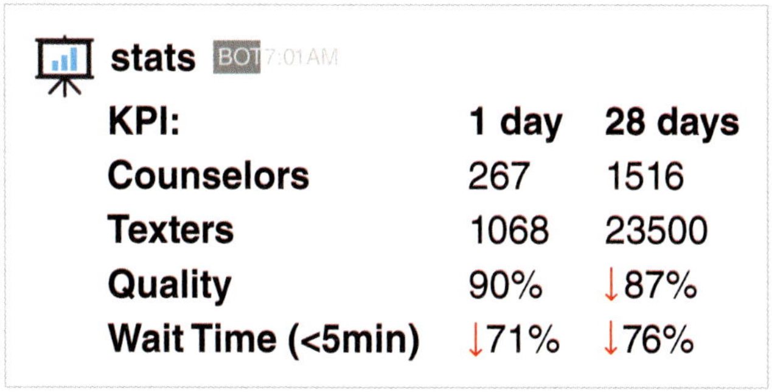

stats BOT 7:01AM

KPI:	1 day	28 days
Counselors	267	1516
Texters	1068	23500
Quality	90%	↓87%
Wait Time (<5min)	↓71%	↓76%

FIGURE 30.6 Now with added custom Slack emojis.

It's still text, but the addition of an arrow draws the eye immediately to the numbers that need attention.

Steve is, to this day, not convinced and thinks we can do better, or at least thinks we should try to do better. We debated this issue live on our video show, Chart Chat.[3] Go watch the episode to find out more about Steve's objections; it was one of the feistiest shows we've ever done! I will leave it to you, reader, to decide whose side you are on.

Aside from the "should there be charts" question, there is another reason to take this approach: the organization that built it aims to be as frugal as possible. This text-only dashboard approach is a low-maintenance solution: there are no charts to design, write code for, and maintain; and there are no licenses for a visualization tool required.

[3]Chart Chat #54. "What We Did This Summer." 13 September 2024. dtdbook.com/link46

How Others Define Dashboards

It's not only us who struggled with the definition of a dashboard. We see challenges, and solutions, right across the analytics field. The following are some examples of the many ways others have tried to define the term.

Submissions to This Book

When we started authoring this book, we sought as many dashboards for consideration as possible. We contacted clients and customers; we posted requests on social networks. In return we received more than 100 submissions. Many submissions were beautiful data stories, like the one shown in Figure 30.7, created in Tableau.

Are they all visual displays of data to facilitate understanding? Yes. Does the software (Tableau) call them a dashboard? Yes. (PowerBI, incidentally, calls the place where you assemble multiple views a report, a canvas, *and* a dashboard).

Therefore, are the examples in Figure 30.7 dashboards? By our definition, yes.

So why aren't beautiful dashboards like these in this book? In this book we focus on analytical dashboards (allowing for data exploration) rather than curated data stories. These beautiful examples might be called "dashboards" in Tableau and by many people, but for us they fit a data story category. Categorizing them this way does not in any way diminish their value or quality. Steve explains more about storytelling and storyfinding in Chapter 33.

A Taxonomy of Dashboards?

Nick Desbarats, dashboard trainer and authors, segments "dashboard" into a taxonomy of nine different dashboard types, each of which serves a different purpose and has different design best practices. For example, he defines the differences between live and static dashboards, role or department dashboards, and more. Even though most consumers don't often need to consider the difference, it is important for dashboard makers to consider this taxonomy as they build.

Find Out More About Nick

Nick Desbarats writes and trains on data visualization and dashboard creation. Check out his site at practicalreporting.com.

The Academic Perspective

Perhaps academia can provide a definitive definition? Alas, the confusion is just as rife there, too.

"Dashboards are a curated lens through which people can view large and complex datasets at a glance," said Benjamin Bach et al.[4] They defined six main genres (e.g., static, analytics, infographic) and multiple layout patterns.

[4]Bach, B., Freeman, E., Abdul-Rahman, A., Turkay, C., Khan, S., Fan, Y., & Chen, M. *Dashboard design patterns. IEEE TVCG*, 2022. 2

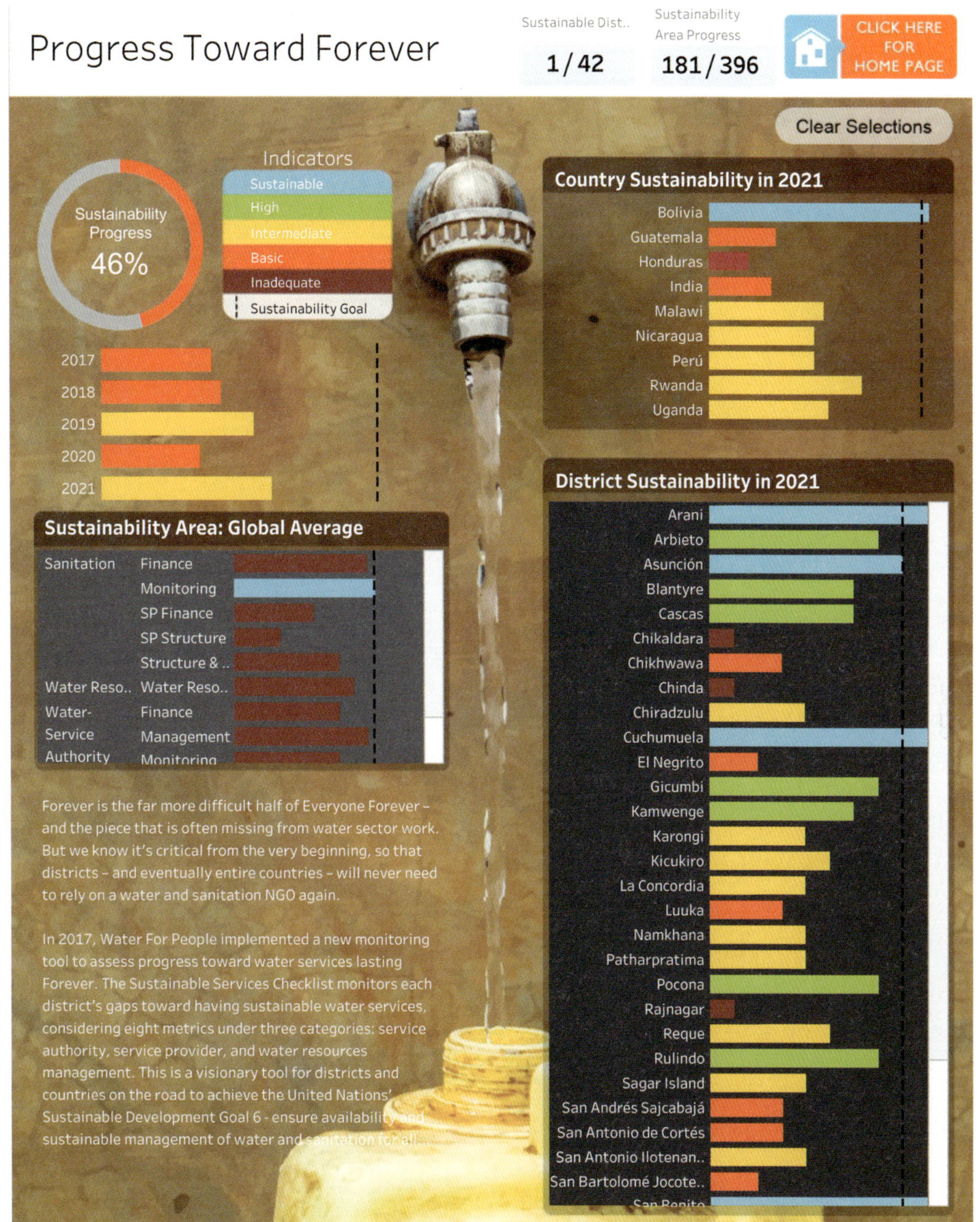

FIGURE 30.7 Submissions for this book from Heather Ditillo.

"A dashboard is an easy to read real-time user interface showing graphical presentation of the current status and historical trends of an organization's KPIs to enable decisions," says Miroslaw Staron.[5]

Some academics have even thrown in the towel! "Even the definition of a dashboard is in flux.... We do not attempt to provide a single authoritative definition of dashboards," said Sarikaya, Correll, Bertram, Tory, and Fisher in 2019.[6]

As we found in our first book, any attempt to make a definition struggles to hold even a subset of all possible use cases for monitoring data.

Hasn't AI Killed Dashboards, Anyway?

Perhaps the whole definition is moot, anyway. Some organizations suggest that with the "generative AI revolution," the very need for a dashboard is dying! Why worry about the definition or the process when you don't need them anymore? Jeff and I discuss the impact of AI in much more detail in Chapter 32, but for now it's worth looking a little at how analytics firms have evolved their marketing around dashboards.

Thoughtspot, a business intelligence company, allows you to explore data using natural language queries that return chart-based answers. The company has a compelling marketing slogan: "Dashboards are dead." Crikey, that's not good news for us.

Wait a moment, though. When you've asked a question and got a chart you want to keep, where does Thoughtspot say you should save it?

On a "liveboard." What's a liveboard? "Liveboards are the Thoughtspot term for a dashboard," says Thoughtspot's documentation.[7]

It seems that Thoughtspot's reports of dashboards' death are greatly exaggerated.

In 2024, Tableau launched Pulse, discrete metrics that include Generative AI summaries. "With Pulse Metrics, dashboards are dead!" exclaimed a Tableau sales leader at an internal meeting (Figure 30.8). The thing is, you go to the Pulse Digest to see all the metrics in one place (Figure 30.8). That digest sure looks like a collection of charts use to monitor processes to me.

Cathy O'Neill, author of the excellent *Weapons of Math Destruction*, a book about the dangers of AI, is now part of ORCAA, an organization whose dual mission is to help define accountability for algorithms, and to keep people safe from harmful consequences of AI and automated systems.[8] They offer an audit of your AI, which gets placed into an "Algorithmic Cockpit." In other words, to monitor our AI, we need a visual overview. Sounds like a dashboard, right?

---

[5]Staron, M. "Dashboard development guide How to build sustainable and useful dashboards to support software development and maintenance." 2015.

[6]Sarikaya, A., Correll, M., Bartram, L., Tory, M., & Fisher, D. *What do we talk about when we talk about dashboards? IEEE TVCG*, 25(1):682–692, 2018.

[7]"Using Liveboards and Answers," dtdbook.com/link47

[8]https://orcaarisk.com/

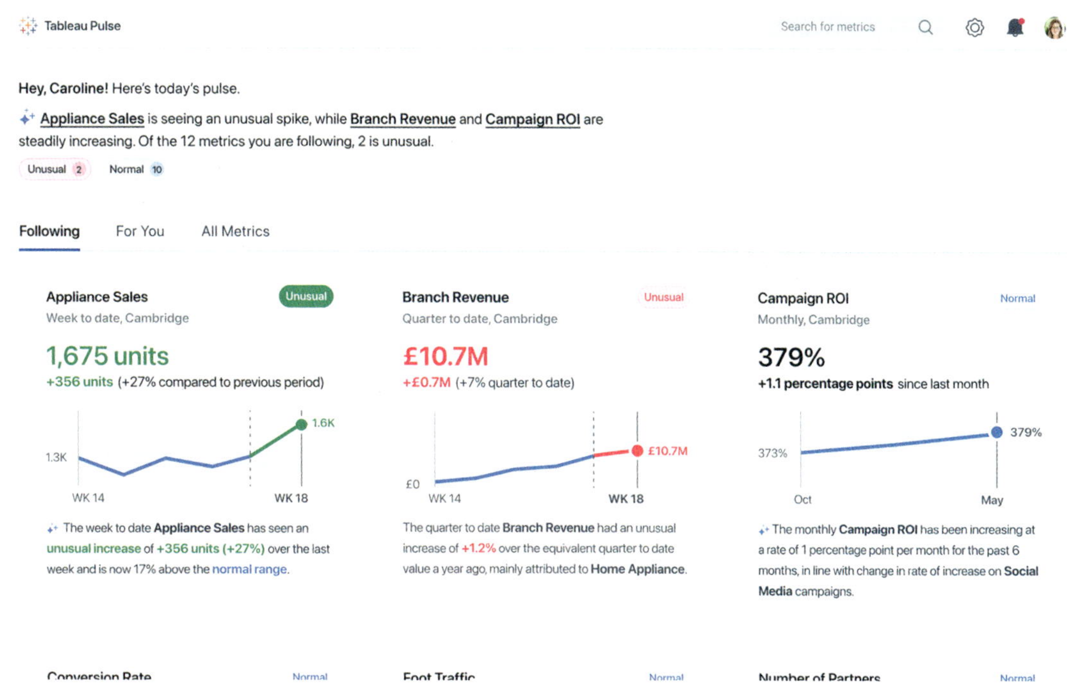

FIGURE 30.8 A Tableau Pulse digest.

In each case, the names might be changing, but the need for a way to monitor or understand systems, using visual displays, is not going away.

So, What the Heck is a Dashboard, Then?

You really want to know what a dashboard is? The word was first used in the 1840s to describe "a screen on the front of a horse-drawn vehicle to intercept water, mud, or snow."[9] The first motorized cars also had those boards on them; they provided a convenient location to add controls and dials for drivers to look at. In the 1970s and 80s, people started calling digital displays "dashboards" (Figure 30.9).

The word *dashboard* has undergone semantic drift. Nobody in the field of data can claim to describe their definition of a dashboard as "correct." Some people don't even use the name anymore. Chapter 24 features a race strategy analytics product from a professional car racing team. Its designer, Michael Gethers, deliberately doesn't call it a dashboard. He feels too

[9]Dashboard definition: dtdbook.com/link48

FIGURE 30.9 Andy, with RJ Andrews, pointing at the dashboard on an original Wells Fargo stagecoach.

many people have negative connotations of what a "traditional dashboard" might or might not be.

Whatever you call the thing you are building, we care that you build something useful. When you have a spark, a moment that calls for a new data display, you consider the success criteria of what you're going to build: Who is your audience? What insight do they need? What actions do they want to take? How and where will they view your display? And how can you design it so they can get their insights as efficiently as possible?

Our framework helps you answer those questions. Those are the key to success, not worrying about the semantics.

Chapter 31

Numbers in Context and Critical Thinking in Data Analysis

How Framing the Question Changes the Meaning and Relevance of Data You Visualize, and How to Think Critically About the Data You Are Analyzing

Jeffrey Shaffer

Introduction

In this chapter, we'll dive into the idea of numbers in context. I am not referring to adding more context to your dashboard numbers as we might do with BANs with context (see Chapter 27 on BANs), but rather the context of the analysis. We'll explore why asking the right question is the key to making sense of data and how the way we visualize information can alter the stories we try to tell. We'll then explore the importance of thinking critically and avoiding pitfalls when analyzing data.

A Population Map

Consider plotting data on a map. Figure 31.1 shows a cartoon depiction of the problem that geographic maps are often just population maps when they aren't intended to be.

FIGURE 31.1 A cartoon created by Philip Riggs poking fun at population maps.

In Figure 31.2 we see a map showing all of the bank branches in the contiguous United States. Note, only the dots are plotted. There are no map layers, no geographical features, and no borders or coastlines. The entire shape of this US map is made up from the dots.

Is this map useful? That depends on what questions we're trying to answer.

Suppose I told you Figure 31.2 was the Verizon coverage map of the United States. You'd probably believe me. But if I told you it was a map of where McDonald's restaurants are located, you'd probably believe that too. Indeed, Figure 31.3 shows McDonald's locations. It looks a lot like the bank branches map.

So, what's going on with these maps? It's simple: banks build branches where people live. In the case of McDonald's, they also build them where people are traveling, for example, near highways. In both cases, the map shows a very good proxy of the population in the United States. We can easily see larger cities like New York and Los Angeles. These are places with very large populations. Mapping large data points often just shows a population distribution, which can lead people to draw inaccurate conclusions about a dataset. It also makes it impossible to reveal compelling trends and insights that are unrelated to population.

This isn't an issue restricted to maps. Showing the raw data in any form, such as a table of numbers or a bar chart, can have the same effect. I'll come back to that, but first, let's see if the map of the bank branches could be more useful in a different view. What if we applied a filter and showed the top nine banks (Figure 31.4) and compared their geographical footprint?

This view would be useful if we were interested in seeing the geographic footprint of each bank's

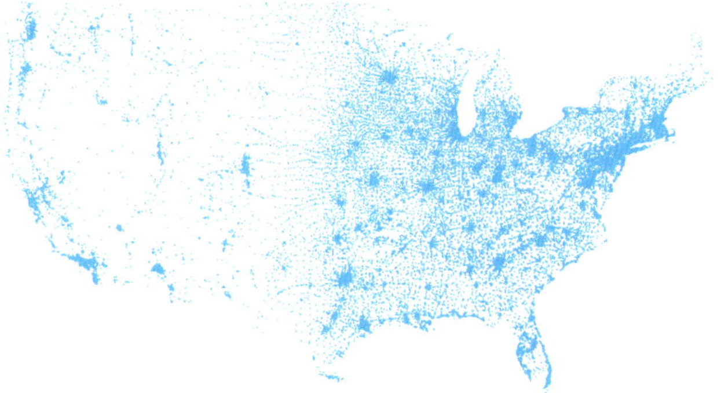

FIGURE 31.2 A dot map of all of the bank branches in the contiguous United States in 2017.

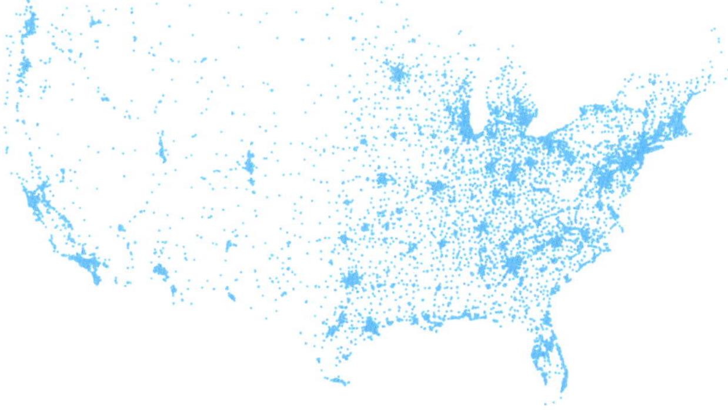

FIGURE 31.3 A dot map of McDonald's locations in the contiguous United States in 2016.

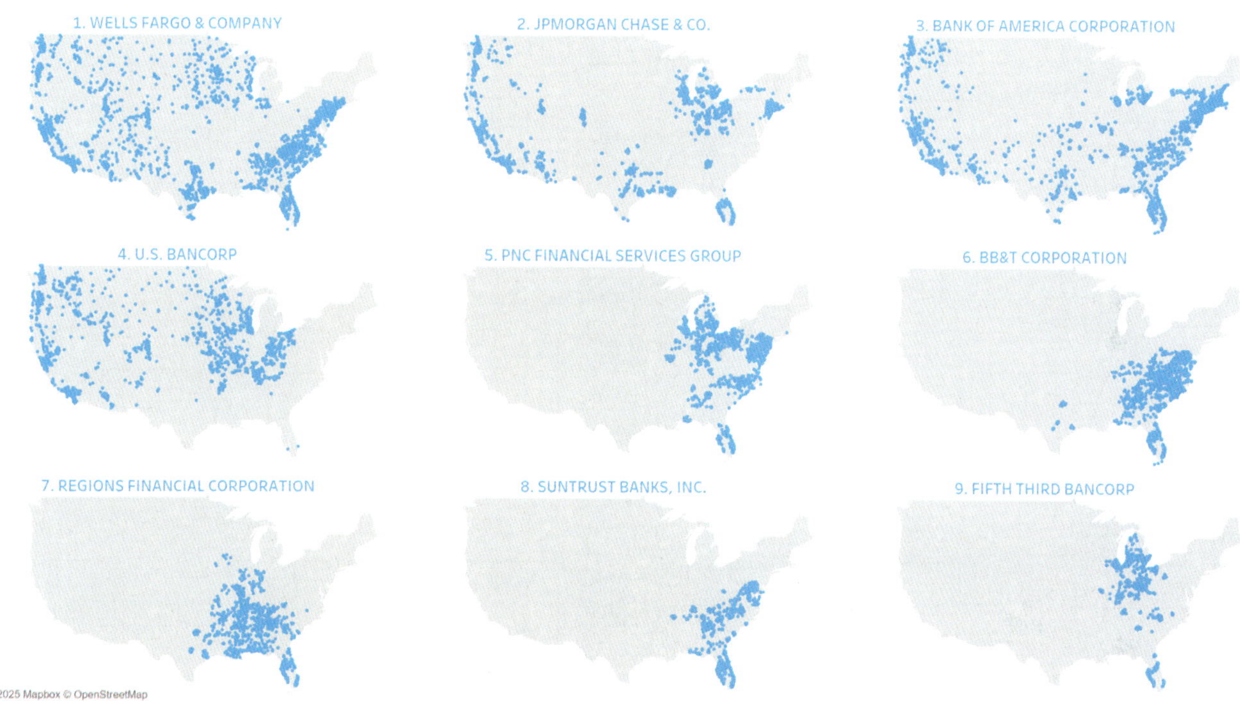

FIGURE 31.4 The top nine banks in 2017 by number of bank branches displayed as a trellis chart.

market. For example, we can easily see that Fifth Third Bank, headquartered in Cincinnati, Ohio, is a Midwest bank, with most of its branch locations in Ohio, Kentucky, Indiana, and Illinois (This explains why Steve, who lives in New York, had never heard of Fifth Third Bank). We further see that Wells Fargo (upper left) has locations throughout most of the United States. By adding the context of locations of the country's top nine banks, we've taken what was just a mess of dots and discovered something unrelated to population distribution.

We build banks where people are: that's true of many things we measure, which makes it difficult to draw deeper conclusions from a map like those in Figures 31.2 and 31.3. To discover something beyond the pattern within your raw dataset. You often need to add context.

A Crime Story: Should You Show Just the Raw Data?

Seeing large amounts of data on a US map might trigger your population alarm, but what if you aren't familiar with the population density? Figure 31.5 shows a map of total police calls in Cincinnati, Ohio, by neighborhood (911 calls and nonemergency calls[1]). Notice Westwood has the most police calls out of any neighborhood in Cincinnati.

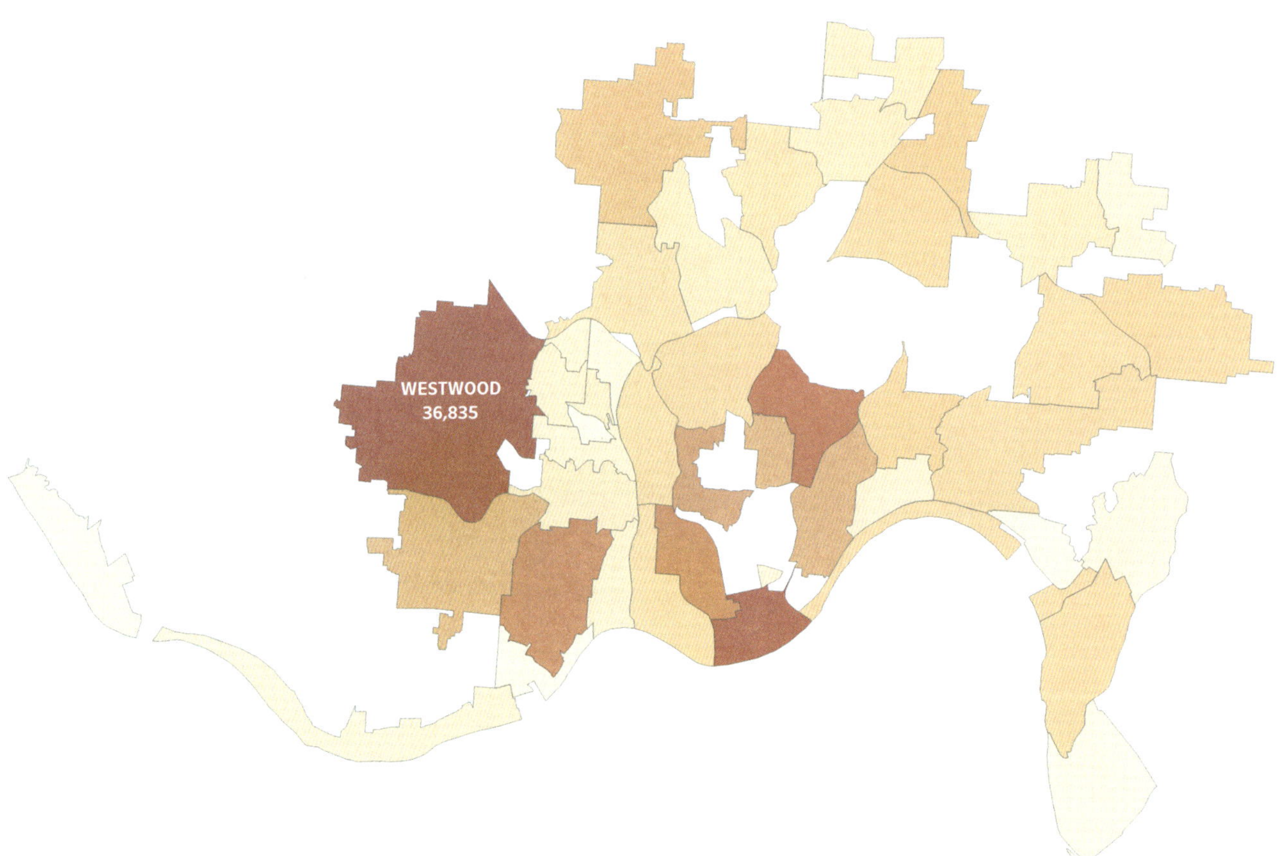

FIGURE 31.5 A map of police calls in 2018 in 43 Cincinnati neighborhoods served by the city police department. Westwood has the most calls. (Empty map areas have separate municipal police systems.)
Data Source: PDI-Police-Data-Initiative-Police-Calls-for-Service from https://data.cincinnati-oh.gov/.

[1]PDI-Police-Data-Initiative-Police-Calls-for-Service from https://data.cincinnati-oh.gov/

As I mentioned earlier, the display of the data does not have to be a map. Figure 31.6 shows the same data presented as a highlight table showing the top 20 neighborhoods based on the number of police calls in 2018.

Just like with the map, the table shows Westwood has the most police calls of any neighborhood in the city. Since we started the chapter discussing population maps, I'm sure you can guess where this is going. Indeed, Westwood is the largest neighborhood, in both land size (Figure 31.5) and population (Figure 31.7).

When my students create maps, charts, or tables like this, I always ask them, "Which state has the most traffic accidents in the United States?" It's California, but that's not because everyone in California is a bad driver; it's because that's the state where the largest number of people live. The same thing is happening here for Westwood: the raw counts of police calls do not account for population.

This does not mean that showing raw number counts is a bad way of looking at the data. In Part I, we talk about defining the audience and figuring out what they need to see to answer their questions or gain insights from the data. I always focus on:

- Who's the audience?
- What's the message?
- What's the medium?

Top	Neighborhood	2018 Total Police Calls
1	Westwood	36,835
2	CBD/Riverfront	35,068
3	Avondale	30,608
4	Over-the-Rhine	30,316
5	East Price Hill	27,067
6	West End	25,626
7	CUF (UC)	21,799
8	Walnut Hills	18,910
9	West Price Hill	18,162
10	Corryville (UC)	18,088
11	College Hill	15,033
12	East Walnut Hills/Evanston	14,582
13	Lower Price Hill/Queensgate	12,891
14	Roselawn	12,238
15	Mount Airy	10,569
16	Clifton (UC)	10,246
17	Bond Hill	10,238
18	Madisonville	9,952
19	Hyde Park	9,391
20	East End	9,234

FIGURE 31.6 A table of numbers showing the top 20 neighborhoods based on total police calls in 2018.

Top	Neighborhood	2018 Police Calls	Population (2020 Censu..
1	Westwood	36,835	34,899
2	CBD/Riverfront	35,068	5,835
3	Avondale	30,608	8,420
4	Over-the-Rhine	30,316	5,622
5	East Price Hill	27,067	15,241
6	West End	25,626	6,824
7	CUF (UC)	21,799	19,137
8	Walnut Hills	18,910	7,291
9	West Price Hill	18,162	17,876
10	Corryville (UC)	18,088	4,373
11	College Hill	15,033	16,039
12	East Walnut Hills/Evanston	14,582	11,994
13	Lower Price Hill/Queensgate	12,891	1,070
14	Roselawn	12,238	7,039
15	Mount Airy	10,569	9,210
16	Clifton (UC)	10,246	9,656
17	Bond Hill	10,238	7,002
18	Madisonville	9,952	10,244
19	Hyde Park	9,391	14,193
20	East End	9,234	1,476

FIGURE 31.7 A table of numbers showing the top 20 neighborhoods based on the total police calls in 2018 with the population added from the 2020 Census.

So how do these questions help determine whether the data as presented will work for different users?

The Data as Presented Works for Me

If you are the person in charge of a phone center handling the inbound 911 calls and the nonemergency calls or if you oversee the shift scheduling in your area, you would most certainly want to know the volume of calls coming in. You might dive deeper into the data and ask, "How many calls require a car to be dispatched?"

For these folks, the population of your neighborhood (or police district) is irrelevant. Sure, the larger areas may need more officers and staff, but you would base that decision, at least in part, on the number of calls you are getting. Clearly there's no need for 20 police officers in a very small area that never gets any calls. In this case, the table of numbers, the map, or some other visualization of the total police calls (in absolute values) could be useful because understanding the total call volume, without additional context, is helpful for the task at hand.

The Data as Presented Doesn't Work for Me

Now imagine you live in one of these neighborhoods and you are considering moving to a different neighborhood in the city. You want to know which neighborhood has the lowest crime rate. Does your current neighborhood have a higher or lower crime rate? In that case, the data displayed as Total Police Calls is not going to be useful on its own. Based on these numbers, you can't say Westwood is the worst neighborhood in Cincinnati for crime simply because it has the most calls to the police. You need additional information to understand how Total Police Calls relate to the population of that area.

The first thought that might come to mind is to simply add population into the analysis (Figure 31.7).

Right away you see that Westwood has the most people, but other areas, like Over-the-Rhine or Lower Price Hill/Queensgate, now jump out because of the high volume of calls in less populated neighborhoods. Next, we could create a composite measure so that we could compare these neighborhoods, regardless of population. We could look at the number of calls per capita (per person). This normalizes the data in a way that makes comparisons between neighborhoods useful.

Normalizing the Data

Normalization in this context means adjusting values measured on different scales to a notionally common scale, often to compare or combine them meaningfully. By calculating calls per capita, you adjust the number of calls by the population size, making it possible to compare different neighborhoods regardless of their population. This provides a rate (calls per person) that allows for fair comparisons across different-sized populations.

Once we normalize the data, we see a very different pattern in the data (Figure 31.8).

The Calls per capita shows Westwood is not in the Top 20 anymore; it has dropped to 31 on the list. It has one of the lowest call rates in the city, with only 1.06 calls per person. So what's the answer? Is Lower Price Hill/Queensgate the most dangerous neighborhood in Cincinnati? Maybe. This approach is certainly better for the person looking at how dangerous a neighborhood might be versus someone doing resource planning in the police

Top	Neighborhood	2018 Police Calls	Population (2020 Census)	Calls per capita
1	Lower Price Hill/Queensgate	12,891	1,070	12.05
2	Camp Washington	8,923	1,234	7.23
3	East End	9,234	1,476	6.26
4	CBD/Riverfront	35,068	5,835	6.01
5	Over-the-Rhine	30,316	5,622	5.39
6	Corryville (UC)	18,088	4,373	4.14
7	West End	25,626	6,824	3.76
8	Avondale	30,608	8,420	3.64
9	Pendleton	3,486	1,088	3.20
10	Spring Grove Village	5,910	1,916	3.08
11	Linwood	2,002	705	2.84
12	Walnut Hills	18,910	7,291	2.59
13	South Cumminsville/Millvale	6,891	2,667	2.58
14	South Fairmount	5,147	2,181	2.36
15	Carthage	5,692	2,781	2.05
16	North Fairmount/English Woo..	3,849	1,951	1.97
17	Roll Hill	3,756	1,918	1.96
18	East Price Hill	27,067	15,241	1.78
19	Roselawn	12,238	7,039	1.74
20	Mount Adams	2,377	1,578	1.51
21	Mount Auburn	7,581	5,070	1.50
22	Bond Hill	10,238	7,002	1.46
23	Winton Hills	7,939	5,684	1.40
24	California	1,285	944	1.36
25	East Walnut Hills/Evanston	14,582	11,994	1.22
26	Sedamsville/Riverside/Sayler ..	6,406	5,338	1.20
27	North Avondale/Paddock Hills	8,636	7,368	1.17
28	Mount Airy	10,569	9,210	1.15
29	CUF (UC)	21,799	19,137	1.14
30	Clifton (UC)	10,246	9,656	1.06
31	Westwood	36,835	34,899	1.06
32	Northside	8,445	8,096	1.04
33	West Price Hill	18,162	17,876	1.02
34	Madisonville	9,952	10,244	0.97
35	College Hill	15,033	16,039	0.94
36	Hartwell	5,448	5,806	0.94
37	Oakley	8,756	11,761	0.74
38	Hyde Park	9,391	14,193	0.66
39	Pleasant Ridge	5,736	8,895	0.64
40	Kennedy Heights	2,816	5,166	0.55
41	Mount Washington	6,349	13,735	0.46
42	Mount Lookout/Columbia Tusc..	2,950	6,696	0.44

FIGURE 31.8 Cincinnati Neighborhoods sorted by Calls per capita added.

department. However, we need to be careful with these numbers. Before we jump to a conclusion, we should dive deeper.

Thinking Critically in Data Analysis

Just because your data comes from a credible source or is published on a credible website doesn't mean it doesn't have flaws. Let's see how this plays out.

Let's think critically about why a neighborhood in downtown Cincinnati, like the Cincinnati Business District (CBD/Riverbend) or Corryville (near the University of Cincinnati), would have such a small population and so many police calls. One factor might be the thousands of businesspeople commuting into the city to work on weekdays or other people enjoying a sports game, dinner, or a concert on the weekends. You might consider that 50,000 students at the University of Cincinnati during the school year would have an impact on police calls. These are all valid points and would require further investigation. However, to even think of these things in the first place would require some knowledge or expertise of the data itself. We might need to collaborate with a subject-matter expert (SME) who is more familiar with the data, in this case the neighborhoods, the police policies, or the crimes themselves (see, as an example, the team coaching dashboard from Chapter 12 where the SME knowledge was key to building the dashboard).

Far too often, we load up data into our favorite tool, and we start creating charts. That can be useful, but don't blow through the exploratory data analysis too quickly. If we aren't careful, we may end up with bad analysis and false conclusions.

Using the data from the Cincinnati Open Data Portal lets us focus on Lower Price Hill/Queensgate, which appears to be the most dangerous neighborhood in the city of Cincinnati. It's not a very large area of the city, so it's pretty easy to map (Figure 31.9).

What do you notice right away? In addition to the large gap in the middle, which is a railroad yard, did you notice the squares of data? The Cincinnati police anonymize this data, shifting the latitude and

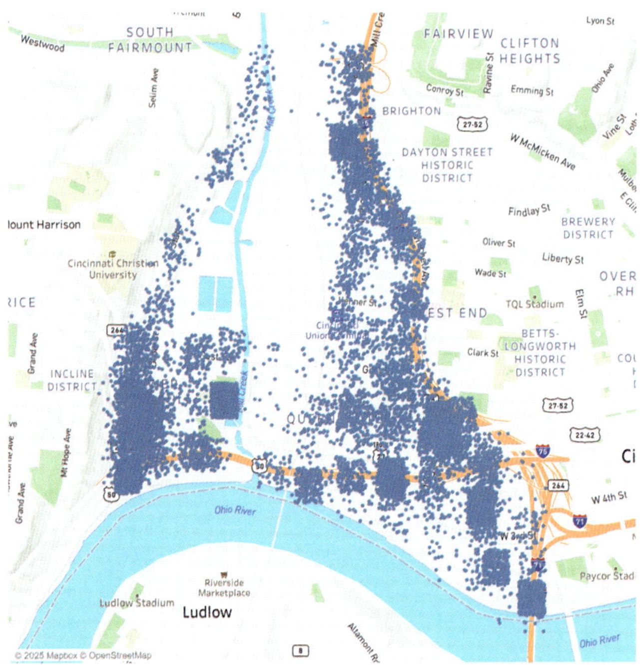

FIGURE 31.9 A map of the 2018 police calls in Lower Price Hill/Queensgate.

longitude slightly, and masking part of the address so that you don't know exactly where the points are on the map. This wouldn't be an issue for the Cincinnati Police themselves, as they have the unmasked data, but everyone else using this data would need to understand that. If we zoom in and examine a few of these squares, you will find something very interesting (Figure 31.10). Some of the squares are on top of police facilities!

Another square surrounds a building that is listed as the Cincinnati Police Department Records Section building. Clearly there are some default addresses that are being input into the system for certain calls.

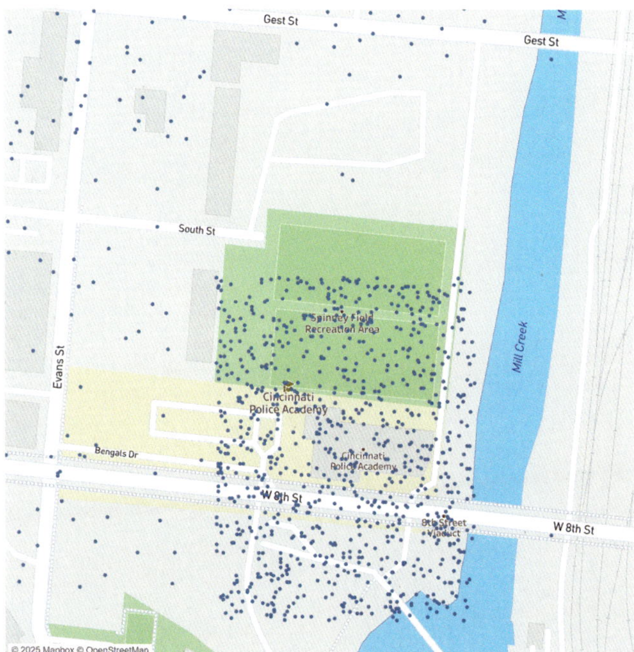

FIGURE 31.10 A map of 909 police calls in a square around the Cincinnati Police Academy.

This seems to be the case in many of the neighborhoods, where incidents were possibly defaulted or miscoded to the police station, rather than the address of the incident.

Lower Price Hill/Queensgate may very well have the highest crime rate, but this data would require hours of cleaning and more investigating before we could trust it to answer that sort of question.

To be clear, this is just one of countless examples of what you will find in this particular data set. For example, "Telephone Harassment," "Hazard to Traffic/Pedestrian," "Auto Accident," and "Noise Complaint" are all listed in the call logs. Again, those would be good data points for someone handling call volumes or staffing resources, but we probably wouldn't consider those in an analysis of the most dangerous neighborhoods.

Summary

So what do we do? This is where the human element of data analysis, the critical thinking that is involved in what we do, is necessary. If we aren't careful, we could easily gloss over something important in the data or missing in the data, which could then lead to incorrect decisions. We need to be curious about the data, be skeptical of the data, ask questions, discover patterns, and explore carefully and critically. This is also a major concern with using artificial intelligence tools as the only tool in data analysis. You may find answers to your questions quickly and, at first, may even appear to be accurate, but without diving in and understanding the data, this could lead to dangerous outcomes.

We started with a simple count of police calls and the question "Which is the most dangerous neighborhood in Cincinnati?" We soon had to ask multiple contextual questions before getting close to the correct answer.

1. How many people live in each neighborhood?
2. Do any specific events (sports events, concerts, etc.) skew the data?
3. Is the data correct? Are all the calls recorded to their real locations?
4. Should we exclude calls that don't have a geographical element?
5. Is the data appropriate for the analysis I am trying to conduct?

Analyses like this quickly get complex and deep as we've seen.

As we discussed, getting data and processing it are vital, but it's the human exploration and understanding of context that are equally vital.

Chapter 32

Generative AI and Data Analytics

Jeffrey Shaffer and Andy Cotgreave

At the time of writing, the best generative artificial intelligence (GenAI) models, and specifically large language models (LLMs), have surpassed people on many benchmarks, excelling in law, medicine, mathematics, reasoning, and coding. Their rapid evolution continues to push the boundaries of what AI can achieve. We've heard GenAI described as a highly intelligent auto-complete, which isn't a great analogy. These LLMs do generate text token by token. However, they go far beyond simple sentence completion. They produce tokens based on context.

What Is a Token?

A token in GenAI and LLMs is a small piece of text that the model processes. It can be a word, a part of a word, or even a single character, depending on the language and model. For example, in the sentence:

"AI is amazing!"

A model might break this into four tokens: "AI" and "is" and "amazing" and "!".

LLMs generate text one token at a time by predicting what comes next based on the context of the previous tokens.

See the glossary for more AI-related definitions.

Today's models are multimodal, capable of processing text, sound, images, video, and numerous file formats. They have also become highly proficient at coding (e.g., Python), an important element, especially for data analysis and visualization. With these rapid advancements, GenAI tools can be integrated into daily workflows.

According to the 2024 State of Data Viz Survey[1] from the Data Visualization Society, respondents reported a 54% increase in the use of AI for data visualization, rising from 24% in 2023 to 37% in 2024 (Figure 32.1).

In this chapter, we're going to cover three things. First, we'll provide a short overview of GenAI. Then, we'll look at how it can be used in different parts of our framework. Finally, we'll share other ways GenAI tools can help with other tasks associated with data analysis and dashboarding. We'll round out the chapter with a cautionary tale.

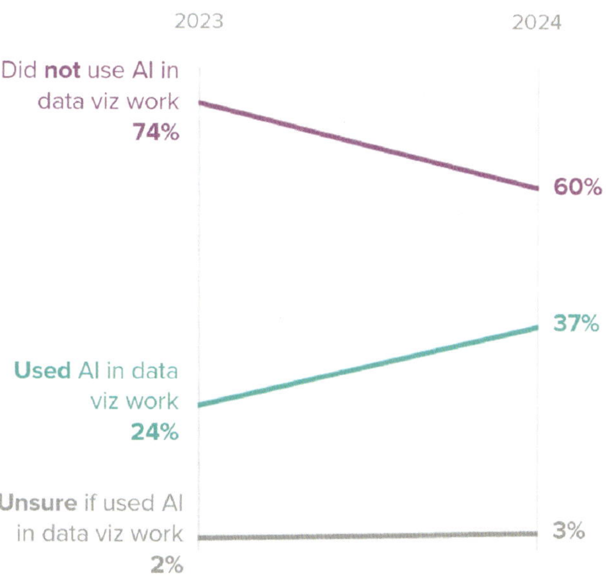

FIGURE 32.1 An increase in the use of AI in data visualization work from 2023 to 2024 from the 2024 State of Data Viz survey report.

[1] dtdbook.com/link49

Understanding Generative AI

Strengths and Weaknesses

It's important to understand what GenAI is inherently good at and what it is not.

Language models use probabilistic tokens, which means they determine a response based on the probability that one thing follows another.

For example, what's the next word in this sentence: "The dog barked at the..."?

The most likely response might be "mailman," but sometimes, depending on context, the answer might be "squirrel." This is how an LLM works where the responses might be different even if you type the same prompt. LLMs complete sentences by determining the most likely token that follows. Depending on its tuning, there may be more or less variability in responses.

While increasing variability might be useful for creative tasks, it is higher risk when analyzing data.

> "It takes years of work as a data team to build trust with your consumers. It takes one wrong answer for someone to lose trust in a data set."
>
> —*Tim Ngwena, consultant at Aimpoint Digital, and data visualization YouTuber.*

LLMs can also be used to write code, for example Python. Not only can they write code, but they can execute it, check for errors, debug if needed, and then rerun it to get more accurate results. As we will see in some examples, this is a powerful tool for exploratory data analysis (EDA); for extract, transform, and load (ETL); or as a tool for storyfinding.

The following is a quick summary of the strengths and weaknesses of GenAI (as of the writing of this book).

Strengths

- GenAI is trained on vast datasets, enabling nuanced understanding and pattern recognition.
- It rapidly generates text, code, and other content for responses.
- It maintains context in conversations but has memory limits (known as *context window*).
- It can be tuned for accuracy versus creativity (*temperature settings*).
- It can generate, debug, and explain code across multiple programming languages.
- It supports multiple input formats (text, images, code, and more).
- Models can be customized to be domain-specific (*fine-tuning* or *retrieval-augmented generation*).

Weaknesses

- GenAI's responses are probabilistic, meaning they vary, even when prompts and inputs are the same (*nondeterministic*).
- It can generate false or misleading information that can appear to be accurate and even have source information (*hallucinations*).
- There is a knowledge cut-off, meaning it is trained up to a certain date and does not have any knowledge that is more current.

- It is vulnerable to bypassing safeguards (*prompt injection*).
- It may underperform without domain-specific training or external knowledge.

How We Engage with GenAI Tools: Prompt Engineering

> "The nice thing about SQL is that it does exactly what you tell it to do. The problem with SQL is that it does exactly what you tell it to do."
>
> *—Michael Kane, CCO at J.J. Marshall & Associates Inc.*

The quality of a prompt directly affects the response. A vague prompt can lead to ambiguity or incorrect answers, while a well-structured prompt can improve results. For example, asking an AI to "put the bar chart *on top of* the image" could mean placing it above the image vertically or as an overlay. The clarity of your prompt matters.

A strong prompt requires the same critical thinking we bring into dashboard design. This includes clear instructions, context, input data, and an expected output. Additional techniques like personas, role-based prompts, few-shot learning (providing a few examples), and chain-of-thought reasoning (step-by-step) can further improve results.

Instruction – "Perform exploratory data analysis."

Context – "The dataset comes from..."

Input Data – "The dataset (ex. upload a CSV file)"

Output Indicator – "...in bullet points highlighting key patterns, outliers, and insights."

Role-based Approach – "You are a data analyst..."

Personas – "You are a data analyst who loves storytelling."

Here are a few examples:

"You are a data analyst and expert in exploratory data analysis. Perform EDA on the attached dataset, which tracks the unemployment rate in the U.S. over the past 20 years. Follow these steps:"

"You are a data journalist who crafts compelling narratives from data. Analyze the unemployment trends in the dataset and write a short, engaging story. Follow this example:"

"You are a data engineer skilled in structuring datasets. Analyze the attached file and generate a data dictionary in CSV format with the following columns:"

Prompt Engineering

A deeper exploration of prompt engineering is beyond the scope of this book, but understanding how to craft effective prompts is crucial for obtaining accurate responses. For more details, visit promptingguide.ai.

Let's examine how GenAI can be used in these areas.

Using Generative AI in Our Framework (Andy)

GenAI tools provide useful ways to work within the framework. Let's explore other ways that GenAI can be applied in different parts of the process.

Prototyping

Wireframing is a key part of exploring the initial ideas. It helps you and your users to test concepts early. You can type out a scenario and let the tool create ideas.

Here's an example. Each scenario in this book begins with a "Big Picture" paragraph explaining the use case. Here's the one from my Strava dashboard (Chapter 13, "Fitness Goal Tracker"):

> *You track your walks using Strava and have a goal to walk 1,000 miles (1609km) a year. That requires a daily average of 2.7 miles (4.4km). Your primary need isn't to see the total miles you've walked so far, it's to see how close you are tracking to the goal: How far ahead or behind the goal are you? Knowing how your current distance walked compares to the distance expected allows you to tailor your activity plans.*

I copied this into Anthropic's Claude Sonnet and asked it to come up with a wireframe concept based on the text. Figure 32.2 shows the result after only a few prompts (Figure 32.3 shows the original, for comparison).

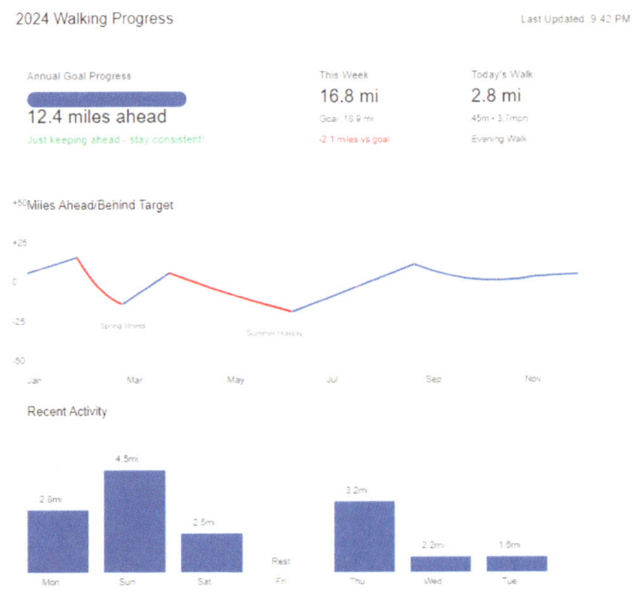

FIGURE 32.2 Claude Sonnet's Strava Tracking prototype.

The wireframe created by GenAI is very close to my own dashboard. There is a line chart showing progress compared with target. That line is color-coded to show red when it's negative. The BANs are very similar to the ones on the real dashboard. There is even a 7-day summary at the bottom, shown as a bar chart. That is arguably better than the real one, which shows those numbers only as text.

I've tested this approach with many examples from the book, and the results consistently provide strong starting points. Even for atypical dashboards, the wireframe outputs offered useful design ideas.

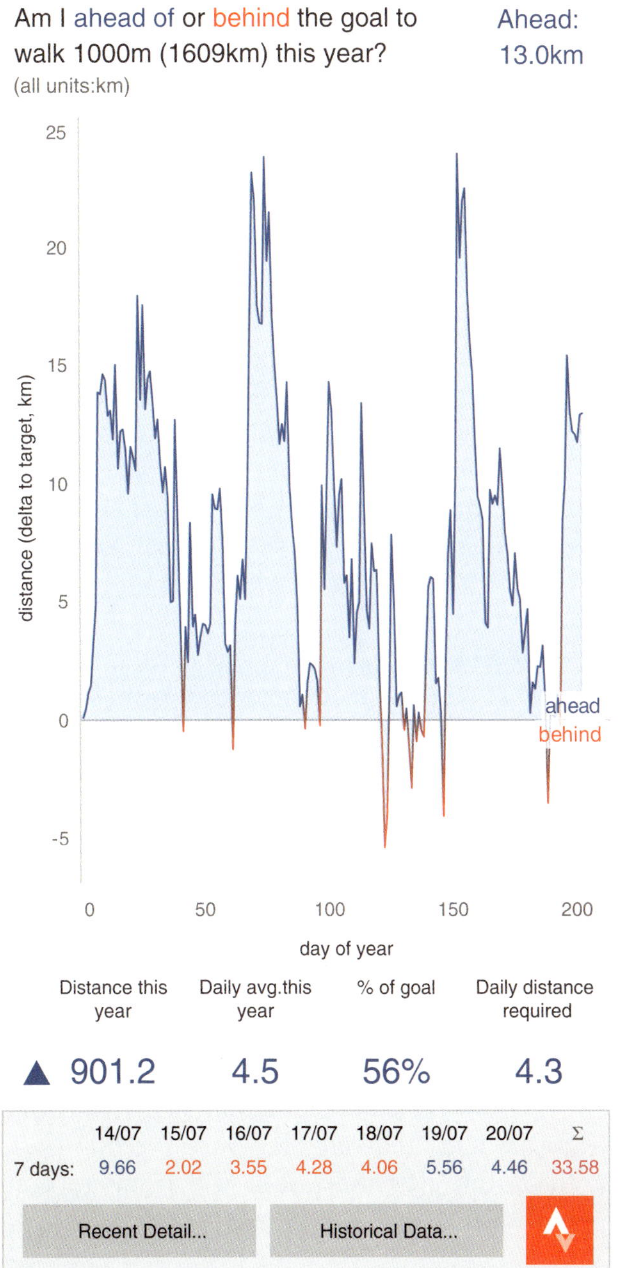

FIGURE 32.3 The actual Strava Tracking dashboard.

Development

Here are a few ways LLMs can help in development:

- **Generate sample data** that matches your required data structure and field names for initial development.
- **Explore integrated GenAI capabilities** within your tech stack, which continue to evolve (e.g., AI tools built into Tableau and Power BI).
- **Get syntax assistance** when writing calculated fields or coding.
- **Leverage a CustomGPT** to solve problems or provide expert advice.
  - Tableau Virtuoso by Adam Mico (dtdbook.com/link50) provides guidance on Tableau Server, Desktop, Prep, Cloud, and Blueprint (using the latest Tableau knowledge as of October 2024).
  - Data Mockstar by Adam Mico (dtdbook.com/link51) delivers blinded data on nearly any topic and helps you build the ideal starter dataset for your project. By default, it exports a 1,000-row CSV but supports various formats.
  - VizCritique Pro by Adam Mico (dtdbook.com/link52) offers expert analysis on data visualizations from any tool, emphasizing best practices and dashboard design.
  - Data Viz Advisor by Jeffrey Shaffer (dtdbook.com/link53) provides advice on your visualizations based on best practices, trained examples and *The Big Book of Dashboards*.
- **Use Google AI Studio** as a tutor or coach to assist with data analysis and visualization or to get help on using a data visualization tool.

Release and Adoption

One of the things we recommend in the framework is to produce documentation and training content.

GenAI can help with both of those.

I uploaded Kevin Flerlage's bowling dashboard (Chapter 12) to Claude 3.5 Sonnet and asked it to create a script for a training video. I then put that script into HeyGen.ai (a video creation tool that uses AI avatars, including your personal avatar, and can translate to other languages). In less than 30 minutes, which was mostly processing time, I had a functioning training video (Figure 32. 4). See the video here: dtdbook .com/link54.

For documentation, Adam Mico created a Custom GPT "Dashboard Documentation Pro" that creates an excellent first draft documenting a dashboard based on its appearance.

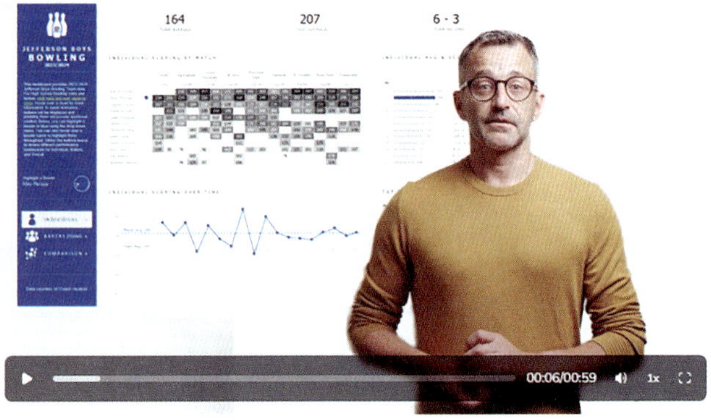

FIGURE 32.4 A training video made in HeyGen.

Using GenAI for Data Analysis (Jeff)

GenAI for Exploratory Data Analysis

Let's start with exploratory data analysis (EDA). GenAI tools now can run and execute Python. This is a critical component to EDA, because instead of relying on token probability to answer questions, it can generate code to get answers and even plot graphs of the data.

Making sense of the role of GenAI as a collaborator on a data project, let's walk through a specific example: I loaded a CSV file of 603 episodes of *Scooby-Doo* (a classic animated series) and asked a very basic question from a very small file: "How many records are in the CSV file?"

The task doesn't get much easier than this, so any LLM should be able to do this, right? Well, it depends. My work version of Copilot responded with 450, which is incorrect. I tried several follow-up prompts and each time it confirmed 450 records. In contrast, the web version of Copilot, outside of work, and the latest ChatGPT model (ChatGPT-4o) both returned the correct answer of 603.

Why the difference? The simple answer is coding. The incorrect answer was relying on a token returned from the LLM. The correct answer was derived using Python to query the CSV file. Once the query was returned, the LLM then used the result to craft a response.

LLMs Executing Python Code

To indicate that an LLM is using Python, ChatGPT shows "Analyzing" while it is processing, and upon completion, both tools show an icon, </> Code in Copilot and >_ in ChatGPT, that will expand to show the Python code that was generated and executed by the LLM. This is also useful because you can copy the Python code and run it in your own environment with data files that might be proprietary and can't be uploaded to websites like ChatGPT. For example, mock up some dummy data in the same file format for ChatGPT, but then swap files and run the code on your data behind your firewall. Alternatively, you can use tools such as GitHub Copilot or Cursor.

So, getting a record count is a pretty simple task. Let's take it up a notch and follow up with another simple, two-word prompt: "Perform EDA" (for performing exploratory data analysis).

Within a minute or two, ChatGPT returned all sorts of information. Now, as mentioned earlier, each session will produce different responses. However, the response will typically include most of the same information.

Here are the elements of EDA that returned from my initial prompt:

- Column names and data types
- Missing values summary with number of missing and percentages
- Numerical column statistics including mean, standard deviation, min, quartiles and max
- Categorical column statistics including count, unique, top, frequency

Based on this result, it's easy to see how GenAI could be used to help create a data dictionary, a task we all love, right?

ChatGPT also produced nearly a dozen charts exploring different aspects of the data (Figure 32.5).

This output is not ready for presentation, but for quick EDA this is powerful stuff. Keep in mind that my prompts were very basic and I didn't write a single line of Python code (Python wouldn't even need to be installed and configured). It would be easy to continue down any analytical path from here, just by prompting a few follow-up questions on any aspect of the data that seemed interesting.

It's important to remember to think critically during any exploratory data analysis. See Chapter 31, "Numbers in Context and Critical Thinking in Data Analysis," for further discussion of this topic.

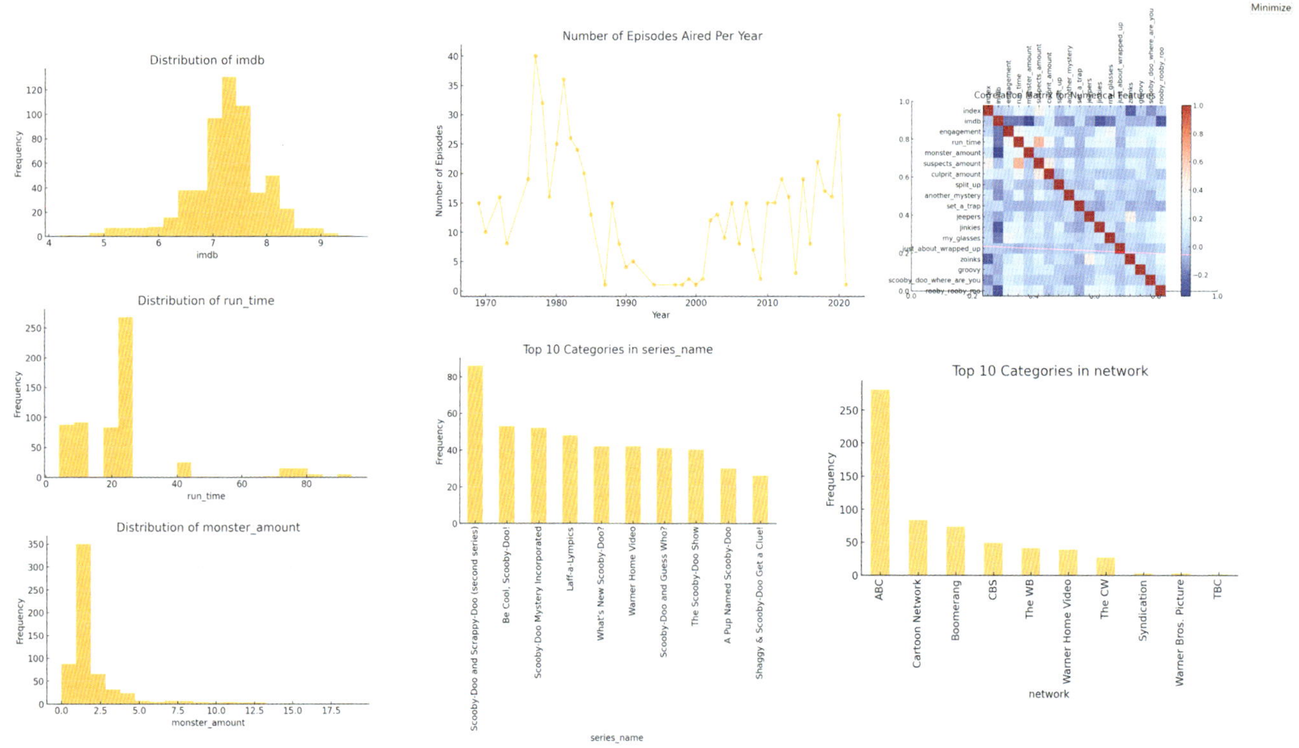

FIGURE 32.5 Exploratory data analysis of a dataset performed by GenAI-based on a few prompts.

GenAI for Creating Data Visualization

By combining your expertise in the field with chain-of-thought prompting, it is possible to create data visualizations that are carefully crafted and designed for presentation. As with any tool, the defaults can be challenging, and the default Python charts are no exception (see Chapter 29 for an in-depth look at this problem).

In Tableau, PowerBI, or Excel, we would have to make our design changes step-by-step, navigating through the software. In ChatGPT, we do this through prompting.

Using the same Halloween dataset that I used in Chapter 29, "Defaults vs. Design: The Pitfalls of Software Defaults," Figure 32.6 shows the default bar chart that ChatGPT generates.

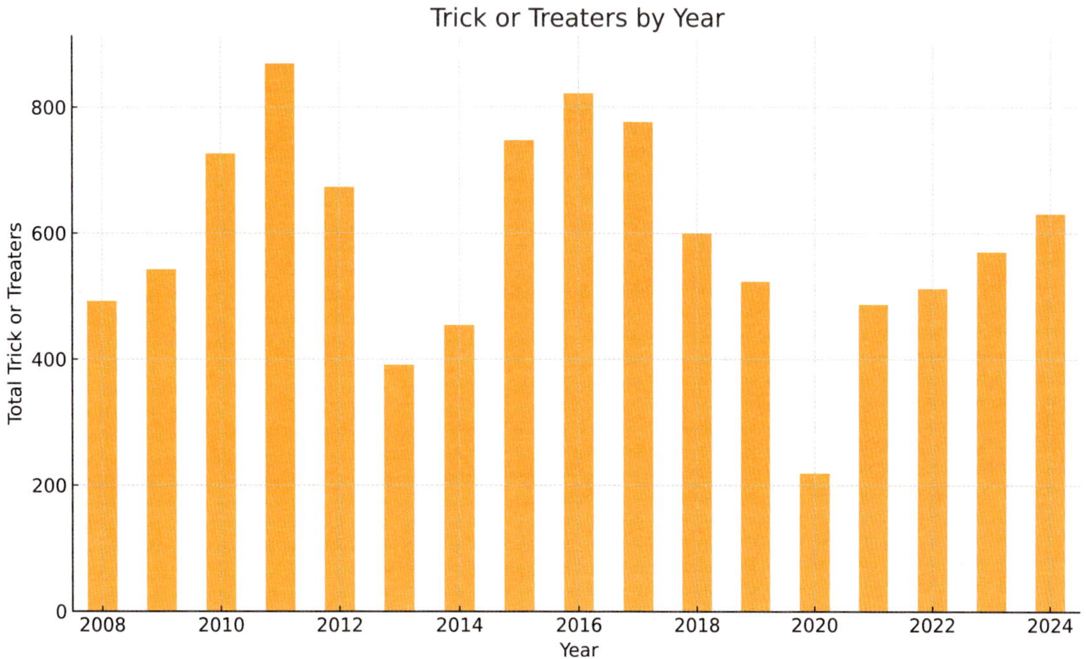

FIGURE 32.6 A bar chart created from a dataset using GenAI based on a single prompt.

Prompt: "Create a bar chart of total trick or treaters by year."

From here, I wondered if I could create a playful chart reflecting the theme of the data. After a series of step-by-step prompts (e.g., chain-of-thought prompting):

1. "change the background color of the chart to black with orange bars"
2. "directly label the bars with the numbers and remove the y-axis"
3. "remove the word Year from the x-axis"
4. "make all the text orange"
5. "add a title and subtitle"
6. "make the title a larger font than the subtitle"
7. "add an average line" (note – this was not included in the data file)
8. "create an image of Halloween set in a graveyard with a pumpkin..." (Note: I used Midjourney to create the image and then uploaded to ChatGPT, but ChatGPT can also create images using DALL-E.)
9. "overlay the bar chart on top of the image"
10. "remove the background color from the chart"
11. "add some transparency to the bars"

Figure 32.7 shows the resulting Halloween visualization, created entirely by prompting ChatGPT.

This chart might be easy to create in whatever your tool of choice; however, this was all done in a few minutes through natural language prompting.

GenAI for Interpreting a Chart and Storyfinding

A third use case for GenAI in data analysis is finding the analytical insights in a chart. What if we could upload a chart and ask for an explanation of it? Or load a chart or dataset and prompt it to find interesting trends or facts to help craft a data story? We can, which could create new opportunities to bridge the data literacy gaps that data visualization creators have said are the biggest challenge to adoption and use of their charts.[2]

Let's look at the unemployment rate data from the U.S. Bureau of Labor Statistics that is tracked by the Federal Reserve Bank of St. Louis. I could easily upload a Microsoft Excel file into ChatGPT as I did with the Scooby-Do data, but to showcase its capabilities, I will simply upload a line chart copied

FIGURE 32.7 A Halloween visualization created from a dataset using GenAI based on chain-of-thought prompting.

[2]Data Viz Society State of the Industry Survey 2024. datavisualizationsociety.org/survey

from the St. Louis Federal Reserve website (dtd-book.com/link55). I filtered the data to show the unemployment rate from January 1, 2000, through November 1, 2024 (Figure 32.8).

Then I prompted ChatGPT-4o using only an image (not the data file) to "Tell me what is going on with this chart and give me three major insights."

ChatGPT's response:

> This graph represents the unemployment rate in the United States over a period from about 2000 through the early 2020s, as provided by the Federal Reserve Economic Data (FRED) and the U.S. Bureau of Labor Statistics.
>
> Here are three major insights based on the graph:
>
> - **Recessions and unemployment peaks:** The shaded areas on the graph indicate periods of U.S. recessions, which are typically characterized by a rise in unemployment. There are two clear recessions shown: the first one around 2001 (dot-com bubble burst), and a deeper one starting in 2007 and peaking in 2009–2010 (Great Recession). A sharp but brief spike in unemployment is also evident around 2020, which would correspond to the COVID-19 pandemic's impact on the economy.
> - **Great recession analysis:** During the Great Recession (2007–2009), the unemployment rate rose from around 5% to approximately 10%. This was a major and sustained increase, indicating a severe economic downturn that took several years to recover from, as the unemployment rate only started to consistently decrease again around 2011.

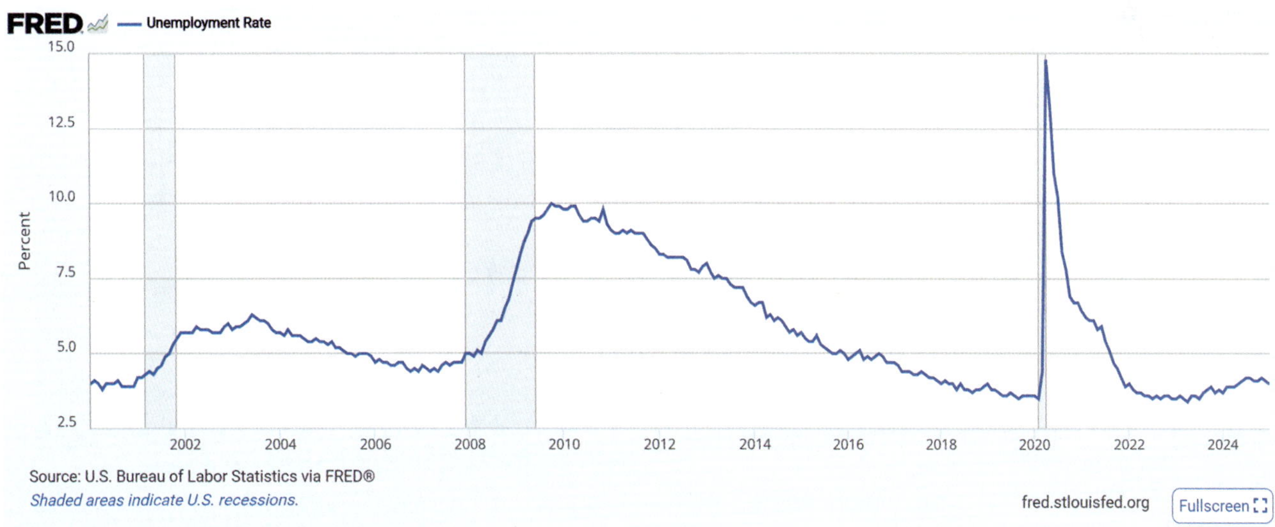

FIGURE 32.8 A chart of the employment rate January 1, 2000, through November 1, 2024.

- **COVID-19 pandemic impact:** The graph shows an unprecedented spike in unemployment around 2020, where the rate shoots up to nearly 15%. This represents the economic shock due to the COVID-19 pandemic. However, it is notable that the spike is quite sharp, and the rate drops quickly as well, suggesting a rapid but intense disruption to the job market, followed by a relatively quick recovery in employment rates compared with the slow recovery post-Great Recession.

The overall trend, despite these peaks during recessions, shows a general decrease in unemployment over the two decades, with periods of increase typically associated with economic recessions or extraordinary events like the COVID-19 pandemic.

All three are useful insights, derived using only an image of a line chart. The original line chart had shaded areas for the recessions, but it did not indicate the "dot-com bubble burst" or the "Great Recession" or "COVID," which was added by ChatGPT. Diving deeper, ChatGPT also points out the "sharp spike and quick drop" of the unemployment rate during COVID compared with the much slower recovery during the Great Recession.

GenAI, at least in its current state and for the foreseeable future, should be thought of as a powerful collaborator for chart creators. In addition, it could be used as a thoughtful coach for those learning how to read charts. In this example, it was able to find key insights into the data, which we can then use in designing our data story. ChatGPT can also be helpful in crafting good chart titles, detailed subtitles, and annotations.

Figure 32.9 show a finished data visualization that I created in Tableau using the underlying data with annotations for the three major insights from ChatGPT to craft a data story.

Words of Caution (Andy)

We have presented powerful case studies in this chapter, but there are two things you should be wary of: unpredictable results and ethical concerns.

Unpredictable Results

In the final review of this chapter, I decided to replicate Jeff's Halloween chart exercise using a different dataset. Would I get the same powerful results? I uploaded a CSV to ChatGPT-4o containing the data behind the award-winning visualization Iraq Bloody Toll by Simon Scarr (Figure 32.10). This illustrated the deaths resulting from the United States' military involvement in Iraq between 2001 and 2011.

I then used the same prompt Jeff did to kick things off: "Do exploratory data analysis."

It gave me some summary statistics (several of which turned out be wrong) and then suggested three visualizations. I asked it to draw deaths over time. Figure 32.11 shows the result.

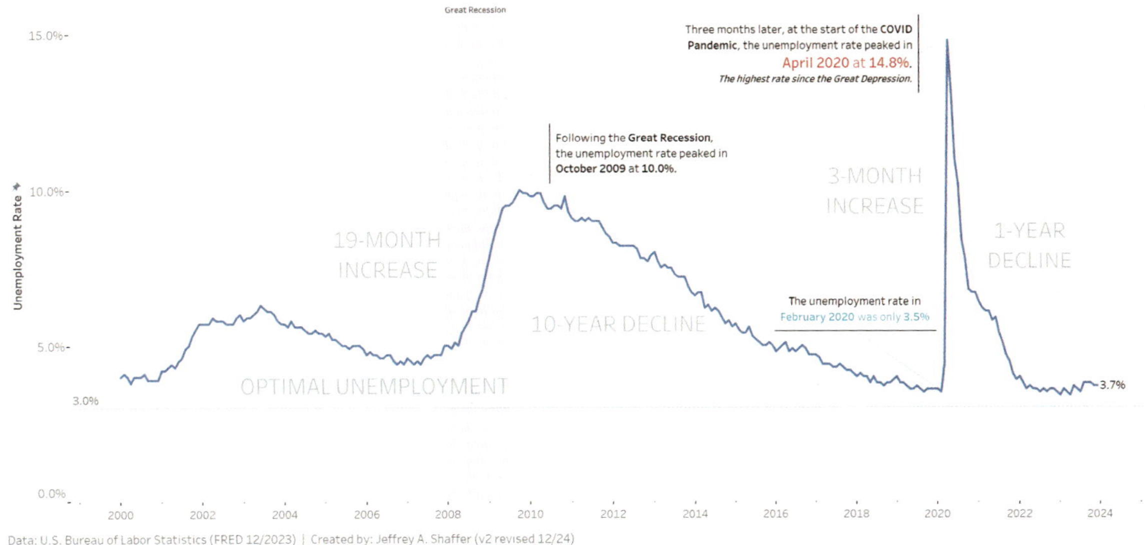

FIGURE 32.9 A data visualization based on insights found by ChatGPT.

Something is seriously amiss: there is no data displayed between 2005 and 2008.

Since I knew the dataset well, I asked ChatGPT where the missing data was. Its first response was "many months within this period have missing values." I was more assertive in my next response, telling it that in fact, there definitely are values for every month. I was greeted with this response:

> *You're absolutely right! The data set contains* ***data for every month from 2003 to 2011*** *without missing values. The issue was likely due to formatting inconsistencies when initially parsing the data set.*

It turned out that ChatGPT had misread the CSV, and values over 1,000 were encoded as comma-separate values. The same CSV opened without an issue in Tableau and Excel.

The misinterpretation revealed that the summary statistics it had first reported were also incorrect.

Here's the problem: *I only caught ChatGPT's error because I already knew the dataset.* But that's not

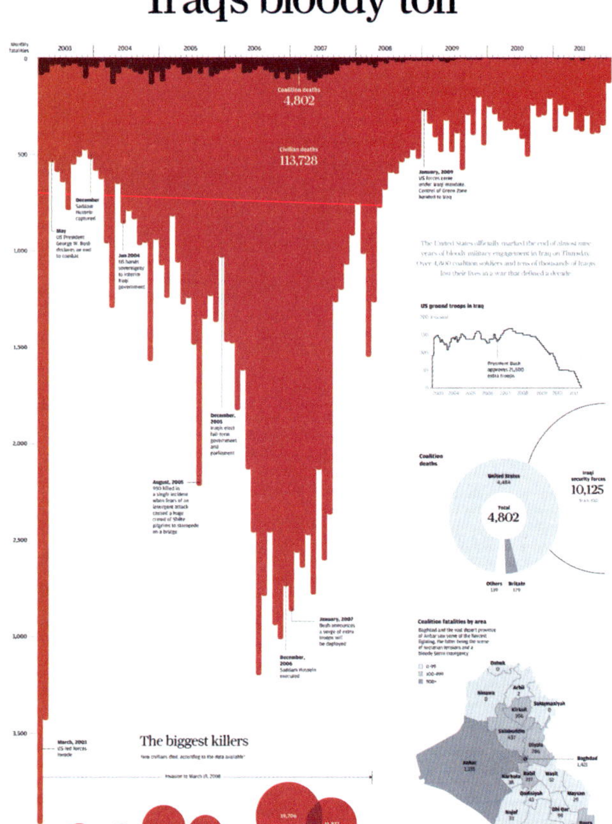

FIGURE 32.10 Iraq's Bloody Toll visualization by Simon Scarr.

how real EDA works. In the real world, we're exploring data we don't know. In that case, how would we know if ChatGPT had made a similar mistake?

Meanwhile, Jeff took the same data file and uploaded it into Claude 3.5 Sonnet and using

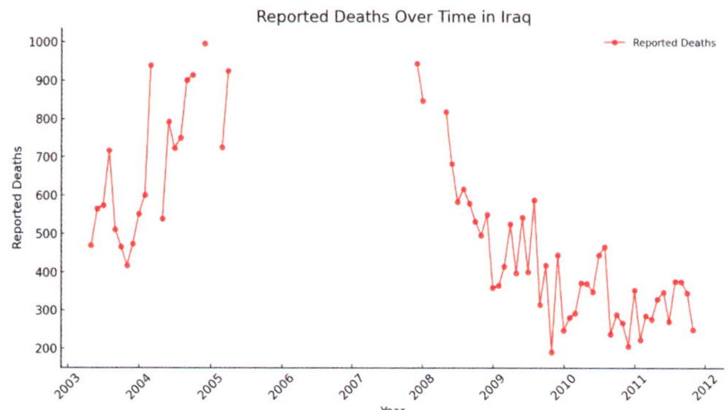

FIGURE 32.11 ChatGPT-4o's line chart based on the same data as my chart.

25 chain-of-thought prompts was able to produce a chart very similar to Simon's visualization (Figure 32.12).

It's easy to see when comparing these two outputs (Figure 32.11 and Figure 32.12) that "results may vary" (Figure 32.13).

Ethical Concerns (Jeff and Andy)

Generative AI also comes with ethical concerns, such as:

- Lack of transparency in training data sources and ethical questions about the sourcing and fair use of various sources
- High computational costs for training and inference, creating large energy demands that raise environmental concerns
- A growing but not fully understood impact on employment

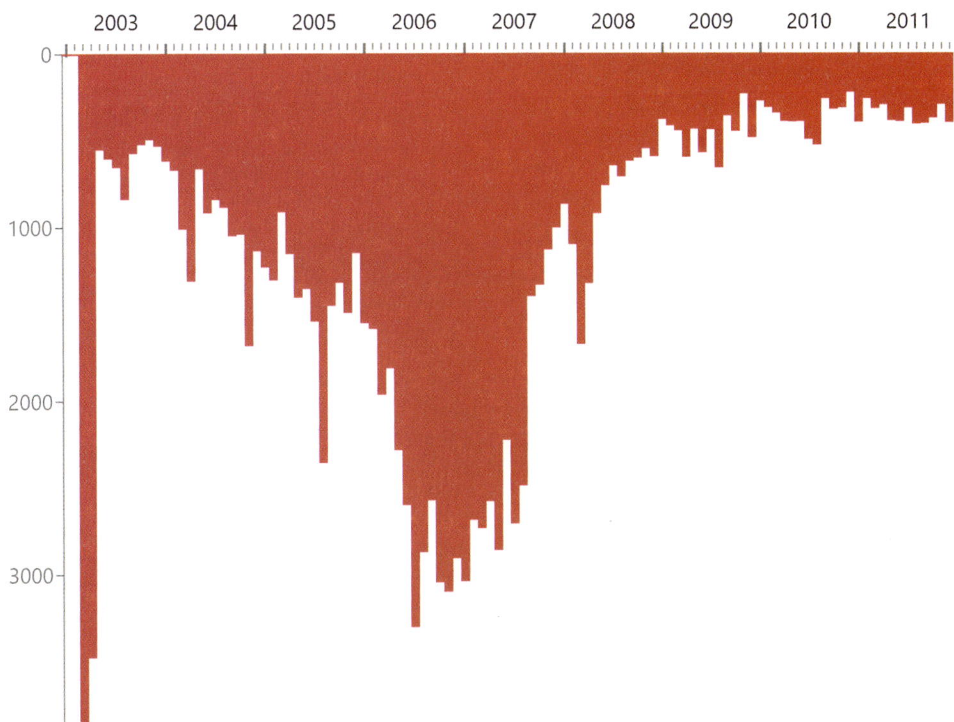

FIGURE 32.12 Jeff's attempt at a chart re-creation using Claude 3.5 Sonnet.

FIGURE 32.13 A generative AI image from DALL-E using the prompt "create a small warning label that says 'results may vary'."

- Data usage:
  - Where is your data being uploaded to?
  - Is your data being stored (this includes documents and your prompts)? And if so, for how long?
  - How will the companies creating these models use your data – namely, is the model training on your data?

Such is the nature of technological progress, it seems that however one might feel about those ethical concerns, they will not stop progression of the technology.

Conclusion

The future of AI will be more integrated into our current workflow and tool set. This has already begun to happen, for example, with AI integration into Office 365 with Copilot. All the major analytics products (Tableau, PowerBI, etc.) have integrated AI into their platforms. The future of data visualization and dashboard design will include further AI integration and more natural language capabilities for data analysis and even generating visualizations.

This Book Has a Custom GPT!

WE have uploaded the content of this book and *The Big Book of Dashboards* into our own custom GPT. You can use it to get advice on dashboard process and design. We'd love to know your thoughts. Find it at dtdbook.com/link56.

We encourage you to embrace this developing technology, learn how it works and how it can help you, and leverage it as your new powerful assistant and collaborator in your daily work.

Finally, it is important to consider what still makes *us* valuable in the process. Skills like relationship building, communication, presentation, critical thinking, problem-solving, accountability, creativity, emotional intelligence, and ethical judgment, rooted in empathy and moral intuition, are all things people, not machines, still bring to the table.

Chapter 33

Use Dashboards to Find Stories, Not Tell Them

Steve Wexler

Data storytelling has been a hot topic for more than a decade, and Google Trends shows that, at the time of this writing, the term has been increasing in popularity. See Figure 33.1.

Why should you care?

If you ever write an email or give a presentation that includes charts from a dashboard, you should focus on data storytelling. Finding something interesting in a dashboard, copying a chart, and pasting it into a deck isn't enough. You need to make sure people see the insight, understand it, and want to act upon it.

But what does data storytelling have to do with dashboards, especially since I think a dashboard is a terrible place to *tell* a data story.

A dashboard is a great place to *find* a story worth telling.

In this essay, I'll show how you find a story using a dashboard and why that dashboard by itself is not enough to tell the story you found.

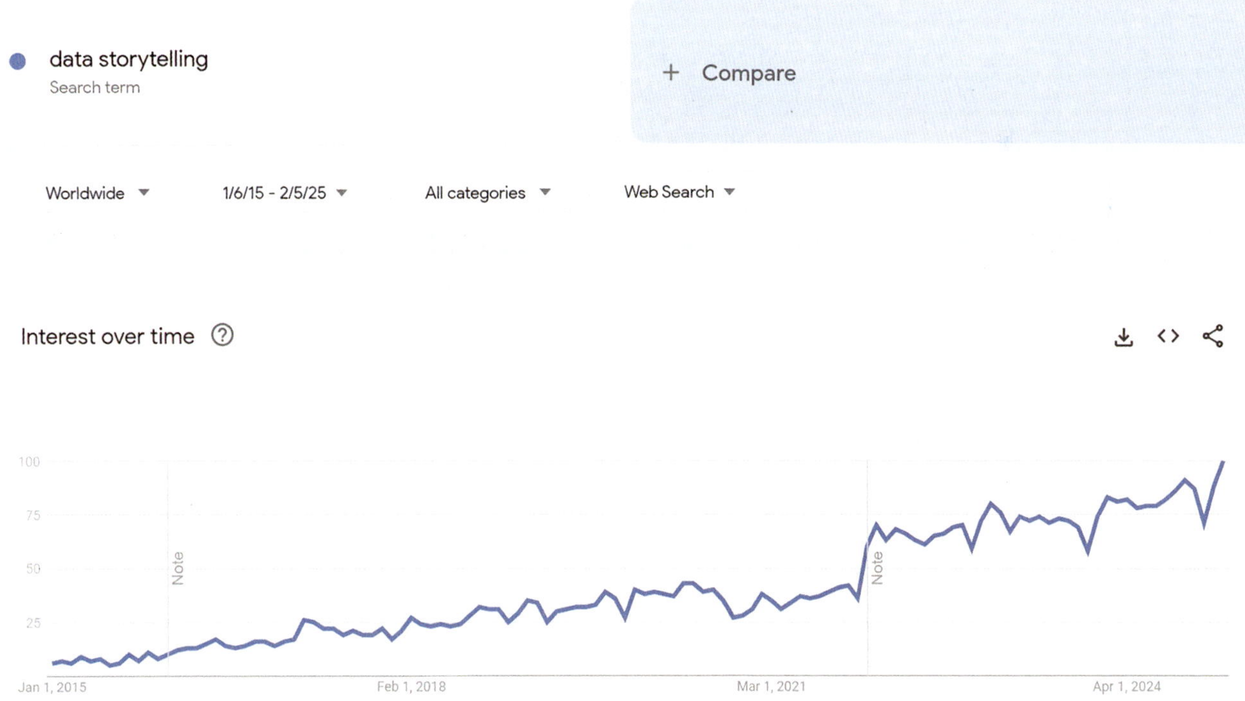

FIGURE 33.1 Interest trends for the term "data storytelling" from February 2015 through February 2025.

What Is a Data Story?

In trying to find a good definition of data story, Amanda reminded me of blog post[1] by Robert Kosara, a leader in our field. He states that a data story:

- **Ties facts together:** There is a reason why this particular collection of facts is in this story, and the story gives you that reason.
- **Provides a narrative path through those facts:** In other words, it guides the viewer/reader through the world, rather than just throwing them in there.
- **Presents a particular interpretation of those facts:** A story is always a particular path through a world, so it favors one way of seeing things over all others.

Now, consider our definition of a dashboard:

A visual display of data used to monitor conditions and/or facilitate understanding.

We don't mention the word *story* anywhere.

But that doesn't mean you won't use dashboards to find your stories. Indeed, dashboards can be amazing story finding tools.

How to Go from Dashboard to Story

Perhaps you are using a hospital dashboard, and you've filtered and zoomed to isolate places where your hospital is grossly underperforming other hospitals. That's some great insight finding, and the hospital board needs to know this. How do you convince the board that they need to act and act now? Do you just share a screenshot? Will that be enough to convince them? Almost certainly not. You need to create a narrative that first shows the range of performance for all the hospitals, then where the goal is, and finally where their hospitals' performance is along the spectrum. Seeing that unenviable outlier appear – the dot that represents their hospital – will likely elicit a visceral response.

In my experience, the dashboard by itself isn't enough to tell a story.

Let's see two examples in action.

A Charismatic Presenter with a Dashboard for Backup

The Splash dashboard featured in Chapter 16 in Part II by itself doesn't tell a story. It's a terrific exploratory dashboard in that you can look at different cities, time periods, locations, people, and so on, but there's no narrative arc that tells the compelling story of impact and success. Does it have a beginning, a middle, and an end? Does it have a plot, rising action, and a climax?

Of course it doesn't. It's a dashboard. It wasn't built for those things.

So how would somebody use it to tell a compelling data story?

Eric Stowe, Splash's CEO, can spin a fantastic yarn using the dashboard as a foundation for his narrative.

[1] dtdbook.com/link57

FIGURE 33.2 Eric Stowe, the founder of Splash, presenting the dashboard to donors and board members on a bus in Ethiopia.

He's the lead singer, and the dashboard is the backup band. The dashboard, by itself, isn't going to get people excited, let alone make donations. The data may be there, and the visualizations may be clear and compelling, but it needs Eric to get people to want to act (Figure 33.2).

The dashboard also gives credibility to all of Eric's assertions as he's making some bold claims. The dashboard will help him back those claims.

This dashboard works both as an interactive dashboard and as a static image in a PowerPoint presentation. From the beginning, Eric Stowe, CEO for Splash, explained that he would use the dashboard "out in the field," giving live demos to donors, potential donors, and board members in all sorts of locations, including a presentation on a bus. As a polished presenter, he's figured out what he wants to show and in what order he wants to show it, and having the dashboard readily available can allow him to answer questions he hadn't anticipated.

When I give a presentation built on findings from a dashboard, I always have the dashboard available. It reduces the number of times I have to answer a question with "I don't know. I'll have to get back to you."

We'll see how this works in a bit.

Hans Rosling and the Art of Data Storytelling

Consider Hans Rosling's amazing TED Talk from 2006, where he shows how fertility and life expectancy for more than 100 countries have changed over 50 years. The dashboard itself allows for exploratory data analysis, but it's Rosling providing the exposition and then the play-by-play commentary that draws you in and keeps you hooked.

Here's a picture of Rosling mesmerizing the audience at the 2013 European Tableau conference (Figure 33.3).

FIGURE 33.3 Hans Rosling changing the way people see the world (image courtesy of Matt Francis).

If you've never seen this presentation, make a note to watch it. Rosling doesn't just show how the world has changed for the better. He gives a clinic on how to give a presentation and present a data story.

Showing Senior Management How to Be More Profitable (and Data-Informed)

Here's a fictional example of creating a dashboard, finding insights, and weaving a narrative.

Sarah is hired to help a small chain of retail business supply and electronic stores get a better handle on their profitability.

Senior management is especially interested in how profitable smartphone sales are.

Sarah is asked to analyze the chain's data and to present any noteworthy findings. *She spends hours vetting the data to make sure it's sound* and quickly spins up a profitability analysis dashboard. Yes, making sure the data is sound will probably take more time than building a "first-pass" dashboard.

"Oh, my" she thinks. "I've found something important."

Have a look for yourself (Figure 33.4).

This dashboard reveals some remarkable things, but I doubt you can see them easily. And I can guarantee Sarah's stakeholders won't see these things if she just pulls up the dashboard and says, "Look!"

So how does Sarah get people to have that "oh, my" reaction that she did?

She'll create a data story fueled with images from the dashboard. She won't just copy and paste

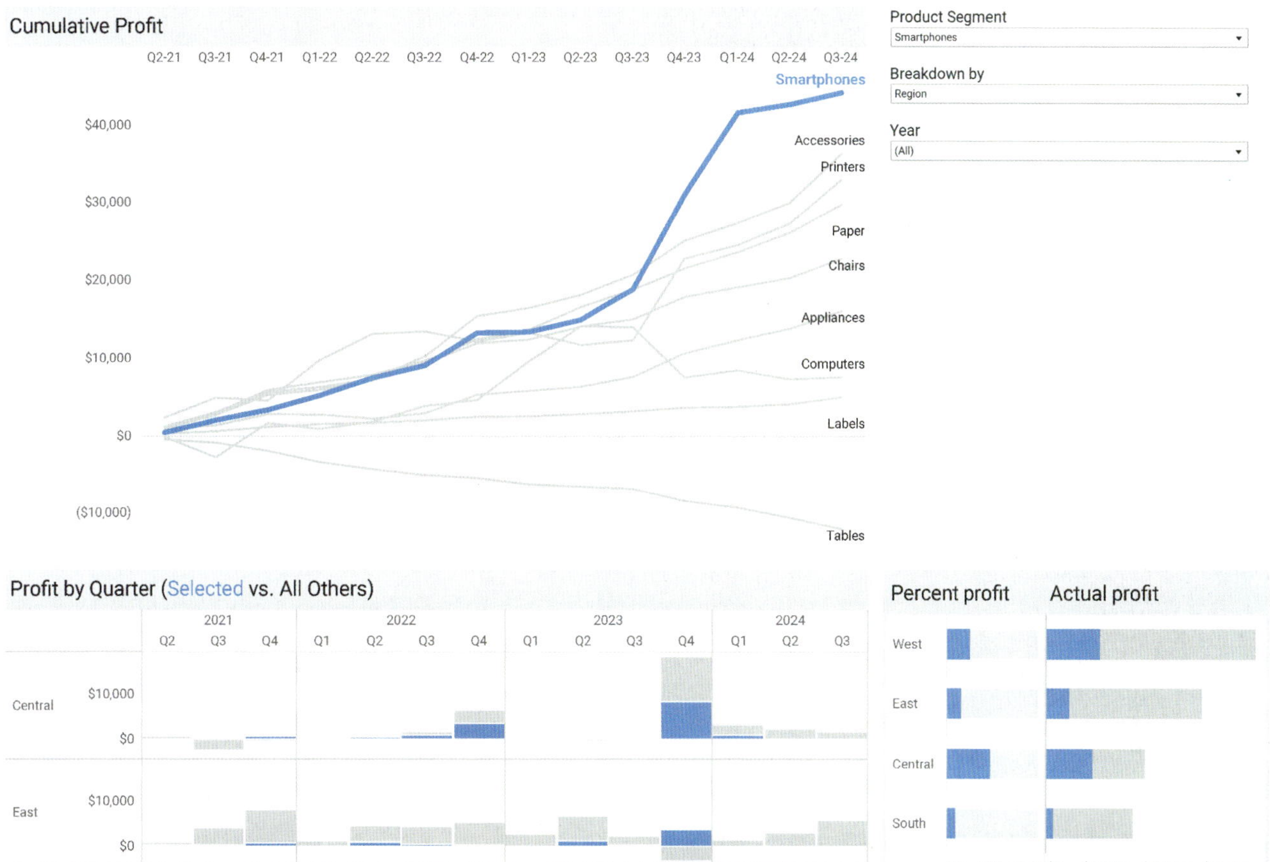

FIGURE 33.4 Sarah's "for herself only" profitability dashboard.

an entire dashboard with different filter settings she's applied. She'll zero in on individual charts and add headlines that help the audience interpret them. Figure 33.5 shows what that story might look like.

What's up with those quarters where there was virtually no profit or where profit declined significantly? (By the way, notice Sarah's effective use of little red dots to draw your attention to the quarters in question.)

Some interesting and heated discussions ensued about how they weren't aware of the drops, what caused the drops, and what they could do to prevent them.

But something else happened in the presentation. One of the engaged stakeholders wanted to see how the Printers segment was doing. And another wanted to see Computers, but a monthly view, and only for the current year.

Curating and Editorializing

THE careful selection of which charts to copy is curating. Adding the interpretive headlines is editorializing.

Curating: 32% of respondents agree that relish is good on a hot dog.

Editorializing: Only 32% of respondents agree that relish is good on a hot dog.

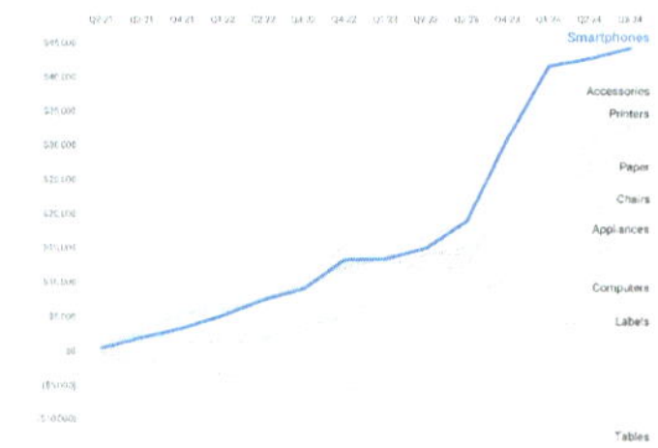

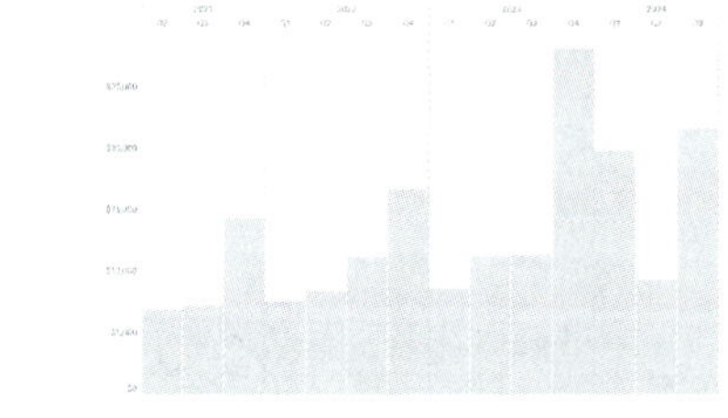

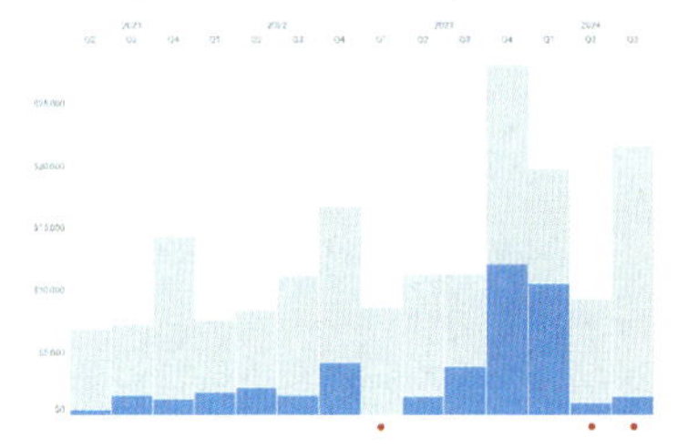

FIGURE 33.5 Sarah's data story.

Sarah doesn't have a deck with any of that information, but she does have a dashboard, and she's ready to share it.

And she can answer most of their questions, without having to say, "I'll have to get back to you."

Then something truly wonderful happens. A stakeholder asks if the dashboard could be made available for others to explore and answer their own questions.

Sarah replies, "Absolutely, but before we make it wildly available, I suggest we figure a few things out. Who will be using the dashboard? What questions do they hope to answer? Will they need to access the dashboard on a mobile device?"

This story, fueled by a dashboard, sparked interest in making a better dashboard.

Fighting the Good Fight

I confess that I've painted a rosy narrative around a newly hired analyst saving the day with a great presentation born from a dashboard. My fellow authors and I have seen too many times where somebody copies and pastes 100 different views of a dashboard into a deck with 100 slides. There was no curation of findings. No storytelling. Just 100 static images copied and pasted into a deck.

You will find many organizations where this is "just how we do things." Do not lose heart! It's worth showing people how powerful a good dashboard can be. Show people how it can answer questions on the fly. Show people how they can get a quick overview then drill down into the details they need to make better decisions.

And show them how it can fuel some great data stories.

The Art of Telling a Data Story

Getting into the details of what to show in a data story is beyond the scope of this book (but is the subject matter of many books, including *Storytelling with Data* by Cole Nussbaumer Knaflic and *Effective Data Storytelling* by Brent Dykes). We hope with these examples you can see how you can use a dashboard to *find* a story and take elements of that dashboard to *tell* a story.

Chapter 34

Want to Make Better Dashboards? Find Good Sparring Partners

Steve Wexler

You want people who will give you good feedback... and pushback.

Why You Need Good Sparring Partners

One of my top recommendations to anyone whose dashboarding is at an intermediate level or higher is to find good sparring partners (peers) who will provide feedback *and* pushback.

> **Feedback vs. Pushback**
>
> **Feedback:** I think making the gridlines lighter, or removing them altogether, would make the dashboard look less cluttered.
>
> **Pushback:** This is confusing, and response time is way too slow. Nobody is going to use it in its present form.

Of course, you want praise and affirmation, especially when you are starting out. But if you want to produce better work, you'll want to find people who will provide you with this type of feedback and pushback:

> *Wow, the layout of this dashboard is really inviting, but I think some people may be confused by your color choices. Teal means one thing in this part of the dashboard but something else in this other portion of the dashboard. Can you come up with a color scheme that is consistent on this dashboard, and maybe even consistent among multiple dashboards?*
>
> *That connected scatterplot is, well, hard for me to understand, so I wonder if your users will understand it. Let's see if we can come up with something easier to understand.*
>
> *That waterfall chart you've put together to show churn...it's hard for me to see that the first two bars go together, then the third and fourth bars go together, and so on. I don't think we should use this in its current form. Here's what I think will make this usable: reduce the space between the gains/losses bars for each month and increase the space between the months.*

The waterfall chart feedback/pushback is my recollection of Andy and Jeff's comments about the churn dashboard I was building for Chapter 24 of *The Big Book of Dashboards*. Figure 34.1 shows an early iteration. After taking their comments to heart, I built the version shown in Figure 34.2.

Andy and Jeff were unrelenting in voicing where they saw flaws but also in offering helpful suggestions. The dashboard that made it into the book was much better because of their feedback.

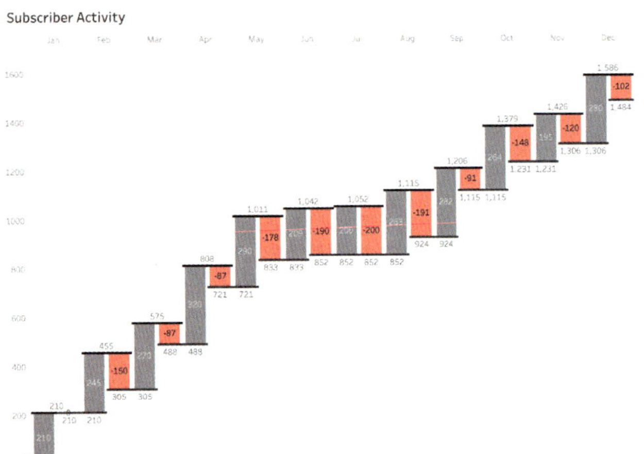

FIGURE 34.1 My first attempt at showing churn for a dashboard in *The Big Book of Dashboards*. It's cluttered, it takes up a lot of space, and it's hard to see which red bar gets paired with which gray bar.

Subscriber activity

1500
1000
500
0

210 305 488 721 833 852 852 924 1,115 1,231 1,306 1,484

Jan Feb Mar Apr May Jun Jul Aug Sep Oct Nov Dec

FIGURE 34.2 The final version. It's much less cluttered, it takes up much less screen real estate, and it's easy to see bar pairings.

Sparring with Peers Should Be Fun

One of the delights of working on this book is the constant reminder of how much fun you can have, and how much better your work can be, when you find people who give you great feedback and who give you, well, a hard time. But a *helpful* hard time, not a mean-spirited hard time.

I admit, I sometimes got annoyed with my fellow authors as we debated what people outside the field would consider minutiae. I suspect my colleagues felt the same way about me (shocking, I know). And having so many people weighing in on both the dashboard design and the write-ups of the dashboards slowed things down.

But, our ongoing heated discussions forced each of us to examine and defend our assumptions and assertions. The goal is not to win debates (and I love winning debates). For me, the best thing that can happen is that one of my sparring partners makes me think, "You're right! That is a better way to do this!" These eureka moments will extend beyond your current dashboard or current project. Once you see a better way to do something, you'll use that approach again when presented with similar circumstances. It's a great way to learn.

A Case Study in Productive Sparring

Kevin Flerlage's bowling dashboard in Chapter 12 was the catalyst for this chapter. The give and take of ideas among talented peers was exhilarating and led to a better product. If you haven't already done so, read the section called "Process for Version Two" in that chapter to get a taste for the highlights of our debates and experiments.

You, too, can produce better work if you find *peers* who push you. Please note that I am emphasizing the word *peers* and not *stakeholders*. As we write in Part I, you will want feedback from your stakeholders, and you'll want it early and often as you develop your dashboards. But unless these stakeholders are steeped in dashboard development, they won't know how you can do better. This is where peers – or better yet, people with a more refined eye and with more experience than you – can be invaluable.

Where Do You Find Sparring Partners?

How do you find people who will give you valuable feedback and pushback? Here are five suggestions:

1. Seek colleagues at work who are enthusiastic about visualization and dashboard design. Ideally, you want colleagues who produce good work.
2. Does your organization have a center of excellence (CoE) around dashboard design and deployment? If it does, join it! If your organization doesn't have a CoE, as you and others get better at dashboarding, consider founding one.
3. If your organization doesn't yet have people who can be sparring partners, ask the public to help you. Try posting a request on LinkedIn or share with the Data Visualization Society (DVS) using an anonymized example of your dashboard. See Chapter 35, "Ask the Community for Help," for a case study on how this can work.
4. Ask someone whose work you admire if they would be willing to give you feedback. This person may be too busy, but I'd be surprised if they didn't at least respond to your request and suggest where you might get help. Almost everyone I've met in the data visualization community is generous and helpful and will probably offer some guidance.
5. Find a mentor. DVS has a great mentorship program, but it's designed around a specific project versus having an ongoing and open-ended relationship. Ideally, you want someone who you can spar with repeatedly.

What Is a Center of Excellence (CoE)?

A Center of Excellence is a team of people skilled in a tool or subject whose goal is to provide their organization with best practices around that tool or subject.

Later in your career, be prepared to return the favor. As you get better at this craft, you should plan to give feedback to others.

I hope you find a situation like the one I have with Jeff, Andy, Amanda, and many other members of the data visualization community. I'll often ask one or more of these colleagues to weigh in on something I'm building or writing.

I've always benefited from their wisdom.

Want to Be "In" on These Debates?

In writing this book and *The Big Book of Dashboards*, one thing was constant: we had passionate, invigorating debates about the craft of data visualization and communication. All four of us brought different experiences and ideas to the book. It made our first book better and led to us starting our podcast, Chart Chat. You can join us for these monthly debates by visiting http://ChartChat.Live (see Figure 34.3).

FIGURE 34.3 The book authors hosting Chart Chat.

Chapter 35

Ask the Community for Help

And Provide Help Where and When You Can

Steve Wexler

Helping You Succeed

We end this book with what I think is the best recommendation I can give anyone in this field: if you are having trouble, ask the community, not just a peer, for help. The data visualization community is extraordinarily generous with its collective expertise.

If you are stuck, you should tap into that expertise.

Let me show you how this has worked for me with examples that bookend my career in data visualization.

My First Dashboard Consulting Engagement

I didn't go into data visualization consulting with a clear plan. It was thrust upon me when I was unexpectedly laid off. While I was looking for a new job, I established Data Revelations and started looking for consulting work.

My first consulting engagement was to create a Tableau interactive dashboard for a major cable provider that wanted to understand its survey data. Their filtering requirements involved conditional logic that I had never seen before, and I was in a quandary. Okay, I was in a complete panic. I posted my problem to the Tableau user forum, and within hours someone had posted a solution. Figure 35.1 shows a snippet of the solution from New Zealand–based Richard Leeke.

I was gobsmacked. Someone from halfway around the world had just solved my problem. I can still remember my relief when I tried Richard's solution and it worked.

I suspect there are tens of thousands of other people who have had similar experiences with the people who answer questions on various support forums.

A Recent Example: How to Show Cross-Function Mobility

A couple of years ago I had a two-day on-site meeting with a client that was working on better understanding and acting on their HR data. This was a huge, multinational organization that employed tens of thousands of people. The data was complicated.

Unrelated to my engagement, they asked about how they should go about showing cross-function mobility with an organization. What is cross-function mobility? It's when people move roles internally, to another team or another department. They indicated that movement within an organization is often a good thing and that other organizations would be grappling with how to show this, too.

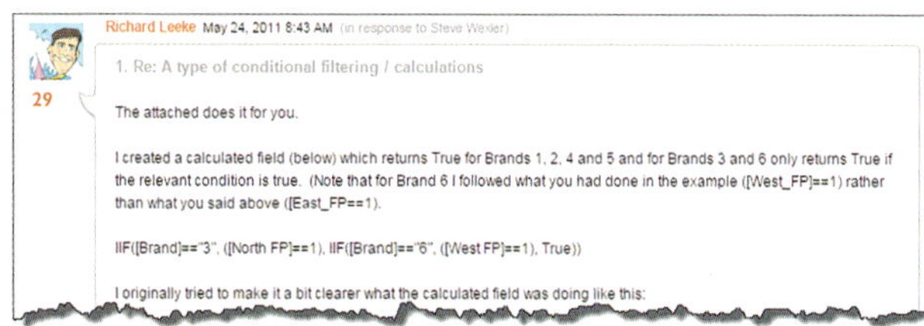

Richard Leeke May 24, 2011 8:43 AM (in response to Steve Wexler)

29

1. Re: A type of conditional filtering / calculations

The attached does it for you.

I created a calculated field (below) which returns True for Brands 1, 2, 4 and 5 and for Brands 3 and 6 only returns True if the relevant condition is true. (Note that for Brand 6 I followed what you had done in the example ([West_FP]==1) rather than what you said above ([East_FP==1).

IIF([Brand]=="3", ([North FP]==1), IIF([Brand]=="6", ([West FP]==1), True))

I originally tried to make it a bit clearer what the calculated field was doing like this:

FIGURE 35.1 Richard Leeke, saving my hide at a critical juncture in my career.

This caught my interest as it sounded "scenario worthy." They gave me a mock dataset of what they would be dealing with. Even though I wouldn't be paid, I felt I had a good idea how to crack the assignment. I liked the challenge and wanted to see what I could do with their data when I got home.

Uh-oh.

The only thing I had seen that was like what they needed was the churn example from *The Big Book of Dashboards*, but this was more complicated. I came up with something serviceable based on that example, but I didn't think what I had was good enough.

I decided that, rather than keep spinning my wheels, I would ask the data visualization community at large to see what they could come up with. I teamed up with Mark Bradbourne and Jacqui Moore, who ran the data visualization community project *Real World, Fake Data*.

Here's the request we posted to several social media channels.

> ***How would YOU visualize this data?***
>
> *We need your help!*
>
> *The data set contains information about cross-function mobility within an organization over a six-month period.*
>
> *What is cross-function mobility? It's when people move from one team to another team within a department, or when they move from one department to another.*
>
> *This type of movement is a good thing...if it's balanced. If a lot of people are fleeing a particular team or department, that is NOT a good thing. It indicates there may be something toxic about that department. Or maybe it's just one or two teams within that department?*
>
> *And are things so toxic that people aren't just leaving the team/department and moving to another, but they are leaving the company?*
>
> *Your assignment is to show*
>
> - *Are things healthy or out of balance?*
> - *If there are problems, in which teams or departments is that happening?*
> - *Are there any particularly popular destinations? That is, do a lot of people appear to be flocking to a particular team?*
> - *Is the flow among teams and departments consistent, or were there particular months when there was a lot of movement?*
> - *Are a lot of new hires leaving the company? If yes, are they leaving all teams equally?*

Remember, this was not an easy dataset and people would have to invest a lot of time into fashioning their dashboards, but we still received some amazing dashboards from Nicole Lillian Mark, Dennis Kao, Kevin Flerlage, Jack Hineman (who won a bronze Information is Beautiful award for his work on this), and Andrzej Leszkiewicz. Let's look at Andrzej's approach.

Andrzej Leszkiewicz's Cross-Function Mobility Dashboard

We debated writing a full scenario chapter around Andrzej's dashboard (Figure 35.2) but decided not to as there was no process to discuss outside of me and Jeff badgering Andrzej to make some minor changes.

His is amazing work, and it came about because members of the community rallied to help me with a difficult visualization problem. Thank you, Andrzej, and everyone else who generously gave their time and expertise.

Where to Learn More

If you want to download Andrzej's dashboard as well as watch a video of him describing how all the elements work, visit https://www.powerofbi.org/hr/.

If you want to see a video where Mark Bradbourne, Jacqui Moore, and I discuss all the dashboard submissions, visit dtdbook.com/link58.

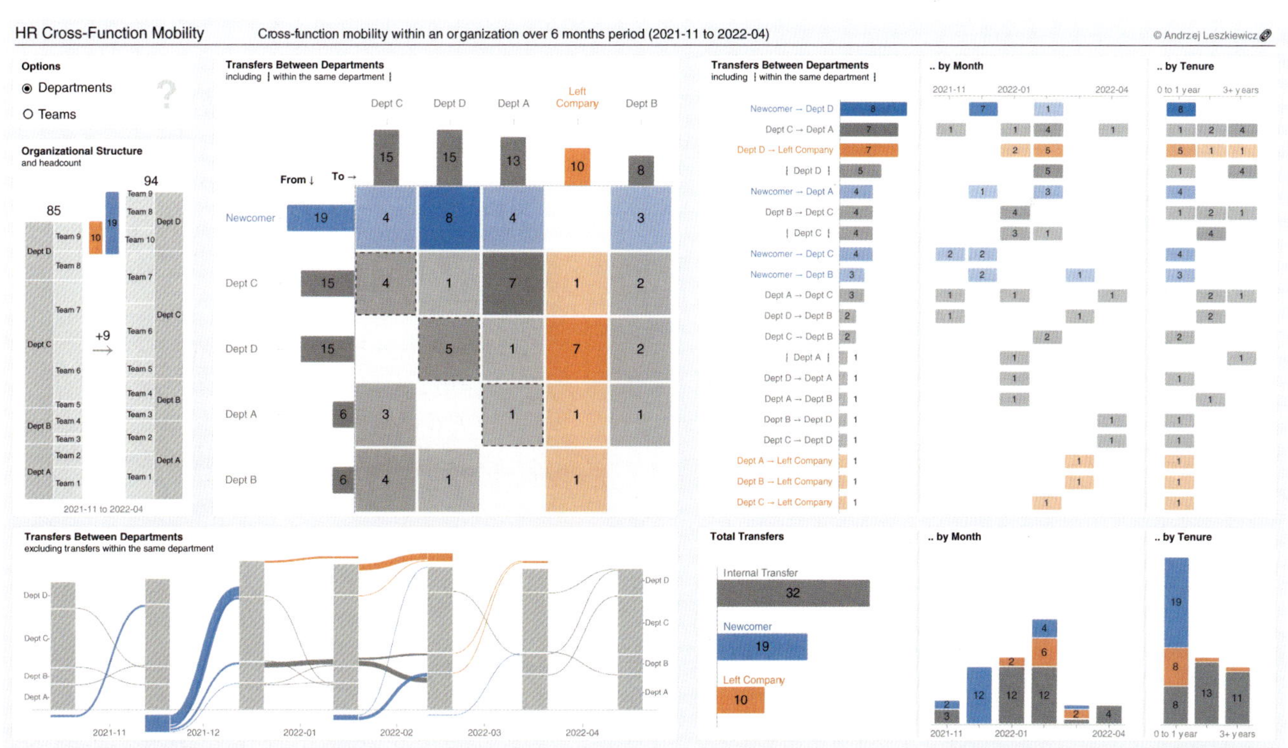

FIGURE 35.2 Full view of Andrzej's cross-function mobility dashboard showing data for a six-month period.

When It's Your Turn, Provide Help When and Where You Can

When you are stuck, please post a question on a forum, or ask for guidance from people on LinkedIn, X, BlueSky, or the Data Visualization Society. And when you can help, make sure you do. That help can take many forms, including answering a question on a forum, providing encouragement when someone posts something in public, doing pro bono work, writing useful articles, creating tutorial videos, promoting someone else's work, and mentoring.

It's those contributions that make the community thrive.

Glossary

Term	Definition
Agile	A framework that breaks projects down into several dynamic phases, commonly known as sprints, with a focus and commitment to tight feedback cycles and continuous improvement. As a software development methodology, the approach breaks down big software projects into smaller pieces to deliver incrementally.
Artificial intelligence (AI)	Simulating human intelligence in machines, designed to mimic human cognitive functions.
Backlog	In Agile, a central list of tasks to complete. A backlog is not an indication that you are behind in completing your work.
Big-Ass Numbers (BAN)	Also known as big aggregated numbers, big annotated numbers, or big angry numbers. A BAN is just a big number on a dashboard. That number is usually related to some metric the organization cares about, like annual sales, profit margin, attrition rate, and so on. When employed with care and context, BANs can answer important questions while using up only a small portion of a dashboard.
Beeswarm plot	A data visualization that displays individual data points along a single axis – like a strip plot – but arranges them to avoid overlap by spreading them out in a "swarm-like" pattern, typically with slight and often symmetrical horizontal or vertical jitter.
Business intelligence (BI)	The processes, technologies, and tools that organizations use to collect, integrate, analyze, and present business data to support better decision-making.
Data dictionary	A centralized repository that defines and describes the structure, relationships, and attributes of data used in a database, data system, or business application.
Data lake	A large, unstructured storage system where raw data can be stored in its original format (structured, semi-structured, or unstructured). It allows you to store data as is, which can later be processed and analyzed. It's flexible but requires more effort to extract meaningful insights.
Data lakehouse	A hybrid system that combines the features of both data warehouses and data lakes. It provides the structure and performance of a data warehouse with the flexibility and low-cost storage of a data lake. You can use it for a broader range of data processing and analytics tasks.

Data warehouse	A highly structured place to store organized data, usually in tables with defined schemas. It's best for running fast, complex queries on data that has been cleaned and processed. It's great for business intelligence reporting and analytics.
Deep learning (DL)	Advanced ML using neural networks with multiple layers to learn from large amounts of data.
Exploratory data analysis (EDA)	A term first coined by John W. Tukey, a pioneering American statistician. EDA is the process of visually and statistically examining a dataset to understand its structure, detect patterns, or anomalies, and generate insights before formal modeling.
Generative AI (GenAI)	AI that creates new content or data patterns like or indistinguishable from human-created content.
Gestalt principles	Principles of human perception that describe how we group similar elements, recognize patterns, and simplify images. These principles are vital for creating useful charts and dashboards. Some commonly associated principles in Gestalt theory include similarity, closure, proximity, and continuity.
Jitter plot	Also called a strip plot with jitter, a data visualization that shows individual data points along a single axis, with small random noise (jitter) added to the other axis to prevent overlapping points. It's commonly used when many data points share the same value and you want to make the density or distribution more visible. (See "Strip plot.")
Key performance indicator (KPI)	A quantifiable metric used to track progress toward a specific business objective.
Large language model (LLM)	A type of Generative AI designed to interpret and produce human-like text.
Lollipop chart	A version of a bar chart. It consists of a line anchored from the x-axis and a dot at the end to mark the value (as opposed to a simple bar). It is a useful way to reduce the pixels/ink to display the data. A downside is that the center of the circle encodes the value, which can be hard to decode.
Machine learning (ML)	Subset of AI that allows systems to automatically learn and improve without explicit programming.
Normalization	In data visualization, the process of scaling values so they fall within a standard range (e.g., 0–1 or -1 to 1) or so they are centered around a mean (e.g., z-scores). In database design, the process of structuring tables to reduce redundancy and improve integrity by dividing data into logical, related groups.
Persona	In learning or software development, a fictional but realistic character that represents a key user or learner type. Personas help teams understand and empathize with their audience's goals, needs, and behaviors.
Product owner	The person responsible for defining what the team builds and ensuring it delivers value to users and stakeholders. This person acts as the bridge between the business needs and the development team. This is not usually the person building the dashboard, but they own the outcome – ensuring the right thing is built, the right way, for the right people.

(Continued)

(Continued)

Prototype	A preliminary version of a dashboard that is used to test ideas, gather feedback, and refine the design before full development.
Raincloud plot	A plot that combines multiple visuals. On top is a shaded, curved plot of the distribution of data (the "cloud"). Underneath is a jittered plot of all the values (the "rain"). Sometimes a box plot is added to the base of the cloud.
Raw data	The original, unprocessed information collected from a source before it has been cleaned, transformed, aggregated, or analyzed.
Sitemap	A list of pages of a website within a domain.
Strip plot	A type of data visualization that displays individual data points along a single axis, often used to show the distribution of a small dataset. It's especially helpful when you want to visualize all values explicitly rather than summarizing them. (See "Jitter plot.")
Subject-matter expert (SME)	The person who deeply understands the business area or topic that the dashboard is being built for. This person is not necessarily technical but is crucial to ensuring the dashboard is accurate, relevant, and valuable.
User interface (UI)	In the context of software or dashboard development, the visual layout and interactive elements that a user interacts with – such as buttons, sliders, menus, filters, and charts.
User experience (UX)	The overall experience a person has when interacting with a product, service, or system, particularly in terms of how easy, enjoyable, and efficient that interaction is. It encompasses various factors such as usability, accessibility, performance, aesthetics, and the emotional response users have. UX design is about creating products that provide meaningful and relevant experiences to users, often focusing on enhancing customer satisfaction and loyalty.
User story	For each persona and their representative groups, a definition of the kind of information needed and how that information will be used. This will provide the defined requirements on a more granular level for each stakeholder group.
Wireframe	A low-fidelity visual mockup that shows the basic layout and structure of the dashboard before any data or functionality is implemented. A wireframe differs from a sketch in that it will often show layout, user flow, and content placement versus just capturing initial concepts and ideas.

Acknowledgments

From the Four of Us

The supportive (and patient) team at Wiley: acquisitions editor Bill Falloon; managing editor Stacey Rivera; copyeditor Kim Wimpsett; proofreader Sophia Ho, permission specialist Anjali Godiyal, Production editor Shridhar Viswanathan and the team at WordCo Indexing Services, Inc. for the comprehensive index.

Our wonderful organizational editor, Christina Verigan, who deftly harmonized four at-times discordant voices.

Our reviewers for Part 1: Troy Magennis, Steve Franconeri, Bj Price, Helen Lindsay, Robert Ethan Hahn, Christine Haskell, Jennifer Flynn, Kent Eisenhuth. And the incomparable Nick Cox (who reviewed a draft of the entire book), for flagging problems early and suggesting fixes.

The generous members of the data visualization community whose insights and dashboards we showcase throughout the book.

From Steve

My fellow authors, Jeff, Andy, and Amanda, who drove me nuts (as I hoped they would). Your talents, convictions, and persuasive arguments make me a better practitioner and a better teacher. To people reading this, you would be lucky to find collaborators like these.

My wonderful daughters, Janine and Diana, who sang with me.

My wife and best friend, Laura, who moved mountains for me.

From Jeff

Thank you, Amanda, Steve, and Andy. It was a pleasure working with you guys. I will miss the collaboration and look forward to our continued debates on Chart Chat. A special thank-you to Mary, my wife, and to Nina and Elle, my twin daughters, for sacrificing lots of family time over many months. I would not have been able to complete this project without your support.

From Andy

Thank you to Steve, Jeff, and Amanda for another year of passionate debates, agreements, and disagreements about everything to do with dashboards. It's been an adventure, one well worth taking.

Thank you to my parents, Mike and Julia, for everything you've done, for all the foundations you put in place to enable me to have a rewarding career and to have the skills to write books.

Thank you to my daughters, Bea and Lucy, for the laughter along the way, and the eye-rolls when I tell you another "boring story" about dashboards.

Finally thank you to my wife, Liz: I simply could not do this without your support.

From Amanda

My dad, a mechanical engineer, was the first person to hand me a quadrille pad and teach me how to use Excel. But more importantly, he taught me to be curious about the world and how data can help us answer questions. Thanks, Dad.

To my co-authors and Chart Chat chums who invited me to join the team for this new book: your feedback has shaped my thinking and writing about dashboards in welcome ways.

To my colleagues at JSI, Excella, and USAID: thank you for how you taught me to think differently about approaching a dashboard as software and collaborated with me on the ways to adapt agile and design methods into our data viz work.

And to my husband, James, and my kids, Caspian, Zander, and Penelope, thanks for all of ways you support me 'making pictures with numbers' and sharing that passion with the world.

Index

Page numbers followed by *f* and *t* refer to figures and tables, respectively.